# *The* WESTERN HERITAGE

# Why Do You Need This New Edition?

## 6 good reasons why you should buy this new edition of *The Western Heritage: Teaching and Learning Classroom Edition!*

1. A new introductory essay titled "What Is the Western Heritage?" introduces students to the concept of Western civilization as it has changed over the centuries and provides instructors with an opportunity to debate the concept and its implications with students.

2. Each chapter includes a dynamic new feature called "Compare & Connect" that juxtaposes two or more documents, in some cases including visual documents, in which an important question is debated. These features are intended to encourage students to debate different points of view in class, to learn to read and evaluate differing viewpoints, or to analyze documentary and visual evidence. An interactive version of this feature is available on www.myhistorylab.com.

3. A new chapter, "The Age of Western Imperialism" (Chapter 25), provides an in-depth global overview of nineteenth-century Western imperial expansion. Topics covered in this chapter include the nineteenth-century shift in Western imperial ventures from the Americas to Africa and Asia, the significance of the British Empire, British imperial rule in India, the New Imperialism, the partition of Africa, the role of missionaries in European colonialism, the relationship of technology and science to imperialism, and international colonial rivalries.

4. The new chapter on Western imperialism has led to a streamlining of the chapter titled "Alliances, War, and a Troubled Peace" (Chapter 26), which covers World War I and its aftermath and includes more extensive comments on the colonial ramifications of the peace settlement.

5. The new edition features a single, more sharply focused chapter on the twentieth-century interwar years titled "The Interwar Years: The Challenge of Dictators and Depression" (Chapter 27).

6. The two closing chapters of the book (Chapters 29 and 30) carry the narrative through important recent events such as the Russian invasion of Georgia and the collapse of financial institutions in Europe and the United States in the fall of 2008.

# The WESTERN HERITAGE

**TEACHING AND LEARNING CLASSROOM EDITION**

BRIEF SIXTH EDITION

VOLUME 1: TO 1740

## Donald Kagan
YALE UNIVERSITY

## Steven Ozment
HARVARD UNIVERSITY

## Frank M. Turner
YALE UNIVERSITY

**Prentice Hall**

Boston   Columbus   Indianapolis   New York   San Francisco   Upper Saddle River
Amsterdam   Cape Town   Dubai   London   Madrid   Milan   Munich
Paris   Montreal   Toronto   Delhi   Mexico City   Sao Paulo   Sydney
Hong Kong   Seoul   Singapore   Taipei   Tokyo

**VP, Editorial Director:** Leah Jewell
**Executive Editor:** Charles Cavaliere
**Editorial Project Manager:** Rob DeGeorge
**Production Project Manager:** Lynn Savino Wendel
**Editorial Assistant:** Lauren Aylward
**Director of Marketing:** Brandy Dawson
**Senior Managing Editor:** Ann Marie McCarthy
**Copy Editor:** Martha Williams
**Proofreader:** Donna Mulder
**Senior Operations Supervisor:** Mary Ann Gloriande
**Senior Art Director:** Maria Lange
**Text Designer:** Jill Little
**Cover Designer:** John Christiana/Corrin Skidds
**AV Project Manager:** Mirella Signoretto

**Manager, Visual Research:** Beth Brenzel
**Manager, Rights and Permissions:** Zina Arabia
**Image Permission Coordinator:** Michelina Viscusi
**Manager, Cover Visual Research & Permissions:** Karen Sanatar
**Cover Art:** Karl Marx/Bettmann/Corbis
**Media Director:** Brian Hyland
**Lead Media Project Manager:** Sarah Kinney
**Supplements Editor:** Emsal Hasan
**Composition, Full-Service Project Management:** Rebecca Dunn, Prepare, Inc.
**Printer/Binder:** Courier, Kendallville
**Cover Printer:** Lehigh-Phoenix Color

This book was set in 10/13 Goudy Regular.

Credits and acknowledgments borrowed from other sources and reproduced, with permission, in this textbook appear on appropriate page within text.

**Library of Congress Cataloging-in-Publication Data**

Kagan, Donald.
  The Western heritage/Donald Kagan, Steven Ozment, Frank M. Turner. —Teaching and learning classroom edition, Brief 6th ed.
    p. cm.
  "Combined volume."
  Includes bibliographical references and index.
  ISBN 978-0-205-72891-6 (combined)—ISBN 978-0-205-73210-4 (exam)—ISBN 978-0-205-72892-3 (volume one)—
  ISBN 978-0-205-72893-0 (volume two)
  1. Civilization, Western—History—Textbooks.   I. Ozment, Steven E.   II. Turner, Frank M. (Frank Miller), 1944   III. Title.
CB245.K28 2010b
909'.09821–dc22                              2009014281

10 9 8 7 6 5

**Prentice Hall**
is an imprint of

www.pearsonhighered.com

ISBN 10: 0-205-72892-8
ISBN 13: 978-0-205-72892-3

BRIEF CONTENTS

v

## PART 3 Europe in Transition, 1300–1750

## 9 The Late Middle Ages: Social and Political Breakdown (1300–1453)    222

## 10 Renaissance and Discovery    242

## 11 The Age of Reformation    270

## 12 The Age of Religious Wars    298

## 13 European State Consolidation in the Seventeenth and Eighteenth Centuries    320

# PREFACE

Students undertaking the study of the Western heritage on the threshold of the second decade of the twenty-first century do so at a remarkable historical moment. In 2008, the United States elected its first African American president, a Democrat backed by larger Democratic congressional majorities pledged to undertaking major new policy directions at home and abroad. Both the Western and non-Western worlds confront a changing global economy that gave birth to a financial crisis with the most serious implications for economic stability since the 1930s. The August 2008 invasion of Georgia by Russian Federation troops signaled the possibility of a move from a period of relative quietude to one of military resurgence that may bring into question numerous strategic military assumptions that prevailed for almost two decades after the collapse of the Soviet Union. The United States and Western Europe, after several years of controversial military engagement in Iraq and Afghanistan, continue efforts to reshape foreign policy with an emphasis on diplomacy instead of preemptive warfare. Christians in the Northern and Southern Hemispheres continue to be sharply divided as they debate the character of their faith and its relationship to other faiths and the social questions of the day. A growing consensus of opinion recognizes the dangers posed by environmental change.

The authors of this volume continue to believe that the heritage of Western civilization remains a major point of departure for understanding and defining the challenges of this no longer new century. The unprecedented globalization of daily life that is a hallmark of our era has occurred largely through the spread of Western influences. From the sixteenth century onward, the West has exerted vast influences throughout the globe for both good and ill, and today's global citizens continue to live in the wake of that impact. It is the goal of this book to introduce its readers to the Western heritage, so that they may be better informed and more culturally sensitive citizens of the increasingly troubled and challenging global age. The events of recent years and the hostility that has arisen in many parts of the world to the power and influence of the West require new efforts to understand how the West sees itself and how other parts of the world see the West.

Since *The Western Heritage* first appeared, we have sought to provide our readers with a work that does justice to the richness and variety of Western civilization and its many complexities. We hope that such an understanding of the West will foster lively debate about its character, values, institutions, and global influence. Indeed, we believe such a critical outlook on their own culture has characterized the peoples of the West since the dawn of history. Through such debates we define ourselves and the values of our culture. Consequently, we welcome the debate and hope that *The Western Heritage: Teaching and Learning Classroom Edition*, Brief Sixth Edition, can help foster an informed discussion through its history of the West's strengths and weaknesses, and the controversies surrounding Western history. To further that debate, we have included a new introductory essay entitled "What Is the Western Heritage?" to introduce students to the concept of the West and to allow instructors and students to have a point of departure for debating this concept in their course of study.

We also believe that any book addressing the experience of the West must also look beyond its historical European borders. Students reading this book come from a wide variety of cultures and experiences. They live in a world of highly interconnected economies and instant communication between cultures. In this emerging multicultural society it seems both appropriate and necessary to recognize how Western civilization has throughout its history interacted with other cultures, both influencing and being influenced by them. For this reason, we have introduced to this edition a new chapter on the nineteenth-century European age of imperialism. Further examples of Western interaction with other parts of the world, such as with Islam, appear throughout the text.

In this edition as in past editions, our goal has been to present Western civilization fairly, accurately, and in a way that does justice to this great, diverse legacy of human enterprise. History has many facets, no single one of which can alone account for the others. Any attempt to tell the story of the West from a single overarching perspective, no matter how timely, is bound to neglect or suppress some important parts of this story. Like all other authors of introductory texts, we have had to make choices, but we have attempted to provide the broadest possible introduction to Western civilization.

## GOALS OF THE TEXT

Our primary goal has been to present a strong, clear, narrative account of the central developments in Western history. We have also sought to call attention to certain critical themes:

- The capacity of Western civilization, from the time of the Greeks to the present, to transform itself through self-criticism.

- The development in the West of political freedom, constitutional government, and concern for the rule of law and individual rights.

- The shifting relations among religion, society, and the state.

- The development of science and technology and their expanding impact on Western thought, social institutions, and everyday life.

- The major religious and intellectual currents that have shaped Western culture.

We believe that these themes have been fundamental in Western civilization, shaping the past and exerting a continuing influence on the present.

**Flexible Presentation**    *The Western Heritage: Teaching and Learning Classroom Edition,* Brief Sixth Edition, is designed to accommodate a variety of approaches to a course in Western civilization, allowing teachers to stress what is most important to them. Some teachers will ask students to read all the chapters. Others will select among them to reinforce assigned readings and lectures. We believe the "Compare & Connect" and "Encountering the Past" features may also be adopted selectively by instructors for purposes of classroom presentation and debate and as the basis for short written assignments.

**Integrated Social, Cultural, and Political History**
*The Western Heritage* provides one of the richest accounts of the social history of the West available today, with strong coverage of family life, the changing roles of women, and the place of the family in relation to broader economic, political, and social developments. This coverage reflects the explosive growth in social historical research in the past half-century, which has enriched virtually all areas of historical study.

We have also been told repeatedly by teachers that no matter what their own historical specialization, they believe that a political narrative gives students an effective tool to begin to understand the past. Consequently, we have sought to integrate such a strong political narrative with our treatment of the social, cultural, and intellectual factors in Western history.

We also believe that religious faith and religious institutions have been fundamental to the development of the West. No other survey text presents so full an account of the religious and intellectual development of the West. People may be political and social beings, but they are also reasoning and spiritual beings. What they think and believe are among the most important things we can know about them. Their ideas about God, society, law, gender, human nature, and the physical world have changed over the centuries and continue to change. We cannot fully grasp our own approach to the world without understanding the religious and intellectual currents of the past and how they influenced our thoughts and conceptual categories. We seek to recognize the impact of religion in the expansion of the West, including the settlement the Americas in the sixteenth century and the role of missionaries in nineteenth-century Western imperialism.

**Clarity and Accessibility**    Good narrative history requires clear, vigorous prose. As with earlier editions, we have paid careful attention to our writing, subjecting every paragraph to critical scrutiny. Our goal has been to make the history of the West accessible to students without compromising vocabulary or conceptual level. We hope this effort will benefit both teachers and students.

## THE BRIEF SIXTH EDITION

### NEW TO THIS EDITION

- We include a new introductory essay entitled "What Is the Western Heritage?" designed to introduce students to the concept of Western civilization as it has changed over the centuries and at the same to provide instructors the opportunity to debate this concept and its implications with their students.

- Each chapter includes a new feature entitled **"Compare & Connect"** that juxtaposes two or more documents in which an important question is debated or a comparison between a document and an illustration is presented. Each "Compare & Connect" feature contains three to five questions on each of the documents, one of which asks students to make connections between and among the viewpoints presented in the feature. These features are intended to encourage students to debate different points of view in class and to learn to read and evaluate differing viewpoints or to analyze documentary and visual evidence. An interactive version of this feature is available on www.myhistorylab.com.

• An entirely new chapter, "The Age of Western Imperialism" (Chapter 25), provides an in-depth global overview of nineteenth-century Western imperial expansion. Topics covered in this chapter include the nineteenth-century shift in Western imperial ventures from the Americas to Africa and Asia, the significance of the British Empire, British imperial rule in India, the New Imperialism, the partition of Africa, the role of missionaries in European colonialism, the relationship of technology and science to imperialism, and international colonial rivalries.

• The new chapter on imperialism has led to a streamlining of the chapter on World War I and its aftermath as well as more extensive comments on the colonial ramifications of the peace settlement (Chapter 26).

• A single, more sharply focused chapter on the twentieth-century interwar years (Chapter 27) has replaced two longer chapters on this period.

• The two closing chapters of the book (Chapters 29 and 30) carry the narrative through important recent events such as the Russian invasion of Georgia and the collapse of financial institutions in Europe and the United States in the fall of 2008.

## Ongoing Features That Enliven Student Interest and Understanding

**"Encountering the Past"**   Each chapter includes an essay on a significant issue of everyday life or popular culture. These essays explore a variety of subjects, including gladiatorial bouts and medieval games, smoking in early modern Europe, and the politics of rock music in the late twentieth century. These thirty essays, each of which includes an illustration and study questions, expand *The Western Heritage*'s rich coverage of social and cultural history.

**Recent Scholarship**   As in previous editions, changes in this edition reflect our determination to incorporate the most recent developments in historical scholarship and the concerns of professional historians.

**Maps and Illustrations**   To help students understand the relationship between geography and history, approximately half of the maps include relief features. One or two maps in each chapter feature interactive

exercises that can be found in MyHistoryLab. All maps have been carefully edited for accuracy. The text also contains close to 500 color and black and white illustrations, many of which are new to the Brief Sixth Edition.

**Pedagogical Features**   This edition retains the pedagogical features of previous editions, including glossary terms, chapter review questions, and questions accompanying all "Compare & Connect" and "Encountering the Past" features in the text. Each of these features is designed to make the text more accessible to students and to reinforce key concepts.

• **Summary** sections at the end of each chapter summarize the major themes of each chapter.

• **Chapter Review** questions help students focus on and interpret the broader themes of a chapter. These also can be used for class discussion and essay topics.

• **Chronologies** within each chapter help students organize a time sequence for key events.

• **Overview Tables** in each chapter summarize complex issues.

• **Quick Reviews,** found at key places in the margins of each chapter, encourage students to review important concepts.

• **Key Terms,** boldfaced in the text, are listed (with page reference) at the end of each chapter and defined in the book's glossary.

• **Suggested Readings** at the end of the book have been updated with new titles reflecting recent scholarship.

• **Map Explorations** and **Critical-Thinking Questions** prompt students to engage with maps, often in an interactive fashion. Each Map Exploration can be found at www.myhistorylab.com.

**A Note on Dates and Transliterations**   This edition of *The Western Heritage* continues the practice of using B.C.E. (before the common era) and C.E. (common era) instead of B.C. (before Christ) and A.D. (anno Domini, the year of the Lord) to designate dates. We also follow the most accurate currently accepted English transliterations of Arabic words. For example, today *Koran* has been replaced by the more accurate

*Qur'an*; similarly *Muhammad* is preferable to *Mohammed* and *Muslim* to *Moslem*.

## ANCILLARY INSTRUCTIONAL MATERIALS

The ancillary instructional materials that accompany *The Western Heritage: Teaching and Learning Classroom Edition*, Brief Sixth Edition, are designed to reinforce and enliven the richness of the past and inspire students with the excitement of studying the history of Western civilization.

### FOR INSTRUCTORS

*Instructor's Manual*    The *Instructor's Manual* contains chapter summaries, key points and vital concepts, and information on audiovisual resources that can be used in developing and preparing lecture presentations. (ISBN 0-205-73241-0)

**Test Item File**    The Test Item File includes over 1,500 multiple-choice, identification, map, and essay test questions. (ISBN 0-205-73240-2)

**MyTest**    MyTest is a browser-based test management program. The program allows instructors to select items from the Test Item File in order to create tests. It also allows for online testing. (ISBN 0-205-73298-4)

**The Instructor's Resource Center (www.pearsonhighered.com)**    Text-specific materials, such as the Instructor's Manual and the Test Item File, are available for downloading by adopters.

### FOR INSTRUCTORS AND STUDENTS

**myhistorylab MyHistoryLab (www.myhistorylab.com)**    MyHistoryLab provides students with an online package complete with the electronic textbook and numerous study aids. With several hundred primary sources, many of which are assignable and link to a gradebook, pre- and post-tests that link to a gradebook and result in individualized study plans, videos and images, as well as map activities with gradable quizzes, the site offers students a unique, interactive experience that brings history to life. The comprehensive site also includes a History Bookshelf with fifty of the most commonly assigned books in history classes and a History Toolkit with tutorials and helpful links. Other features include gradable assignments and chapter review materials as well as a Test Item File.

### FOR STUDENTS

*The Primary Source: Documents in Western Civilization* **DVD**    This DVD-ROM offers a rich collection of textual and visual sources—many never before available to a wide audience—and serves as an indispensable tool for working with sources. Extensively developed with the guidance of historians and teachers, *Primary Source: Documents in Western Civilization* includes over 800 sources in Western civilization history—from cave art, to text documents, to satellite images of Earth from space. All sources are accompanied by headnotes and focus questions and are searchable by topic, region, or theme. In addition, a built-in tutorial guides students through the process of working with documents. The DVD can be bundled with *The Western Heritage: Teaching and Learning Classroom Edition*, Brief Sixth Edition, at no charge. Please contact your Pearson Arts and Sciences representative for ordering information. (ISBN 0-13-134407-2)

Two-volume print version of *Primary Source: Documents in Western Civilization* is also available:

*Primary Sources in Western Civilization*, Volume 1: *To 1700, Second Edition* (ISBN 0-13-175583-8)

*Primary Sources in Western Civilization*, Volume 2: *Since 1400, Second Edition* (ISBN 0-13-175584-6)

Please contact your Pearson Arts and Sciences representative for ordering information.

*Lives and Legacies: Biographies in Western Civilization*, **Second Edition**    Extensively revised, *Lives and Legacies* includes brief, focused biographies of sixty individuals whose lives provide insight into the key developments of Western civilization. Each biography includes an introduction, prereading questions, and suggestions for additional reading. Available in two volumes:

*Lives and Legacies, Volume 1, Second Edition* (ISBN 0-205-64915-7)

*Lives and Legacies, Volume 2, Second Edition* (ISBN 0-205-64914-9)

**Western Civilization Study Site (www.ablongman.com/longmanwesterncivilization/)**    This course-based, open-access online companion provides both students and professors with links for further research as well as test questions in multiple choice, true/false, and fill-in-the-blank formats.

**Penguin Classics** Selected titles from the renowned Penguin Classics series can be bundled with *The Western Heritage: Teaching and Learning Classroom Edition*, Brief Sixth Edition, for a nominal charge. Please contact your Pearson Arts and Sciences sales representative for details.

***Longman Atlas of Western Civilization*** This 52-page atlas features carefully selected historical maps that provide comprehensive coverage for the major historical periods. Contact your Pearson Arts and Sciences representative for details. (ISBN 0-321-21626-1)

*The Prentice Hall Atlas of Western Civilization*, **Second Edition** Produced in collaboration with Dorling Kindersley, the leader in cartographic publishing, the updated second edition of *The Prentice Hall Atlas of Western Civilization* applies the most innovative cartographic techniques to present Western civilization in all of its complexity and diversity. Copies of the atlas can be bundled with *The Western Heritage: Teaching and Learning Classroom Edition*, Brief Sixth Edition, for a nominal charge. Contact your Pearson Arts and Sciences sales representative for details. (ISBN 0-13-604246-5)

***A Guide to Your History Course: What Every Student Needs to Know*** Written by Vincent A. Clark, this concise, spiral-bound guidebook orients students to the issues and problems they will face in the history classroom. Available at a discount when bundled with *The Western Heritage: Teaching and Learning Classroom Edition*, Brief Sixth Edition. (ISBN 0-13-185087-3)

*A Short Guide to Writing about History*, **Seventh Edition** Written by Richard Marius, late of Harvard University, and Melvin E. Page, Eastern Tennessee State University, this engaging and practical text helps students get beyond merely compiling dates and facts. Covering both brief essays and the documented resource paper, the text explores the writing and researching processes, identifies different modes of historical writing, including argument, and concludes with guidelines for improving style. (ISBN 0-205-67370-8)

**Interpretations of the Western World (www.pearsoncustom.com/custom-library/interpretations-of-the-western-world)** The selections in this customizable database of secondary source readings are grouped together topically so instructors can assign readings that illustrate different points of view on a given historical debate.

## ACKNOWLEDGMENTS

We are grateful to the scholars and teachers whose thoughtful and often detailed comments helped shape this revision:

Mark Baker, California State University, Bakersfield
Fred Baumgartner, Virginia Tech
Jane Bishop, The Citadel, The Military College of South Carolina
Eugene Boia, Cleveland State University
Kristen Burkholder, Oklahoma State University
Joseph Byrnes, Oklahoma State University
Anthony Cardoza, Loyola University, Chicago
Marcus Cox, The Citadel, The Military College of South Carolina
Delores Davison, Foothill College
Paul Deslandes, University of Vermont
Petra DeWitt, University of Missouri, Rolla
Richard Eller, Catawaba Valley Community College
Axel Fair-Schulz, State University of New York at Potsdam
Sean Field, University of Vermont
Shannon Fogg, Missouri S&T
Stephen Gibson, Ranken Technical College
Stephanie Hallock, Harford Community College
Michael Hickey, Bloomsburg University
Anthony Heideman, Range Community College
William Hudon, Bloomsburg University
Terry Jones, Oklahoma State University
Kevin Keating, Broward Community College
Michael Khodarkovsky, Loyola University, Chicago
Martha Kinney, Suffolk County Community College
Helena Krohn, Tidewater Community College
Eugene Larson, Los Angeles Pierce College
Karl Loewenstein, University of Wisconsin, Oshkosh
Arthur Lysiak, Bloomsburg University
William Martin, University of Utah
Lisa McClain, Boise State University
Daniel Miller, University of West Florida
Eva Mo, Meridian Junior College
Michelle Mouton, University of Wisconsin, Oshkosh
Tonia Sharlach Nash, Oklahoma State University
Charles Odahl, Boise State University
Mark Orsag, Doane College
Michael Pascale, SUNY at Suffolk, Farmingdale College
Neal Pease, University of Wisconsin, Milwaukee

Norman Raiford, Greenville Technical College

Pete Rottier, Cleveland State University

Thomas Rowland, University of Wisconsin at Oshkosh

Michael Rutz, University of Wisconsin, Oshkosh

Stephen Ruzicka, University of North Carolina at
    Greensboro

Mark Schumann, Eastern Michigan University

Patrick Speelman, The Citadel, The Military College of
    South Carolina

Frank W. Thackeray, Indiana University Southeast

Daniel Trifan, Missouri Western State University

Miriam Vivian, California State University, Bakersfield

Andrew Zimmerman, George Washington University

We would like to thank the dedicated people who helped produce this new edition. Our acquisitions editor, Charles Cavaliere; our development editor, Gerald Lombardi; our project manager, Rob DeGeorge; our production liaison, Lynn Savino Wendel; Maria Lange, who created the beautiful new design of this edition; Mary Ann Gloriande, our operations specialist; and Rebecca Dunn, production editor.

*D.K.*

*S.O.*

*F.M.T.*

**Donald Kagan** is Sterling Professor of History and Classics at Yale University, where he has taught since 1969. He received the A.B. degree in history from Brooklyn College, the M.A. in classics from Brown University, and the Ph.D. in history from Ohio State University. During 1958–1959 he studied at the American School of Classical Studies as a Fulbright Scholar. He has received three awards for undergraduate teaching at Cornell and Yale. He is the author of a history of Greek political thought, *The Great Dialogue* (1965); a four-volume history of the Peloponnesian war, *The Origins of the Peloponnesian War* (1969); *The Archidamian War* (1974); *The Peace of Nicias and the Sicilian Expedition* (1981); *The Fall of the Athenian Empire* (1987); a biography of Pericles, *Pericles of Athens and the Birth of Democracy* (1991); *On the Origins of War* (1995); and *The Peloponnesian War* (2003). He is coauthor, with Frederick W. Kagan, of *While America Sleeps* (2000). With Brian Tierney and L. Pearce Williams, he is the editor of *Great Issues in Western Civilization*, a collection of readings. He was awarded the National Humanities Medal for 2002 and was chosen by the National Endowment for the Humanities to deliver the Jefferson Lecture in 2004.

**Steven Ozment** is McLean Professor of Ancient and Modern History at Harvard University. He has taught Western Civilization at Yale, Stanford, and Harvard. He is the author of eleven books. *The Age of Reform, 1250–1550* (1980) won the Schaff Prize and was nominated for the 1981 National Book Award. Five of his books have been selections of the History Book Club: *Magdalena and Balthasar: An Intimate Portrait of Life in Sixteenth Century Europe* (1986); *Three Behaim Boys: Growing Up in Early Modern Germany* (1990); *Protestants: The Birth of a Revolution* (1992); *The Burgermeister's Daughter: Scandal in a Sixteenth Century German Town* (1996); and *Flesh and Spirit: Private Life in Early*

*Modern Germany* (1999). His most recent publications are *Ancestors: The Loving Family of Old Europe* (2001); *A Mighty Fortress: A New History of the German People* (2004); and "Why We Study Western Civ," *The Public Interest 158* (2005).

**Frank M. Turner** is John Hay Whitney Professor of History at Yale University and Director of the Beinecke Rare Book and Manuscript Library at Yale University, where he served as University Provost from 1988 to 1992. He received his B.A. degree at the College of William and Mary and his Ph.D. from Yale. He has received the Yale College Award for Distinguished Undergraduate Teaching. He has directed a National Endowment for the Humanities Summer Institute. His scholarly research has received the support of fellowships from the National Endowment for the Humanities and the Guggenheim Foundation and the Woodrow Wilson Center. He is the author of *Between Science and Religion: The Reaction to Scientific Naturalism in Late Victorian England* (1974); *The Greek Heritage in Victorian Britain* (1981), which received the British Council Prize of the Conference on British Studies and the Yale Press Governors Award; *Contesting Cultural Authority: Essays in Victorian Intellectual Life* (1993); and *John Henry Newman: The Challenge to Evangelical Religion* (2002). He has also contributed numerous articles to journals and has served on the editorial advisory boards of *The Journal of Modern History, Isis*, and *Victorian Studies*. He edited *The Idea of a University* by John Henry Newman (1996); *Reflections on the Revolution in France* by Edmund Burke (2003); and *Apologia Pro Vita Sua* and *Six Sermons by John Henry Newman* (2008). Between 1996 and 2006, he served as a Trustee of Connecticut College and between 2004 and 2008 as a member of the Connecticut Humanities Council. In 2003, Professor Turner was appointed Director of the Beinecke Rare Book and Manuscript Library at Yale University.

# WHAT IS THE WESTERN HERITAGE?

This book invites students and instructors to explore the Western Heritage. What is that heritage? The Western Heritage emerges from an evolved and evolving story of human actions and interactions, peaceful and violent, that arose in the eastern Mediterranean and then spread across the western Mediterranean into northern Europe and eventually to the American continents, and in their broadest impact, to the peoples of Africa and Asia as well.

The Western Heritage as a distinct portion of world history descends from the ancient Greeks. They saw their own political life based on open discussion of law and policy as different from that of Mesopotamia, Persia, and Egypt, where kings ruled without regard to public opinion. The Greeks invented the concept of citizenship, defining it as engagement in some form of self-government. Furthermore, through their literature and philosophy, the Greeks established the conviction, which became characteristic of the West, that reason can shape and analyze physical nature, politics, and morality.

The city of Rome, spreading its authority through military conquest across the Mediterranean world, embraced Greek literature and philosophy. Through their conquests and imposition of their law, the Romans created the Western world as a vast empire stretching from Egypt and Syria in the east to Britain in the west. Although the Roman Republic, governed by a Senate and popular political institutions, gave way after civil wars to the autocratic rule of the Roman Empire, the idea of a free republic of engaged citizens governed by public law and constitutional arrangements limiting political authority survived centuries of arbitrary rule by emperors. As in the rest of the world, the Greeks, the Romans, and virtually all other ancient peoples excluded women and slaves from political life and tolerated considerable social inequality.

In the early fourth century C.E., the Emperor Constantine reorganized the Roman Empire in two fundamental ways that reshaped the West. First, he moved the imperial capital from Rome to Constantinople (Istanbul), establishing separate emperors in the east and west. Thereafter, large portions of the western empire became subject to the rulers of Germanic tribes. In the confusion of these times, most of the texts embodying ancient philosophy, literature, and history became lost in the West, and for centuries Western Europeans were intellectually severed from that ancient heritage, which would later be recovered in a series of renaissances, or cultural rebirths, beginning in the eighth century.

Constantine's second fateful major reshaping of the West was his recognition of Christianity as the official religion of the empire. Christianity had grown out of the ancient monotheistic religion of the Hebrew people living in ancient Palestine. With the ministry of Jesus of Nazareth and the spread of his teachings by the Apostle Paul, Christianity had established itself as one of many religions in the empire. Because Christianity was monotheistic, Constantine's official embrace of it led to the eradication of pagan polytheism. Thereafter, the West became more or less coterminous with Latin Christianity, or that portion of the Christian Church acknowledging the Bishop of Rome as its head.

As the emperors' rule broke down, bishops became the effective political rulers in many parts of Western Europe. But the Christian Church in the West never governed without negotiation or conflict with secular rulers, and religious law never replaced secular law. Nor could secular rulers govern if they ignored the influence of the church. Hence, from the fourth century C.E. to the present day, rival claims to political and moral authority between ecclesiastical and political officials have characterized the West.

In the seventh century the Christian West faced a new challenge from the rise of Islam. This new monotheistic religion originating in the teachings of the prophet Muhammad arose on the Arabian Peninsula and spread through rapid conquests across North Africa and eventually into Spain, turning the Mediterranean into what one historian has termed "a Muslim lake." Between the eleventh and the thirteenth centuries, Christians attempted to reclaim the Holy Land from Muslim control in church-inspired military crusades that still resonate negatively in the Islamic world.

It was, however, in the Muslim world that most of the texts of ancient Greek and Latin learning survived and were studied, while intellectual life languished in the West. Commencing in the twelfth century, knowledge of those texts began to work its way back into Western Europe. By the fourteenth century European thinkers redefined themselves and their intellectual ambitions by recovering the literature and science

In his painting *The School of Athens*, the great Italian Renaissance painter Raphael portrayed the ancient Greek philosopher Plato and his student Aristotle engaged in debate. Plato, who points to the heavens, believed in a set of ideal truths that exists in its own realm distinct from the earth. Aristotle urged that all philosophy must be in touch with lived reality and confirms this position by pointing to the earth. Such debate has characterized the intellectual, political, and social experience of the West. Indeed, the very concept of "Western Civilization" has itself been subject to debate, criticism, and change over the centuries.
© Scala/Art Resource, NY

from the ancient world, reuniting Europe with its Graeco-Roman past.

From the twelfth through the eighteenth centuries, a new European political system slowly arose based on centralized monarchies characterized by large armies, navies, and bureaucracies loyal to the monarch and by the capacity to raise revenues. Whatever the personal ambitions of individual rulers, for the most part these monarchies recognized both the political role of local or national assemblies drawn from the propertied elites and the binding power of constitutional law on themselves. Also, in each of these monarchies, church officials and church law played important roles in public life. The monarchies, their military, and their expanding commercial economies became the basis for the extension of European and Western influence around the globe.

In the late fifteenth and early sixteenth centuries, two transforming events occurred. The first was the European discovery and conquest of the American continents, thus opening the Americas to Western institutions, religion, and economic exploitation. Over time the labor shortages of the Americas led to the forced migration of millions of Africans as slaves to the "New World." By the mid–seventeenth century, the West consequently embraced the entire transatlantic world and its multiracial societies.

Second, shortly after the American encounter, a religious schism erupted within Latin Christianity. Reformers rejecting both many medieval Christian doctrines as unbiblical and the primacy of the Pope in Rome established Protestant churches across much of northern Europe. As a consequence, for almost two centuries religious warfare between Protestants and Roman

Catholics overwhelmed the continent as monarchies chose to defend one side or the other. This religious turmoil meant that the Europeans who conquered and settled the Americas carried with them particularly energized religious convictions, with Roman Catholics dominating Latin America and English Protestants most of North America.

By the late eighteenth century, the idea of the West denoted a culture increasingly dominated by two new forces. First, science arising from a new understanding of nature achieved during the sixteenth and seventeenth centuries persuaded growing numbers of the educated elite that human beings can rationally master nature for ever-expanding productive purposes improving the health and well-being of humankind. From this era to the present, the West has been associated with advances in technology, medicine, and scientific research. Second, during the eighteenth century, a drive for economic improvement that vastly increased agricultural production and then industrial manufacturing transformed economic life, especially in Western Europe and later the United States. Both of these economic developments went hand in hand with urbanization and the movement of the industrial economy into cities where the new urban populations experienced major social dislocation.

During these decades certain Western European elites came to regard advances in agricultural and manufacturing economies that were based on science and tied to commercial expansion as "civilized" in contrast to cultures that lacked those characteristics. From these ideas emerged the concept of Western Civilization defined to suggest that peoples dwelling outside Europe or inside Europe east of the Elbe River were less than civilized. Whereas Europeans had once defined themselves against the rest of the world as free citizens and then later as Christians, they now defined themselves as "civilized." Europeans would carry this self-assured superiority into their nineteenth- and early-twentieth-century encounters with the peoples of Asia, Africa, and the Pacific.

During the last quarter of the eighteenth century, political revolution erupted across the transatlantic world. The British colonies of North America revolted. Then revolution occurred in France and spread across much of Europe. From 1791 through 1830, the Wars of Independence liberated Latin America from its European conquerors. These revolutions created bold new modes of political life, rooting the legitimacy of the state in some form of popular government and generally written constitutions. Thereafter, despite the presence of authoritarian governments on the European continent, the idea of the West, now including the new republics of the United States and Latin America, became associated with liberal democratic governments.

Furthermore, during the nineteenth century, most major European states came to identify themselves in terms of nationality—language, history, and ethnicity—rather than loyalty to a monarch. Nationalism eventually inflamed popular opinion and unloosed unprecedented political ambition by European governments.

These ambitions led to imperialism and the creation of new overseas European empires in the late nineteenth century. For the peoples living in European-administered Asian and African colonies, the idea and reality of the West embodied foreign domination and often disadvantageous involvement in a world economy. When in 1945 the close of World War II led to a sharp decline in European imperial authority, colonial peoples around the globe challenged that authority and gained independence. These former colonial peoples, however, often still suspected the West of seeking to control them. Hence, anticolonialism like colonialism before it redefined the West far from its borders.

Late-nineteenth-century nationalism and imperialism also unleashed with World War I in 1914 unprecedented military hostilities among European nations that spread around the globe, followed a quarter-century later by an even greater world war. As one result of World War I, revolution occurred in Russia with the establishment of the communist Soviet Union. During the interwar years a Fascist Party seized power in Italy and a Nazi Party took control of Germany. In response to these new authoritarian regimes, Western European powers and the United States identified themselves with liberal democratic constitutionalism, individual freedom, commercial capitalism, science and learning freely pursued, and religious liberty, all of which they defined as the Western Heritage. During the Cold War, conceived of as an East-West, democratic versus communist struggle that concluded with the collapse of the Soviet Union in 1991, the Western powers led by the United States continued to embrace those values in conscious opposition to the Soviet government, which since 1945 had also dominated much of Eastern Europe.

Since 1991, the West has again become redefined in the minds of many people as a world political and economic order dominated by the United States. Europe clearly remains the West, but political leadership has moved to North America. That American domination and recent American foreign policy have led throughout the West and elsewhere to much criticism of the United States.

Such self-criticism itself embodies one of the most important and persistent parts of the Western Heritage. From the Hebrew prophets and Socrates to the critics of European imperialism, American foreign policy, social inequality, and environmental devastation, voices in the West have again and again been raised to criticize often in the most strident manner the policies of Western governments and the thought, values, social conditions, and inequalities of Western societies.

Consequently, we study the Western Heritage not because the subject always or even primarily presents an admirable picture, but because the study of the Western Heritage like the study of all history calls us to an integrity of research, observation, and analysis that clarifies our minds and challenges our moral sensibilities. The challenge of history is the challenge of thinking, and it is to that challenge that his book invites its readers.

## QUESTIONS

1. How have people in the West defined themselves in contrast with civilizations of the ancient East, and later in contrast with Islamic civilization, and still later in contrast with less economically developed regions of the world? Have people in the West historically viewed their own civilization to be superior to civilizations in other parts of the world? Why or why not?

2. How did the Emperor Constantine's adoption of Christianity as the official religion of the Roman Empire change the concept of the West? Is the presence of Christianity still a determining characteristic of the West?

3. How has the geographical location of what has been understood as the West changed over the centuries?

4. In the past two centuries Western nations established empires around the globe. How did these imperial ventures and the local resistance to them give rise to critical definitions of the West that contrasted with the definitions that had developed in Europe and the United States? How have those non-Western definitions of the West contributed to self-criticism within Western nations?

5. How useful is the concept of Western civilization in understanding today's global economy and global communications made possible by the Internet? Is the idea of Western civilization synonymous with the concept of modern civilization? Do you think the concept of the West will once again be redefined ten years from now?

To view a video of the authors discussing the Western heritage, go to www.myhistorylab.com

# The
# WESTERN
# HERITAGE

# 1

# The Birth of Civilization

**This depiction of the Pharaoh Tutankahmun** (r. 1336–1327 B.C.E.) and his queen comes from his tomb, which was discovered in the 1920s. "King Tut" died at the age of eighteen.

Robert Frerck/Odyssey Production/Woodfin Camp & Associates

**How did Egyptian pharaohs use clothing, decoration, and ritual to emphasize their divine status?**

3

For hundreds of thousands of years, human beings lived by hunting and gathering what nature spontaneously provided. Only some 10,000 years ago did they begin to cultivate plants, domesticate animals, and settle in permanent communities. About 5,000 years ago, the Sumerians, who lived near the confluence of the Tigris and Euphrates Rivers (a region Greek geographers called "Mesopotamia," i.e., "between-rivers"), and the Egyptians who dwelt in the Nile Valley pioneered civilization. By the fourteenth century B.C.E., powerful empires had arisen and were struggling for dominance of the civilized world, but one of the region's smaller states probably had greater influence on the course of Western civilization. The modern West's major religions (Judaism, Christianity, and Islam) are rooted in the traditions of ancient Israel. ■

# EARLY HUMANS AND THEIR CULTURE

**HOW DID** life in the Neolithic Age differ from the Paleolithic?

**Homo sapiens** Our own species, which dates back roughly 200,000 years.

**culture** Way of life invented by a group and passed on by teaching.

**Paleolithic** Greek for "old stone"; the earliest period in cultural development that began with the first use of stone tools about a million years ago and continued until about 10,000 B.C.E.

Scientists estimate that creatures very much like humans appeared perhaps 3 to 5 million years ago, probably in Africa. Some 1 to 2 million years ago, erect and tool-using early humans spread over much of Africa, Europe, and Asia. Our own species, **Homo sapiens**, probably emerged some 200,000 years ago, and the earliest remains of fully modern humans date to about 90,000 years ago.

Humans, unlike other animals, are cultural beings. **Culture** may be defined as the ways of living built up by a group and passed on from one generation to another. It includes behavior such as courtship or child-rearing practices; material things such as tools, clothing, and shelter; and ideas, institutions, and beliefs. Because culture is learned and not inherited, it permits rapid adaptation to changing conditions, making possible the spread of humanity to almost all the lands of the globe.

## THE PALEOLITHIC AGE

Anthropologists designate early human cultures by their tools. The earliest period—the **Paleolithic** (from Greek, "old stone")—dates from the earliest use of stone tools some 1 million years ago to about 10,000 B.C.E. During this immensely long period, people were hunters, fishers, and gatherers, but not producers, of food. They learned to make and use increasingly sophisticated tools of stone and perishable materials like wood; they learned to make and control fire; and they acquired language and the ability to use it to pass on what they had learned.

These early humans, dependent on nature for food and vulnerable to wild beasts and natural disasters, may have developed responses to the world rooted in fear of the unknown—of the uncertainties of human life or the overpowering forces of nature. Evidence of religious faith and practice, as well as of magic, goes as far back as archaeology can take us. The sense that there is more to the world than meets the eye—in other words, the religious response to the world—seems to be as old as humankind.

The style of life and the level of technology of the Paleolithic period could support only a sparsely settled society. If hunters were too numerous, game would not suffice. In Paleolithic times, people were subject to the same natural and ecological constraints that today maintain a balance between wolves and deer in Alaska.

Evidence from Paleolithic art and from modern hunter-gatherer societies suggests that human life in the Paleolithic Age was probably characterized by a division of labor by sex. Men engaged in hunting, fishing, making tools and weapons, and fighting against other families, clans, and tribes. Women, less mobile because of childbearing, gathered nuts, berries, and wild grains, wove baskets, and made clothing. Women gathering food probably discovered how to plant and care for seeds. This knowledge eventually made possible the development of agriculture and animal husbandry.

# THE NEOLITHIC AGE

Only a few Paleolithic societies made the initial shift from hunting and gathering to agriculture. Anthropologists and archaeologists disagree as to why, but however it happened, some 10,000 years ago parts of what we now call the Near East began to change from a nomadic hunter-gatherer culture to a more settled agricultural one. This period is called the **Neolithic Age** (from Greek, "new stone"). Productive animals, such as sheep and goats, and food crops, such as wheat and barley, were first domesticated in the mountain foothills where they already lived or grew in the wild. Once domestication had taken place, people could move to areas where these plants and animals did not occur naturally, such as the river valleys of the Near East. The invention of pottery during the Neolithic Age enabled people to store surplus foods and liquids and to transport them, as well as to cook agricultural products that were difficult to eat or digest raw. Cloth was made from flax and wool. Crops required constant care from planting to harvest, so Neolithic farmers built permanent dwellings. Houses in a Neolithic village were normally all the same size and were built on the same plan, suggesting that most Neolithic villagers had about the same level of wealth and social status. A few items, such as stones and shells, were traded long distance, but Neolithic villages tended to be self-sufficient.

Two larger Neolithic settlements do not fit this village pattern. One was found at Çatal Höyük, in a fertile agricultural region about 150 miles south of Ankara, the capital of present-day Turkey. This was a large town covering over fifteen acres, with a population probably well over 6,000 people. The houses were clustered so closely that they had no doors, but were entered by ladders from the roofs. The agriculture, arts, and crafts of this town were astonishingly diversified and at a much higher level of attainment than other, smaller settlements of the period. The site of Jericho, an oasis around a spring near the Dead Sea, was occupied as early as 12,000 B.C.E. The inhabitants of Neolithic Jericho had a mixed agricultural, herding, and hunting economy and may have traded salt. These two sites show that the economy and the settlement patterns of the Neolithic period may be more complicated than many scholars have thought.

Throughout the Paleolithic Age, the human population had been small and relatively stable. The shift from food gathering to food production may not have been associated with an immediate change in population, but over time in the regions where agriculture and animal husbandry appeared, the number of human beings grew at an unprecedented rate. One reason for this is that farmers usually had larger families than hunters. When animals and plants were domesticated and brought to the river valleys, the relationship between human beings and nature was changed forever. People had learned to control nature, a vital prerequisite for the emergence of civilization. Some scholars refer to the dramatic changes in subsistence, settlement, technology, and population of this time as the Neolithic Revolution.

# THE BRONZE AGE AND THE BIRTH OF CIVILIZATION

Neolithic agricultural villages and herding cultures gradually replaced Paleolithic culture in much of the world. Then another major shift occurred, first in the plains along the Tigris and Euphrates Rivers in the region the Greeks and Romans called Mesopotamia (modern Iraq), later in the valley of the Nile River in Egypt, and somewhat later in India and the Yellow River basin in China. This shift was associated initially with the growth of towns alongside villages, creating a hierarchy of larger and smaller settlements in the same region. Some towns then grew into much larger urban centers and often drew population into them, so that nearby villages and towns

**At Ain Ghazal,** a Neolithic site in Jordan, several pits contained male and female statues made of clay modeled over a reed framework. Similar figures have been found at Jericho and other sites, all from the same period, about 8500–7000 B.C.E. They were probably used in religious rituals, perhaps connected with ancestor worship, as were plastered skulls, masks, carved heads, and other artifacts.

Archaeological Museum, Amman, Jordan, kingdom. Photograph © Erich Lessing, Art Resource, NY

**What clues might such statues offer about the nature of Neolithic religion?**

**Neolithic Age** "New stone" age, dating back 10,000 years to when people living in some parts of the Middle East made advances in the production of stone tools and shifted from hunting and gathering to agriculture.

declined. The urban centers, or cities, usually had monumental buildings, such as temples and fortifications. These were vastly larger than individual houses and could be built only by the sustained effort of hundreds and even thousands of people over many years. Elaborate representational artwork appeared, sometimes made of rare and imported materials. New technologies, such as smelting and the manufacture of metal tools and weapons, were characteristic of urban life. Commodities, like pottery and textiles that had been made in individual houses in villages, were mass produced in cities, which also were characterized by social stratification—that is, the grouping of people into classes based on factors such as control of resources, family, religious or political authority, and personal wealth. The earliest writing is also associated with the growth of cities.

These attributes—urbanism; technological, industrial, and social change; long-distance trade; and new methods of symbolic communication—are defining characteristics of the form of human culture called **civilization**. At about the time the earliest civilizations were emerging, someone discovered how to combine tin and copper to make a stronger and more useful material—bronze. Archaeologists coined the term **Bronze Age** to refer to the period 3100 to 1200 B.C.E. in the Near East and eastern Mediterranean.

**civilization** Stage in the evolution of organized society that has among its characteristics urbanism, long-distance trade, writing systems, and accelerated technological and social development.

**Bronze Age** (3100–1200 B.C.E.) Began with the increasing importance of metal that also ended the Stone Ages.

**Ötzi is the nickname** scientists have given to the remains of the oldest mummified human body yet discovered. This reconstruction shows his probable appearance and the clothing and weapons found on and with him.
Wieslav Smetek/Stern/Black Star

**What light does the practice of mummification shed on Neolithic beliefs about the afterlife?**

# EARLY CIVILIZATIONS TO ABOUT 1000 B.C.E.

**WHY DID** the first cities develop?

By 4000 B.C.E., people had settled in large numbers in the river-watered lowlands of Mesopotamia and Egypt. By about 3000 B.C.E., when the invention of writing gave birth to history, urban life and the organization of society into centralized states were well established in the valleys of the Tigris and Euphrates Rivers in Mesopotamia and of the Nile River in Egypt.

## MESOPOTAMIAN CIVILIZATION

The first civilization appears to have arisen in Mesopotamia. The region is divided into two ecological zones, roughly north and south of modern Baghdad. In the south (Babylonia), irrigation is vital; in the north (later Assyria), agriculture is possible with rainfall and wells. The oldest Mesopotamian cities seem to have been founded by a people called the Sumerians during the fourth millennium B.C.E. in the land of Sumer, which is the southern half of Babylonia. By 3000 B.C.E., the Sumerian city of Uruk was the largest city in the world. (See Map 1–1.) Colonies of people from Uruk built cities and outposts in northern Syria and southern Anatolia.

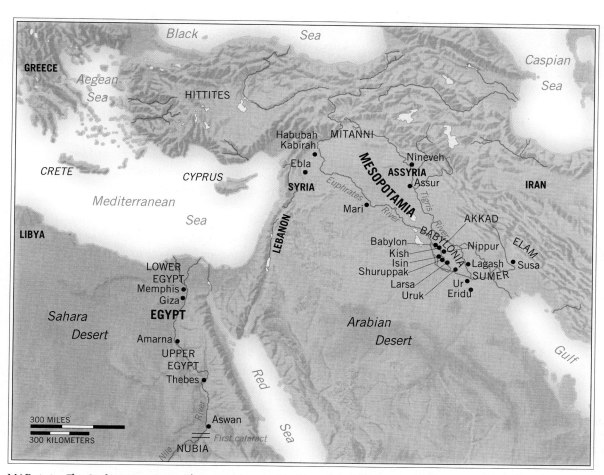

MAP 1–1 **The Ancient Near East** There were two ancient river-valley civilizations. Egypt was united into a single state, and Mesopotamia was long divided into a number of city-states.

**Based on** this map, what might explain why independent city-states were spread out in Mesopotamia while Egypt remained united in a single state?

From about 2800 to 2370 B.C.E., in what is called the Early Dynastic period, several Sumerian city-states, independent political units consisting of a major city and its surrounding territory, existed in southern Mesopotamia, arranged in north-south lines along the major watercourses. Among these cities were Uruk, Ur, Nippur, Shuruppak, and Lagash. Some of the city-states formed leagues among themselves that apparently had both political and religious significance. Quarrels over water and agricultural land led to incessant warfare, and in time, stronger towns and leagues conquered weaker ones and expanded to form kingdoms ruling several city-states.

Peoples who, unlike the Sumerians, mostly spoke Semitic languages (that is, languages in the same family as Arabic and Hebrew) occupied northern Mesopotamia and Syria. Many of these Semitic peoples absorbed aspects of Sumerian culture, especially writing. In northern Babylonia, the Mesopotamians believed the large city of Kish had the first kings in history. In the far east of this territory, not far from modern Baghdad, a people known as the Akkadians established their own kingdom at a capital city called Akkade, under their first king, Sargon, who had been a servant of the king of Kish.

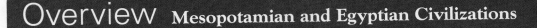

# Overview   Mesopotamian and Egyptian Civilizations

| | MESOPOTAMIA | EGYPT |
|---|---|---|
| **GOVERNMENT** | Different kinds of monarchies appeared in different times and places. Sumerian kings led armies; northern Assyrian kings were the chief priests; and, in the south, Babylonian kings and priests held separate offices. | *Nomarchs*, regional governors whose districts were called *nomes*, handled important local issues such as water management. However, Old Kingdom pharaohs held much of the power and resources. |
| **LANGUAGE AND LITERATURE** | Sumerians developed the world's first system of writing, *cuneiform*. Sumerian scribes had to learn several thousand characters; some stood for words, others for sounds. | Writing first appears in Egypt about 3000 B.C.E., the impetus most likely derived from Mesopotamian *cuneiform*. This writing system, *hieroglyphs*, was highly sophisticated, involving hundreds of picture signs. |
| **RELIGION** | The Mesopotamians were *polytheists*, worshipping many gods and goddesses, most of whom represented phenomena of nature (storms, earthquakes, etc.). The gods were grouped into families, heaven being organized like a community. | Egyptians had three different myths to explain the origin of the world, and each featured a different creator-god. Gods were represented in both human and animal form. Egyptians placed great trust in magic, oracles, and amulets to ward off evil. |
| **SOCIETY** | Parents usually arranged marriages. A marriage started out monogamous, but husbands could take a second wife. Women could own their own property and do business on their own. | Women's prime roles were connected with the management of the household. They could not hold office, go to scribal schools, or become artisans. Royal women often wielded considerable influence. In art, royal and nonroyal women are usually shown smaller than the male figures. |
| **SLAVERY** | The two main forms of slavery were chattel and debt slavery. Chattel slaves were bought and had no legal rights. Debt slaves, more common than chattel slaves, could not be sold, but they could redeem their freedom by paying off the loan. | Slaves did not become numerous in Egypt until the Middle Kingdom (about 2000 B.C.E.). Black Africans and Asians were captured in war and brought back as slaves. Slaves could be freed, but manumission was rare. |

The Akkadians conquered all the Sumerian city-states and invaded southwestern Iran and northern Syria. This was the first empire in history, having a heartland, provinces, and an absolute ruler. Sargon's name became legendary as the first great conqueror of history. His grandson, Naram-Sin, ruled from the Persian Gulf to the Mediterranean Sea, with a standardized administration, unheard-of wealth and power, and a grand style that to later Mesopotamians was a high point of their history. External attack and internal weakness destroyed the Akkadian Empire, but several smaller states flourished independently, notably Lagash in Sumer, under its ruler Gudea.

About 2125 B.C.E., the Sumerian city of Ur rose to dominance, and the rulers of the Third Dynasty of Ur established an empire built on the foundation of the Akkadian Empire, but far smaller. In this period, Sumerian culture and literature flourished. Epic poems were composed, glorifying the deeds of the ancestors of the kings of Ur. A highly centralized administration kept detailed records of agriculture, animal husbandry, commerce, and other matters. After little more than a century of prominence, the kingdom of Ur disintegrated in the face of famine and invasion. From the east, the Elamites attacked the city of Ur and captured the king. From the north and west, a Semitic-speaking people, the Amorites, invaded Mesopotamia in large numbers, settling around the Sumerian cities and eventually founding their own dynasties in some of them, such as at Uruk, Babylon, Isin, and Larsa.

For some time after the fall of Ur, there was relative peace in Babylonia under the Amorite kings of Isin, who used Sumerian at their court and considered themselves the successors of the kings of Ur. Eventually, another Amorite dynasty at the city of Larsa contested control of Babylonia, and a period of warfare began. A powerful

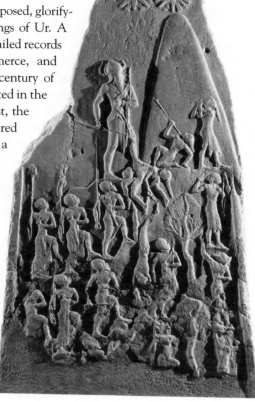

**The Victory Stele of Naram-Sin,** the Akkadian ruler, commemorates the king's campaign (ca. 2230 B.C.E.) against the Lullubi, a people living in the northern Zagros Mountains, along the eastern frontier of Mesopotamia. Kings set up monuments like this one in the courtyards of temples to record their deeds. They were also left in remote corners of the empire to warn distant peoples of the death and enslavement awaiting the king's enemies (pink sandstone).

Victory stele of Naram-Sin, King of Akkad, over the mountain-dwelling Lullubi, Mesopotamian, Akkadian Period, c. 2230 BC (pink sandstone). Louvre, Paris, France/The Bridgeman Art Library International Ltd.

**What do such monuments tell us about how Akkadian kings wanted to be seen by their subjects?**

**The Royal Standard of Ur,** a mosaic that dates from about 2750 B.C.E., shows officials from the Sumerian city of Ur celebrating a military victory as animals are brought in to be slaughtered for a feast.

British Museum, London, UK/Bridgeman Art Library

**Why did Sumerian kings go to war? What was the most important job of a king? Warrior, judge, priest, administrator?**

**Code of Hammurabi**

Stele of the Code of Laws of Hammurabi.
c. 1792-1750 BCE. Diorite. 225 x 65 cm. Found at
Susa. Photo: Ch. Larrieu. Reunion des Musées
Nationaux et Ecoli du Louvre, Paris/ Art Resource, NY

**How did the Code of Hammurabi reflect the social and political structure of Mesopotamia?**

**cuneiform**    Developed by the Sumerians as the very first writing system ever used, it used several thousand characters, some of which stood for words and some for sounds.

new dynasty at Babylon defeated Isin, Larsa, and other rivals and dominated Mesopotamia for nearly 300 years. Its high point was the reign of its most famous king, Hammurabi (r. ca. 1792–1750 B.C.E.), best known today for the collection of laws that bears his name. Hammurabi destroyed the great city of Mari on the Euphrates and created a kingdom embracing most of Mesopotamia.

The Code of Hammurabi reveals a society divided by class. There were nobles, commoners, and slaves, and the law did not treat all of them equally. In general, punishments were harsh, based literally on the principle of "an eye for an eye, a tooth for a tooth." Disputes over property and other complaints were heard in the first instance by local city assemblies of leading citizens and heads of families. Professional judges heard cases for a fee and held court near the city gate. In Mesopotamian trials, witnesses and written evidence had to be produced and a written verdict issued. False testimony was punishable by death. Cases of capital punishment could be appealed to the king. Hammurabi was closely concerned with the details of his kingdom, and his surviving letters often deal with minor local disputes.

About 1600 B.C.E., the Babylonian kingdom fell apart under the impact of invasions from the north by the Hittites, Hurrians, and Kassites, all non-Mesopotamian peoples.

**Government**    From the earliest historical records, it is clear that the Sumerians were ruled by monarchs in some form. The type of rule varied at different times and places. In later Assyria, for example, the king served as chief priest; in Babylonia, the priesthood was separate from royalty. Royal princesses were sometimes appointed as priestesses of important gods.

The government and the temples cultivated large areas of land to support their staffs and retinue. Laborers of low social status who were given rations of raw foods and other commodities to sustain them and their families did some of the work on this land. Citizens leased some land for a share of the crop and a cash payment. The government and temples owned large herds of sheep, goats, cattle, and donkeys. The Sumerian city-states exported wool and textiles to buy metals, such as copper, that were not available in Mesopotamia. Families and private individuals often owned their own farmland or houses in the cities, which they bought and sold as they liked.

**Writing and Mathematics**    Government, business, and scholarship required a good system of writing. The Sumerians invented the writing system now known as **cuneiform** (from the Latin *cuneus*, "wedge") because of the wedge-shaped marks they made by writing on clay tablets with a cut reed stylus. The Sumerian writing system used several thousand characters, some of which stood for words and some for sounds. Sumerian and Babylonian schools emphasized language and literature, accounting, legal practice, and mathematics, especially geometry, along with memorization of much abstract knowledge that had no relevance to everyday life. The ability to read and write was restricted to an elite who could afford to go to school. Success in school, however, and factors such as good family connections meant a literate Sumerian could find employment as a clerk, surveyor, teacher, diplomat, or administrator.

The Sumerians also began the development of mathematics. By the time of Hammurabi, the Mesopotamians were expert in many types of mathematics, including mathematical astronomy. The calendar the Mesopotamians used had twelve lunar months of thirty days each. To keep it in accordance with the solar year and the seasons, the Mesopotamians occasionally introduced a thirteenth month.

**Religion**    The Sumerians and their successors worshiped many gods and goddesses. They were visualized in human form, with human needs and weaknesses. Most of the gods were identified with some natural phenomenon such as the sky, fresh water, or storms. They differed from humans in their greater power, sublime position in the universe, and immortality. The Mesopotamians believed the human race was created to serve the gods and to relieve the gods of the necessity of providing for themselves. The gods were considered universal, but also residing in specific places, usually one important god or goddess in each city. The Mesopotamians were religiously tolerant and readily accepted the possibility that different people might have different gods.

The Mesopotamians had a vague and gloomy picture of the afterworld. The winged spirits of the dead were recognizable as individuals. They were confined to a dusty, dark netherworld, doomed to perpetual hunger and thirst unless someone offered them food and drink. Some spirits escaped to haunt human beings. There was no preferential treatment in the afterlife for those who had led religious or virtuous lives— everyone was in equal misery. Mesopotamian religion focused on problems of this world and how to lead a good life before dying. (See "Encountering the Past: Divination in Ancient Mesopotamia," page 14.)

Religion played a large part in the literature and art of Mesopotamia. Epic poems told of the deeds of the gods, such as how the world was created and organized, of a great flood the gods sent to wipe out the human race, and of the hero-king Gilgamesh, who tried to escape death by going on a fantastic journey to find the sole survivor of the great flood. (See "Compare & Connect: The Great Flood," on pages 12–13.) There were also many literary and artistic works that were not religious in character, so we should not imagine religion dominated all aspects of the Mesopotamians' lives. Religious architecture took the form of great temple complexes in the major cities. The most imposing religious structure was the *ziggurat*, a tower in stages, sometimes with a small chamber on top.

**Society**   Hundreds of thousands of cuneiform texts from the early third millennium B.C.E. until the third century B.C.E. give us a detailed picture of how peoples in ancient Mesopotamia conducted their lives and of the social conditions in which they lived.

Categorizing the laws of Hammurabi according to the aspects of life with which they deal reveals much about Babylonian life in his time. The third largest category of laws deals with commerce, relating to such issues as contracts, debts, rates of interest, security, and default. Business documents of Hammurabi's time show how people invested their money in land, moneylending, government contracts, and international trade. Some of these laws regulate professionals, such as builders, judges, and surgeons. The second largest category of laws deals with land tenure, especially land given by the king to soldiers and marines in return for their service. The letters of Hammurabi that deal with land tenure show he was concerned to uphold the individual rights of landholders against powerful officials who tried to take their land from them. The largest category of laws relates to the family and its maintenance and protection, including marriage, inheritance, and adoption.

Parents usually arranged marriages, and betrothal was followed by the signing of a marriage contract. The bride usually left her own family to join her husband's. The husband-to-be could make a bridal payment, and the father of the bride-to-be provided a dowry for his daughter in money, land, or objects. A marriage started out monogamous, but a husband whose wife was childless or sickly could take a second wife. Sometimes husbands also sired children from domestic slave women. Women could possess their own property and do business on their own. Women divorced by their husbands without good cause could get their dowry back. A woman seeking divorce

**QUICK REVIEW**

**Mesopotamian Religion**

- ◆ Mesopotamians produced a large body of sacred literature
- ◆ *Ziggurat*: a huge terraced mound of mudbricks topped by a temple
- ◆ Gods were grouped into families and heaven was organized like a human community

# THE GREAT FLOOD

Stories of a great deluge appeared in many cultures at various times in the ancient world. In the Mesopotamian world the earliest known story of a great flood sent by the gods to destroy mankind appeared in the Sumerian civilization. Later the story was included in the Gilgamesh epic in a Semitic language. The great flood of Noah's time appears in the book of Genesis in the Hebrew Bible.

1. In what ways is the story from the *Epic of Gilgamesh* similar to the Story of Noah in the Hebrew Bible?

2. How is the account of a great flood in the Story of Noah different from that in the *Epic of Gilgamesh*?

3. What is the significance of the similarities and differences between the two accounts?

## I. THE BABYLONIAN STORY OF THE FLOOD

*The passage that follows is part of the Babylonian* Epic of Gilgamesh. *An earlier independent Babylonian story of the flood suggested that the gods sent a flood because there were too many people on the earth. A version of this story was later combined with the* Epic of Gilgamesh, *about a legendary king who became terrified of death when his best friend and companion died. After many adventures, Gilgamesh crossed the distant ocean and the "waters of death" to ask Utanapishtim, who, with his wife, was the only survivor of the great flood, the secret of eternal life. In response, Utanapishtim narrated the story of the great flood to show that his own immortality derived from a onetime event in the past, so Gilgamesh could not share his destiny.*

Six days and seven nights
The wind continued, the deluge and windstorm
  levelled the land.
When the seventh day arrived,
The windstorm and deluge left off their battle,
Which had struggled, like a woman in labor.
The sea grew calm, the tempest stilled, the deluge
  ceased.
I looked at the weather, stillness reigned,
And the whole human race had turned into clay.
The landscape was flat as a rooftop.
I opened the hatch, sunlight fell upon my face.
Falling to my knees, I sat down weeping,
Tears running down my face.
I looked at the edges of the world, the borders of the sea,
At twelve times sixty double leagues the periphery
  emerged.
The boat had come to rest on Mount Nimush,
Mount Nimush held the boat fast, not letting it move.
One day, a second day Mount Nimush held the boat
  fast, not letting it move.
A third day, a fourth day Mount Nimush held the boat
  fast, not letting it move.
A fifth day, a sixth day Mount Nimush held the boat
  fast, not letting it move.
When the seventh day arrived,
I brought out a dove and set it free.
The dove went off and returned,
No landing place came to its view, so it turned back.
I brought out a swallow and set it free,
The swallow went off and returned,

No landing space came to its view, so it turned back.
I brought out a raven and set it free.
The raven went off and saw the ebbing of the waters.
It ate, preened, left droppings, did not turn back.
I released all to the four directions,
I brought out an offering and offered it to the four
  directions.
I set up an incense burner on the summit of the
  mountain,
I arranged seven and seven cult vessels,
I heaped reeds, cedar, and myrtle in their bowls.
The gods smelled the savor,
The gods smelled the sweet savor,
The gods crowded round the sacrificer like flies.
As soon as the Belet-ili arrived,
She held up the great fly-ornaments that Anu had
  made in his ardor:
'O ye gods, as surely as I shall not forget these lapis
  pendants on my neck,
'I shall be mindful of these days and not forget, not ever!
'The gods should come to the incense burner,
'But Enlil should not come to the incense burner,
'For he, irrationally, brought on the flood,
'And marked my people for destruction!'
As soon as Enlil arrived,
He saw the boat, Enlil flew into a rage,
He was filled with fury at the gods:
'Who came through alive? No man was to survive
  destruction!'
Ninurta made ready to speak,
Said to the valiant Enlil:

'Who but Ea could contrive such a thing?
'For Ea alone knows every artifice.'
Ea made ready to speak,
Said to the valiant Enlil:
'You, O valiant one, are the wisest of the gods,
'How could you, irrationally, have brought on the flood?
'Punish the wrong-doer for his wrong-doing,
    'Punish the transgressor for his transgression,
      'But be lenient, lest he be cut off,
        'Bear with him, lest he [. . .].
      'Instead of your bringing on a flood,
      'Let the lion rise up to diminish the human race!
      'Instead of your bringing on a flood,
        'Let the wolf rise up to diminish the human race!
      'Instead of your bringing on a flood,
        'Let famine rise up to wreak havoc in the land!
      'Instead of your bringing on a flood,
      'Let pestilence rise up to wreak havoc in the land!
    'It was not I who disclosed the secret of the great gods,
    'I made Atrahasis have a dream and so he heard the
      secret of the gods.
'Now then, make some plan for him.'
  Then Enlil came up into the boat,
  Leading me by the hand, he brought me up too.
He brought my wife up and had her kneel beside me.
He touched our brows, stood between us to bless us:
'Hitherto Utanapishtim has been a human being,
'Now Utanapishtim and his wife shall become like us gods.
'Utanapishtim shall dwell far distant at the source of
  the rivers.'

**The Flood Tablet (Tablet XI),** which relates part of the *Epic of Gilgamesh.* The eleventh tablet describes the meeting of Gilgamesh and Utanapishtim who, along with his wife, survived a great flood that destroyed the rest of humankind.

Art Resource/The British Museum Great Court Ltd. © Copyright The British Museum

**What does the fact that the *Epic of Gilgamesh* was inscribed on a tablet tell us about its place in Mesopotamian culture?**

Source: "The Babylonian Story of the Flood" from *The Babylonian Epic of Gilgamesh,* in *The Epic of Gilgamesh,* trans. by Benjamin R. Foster. Copyright © 2001 by W.W. Norton & Company. Used by permission of W.W. Norton & Company, Inc.

## II. NOAH'S FLOOD – GENESIS 7.11–9.11

In the six hundredth year of Noah's life, in the second month, on the seventeenth day of the month, on that day all the fountains of the great deep burst forth, and the windows of the heavens were opened. The rain fell on the earth forty days and forty nights. . . .

At the end of forty days Noah opened the window of the ark that he had made and sent out the raven; and it went to and fro until the waters were dried up from the earth. Then he sent out the dove from him, to see if the waters had subsided from the face of the ground; but the dove found no place to set its foot, and it returned to him to the ark, for the waters were still on the face of the whole earth. So he put out his hand and took it and brought it into the ark with him. He waited another seven days, and again he sent out the dove from the ark; and the dove came back to him in the evening, and there in its beak was a freshly plucked olive leaf; so Noah knew that the waters had subsided from the earth. Then he waited another seven days, and sent out the dove; and it did not return to him any more. . . .

Then God said to Noah and to his sons with him, "As for me, I am establishing my covenant with you and your descendants after you, and with every living creature that is with you, the birds, the domestic animals, and every animal of the earth with you, as many as came out of the ark. I establish my covenant with you, that never again shall all flesh be cut off by the waters of a flood, and never again shall there be a flood to destroy the earth."

# ENCOUNTERING THE PAST

## DIVINATION IN ANCIENT MESOPOTAMIA

*Mesopotamians believed the world was full of omens— events that, if properly interpreted, would enable them to predict the future. They did not view the future as a predestined, unalterable fate, but they assumed that if they knew what was going to happen, appropriate rituals and planning would enable them to head off unfavorable developments. Divination is the practice of foretelling the future by magical or occult means, and the Mesopotamians were pioneers of the art.*

One of the earliest and most trusted divination methods involved the examination of the entrails of the animals offered at religious sacrifices. Deformities of organs were believed to be warnings from the gods. Clay models were made of these organs, and together with a report of the events they were believed to have predicted, these models were preserved in a kind of reference library for temple diviners.

Animal sacrifice was expensive and used most commonly by the state. Ordinary Mesopotamians relied on more economical methods to obtain the information they needed to plan for their futures. The seers who served them examined patterns made by the smoke of burning incense or oil poured onto water. Chance remarks of strangers, facial features, dreams, and birth defects were all considered significant. The movements of the heavenly bodies were believed to be extremely portentous for events on earth. Mesopotamian faith in astrology had the positive effect of gathering data that led to advances in astronomy. Any divergence from what were considered normal forms or patterns was considered a portent of disaster and called for prayers and magic to ward off suspected dangers.

**Ancient Mesopotamians used** astrology to predict the future. This calendar from the city of Uruk dates from the first millennium B.C.E. and is based on careful observation of the heavens.

Astrological calendar. From Uruk, Mesopotamia. Babylonian, 1st mill. B.C.E. Museum of Oriental Antiquities, Istanbul, Turkey. Photograph © Erich Lessing/Art Resource, NY

**How did belief in the ability of humans to divine the future promote the study of astronomy in Mesopotamia?**

HOW DID the Mesopotamians try to predict the future, and what did they do with the information they obtained?

could also recover her dowry if her husband could not convict her of wrongdoing. A married woman's place was thought to be in the home, but hundreds of letters between wives and husbands show them as equal partners in the ventures of life. Single women who were not part of families could set up in business on their own, often as tavern owners or moneylenders, or could be associated with temples, sometimes working as midwives and wet nurses, or taking care of orphaned children.

**Slavery: Chattel Slaves and Debt Slaves** There were two main types of slavery in Mesopotamia: chattel and debt slavery. Chattel slaves were bought like any other piece of property and had no legal rights. They were often non-Mesopotamians bought from slave merchants. Prisoners of war could also be enslaved. Chattel slaves were expensive luxuries during most of Mesopotamian history. They were used in domestic service rather than in production, such as fieldwork. A wealthy household might have five or six slaves, male and female.

Debt slavery was more common than chattel slavery. If debtors had pledged themselves or members of their families as surety for a loan, they became the slave of the creditor; their labor went to pay the interest on the loan. Debt slaves could not be sold but could redeem their freedom by paying off the loan. True chattel slavery did not become common until the Neo-Babylonian period (612–539 B.C.E.).

Although laws against fugitive slaves or slaves who denied their masters were harsh, Mesopotamian slavery appears enlightened compared with other slave systems in history. Slaves were generally of the same people as their masters. They had been enslaved because of misfortune from which their masters were not immune, and they generally labored alongside them. Slaves could engage in business and, with certain restrictions, hold property. They could marry free men or women, and the resulting children would normally be free. A slave who acquired the means could buy his or her freedom. Children of a slave by a master might be allowed to share his property after his death. Nevertheless, slaves were property, subject to an owner's will and had little legal protection.

## EGYPTIAN CIVILIZATION

As Mesopotamian civilization arose in the valley of the Tigris and Euphrates, another great civilization emerged in Egypt, centered on the Nile River. From its sources in Lake Victoria and the Ethiopian highlands, the Nile flows north some 4,000 miles to the Mediterranean. Ancient Egypt included the 750-mile stretch of smooth, navigable river from Aswan to the sea. South of Aswan the river's course is interrupted by several cataracts—rocky areas of rapids and whirlpools.

The Egyptians recognized two sets of geographical divisions in their country. **Upper** (southern) **Egypt** consisted of the narrow valley of the Nile. **Lower** (northern) **Egypt** referred to the broad triangular area, named by the Greeks after their letter "delta," formed by the Nile as it branches out to empty into the Mediterranean. They also made a distinction between what they termed the "black land," the dark fertile fields along the Nile, and the "red land," the desert cliffs and plateaus bordering the valley.

**Upper Egypt**   Narrow valley extending 650 miles from Aswan to the border of Lower Egypt.

**Lower Egypt**   The Nile's 100-mile deep, triangularly shaped delta.

The Nile alone made agriculture possible in Egypt's desert environment. Each year the rains of central Africa caused the river to rise over its floodplain, cresting in September and October. In places the plain extends several miles on either side; elsewhere the cliffs slope down to the water's edge. When the floodwaters receded, they left a rich layer of organically fertile silt. The construction and maintenance of canals, dams, and irrigation ditches to control the river's water, together with careful planning and organization of planting and harvesting, produced an agricultural prosperity unmatched in the ancient world.

The Nile served as the major highway connecting Upper and Lower Egypt. There was also a network of desert roads running north and south, as well as routes across the eastern desert to the Sinai and the Red Sea. Other tracks led to oases in the western desert. Thanks to geography and climate, Egypt was more isolated and enjoyed far more security than Mesopotamia. This security, along with the predictable flood calendar, gave

## MAJOR PERIODS IN MESOPOTAMIAN AND EGYPTIAN HISTORY

**MESOPOTAMIA**

| | |
|---|---|
| ca. 3500 B.C.E. | Cities appear |
| ca. 2800–2370 B.C.E. | First Dynasties |
| 2370–2205 B.C.E. | Sargon's empire |
| 2125–2027 B.C.E. | III Dynasty of Ur |
| 1792–1750 B.C.E. | Reign of Hammurabi |
| ca. 1600 B.C.E. | Fall of Amoritic Babylon |

**EGYPT**

| | |
|---|---|
| ca. 3100–2700 B.C.E. | Early Dynastic Period (dynasties I–II) |
| ca. 2700–2200 B.C.E. | The Old Kingdom (dynasties III–VI) |
| 2200–2025 B.C.E. | I Intermediate Period (dynasties VII–XI) |
| 2025–1630 B.C.E. | The Middle Kingdom (dynasties XII–XIII) |
| 1630–1550 B.C.E. | II Intermediate Period (dynasties XIV–XVII) |
| 1550–1075 B.C.E. | The New Kingdom (dynasties XVIII–XX) |

**pharaoh**    The god-king of ancient Egypt.

Egyptian civilization a more optimistic outlook than the civilizations of the Tigris and Euphrates, which were more prone to storms, flash floods, and invasions.

The 3,000-year span of ancient Egyptian history is traditionally divided into 31 royal dynasties, from the first, said to have been founded by Menes, the king who originally united Upper and Lower Egypt, to the last, established by Alexander the Great, who conquered Egypt in 332 B.C.E. (as we see in Chapter 3).

The unification of Upper and Lower Egypt was vital, for it meant the entire river valley could benefit from an unimpeded distribution of resources. Three times in its history, Egypt experienced a century or more of political and social disintegration, known as Intermediate Periods. During these eras, rival dynasties often set up separate power bases in Upper and Lower Egypt until a strong leader reunified the land.

**The Old Kingdom (2700–2200 B.C.E.)**    The Old Kingdom represents the culmination of the cultural and historical developments of the Early Dynastic period. For over four hundred years, Egypt enjoyed internal stability and great prosperity. During this period, the **pharaoh** was a king who was also a god. From his capital at Memphis, the god-king administered Egypt according to set principles, prime among them being *maat*, an ideal of order, justice, and truth. In return for the king's building and maintaining temples, the gods preserved the equilibrium of the state and ensured the king's continuing power, which was absolute. Since the king was obligated to act infallibly in a benign and beneficent manner, the welfare of the people of Egypt was automatically guaranteed and safeguarded.

Nothing better illustrates the nature of Old Kingdom royal power than the pyramids built as pharaonic tombs. Beginning in the Early Dynastic period, kings constructed increasingly elaborate burial complexes in Upper Egypt. Djoser, a Third Dynasty king, was the first to erect a monumental six-step pyramid of hard stone. Subsequent pharaohs built other stepped pyramids until Snefru, the founder of the Fourth Dynasty, converted a stepped to a true pyramid over the course of putting up three monuments.

His son Khufu (Cheops in the Greek version of his name) chose the desert plateau of Giza, south of Memphis, as the site for the largest pyramid ever constructed. Its dimensions are prodigious: 481 feet high, 756 feet long on each side, and its base covering 13.1 acres. The pyramid is made of 2.3 million stone blocks averaging 2.5 tons each. It is also a geometrical wonder, deviating from absolutely level and square only by the most minute measurements using the latest modern devices. Khufu's successors, Khafre (Chephren) and Menkaure (Mycerinus), built equally perfect pyramids at Giza, and together, the three constitute one of the most extraordinary achievements in human history.

The pyramids are remarkable not only for the great technical skill they demonstrate, but also for the concentration of resources they represent. They are evidence that the pharaohs controlled vast wealth and had the power to focus and organize enormous human effort over the years it took to build each pyramid. They also provide a visible indication of the nature of the Egyptian state: The pyramids, like the pharaohs, tower above the land; the low tombs at their base, like the officials buried there, seem to huddle in relative unimportance.

Originally, the pyramids and their associated cult buildings contained statuary, offerings, and all the pharaoh needed for the afterlife. Despite great precautions and ingenious concealment methods, tomb robbers took nearly everything, leaving little for modern archeologists to recover. Several full-size wooden boats have been found, however, still in their own graves at the base of the pyramids, ready for the pharaoh's journeys in the next world. Recent excavations have uncovered remains of the large town built to house the thousands of pyramid builders, including the farmers who worked at Giza during the annual flooding of their fields.

Numerous officials, both members of the royal family and nonroyal men of ability, aided the god-kings. The highest office was the *vizier* (a modern term from Arabic). Central offices dealing with granaries, surveys, assessments, taxes, and salaries administered the land. Water management was local rather than on a national level. Upper and Lower Egypt were divided into **nomes**, or districts, each governed by a *nomarch*, or governor, and his local officials. The kings could also appoint royal officials to oversee groups of *nomes* or to supervise pharaonic landholdings throughout Egypt.

**nomes**  Egyptian districts ruled by regional governors who were called nomarchs.

**The First Intermediate Period and Middle Kingdom (2200–1786 B.C.E.)**  Toward the end of the Old Kingdom, for a combination of political and economic reasons, absolute pharaonic power waned as the nomarchs and other officials became more independent and influential. About 2200 B.C.E., the Old Kingdom collapsed and gave way to the decentralization and disorder of the First Intermediate Period, which lasted until about 2052 B.C.E. Eventually, the kings of Dynasty 11, based in Thebes in Upper Egypt, defeated the rival Dynasty 10, based in a city south of Giza.

Amunemhet I, the founder of Dynasty 12 and the Middle Kingdom, probably began his career as a successful vizier under an Eleventh Dynasty king. After reuniting Upper and Lower Egypt, he turned his attention to making three important and long-lasting administrative changes. First, he moved his royal residence from Thebes to a brand-new town, just south of the old capital at Memphis, signaling a fresh start rooted in past glories. Second, he reorganized the nome structure by more clearly defining the nomarchs' duties to the state, granting them some local autonomy within the royal structure. Third, he established a co-regency system to smooth transitions from one reign to another.

Yet the events of the First Intermediate Period had irrevocably changed the nature of Egyptian kingship. Gone was the absolute, distant god-king; the king was now more directly concerned with his people. In art, instead of the supremely confident faces of the Old Kingdom pharaohs, the Middle Kingdom rulers seem thoughtful, careworn, and brooding.

Egypt's relations with its neighbors became more aggressive during the Middle Kingdom. To the south, royal fortresses were built to control Nubia and the growing trade in African resources. To the north and east, Syria and Palestine increasingly came under Egyptian influence, even as fortifications sought to prevent settlers from the Levant from moving into the Delta.

**The Second Intermediate Period and the New Kingdom (1630–1075 B.C.E.)**  For some unknown reason, during Dynasty 13, the kingship changed hands rapidly and the western Delta established itself as an independent Dynasty 14, ushering in the Second Intermediate Period. The eastern Delta, with its expanding Asiatic populations, came under the control of the Hyksos (Dynasty 15) and minor Asiatic kings (Dynasty 16). Meanwhile, the Dynasty 13 kings left their northern capital and regrouped in Thebes (Dynasty 17).

Though much later sources describe the Hyksos ("chiefs of foreign lands" in Egyptian) as ruthless invaders from parts unknown, they were almost certainly Amorites from the Levant, part of the gradual infiltration of the Delta during the Middle Kingdom. After nearly a century of rule, the Hyksos were expelled, a process begun by Kamose, the last king of Dynasty 17, and completed by his brother Ahmose, the first king of Dynasty 18 and the founder of the New Kingdom.

**The pyramids of Giza.**

Peter Wilson © Dorling Kindersley

During Dynasty 18, Egypt pursued foreign expansion with renewed vigor. Military expeditions reached as far north as the Euphrates in Syria, with frequent campaigns in the Levant. To the south, major Egyptian temples were built in the Sudan, almost 1,300 miles from Memphis. Egypt's economic and political power was at its height.

Egypt's position was reflected in the unprecedented luxury and cosmopolitanism of the royal court and in the ambitious palace and temple projects undertaken throughout the country. Perhaps to foil tomb robbers, the Dynasty 18 pharaohs were the first to cut their tombs deep into the rock cliffs of a desolate valley in Thebes, known today as the Valley of the Kings. To date, only one intact royal tomb has been discovered there, that of the young Dynasty 18 king Tutankhamun, and even it had been disturbed shortly after his death. The thousands of goods buried with him, many of them marvels of craftsmanship, give an idea of Egypt's material wealth during this period.

Following the premature death of Tutankhamun in 1323 B.C.E., a military commander named Horemheb assumed the kingship, which passed in turn to his own army commander, Ramses I. The pharaohs Ramessides of Dynasty 19 undertook numerous monumental projects, among them Ramses II's rock-cut temples at Abu Simbel, south of the First Cataract, which had to be moved to a higher location when the Aswan High Dam was built in the 1960s. There and elsewhere, Ramses II left textual and pictorial accounts of his battle in 1285 B.C.E. against the Hittites at Kadesh on the Orontes in Syria. Sixteen years later, the Egyptians and Hittites signed a formal peace treaty, forging an alliance against an increasingly volatile political situation in the Mideast and eastern Mediterranean during the thirteenth century B.C.E.

Merneptah, one of the hundred offspring of Ramses II, held off a hostile Libyan attack, as well as incursions by the Sea Peoples, a loose coalition of Mediterranean raiders who seem to have provoked and taken advantage of unsettled conditions. One of Merneptah's inscriptions commemorating his military triumphs contains the first known mention of Israel.

Despite his efforts, by the end of Dynasty 20, Egypt's period of imperial glory had passed. The next thousand years witnessed a Third Intermediate Period, a Saite Renaissance, Persian domination, conquest by Alexander the Great, the Ptolemaic period, and finally, defeat at the hands of Rome in 30 B.C.E.

**Language and Literature**    Writing first appears in Egypt about 3000 B.C.E. The writing system, dubbed **hieroglyphics** ("sacred carvings") by the Greeks, was highly sophisticated, involving hundreds of picture signs that remained relatively constant in the way they were rendered for over 3,000 years. A cursive version of hieroglyphics was used for business documents and literary texts, which were penned rapidly in black and red ink. The Egyptian language, part of the Afro-Asiatic (or Hamito-Semitic) family, evolved through several stages—Old, Middle, and Late Egyptian, Demotic, and Coptic—thus giving it a history of continuous recorded use well into the medieval period.

Egyptian literature includes narratives, myths, books of instruction in wisdom, letters, religious texts, and poetry, written on papyri, limestone flakes, and postherds. Unfortunately only a small fraction of this enormous literature has survived, and many texts are incomplete.

**Religion: Gods and Temples**    Egyptian religion encompasses a multitude of concepts that often seem mutually contradictory to us. Three separate explanations for the origin of the universe were formulated, each based in the philosophical traditions of a venerable Egyptian city.

The Egyptian gods, or pantheon, similarly defy neat categorization, in part because of the common tendency to combine the character and function of one or more

**hieroglyphics**    ("sacred carving") Greek name for Egyptian writing. The writing was often used to engrave holy texts on monuments.

gods. Amun, one of the eight entities in the Hermopolitan cosmogony, provides a good example. Thebes, Amun's cult center, rose to prominence in the Middle Kingdom. In the New Kingdom, Amun was elevated above his seven cohorts and took on aspects of the sun god Re to become Amun-Re.

Not surprisingly in a nearly rainless land, solar cults and mythologies were highly developed. Much thought was devoted to conceptualizing what happened as the sun god made his perilous way through the underworld in the night hours between sunset and sunrise.

The Eighteenth Dynasty was one of several periods during which solar cults were in ascendancy. Early in his reign, Amunhotep IV promoted a single, previously minor aspect of the sun, the Aten ("disk") above Re himself and the rest of the gods. He declared that the Aten was the creator god who brought life to humankind and all living beings, with himself and his queen Nefertiti the sole mediators between the Aten and the people. For religious and political reasons still imperfectly understood, he went further, changing his name to Akhenaten ("the effective spirit of the Aten"), building a new capital called Akhetaten ("the horizon of the Aten") near Amarma north of Thebes, and chiseling out the name of Amun from inscriptions everywhere. Shortly after his death, Amarna was abandoned and partially razed. During the reigns of Akhenaten's successors, Tutankhamun (born Tutankhaten) and Horemheb, Amun was restored to his former position, and Akhenaten's monuments were defaced and even demolished.

In representations, Egyptian gods have human bodies, possess human or animal heads, and wear crowns, celestial disks, or thorns. The lone exception is the Aten, made nearly abstract by Akhenaten, who altered its image to a plain disk with solar rays ending in small hands holding the hieroglyphic sign for life to the nostrils of Akhenaten and Nefertiti. The gods were thought to reside in their cult centers, where, from the New Kingdom on, increasingly ostentatious temples were built, staffed by full-time priests. Though the ordinary person could not enter a temple precinct, great festivals took place for all to see. During Amun's major festival of Opet, the statue of the god traveled in a divine boat along the Nile, whose banks were thronged with spectators.

**Worship and the Afterlife**    For most Egyptians, worship took place at small local shrines. They left offerings to the chosen gods, as well as votive inscriptions with simple prayers. Private houses often had niches containing busts for ancestor worship and statues of household deities. The Egyptians strongly believed in the power of magic, dreams, and oracles, and they possessed a wide variety of amulets to ward off evil.

The Egyptians thought the afterlife was full of dangers, which could be overcome by magical means, among them the spells in the *Book of the Dead*. The goals were to join and be identified with the gods, especially Osiris, or to sail in the "boat of millions." Originally only the king could hope to enjoy immortality with the gods, but gradually this became available to all. Since the Egyptians believed the preservation of the body was essential for continued existence in the afterlife, early on they developed mummification, a process that took seventy days by the New Kingdom. How lavishly tombs were prepared and decorated varied over the course of Egyptian history and in accordance with the wealth of a family.

**Women in Egyptian Society**    It is difficult to assess the position of women in Egyptian society, because our pictorial and textual evidence comes almost entirely from male sources. Women's prime roles were connected with the management of the household. They could not hold office, go to scribal schools, or become artisans. Nevertheless, women could own and control property, sue for divorce, and, at least in theory, enjoy equal legal protection.

**An elaborately decorated mummy coffin.**

Peter Hayman © Dorling Kindersley

***The Book of the Dead.*** The Egyptians believed in the possibility of life after death through the god Osiris. Aspects of each person's life had to be tested by forty-two assessor-gods before the person could be presented to Osiris. In the scene from a papyrus manuscript of the *Book of the Dead*, the deceased and his wife (on the left) watch the scales of justice weighing his heart (on the left side of the scales) against the feather of truth. The jackal-headed god Anubis also watches the scales, and the ibis-headed god Thoth keeps the record.

British Museum, London, UK/The Bridgeman Art Library International Ltd.

**How did Egyptian beliefs about the afterlife differ from those of the Mesopotamians?**

Royal women often wielded considerable influence, particularly in the Eighteenth Dynasty. The most remarkable was Hatshepsut, daughter of Thutmosis I and widow of Thutmosis II, who ruled as pharaoh for nearly twenty years. Many Egyptian queens held the title "god's wife of Amun," a power base of great importance.

**Slaves** Slaves did not become numerous in Egypt until the growth of Egyptian imperial power in the Middle Kingdom (2052–1786 B.C.E.). During that period, black Africans from Nubia to the south and Asians from the east were captured in war and brought back to Egypt as slaves. The great period of Egyptian imperial expansion, the New Kingdom (1550–1075 B.C.E.), vastly increased the number of slaves and captives in Egypt. Sometimes an entire people was enslaved, as the Bible says the Hebrews were.

Slaves in Egypt performed many tasks. They labored in the fields with the peasants, in the shops of artisans, and as domestic servants. Others worked as policemen and soldiers. Many slaves labored to erect the great temples, obelisks, and other huge monuments of Egypt's imperial age. Slaves could be freed in Egypt, but manumission seems to have been rare. Nonetheless, former slaves were not set apart and could expect to be assimilated into the mass of the population.

# ANCIENT NEAR EASTERN EMPIRES

**WHAT WERE** the great empires of the ancient Near East?

In the time of Dynasty 18 in Egypt, new groups of peoples had established themselves in the Near East: the Kassites in Babylonia, the Hittites in Asia Minor, and the Mitannians in northern Syria and Mesopotamia. (See Map 1–2.) The Kassites and Mitanni-

## MAP EXPLORATION

Interactive map: To explore this map further, go to www.myhistorylab.com

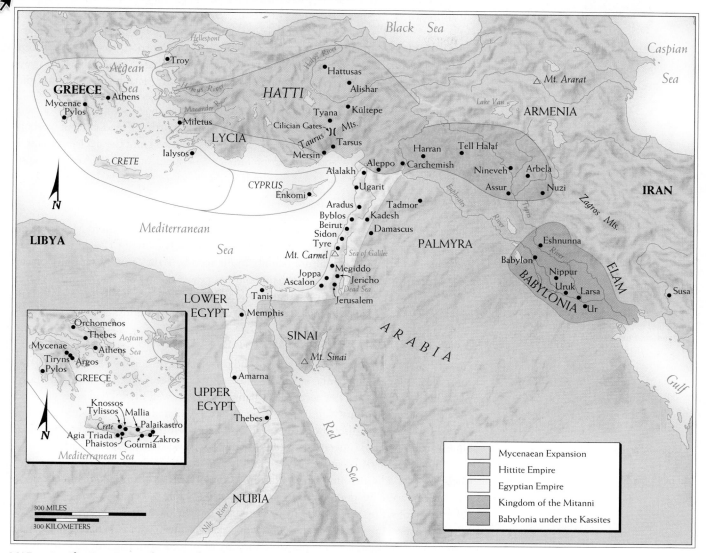

**MAP 1–2   The Near East and Greece about 1400 B.C.E.**    About 1400 B.C.E., the Near East was divided among four empires. Egypt extended south to Nubia and north through Palestine and Phoenicia. The Kassites ruled in Mesopotamia, the Hittites in Asia Minor, and the Mitannians in Assyrian lands. In the Aegean, the Mycenaean kingdoms were at their height.

**Based on** the locations of the various states that had risen by the fifteenth century B.C.E., what were these new states dependent on, geographically, to succeed?

ans were warrior peoples who ruled as a minority over more civilized folk and absorbed their culture. The Hittites established a kingdom of their own and forged an empire that lasted some two hundred years.

## THE HITTITES

The Hittites were an Indo-European people, speaking a language related to Greek and Sanskrit. By about 1500 B.C.E., they established a strong, centralized government with

**Statue of Hatshepsut**

"Statue of Hatshepsut." Red Granite. Dynasty 18, 1490–1480 B.C. (Egyptian). The Metropolitan Museum of Art, Rogers Fund and Edward S. Harkness Gift, 1929. (29.3.1)

**Why were so many of the official statues and other depictions of Hatshepsut destroyed after her death?**

a capital at Hattusas (near Ankara, the capital of modern Turkey). Between 1400 and 1200 B.C.E., they emerged as a leading military power in the Mideast and contested Egypt's ambitions to control Palestine and Syria. This struggle culminated in a great battle between the Egyptian and Hittite armies at Kadesh in northern Syria (1285 B.C.E.) and ended as a standoff. The Hittites adopted Mesopotamian writing and many aspects of Mesopotamian culture, especially through the Hurrian peoples of northern Syria and southern Anatolia. The Hittite kingdom disappeared by 1200 B.C.E., swept away in the general invasions and collapse of the Mideastern nation-states at that time.

**The Discovery of Iron**    An important technological change took place in northern Anatolia, somewhat earlier than the creation of the Hittite Kingdom, but perhaps within its region. This was the discovery of how to smelt iron and the decision to use it to manufacture weapons and tools in preference to copper or bronze. Archaeologists refer to the period after 1100 B.C.E. as the Iron Age.

## THE ASSYRIANS

The Assyrians were originally a people living in Assur, a city in northern Mesopotamia on the Tigris River. They spoke a Semitic language closely related to Babylonian. They had a proud, independent culture heavily influenced by Babylonia. Assur had been an early center for trade but emerged as a political power during the fourteenth century B.C.E. The first Assyrian empire spread north and west but was brought to an end in the general collapse of Near Eastern states at the end of the second millennium.

## THE SECOND ASSYRIAN EMPIRE

After 1000 B.C.E., the Assyrians began a second period of expansion, and by 665 B.C.E., they controlled all of Mesopotamia, much of southern Asia Minor, Syria, Palestine, and Egypt to its southern frontier. They succeeded, thanks to a large, well-disciplined army and a society that valued military skills. Some Assyrian kings boasted of their atrocities, so their names inspired terror throughout the Near East. They constructed magnificent palaces at Nineveh and Nimrud (near modern Mosul, Iraq), surrounded by parks and gardens.

The Assyrians organized their empire into provinces with governors, military garrisons, and administration for taxation, communications, and intelligence. Important officers were assigned large areas of land throughout the empire, and agricultural colonies were set up in key regions to store up supplies for military actions beyond the frontiers. Vassal kings had to send tribute and delegations to the Assyrian capital every year. Tens of thousands of people were forcibly displaced from their homes and resettled in other areas of the empire, partly to populate sparsely inhabited regions, partly to diminish resistance to Assyrian rule. People of the kingdom of Israel, which the Assyrians invaded and destroyed, were among them.

The empire became too large to govern efficiently. The last years of Assyria are obscure, but civil war apparently divided the country. The Medes, a powerful people from western and central Iran, had been expanding across the Iranian plateau. The Medes attacked Assyria and were joined by the Babylonians, who had always been restive under Assyrian rule, under the leadership of a general named Nebuchadnezzar. They eventually destroyed the Assyrian cities, including Nineveh in 612 B.C.E., so thoroughly that Assyria never recovered.

## THE NEO-BABYLONIANS

The Medes did not follow up on their conquests, so Nebuchadnezzar took over much of the Assyrian Empire. Under him and his successors, Babylon grew into one of the greatest cities of the world. Nebuchadnezzar's dynasty did not last long, and the government passed to various men in rapid succession. The last independent king of Babylon set up a second capital in the Arabian desert and tried to force the Babylonians to honor the Moon-god above all other gods. He allowed dishonest or incompetent speculators to lease huge areas of temple land for their personal profit. These policies proved unpopular—some said that the king was insane—and many Babylonians may have welcomed the Persian conquest that came in 539 B.C.E. After that, Babylonia began another, even more prosperous phase of its history as one of the most important provinces of another great Eastern empire, that of the Persians.

# THE PERSIAN EMPIRE

The great Persian Empire arose in the region now called Iran. (See Map 1–3.) The ancestors of the people who would rule it spoke a language from the Aryan branch of the family of Indo-European languages, related to the Greek spoken by the Hellenic peoples and the Latin of the Romans. The most important collections of tribes among them were the Medes and the Persians, peoples so similar in language and customs that the Greeks used both names interchangeably.

**WHAT WERE** the Persian rulers' attitudes toward the cultures they ruled?

## MAP EXPLORATION

Interactive map: To explore this map further, go to **www.myhistorylab.com**

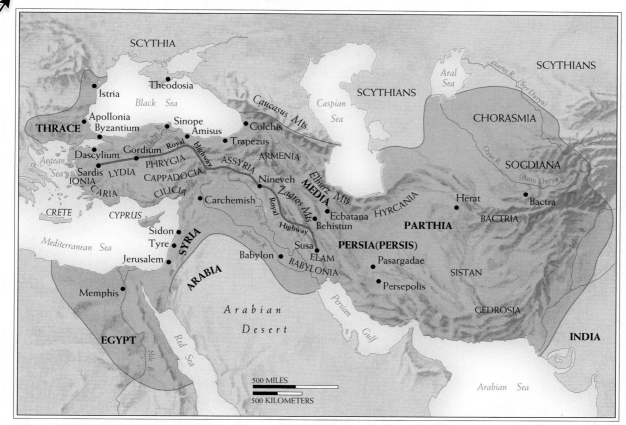

**MAP 1–3   The Achaemenid Persian Empire**   The empire created by Cyrus had reached its fullest extent under Darius when Persia attacked Greece in 490 B.C.E. It extended from India to the Aegean, and even into Europe, encompassing the lands formerly ruled by Egyptians, Hittites. Babylonians, and Assyrians.

**What strategies** did the Persians use in their efforts to rule such a large and diverse empire?

Until the middle of the sixth century, the Persians were subordinate to the Medes, but when Cyrus II (called the Great) became King of the Persians (r. 559–530 B.C.E.), their positions were reversed. About 550 B.C.E., Cyrus captured the capital at Ecbatana and united the Medes and Persians under his own rule.

## CYRUS THE GREAT

Cyrus quickly expanded his power. The territory he inherited from the Medes touched on Lydia, ruled by the rich and powerful king Croesus. Croesus controlled western Asia Minor, having conquered the Greek cities of the coast about 560 B.C.E. Made confident by his victories, by alliances with Egypt and Babylon, and by what he thought was a favorable signal from the Greek oracle of Apollo at Delphi, he invaded Persian territory in 546 B.C.E. Cyrus achieved a decisive victory, capturing Croesus and his capital city of Sardis. By 539 B.C.E. he had conquered the Greek cities, and extended his power as far to the east as the Indus valley and modern Afghanistan. In that same year he captured Babylon.

Unlike the harsh Babylonian and Assyrian conquerors who preceded him, Cyrus pursued a policy of toleration and restoration. He did not impose the Persian religion but claimed to rule by the favor of the Babylonian god. Instead of deporting defeated peoples from their native lands and destroying their cities, he rebuilt their cities and allowed the exiles to return. This policy, followed by his successors, was effective but not as gentle as it might seem. Wherever they ruled, Cyrus and his successors demanded tribute from their subjects and military service, enforcing these requirements strictly and sometimes brutally.

## DARIUS THE GREAT

Cyrus's son Cambyses succeeded to the throne in 529 B.C.E. His great achievement was the conquest of Egypt, establishing it as a satrapy (province) that ran as far west as Lybia and as far south as Ethiopia. On Cambyses's death in 522 B.C.E., a civil war roiled much of the Persian Empire. Darius emerged as the new emperor in 521 B.C.E.

**Darius.**    Persian nobles pay homage to King Darius in this relief from the treasury at the Persian capital of Persepolis. Darius is seated on the throne: his son and successor Xerxes stands behind him. Darius and Xerxes are carved in larger scale to indicate their royal status.

Courtesy of the Oriental Institute of the University of Chicago

**What was the relationship between the Persian Empire and its subjects' kingdoms?**

Darius's long and prosperous reign lasted until 486 B.C.E., during which he brought the empire to its greatest extent. To the east he added new conquests in northern India. In the west he sought to conquer the nomadic people called Scythians who roamed around the Black Sea. For this purpose he crossed into Europe over the Hellespont (Dardanelles) to the Danube River and beyond, taking possession of Thrace and Macedonia on the fringes of the Greek mainland. In 499 B.C.E., the Ionian Greeks of western Asia Minor rebelled, launching the wars between Greeks and Persians that would not end until two decades later. (See Chapter 2.)

## GOVERNMENT AND ADMINISTRATION

Like the Mesopotamian kingdoms, the Persian Empire was a hereditary monarchy that claimed divine sanction from the god **Ahura Mazda**. The ruler's title was *Shahanshah*, "king of kings." In theory all the land and the peoples in the empire belonged to him as absolute monarch, and he demanded tribute and service for the use of his property. In practice he depended on the advice and administrative service of aristocratic courtiers, ministers, and provincial governors, the satraps.

The empire was divided into twenty-nine satrapies. The satraps were allowed considerable autonomy. They ruled over civil affairs and commanded the army in war, but the king exercised several means of control. In each satrapy he appointed a secretary and a military commander. He also chose inspectors called "the eyes and ears of the king" who traveled throughout the empire reporting on what they learned in each satrapy. Their travels and those of royal couriers were made swifter and easier by a system of excellent royal roads. Ruling over a vast empire whose people spoke countless different languages, the Persians did not try to impose their own, but instead adopted Aramaic, the most common language of Middle Eastern commerce, as the imperial tongue. This practical decision simplified both civil and military administration.

Medes and Persians made up the core of the army. Royal schools trained aristocratic Median and Persian boys as military officers and imperial administrators. The officers commanded not only the Iranian troops but also drafted large numbers of subject armies when needed.

## RELIGION

Persia's religion was different from that of its neighbors and subjects. Its roots lay in the Indo-European traditions of the Vedic religion that Aryan peoples brought into India about 1500 B.C.E. Their religious practices included animal sacrifices and a reverence for fire. Although the religion was polytheistic, its chief god Ahura Mazda, the "Wise Lord," demanded an unusual emphasis on a stern ethical code. It took a new turn with the appearance of Zarathushtra, a Mede whom the Greeks called Zoroaster, perhaps as early as 1000 B.C.E., as tradition states, although some scholars place him about 600 B.C.E. He was a great religious prophet and teacher who changed the traditional Aryan worship.

Zarathushtra's reform made Ahura Mazda the only god, dismissing the others as demons not to be worshipped but fought. There would be no more polytheism and no sacrifices. Zarathushtra insisted that the people should reject the "Lie" (*druj*) and speak only the "Truth" (*asha*), portraying life as an unending struggle between two great forces, Ahura Mazda, the creator and only god, representing goodness and light, and Ahriman, a demon, representing darkness and evil.

Traditions and legends about Zarathustra as well as law, liturgy, and the teachings of the prophet are contained in the *Avesta*, the sacred book of the Persians. By the middle of the sixth century B.C.E., Zoroastrianism had become the chief religion of the Persians.

**Ahura Mazda**   The chief deity of Zoroastrianism, the native religion of Persia. Ahura Mazda is the creator of the world, the source of light, and the embodiment of good.

## ART AND CULTURE

The Persians learned much from the people they encountered and those they conquered, especially from Mesopotamia and Egypt, but they shaped it to fit comfortably on a Persian base. A good example is to be found in their system of writing. They adapted the **Aramaic** alphabet of the Semites to create a Persian alphabet and used the cuneiform symbols of Babylon to write the Old Persian language they spoke. They borrowed their calendar from Egypt. Persian art and architecture contain similar elements of talents and styles borrowed from other societies and blended with Persian traditions to serve Persian purposes.

**Aramaic**   Semitic language spoken widely throughout the Middle East in antiquity.

# PALESTINE

**HOW WAS** Hebrew monotheism different from Mesopotamian and Egyptian polytheism?

None of the powerful kingdoms of the ancient Near East had as much influence on the future of Western civilization as the small stretch of land between Syria and Egypt, the land called Palestine for much of its history. The three great religions of the modern world outside the Far East—Judaism, Christianity, and Islam—trace their origins, at least in part, to the people who arrived there a little before 1200 B.C.E. The book that recounts their experiences is the Hebrew Bible.

## THE CANAANITES AND THE PHOENICIANS

Before the Israelites arrived in their promised land, it was inhabited by groups of people speaking a Semitic language called Canaanite. The Canaanites lived in walled cities and were farmers and seafarers. The Canaanites, like the other peoples of Syria-Palestine, worshipped many gods, especially gods of weather and fertility, whom they thought resided in the clouds atop the high mountains of northern Syria. The invading Israelites destroyed various Canaanite cities and holy places and may have forced some of the population to move north and west, though Canaanite and Israelite culture also intermingled.

The **Phoenicians** were the descendants of the Canaanites and other peoples of Syria-Palestine, especially those who lived along the coast. They played an important role in Mediterranean trade, sailing to ports in Cyprus, Asia Minor, Greece, Italy, France, Spain, Egypt, and North Africa, as far as Gibraltar and possibly beyond. They founded colonies throughout the Mediterranean as far west as Spain. The most famous of these colonies was Carthage, near modern Tunis in North Africa. Sitting astride the trade routes, the Phoenician cities were important sites for the transmission of culture from east to west. The Greeks, who had long forgotten their older writing system of the Bronze Age, adopted a Phoenician version of the Canaanite alphabet that is the origin of our present alphabet.

**Phoenicians**   Seafaring people (Canaanites and Syrians) who scattered trading colonies from one end of the Mediterranean to the other.

## THE ISRAELITES

The history of the Israelites must be pieced together from various sources. They are mentioned only rarely in the records of their neighbors, so we must rely chiefly on their own account, the Hebrew Bible. This is not a history in our sense, but a complicated collection of historical narrative, pieces of wisdom, poetry, law, and religious witness. Scholars of an earlier time tended to discard it as a historical source, but the most recent trend is to take it seriously while using it with caution.

According to tradition, the patriarch Abraham came from Ur and wandered west to tend his flocks in the land of the Canaanites. Some of his people settled there, and others wandered into Egypt. By the thirteenth century B.C.E., led by Moses, they had left Egypt and wandered in the desert until they reached and conquered Canaan. They established a united kingdom that reached its peak under David and Solomon in the tenth century B.C.E. The sons of Solomon could not maintain the unity of the kingdom, and it split into two parts: Israel in the north and Judah, with its capital at Jerusalem, in the south. The rise of the great empires brought disaster to the Israelites. The northern kingdom fell to the Assyrians in 722 B.C.E., and its people—the **ten lost tribes**—were scattered and lost forever. Only the kingdom of Judah remained. It is from this time that we may call the Israelites Jews.

In 586 B.C.E., Judah was defeated by the Neo-Babylonian king Nebuchadnezzar II. He destroyed the great temple built by Solomon and took thousands of hostages off to Babylon. When the Persians defeated Babylonia, they ended this Babylonian captivity of the Jews and allowed them to return to their homeland. After that, the area of the old kingdom of the Jews in Palestine was dominated by foreign peoples for some 2,500 years, until the establishment of the State of Israel in 1948 C.E.

**Exile of the Israelites.** In 722 B.C.E. the northern part of Jewish Palestine, the kingdom of Israel, was conquered by the Assyrians. Its people were driven from their homeland and exiled all over the vast Assyrian Empire. This wall carving in low relief comes from the palace of the Assyrian king Sennacherib at Nineveh. It shows the Jews with their cattle and baggage going into exile.

Relief, Israel, 10th–6th Century: Judean exiles carrying provisions. Detail of the Assyrian conquest of the Jewish fortified town of Lachish (battle 701 B.C.). Part of a relief from the palace of Sennacherib at Niniveh, Mesopotamia (Iraq). British Museum, London, Great Britain. © Erich Lessing/Art Resource, NY.

**What did the Assyrians hope to gain by exiling the Israelites?**

**ten lost tribes** Israelites who were scattered and lost to history when the northern kingdom of Israel fell to the Assyrians in 722 B.C.E.

## THE JEWISH RELIGION

The fate of the small nation of Israel would be of little interest were it not for its unique religious achievement. The great contribution of the Jews is the development of **monotheism**—the belief in one universal God, the creator and ruler of the universe. The Jewish God is neither a natural force nor like human beings or any other creatures; he is so elevated, that those who believe in him may not picture him in any form. The faith of the Jews is given special strength by their belief that God made a covenant with Abraham that his progeny would be a chosen people who would be rewarded for following God's commandments and the law he revealed to Moses.

**monotheism** Having faith in a single God.

Like the teachings of Zarathushtra in Iran, Jewish religious thought included a powerful ethical element. God is a severe, but just, judge. Ritual and sacrifice are not enough to achieve his approval. People must be righteous, and God himself appears to be bound to act righteously. The Jewish prophetic tradition was a powerful ethical force. The prophets constantly criticized any falling away from the law and the path of righteousness. They placed God in history, blaming the misfortunes of the Jews on God's righteous and necessary intervention to punish the people for their misdeeds. The prophets also promised the redemption of the Jews if they repented, however. The prophetic tradition expected the redemption to come in the form of a Messiah who would restore the house of David. Christianity, emerging from this tradition, holds that Jesus of Nazareth was that Messiah.

Jewish religious ideas influenced the future development of the West, both directly and indirectly. The Jews' belief in an all-powerful creator (who is righteous himself and demands righteousness and obedience from humankind) and a universal God (who is the father and ruler of all peoples) is a critical part of the Western heritage.

# GENERAL OUTLOOK OF MIDEASTERN CULTURES

**WHAT SOCIAL** and political contrasts existed between ancient Middle Eastern and Greek civilizations?

Our brief account of the history of the ancient Mideast so far reveals that its various peoples and cultures were different in many ways. Yet the distance between all of them and the emerging culture of the Greeks (Chapter 2) is striking. We can see this distance best by comparing the approach of the other cultures to several fundamental human problems with that of the Greeks: What is the relationship of humans to nature? To the gods? To each other? These questions involve attitudes toward religion, philosophy, science, law, politics, and government. Unlike the Greeks, the civilizations of the Mideast seem to have these features in common: Once established, they tended toward cultural uniformity and stability. Reason, though employed for practical and intellectual purposes, lacked independence from religion and the high status to challenge the most basic received ideas. The standard form of government was a monarchy; republics were unknown. Rulers were considered divine or the appointed spokesmen for divinity. Religious and political institutions and beliefs were thoroughly intertwined. Government was not subject to secular, reasoned analysis but rested on religious authority, tradition, and power. Individual freedom had no importance.

## HUMANS AND NATURE

For the peoples of the Mideast, there was no simple separation between humans and nature or even between animate creatures and inanimate objects. Humanity was part of a natural continuum, and all things partook of life and spirit. These peoples imagined that gods more or less in the shape of humans ruled a world that was irregular and unpredictable, subject to divine whims. The gods were capricious because nature seemed capricious.

Humanity's function was merely to serve the gods. In a world ruled by powerful deities, human existence was precarious. Disasters that we would think human in origin, the Mesopotamians saw as the product of divine will. In such a universe, humans could not hope to understand nature, much less control it. At best, they could try by magic to use uncanny forces against others.

## HUMANS AND THE GODS, LAW, AND JUSTICE

Human relationships to the gods were equally humble. There was no doubt that the gods could destroy human beings and might do so at any time for no good reason. Humans could—and, indeed, had to—try to win the gods over by prayers and sacrifices, but there was no guarantee of success. The gods were bound by no laws and no morality. The best behavior and the greatest devotion to the cult of the gods were no defense against the divine and cosmic caprice.

In the earliest civilizations, human relations were guided by laws, often set down in written codes. The basic question about law concerned its legitimacy: Why, apart from the lawgiver's power to coerce obedience, should anyone obey the law? For Old Kingdom Egyptians, the answer was simple: The king was bound to act in accordance with *maat*, and so his laws were righteous. For the Mesopotamians, the answer was almost the same: The king was a representative of the gods, so the laws he set forth were authoritative.

The Hebrews introduced some important new ideas. Their unique God was capable of great anger and destruction, but he was open to persuasion and subject to morality. He was therefore more predictable and comforting, for all the terror of his wrath. The biblical version of the flood story, for instance, reveals the great difference between the Hebrew God and the Babylonian deities. The Hebrew God was powerful and wrathful, but he was not arbitrary. He chose to destroy his creatures for their moral failures.

Such a world offers the possibility of order in the universe and on this earth. There is also the possibility of justice among human beings, for the Hebrew God had provided his people with law. Through his prophet Moses, he had provided humans with regulations that would enable them to live in peace and justice. If they would abide by the law and live upright lives, they and their descendants could expect happy and prosperous lives. This idea was different from the uncertainty of the Babylonian view, but like it and its Egyptian partner, it left no doubt of the certainty of the divine. Cosmic order, human survival, and justice all depended on God.

# TOWARD THE GREEKS AND WESTERN THOUGHT

Greek thought offered different approaches and answers to many of the concerns we have been discussing. Calling attention to some of those differences will help convey the distinctive outlook of the Greeks and the later cultures within Western civilization that have drawn heavily on Greek influence.

**WHY WAS** Greek rationalism such an important break with earlier intellectual traditions?

Greek ideas had much in common with the ideas of earlier peoples. The Greek gods had most of the characteristics of the Mesopotamian deities. Magic and incantations played a part in the lives of most Greeks, and Greek law, like that of earlier peoples, was usually connected with divinity. Many, if not most, Greeks in the ancient world must have lived their lives with notions similar to those other peoples held. The surprising thing is that some Greeks developed ideas that were strikingly different and, in so doing, set part of humankind on an entirely new path.

As early as the sixth century B.C.E., some Greeks living in the Ionian cities of Asia Minor raised questions and suggested answers about the nature of the world that produced an intellectual revolution. In their speculations, they made guesses that were completely naturalistic and made no reference to supernatural powers. By putting the question of the world's origin in a naturalistic form, the Greeks may have begun the unreservedly rational investigation of the universe and, in so doing, initiated both philosophy and science.

This rationalistic, skeptical way of thinking carried over into practical matters. The school of medicine led by Hippocrates of Cos (about 400 B.C.E.) attempted to understand, diagnose, and cure disease without any attention to supernatural forces. By the fifth century B.C.E., the historian Thucydides could analyze and explain human behavior completely in terms of human nature and chance, leaving no place for the gods or supernatural forces. The same absence of divine or supernatural forces characterized Greek views of law and justice. Most Greeks, of course, liked to think that, in a vague way, law came ultimately from the gods. In practice, however, and especially in the democratic states, they knew that laws were made by humans and should be obeyed because they represented the expressed consent of the citizens.

# SUMMARY

## HOW DID life in the Neolithic Age differ from the Paleolithic?

**Early Humans and Their Culture** During the Paleolithic period, humans lived by hunting, fishing, and gathering food. They used tools, fire, and language; they believed in the supernatural. Around 10,000 B.C.E., humans started domesticating animals and plants for food. This Neolithic Revolution, which took place at different times in different parts of the world, was based on different crops in different environments. Civilization emerged, first in Mesopotamia, approximately during the Bronze Age, 3100 to 1200 B.C.E. *page 4*

## WHY DID the first cities develop?

**Early Civilizations to about 1000 B.C.E.** Around 3000 B.C.E., civilizations along the Tigris and Euphrates Rivers in Mesopotamia, and the Nile River in Egypt, started to produce written records. Civilization in southern Mesopotamia was founded by Sumerians. Semitic Akkadians from northern Babylonia established the first empire in history; Sumerians returned to power in the Third Dynasty of Ur. Egypt's pharaohs united lands along the Nile. Hieroglyphs and tombs have left us an extensive record of life in ancient Egypt. *page 6*

## WHAT WERE the great empires of the ancient Middle East?

**Ancient Near Eastern Empires** Between about 1400 B.C.E. and 500 B.C.E., new peoples and empires emerged in the Middle East. The Kassites and Mitannians were warrior peoples who ruled over the inhabitants of Babylonia and northern Syria/Mesopotamia, respectively. The Hittites based an empire in what is now Turkey. The Assyrian military supported a large Middle Eastern empire that lasted for almost half a millennium. Nebuchadnezzar overthrew the Assyrians and established a short-lived Neo-Babylonian dynasty. *page 20*

## WHAT WERE the Persian rulers' attitudes toward the cultures they ruled?

**The Persian Empire** In the late sixth and early fifth centuries B.C.E., the Persian Empire reached the height of its power and geographical expansion under Cyrus the Great and Darius the Great. By assimilating cultures and peoples, the empire successfully combined a measure of autonomy among its twenty-nine satrapies (provinces) with a centralized authority based on the king's rule as a semidivine autocrat. Tolerance of other religions, use of the common language of Aramaic and existing writing systems, and an efficient communications system contributed to the Persians' imperial power. The Persian Empire was also built on the use of non-Persian soldiers and the art, architecture, and raw materials of its conquered lands. *page 23*

## HOW WAS Hebrew monotheism different from Mesopotamian and Egyptian polytheism?

**Palestine** Judaism, Christianity, and Islam all owe many of their beliefs and practices to the Israelites who settled in Palestine before 1200 B.C.E. Israelites under Moses conquered Canaan in the thirteenth century B.C.E., and their kingdom reached its peak in the tenth century B.C.E. in the reigns of David and Solomon before splintering. Polytheistic Canaanites had lived in Syria-Palestine and through the coastal Phoenicians gave the Greeks the predecessor of the alphabet we use today. *page 26*

## WHAT SOCIAL and political contrasts existed between ancient Middle Eastern and Greek civilizations?

**General Outlook of Mideastern Cultures** Most people of the ancient Mideast believed humans were inseparable from nature, and the gods were powerful and capricious. The Hebrew God reflected a different perspective on humanity's relationship with nature and with divine power. All the ancient Middle Eastern attitudes toward religion, philosophy, science, and society in general differ markedly from what we will learn about the Greeks. *page 28*

## WHY WAS Greek rationalism such an important break with earlier intellectual traditions?

**Toward the Greeks and Western Thought** By the sixth century B.C.E., some Greeks started thinking about the world in ways that became the hallmark of Western civilization: They began to seek naturalistic, rational explanations for material phenomena and human behavior. Philosophy and science, as we understand them, could only develop once the Greeks had discarded supernatural explanations and reliance on divine intervention as ways of understanding the world. By the fifth century B.C.E., Greek thinkers had inaugurated the study of medicine and history, and by the fourth century B.C.E., Greek law and democracy had begun to evolve into forms recognizable to us. *page 29*

# REVIEW QUESTIONS

1. How was life during the Paleolithic Age different from life during the Neolithic Age? What advances account for the difference? Were these advances so significant that they warrant referring to the Neolithic as a revolutionary era?

2. What differences do you see in the political and intellectual outlooks of the Egyptian and Mesopotamian civilizations? How do their religious views compare? What influence did geography have on their religious outlooks?

3. What was significant about Cyrus the Great and Darius the Great? During their reigns, how did the Persians treat the cultures and peoples of subject lands?

4. What role did religious faith play in the political history of the Jews? Why did Middle Eastern civilizations regard the concept of Hebrew monotheism as a radical idea?

5. How did Greek thinkers diverge from the intellectual traditions of the Middle East? What new kinds of questions did Greeks ask?

## KEY TERMS

**Ahura Mazda** (p. 25)
**Aramaic** (p. 26)
**Bronze Age** (p. 6)
**civilization** (p. 6)
**culture** (p. 4)
**cuneiform** (p. 10)
**hieroglyphics** (p. 18)
*Homo sapiens* (p. 4)
**Lower Egypt** (p. 15)

**monotheism** (p. 27)
**Neolithic Age** (p. 5)
*nomes* (p. 17)
**Paleolithic** (p. 4)
**pharaoh** (p. 16)
**Phoenicians** (p. 26)
**ten lost tribes** (p. 27)
**Upper Egypt** (p. 15)

For additional learning resources related to this chapter, please go to **www.myhistorylab.com**

PEARSON
myhistorylab

# 2

# The Rise of Greek Civilization

**In 1972, this striking bronze statue** was found off the coast of Riace, southern Italy. Possibly a votive statue from the sanctuary of Delphi in Greece, it may have been the work of the sculptor Phidias (ca. 490–430 B.C.E.).

**In what ways does this statue reflect the confident worldview of the Ancient Greeks?**

**Minoan**   Civilization of Crete (2100–1150 B.C.E.), and the Aegean's first civilization, named for a legendary king on the island.

**Mycenaean**   Civilization occupying mainland Greece during the Late Helladic era (1580–1150 B.C.E.).

**This statuette of a female** with a snake in each of her hands is thought to represent either the Minoan snake goddess herself or one of her priestesses performing a religious ritual. It was found on Crete and dates from around 1600 B.C.E.

Max Alexander/Dorling Kindersley © Archaeological Receipts Fund (TAP)

**What might goddess worship tell us about gender roles in ancient Crete?**

**A**bout 2000 B.C.E., *Greek-speaking peoples settled the lands surrounding the Aegean Sea and established communities that made major contributions to the Western heritage. The Greeks' location at the eastern end of the Mediterranean put them in touch, early in their history, with Mesopotamia, Egypt, Asia Minor, and Syria-Palestine. The Greeks acknowledged debts to the cultures of these regions but were conscious (and proud) of the ways in which their way of life was unique.* ■

# THE BRONZE AGE ON CRETE AND ON THE MAINLAND TO ABOUT 1150 B.C.E.

**IN WHAT** ways were the Minoan and Mycenaean civilizations different?

The Bronze Age civilizations in the region the Greeks would rule arose on the island of Crete, on the islands of the Aegean, and on the mainland of Greece. Crete was the site of the earliest Bronze Age settlements, and modern scholars have called the civilization that arose there **Minoan**, after Minos, the legendary king of Crete. A later Bronze Age civilization was centered at the mainland site of Mycenae and is called **Mycenaean**.

## THE MINOANS

With Greece to the north, Egypt to the south, and Asia to the east, Crete was a cultural bridge between the older civilizations and the new one of the Greeks. The Bronze Age came to Crete not long after 3000 B.C.E., and the Minoan civilization, which powerfully influenced the islands of the Aegean and the mainland of Greece, arose in the third and second millennia B.C.E.

The Minoans produced a civilization that was new and unique in its character and beauty. Its most striking creations are the palaces uncovered at such sites as Phaestus, Haghia Triada, and, most important, Cnossus. Each of these palaces was built around a central court surrounded by a labyrinth of rooms. Some sections of the palace at Cnossus were four stories high. The palace design and the paintings show the influence of Syria, Asia Minor, and Egypt, but the style and quality are unique to Crete.

In contrast to the Mycenaean cities on the mainland of Greece, Minoan palaces and settlements lacked strong defensive walls. This evidence that the Minoans built without defense in mind has raised questions and encouraged speculation. Some scholars, pointing also to evidence that Minoan religion was more matriarchal than the patriarchal religion of the Mycenaeans and their Greek descendants, have argued that the civilizations of Crete, perhaps reflecting the importance of women, were inherently more tranquil and pacific than others. An earlier and different explanation for the absence of fortifications was that the protection provided by the sea made them unnecessary. The evidence is not strong enough to support either explanation, and the mystery remains.

Along with palaces, paintings, pottery, jewelry, and other valuable objects, excavations have revealed clay writing tablets like those found in Mesopotamia. The tablets, preserved accidentally when a great fire that destroyed the royal palace at Cnossus hardened them, have three distinct kinds of writing on them: a kind of picture writing called *hieroglyphic*, and two different linear scripts called Linear A and Linear B. The languages of the two other scripts remain unknown, but Linear B proved to be an early form of Greek. The contents of the tablets, primarily inventories, reveal an organization centered on the palace and ruled by a king who was supported by an extensive bureaucracy that kept remarkably detailed records.

This sort of organization is typical of early civilizations in the Near East, but as we shall see, is nothing like that of the Greeks after the Bronze Age. Yet the inventories were written in a form of Greek. If they controlled Crete throughout the Bronze Age, why should Minoans, who were not Greek, have written in a language not their own? This question raises the larger one of what the relationship was between Crete and the Greek mainland in the Bronze Age and leads us to an examination of mainland culture.

## THE MYCENAEANS

In the third millennium B.C.E.—the Early Helladic Period—most of the Greek mainland, including many of the sites of later Greek cities, was settled by people who used metal, built some impressive houses, and traded with Crete and the islands of the Aegean. The names they gave to places, names that were sometimes preserved by later invaders, make it clear they were not Greeks and they spoke a language that was not Indo-European (the language family to which Greek belongs). Not long after the year 2000 B.C.E., many of these Early Helladic sites were destroyed by fire, some were abandoned, and still others appear to have yielded peacefully to an invading people. These signs of invasion probably signal the arrival of the Greeks and the advent of a civilization historians have named Mycenaean for Mycenae, one of its cities. The presence of the Greek Linear B tablets at Cnossus suggests that Greek invaders also established themselves in Crete, and there is good reason to believe that at the height of Mycenaean power (1400–1200 B.C.E.), Crete was part of the Mycenaean world.

**Mycenaean Culture**   The Mycenaean people were warriors, as their art, architecture, and weapons reveal. The success of their campaigns and the defense of their territory required strong central authority, and all available evidence shows that the kings provided it. Their palaces, in which the royal family and its retainers lived, were located within the walls; most of the population lived outside the walls. As on Crete, paintings usually covered the palace walls, but instead of peaceful landscapes and games, the Mycenaean murals depicted scenes of war and boar hunting.

About 1500 B.C.E., Mycenaean kings were constructing *tholos* tombs. These large, beehivelike chambers were built of enormous well-cut and fitted stones and were approached by an unroofed passage (*dromos*) cut horizontally into the side of the hill. Only a strong king whose wealth was great, whose power was unquestioned, and who commanded the labor of many people could undertake such a project. His wealth probably came from plundering raids, piracy, and trade.

**The citadel of Mycenae**, a major center of the Greek civilization of the Bronze Age, was built of enormously heavy stones. The lion gate at its entrance was built in the thirteenth century B.C.E.

Joe Cornish/Dorling Kindersley © Archaeological Receipts Fund (TAP)

**Why did the Mycenaeans devote so much time and energy to the construction of heavily fortified outposts?**

**The Rise and Fall of Mycenaean Power**    At the height of their power (1400–1200 B.C.E.), the Mycenaeans were prosperous and active. They enlarged their cities, expanded their trade, and even established commercial colonies in the East. Sometime about 1250 B.C.E., they probably sacked Troy, on the coast of northwestern Asia Minor, giving rise to the epic poems of Homer—the *Iliad* and the *Odyssey*. (See Map 2–1.) Around 1200 B.C.E., however, the Mycenaean world showed signs of trouble, and by 1100 B.C.E., it was gone. Its palaces were destroyed, many of its cities were abandoned, and its art, way of life, and system of writing were buried and forgotten.

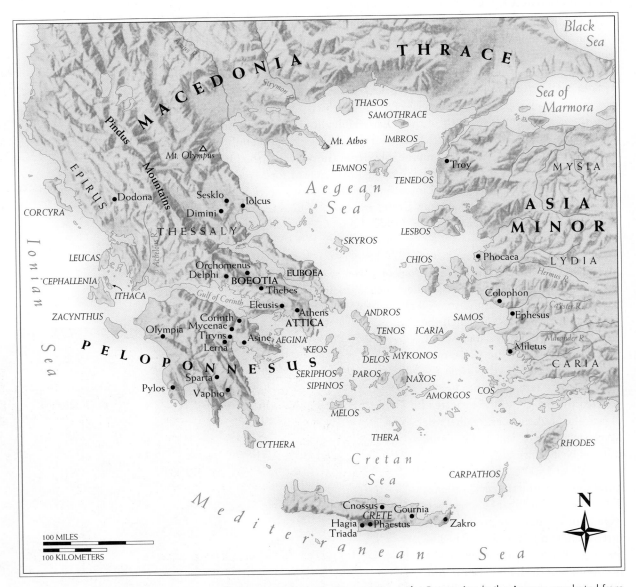

MAP 2–1    **The Aegean Area in the Bronze Age**    The Bronze Age in the Aegean area lasted from about 1900 to about 1100 B.C.E. Its culture on Crete is called Minoan and was at its height about 1900–1400 B.C.E. Bronze Age Helladic culture on the mainland flourished from about 1600–1200 B.C.E.

**What societal** differences between the Mycenaean civilization on mainland Greece and the Minoan civilization of Crete might be a direct result of the geographic differences between the two civilizations?

What happened? Some recent scholars, not-ing evidence that the Aegean island of Thera (modern Santorini) suffered a massive volcanic explosion in the middle to late second millennium B.C.E., have suggested that this natural disaster was responsible. However, the Mycenaean towns were not destroyed all at once; many fell around 1200 B.C.E., but some flourished for another century, and the Athens of the period was never destroyed or abandoned. No theory of natural disaster can ac-count for this pattern, leaving us to seek less dra-matic explanations for the end of Mycenaean civilization.

**The Dorian Invasion**   Some scholars have sug-gested that piratical sea raiders, known as Dorians, destroyed Pylos and, perhaps, other sites on the mainland. Archaeology has not provided material evidence of whether there was a single Dorian inva-sion or a series of them, and it is impossible as yet to say with any certainty what happened at the end of

## CHRONOLOGY OF THE RISE OF GREECE

| | |
|---|---|
| ca. 2900–1150 B.C.E. | Minoan period |
| ca. 1900 B.C.E. | Arrival of the Greeks on the mainland |
| ca. 1600–1150 B.C.E. | Mycenaean period |
| ca. 1250 B.C.E. | Sack of Troy |
| ca. 1200–1150 B.C.E. | Fall of the Mycenaean kingdoms |
| ca. 1150–750 B.C.E. | The Greek Dark Ages |
| ca. 750–500 B.C.E. | Greek colonial expansion |
| ca. 725 B.C.E. | Homer flourished |
| ca. 700 B.C.E. | Hesiod flourished |
| ca. 650 B.C.E. | Spartan constitution militarizes the state |
| 546–510 B.C.E. | Athenian tyranny of Pisistratus and Hippias |
| 508 B.C.E. | Clisthenes inaugurates Athenian democracy |
| 499 B.C.E. | Miletus rebels against Persia |
| 490 B.C.E. | Persian Wars: Darius |
| 480–479 B.C.E. | Persian Wars: Xerxes |

the Bronze Age in the Aegean. The chances are good, however, that Mycenaean civiliza-tion ended gradually over the century between 1200 B.C.E. and 1100 B.C.E. Its end may have been the result of internal conflicts among the Mycenaean kings combined with continuous pressure from outsiders, who raided, infiltrated, and eventually dominated Greece and its neighboring islands. There is reason to believe that Mycenaean society suffered internal weaknesses due to its organization around the centralized control of mil-itary force and agricultural production. This rigid organization may have deprived it of flexibility and vitality, leaving it vulnerable to outside challengers.

# THE GREEK "MIDDLE AGES" TO ABOUT 750 B.C.E.

**WHAT WERE** the Greek Dark Ages?

The immediate effects of the Dorian invasion were disastrous for the inhabitants of the Mycenaean world. The palaces and the kings and bureaucrats who managed them were destroyed. The wealth and organization that had supported the artists and merchants were likewise swept away by a barbarous people who did not have the knowledge or so-cial organization to maintain them. The chaos resulting from the collapse of the rigid-ly controlled palace culture produced severe depopulation and widespread poverty that lasted for a long time.

## GREEK MIGRATIONS

Another result of the invasion was the spread of the Greek people eastward from the mainland to the Aegean islands and the coast of Asia Minor. The Dorians themselves, after occupying most of the Peloponnesus, occupied the southern Aegean islands and the southern part of the Anatolian coast.

These migrations made the Aegean a Greek lake. The fall of the advanced Mi-noan and Mycenaean civilizations, however, virtually ended trade with the old civiliza-tions of the Near East, nor was there much internal trade among the different parts of Greece. The Greeks were forced to turn inward, and each community was left largely to its own devices.

*Iliad*   Homer's poem narrates a dispute between Agamemnon the king and his warrior Achilles, whose honor is wounded and then avenged.

*Odyssey*   Homer's epic poem tells of the wanderings of the hero Odysseus.

*arete*   The highest virtue in Homeric society: the manliness, courage, and excellence that equipped a hero to acquire and defend honor.

**Black-Figure Hydria** Five women filling hydriae in a fountain house.

"Hydria (water jug)". Greek, Archaic period, ca. 520 B.C. Athens, Attica, Greece the Priam Painter. Ceramic, black-figure, H: 0.53 cm Diam (with handles): 0.37 cm. William Francis Warden Fund. ©2004 Museum of Fine Arts, Boston

**What place did women have in the Ancient Greek household?**

# THE AGE OF HOMER

For a picture of society in these "Dark Ages," the best source is Homer. His epic poems, the **Iliad** and the **Odyssey**, emerged from a tradition of oral poetry whose roots extend into the Mycenaean Age. Although the poems tell of the deeds of Mycenaean Age heroes, the world they describe clearly differs from the Mycenaean world. Homer's heroes are not buried in *tholos* tombs but are cremated; they worship gods in temples, whereas the Mycenaeans had no temples; they have chariots but do not know their proper use in warfare. Certain aspects of the society described in the poems appear instead to resemble the world of the tenth and ninth centuries B.C.E., and other aspects appear to belong to the poet's own time, when population was growing at a swift pace and prosperity was returning, thanks to changes in Greek agriculture, society, and government.

**Government and Society**   In the Homeric poems, the power of the kings is much less than that of the Mycenaean rulers. Homeric kings had to consult a council of nobles before they made important decisions. The nobles felt free to discuss matters in vigorous language and in opposition to the king's wishes. The king could ignore the council's advice, but it was risky for him to do so.

Only noblemen had the right to speak in council, but the common people could not be entirely ignored. If a king planned a war or a major change of policy during a campaign, he would not fail to call the common soldiers to an assembly; they could listen and express their feelings by acclamation, though they could not take part in the debate.

Homeric society, nevertheless, was sharply divided into classes, the most important division being the one between nobles and everyone else. Birth determined noble status, and wealth usually accompanied it. Below the nobles were three other classes: *thetes*, landless laborers, and slaves. We do not know whether the *thetes* owned the land they worked outright (and so were free to sell it) or worked a hereditary plot that belonged to their clan (and was, therefore, not theirs to dispose of as they chose). The worst condition was that of the free, but landless, hired agricultural laborer. The slave, at least, was attached to a family household and so was protected and fed. In a world where membership in a settled group gave the only security, the free laborers were desperately vulnerable. Slaves were few in number and were mostly women, who served as maids and concubines.

**Homeric Values**   The Homeric poems reflect an aristocratic code of values that powerfully influenced all future Greek thought. Those values were physical prowess; courage; fierce protection of one's family, friends, property; and, above all, personal honor and reputation. Achilles, the great hero of the *Iliad*, refuses to fight in battle, allowing his fellow Greeks to be slain and almost defeated, because Agamemnon has wounded his honor by taking away his battle prize. He returns not out of a sense of duty to the army, but to avenge the death of his dear friend Patroclus.

The highest virtue in Homeric society was *arete*—manliness, courage in the most general sense, and the excellence proper to a hero. This quality was best revealed in a contest, or *agon*. Homeric battles are not primarily group combats, but a series of individual contests between great champions. One of the prime forms of entertainment is the athletic contest, and such a contest celebrates the funeral of Patroclus.

The central ethical idea in Homer can be found in the instructions that Achilles' father gives him when he sends him off to fight at Troy: "Always be the best and distinguished above others." Here in a nutshell we have the chief values of the aristocrats of Homer's world: to vie for individual supremacy in *arete* and to defend and increase the honor of the family.

**Women in Homeric Society**   In the world described by Homer, the role of women was chiefly to bear and raise children, but the wives of the heroes also had a respected position, presiding over the household, overseeing the servants, and safeguarding the family property. They were prized for their beauty, constancy, and skill at weaving. Unlike Greek women in later centuries, the women of the higher class depicted in Homer are seen moving freely about their communities in town and country. They have a place alongside their husbands at the banquets in the great halls and take part in the conversation.

# THE *POLIS*

The characteristic Greek institution was the *polis* (plural *poleis*). The common translation of that word as "city-state" is misleading, for it says both too much and too little. All Greek *poleis* began as little more than agricultural villages or towns, and many stayed that way, so the word "city" is inappropriate. All of them were states, in the sense of being independent political units, but they were much more than that. The *polis* was thought of as a community of relatives; all its citizens, who were theoretically descended from a common ancestor, belonged to subgroups, such as fighting brotherhoods or *phratries*, clans, and tribes, and worshipped the gods in common ceremonies.

Aristotle argued that the *polis* was a natural growth and the human being was by nature "an animal who lives in a *polis*." Humans alone have the power of speech and from it derive the ability to distinguish good from bad and right from wrong, "and the sharing of these things is what makes a household and a *polis*." Without law and justice, human beings are the worst and most dangerous of the animals. With them, humans can be the best, and justice exists only in the *polis*. These high claims were made in the fourth century B.C.E., hundreds of years after the *polis* came into existence, but they accurately reflect an attitude that was present from the first.

**DESCRIBE THE** *polis* and how it affected society and government.

**Entrance to Acrocorinth with its three gateways.**

Joe Cornish © Dorling Kindersley

## DEVELOPMENT OF THE *POLIS*

Originally the word *polis* referred only to a citadel—an elevated, defensible rock to which the farmers of the neighboring area could retreat in case of attack. The **Acropolis** in Athens and the hill called Acrocorinth in Corinth are examples. For some time, such high places and the adjacent farms made up the *polis*. The towns grew gradually and without planning, as their narrow, winding, and disorderly streets show. For centuries they had no walls. Unlike the city-states of the Near East, they were not placed for commercial convenience on rivers or the sea. Nor did they grow up around a temple to serve the needs of priests and to benefit from the needs of worshippers. The availability of farmland and of a natural fortress determined their location. They were placed either well inland or far enough away from the sea to avoid piratical raids. Only later and gradually did the **agora**—a marketplace and civic center—appear within the *polis*. The *agora* was to become the heart of the Greeks' remarkable social life, distinguished by conversation and argument carried on in the open air.

Some *poleis* probably came into existence early in the eighth century B.C.E. The institution was certainly common by the middle of the century, for all the colonies that were established by the Greeks in the years after 750 B.C.E. took the form of the *polis*. Once the new institution had been fully established, true monarchy disappeared. The original form of the *polis* was an aristocratic republic dominated by the nobility through its council of nobles and its monopoly of the magistracies. About 750 B.C.E., coincident with the development of the *polis*, the Greeks borrowed a writing system from one of

**Acropolis**   At the center of the city of Athens, the most famous example of a citadel.

**agora**   Place for markets and political assemblies.

the Semitic scripts and added vowels to create the first true alphabet. This new Greek alphabet was easier to learn than any earlier writing system, leading to a much wider literacy.

## THE *HOPLITE* PHALANX

A new military technique was crucial to the development of the *polis*. In earlier times, small troops of cavalry and individual "champions" who first threw their spears and then came to close quarters with swords may have borne the brunt of fighting. Toward the end of the eighth century B.C.E., however, the **hoplite** phalanx came into being and remained the basis of Greek warfare thereafter.

**hoplite**    A true infantry soldier that began to dominate the battlefield in the late eighth century B.C.E.

The *hoplite* was a heavily armed infantryman who fought with a spear and a large shield. Most scholars believe that these soldiers were formed into a phalanx in close order, usually at least eight ranks deep, although some argue for a looser formation. As long as the *hoplites* fought bravely and held their ground, there would be few casualties and no defeat, but if they gave way, the result was usually a rout. All depended on the discipline, strength, and courage of the individual soldier. At its best, the phalanx could withstand cavalry charges and defeat infantries not as well protected or disciplined. Until defeated by the Roman legion, it was the dominant military force in the eastern Mediterranean.

**phalanx**    Tight military formation of men eight or more ranks deep.

In every way, the phalanx was a communal effort that relied not on the extraordinary actions of the individual, but on the courage of a considerable portion of the citizenry. This style of fighting produced a single, decisive battle that reduced the time lost in fighting other kinds of warfare; it spared the houses, livestock, and other capital of the farmer-soldiers who made up the phalanx, and it also reduced the number of casualties. It perfectly suited the farmer-soldier-citizen, who was the backbone of the *polis*, and, by keeping wars short and limiting their destructiveness and expense, it helped the *polis* prosper.

The phalanx and the *polis* arose together, and both heralded the decline of the kings. The phalanx, however, was not made up only of aristocrats. Most of the *hoplites* were farmers working small holdings. The immediate beneficiaries of the royal decline were the aristocrats, but because the existence of the *polis* depended on small farmers, their wishes could not long be wholly ignored. The rise of the *hoplite* phalanx created a bond between the aristocrats and the yeomen family farmers who fought in it. This bond helps explain why class conflicts were muted for some time. It also guaranteed, however, that the aristocrats, who dominated at first, would not always be unchallenged.

# EXPANSION OF THE GREEK WORLD

**HOW AND** why did the Greeks colonize large parts of the Mediterranean?

From the middle of the eighth century B.C.E. until well into the sixth century B.C.E., the Greeks vastly expanded their territory, their wealth, and their contacts with other peoples. A burst of colonizing activity placed *poleis* from Spain to the Black Sea. (See Map 2–2.)

## THE GREEK COLONY

The Greeks did not lightly leave home to join a colony. The voyage by sea was dangerous and uncomfortable, and at the end of it were uncertainty and danger. Only powerful pressures like overpopulation and hunger for land drove thousands from their homes to establish new *poleis*.

## MAP EXPLORATION

Interactive map: To explore this map further, go to **www.myhistorylab.com**

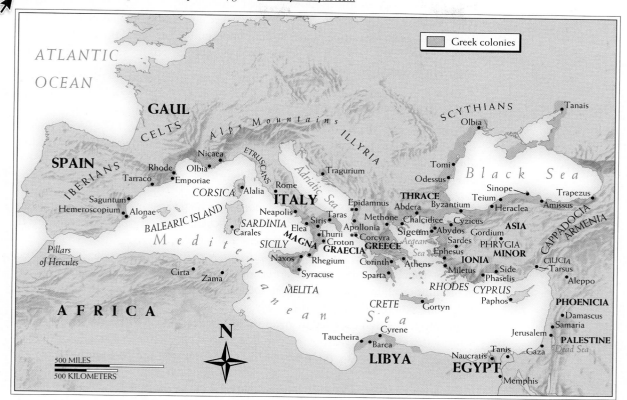

**MAP 2–2   Greek Colonization**   The height of Greek colonization was between about 750 and 550 B.C.E. Greek colonies stretched from the Mediterranean coasts of Spain and Gaul (modern France) in the west to the Black Sea and Asia Minor in the east.

**Note the** area of penetration in the various colonized areas on this map. How is this indicative of a colonization achieved mainly by means of the sea?

The colony, although sponsored by the mother city, was established for the good of the colonists rather than for the benefit of those they left behind. The colonists tended to divide the land they settled into equal shares, reflecting an egalitarian tendency inherent in the ethical system of the yeoman farmers in the mother cities. Most colonies, though independent, were friendly with their mother cities. Each might ask the other for aid in time of trouble and expect to receive a friendly hearing, although neither was obligated to help the other.

Colonization had a powerful influence on Greek life. By relieving the pressure of a growing population, it provided a safety valve that allowed the *poleis* to escape civil wars. By confronting the Greeks with the differences between themselves and the new peoples they met, colonization gave them a sense of cultural identity and fostered a **Panhellenic** ("all-Greek") spirit that led to the establishment of common religious festivals. The most important ones were at Olympia, Delphi, Corinth, and Nemea.

Colonization also encouraged trade and industry. The influx of new wealth from abroad and the increased demand for goods from the homeland stimulated a more intensive use of the land and an emphasis on crops for export, chiefly the olive and the

**Panhellenic ("all Greek")**   Sense of cultural identity that all Greeks felt in common with one another.

wine grape. The manufacture of pottery, tools, weapons, and fine artistic metalwork, as well as perfumed oil, the soap of the ancient Mediterranean world, was likewise encouraged. New opportunities allowed some men, sometimes outside the nobility, to become wealthy and important. The new rich became a troublesome element in the aristocratic *poleis*, for, although increasingly important in the life of their states, the ruling aristocrats barred them from political power, religious privileges, and social acceptance. These conditions soon created a crisis in many states.

## THE TYRANTS (ABOUT 700–500 B.C.E.)

In some cities—perhaps only a small percentage of the more than 1,000 Greek *poleis*—the crisis produced by new economic and social conditions led to or intensified factional divisions within the ruling aristocracy. Between 700 and 500 B.C.E., the result was often the establishment of a tyranny.

**The Rise of Tyranny**    A tyrant was a monarch who had gained power in an unorthodox or unconstitutional, but not necessarily wicked, way and who exercised a strong one-man rule that might well be beneficent and popular.

The founding tyrant was usually a member of the ruling aristocracy who either had a personal grievance or led an unsuccessful faction. He often rose to power because of his military ability and support from the *hoplites*. He generally had the support of the politically powerless group of the newly wealthy and of the poor farmers. When he took power, he often expelled many of his aristocratic opponents and divided at least some of their land among his supporters. He pleased his commercial and industrial supporters by destroying the privileges of the old aristocracy and by fostering trade and colonization.

The tyrants presided over a period of population growth that saw an increase especially in the number of city dwellers. They responded with a program of public works that included the improvement of drainage systems, care for the water supply, the construction and organization of marketplaces, the building and strengthening of city walls, and the erection of temples. They introduced new local festivals and elaborated the old ones. They patronized the arts, supporting poets and artisans with gratifying results. All this activity contributed to the tyrant's popularity, to the prosperity of his city, and to his self-esteem.

**The End of the Tyrants**    By the end of the sixth century B.C.E., tyranny had disappeared from the Greek states and did not return in the same form or for the same reasons. The last tyrants were universally hated for their cruelty and repression. They left bitter memories in their own states and became objects of fear and hatred everywhere.

Besides the outrages individual tyrants committed, the very concept of tyranny was inimical to the idea of the *polis*. The notion of the *polis* as a community to which every member must be responsible, the connection of justice with that community, and the natural aristocratic hatred of monarchy all made tyranny seem alien and offensive. The rule of a tyrant, however beneficent, was arbitrary and unpredictable. Tyranny came into being in defiance of tradition and law, and the tyrant governed without either. He was not answerable in any way to his fellow citizens.

From a longer perspective, however, the tyrants made important contributions to the development of Greek civilization. They encouraged economic changes that helped secure the future prosperity of Greece. They increased communication with the rest of the Mediterranean world and cultivated crafts and technology, as well as arts and literature. Most important of all, they broke the grip of the aristocracy and put the productive powers of the most active and talented of its citizens fully at the service of the *polis*.

**QUICK REVIEW**

**Greek Tyranny**

- Tyrants were men who took power through illegal means
- Rule was not always oppressive
- Tyrannies faded away around the sixth century B.C.E.

# THE MAJOR STATES

Generalization about the *polis* becomes difficult not long after its appearance, for although the states had much in common, some of them developed in unique ways. Sparta and Athens, which became the two most powerful Greek states, had especially unusual histories.

## SPARTA

At first Sparta—located on the **Peloponnesus**, the southern peninsula of Greece— seems not to have been strikingly different from other *poleis*. About 725 B.C.E., however, the pressure of population and land hunger led the Spartans to launch a war of conquest against their western neighbor, Messenia. The First Messenian War gave the Spartans as much land as they would ever need. The reduction of the Messenians to the status of serfs, or **Helots**, meant the Spartans did not even need to work the land that supported them.

The turning point in Spartan history came about 650 B.C.E., when, in the Second Messenian War, the Helots rebelled with the help of Argos and other Peloponnesian cities. After they had suppressed the revolt, the Spartans were forced to reconsider their way of life. They could not expect to keep down the Helots, who outnumbered them perhaps ten to one, and still maintain the old free and easy habits typical of most Greeks. Faced with the choice of making drastic changes and sacrifices or abandoning their control of Messenia, the Spartans chose to turn their city forever after into a military academy and camp.

**Spartan Society**   The new system that emerged late in the sixth century B.C.E. exerted control over each Spartan from birth, when officials of the state decided which infants were physically fit to survive. At the age of seven, the Spartan boy was taken from his mother and turned over to young instructors. He was trained in athletics and the military arts and taught to endure privation, to bear physical pain, and to live off the country, by theft if necessary. At twenty, the Spartan youth was enrolled in the army, where he lived in barracks with his companions until the age of thirty. Marriage was permitted, but a strange sort of marriage it was, for the Spartan male could visit his wife only infrequently and by stealth. At thirty he became a full citizen, an "equal." Military service was required until the age of sixty; only then could the Spartan retire to his home and family.

This educational program extended to women, too, although they were not given military training. Like males, female infants were examined for fitness to survive. Girls were given gymnastic training, were permitted greater freedom of movement than among other Greeks, and were equally indoctrinated with the idea of service to Sparta.

The entire system was designed to change the natural feelings of devotion to family and children into a more powerful commitment to the *polis*. Privacy, luxury, and even comfort were sacrificed to the purpose of producing soldiers whose physical powers, training, and discipline made them the best in the world. Nothing that might turn the mind away from duty was permitted.

**Spartan Government**   The Spartan constitution was mixed, containing elements of monarchy, oligarchy, and democracy. There were two kings, whose power was limited by law and also by the rivalry that usually existed between the two royal houses. Their functions were chiefly religious and military. A Spartan army rarely left home without a king in command.

**HOW WERE** the government and politics of Athens different from those of Sparta?

**Peloponnesus**   Southern half of the Greek peninsula.

**Helots**   Slaves to the Spartans who revolted and nearly destroyed Sparta in 650 B.C.E.

**A large Spartan plate** from the second quarter of the sixth century B.C.E.
Hirmer Fotoarchiv

**How did Spartan society differ from that of other Greek city-states?**

**A spartan warrior.**
Nick Nicholls © The British Museum

A council of elders, consisting of twenty-eight men over the age of sixty, elected for life, and the kings, represented the oligarchic element. These elders had important judicial functions, sitting as a court in cases involving the kings. They also were consulted before any proposal was put before the assembly of Spartan citizens.

The Spartan assembly consisted of all males over thirty. This was thought to be the democratic element in the constitution, but its membership included only a small percentage of the entire population. Theoretically, they were the final authority, but in practice, only magistrates, elders, and kings participated in debate, and voting was usually by acclamation. Therefore, the assembly's real function was to ratify decisions already made or to decide between positions favored by the leading figures.

**The Peloponnesian League**   By about 550 B.C.E., the Spartan system was well established, and its limitations were plain. Suppression of the Helots required all the effort and energy that Sparta had. The Spartans could expand no further, but they could not allow unruly independent neighbors to cause unrest that might inflame the Helots.

When the Spartans defeated Tegea, their northern neighbor, they imposed an unusual peace. Instead of taking away land and subjugating the defeated state, Sparta left the Tegeans their land and their freedom. In exchange, they required the Tegeans to follow the Spartan lead in foreign affairs and to supply a fixed number of soldiers to Sparta on demand. This became the model for Spartan relations with the other states in the Peloponnesus. Soon Sparta was the leader of an alliance that included every Peloponnesian state but Argos; modern scholars have named this alliance the Peloponnesian League. It provided Sparta with security and made it the most powerful *polis* in Hellenic history.

## ATHENS

**Attica**   Region (about 1,000 square miles) that Athens dominated.

Athens—located in **Attica**—was slow to come into prominence and to join in the new activities that were changing the more advanced states. The reasons were several: Athens was not situated on the most favored trade routes of the eighth and seventh centuries B.C.E.; its large area (about 1,000 square miles) allowed population growth without great pressure; and the many villages and districts within this territory were not fully united into a single *polis* until the seventh century B.C.E.

**Aristocratic Rule**   In the seventh century B.C.E., Athens was a typical aristocratic *polis*. Its people were divided into four tribes and into several clans and brotherhoods (*phratries*). The aristocrats held the most land and the best land, and dominated religious and political life. The **Areopagus**, a council of nobles deriving its name from the hill where it held its sessions, governed the state. Annually the council elected nine magistrates, called *archons*, who joined the Areopagus after their year in office. Because the *archons* served for only a year, were checked by their colleagues, and looked forward to a lifetime as members of the Areopagus, the aristocratic Areopagus, not the *archons*, was the true master of the state.

**Areopagus**   Council heading Athens's government comprised of a group of nobles that annually chose the city's nine *archons*, the magistrates who administered the *polis*.

**Pressure for Change**   In the seventh century B.C.E., the peaceful life of Athens was disturbed, in part by quarrels within the nobility and in part by the beginnings of an agrarian crisis. In 621 B.C.E., a man named Draco was given special authority to codify and publish laws for the first time. Draco's work was probably limited to laws concerning homicide and was aimed at ending blood feuds between clans, but it set an important precedent: The publication of laws strengthened the hand of the state against the local power of the nobles.

The root of Athens's troubles was agricultural. Many Athenians worked family farms, from which they obtained most of their living. It appears that they planted wheat, the staple crop, year after year without rotating fields or using enough fertilizer. Shifting to more intensive agricultural techniques and to the planting of fruit and olive trees and grapevines required capital, leading the less successful farmers to acquire excessive debt. Inevitably, many Athenians defaulted and were enslaved. Revolutionary pressures grew among the poor, who began to demand the abolition of debt and a redistribution of the land.

**Reforms of Solon**   In the year 594 B.C.E., as tradition has it, the Athenians elected Solon as the only *archon*, with extraordinary powers to legislate and revise the constitution. Immediately, he attacked the agrarian problem by canceling current debts and forbidding future loans secured by the person of the borrower. He helped bring back many Athenians enslaved abroad and freed those in Athens enslaved for debt.

In the short run, therefore, Solon did resolve the economic crisis, but his other economic actions had profound success in the long run. He forbade the export of wheat and encouraged that of olive oil. This policy had the initial effect of making wheat more available in Attica and encouraging the cultivation of olive oil and wine as cash crops. By the fifth century B.C.E., the cultivation of cash crops had become so profitable that much Athenian land was diverted from grain production, and Athens became dependent on imported wheat. Solon also changed the Athenian standards of weights and measures to conform with those of Corinth and Euboea and the cities of the east. This change also encouraged commerce and turned Athens in the direction that would lead it to great prosperity in the fifth century B.C.E. Solon also encouraged industry by offering citizenship to foreign artisans.

Solon also changed the constitution. Citizenship had previously been the privilege of all male adults whose fathers were citizens; to their number he added those immigrants who were tradesmen and merchants. All these Athenian citizens were divided into four classes on the basis of wealth, measured by annual agricultural production. The two highest classes alone could hold the *archonship*, the chief magistracy in Athens, and sit on the Areopagus.

Men of the third class were allowed to serve as *hoplites*. They could be elected to a council of 400 chosen by all the citizens, 100 from each tribe. The *thetes* made up the last class. They voted in the assembly for the *archons* and the council members and on any other business brought before them by the *archons* and the council. They also sat on a new popular court established by Solon. This new court was recognized as a court of appeal, and by the fifth century B.C.E., almost all cases came before it. In Solon's Athens, as everywhere in the world before the twentieth century, women took no part in the political or judicial process.

**Pisistratus the Tyrant**   Solon's efforts to avoid factional strife failed. Within a few years contention reached such a degree that no *archons* could be chosen. Out of this turmoil emerged the first Athenian tyranny. Pisistratus, a nobleman, leader of a faction, and military hero, briefly seized power in 560 B.C.E. and again in 556 B.C.E., but each time his support was inadequate, and he was driven out. At last, in 546 B.C.E., he came back at the head of a mercenary army from abroad and established a successful tyranny.

Pisistratus sought to increase the power of the central government at the expense of the nobles, but he made no formal change in the Solonian constitution. The assembly, councils, and courts met; the magistrates and councils were elected. Pisistratus merely saw to it that his supporters dominated these bodies. The intended effect was to

**Bust of Solon.**

Bust of Solon. Rudolf Lesch Fine Arts Inc., New York, New York.

blunt the sharp edge of tyranny with the appearance of a constitutional government. The unintended effect was to give the Athenians more experience in the procedures of self-government and a growing taste for it.

**Spartan Intervention**   Pisistratus was succeeded by his oldest son, Hippias, who followed his father's ways at first. In 514 B.C.E., however, his brother Hipparchus was murdered as a result of a private quarrel. Hippias became nervous, suspicious, and harsh. Led by their ambitious king, Cleomenes I, the Spartans marched into Athenian territory in 510 B.C.E. and deposed Hippias, who went into exile to the Persian court. The tyranny was over.

The Spartans must have hoped to leave Athens in friendly hands, and indeed Cleomenes' friend Isagoras held the leading position in Athens after the withdrawal of the Spartan army. Isagoras, however, faced competitors, chief among them Clisthenes. Clisthenes lost out in the initial political struggle among the noble factions. Clisthenes then took an unprecedented action—he turned to the people for political support and won it with a program of great popular appeal. In response, Isagoras called in the Spartans again who drove Clisthenes out. But the people refused to tolerate an aristocratic restoration and drove out the Spartans and Isagoras with them. Clisthenes and his allies returned, ready to put their program into effect.

**Clisthenes, the Founder of Democracy**   A central aim of Clisthenes' reforms was to diminish the influence of traditional localities and regions in Athenian life, for these were an important source of power for the nobility and of factions in the state. In 508 B.C.E., he made the *deme*, the equivalent of a small town in the country or a ward in the city, the basic unit of civic life. The *deme* was a purely political unit that elected its own officers. The distribution of *demes* in each tribe guaranteed that no region would dominate any of them.

A new council of 500 replaced the Solonian council of 400. The council's main responsibility was to prepare legislation for the assembly to discuss, but it also had important financial duties and received foreign emissaries. Final authority in all things rested with the assembly of all adult male Athenian citizens. Debate in the assembly was free and open; any Athenian could submit legislation, offer amendments, or argue the merits of any question.

As a result of the work of Solon, Pisistratus, and Clisthenes, Athens entered the fifth century B.C.E. well on the way to prosperity and democracy. It was much more centralized and united than it had been, and it was ready to take its place among the major states that would lead the defense of Greece against the dangers that lay ahead.

**QUICK REVIEW**

**Clisthenes' Democracy**

- Clisthenes sought to weaken his opponents by dividing Attica into *demes*
- Increased Solon's council from four to five hundred
- All adult male Athenians were members of the popular assembly

# LIFE IN ARCHAIC GREECE

**WHAT ROLE** did religion play in the lives of ordinary Greeks?

## SOCIETY

As the "Dark Ages" ended, the features that would distinguish Greek society thereafter took shape. The artisan and the merchant grew more important as contact with the non-Hellenic world became easier. Most people, however, continued to make their living from the land.

**Farmers**   Ordinary country people rarely leave a written record of their thoughts or activities, and we have no such record from ancient Greece. The poet Hesiod (ca. 700 B.C.E.), however, was certainly no aristocrat. He presented himself as a small farmer, and his *Works and Days* gives some idea of the life of such a farmer. The crops included grain—chiefly barley, but also wheat; grapes for making wine; olives for food and oil; green vegetables, especially the bean; and some fruit. Sheep and goats provided milk and cheese. He and small farmers like him tasted meat chiefly from sacrificial animals at festivals.

These farmers worked hard to make a living. The hardest work came in October, at the start of the rainy season, the time for the first plowing. Autumn and winter were the time for cutting wood, building wagons, and making tools. Late winter was the time to tend to the vines, May was the time to harvest the grain, July to winnow and store it. Only at the height of summer's heat did Hesiod allow for rest, but when September came, it was time to harvest the grapes. As soon as that task was done the cycle started again.

**Aristocrats**   Most aristocrats were rich enough to employ many hired laborers, sometimes sharecroppers, and sometimes even slaves, to work their extensive lands. They could therefore enjoy leisure for other activities. The center of aristocratic social life was the drinking party, or *symposium*. The sessions began with prayers and libations to the gods. Usually there were games, such as dice or *kottabos*, in which wine was flicked from the cups at different targets. Sometimes dancing girls or flute girls offered entertainment. Frequently the aristocratic participants provided their own amusements with songs, poetry, or even philosophical disputes. Characteristically, these took the form of contests, with some kind of prize for the winner, for aristocratic values continued to emphasize competition and the need to excel, whatever the arena.

This aspect of aristocratic life appears in the athletic contests that became widespread early in the sixth century. The games included running events; the long jump; the discus and javelin throws; the pentathlon, which included all of these; boxing; wrestling; and the chariot race. Only the rich could afford to raise, train, and race horses, so the chariot race was a special preserve of aristocracy. The nobility also especially favored wrestling, and the *palaestra*, or fields, where they practiced became an important social center for the aristocracy. The contrast between the hard, drab life of the farmers and the leisured and lively one of the aristocrats could hardly have been greater. (See "Encountering the Past: Greek Athletics," page 48.)

## RELIGION

Like most ancient peoples, the Greeks were **polytheists**, and religion played an important part in their lives. Much of Greek art and literature was closely connected with religion, as was the life of the *polis* in general.

**Olympian Gods**   The Greek pantheon consisted of the twelve gods who lived on Mount Olympus, led by Zeus, the father of the Gods. These gods were seen as behaving much like mortals, with all the foibles of humans, except they were superhuman in these as well as in their strength and immortality. In contrast, Zeus, at least, was seen as a source of human justice, and even the Olympians were understood to be subordinate to the Fates. Each *polis* had one of the Olympians as its guardian deity and worshipped that god in its own special way, but all the gods were Panhellenic.

**Immortality and Morality**   Besides the Olympians, the Greeks also worshipped countless lesser deities connected with local shrines. They even worshipped human heroes, real or legendary, who had accomplished great deeds and had earned immortality and divine status. The worship of these deities was not a very emotional experience. It was a matter of offering prayer, libations, and gifts in return for protection and favors from the god during the lifetime of the worshipper. The average human had no hope of immortality, and these devotions involved little moral teaching.

**An amphora decorated with a symposium scene.**
Ashmolean Museum, University of Oxford, UK/The Bridgeman Art Library

*symposium*   A men's drinking party at the center of aristocratic social life in archaic Greece.

**polytheists**   Worshippers of many gods

# ENCOUNTERING THE PAST

## GREEK ATHLETICS

*Athletic contests were an integral part of Greek civilization throughout its entire history. They were much more than entertainments. They were religious festivals in which the Greeks celebrated the virtues and attitudes that they considered central to their way of life. International or Panhellenic ("all-Greek") contests were scheduled in alternating annual cycles. The most prestigious of these were the games that began to be celebrated in honor of Zeus at the southern mainland city of Olympia in 776 B.C.E.*

*The Greeks' primary interest was not team sports, but contests in which individuals could prove their su-periority. Races of various lengths were the heart of Olympic competition, but there were also field events such as discus and javelin throws and combat sports such as wrestling and boxing. Only male athletes were admitted to the games, and by the fifth century B.C.E., all contestants (except those in a race in full armor) competed nude. The official prizes were simple wreaths, but poleis lavishly rewarded the native sons who brought home these tokens of victory.*

WHY DID the Greeks prefer individual contests to team sports? What motivated them to train and compete?

**A foot race,** probably a sprint, at the Panathenaic Games in Athens, ca. 530 B.C.E.

National Archives and Records Administration

**Why was public athletic competition so important to Ancient Greek men? What values were highlighted by such competitions?**

Most Greeks seem to have held to the commonsense notion that justice lay in paying one's debts. They thought that civic virtue consisted of worshipping the state deities in the traditional way, performing required public services, and fighting in defense of the state. To them, private morality meant to do good to one's friends and harm to one's enemies.

**The Cult of Delphian Apollo**   In the sixth century B.C.E., the influence of the cult of Apollo at Delphi and of his oracle there became great. The oracle was the most important of several that helped satisfy the human craving for a clue to the future. The priests of Apollo preached moderation; the two famous sayings identified with Apollo—"Know thyself" and "Nothing in excess"—exemplified their advice. Humans needed self-control (*sophrosynēe*). Its opposite was arrogance (**hubris**), brought on by excessive wealth or good fortune. *Hubris* led to moral blindness and, finally, to divine vengeance. This theme of moderation and the dire consequences of its absence was central to Greek popular morality and appears frequently in Greek literature.

*hubris*   Arrogance produced by excessive wealth or good fortune.

**The Cult of Dionysus and the Orphic Cult**   The somewhat cold religion of the Olympian gods and of the cult of Apollo did little to assuage human fears or satisfy human hopes and passions. For these needs, the Greeks turned to other deities and rites. Of these deities, the most popular was Dionysus, a god of nature and fertility, of the grapevine, drunkenness, and sexual abandon. The Orphic cult, named after its supposed founder, the mythical poet Orpheus, provided its followers with more hope than did the worship of the twelve Olympians. Cult followers are thought to have refused to kill animals or eat their flesh and to have believed in the transmigration of souls, which offered the prospect of some form of life after death.

## POETRY

The poetry of the sixth century B.C.E. also reflected the great changes sweeping through the Greek world. The lyric style—poetry meant to be sung, either by a chorus or by one person—predominated. Sappho of Lesbos, Anacreon of Teos, and Simonides of Cos composed personal poetry, often relating the pleasure and agony of love. Alcaeus of Mytilene, an aristocrat driven from his city by a tyrant, wrote bitter invective.

Perhaps the most interesting poet of the century from a political point of view was Theognis of Megara. Theognis was the spokesperson for the old, defeated aristocracy of birth. He divided everyone into two classes, the noble and the base; the former were the good, the latter, bad. Those nobly born must associate only with others like themselves if they were to preserve their virtue; if they mingled with the base, they became base. Those born base, however, could never become noble. Only nobles could aspire to virtue and possessed the critical moral and intellectual qualities—respect or honor and judgment. These qualities could not be taught; they were innate. Even so, they had to be carefully guarded against corruption by wealth or by mingling with the base.

**This Attic cup** from the fifth century B.C.E. shows the two great poets from the island of Lesbos, Sappho (center) and Alcaeus (far left).

Hirmer Fotoarchiv

**What role did poetry play in Ancient Greek culture?**

Intermarriage between the noble and the base was especially condemned. Such ideas remained alive in aristocratic hearts throughout the next century and greatly influenced later thinkers, Plato among them.

# THE PERSIAN WARS

**WHAT WAS** the significance of the wars between the Greeks and the Persians?

The Greeks' period of fortunate isolation and freedom ended in the sixth century B.C.E. They had established colonies along most of the coast of Asia Minor from as early as the eleventh century B.C.E. The colonies maintained friendly relations with the mainland but developed a flourishing economic and cultural life independent of their mother cities and of their eastern neighbors. In the middle of the sixth century B.C.E., however, these Greek cities of Asia Minor came under the control of Lydia and its king, Croesus (ca. 560–546 B.C.E.).

## THE IONIAN REBELLION

The Ionian Greeks (those living on the central part of the west coast of Asia Minor and nearby islands) had been moving toward democracy and were not pleased to find themselves under the monarchical rule of Persia. That rule, however, was not overly burdensome at first. The Persians ruled the Greek cities through local individuals, who governed their cities as "tyrants." Most of the tyrants, however, were not harsh, the Persian tribute was not excessive, and the Greeks enjoyed general prosperity. Neither the death of the Persian king Cyrus the Great fighting on a distant frontier in 530 B.C.E., nor the suicide of his successor Cambyses, nor the civil war that followed it in 522–521 B.C.E. produced any disturbance in the Greek cities. When Darius emerged as Great King in 521 B.C.E., he found **Ionia** perfectly obedient.

**Ionia**   Western coast of Asia Minor.

The private troubles of the ambitious tyrant of Miletus, Aristagoras, ended this calm. He had urged a Persian expedition against the island of Naxos; when it failed, he feared the consequences and organized the Ionian rebellion of 499 B.C.E. To gain support, he overthrew the tyrannies and proclaimed democratic constitutions. Then he turned to the mainland states for help, petitioning first Sparta, the most powerful Greek state. The Spartans, however, would have none of Aristagoras's promises of easy victory and great wealth.

Aristagoras next sought help from the Athenians, who were related to the Ionians and had close ties of religion and tradition with them. Besides, Hippias, the deposed tyrant of Athens, was an honored guest at the court of Darius, who had already made it plain that he favored the tyrant's restoration. The Persians, moreover, controlled both sides of the Hellespont, the route to the grain fields beyond the Black Sea that were increasingly vital to Athens. Perhaps some Athenians already feared that a Persian attempt to conquer the Greek mainland was only a matter of time. The Athenian assembly agreed to send a fleet of twenty ships to help the rebels. The Athenian expedition was strengthened by five ships from Eretria in Euboea, which participated out of gratitude for past favors.

In 498 B.C.E., the Athenians and their allies made a surprise attack on Sardis, the old capital of Lydia and now the seat of the *satrap*, and burned it. This action caused the revolt to spread throughout the Greek cities of Asia Minor outside Ionia, but the Ionians could not follow it up. The Athenians withdrew and took no further part. Gradually the Persians reimposed their will. In 495 B.C.E., they defeated the Ionian fleet at Lade, and in the next year they wiped out Miletus. The Ionian rebellion was over.

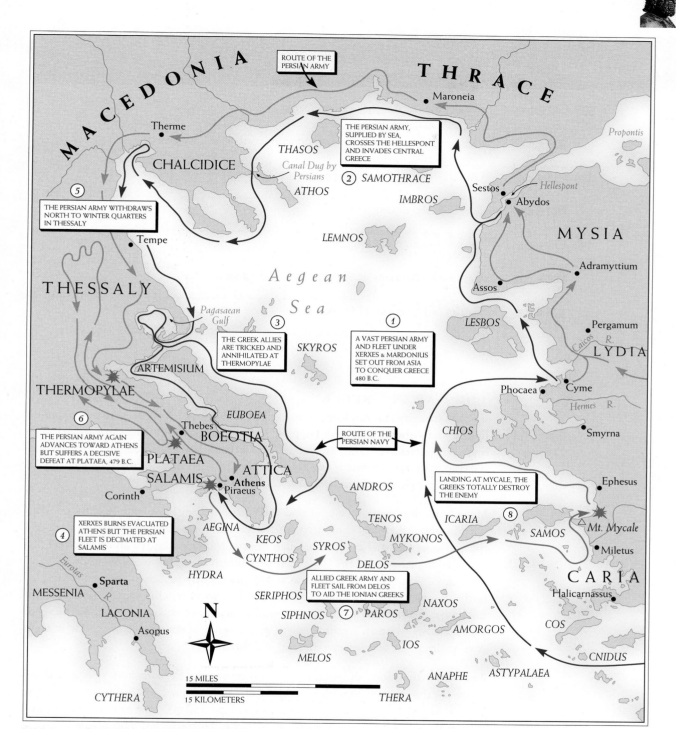

**MAP 2–3   The Persian Invasion of Greece**   This map traces the route taken by the Persian king Xerxes in his invasion of Greece in 480 B.C.E. The gray arrows show movements of Xerxes' army, the purple arrows show movements of his navy, and the green arrows show movements of the Greek army and navy.

**Although Xerxes'** army had superior numbers, how did Greece's geography favor the Greek cities over the Persians?

## Overview  The Greek Wars Against Persia

| | |
|---|---|
| **560–546 B.C.E.** | Greek cities of Asia Minor conquered by Croesus of Lydia |
| **546 B.C.E.** | Cyrus of Persia conquers Lydia and gains control of Greek cities |
| **499–494 B.C.E.** | Greek cities rebel (Ionian rebellion) |
| **490 B.C.E.** | Battle of Marathon |
| **480–479 B.C.E.** | Xerxes' invasion of Greece |
| **480 B.C.E.** | Battles of Thermopylae, Artemisium, and Salamis |
| **479 B.C.E.** | Battles of Plataea and Mycale |

## THE WAR IN GREECE

In 490 B.C.E., the Persians launched an expedition directly across the Aegean to punish Eretria and Athens, to restore Hippias, and to gain control of the Aegean Sea. (See Map 2–3 on page 51.) They landed their infantry and cavalry forces first at Naxos, destroying it for its successful resistance in 499 B.C.E. Then they destroyed Eretria and deported its people deep into the interior of Persia.

**Marathon**   Rather than submit and accept the restoration of the hated tyranny of Hippias, the Athenians chose to resist the Persian forces bearing down on them and risk the same fate that had just befallen Eretria. Miltiades, an Athenian who had fled from Persian service, led the city's army to confront the Persians at Marathon.

A Persian victory at Marathon would have destroyed Athenian freedom and led to the conquest of all the mainland Greeks. The greatest achievements of Greek culture, most of which lay in the future, would never have occurred. But the Athenians won a decisive victory, instilling them with a sense of confidence and pride in their *polis*, their unique form of government, and themselves.

**The Great Invasion**   Internal troubles prevented the Persians from taking swift revenge for their loss at Marathon. Almost ten years elapsed before Darius's successor, Xerxes, in 481 B.C.E., gathered an army of at least 150,000 men and a navy of more than 600 ships to conquer Greece. In Athens, Themistocles, who favored making Athens into a naval power, had become the leading politician. During his *archonship* in 493 B.C.E., Athens had already built a fortified port at Piraeus. A decade later the Athenians came upon a rich vein of silver in the state mines, and Themistocles persuaded them to use the profits to increase their fleet. By 480 B.C.E., Athens had over 200 ships, the backbone of a navy that was to defeat the Persians.

Of the hundreds of Greek states, only thirty-one—led by Sparta, Athens, Corinth, and Aegina—were willing to fight as the Persian army gathered south of the Hellespont. In the spring of 480 B.C.E., Xerxes launched his invasion. The Persian strategy was to march into Greece, destroy Athens, defeat the Greek army, and add the Greeks to the number of Persian subjects. The huge Persian army needed to keep in touch with the fleet for supplies. If the Greeks could defeat the Persian navy, the army could not remain in Greece long. Themistocles knew that the Aegean was subject to sudden devastating storms. His strategy was to delay the Persian army and then to bring on the kind of naval battle he might hope to win. (See "Compare & Connect: Greek Strategy in the Persian War," on pages 54–55.)

The Greek League, founded specifically to resist this Persian invasion, met at Corinth as the Persians were ready to cross the Hellespont. They chose Sparta as leader and first confronted the Persians at Thermopylae, the "hot gates," on land and off Artemisium at sea. The opening between the mountains and the sea at Thermopylae was so narrow that a small army could hold it against a much larger one. The Spartans sent their king, Leonidas, with 300 of their own citizens and enough allies to make a total of about 9,000.

Severe storms wrecked many Persian ships while the Greek fleet waited safely in a protected harbor. Then Xerxes attacked Thermopylae, and for two days the Greeks butchered his best troops without serious loss to themselves. On the third day, however, a traitor showed the Persians a mountain trail that permitted them to come on the Greeks from behind. Many allies escaped, but Leonidas and his 300 Spartans all died fighting. At about the same time, the Greek and Persian fleets fought an indecisive battle at Artemisium. The fall of Thermopylae, however, forced the Greek navy to withdraw. The Persian army moved into Attica and burned Athens.

**Defeating the Persians**   A sea battle in the narrow waters to the east of the island of Salamis, to which the Greek fleet withdrew after the battle at Artemisium, decided the fate of Greece. Because the Greek ships were fewer, slower, and less maneuverable than those of the Persians, the Greeks put soldiers on their ships and relied chiefly on hand-to-hand combat. In the ensuing battle the Persians lost more than half their ships and retreated to Asia with a good part of their army, but the danger was not over yet.

The Persian general Mardonius spent the winter in central Greece, and in the spring he unsuccessfully tried to win the Athenians away from the Greek League. The Spartan regent, Pausanias, then led the largest Greek army up to that time to confront Mardonius in Boeotia. At Plataea, in the summer of 479 B.C.E., the Persians suffered a decisive defeat.

Meanwhile the Ionian Greeks urged King Leotychidas, the Spartan commander of the fleet, to fight the Persian fleet. At Mycale, on the coast of Samos, Leotychidas destroyed the Persian camp and its fleet. The Persians fled the Aegean and Ionia. For the moment, at least, the Persian threat was gone.

# GREEK STRATEGY IN THE PERSIAN WAR

In the summer of 480 B.C.E., Xerxes, Great King of Persia, took an enormous invading army into Greece. During the previous year those Greeks who meant to resist met to plan a defense. After abandoning an attempt to make a stand at Tempe in Thessaly, they fell back to central Greece, at Thermopylae on land and Artemisium at sea. Herodotus is our main source and his account of the Greek strategy is not clear. How did the Greeks hope to check the Persians? Did they hope to stop them for good at Thermopylae, or was the idea to force a sea battle at Artemisium? Were both the army and the fleet intended only to fight holding actions until the Athenians fled to Salamis and the Peloponnesus? Scholars have long argued these questions, which have been sharpened by the discovery of the "Themistocles Decree," an inscription from the third century B.C.E. which purports to be an Athenian decree passed in 480 before the Battle of Artemisium. The authenticity of the decree is still in question, but if it reflects a reliable tradition it must influence our view in important ways.

## QUESTIONS

1. In Herodotus's account what is the state of the Athenian preparation?

2. What light does it reflect on the original Greek strategy for the war?

3. Was the Themistocles Decree passed before or after the battle at Thermopylae? What light does this decree shed on Greek strategy?

4. How do the two documents compare?

5. Are they incompatible?

## I. THE ACCOUNT OF HERODOTUS

*In this passage Herodotus describes Athens after the Greek defeat at Thermopylae.*

Meanwhile, the Grecian fleet, which had left Artemisium, proceeded to Salamis, at the request of the Athenians, and there cast anchor. The Athenians had begged them to take up this position, in order that they might convey their women and children out of Attica, and further might deliberate upon the course which it now behooved them to follow. Disappointed in the hopes which they had previously entertained, they were about to hold a council concerning the present posture of their affairs. For they had looked to see the Peloponnesians drawn up in full force to resist the enemy in Boeotia, but found nothing of what they had expected; nay, they learnt that the Greeks of those parts, only concerning themselves about their own safety, were building a wall across the Isthmus, and intended to guard the Peloponnese, and let the rest of Greece take its chance. These tidings caused them to make the request whereof I spoke, that the combined fleet should anchor at Salamis.

So while the rest of the fleet lay to off this island, the Athenians cast anchor along their own coast. Immediately upon their arrival, proclamation was made, that every Athenian should save his children and household as he best could; whereupon some sent their families to Aegina, some to Salamis, but the greater number to Troezen. This removal was made with all possible haste, partly from a desire to obey the advice of the oracle, but still more for another reason. The Athenians say they have in their acropolis a huge serpent which lives in the temple, and is the guardian of the whole place. Nor do they only say this, but, as if the serpent really dwelt there, every month they lay out its food, which consists of a honey-cake. Up to this time the honey-cake had always been consumed; but now it lay untouched. So the priestess told the people what had happened; whereupon they left Athens the more readily, since they believed that the goddess had abandoned the citadel.

Source: Herodotus, *Histories*, trans. by George Rawlinson, 8.40.41.

## II. THE THEMISTOCLES DECREE

### The Gods

Resolved by the Council and the People

Themistocles, son of Neokles, of Phrearroi, made the motion:

To entrust the city to Athena the Mistress of Athens and to all the other Gods to guard and defend from the Barbarian for the sake of the land. The Athenians themselves and the foreigners who live in Athens are to send their children and women to safety in Troizen, their protector being Pittheus, the founding hero of the land. They are to send the old men and their movable possessions to safety on Salamis. The treasurers and priestesses are to remain on the acropolis guarding the property of the gods.

All the other Athenians and foreigners of military age are to embark on the 200 ships that are ready and defend against the Barbarian for the sake of their own freedom and that of the rest of the Greeks along with the Lakedaimonians, the Korinthians. the Aiginetans, and all others who wish to share the danger.

The generals are to appoint, starting tomorrow, 200 trierarchs [captains], one to a ship, from among those who have land and house in Athens and legitimate children and who are not older than fifty; to these men the ships are to be assigned by lot. They are to enlist marines, 10 to each ship, from men between the ages of twenty and thirty, and four archers. They are to distribute the servicemen [the marines and archers] by lot at the same time as they assign the trierarchs to the ships by lot. The generals are to write up the rest ship by ship on white boards, (taking) the Athenians from the lexiarchic registers, the foreigners from those registered with the polemarch. They are to write them up assigning them by divisions, 200 of about one hundred (men) each, and to write above each division the name of the trireme and of the trierarch and the servicemen, so that they may know on which trireme each division is to embark. When all the divisions have been composed and allotted to the triremes, the Council and the generals are to man all the 200 ships, after sacrificing a placatory offering to Zeus the Almighty and Athena and Nike and Poseidon the Securer.

When the ships have been manned, with 100 of them they are to meet the enemy at Artemision in Euboia, and with the other 100 they are to lie off Salamis and the coast of Attica and keep guard over the land. In order that all Athenians may be united in their defense against the Barbarian those who have been sent into exile for ten years are to go to Salamis and to stay there until the People come to some decision about them, while those who have been deprived of citizen rights are to have their rights restored . . .

Source: "Waiting for the Barbarian, Greece and Rome," second series, 8 trans. by Michael H. Jameson (Oxford, 1961), pp. 5–18. By permission of the Oxford University Press.

**A Greek *hoplite* attacking a Persian soldier.** The contrast between the Greek's metal body armor, large shield, and long spear and the Persian's cloth and leather garments indicates one reason the Greeks won. This Attic vase was found on Rhodes and dates from ca. 475 B.C.E.

Greek. Vase, Red-figured. Attic. ca. 480–470 B.C. Neck amphora, Nolan type. Side 1: "Greek warrior attacking a Persian." Said to be from Rhodes. Terracotta. H. 13-11/16 in. The Metropolitan Museum of Art, Rogers Fund, 1906. (06.1021.117) Photograph © 1986 The Metropolitan Museum of Art

**How did conflict with Persia shape the image Greeks had of themselves and their society?**

# SUMMARY

## IN WHAT ways were the Minoan and Mycenaean civilizations different?

**The Bronze Age on Crete and on the Mainland to about 1150 B.C.E.** During the Bronze Age, the Minoan and Mycenaean civilizations ruled over the Greek mainland and Aegean islands. The Minoan civilization on Crete is renowned for its beautiful palaces. They were the organizational center of Minoan society, and Minoan kings employed a large bureaucracy. The lack of defensive walls is a notable feature of Minoan settlements. On the Greek mainland, starting around 1600 B.C.E., the Mycenaean culture was warlike and ruled by strong kings. Mycenaeans traded widely. Historians and archaeologists have suggested various explanations for the fact that, by 1100 B.C.E., the Mycenaean culture had disappeared. *page 34*

## WHAT WERE the Greek Dark Ages?

**The Greek "Middle Ages" to about 750 B.C.E.** The Dorian invasion destroyed the Mycenaean palace culture. The Greek peoples spread around the Aegean. Trade diminished; writing and other arts disappeared. Oral poetry flourished, and Homer's *Iliad* and *Odyssey* provide both great stories and insights into life in the Greek "Dark Ages." The aristocratic values of the tenth and ninth centuries B.C.E. idealized the individual hero. *page 37*

## DESCRIBE THE *polis* and how it affected society and government.

**The *Polis*** Greek social and political values are exemplified in the Greeks' characteristic form of community, the *polis*. Early *poleis* developed around 800 B.C.E. in locations that featured fertile farmland and, nearby, natural defensive positions. Later *poleis* always included an *agora*, a marketplace and civic center. *Polis* society was made possible by a new military technology, the *hoplite* phalanx. The power of the kings and, later, the aristocrats was undermined by the emergence of the farmer-soldier-citizen in the *polis*. *page 39*

## HOW AND why did the Greeks colonize large parts of the Mediterranean?

**Expansion of the Greek World** For about two centuries starting around 750 B.C.E., the Greeks colonized widely throughout the Mediter-

ranean world. Trade became an increasingly important part of the Greek economy. Exposure to other peoples and cultures fostered consciousness of Greek cultural identity and led to Panhellenic feelings. In some *poleis*, new social and economic conditions led to rule by tyrants. But by late in the sixth century B.C.E., tyrants had lost favor with the populace, and by the end of the century, they were gone. *page 40*

## HOW WERE the government and politics of Athens different from those of Sparta?

**The Major States** The two most powerful Greek *poleis*, Sparta and Athens, developed differently. Starting around 725 B.C.E., Sparta gained land and power over the Messenians through warfare. Late in the sixth century B.C.E., Spartan society was reorganized along military lines to ensure that Sparta could continue its hold over Messenia. By 500 B.C.E., Sparta headed a Peloponnesian League, a mighty military alliance. In Athens, meanwhile, political and economic innovations included the publication of laws; by the fifth century B.C.E., prosperity and democracy had taken root in Athens. *page 43*

## WHAT ROLE did religion play in the lives of ordinary Greeks?

**Life in Archaic Greece** Social class shaped everyday life for the ancient Greeks. Greeks were polytheistic, worshipping the Olympian gods and other deities through sacrifices and athletic contests. Lyric poetry treated topics ranging from love to politics. *page 46*

## WHAT WAS the significance of the wars between the Greeks and the Persians?

**The Persian Wars** Cyrus the Great came to power in Persia in 559 B.C.E. and set about unifying and expanding his territory. For almost a century, starting around 550 B.C.E. and continuing into the mid–fifth century B.C.E., Greece faced intermittent military challenges from the Persian Empire. After Lydia came under Persian rule in 546 B.C.E., the Ionian Greeks sought military assistance from first the Spartans (who refused to get involved) and then the Athenians, who in 498 B.C.E. helped them in a short-lived revolt. Eventually the Persians withdrew from the Aegean Sea and Ionia. *page 50*

# REVIEW QUESTIONS

1. How were the Minoan and the Mycenaean civilizations similar? How were they different?

2. What was a *polis*? What role did geography play in its development? What contribution did it make to the development of Hellenic civilization?

3. How did the political, social, and economic institutions of Athens and Sparta compare around 500 B.C.E.? What explains Sparta's uniqueness? How did Athens make the transition from aristocracy to democracy?

4. Why did the Greeks and Persians go to war in 490 and 480 B.C.E.? Why were the Greeks victorious over the Persians?

## KEY TERMS

**Acropolis** (p. 39)
*agora* (p. 39)
**Areopagus** (p. 44)
*arete* (p. 38)
**Attica** (p. 44)
**Helots** (p. 43)
*hoplite* (p. 40)
*hubris* (p. 48)
*Iliad* (p. 38)

**Ionia** (p. 49)
**Minoan** (p. 34)
**Mycenaean** (p. 34)
*Odyssey* (p. 38)
**Panhellenic ("all Greek")** (p. 41)
**Peloponnesus** (p. 43)
**phalanx** (p. 40)
**polytheists** (p. 47)
*symposium* (p. 47)

For additional learning resources related to this chapter, please go to **www.myhistorylab.com**

myhistorylab

# 3

# Classical and Hellenistic Greece

**The Winged Victory of Samothrace.** This is one of the great masterpieces of Hellenistic sculpture. It appears to be the work of the Rhodian sculptor Pythokritos, about 200 B.C.E. The statue stood in the Sanctuary of the Great Gods on the Aegean island of Samothrace on a base made in the shape of a ship's prow. The goddess is seen as landing on the ship to crown its victorious commander and crew.

*The Nike of Samothrace*, goddess of victory. Marble figure (190 B.C.E.) from Rhodos, Greece. Height 328 cm, MA 2369, Louvre, Dpt. des Antiquités Grecques/Romaines, Paris, France. Photograph © Erich Lessing/Art Resource, NY

**How were Greek cultural values reflected in *The Winged Victory of Samothrace*?**

*The Greeks' remarkable victory over the Persians (480–479 B.C.E.) marked the start of an era of great achievement. Fear of another Persian incursion into the Aegean led the Greeks to contemplate some kind of arrangement for their joint defense. The Spartans refused to make commitments that would take them away from their homeland, but the Athenians were eager for leadership opportunities. They negotiated a military alliance called the Delian League. It laid the foundation for an Athenian Empire, and fear of Athenian expansion led other states to ally with Sparta. The Greek world was polarized and finally erupted in a self-destructive civil war. In 338 B.C.E., Philip of Macedon intervened, took control, and ended the era of the independent polis.* ▨

## AFTERMATH OF VICTORY

**WHAT LED** to the foundation of the Delian League?

The unity of the Greeks had shown strain even in the life-and-death struggle against the Persians. Within two years of the Persian retreat, it gave way almost completely and yielded to a division of the Greek world into two spheres of influence dominated by Sparta and Athens. The need of the Ionian Greeks to obtain and defend their freedom from Persia and the desire of many Greeks to gain revenge and financial reparation for the Persian attack brought on the split. (See Map 3–1.)

### THE DELIAN LEAGUE AND THE RISE OF CIMON

Sparta had led the Greeks to victory, and it was natural to look to the Spartans to continue the campaign against Persia. But Sparta was ill-suited to the task, which required both a long-term commitment far from the Peloponnesus and continuous naval action.

Athens had become the leading naval power in Greece, and the same motives that had led the Athenians to support the Ionian revolt prompted them to try to drive the Persians from the Aegean and the Hellespont. The Ionians were at least as eager for the Athenians to take the helm as the Athenians were to accept the responsibility and opportunity.

**MAP 3–1    Classical Greece**    Greece in the Classical period (ca. 480–338 B.C.E.) centered on the Aegean Sea. Although there were important Greek settlements in Italy, Sicily, and all around the Black Sea, the area shown in this general reference map embraced the vast majority of Greek states.

**Why was** Athens not able to control its vast empire? What are some of the factors that led to its decline?

In the winter of 478–477 B.C.E., the islanders and the Greeks from the coast of Asia Minor and other Greek cities on the Aegean met with the Athenians on the sacred island of Delos and swore oaths of alliance. The aims of this new **Delian League** were to free those Greeks who were under Persian rule, to protect all against a Persian return, and to obtain compensation from the Persians by attacking their lands and taking booty. An assembly in which each state, including Athens, had one vote was supposed to determine league policy. Athens, however, was clearly designated the leader.

**Delian League**    Pact joined in 478 B.C.E. by Athenians and other Greeks to continue the war with Persia.

From the first, the league was remarkably successful. The Persians were driven from Europe and the Hellespont, and the Aegean was cleared of pirates. In 467 B.C.E., a great victory at the Eurymedon River in Asia Minor routed the Persians and added several cities to the league.

Cimon, son of Miltiades, the hero of Marathon, became the leading Athenian soldier and statesman soon after the war with Persia. Cimon, who was to dominate Athenian politics for almost two decades, pursued a policy of aggressive attacks on Persia and friendly relations with Sparta. Cimon led the Athenians and the Delian League to victory after victory, and his own popularity grew with his successes.

# THE FIRST PELOPONNESIAN WAR: ATHENS AGAINST SPARTA

In 465 B.C.E., the island of Thasos rebelled from the Delian League, and Cimon put the rebellion down after a siege of more than two years. When Cimon returned to Athens from Thasos, he was charged with taking bribes for having refrained from conquering Macedonia, although conquering Macedonia had not been part of his assignment. He was acquitted; the trial was only a device by which his political opponents tried to reduce his influence. Their program at home was to undo the gains made by the Areopagus and bring about further democratic changes. In foreign policy, Cimon's enemies wanted to break with Sparta and contest its claim to leadership over the Greeks. The head of this faction was Ephialtes.

WHAT WAS the cause of the Peloponnesian War, and what was the end result?

## THE BREACH WITH SPARTA

When the Thasians began their rebellion, they asked Sparta to invade Athens the next spring, and the *ephors*, the annual magistrates responsible for Sparta's foreign policy, agreed. An earthquake, however, accompanied by a rebellion of the Helots that threatened the survival of Sparta, prevented the invasion. The Spartans asked their allies, the Athenians among them, for help, and Cimon persuaded the Athenians to send it. While Cimon was in the Peloponnesus helping the Spartans, Ephialtes stripped the Areopagus of almost all its power. In 462 B.C.E., Ephialtes was assassinated, and Pericles replaced him as leader of the democratic faction. In the spring of 461 B.C.E., Cimon was ostracized, and Athens made an alliance with Argos, Sparta's traditional enemy. Almost overnight, Cimon's domestic and foreign policies had been overturned.

## THE DIVISION OF GREECE

The new regime at Athens, led by Pericles and the democratic faction, was confident and ambitious. When Megara, getting the worst of a border dispute with Corinth, withdrew from the Peloponnesian League, the Athenians accepted the Megarians as

**Peloponnesian Wars**   Series of wars between Athens and Sparta beginning in 460 B.C.E.

allies. Sparta, however, resented the defection of Megara to Athens, leading to the outbreak of the first of the **Peloponnesian Wars**, the first phase in a protracted struggle between Athens and Sparta. The Athenians conquered Aegina and gained control of Boeotia. At this moment Athens was supreme and apparently invulnerable, controlling the states on its borders and dominating the sea. (See Map 3–2.)

About 455 B.C.E., however, the tide turned. A disastrous defeat met an Athenian fleet that had gone to aid an Egyptian rebellion against Persia. The great loss of men, ships, and prestige caused rebellions in the empire, forcing Athens to make a truce in Greece to subdue its allies in the Aegean. In 449 B.C.E., the Athenians ended the war against Persia.

In 446 B.C.E., the war on the Greek mainland broke out again. Rebellions in Boeotia and Megara removed Athens's land defenses and brought a Spartan invasion. Rather than fight, Pericles, the commander of the Athenian army, agreed to a peace of thirty years by the terms of which he abandoned all Athenian possessions on the Greek mainland outside of Attica. In return, the Spartans gave formal recognition to the Athenian Empire. From then on, Greece was divided into two power blocs: Sparta with its alliance on the mainland, and Athens ruling its empire in the Aegean.

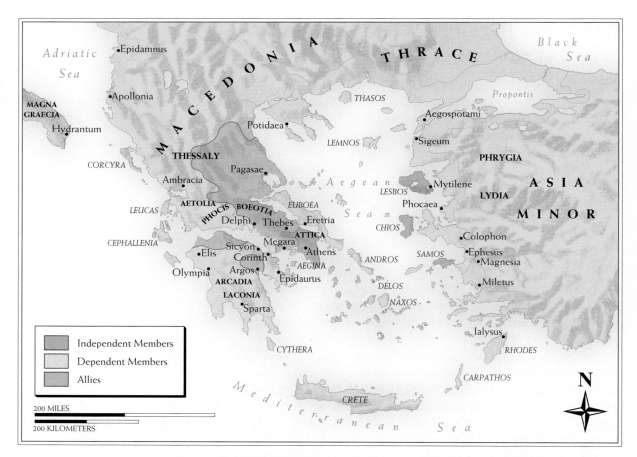

**MAP 3–2   The Athenian Empire about 450 B.C.E.**   The Athenian Empire at its fullest extent. We see Athens and the independent states that provided manned ships for the imperial fleet but paid no tribute; dependent states that paid tribute; and states allied to, but not actually in, the empire.

**Why would** some of the weakest and most dependent Greek states be located in Asia Minor and Thrace?

# CLASSICAL GREECE

## THE ATHENIAN EMPIRE

Because of the peace with Persia, the Athenians were compelled to find a new justification for their empire. They called for a Panhellenic congress to meet at Athens to discuss rebuilding the temples the Persians had destroyed and to consider how to maintain freedom of the seas. When Sparta's reluctance to participate prevented the congress, Athens felt free to continue to collect funds from the allies, both to maintain its navy and to rebuild the Athenian temples. Athenian propaganda suggested that henceforth the allies would be treated as colonies and Athens as their mother city, the whole to be held together by good feeling and common religious observances.

There is little reason, however, to believe the allies were taken in or were truly content with their lot. Nothing could cloak the fact that Athens was becoming the master and its allies mere subjects. The change from alliance to empire came about because of the pressure of war and rebellion and largely because the allies were unwilling to see to their own defense. Although the empire had many friends among the lower classes and the democratic politicians in the subject cities, it was seen more and more as a tyranny. Athenian prosperity and security, however, had come to depend on the empire, and the Athenians were determined to defend it.

## ATHENIAN DEMOCRACY

Even as the Athenians were tightening their control over their empire, they were expanding democracy at home. Under the leadership of Pericles, they evolved the freest government the world had yet seen.

**Democratic Legislation**   Legislation was passed making the *hoplite* class eligible for the *archonship*, and, in practice, no one was thereafter prevented from serving in this office on the basis of his property class. Pericles himself proposed a law introducing pay for jury members, opening that important duty to the poor. Circuit judges were reintroduced, a policy making swift impartial justice available even to the poorest residents in the countryside.

Finally, Pericles himself introduced a bill limiting citizenship to those who had two citizen parents. Democracy was defined as the privilege of those who held citizenship, making citizenship a valuable commodity. Limiting it increased its value. Women, resident aliens, and slaves were also denied participation in government in all the Greek states.

(a)  (b)

**An Athenian silver** four-drachma coin (tetradrachm) from the fifth century B.C.E. (440–430 B.C.E.). On the front (a) is the profile of Athena and on the back (b) is her symbol of wisdom, the owl. The silver from which the coins were struck came chiefly from the state mines at Sunium in southern Attica.

Hirmer Fotoarchiv

**How did the Athenians use economic exploitation to transform the Delian League into the Athenian Empire?**

**How Did the Democracy Work?**   Within the citizen body, the extent of Athenian democracy was remarkable. The popular assembly—a collection of the people, not their representatives—had to approve every decision of the state. Every judicial decision was subject to appeal to a popular court chosen from an annual panel of jurors widely representative of the Athenian population. (See "Encountering the Past, Going to Court in Athens.") Most officials were selected by lot without regard to class. All public officials were subject to scrutiny before taking office and could be called to account or be removed from office during their tenure. They were held to compulsory

# ENCOUNTERING THE PAST

## GOING TO COURT IN ATHENS

The Athenians placed the administration of justice directly into the hands of their fellow citizens, including the poorest ones. Each year 6,000 Athenian males, between a quarter and a fifth of the citizen body, signed on to a panel. (Because women were not considered citizens, they were not allowed to sit on juries or sue in the courts.) From this panel on any given day, jurors were assigned to specific courts and cases. The usual size of a jury was 501, although there were juries of from 51 to as many as 1,501 members.

Unlike in a modern American court, there was no public prosecutor, no lawyers at all, and no judge. The jury was everything. Private citizens registered complaints and argued their own cases. In deciding fundamental matters of justice and fairness, the Athenian democrat put little faith in experts.

In the courtroom the plaintiff and defendant would each present his case for himself, rebut his opponent, cite the relevant laws and precedents, produce witnesses, and sum up. No trial lasted more than a day. The jury did not deliberate but just voted by secret ballot. A simple majority decided the verdict. If a penalty was called for and not prescribed by law (as few were), the plaintiff proposed one penalty, and the defendant a different one. The jury voted to choose one of these but could not propose any other. Normally, this process led both sides to suggest moderate penalties, for an unreasonable suggestion would alienate the jury. To further deter frivolous lawsuits, the plaintiff had to pay a large fine if he did not win a stated percentage of the jurors' votes.

The Athenian system of justice had obvious flaws. Decisions could be quirky and unpredictable because they were unchecked by precedent. Juries could be prejudiced, and the jurors had no defense except their own intelligence and knowledge against

speakers who cited laws incorrectly and distorted history. Speeches—unhampered by rules of evidence and relevance, and without the discipline judges impose—could be fanciful, false, and deceptive.

For all its flaws, however, the Athenian system was simple, speedy, open, and easily understood by the citizens. It counted, as always, on the common sense of the ordinary Athenian, and contained provisions aimed at producing moderate penalties and deterring unreasonable lawsuits. No legal technicalities or experts came between the citizens and their laws.

**Water Clock and Jury Ballots.** Participants in an Athenian trial could speak for only a limited time. A water clock (*clepsydra*) like this kept the time. In front of it are two ballots used by the jurors to vote in favor of the plaintiff or the defendant.

Picture Desk/The Art Archive/Agora Museum Athens/Dagli Orti

**What characteristics of Athenian democracy were revealed by the conduct of Athenian justice?**

WHAT WERE the advantages and disadvantages of the Athenian justice system? Do you think it would lead to fair and just results?

examination and accounting at the end of their term. There was no standing army, no police force, open or secret, and no way to coerce the people.

Pericles was elected to the generalship fifteen years in a row and thirty times in all, not because he was a dictator but because he was a persuasive speaker, a skillful politician, a respected military leader, an acknowledged patriot, and patently incorruptible. When he lost the people's confidence, they did not hesitate to depose him from office. In 443 B.C.E., however, he stood at the height of his power. The defeat of the Athenian fleet in the Egyptian campaign and the failure of Athens's continental campaigns had persuaded him to favor a conservative policy, seeking to retain the empire in the Aegean and live at peace with the Spartans. It was in this direction that he led Athens's imperial democracy in the years after the First Peloponnesian War. (See "Compare & Connect: Athenian Democracy—Pro and Con," on pages 66–67.)

## THE WOMEN OF ATHENS: LEGAL STATUS AND EVERYDAY LIFE

Men dominated Greek society, like most societies all over the world throughout history. This was true of the democratic city of Athens in the great days of Pericles, in the fifth century B.C.E., no less than of any other Greek city. The actual position of women in classical Athens, however, has been the subject of much controversy.

The bulk of the evidence, coming from the law, from philosophical and moral writings, and from information about the conditions of daily life and the organization of society, shows that women were excluded from most aspects of public life. They could not vote, could not take part in the political assemblies, could not hold public office, and could not take any direct part in politics.

In the private aspects of life women were always under the control of a male guardian—a father, a husband, or some other male relative.

The main function and responsibility of a respectable Athenian woman of a citizen family was to produce male heirs for the *oikos*, or household, of her husband. Because the pure and legitimate lineage of the offspring was important, women were carefully segregated from men outside the family and were confined to the women's quarters in the house. The only public function of women—an important one—was in the various rituals and festivals of the state religion. Apart from these activities, Athenian women were expected to remain at home out of sight, quiet, and unnoticed. Pericles told the widows and mothers of the Athenian men who died in the first year of the Peloponnesian War only this: "Your great glory is not to fall short of your natural character, and the greatest glory of women is to be least talked about by men, whether for good or bad."

The picture of the legal status of women derived from these sources is largely accurate. It does not fit well, however, with other evidence from mythology, from pictorial art, and from the tragedies and comedies by the great Athenian dramatists. These often show women as central characters and powerful figures in both the public and the private spheres, suggesting that Athenian women may have played a more complex role than their legal status suggests.

**An Exceptional Woman: Aspasia**  Pericles' life did not conform to his own prescription. After divorcing his first wife, he entered a liaison that was unique in his time, to a woman who was, in her own way, as remarkable as the great Athenian leader. His companion was Aspasia, a young woman who had left her native Miletus

# ATHENIAN DEMOCRACY—PRO AND CON

The first democracy in the world's history appeared in Athens at the end of the sixth century B.C.E. By the middle of the fifth century the Athenian constitution had broadened to give all adult males participation in all aspects of government.

Although most Greek states remained oligarchic, some adopted the Athenian model and became democratic, but democracy was harshly criticized by members of the upper classes, traditionalists, and philosophers. In the following documents Pericles, the most famous Athenian political leader, and an anonymous pamphleteer present contrasting evaluations of the Athenian democracy.

## QUESTIONS

1. What virtues does Pericles find in the Athenian constitution?

2. Against what criticisms is he defending it?

3. What are the author's objections to democracy?

4. How would a defender of the Athenian constitution and way of life meet his complaints?

5. To what extent do these descriptions agree?

6. How do they disagree?

## I. PERICLES' FUNERAL ORATION

*In 431 B.C.E., the first year of the Peloponnesian War, Pericles delivered a speech to honor and commemorate the Athenian soldiers who died in the fighting. A key part of it was the praise of the Athenian democratic constitution, which, he argued, justified the sacrifice they had made.*

Our constitution does not copy the laws of neighbouring states; we are rather a pattern to others than imitators ourselves. Its administration favours the many instead of the few; this is why it is called a democracy. If we look to the laws, they afford equal justice to all in their private differences; if to social standing, advancement in public life falls to reputation for capacity, class considerations not being allowed to interfere with merit; nor again does poverty bar the way, if a man is able to serve the state, he is not hindered by the obscurity of his condition. The freedom which we enjoy in our government extends also to our ordinary life. There, far from exercising a jealous surveillance over each other, we do not feel called upon to be angry with our neighbour for doing what he likes, or even to indulge in those injurious looks which cannot fail to be offensive, although they inflict no positive penalty. But all this ease in our private relations does not make us lawless as citizens. Against this fear is our chief safeguard, teaching us to obey the magistrates and the laws, particularly such as regard the protection of the injured, whether they are actually on the statute book, or belong to that code which, although unwritten, yet cannot be broken without acknowledged disgrace.

Source: Thucydides, *The Peloponnesian War* 2.37, trans. by Richard Crawley.

## II. ATHENIAN DEMOCRACY: AN UNFRIENDLY VIEW

*The following selection comes from an anonymous pamphlet thought to have been written in the midst of the Peloponnesian War. Because it has come down to us among the works of Xenophon, but cannot be his work, it is sometimes called "The Constitution of the Athenians" by Pseudo-Xenophon. It is also common to refer to the unknown author as "The Old Oligarch"—although neither his age nor his purpose is known—because of the obviously anti-democratic tone of the work. Such opinions were common among members of the upper classes in Athens late in the fifth century* B.C.E. *and thereafter.*

Now, in discussing the Athenian constitution, I cannot commend their present method of running the state, because in choosing it they preferred that the masses should do better than the respectable citizens; this, then, is my reason for not commending it. Since, however, they have made this choice, I will demonstrate how well they preserve their constitution and handle the other affairs for which the rest of the Greeks criticize them.

Again, some people are surprised at the fact that in all fields they give more power to the masses, the poor, and the common people than they do to the respectable elements of society, but it will become clear that they preserve the democracy by doing precisely this. When the poor, the ordinary people, and the lower classes flourish and increase in numbers, then the power of the democracy will be increased; if, however, the rich and the respectable flourish, the democrats increase the strength of their opponents. Throughout the world the aristocracy are opposed to democracy, for they are naturally least liable to loss of self-control and injustice and most meticulous in their regard for what is respectable, whereas the masses display extreme ignorance, indiscipline, and wickedness, for poverty gives them a tendency towards the ignoble, and in some cases the lack of money leads to their being uneducated and ignorant.

It may be objected that they ought not to grant each and every man the right of speaking in the Ekklesia and serving on the Boule, but only the ablest and best of them; however, in this also they are acting in their own best interests by allowing the mob also a voice. If none but the respectable spoke in the Ekklesia and the Boule, the result would benefit that class and harm the masses; as it is, anyone who wishes rises and speaks, and as a member of the mob he discovers what is to his own advantage and that of those like him.

But someone may say: "How could such a man find out what was advantageous to himself and the common people?" The Athenians realize that this man, despite his ignorance and badness, brings them more advantage because he is well-disposed to them than the ill-disposed, respectable man would, despite his virtue and wisdom. Such practices do not produce the best city, but they are the best way of preserving democracy. For the common people do not wish to be deprived of their rights in an admirably governed city, but to be free and to rule the city; they are not disturbed by inferior laws, for the common people get their strength and freedom from what you define as inferior laws.

**Pericles** (ca. 495–429 B.C.E.) was the leading statesman of Athens for much of the fifth century. This is a Roman copy in marble of the Greek bronze bust that was probably cast in the last decade of Pericles' life.

Library of Congress

**What does the sustained power of Pericles tell us about Athenian democracy?**

Source: *Aristotle and Xenophon on Democracy and Oligarchy*, trans. with introductions and commentary by J. M. Moore (Berkeley and Los Angeles: University of California Press, 1975), pp. 37–38.

**The Acropolis was** both the religious and civic center of Athens. In its final form it is the work of Pericles and his successors in the late fifth century B.C.E. This photograph shows the Parthenon and to its left, the Erechtheum.

Meredith Pillon, Greek National Tourism Organization

**Why did Pericles devote so much energy and so many resources to the construction of public buildings and monuments?**

and come to live in Athens. The ancient writers refer to her as a *hetaira*, a kind of high-class courtesan who provided men with both erotic and other kinds of entertainment.

Aspasia represented something completely different from Athenian women. She was not a child, not a sheltered and repressed creature confined to the narrow world of slave women, children, and female relatives, but a beautiful, independent, brilliantly witty young woman capable of holding her own in conversation with the best minds in Greece and of discussing and illuminating any question with her husband. There can be no doubt that Pericles loved her passionately. He took her into his house, and whether or not they were formally and legally married, he treated her as his one and only beloved wife.

## SLAVERY

The Greeks had some form of slavery from the earliest times, but true chattel slavery was initially rare. The most common forms of bondage were different kinds of serfdom in relatively backward areas such as Crete, Thessaly, and Sparta. Another early form of bondage involving a severe, but rarely permanent, loss of freedom resulted from default in debt.

True chattel slavery began to increase about 500 B.C.E. and remained important to Greek society thereafter. The main sources of slaves were war captives and the captives of pirates. Like the Chinese, Egyptians, and many other peoples, the Greeks regarded foreigners as inferior, and most slaves working for the Greeks were foreigners.

The chief occupation of the Greeks, as of most of the world before our century, was agriculture. Most Greek farmers worked small holdings too poor to support even one slave, but some had one or two slaves to work alongside them. The upper classes had larger farms that were let out to free tenant farmers or were worked by slaves, generally under an overseer who was himself a slave.

Larger numbers of slaves labored in industry, especially in mining. Most manufacturing was on a small scale, with shops using one, two, or a handful of slaves. Slaves worked as craftsmen in almost every trade, and, like agricultural slaves on small farms, they worked alongside their masters. Many slaves were domestic servants or shepherds. Publicly held slaves served as policemen, prison attendants, clerks, and secretaries.

The number of slaves in ancient Greece and their importance to Greek society are the subjects of controversy. We have no useful figures of the absolute number of slaves or their percentage of the free population in the classical period (fifth and fourth centuries B.C.E.), and estimates range from 20,000 to 100,000. Accepting the mean between the extremes, 60,000, and estimating the free population at its height at about 40,000 households, would yield a figure of fewer than two slaves per family. Estimates suggest that only a quarter to a third of free Athenians owned any slaves at all.

## RELIGION IN PUBLIC LIFE

In Athens, as in the other Greek states, religion was more a civic than a private matter. Participation in the rituals of the state religion was not a matter of faith, but of patriotism and good citizenship. In its most basic form, it had little to do with morality. Greek religion emphasized not moral conduct to orthodox belief, but the faithful practice of rituals meant to win the favor of the gods. To fail to carry out these duties or to attack the gods in any way was seen as a blow against the state and was severely punished.

Famous examples of such blasphemies and their punishment occurred late in the fifth and early in the fourth centuries B.C.E. The best known is the case of the philosopher Socrates. In 399 B.C.E., Socrates was convicted of not honoring the state's gods and of introducing new divinities, and he was put to death. This was connected with the further charge of corrupting the youths, both acts believed to do harm to the well-being of Athens. In ancient Greece there was no thought of separating religion from civic and political life.

# THE GREAT PELOPONNESIAN WAR

During the first decade after the Thirty Years' Peace of 445 B.C.E., the willingness of each side to respect the new arrangements was tested and not found wanting. About 435 B.C.E., however, a dispute in a remote and unimportant part of the Greek world ignited a long and disastrous war that shook the foundations of Greek civilization.

**HOW DID** the Peloponnesian War affect the faith in the *polis*?

## CAUSES

The spark that ignited the conflict was a civil war at Epidamnus, a Corcyraean colony on the Adriatic. This civil war caused a quarrel between Corcyra (modern Corfu) and its mother city and traditional enemy, Corinth, an ally of Sparta. The Corcyraean fleet was second in size only to that of Athens, and the Athenians feared that its capture by Corinth would threaten Athenian security. As a result, they made an alliance with the previously neutral Corcyra, angering Corinth and leading to a series of crises in 433–432 B.C.E. that threatened to bring the Athenian Empire into conflict with the Peloponnesian League.

In the summer of 432 B.C.E., the Spartans met to consider the grievances of their allies. Persuaded, chiefly by the Corinthians, that Athens was an insatiably aggressive power seeking to enslave all the Greeks, they voted for war. In the spring of 431 B.C.E., its army marched into Attica, the Athenian homeland.

## STRATEGIC STALEMATE

The Spartan strategy was traditional: to invade the enemy's country and threaten the crops, forcing the enemy to defend them in a *hoplite* battle. Such a battle the Spartans were sure to win because they had the better army and they outnumbered the Athenians at least two to one. Any ordinary *polis* would have yielded or fought and lost.

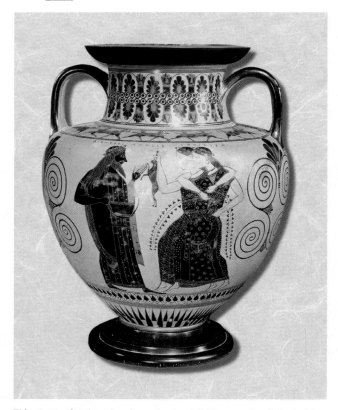

**This storage jar** *(amphora)*, made about 540 B.C.E., is attributed to the anonymous Athenian master artist called the Amasis painter. It shows Dionysus, the god of wine, revelry, and fertility, with two of his ecstatic female worshippers called maenads.

Cliché Bibliothèque Nationale de France—Paris

**What role did the gods play in the daily life of Classical Athens?**

Athens, however, had an enormous navy, an annual income from the empire, a vast reserve fund, and long walls that connected the fortified city with the fortified port of Piraeus.

The Athenians' strategy was to allow devastation of their own land to prove that Spartan invasions could not hurt Athens. At the same time, the Athenians launched seaborne raids on the Peloponnesian coast to hurt Sparta's allies. Pericles expected that within a year or two—three at most—the Peloponnesians would become discouraged and make peace, having learned their lesson.

The plan required restraint and the leadership only a Pericles could provide. In 429 B.C.E., however, after a devastating plague and a political crisis that had challenged his authority, Pericles died. After his death, no dominant leader emerged to hold the Athenians to a consistent policy. Two factions vied for influence: One, led by Nicias, wanted to continue the defensive policy, and the other, led by Cleon, preferred a more aggressive strategy. In 425 B.C.E., the aggressive faction was able to win a victory that changed the course of the war. Four hundred Spartans surrendered. Sparta offered peace at once to get them back. The great victory and the prestige it brought Athens made it safe to raise the imperial tribute, without which Athens could not continue to fight. The Athenians indeed wanted to continue, for the Spartan peace offer gave no adequate guarantee of Athenian security.

In 424 B.C.E., the Athenians undertook a more aggressive policy. They sought to make Athens safe by conquering Megara and Boeotia. Both attempts failed, and defeat helped discredit the aggressive policy, leading to a truce in 423 B.C.E. Meanwhile, Sparta's ablest general, Brasidas, took a small army to Thrace and Macedonia. He captured Amphipolis, the most important Athenian colony in the region. In 422 B.C.E., Cleon led an expedition to undo the work of Brasidas. At Amphipolis, both he and Brasidas died in battle. The removal of these two leaders of the aggressive factions in their respective cities paved the way for the Peace of Nicias, named for its chief negotiator, which was ratified in the spring of 421 B.C.E.

## THE FALL OF ATHENS

The peace, officially supposed to last fifty years and, with a few exceptions, guarantee the status quo, was in fact fragile. Neither side carried out all its commitments, and several of Sparta's allies refused ratification. In 415 B.C.E., Alcibiades persuaded the Athenians to attack Sicily to bring it under Athenian control. This ambitious and unnecessary undertaking ended in disaster in 413 B.C.E., when the entire expedition was destroyed. It shook Athens's prestige, reduced its power, provoked rebellions, and brought the wealth and power of Persia into the war on Sparta's side.

It is remarkable that the Athenians could continue fighting despite the disaster. Their allies rebelled, however, and Persia paid for fleets to sustain them. When its fleet was caught napping and was destroyed at Aegospotami in 405 B.C.E., Athens could not build another. The Spartans, under Lysander, a clever and ambitious general who was responsible for obtaining Persian support, cut off the food supply through the Hellespont, and the Athenians were starved into submission. In 404 B.C.E., they surrendered unconditionally; the city walls were dismantled, Athens was permitted no fleet, and the empire was gone. The Great Peloponnesian War was over.

# COMPETITION FOR LEADERSHIP IN THE FOURTH CENTURY B.C.E.

Athens's defeat did not bring domination to the Spartans. Instead, the period from 404 B.C.E. until the Macedonian conquest of Greece in 338 B.C.E. was a time of intense rivalry among the Greek cities, each seeking to achieve leadership and control over the others.

**HOW DID** Athens and Sparta compete for leadership in the Greek world?

## THE HEGEMONY OF SPARTA

The collapse of the Athenian Empire created a vacuum of power in the Aegean and opened the way for Spartan leadership or hegemony. Under the leadership of Lysander, the Spartans made a mockery of their promise to free the Greeks by stepping into the imperial role of Athens in the cities along the European coast and the islands of the Aegean. In most of the cities, Lysander installed a board of ten local oligarchs loyal to him and supported them with a Spartan garrison. Tribute brought in an annual revenue almost as great as that the Athenians had collected.

The increasing arrogance of Sparta's policies alienated some of its allies, especially Thebes and Corinth. In 404 B.C.E., Lysander installed an oligarchic government in Athens. Democratic exiles took refuge in Thebes and Corinth and raised an army to challenge the oligarchy. Sparta's conservative king, Pausanias, replaced Lysander, arranging a peaceful settlement and, ultimately, the restoration of democracy. Thereafter, Athenian foreign policy remained under Spartan control, but otherwise Athens was free.

In 405 B.C.E., Darius II of Persia died and was succeeded by Artaxerxes II. His younger brother, Cyrus, received Spartan help in recruiting a Greek mercenary army to help him contest the throne. The Greeks marched inland as far as Mesopotamia, where they defeated the Persians at Cunaxa in 401 B.C.E., but Cyrus was killed in the battle. The Greeks were able to march back to the Black Sea and safety; their success revealed the potential weakness of the Persian Empire.

The Greeks of Asia Minor had supported Cyrus and were now afraid of Artaxerxes' revenge. The Spartans accepted their request for aid and sent an army into Asia, attracted by the prospect of prestige, power, and money. In 396 B.C.E., the command of Sparta's army was given to a new king, Agesilaus, who dominated Sparta until his death in 360 B.C.E.

Agesilaus collected much booty and frightened the Persians. They sent a messenger with money and promises of further support to friendly factions in all of the Greek states likely to help them against Sparta. By 395 B.C.E., Thebes was able to organize an alliance that included Argos, Corinth, and a resurgent Athens. The result was the Corinthian War (395–387 B.C.E.), which put an end to Sparta's Asian adventure. In 394 B.C.E., the Persian fleet destroyed Sparta's maritime empire. Meanwhile, the Athenians rebuilt their walls, enlarged their navy, and even recovered some of their lost empire in the Aegean. The war ended when the exhausted Greek states accepted a peace dictated by the Great King of Persia.

The Persians, frightened now by the recovery of Athens, turned the management of Greece over to Sparta. Agesilaus broke up all alliances except the Peloponnesian League. He used or threatened to use the Spartan army to interfere in other *poleis* and put friends of Sparta in power within them. Sparta reached a new level of lawless arrogance in 382 B.C.E., when it seized Thebes during peacetime without warning or pretext. In 379 B.C.E., a Spartan army made a similar attempt on Athens. That action persuaded the Athenians to join with Thebes, which had rebelled from Sparta a few months earlier, to wage war on the Spartans. In 371 B.C.E., the Thebans, led by their great generals Pelopidas and Epaminondas, defeated the Spartans at Leuctra. The Theban victory brought the end of Sparta as a power of the first rank.

## THE HEGEMONY OF THEBES: THE SECOND ATHENIAN EMPIRE

Thebes's power after its victory at Leuctra lay in its democratic constitution, its control over Boeotia, and its two outstanding and popular generals. One of these generals, Pelopidas, died in a successful attempt to gain control of Thessaly. The other, Epaminondas, made Thebes dominant over all of Greece north of Athens and the Corinthian Gulf and challenged the reborn Athenian Empire in the Aegean. All this activity provoked resistance, and by 362 B.C.E., Thebes faced a Peloponnesian coalition as well as Athens. Epaminondas, once again leading a Boeotian army into the Peloponnesus, confronted this coalition at the Battle of Mantinea. His army was victorious, but Epaminondas himself was killed, and Theban dominance died with him.

The Second Athenian Confederation, which Athens had organized in 378 B.C.E., was aimed at resisting Spartan aggression in the Aegean. Its constitution avoided the abuses of the Delian League, but the Athenians soon began to repeat them anyway. This time, however, they did not have the power to put down resistance. When the collapse of Sparta and Thebes and the restraint of Persia removed any reason for voluntary membership, Athens's allies revolted. By 355 B.C.E., Athens had to abandon most of the empire. After two centuries of almost continuous warfare, the Greeks returned to the chaotic disorganization that characterized the time before the founding of the Peloponnesian League.

### THE COMPETITION FOR LEADERSHIP OF GREECE

| | |
|---|---|
| 479 B.C.E. | Battles of Plataea and Mycale |
| 478–477 B.C.E. | Formation of the Delian League |
| 465–463 B.C.E. | Thasos attempts to leave the league |
| 462 B.C.E. | Pericles begins to lead Athens |
| 460–445 B.C.E. | First Peloponnesian War |
| 454 B.C.E. | Athens is defeated in Egypt |
| 449 B.C.E. | Athens makes peace with Persia |
| 435 B.C.E. | Corinth attacks Corcyra |
| 432–404 B.C.E. | Great Peloponnesian War |
| 421 B.C.E. | Peace of Nicias |
| 415–413 B.C.E. | Athens's Sicilian campaign |
| 404 B.C.E. | Sparta defeats Athens |
| 404–403 B.C.E. | Thirty Tyrants govern Athens |
| 382 B.C.E. | Sparta seizes Thebes |
| 378 B.C.E. | Second Athenian Confederation |
| 371 B.C.E. | Thebes defeats Sparta at Leuctra |
| 362 B.C.E. | End of Theban hegemony |
| 338 B.C.E. | Philip of Macedon dominates Greece |
| 336–323 B.C.E. | Reign of Alexander the Great |

# THE CULTURE OF CLASSICAL GREECE

**WHAT ARE** the achievements of Classical Greece?

The repulse of the Persian invasion released a flood of creative activity in Greece that was rarely, if ever, matched anywhere at any time. The century and a half between the Persian retreat and the conquest of Greece by Philip of Macedon (479–338 B.C.E.) produced achievements of such quality as to justify the designation of that era as the Classical Period. Ironically, we often use the term *classical* to suggest calm and serenity, but the word that best describes Greek life, thought, art, and literature in this period is *tension*.

## THE FIFTH CENTURY B.C.E.

Two sources of tension contributed to the artistic outpouring of fifth-century B.C.E. Greece. One arose from the conflict between the Greeks' pride in their accomplishments and their concern that overreaching would bring retribution. The second source of tension was the conflict between the soaring hopes and achievements of individuals and the claims and limits their fellow citizens in the *polis* put on them. These tensions were felt throughout Greece. They had the most spectacular consequences, however, in Athens in its Golden Age, the time between the Persian and the Peloponnesian wars.

**Attic Tragedy**   Nothing reflects Athens's concerns better than Attic tragedy, which emerged as a major form of Greek poetry in the fifth century B.C.E. The tragedies were presented in a contest as part of the public religious observations in honor of the god Dionysus. The festivals in which they were shown were civic occasions.

Attic tragedy served as a forum in which the poets raised vital issues of the day, enabling the Athenian audience to think about them in a serious, yet exciting, context. On rare occasions, the subject of a play might be a contemporary or historic event, but almost always it was chosen from mythology. Until late in the century, the tragedies always dealt solemnly with difficult questions of religion, politics, ethics, morality, or some combination of these. The plays of the dramatists Aeschylus and Sophocles, for example, follow this pattern. The plays of Euripides, written toward the end of the century, are less solemn and more concerned with individual psychology.

**Old Comedy**   Comedy was introduced into the Dionysian festival early in the fifth century B.C.E. Cratinus, Eupolis, and the great master of the genre called Old Comedy, Aristophanes (ca. 450–385 B.C.E.), the only one from whom we have complete plays, wrote political comedies. They were filled with scathing invective and satire against such contemporary figures as Pericles, Cleon, Socrates, and Euripides.

**Architecture and Sculpture**   The great architectural achievements of Periclean Athens, as much as Athenian tragedy, illustrate the magnificent results of the union and tension between religious and civic responsibilities, on the one hand, and the transcendent genius of the individual artist, on the other. Beginning in 448 B.C.E. and continuing to the outbreak of the Great Peloponnesian War, Pericles undertook a great building program on the Acropolis. The income from the empire paid for it. Pericles' main purpose seems to have been to represent visually the greatness and power of Athens, by emphasizing intellectual and artistic achievement—civilization rather than military and naval power. It was as though these buildings were tangible proof of Pericles' claim that Athens was "the school of Hellas"—that is, the intellectual center of all Greece.

**Philosophy**   The tragic dramas, architecture, and sculpture of the fifth century B.C.E. all indicate an extraordinary concern with human beings—their capacities, their limits, their nature, and their place in the universe. The same concern is clear in the development of philosophy.

To be sure, some philosophers continued the speculation about the nature of the cosmos (as opposed to human nature) that began with Thales in the sixth century B.C.E. Parmenides of Elea and his pupil Zeno, in opposition to the earlier philosopher Heraclitus, argued that change was only an illusion of the senses. Reason and reflection showed that reality was fixed and unchanging, because it seemed evident that nothing could be created out of nothingness. Empedocles of Acragas further advanced such fundamental speculations by identifying four basic elements: fire, water, earth, and air. Like Parmenides, he thought that reality was permanent, but he thought it was not immobile; two primary forces, he contended, love and strife—or, as we might say, attraction and repulsion—moved the four elements.

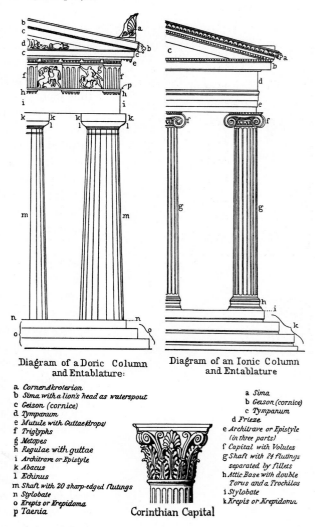

**Diagram of a Doric Column and Entablature**

a  Corner Akroterion
b  Sima with a lion's head as waterspout
c  Geison (cornice)
d  Tympanum
e  Mutule with Guttae (drops)
f  Triglyphs
g  Metopes
h  Regulae with guttae
i  Architrave or Epistyle
k  Abacus
l  Echinus
m  Shaft with 20 sharp-edged flutings
n  Stylobate
o  Krepis or Krepidoma
p  Taenia

**Diagram of an Ionic Column and Entablature**

a  Sima
b  Geison (cornice)
c  Tympanum
d  Frieze
e  Architrave or Epistyle (in three parts)
f  Capital with Volutes
g  Shaft with 24 flutings separated by fillets
h  Attic Base with double Torus and a Trochilos
i  Stylobate
k  Krepis or Krepidoma

**Corinthian Capital**

**The three orders** of Greek architecture, Doric, Ionic, and Corinthian, have had an enduring impact on Western architecture.

**What role did public spaces play in Athenian life?**

Empedocles' theory is clearly a step on the road to the atomist theory of Leucippus of Miletus and Democritus of Abdera. According to this theory, the world consists of innumerable tiny, solid, indivisible, and unchangeable particles—or "atoms"—that move about in the void. The size of the atoms and the arrangements they form when joined produce the secondary qualities that our senses perceive, such as color and shape. These secondary qualities are merely conventional—the result of human interpretation and agreement—unlike the atoms themselves, which are natural.

Previous to the atomists, Anaxagoras of Clazomenae, an older contemporary and a friend of Pericles, had spoken of tiny fundamental particles called *seeds*, which were put together on a rational basis by a force called *nous*, or "mind." Anaxagoras was thus suggesting a distinction between matter and mind. The atomists, however, regarded "soul," or mind, as material and believed purely physical laws guided everything. In these conflicting positions, we have the beginning of the enduring philosophical debate between materialism and idealism.

These speculations were of interest to few people, and in fact, most Greeks were suspicious of them. A group of professional teachers who emerged in the mid-fifth century began a far more influential debate. Called *Sophists*, they traveled about and received pay for teaching such practical techniques of persuasion as rhetoric, dialectic, and argumentation. Reflecting the human focus characteristic of fifth-century thought, they refrained from speculations about the physical universe, instead applying reasoned analysis to human beliefs and institutions. In doing so, they identified a central problem of human social life and the life of the *polis*: the conflict between nature and custom, or law. The more traditional among them argued that law itself was in accord with nature and was of divine origin, a view that fortified the traditional beliefs of the *polis*.

Others argued, however, that laws were merely the result of convention—an agreement among people—and not in accord with nature. The laws could not pretend to be a positive moral force but merely had the negative function of preventing people from harming each other. The most extreme Sophists argued that law was contrary to nature, a trick whereby the weak control the strong.

**History**    The first prose literature in the form of history was Herodotus's account of the Persian War. "The father of history," as he has been deservedly called, was born shortly before the outbreak of the war. His account goes far beyond all previous chronicles, genealogies, and geographical studies and attempts to explain human actions and to draw instruction from them.

Although his work was completed about 425 B.C.E. and shows a few traces of Sophist influence, its spirit is that of an earlier time. Herodotus accepted the evidence of legends and oracles, although not uncritically, and often explained human events in terms of divine intervention. Yet the *History* is typical of its time in celebrating the crucial role of human intelligence. Nor was Herodotus unaware of the importance of institutions. His pride in the superiority of the Greek *polis*, in the discipline it inspired in its citizen soldiers, and in the superiority of the Greeks' voluntary obedience to law over the Persians' fear of punishment is unmistakable.

Thucydides, the historian of the Peloponnesian War, was born about 460 B.C.E. and died a few years after the end of the Great Peloponnesian War. He was very much a product of the late fifth century B.C.E. His work, which was influenced by the secular, human-centered, skeptical rationalism of the Sophists, also reflects the scientific attitude of the school of medicine named for his contemporary, Hippocrates of Cos.

The Hippocratic school, known for its pioneering work in medicine and scientific theory, emphasized an approach to the understanding, diagnosis, and treatment of disease that combined careful observation with reason. In the same way, Thucydides took pains to achieve factual accuracy and tried to use his evidence to discover meaningful patterns of human behavior. His work has proved to be, as he hoped, "a possession forever." Its description of the terrible civil war between the two basic kinds of *poleis* is a final and fitting example of the tension that was the source of both the greatness and the decline of Classical Greece.

## THE FOURTH CENTURY B.C.E.

Historians often speak of the Peloponnesian War as the crisis of the *polis* and of the fourth century B.C.E. as the period of its decline. The Greeks of the fourth century B.C.E. did not know, however, that their traditional way of life was on the verge of destruction. Still, thinkers recognized that they lived in a time of troubles, and they responded in various ways. Some looked to the past and tried to shore up the weakened structure of the *polis*; others tended toward despair and looked for new solutions; and still others averted their gaze from the public arena altogether. All these responses are apparent in the literature, philosophy, and art of the period.

**Drama**    The tendency of some to turn away from the life of the *polis* and inward to everyday life, the family, and their own individuality is apparent in the poetry of the fourth century B.C.E. A new genre, called Middle Comedy, replaced the political subjects and personal invective of the Old Comedy with a comic-realistic depiction of daily life, plots of intrigue, and a mild satire of domestic situations. Significantly, the role of the chorus, which in some way represented the *polis*, was diminished quite a bit. These trends all continued and were carried even further in the New Comedy. Its leading playwright, Menander (342–291 B.C.E.), completely abandoned mythological subjects in favor of domestic tragicomedy.

Tragedy faded as a robust and original form. It became common to revive the great plays of the previous century. No tragedies written in the fourth century B.C.E. have been preserved. The plays of Euripides, which rarely won first prize when first

### QUICK REVIEW
**Heredotus**

- "Father of history"
- Assigned human intelligence a crucial role in determining the course of events
- Credited Greece's victory over Persia to citizens' love of liberty

**The theater at** Epidaurus was built in the fourth century B.C.E. The city contained the Sanctuary of Asclepius, a god of healing, and drew many visitors who packed the theater at religious festivals.

Hirmer Fotoarchiv

**What was the relationship between religion and theater in Classical Athens?**

**The striding god** from Artemisium is a bronze statue dating from about 460 B.C.E. It was found in the sea near Artemisium, the northern tip of the large Greek island of Euboea, and is now on display in the Athens archaeological museum. Exactly whom he represents is not known. Some have thought him to be Poseidon holding a trident; others believe he is Zeus hurling a thunderbolt. In either case, he is a splendid representative of the early Classical Period of Greek sculpture.

National Archaeological Museum, Athens

**What does the striding god tell us about Classical Greek attitudes toward the male human body?**

**Academy**    School founded by Plato in Athens to train statesmen and citizens.

produced for Dionysian festival competitions, became increasingly popular in the fourth century and after. Euripides was less interested in cosmic confrontations of conflicting principles than in the psychology and behavior of individual human beings.

**Sculpture**    The same movement away from the grand, the ideal, and the general, and toward the ordinary, the real, and the individual is apparent in the development of Greek sculpture. To see these developments, one has only to compare the statue of the striding god from Artemisium (ca. 460 B.C.E.), thought to be either Zeus on the point of releasing a thunderbolt or Poseidon about to throw his trident, or the Doryphoros of Polycleitus (ca. 450–440 B.C.E.) with the Hermes of Praxiteles (ca. 340–330 B.C.E.) or the Apoxyomenos attributed to Lysippus (ca. 330 B.C.E.).

## PHILOSOPHY AND THE CRISIS OF THE *POLIS*

**Socrates**    Probably the most complicated response to the crisis of the *polis* may be found in the life and teachings of Socrates (469–399 B.C.E.). Because he wrote nothing, our knowledge of him comes chiefly from his disciples Plato and Xenophon and from later tradition. Socrates was committed to the search for truth and for the knowledge about human affairs that he believed reason could discover. His method was to question and cross-examine men, particularly those reputed to know something, such as craftsmen, poets, and politicians.

The result was always the same. Those Socrates questioned might have technical information and skills but seldom had any knowledge of the fundamental principles of human behavior. It is understandable that Athenians so exposed should be angry with their examiner, and it is not surprising they thought Socrates was undermining the beliefs and values of the *polis*. Socrates' unconcealed contempt for democracy, which seemingly relied on ignorant amateurs to make important political decisions without any certain knowledge, created further hostility. Moreover, his insistence on the primacy of his own individualism and his determination to pursue philosophy even against the wishes of his fellow citizens reinforced this hostility and the prejudice that went with it.

In 399 B.C.E., an Athenian jury condemned him to death on the charges of bringing new gods into the city and of corrupting the youth. His dialectical inquiries had angered many important people. He was given a chance to escape but, as Plato's *Crito* tells us, he refused to do so because of his veneration of the laws. Socrates' career set the stage for later responses to the travail of the *polis*. He recognized its difficulties and criticized its shortcomings, and he turned away from an active political life, but he did not abandon the idea of the *polis*. He fought as a soldier in its defense, obeyed its laws, and sought to put its values on a sound foundation by reason.

**Plato**    Plato (429–347 B.C.E.) was by far the most important of Socrates' associates and is a perfect example of the pupil who becomes greater than his master. He was the first systematic philosopher and therefore the first to place political ideas in their full philosophical context. Plato came from a noble Athenian family, and he looked forward to an active political career until the excesses of the Thirty Tyrants and the execution of Socrates discouraged him from that pursuit.

In 386 B.C.E., he founded the **Academy**, a center of philosophical investigation and a school for training statesmen and citizens. It had a powerful impact on Greek thought and lasted until the emperor Justinian closed it in the sixth century C.E.

Like Socrates, Plato firmly believed in the *polis* and its values. Its virtues were order, harmony, and justice, and one of its main objects was to produce good people. Like his master, Plato thought the *polis* was in accord with nature. He accepted Socrates' doctrine of the identity of virtue and knowledge. He made it plain what that knowledge was: *episteme*—science—a body of true and unchanging wisdom open to only a few philosophers, whose training, character, and intellect allowed them to see reality. Only such people were qualified to rule; they would prefer the life of pure contemplation but would accept their responsibility and take their turn as philosopher kings. The training of such an individual required a specialization of function and a subordination of that individual to the community even greater than that at Sparta. This specialization would lead to Plato's definition of justice: Each person should do only that one thing to which his or her nature is best suited.

Plato understood that the *polis* of his day suffered from terrible internal stress, class struggle, and factional divisions. His solution, however, was not that of some Greeks—that is, conquest and resulting economic prosperity. For Plato, the answer was in moral and political reform. The way to harmony was to destroy the causes of strife: private property, the family—anything, in short, that stood between the individual citizen and devotion to the *polis*.

Concern for the redemption of the *polis* was at the heart of Plato's system of philosophy. He began by asking the traditional questions: What is a good man, and how is he made? The goodness of a human being belonged to moral philosophy, and when goodness became a function of the state, it became political philosophy. Because goodness depended on knowledge of the good, it required a theory of knowledge and an investigation of what kind of knowledge goodness required. The answer must be

# Overview   **The Three Great Greek Intellectuals**

| | |
|---|---|
| **SOCRATES (469–399 B.C.E.)** | One of the first Greek intellectuals to recognize the shortcomings of the *polis*. He believed in the existence of truth and the power of reason to discover it. He made no attempt to conceal his contempt for Athenian democracy—a political system that he said empowered the ignorant to make decisions about things they did not understand. Socrates was eventually tried and executed for undercutting the Athenian way of life. |
| **PLATO (429–347 B.C.E.)** | The most important of Socrates' followers, he was the first to formulate a consistent worldview and a method for exploring all of life's fundamental questions. Like Socrates, Plato believed in the *polis* and saw it as consistent with humanity's social nature. He established the Academy in 386 B.C.E., a school for training statesmen and citizens. Plato believed power should be entrusted to philosophers only and that the *polis* could only be redeemed by improving its ability to produce good citizens. |
| **ARISTOTLE (384–322 B.C.E.)** | The most prominent of Plato's students, he founded the Lyceum (the school of the Peripatetics). Unlike Plato's students at the Academy, Aristotle's students gathered, ordered, and analyzed data from all fields of knowledge. He wrote on logic, physics, astronomy, biology, ethics, rhetoric, literary criticism, and politics. Aristotle believed human beings are social creatures and that the *polis* was necessary to realize their potential. He also stated that a moderate constitution was necessary to create a state dominated by the middle class, not by the rich or the poor. |

metaphysical and so required a full examination of metaphysics. Even when the philosopher knew the good, however, the question remained how the state could bring its citizens to the necessary comprehension of that knowledge. The answer required a theory of education. Even purely logical and metaphysical questions, therefore, were subordinate to the overriding political questions. In this way, Plato's need to find a satisfactory foundation for the beleaguered *polis* contributed to the birth of systematic philosophy.

**Aristotle**    Aristotle (384–322 B.C.E.) was a pupil of Plato's and owed much to the thought of his master, but his different experience and cast of mind led him in new directions. He was born at Stagirus, the son of the court doctor of neighboring Macedon. As a young man, he went to Athens to study at the Academy, where he stayed until Plato's death. Then he joined a Platonic colony at Assos in Asia Minor, and from there he moved to Mytilene. In both places he did research in marine biology, and biological interests played a large part in all his thoughts. In 342 B.C.E., Philip, the king of Macedon, appointed him tutor to his son, the young Alexander. (See "The Hellenistic World," page 79.)

In 336 B.C.E., Aristotle returned to Athens, where he founded his own school, the **Lyceum**. Unlike the Academy, the members of the Lyceum took little interest in mathematics and were concerned with gathering, ordering, and analyzing all human knowledge. Almost all of what we possess of their work is in the form of philosophical and scientific studies, whose loose organization and style suggest they were lecture notes. The range of subjects treated is astonishing, including logic, physics, astronomy, biology, ethics, rhetoric, literary criticism, and politics.

In each field, the method is the same. Aristotle began with observation of the empirical evidence, which in some cases was physical and in others was common opinion. To this body of information, he applied reason and discovered inconsistencies or difficulties. To deal with these, he introduced metaphysical principles to explain the problems or to reconcile the inconsistencies.

His view on all subjects, like Plato's, was teleological; that is, both Plato and Aristotle recognized purposes apart from and greater than the will of the individual human being. Plato's purposes, however, were contained in ideas, or forms, that were transcendental concepts outside the experience of most people. For Aristotle, the purposes of most things were easily inferred by observation of their behavior in the world. Aristotle's most striking characteristics are his moderation and his common sense. His epistemology finds room for both reason and experience; his metaphysics gives meaning and reality to both mind and body; his ethics aims at the good life, which is the contemplative life, but recognizes the necessity for moderate wealth, comfort, and pleasure.

All these qualities are evident in Aristotle's political thought. Like Plato, he opposed the Sophists' assertion that the *polis* was contrary to nature and the result of mere convention. His response was to apply to politics the teleology he saw in all nature. In his view, matter existed to achieve an end, and it developed until it achieved its form, which was its end. There was constant development from matter to form, from potential to actual. Therefore, human primitive instincts could be seen as the matter out of which the human's potential as a political being could be realized. The *polis* made individuals self-sufficient and allowed the full realization of their potentiality. It was therefore natural.

It was also the highest point in the evolution of the social institutions that serve the human need to continue the species—marriage, household, village, and, finally, *polis*. For Aristotle, the purpose of the *polis* was neither economic nor military, but moral. According to Aristotle, "The end of the state is the good life" (*Politics* 1280b), the life lived "for the sake of noble actions" (1281a), a life of virtue and morality.

Characteristically, Aristotle was less interested in the best state—the utopia that required philosophers to rule it—than in the best state that was practically possible, one that

**Lyceum**    School founded by Aristotle in Athens that focused on the gathering and analysis of data from all fields of knowledge.

would combine justice with stability. The constitution for that state he called *politeia*, not the best constitution, but the next best, the one most suited to, and most possible for most states. Its quality was moderation, and it naturally gave power to neither the rich nor the poor, but to the middle class, which must also be the most numerous. The middle class possessed many virtues; because of its moderate wealth, it was free of the arrogance of the rich and the malice of the poor. For this reason, it was the most stable class.

The stability of the constitution also came from its being a mixed constitution, blending in some way the laws of democracy and of oligarchy. Aristotle's scheme was unique because of its realism and the breadth of its vision. Aristotle combined the practical analysis of political and economic realities with the moral and political purposes of the traditional defenders of the *polis*. The result was a passionate confidence in the virtues of moderation and of the middle class, and the proposal of a constitution that would give it power. It is ironic that the ablest defense of the *polis* came soon before its demise.

# THE HELLENISTIC WORLD

The term **Hellenistic** was coined in the nineteenth century to describe the period of three centuries during which Greek culture spread far from its homeland to Egypt and deep into Asia. The new civilization formed in this expansion was a mixture of Greek and Near Eastern elements, although the degree of mixture varied from time to time and place to place. The Hellenistic world was larger than the world of Classical Greece, and its major political units were much larger than the city-states, though these persisted in different forms. The new political and cultural order had its roots in the rise to power of a Macedonian dynasty that conquered Greece and the Persian Empire in two generations.

**WHO WAS** Alexander the Great and what was his legacy?

**Hellenistic** Term that describes the cosmopolitan civilization, established under the Macedonians, that combined aspects of Greek and Middle Eastern cultures.

## THE MACEDONIAN CONQUEST

The quarrels among the Greeks brought on defeat and conquest by a new power that suddenly rose to eminence in the fourth century B.C.E.: the kingdom of Macedon (see Map 3–1, page 60). By Greek standards, Macedon was a backward, semibarbaric land. It had no *poleis* and was ruled loosely by a king. A council of nobles checked the royal power and could reject a weak or incompetent king. Hampered by constant wars with the barbarians, internal strife, loose organization, and lack of money, Macedon played no great part in Greek affairs up to the fourth century B.C.E.

The Macedonians were of the same stock as the Greeks and spoke a Greek dialect, and the nobles, at least, thought of themselves as Greeks. The kings claimed descent from Heracles and the royal house of Argos. They tried to bring Greek culture into their court and won acceptance at the Olympic games. If a king could be found to unify this nation, it was bound to play a greater part in Greek affairs.

**Philip of Macedon**  That king was Philip II (r. 359–336 B.C.E.), who, although still under thirty, took advantage of his appointment as regent to overthrow his infant nephew and make himself king. His talents for war and diplomacy and his boundless ambition made him the ablest king in Macedonian history. Using both diplomatic and military means, he pacified the tribes on his frontiers and strengthened his own hold on the throne. Then he began to undermine Athenian control of the northern Aegean. He took Amphipolis, which gave him control of gold and silver mines. The income allowed him to found new cities, to bribe politicians in foreign towns, and to reorganize his army into the finest fighting force in the world.

**The Macedonian Army**  Philip created a versatile and powerful army that was at once national and professional, unlike the amateur armies of citizen-soldiers who fought for

**Hermes and Dionysus**

Praxiteles (c. 400–300 B.C.E.), *Hermes and Dionysus* c. 350–330 B.C.E. National Archeological Museum, Olympia. Scala/ Art Resource, NY

**In what ways does the sculpture represent a departure from earlier Classical works?**

the individual *poleis*. The infantry was drawn from among Macedonian farmers and the frequently rebellious Macedonian hill people. In time, these two elements were integrated to form a loyal and effective national force. Infantrymen were armed with thirteen-foot pikes instead of the more common nine-foot pikes and stood in a more open phalanx formation than the *hoplite* phalanx of the *poleis*. The effectiveness of this formation depended more on the skillful use of the pike than the weight of the charge. In Macedonian tactics, the role of the phalanx was not to be the decisive force, but to hold the enemy until a massed cavalry charge could strike a winning blow on the flank or into a gap. The cavalry was made up of Macedonian nobles and clan leaders, called Companions, who lived closely with the king and developed a special loyalty to him.

Philip also employed mercenaries who knew the latest tactics used by mobile light-armed Greek troops and were familiar with the most sophisticated siege machinery known to the Greeks. With these mercenaries, and with draft forces from among his allies, he could expand on his native Macedonian army of as many as 40,000 men.

**The Invasion of Greece**    So armed, Philip turned south toward central Greece. Since 355 B.C.E., the Phocians had been fighting against Thebes and Thessaly. Philip gladly accepted the request of the Thessalians to be their general, defeated Phocis, and treacherously took control of Thessaly. Swiftly he turned northward again to Thrace and gained domination over the northern Aegean coast and the European side of the straits to the Black Sea. This conquest threatened the vital interests of Athens, which still had a formidable fleet of three hundred ships.

The Athens of 350 B.C.E. was not the Athens of Pericles. It had neither imperial revenue nor allies to share the burden of war, and its own population was smaller than in the fifth century. The Athenians, therefore, were reluctant to go on expeditions themselves or even to send out mercenary armies under Athenian generals, for they had to be paid out of taxes or contributions from Athenian citizens.

The leading spokesman against these tendencies and the cautious foreign policy that went with them was Demosthenes (384–322 B.C.E.), one of the greatest orators in Greek history. He was convinced that Philip was a dangerous enemy to Athens and the other Greeks. He spent most of his career urging the Athenians to resist Philip's encroachments. He was right, for beginning in 349 B.C.E., Philip attacked several cities in northern and central Greece and firmly planted Macedonian power in those regions.

The years between 346 B.C.E. and 340 B.C.E. were spent in diplomatic maneuvering, each side trying to win useful allies. At last, Philip attacked Perinthus and Byzantium, the lifeline of Athenian commerce; in 340 B.C.E., he besieged both cities and declared war. The Athenian fleet saved both, and so in the following year, Philip marched into Greece. Demosthenes performed wonders in rallying the Athenians and winning Thebes over to the Athenian side. In 338 B.C.E., however, Philip defeated the allied forces at Chaeronea in Boeotia. The decisive blow in this great battle was a cavalry charge led by Alexander, the eighteen-year-old son of Philip.

**The Macedonian Government of Greece**    The Macedonian settlement of Greek affairs was not as harsh as many had feared, although in some cities the friends of Macedon came to power and killed or exiled their enemies. Athens was spared from attack on the condition that it give up what was left of its empire and follow the lead of Macedon. The rest of Greece was arranged so as to remove all dangers to Philip's rule. To guarantee his security, Philip placed garrisons at Thebes, Chalcis, and Corinth.

In 338 B.C.E., Philip called a meeting of the Greek states to form the federal League of Corinth. The constitution of the league provided for autonomy, freedom from tribute and garrisons, and suppression of piracy and civil war. The league delegates would make foreign policy in theory without consulting their home governments or Philip. All this was a facade; not only was Philip of Macedon president of the league, but he was also its ruler. The defeat at Chaeronea ended Greek freedom and autonomy. Although it maintained its form and way of life for some time, the *polis* had lost control of its own affairs and the special conditions that had made it unique.

Philip did not choose Corinth as the seat of his new confederacy simply from convenience or by accident. It was at Corinth that the Greeks had gathered to resist a Persian invasion almost 150 years earlier. And it was there in 337 B.C.E. that Philip announced his intention to invade Persia in a war of liberation and revenge, as leader of the new league. In the spring of 336 B.C.E., however, as he prepared to begin the campaign, Philip was assassinated.

## ALEXANDER THE GREAT

Philip's first son, Alexander III (356–323 B.C.E.), later called Alexander the Great, succeeded his father at the age of twenty. The young king also inherited his father's daring plans to conquer Persia.

**The Conquest of the Persian Empire**   The Persian Empire was vast and its resources enormous. The usurper Cyrus and his Greek mercenaries, however, had shown it to be vulnerable when they penetrated deep into its interior in the fourth century B.C.E. Its size and disparate nature made it hard to control and exploit. Its rulers faced constant troubles on its far-flung frontiers and intrigues within the royal palace. Throughout the fourth century, they had used Greek mercenaries to suppress uprisings. At the time of Philip II's death in 336 B.C.E., a new and inexperienced king, Darius III, was ruling Persia. Yet with a navy that dominated the sea, a huge army, and vast wealth, it remained a formidable opponent.

In 334 B.C.E., Alexander crossed the Hellespont into Asia. His army consisted of about 30,000 infantry and 5,000 cavalry; he had no navy and little money. These facts determined his early strategy—he must seek quick and decisive battles to gain money and supplies from the conquered territory, and he must move along the coast to neutralize the Persian navy by depriving it of ports.

Alexander met the Persian forces of Asia Minor at the Granicus River, where he won a smashing victory in characteristic style. (See Map 3–3, page 82.) He led a cavalry charge across the river into the teeth of the enemy on the opposite bank. He almost lost his life in the process, but he won the devotion of his soldiers. That victory left the coast of Asia Minor open. Alexander captured the coastal cities, thus denying them to the Persian fleet.

In 333 B.C.E., Alexander marched inland to Syria, where he met the main Persian army under King Darius at Issus. Alexander himself led the cavalry charge that broke the Persian line and sent Darius fleeing into central Asia Minor. He continued along the coast and captured previously impregnable Tyre after a long and ingenious siege, putting an end to the threat of the Persian navy. He took Egypt with little trouble and was greeted as liberator, pharaoh, and son of Re (an Egyptian god whose Greek equivalent was Zeus). At Tyre, Darius sent Alexander a peace offer, yielding his entire empire west of the Euphrates River and his daughter in exchange for an alliance and an end to the invasion. But Alexander aimed at conquering the whole empire and probably whatever lay beyond.

In the spring of 331 B.C.E., Alexander marched into Mesopotamia. At Gaugamela, near the ancient Assyrian city of Nineveh, he met Darius, ready for a last stand. Once again, Alexander's tactical genius and personal leadership carried the day. The Persians were broken, and Darius fled once more. Alexander entered Babylon, again hailed as liberator and king.

Interactive map: To explore this map further, go to www.myhistorylab.com

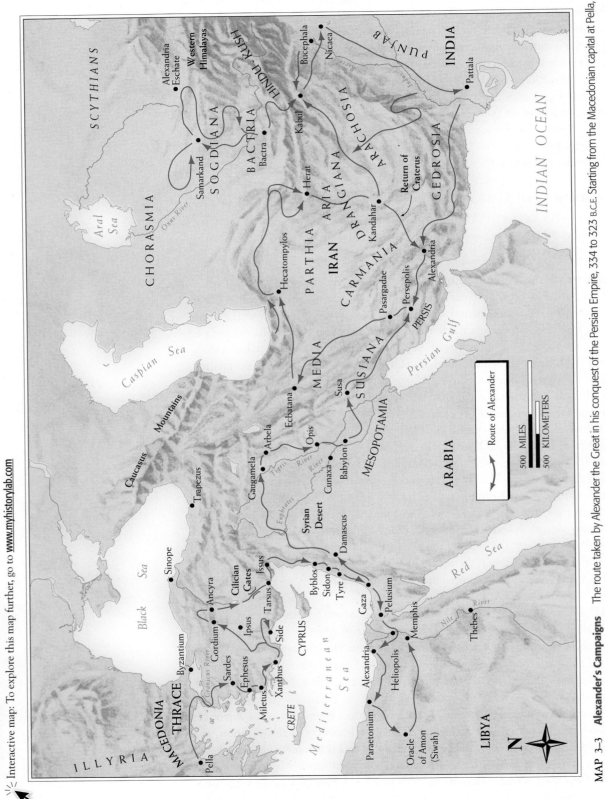

**MAP 3–3   Alexander's Campaigns**   The route taken by Alexander the Great in his conquest of the Persian Empire, 334 to 323 B.C.E. Starting from the Macedonian capital at Pella, he reached the Indus Valley before being turned back by his own restive troops. He died of fever in Mesopotamia.

**Before crossing** into Mesopotamia, what considerations determined Alexander's route? Was his aim merely to defeat the Persians?

In January 330 B.C.E., he came to Persepolis, the Persian capital, which held splendid palaces and the royal treasury. This bonanza ended his financial troubles and put a vast sum of money into circulation, with economic consequences that lasted for centuries. After a stay of several months, Alexander burned Persepolis to dramatize the destruction of the native Persian dynasty and the completion of Hellenic revenge for the earlier Persian invasion of Greece.

The new regime could not be secure while Darius lived, so Alexander pursued him eastward. Just south of the Caspian Sea, he came on the corpse of Darius, killed by his relative Bessus. The Persian nobles around Darius had lost faith in him and had joined in the plot. The murder removed Darius from Alexander's path, but now he had to catch Bessus, who proclaimed himself successor to Darius. The pursuit of Bessus (who was soon caught), combined with his own great curiosity and longing to go to the most distant places, took Alexander to the frontier of India.

In 327 B.C.E., Alexander took his army through the Khyber Pass in an attempt to conquer the lands around the Indus River (modern Pakistan). He reduced the king of these lands, Porus, to vassalage but pushed on in the hope of reaching the river called Ocean that the Greeks believed encircled the world. Finally, his weary men refused to go on. By the spring of 324 B.C.E., the army was back at the Persian Gulf and celebrated in the Macedonian style, with a wild spree of drinking.

**The Death of Alexander**   Alexander was filled with plans for the future: for the consolidation and organization of his empire; for geographical exploration; for building new cities, roads, and harbors; and perhaps for further conquests in the west. There is even some evidence that he asked to be deified and worshiped as a god, although we cannot be sure if he really did so or why. In June 323 B.C.E., however, he was overcome by a fever and died in Babylon at the age of thirty-three. His memory has never faded, and he soon became the subject of myth, legend, and romance. From the beginning, estimates of him have varied. Some have seen in him a man of grand and noble vision who transcended the narrow limits of Greek and Macedonian ethnocentrism and sought to realize the solidarity of humankind in a great world state. Others have seen him as a calculating despot, given to drunken brawls, brutality, and murder.

The truth is probably somewhere in between. Alexander was one of the greatest generals the world has seen; he never lost a battle or failed in a siege, and with a modest army he conquered a vast empire. He had rare organizational talents, and his plan for creating a multinational empire was the only intelligent way to consolidate his conquests. He established many new cities—seventy, according to tradition—mostly along trade routes. These cities encouraged commerce and prosperity and introduced Hellenic civilization into new areas. It is hard to know if even Alexander could have held together the vast new empire he had created, but his death proved that only he would have had a chance to succeed.

## THE SUCCESSORS

Nobody was prepared for Alexander's sudden death, and a weak succession further complicated affairs. His able and loyal Macedonian generals at first hoped to preserve the empire for the Macedonian royal house, and to this end they appointed themselves governors of the various provinces of the empire. The conflicting ambitions of these strong-willed men, however, led to prolonged warfare among them. In these conflicts three of the original number were killed, and all of the direct members of the Macedonian royal house were either executed or murdered. In 306 and 305 B.C.E., the surviving governors proclaimed themselves kings of their various holdings.

Three of these Macedonian generals founded dynasties of significance in the spread of Hellenistic culture:

- Ptolemy I, 367–283 B.C.E.; founder of Dynasty 31 in Egypt, the Ptolemies, of whom Cleopatra, who died in 30 B.C.E., was the last
- Seleucus I, 358–280 B.C.E.; founder of the Seleucid Dynasty in Mesopotamia
- Antigonus I, 382–301 B.C.E.; founder of the Antigonid Dynasty in Asia Minor and Macedon

For the first 75 years or so after the death of Alexander, the world ruled by his successors enjoyed considerable prosperity. The vast sums of money that he and they put into circulation greatly increased the level of economic activity. The opportunities for service and profit in the East attracted many Greeks and relieved their native cities of some of the pressure of the poor. The opening of vast new territories to Greek trade, the increased demand for Greek products, and the new availability of desired goods, as well as the conscious policies of the Hellenistic kings, all helped the growth of commerce.

The new prosperity, however, was not evenly distributed. The urban Greeks, the Macedonians, and the Hellenized natives who made up the upper and middle classes lived in comfort and even luxury, but the rural native peasants did not. Unlike the independent men who owned and worked the relatively small and equal lots of the *polis* in earlier times, Hellenistic farmers were reduced to subordinate, dependent peasant status, working on large plantations of decreasing efficiency. During prosperous times these distinctions were bearable, although even then there was tension between the two groups. After a while, however, the costs of continuing wars, inflation, and a gradual lessening of the positive effects of the introduction of Persian wealth all led to economic crisis. The kings bore down heavily on the middle classes, who were skilled at avoiding their responsibilities, however. The pressure on the peasants and the city laborers became great too, and they responded by slowing down their work and even by striking. In Greece, economic pressures brought clashes between rich and poor, demands for the abolition of debt and the redistribution of land, and even, on occasion, civil war.

These internal divisions, along with international wars, weakened the capacity of the Hellenistic kingdoms to resist outside attack. By the middle of the second century B.C.E., they had all, except for Egypt, succumbed to an expanding Italian power, Rome. The two centuries between Alexander and the Roman conquest, however, were of great and lasting importance. They saw the entire eastern Mediterranean coast, Greece, Egypt, Mesopotamia, and the old Persian Empire formed into a single political, economic, and cultural unit.

## HELLENISTIC CULTURE

**HOW DID** Hellenistic culture differ from the culture of Classical Greece?

The career of Alexander the Great marked a significant turning point in Greek thought as it was represented in literature, philosophy, religion, and art. His conquests and the establishment of the successor kingdoms put an end to the central role of the *polis* in Greek life and thought. Deprived of control of their foreign affairs, and with a foreign monarch determining their important internal arrangements, the post-Classical cities lost the political freedom that was basic to the old outlook. They were cities, perhaps—in a sense, even city-states—but not *poleis*. As time passed, they changed from sovereign states to municipal towns merged into military empires. Never again in antiquity would there be either a serious attack on or defense of the *polis*, for its importance was gone. For the most part, the Greeks after Alexander turned away from political solutions for their problems. Instead, they sought personal responses to their hopes and fears, particularly in religion, philosophy, and magic. The confident, sometimes arrogant, humanism of the fifth century B.C.E. gave way to a kind of resignation to fate, a recognition of helplessness before forces too great for humans to manage.

## PHILOSOPHY

These developments are noticeable in the changes that overtook the established schools of philosophy as well as in the emergence of two new and influential groups of philosophers: the Epicureans and the Stoics. Athens's position as the center of philosophical studies was reinforced, for the Academy and the Lyceum continued in operation, and the new schools were also located in Athens. The Lyceum turned gradually away from the universal investigations of its founder, Aristotle, even from his scientific interests, to become a center chiefly of literary and especially historical studies.

The Academy turned even further away from its tradition. It adopted the systematic Skepticism of Pyrrho of Elis. Under the leadership of Arcesilaus and Carneades, the Skeptics of the Academy became skilled at pointing out fallacies and weaknesses in the philosophies of the rival schools. They thought that nothing could be known and so consoled themselves and their followers by suggesting that nothing mattered. It was easy for them, therefore, to accept conventional morality and the world as it was.

**The Epicureans**   Epicurus of Athens (342–271 B.C.E.) formulated a new teaching, embodied in the school he founded in his native city in 306 B.C.E. His philosophy conformed to the mood of the times in that its goal was not knowledge, but human happiness, which he believed a style of life based on reason could achieve. He took sense perception to be the basis of all human knowledge. The reality and reliability of sense perception rested on the acceptance of the physical universe described by the atomists, Democritus and Leucippus. The **Epicureans** proclaimed atoms were continually falling through the void and giving off images that were in direct contact with the senses. These falling atoms could swerve in an arbitrary, unpredictable way to produce the combinations seen in the world.

Epicurus thereby removed an element of determinism that existed in the Democritean system. When a person died, the atoms that composed the body dispersed so the person had no further existence or perception and therefore nothing to fear after death. Epicurus believed the gods existed, but that they took no interest in human affairs. This belief amounted to a practical atheism, and Epicureans were often thought to be atheists.

The purpose of Epicurean physics was to liberate people from their fear of death, of the gods, and of all nonmaterial or supernatural powers. Epicurean ethics were hedonistic, that is, based on the acceptance of pleasure as true happiness. But pleasure for Epicurus was chiefly negative: the absence of pain and trouble. The goal of the Epicureans was *ataraxia*, the condition of being undisturbed, without trouble, pain, or responsibility. Ideally, a man should have enough means to allow him to withdraw from the world and avoid business and public life. Epicurus even advised against marriage and children. He preached a life of genteel, restrained selfishness that might appeal to intellectual men of means but was not calculated to be widely attractive.

**The Stoics**   Soon after Epicurus began teaching in his garden in Athens, Zeno of Citium in Cyprus (335–263 B.C.E.) established the Stoic school. Like the Epicureans, the **Stoics**

**One of the masterpieces** of Hellenistic sculpture, the *Laocoön*. This is a Roman copy. According to legend, Laocoön was a priest who warned the Trojans not to take the Greeks' wooden horse within their city. This sculpture depicts his punishment. Great serpents sent by the goddess Athena, who was on the side of the Greeks, devoured Laocoön and his sons before the horrified people of Troy.

Direzione Generale Musei Vaticani

**How does the sculpture reflect the attitudes and anxieties of Hellenistic Greeks?**

**Epicureans**   People who believed the proper pursuit of humankind is undisturbed withdrawal from the world.

**Stoics**   People who sought freedom from passion and harmony with nature.

sought the happiness of the individual. Quite unlike them, the Stoics proposed a philosophy almost indistinguishable from religion. They believed humans must live in harmony within themselves and with nature; for the Stoics, God and nature were the same. The guiding principle in nature was divine reason (*Logos*), or fire. Every human had a spark of this divinity, and after death it returned to the eternal divine spirit. From time to time the world was destroyed by fire, from which a new world arose.

The aim of humans, and the definition of human happiness, was the virtuous life: a life lived in accordance with natural law. To live such a life required the knowledge only the wise possessed. They knew what was good, what was evil, and what was neither, but "indifferent." According to the Stoics, good and evil were dispositions of the mind or soul: prudence, justice, courage, temperance, and so on, were good, whereas folly, injustice, cowardice, and the like, were evil. Life, health, pleasure, beauty, strength, wealth, and so on, were neutral—morally indifferent—for they did not contribute either to happiness or to misery. Human misery came from an irrational mental contraction—from passion, which was a disease of the soul. The wise sought *apatheia*, or freedom from passion, because passion arose from things that were morally indifferent.

Politically, the Stoics fit well into the new world. They thought of it as a single *polis* in which all people were children of the same God. Although they did not forbid political activity, and many Stoics took part in political life, withdrawal was obviously preferable because the usual subjects of political argument were indifferent. Because the Stoics strove for inner harmony of the individual, their aim was a life lived in accordance with the divine will, their attitude fatalistic, and their goal a form of apathy. They fit in well with the reality of post–Alexandrian life. In fact, Stoicism facilitated the task of creating a new political system that relied not on the active participation of the governed, but merely on their docile submission.

## LITERATURE

Hellenistic literature reflects the new intellectual currents, the new conditions of literary life, and the new institutions created in that period. The center of literary production in the third and second centuries B.C.E. was the new city of Alexandria in Egypt. There the Ptolemies, the monarchs of Egypt during that time, founded the museum—a great research institute where royal funds supported scientists and scholars—and the library, which contained almost half a million papyrus scrolls.

The library contained much of the great body of past Greek literature, most of which has since been lost. The Alexandrian scholars made copies of what they judged to be the best works. They edited and criticized these works from the point of view of language, form, and content, and wrote biographies of the authors. Their work is responsible for the preservation of most of what remains to us of ancient literature.

**The Archimedes Palimpsest** A page from *On Floating Bodies.*

© 2004 Christie's Images, Inc.

**What contributions did Hellenistic thinkers make to mathematics and science?**

## ARCHITECTURE AND SCULPTURE

The advent of the Hellenistic monarchies greatly increased the opportunities open to architects and sculptors. Money was plentiful, rulers sought outlets for conspicuous display, new cities needed to be built and beautified, and the well-to-do wanted objects of art.

The new cities were usually laid out on the grid plan introduced in the fifth century B.C.E. by Hippodamus of Miletus. Temples were built on the classical model, and the covered portico, or *stoa*, became a popular addition to the *agoras* of the Hellenistic towns.

Reflecting the cosmopolitan nature of the Hellenistic world, leading sculptors accepted commissions wherever they were attractive. The result was a certain uniformity of style, although Alexandria, Rhodes, and the kingdom of Pergamum in Asia Minor developed their own distinctive characteristics. For the most part, Hellenistic sculpture moved away from the balanced tension and idealism of the fifth century B.C.E. toward the sentimental, emotional, and realistic mode of the fourth century B.C.E. These qualities are readily apparent in the marble statue called the *Laocoön*, carved at Rhodes in the second century B.C.E. and afterward taken to Rome.

## MATHEMATICS AND SCIENCE

Among the most spectacular and remarkable intellectual developments of the Hellenistic Age were those that came in mathematics and science. The burst of activity in these subjects drew their inspiration from several sources. The stimulation and organization provided by the work of Plato and Aristotle should not be ignored. Alexander's interest in science, evidenced by the scientists he took with him on his expedition and the aid he gave them in collecting data, provided further impetus.

The expansion of Greek horizons geographically and the consequent contacts with Egyptian and Babylonian knowledge were also helpful. Finally, the patronage of the Ptolemies and the opportunity for many scientists to work with one another at the museum at Alexandria provided a unique opportunity for scientific work. The work the Alexandrians did formed the greater part of the scientific knowledge available to the Western world until the scientific revolution of the sixteenth and seventeenth centuries C.E.

Euclid's *Elements* (written early in the third century B.C.E.) remained the textbook of plane and solid geometry until recent times. Archimedes of Syracuse (ca. 287–212 B.C.E.) made further progress in geometry, established the theory of the lever in mechanics, and invented hydrostatics.

These advances in mathematics, once they were applied to the Babylonian astronomical tables available to the Hellenistic world, spurred great progress in astronomy. As early as the fourth century B.C.E., Heraclides of Pontus (ca. 390–310 B.C.E.) had argued that Mercury and Venus circulate around the sun and not Earth. He appears to have made other suggestions leading to a heliocentric theory of the universe. Most scholars, however, give credit for that theory to Aristarchus of Samos (ca. 310–230 B.C.E.), who asserted that the sun, along with the other fixed stars, did not move and that Earth revolved around the sun in a circular orbit and rotated on its axis while doing so. The heliocentric theory ran contrary not only to the traditional view codified by Aristotle, but also to what seemed to be common sense.

Hellenistic scientists mapped the earth as well as the sky. Eratosthenes of Cyrene (ca. 275–195 B.C.E.) calculated the circumference of Earth to within about 200 miles. He wrote a treatise on geography based on mathematical and physical reasoning and the reports of travelers. Despite the new data that were available to later geographers, Eratosthenes' map was in many ways more accurate than the one Ptolemy of Alexandria constructed, which became standard in the Middle Ages.

The Hellenistic Age contributed little to the life sciences, such as biology, zoology, and medicine. Even the sciences that had such impressive achievements to show in the third century B.C.E. made little progress thereafter. In fact, to some extent, there was a retreat from science. Astrology and magic became subjects of great interest as scientific advance lagged.

# SUMMARY

## WHAT LED to the foundation of the Delian League?

**Aftermath of Victory** The tenuous unity the Greeks had shown while fighting against the Persians disintegrated. Sparta and Athens emerged as leaders of two spheres of influence. Sparta was uninterested in continued aggression against Persia. The Athenians and the Ionians shared an interest in driving the Persians out of the Aegean region; with others, they formed the Delian League under Athenian leadership. *page 60*

## WHAT WAS the cause of the Peloponnesian War, and what was the end result?

**The First Peloponnesian War: Athens Against Sparta** Pericles led a democratic, but aggressive, Athens. The Peloponnesian Wars were the manifestation of the conflict between Sparta and Athens. After an initial victory, Athens seemed almost invincible, but soon military defeat abroad and rebellion at home weakened Athens so much that Sparta invaded. Pericles agreed to a thirty peace, abandoning all Athenian possessions on the Greek mainland outside of Attica, but gaining Spartan recognition of the Athenian Empire. *page 61*

## HOW DID democracy work in fifth-century B.C.E. Athens?

**Classical Greece** Athenian government had become more democratic than any previous political system. All male citizens gained important rights, regardless of their property class. The official status of women was severely circumscribed, both in public and in private. Greek art, drama, and mythology suggest that women may have had more freedom and power than a strict reading of the documentary evidence would allow. Before around 500 B.C.E. there was little chattel slavery in Greece—although serfdom and bond slavery were more or less common in various times and places—but later war captives and other foreigners were held as chattel slaves. Slaves worked in agriculture, industry, and households and served as shepherds, policemen, and secretaries. Most Athenians did not own any slaves, and those who did generally owned only a few. *page 63*

## HOW DID the Peloponnesian War affect the faith in the *polis*?

**The Great Peloponnesian War** The Thirty Years' Peace of 445 B.C.E. lasted just over ten years, until a conflict between Corcyra and Corinth drew in their allies, Athens and Sparta, respectively. Sparta violated a clause of the peace that required arbitration of all disagreements between Athens and Sparta, and instead, in 431 B.C.E., invaded Attica. The outnumbered Athenians followed a daring strategy and won an important victory in 425 B.C.E. After a mix of victories and defeats, both sides signed the Peace of Nicias in 421 B.C.E. This peace, too, was short-lived; this time the Athenians were the aggressors, against Sicily, in a disastrous 415 B.C.E. expedition that brought the Persians into the war on Sparta's side. The Athenians fought on, however, until 404 B.C.E., when they surrendered unconditionally. *page 69*

## HOW DID Athens and Sparta compete for leadership in the Greek world?

**Competition for Leadership in the Fourth Century B.C.E.** After defeating Athens, Sparta had a golden opportunity to claim leadership, but Spartan arrogance—among other problems—caused their allies the Persians to turn against them. Theban victory at Leuctra in 371 B.C.E. brought an end to Spartan hegemony. But Theban dominance was short-lived, ending in 362 B.C.E. in a defeat at the hands of the Athenians. Athens, however, repeated many of the same mistakes that had cost it allies in the Delian League, and by 355 B.C.E., Athens again had to abandon most of its empire. Greece descended into chaos. *page 71*

## WHAT ARE the achievements of Classical Greece?

**The Culture of Classical Greece** Classical Greece produced dramas, architecture and sculpture, and philosophical and historical works. The Golden Age of Athens, between the Persian and Peloponnesian Wars, is epitomized by Attic tragedy, including the works of Aeschylus, Sophocles, and Euripedes. The buildings of the Acropolis are the product of Athenian religious and civic sensibility and individual artistry and achievement. Philosophy continued to explore questions about the natural world. Herodotus and Thucydides wrote histories that are models of the genre. Sociopolitical changes brought about by the Peloponnesian War were reflected in drama and sculpture, especially in the philosophical traditions of Socrates, Plato, and Aristotle. *page 72*

## WHO WAS Alexander the Great and what was his legacy?

**The Hellenistic World** Greek culture mixed with Middle Eastern elements and spread throughout the eastern

Mediterranean, Egypt, and far into Asia. This Hellenistic world was largely the result of military conquests by a short-lived, father-and-son Macedonian dynasty. Philip of Macedon introduced tactical innovations into the Macedonian army, and he coupled military force with diplomacy to conquer Greece. In 336 B.C.E., Philip was assassinated and succeeded by his son Alexander. Alexander led his troops to victory in Persia, Egypt, Mesopotamia, and as far as what is now Pakistan. After his death, three of Alexander's generals founded significant dynasties that helped spread Hellenism in Egypt, Mesopotamia, and Asia Minor. Within Greece, class conflict and other internal divisions were exacerbated by the new wealth Alexander's conquests had brought to the region. *page 79*

**HOW DID** Hellenistic culture differ from the culture of Classical Greece?

**Hellenistic Culture** The true *polis* was destroyed by the Macedonian invasion. Greeks turned from the political to the personal. In Athenian philosophy, the Epicureans (whose goal was hedonistic human happiness) and Stoics (who sought happiness through harmony and freedom from passion) gained prominence. Hellenistic Alexandria fostered literature and humanistic scholarship. Hellenistic styles in architecture and sculpture diffused over a wide area. Mathematics and science—especially astronomy—blossomed. *page 84*

# REVIEW QUESTIONS

1. What caused the Great Peloponnesian War? What strategies did Athens and Sparta hope would bring them victory? Why did Sparta win?

2. What were the tensions that characterized Greek life in the Classical Period, and how were they reflected in its art, literature, and philosophy? How does Hellenistic art differ from art of the Classical Period?

3. How and why did Philip II conquer Greece? Why was Athens unable to stop him? Was his success due to Macedon's strength or to the weaknesses of the Greek city-states?

4. What were the consequences of Alexander the Great's early death? What were his lasting achievements? Did he consciously promote Greek civilization, or was he only an egomaniac devoted to endless conquest?

5. What were the most significant elements that made up Hellenistic civilization and culture?

## KEY TERMS

**Academy** (p. 76)
**Delian League** (p. 61)
**Epicureans** (p. 85)
**Hellenistic** (p. 79)

**Lyceum** (p. 78)
**Peloponnesian Wars** (p. 62)
**Stoics** (p. 85)

For additional learning resources related to this chapter, please go to **www.myhistorylab.com**

PEARSON
myhistorylab

# 4

# Rome: From Republic to Empire

**The Pont du Gard,** an aqueduct and bridge, was built in the first century B.C.E. in southern France in Rome's first province beyond the Alps.

Walter S. Clark/Photo Researchers, Inc.

**How did the Romans use their engineering prowess to help bind together their growing empire?**

THE ETRUSCANS *page 92*

**WHO WERE** the Etruscans and how did they influence Rome?

HOW DID ideas about the family influence society and government in early Rome?

**WHAT ROLE** did consuls, the Senate, and the Assembly play in Republican government?

HOW DID contact with the Hellenistic world affect Rome?

**HOW DID** the expansion of Rome change the Republic?

**WHAT EVENTS** led to the fall of the Republic?

*T*he Romans started with a small village in central Italy and went on to unite the peoples of the Western world and sustain the longest period of peace in Western history. By adopting Hellenistic culture and spreading it through their empire, they laid a universal Graeco-Roman foundation for Western civilization. The effects of their achievement are still being felt. ▪

## PREHISTORIC ITALY

The culture of Italy developed late. Paleolithic settlements gave way to the Neolithic mode of life only around 2500 B.C.E. The Bronze Age came around 1500 B.C.E. About 1000 B.C.E., bands of new arrivals—warlike peoples speaking a set of closely related languages we call *Italic*—began to infiltrate Italy from across the Adriatic Sea and around its northern end. By 800 B.C.E., they occupied the highland pastures of the Apennines, and within a short time, they began to challenge the earlier settlers for control of the tempting western plains. It would be the descendants of these tough mountain people—Umbrians, Sabines, Samnites, and Latins—together with others soon to arrive—Etruscans, Greeks, and Celts—who would shape the future of Italy.

## THE ETRUSCANS

**WHO WERE** the Etruscans and how did they influence Rome?

The Etruscans exerted the most powerful external influence on the Romans. Their civilization arose in Etruria (now Tuscany), west of the Apennines between the Arno and Tiber Rivers, about 800 B.C.E. (See Map 4–1.)

### GOVERNMENT

The Etruscans brought civilization with them. Their settlements were self-governing, fortified city-states, of which twelve formed a loose religious confederation. At first, kings ruled these cities, but they were replaced by an agrarian aristocracy, which ruled through a council and elected annual magistrates. The Etruscans were a military ruling

**Much of what** we know of the Etruscans comes from their funery art. This sculpture of an Etruscan couple is part of a sarcophagus.

Sarcophagus of a Couple. Etruscan, 6th B.C.E. Terracotta. H: 114 cm. Louvre, Paris, France. Copyright Erich Lessing/Art Resource, NY

**What contributions did the Etruscans make to Roman culture?**

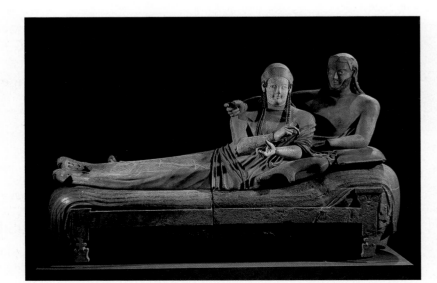

MAP 4–1 **Ancient Italy** This map of ancient Italy and its neighbors before the expansion of Rome shows major cities and towns as well as several geographical regions and the locations of some of the Italic and non-Italic peoples.

**Why, geographically**, was Rome ideal to become the center for Italy's inland communication and trade?

class that exploited the native Italians (the predecessors of the later Italic speakers), who worked the Etruscans' land and mines and served as infantry in Etruscan armies. This aristocracy accumulated wealth through agriculture, industry, piracy, and commerce with the Carthaginians and the Greeks.

## RELIGION

The Etruscans' influence on the Romans was greatest in religion. They imagined a world filled with gods and spirits, many of them evil. To deal with such demons, the Etruscans developed complicated rituals and powerful priesthoods. Divination by sacrifice and omens in nature helped discover the divine will, and careful attention to precise rituals directed by priests helped please the gods. After a while the Etruscans, influenced by the Greeks, worshipped gods in the shape of humans and built temples for them.

## DOMINION

In the seventh and sixth centuries B.C.E., the Etruscan aristocracy expanded their power in Italy and across the sea to Corsica and Elba. They conquered **Latium** (a region that included the small town of Rome) and Campania, where they became neighbors of the Greeks of Naples. In the north, they got as far as the Po Valley. Etruscan power reached its height some time before 500 B.C.E. and then rapidly declined. About 400 B.C.E., Celtic peoples from the area the Romans called **Gaul** (modern France) broke into the Po Valley and drove out the Etruscans. Eventually, even the Etruscan heartland in Etruria lost its independence and was incorporated into Roman Italy.

**Latium** Region located in present-day Italy that included the small town of Rome.

**Gaul** Area that is now modern France.

# ROYAL ROME

Rome was an unimportant town in Latium until the Etruscans conquered it, but its location—fifteen miles from the mouth of the Tiber River at the point at which hills made further navigation impossible—gave it advantages over its Latin neighbors. The island in the Tiber southwest of the Capitoline Hill made the river fordable, so Rome was naturally a center for communication and trade, both east-west and north-south.

**HOW DID** ideas about the family influence society and government in early Rome?

## GOVERNMENT

In the sixth century B.C.E., Rome came under Etruscan control. Led by Etruscan kings, the Roman army, equipped and organized like the Greek phalanx, gained control of most of Latium. An effective political and social order that gave extraordinary power to the ruling figures in both public and private life made this success possible. To their kings the Romans gave the awesome power of **imperium**—the right to issue commands and to enforce them by fines, arrests, and corporal, or even capital, punishment. Although it tended apparently to remain in the same family, kingship was elective. The Roman Senate had to approve the candidate for the office, and a vote of the people gathered in an assembly formally granted the *imperium*. A basic characteristic of later Roman government—the granting of great power to executive officers contingent on the approval of the Senate and, ultimately, the people—was already apparent in this structure.

**imperium** Right held by a Roman king to enforce commands by fines, arrests, and corporal and capital punishment.

The Senate was the second branch of the early Roman government. Ostensibly, the Senate had neither executive nor legislative power; it met only when the king summoned it to advise him. In reality its authority was great, for the senators, like the king, served for life. The Senate, therefore, had continuity and experience, and its members were the most powerful men in the state.

The third branch of government, the curiate assembly, was made up of all citizens, as divided into thirty groups. The assembly met only when the king summoned it; he determined the agenda, made proposals, and recognized other speakers, if any. Usually, the assembly was called to listen and approve.

## FAMILY AND GENDER IN EARLY ROME

The center of Roman life was the family. At its head stood the father, whose power and authority within the family resembled those of the king within the state. Over his children, the father held broad powers analogous to *imperium* in the state. The father was also the chief priest of the family.

Thus, early Roman society was hierarchical and dominated by males. Throughout her life, a woman was under the control of some adult male. Before her marriage it was her father, afterward her husband or, when neither was available, a guardian chosen from one of her male relatives. Nonetheless, women of the upper classes had a position of influence and respect greater than the classical Greeks. Just as the husband was *paterfamilias*, the wife was *materfamilias*. She was mistress within the home, controlling access to the storerooms, keeping the accounts, and supervising the slaves and the raising of the children. She also was part of the family council and a respected adviser on all questions concerning the family.

**Busts of a** Roman couple, from the period of the Republic. Although some have identified the individuals as Cato the Younger and his daughter Porcia, no solid evidence confirms this claim.

Bust of Cato and Porcia. Roman sculpture. Vatican Museums, Vatican State. Photograph © Scala/Art Resource, NY

**How did the Romans view the relationship between husband and wife?**

## CLIENTAGE

Clientage was one of Rome's most important institutions. The patron provided his client with protection, both physical and legal. He gave him economic assistance in the form of a land grant, the opportunity to work as a tenant farmer or a laborer on the patron's land, or simply hand-

## Overview  The Rise of the Plebeians to Equality in Rome

| | |
|---|---|
| **509** B.C.E. | Kings expelled; republic founded |
| **450–449** B.C.E. | Laws of the Twelve Tables published |
| **445** B.C.E. | Plebeians gain right of marriage with patricians |
| **367** B.C.E. | Licinian-Sextian Laws open consulship to plebeians |
| **300** B.C.E. | Plebeians attain chief priesthoods |
| **287** B.C.E. | Laws passed by plebeian assembly made binding on all Romans |

outs. In return, the client would fight for his patron, work his land, and support him politically. Public opinion and tradition reinforced these mutual obligations.

In the early history of Rome, patrons were rich and powerful, whereas clients were poor and weak, but as time passed, rich and powerful members of the upper classes became clients of even more powerful men, chiefly for political purposes. Because the client-patron relationship was hereditary and sanctioned by religion and custom, it played an important part in the life of the Roman Republic.

### PATRICIANS AND PLEBEIANS

In the royal period, a class distinction based on birth divided Roman society in two. The wealthy **patrician** upper class held a monopoly of power and influence. Its members alone could conduct state religious ceremonies, sit in the Senate, or hold office. They formed a closed caste by forbidding marriage outside their own group.

The **plebeian** lower class must have consisted originally of poor, dependent small farmers, laborers, and artisans, the clients of the nobility. As Rome and its population grew, families that were rich, but outside the charmed circle of patricians, grew wealthy. From early times, therefore, there were rich plebeians, and incompetence and bad luck must have produced some poor patricians. The line between the classes and the monopoly of privileges remained firm, nevertheless, and the struggle of the plebeians to gain equality occupied more than two centuries of republican history.

**patricians**   Upper class of Roman families that originally monopolized all political authority. Only they could serve as priests, senators, and magistrates.

**plebeians**   Commoner class of Roman families, usually families of small farmers, laborers, and artisans who were early clients of the patricians.

# THE REPUBLIC

Roman tradition tells us that the outrageous behavior of the last kings led the noble families to revolt in 509 B.C.E., bringing the monarchy to a sudden close and leading to the creation of the Roman Republic.

**WHAT ROLE** did consuls, the Senate, and the Assembly play in Republican government?

### CONSTITUTION

**The Consuls**   The Roman constitution was an unwritten accumulation of laws and customs. The Romans were a conservative people and were never willing to deprive their chief magistrates of the great powers the monarchs had exercised. They elected two patricians to the office of consul and endowed them with *imperium*. Two financial officials called *quaestors*, whose number ultimately reached eight, assisted them. Like the

**consuls** Elected magistrates from patrician families chosen annually to lead the army, oversee the state religion, and sit as judges.

**proconsulships** Extension of terms for consuls who had important work to finish.

**censors** Men of unimpeachable reputation, chosen to carry the responsibility for enrolling, keeping track of, and determining the status and tax liability of each citizen.

kings, the **consuls** led the army, had religious duties, and served as judges. The power of the consuls, however, was limited legally and institutionally as well as by custom.

The power of the consulship was granted not for life, but only for a year. Each consul could prevent any action by his colleague simply by saying no to his proposal, and the consuls shared their religious powers with others. Even the *imperium* was limited. Although the consuls had full powers of life and death while leading an army, within the sacred boundary of the city of Rome, the citizens had the right to appeal all cases involving capital punishment to the popular assembly.

The many checks on consular action tended to prevent initiative, swift action, and change, but this was just what a conservative, traditional, aristocratic republic wanted. Only in the military sphere did divided counsel and a short term of office create important problems. The Romans tried to get around the difficulties by sending only one consul into the field or, when this was impossible, allowing each consul sole command on alternate days. In serious crises, the consuls, with the advice of the Senate, could appoint a *dictator* to the command and could retire in his favor. The *dictator*'s term of office was limited to six months, but his own *imperium* was valid both inside and outside the city without appeal.

These devices worked well enough in the early years of the republic, when Rome's battles were near home. Longer wars and more sophisticated opponents, however, revealed the system's weaknesses and required significant changes. Long campaigns prompted the invention of the **proconsulship** in 325 B.C.E., whereby the term of a consul serving in the field was extended. This innovation contained the seeds of many troubles for the constitution.

The creation of the office of *praetor* also helped provide commanders for Rome's many campaigns. The basic function of the *praetors* was judicial, but they also had *imperium* and served as generals. *Praetors*' terms were also for one year.

At first, the consuls identified citizens and classified them according to age and property. After the middle of the fifth century B.C.E., this job was delegated to a new office, that of *censor*. The Senate elected two **censors** every five years. They conducted a census and drew up the citizen rolls. Their task was not just clerical; the classification of the citizens fixed taxation and status, so the censors had to be men of fine reputation, former consuls. They soon acquired additional powers. By the fourth century B.C.E., they compiled the roll of senators and could strike senators from that roll not only for financial, but also for moral, reasons. As the prestige of the office grew, it became the ultimate prize of a Roman political career.

**Lictors were attendants** of the Roman magistrates who held the power of *imperium*, the right to command. In republican times these magistrates were the consuls, praetors, and proconsuls. The lictors were men from the lower classes—some were even former slaves. They constantly attended the magistrates when the latter appeared in public. The lictors cleared a magistrate's way in crowds and summoned, arrested, and punished offenders for him. They also served as their magistrate's house guard.

Alinari/Art Resource, NY

**How did the lictors serve to reinforce the power and status of Roman magistrates?**

**The Senate and the Assembly** With the end of the monarchy, the Senate became the single continuous, deliberative body in the Roman state, greatly increasing its influence and power. Its members were prominent patricians, often leaders of clans and patrons of many clients. The Senate soon gained control of the state's finances and of foreign policy. Neither magistrates nor popular assemblies could lightly ignore its formal advice.

The most important assembly in the early republic was the *centuriate assembly*, which was, in a sense, the Roman army acting in a political capacity. The assembly elected the consuls and several other magistrates, voted on bills put before it, made decisions of war and peace, and also served as the court of appeal against decisions of the magistrates affecting the life or property of a citizen. In theory, the assembly had final authority, but the Senate exercised great, if informal, influence.

**The Struggle of the Orders** The laws and constitution of the early republic gave to the patricians almost a monopoly of power and privilege. The plebeians undertook a campaign to achieve political, legal, and social equality, and this attempt, which succeeded after two centuries of intermittent effort, is called the *Struggle of the Orders*.

The most important source of plebeian success was the need for their military service. According to tradition, the plebeians, angered by patrician resistance to their demands, withdrew from the city and camped on the Sacred Mount. There they formed a plebeian tribal assembly and elected plebeian **tribunes** to protect them from the arbitrary power of the magistrates. They declared the tribune inviolate and sacrosanct. By extension of his right to protect the plebeians, the tribune gained the power to veto any action of a magistrate or any bill in a Roman assembly or the Senate.

**tribunes** Officials elected by the plebeian tribal assembly given the power to protect plebeians from abuse by patrician magistrates.

Next, the plebeians obtained access to the laws, when early Roman custom in all its harshness and simplicity was codified in the Twelve Tables around 450 B.C.E. In 445 B.C.E., plebeians gained the right to marry patricians. The main prize, the consulship, the patricians did not yield easily. Not until 367 B.C.E. did legislation—the Licinian-Sextian Laws—provide that at least one consul could be a plebeian. Before long, plebeians held other offices—even the dictatorship and the censorship. In 300 B.C.E., they were admitted to the most important priesthoods, the last religious barrier to equality. In 287 B.C.E., the plebeians completed their triumph. They once again withdrew from the city and secured the passage of a law whereby decisions of the plebeian assembly bound all Romans and did not require the approval of the Senate.

It might seem that the Roman aristocracy had given way under the pressure of the lower class. Yet the victory of the plebeians did not bring democracy. An aristocracy based strictly on birth had given way to an aristocracy more subtle, but no less restricted, based on a combination of wealth and birth. A relatively small group of rich and powerful families, both patrician and plebeian, known as *nobiles*, attained the highest offices in the state. The significant distinction was no longer between patrician and plebeian but between the *nobiles* and everyone else.

**QUICK REVIEW**
**The Struggle of the Orders**

◆ Fueled by tensions between plebeians and patricians
◆ Plebeians used power of the army to gain concessions
◆ Plebeians made slow and incremental progress toward greater rights

## THE CONQUEST OF ITALY

Not long after the fall of the monarchy in 509 B.C.E., a coalition of Romans, Latins, and Italian Greeks drove the Etruscans out of Latium for good. Throughout the fifth century B.C.E., the powerful Etruscan city of Veii, only twelve miles north of the Tiber River, raided Roman territory. After a hard struggle and a long siege, the Romans took Veii in 392 B.C.E., more than doubling the size of Rome.

Roman policy toward defeated enemies used both the carrot and the stick. When the Romans made friendly alliances with some, they gained new soldiers for their army. When they treated others more harshly by annexing their land, they achieved a similar end. Service in the Roman army was based on property, and the distribution to poor Romans of conquered land made soldiers of previously useless men. It also gave the poor a stake in Rome and reduced the pressure against its aristocratic regime.

**Gallic Invasion and Roman Reaction** At the beginning of the fourth century B.C.E., a disaster struck. In 387 B.C.E., the Gauls, barbaric Celtic tribes from across the Alps, defeated the Roman army and burned Rome. The Gauls sought plunder, not conquest, so they extorted a ransom from the Romans and returned to the north. Rome's power appeared to be wiped out.

**QUICK REVIEW**
**Roman Italy**

◆ 392 B.C.E.: Rome destroys Veii and seizes its territory
◆ Rome tried to build constructive relationships with conquered Italian cities
◆ Colonies of veteran soldiers established on annexed land

By about 350 B.C.E., however, the Romans were more dominant than ever. Their success in turning back new Gallic raids added to their power and prestige. As the Romans tightened their grip on Latium, the Latins became resentful. In 340 B.C.E., they demanded independence from Rome or full equality and launched a war of independence that lasted until 338 B.C.E. The victorious Romans dissolved the Latin League, and their treatment of the defeated opponents provided a model for the settlement of Italy.

**Roman Policy toward the Conquered**    The Romans did not destroy any of the Latin cities or their people, nor did they treat them all alike. Some near Rome received full Roman citizenship. Others farther away gained municipal status, which gave them the private rights of intermarriage and commerce with Romans, but not the public rights of voting and holding office in Rome. They retained the rights of local self-government and could obtain full Roman citizenship if they moved to Rome. They followed Rome in foreign policy and provided soldiers to serve in the Roman legions.

Still other states became allies of Rome on the basis of treaties, which differed from city to city.

On some of the conquered land, the Romans placed colonies, permanent settlements of veteran soldiers in the territory of recently defeated enemies. The colonists retained their Roman citizenship and enjoyed home rule; in return for the land they had been given, they were a kind of permanent garrison to deter or suppress rebellion. These colonies were usually connected to Rome by a network of military roads. The roads guaranteed that a Roman army could swiftly reinforce an embattled colony or put down an uprising in any weather.

The Roman settlement of Latium reveals even more clearly than before the principles by which Rome was able to conquer and dominate Italy. The excellent army and the diplomatic skill that allowed Rome to separate its enemies help explain its conquests. The reputation for harsh punishment of rebels, and the sure promise that such punishment would be delivered, was made unmistakably clear. But the positive side, represented by Rome's organization of the defeated states, is at least as important. The Romans did not regard the status given each newly conquered city as permanent. They held out to loyal allies the prospect of improving their status—even of achieving the ultimate prize, full Roman citizenship. In so doing, the Romans gave their allies a stake in Rome's future success and a sense of being colleagues, though subordinate ones, rather than subjects. The result, in general, was that most of Rome's allies remained loyal even when put to the severest test.

**Defeated Samnites**    The next great challenge to Roman arms came in a series of wars with a tough mountain people of the southern Apennines, the Samnites. Some of Rome's allies rebelled, and soon the Etruscans and Gauls joined in the war against Rome. But most of the allies remained loyal. In 295 B.C.E., at Sentinum, the Romans defeated an Italian coalition, and by 280 B.C.E., they were masters of central Italy. Their power extended from the Po Valley south to Apulia and Lucania.

Now the Romans were in direct contact with the Greek cities of southern Italy. Roman intervention in a quarrel between Greek cities brought them face to face with Pyrrhus, king of Epirus. He defeated the Romans twice but suffered many casualties. When one of his officers rejoiced at the victory, Pyrrhus told him, "If we win one more battle against the Romans, we shall be completely ruined." This "Pyrrhic victory" led him to withdraw to Sicily in 275 B.C.E. The Greek cities that had hired him were forced to join the Roman confederation. By 265 B.C.E., Rome ruled all Italy as far north as the Po River, an area of 47,200 square miles.

## ROME AND CARTHAGE

The conquest of southern Italy brought the Romans face to face with the great naval power of the western Mediterranean, Carthage. (See Map 4–2.) Late in the ninth century B.C.E., the Phoenician city of Tyre had planted a colony on the coast of northern Africa near modern Tunis, calling it the New City, or Carthage. The city was located on a defensible site and commanded an excellent harbor that encouraged commerce.

Beginning in the sixth century B.C.E., the Carthaginians expanded their domain to include the coast of northern Africa west beyond the Straits of Gibraltar and eastward into Libya. Overseas, they came to control the southern part of Spain, Sardinia, Corsica, Malta, the Balearic Islands, and western Sicily. Carthage profited greatly from the mines of Spain and from an absolute monopoly of trade imposed on the western Mediterranean.

**Rome became a** naval power late in its history to defeat Carthage in the First Punic War (264–241 B.C.E.). This sculpture in low relief shows a Roman ship, propelled by oars, with both ram and soldiers, ready either to ram or board an enemy.

A Roman Warship. Direzione Generale Musei Vaticani

**How did competition for seaborne trade contribute to the outbreak of hostilities between Rome and Carthage?**

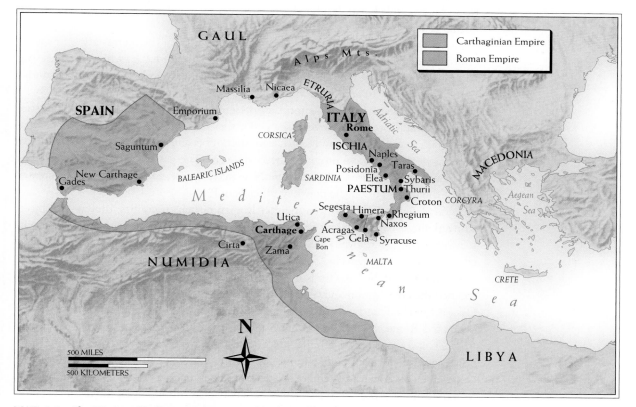

MAP 4–2  **The Western Mediterranean Area During the Rise of Rome**  This map illustrates the theater of conflict between the growing Roman dominions and those of Carthage in the third century B.C.E. The Carthaginian Empire stretched westward from the city (in modern Tunisia) along the North African coast and into southern Spain.

**What economic** and political effects did the Punic Wars have on Rome?

An attack by Hiero, tyrant of Syracuse, on the Sicilian city of Messana just across from Italy, first caused trouble between Rome and Carthage. Messana had been seized by a group of Italian mercenary soldiers who called themselves *Mamertines*, the sons of the war god Mars. When Hiero defeated the Mamertines, some of them called on the Carthaginians to help save their city. Carthage agreed and sent a garrison, for the Carthaginians wanted to prevent Syracuse from dominating the straits. One Mamertine faction, however, fearing that Carthage might take undue advantage of the opportunity, asked Rome for help.

In 264 B.C.E., the request came to the Senate. Because a Punic garrison (the Romans called the Carthaginians *Phoenicians*; in Latin the word is *Poeni* or *Puni*—hence the adjective *Punic*) was in place at Messana, any intervention would be not against Syracuse, but against the mighty empire of Carthage. Unless Rome intervened, however, Carthage would gain control of all Sicily and the straits. The assembly voted to send an army to Messana and expelled the Punic garrison. The First Punic War was on.

**The First Punic War (264–241 B.C.E.)**    The war in Sicily soon settled into a stalemate until the Romans built a fleet to cut off supplies to the besieged Carthaginian cities at the western end of Sicily. When Carthage sent its own fleet to raise the siege, the Romans destroyed it. In 241 B.C.E., Carthage signed a treaty giving up Sicily and the islands between Italy and Sicily; it also agreed to pay a war indemnity in ten annual installments. Neither side was to attack the allies of the other. The peace was realistic and not unduly harsh. If it had been carried out in good faith, it might have brought lasting peace.

A rebellion, however, broke out in Carthage among the mercenaries, newly recruited from Sicily, who now demanded their pay. In 238 B.C.E., while Carthage was still preoccupied with the rebellion, Rome seized Sardinia and Corsica and demanded that Carthage pay an additional indemnity.

The conquest of overseas territory presented the Romans with new administrative problems. Instead of following the policy they had pursued in Italy, they made Sicily a province and Sardinia and Corsica another. It became common to extend the term of the governors of these provinces beyond a year. The governors were unchecked by colleagues and exercised full *imperium*. New magistracies, in effect, were thus created free of the limits put on the power of officials in Rome.

The new populations were neither Roman citizens nor allies; they were subjects who did not serve in the army but paid tribute instead. The old practice of extending citizenship and, with it, loyalty to Rome thus stopped at the borders of Italy. Rome collected taxes on these subjects by "farming" them out at auction to the highest bidder. These innovations were the basis for Rome's imperial organization in the future. In time, they strained the constitution and traditions and threatened the existence of the republic.

After the First Punic War, campaigns against the Gauls and across the Adriatic distracted Rome. Meanwhile Hamilcar Barca, the Carthaginian governor of Spain from 237 B.C.E. until his death in 229 B.C.E., was leading Carthage on the road to recovery. Hamilcar sought to build a Punic Empire in Spain. He improved the ports and the commerce conducted in them, exploited the mines, gained control of the hinterland, won over many of the conquered tribes, and built a strong and disciplined army. Hamilcar's successor, his son-in-law Hasdrubal, pursued the same policies.

**The Second Punic War (218–202 B.C.E.)**    On Hasdrubal's assassination in 221 B.C.E., the army chose as his successor Hannibal, son of Hamilcar Barca. Hannibal was at that time twenty-five years old. He quickly consolidated and extended the Punic Empire in Spain. A few years before his accession, Rome had received an offer of

**QUICK REVIEW**

**Path to War**

◆ Carthage's power expanded throughout western Mediterranean in sixth century B.C.E.

◆ Carthage claimed exclusive rights to trade in the Mediterranean

◆ Conflict over Sicilian city of Messana sparked war

alliance from the people of Saguntum, a Spanish town about one hundred miles south of the Ebro River. The Romans accepted the friendship and the responsibilities it entailed. At first, Hannibal avoided any action against Saguntum, but the Saguntines, confident of Rome's protection, began to interfere with some of the Spanish tribes allied with Hannibal. When the Romans sent an embassy to Hannibal warning him to let Saguntum alone, he ignored the warning and captured the town. The Romans sent an ultimatum to Carthage demanding the surrender of Hannibal. Carthage refused, and Rome declared war in 218 B.C.E.

Between the close of the First Punic War and the outbreak of the Second, Rome had repeatedly provoked Carthage, taking Sardinia in 238 B.C.E. and interfering in Spain, but had not prevented Carthage from building a powerful and dangerous empire in Spain. Hannibal saw to it that the Romans paid the price for these blunders. By September 218 B.C.E., he was across the Alps, in Italy and among the friendly Gauls.

Hannibal defeated the Romans at the Ticinus River and crushed the joint consular armies at the Trebia River. In 217 B.C.E., he outmaneuvered and trapped another army at Lake Trasimene. The key to success, however, would be defection by Rome's allies. Hannibal released Italian prisoners without harm or ransom and moved his army south of Rome to encourage rebellion. But the allies remained firm.

In 216 B.C.E., Hannibal marched to Cannae in Apulia to tempt the Romans into another open fight. They sent off an army of some 80,000 men to meet him. Almost the entire Roman army was wiped out. It was the worst defeat in Roman history. Rome's prestige was shattered, and most of its allies in southern Italy, as well as Syracuse in Sicily, went over to Hannibal. For more than a decade, no Roman army would dare face Hannibal in the field.

Hannibal, however, had neither the numbers nor the supplies to besiege walled cities, nor did he have the equipment to take them by assault. The Romans appointed Publius Cornelius Scipio (237–183 B.C.E.), later called Africanus, to the command in Spain with proconsular *imperium*. Scipio was not yet twenty-five and had held no high office, but he was a general almost as talented as Hannibal. Within a few years, young Scipio had conquered all of Spain and had deprived Hannibal of any hope of help from that region.

In 204 B.C.E., Scipio landed in Africa and forced the Carthaginians to accept a peace, the main clause of which was the withdrawal of Hannibal and his army from Italy. Hannibal had won every battle but lost the war, for he had not counted on the determination of Rome and the loyalty of its allies. Hannibal's return inspired Carthage to break the peace and to risk all in battle. In 202 B.C.E., Scipio and Hannibal faced each other at the Battle of Zama. The generalship of Scipio and the desertion of Hannibal's mercenaries gave the victory to Rome. The new peace terms reduced Carthage to the status of a dependent ally of Rome. Rome now ruled the seas and the entire Mediterranean coast from Italy westward.

## THE REPUBLIC'S CONQUEST OF THE HELLENISTIC WORLD

**The East**  By the middle of the third century B.C.E., the eastern Mediterranean had reached a condition of stability based on a balance of power among the three great Hellenistic kingdoms that allowed an established place even for lesser states. Two aggressive monarchs, Philip V of Macedon (221–179 B.C.E.) and Antiochus III of the Seleucid kingdom (223–187 B.C.E.), threatened this equilibrium, however. Philip and Antiochus moved swiftly, the latter against Syria and Palestine, the former against cities in the Aegean, in the Hellespontine region, and on the coast of Asia Minor.

**QUICK REVIEW**

**Hannibal on the Offensive**

- 218 B.C.E.: crossed Alps and dealt Rome a series of defeats
- 216 B.C.E.: defeated Romans in Battle of Cannae, worst defeat in Roman history
- Victory at Cannae convinced some Roman allies to change sides

## SIGNIFICANT DATES IN ROME'S RISE TO EMPIRE

| | |
|---|---|
| 509 B.C.E. | Republic founded |
| 387 B.C.E. | Gauls sack Rome |
| 338 B.C.E. | Rome defeats the Latin League |
| 295 B.C.E. | Rome defeats the Samnites |
| 287 B.C.E. | "Struggle of the Orders" ends |
| 275 B.C.E. | Pyrrhus abandons Italy to Rome |
| 264–241 B.C.E. | First Punic War |
| 218–202 B.C.E. | Second Punic War |
| 215–205 B.C.E. | First Macedonian War |
| 200–197 B.C.E. | Second Macedonian War |
| 189 B.C.E. | Rome defeats Antiochus |
| 172–168 B.C.E. | Third Macedonian War |
| 149–146 B.C.E. | Third Punic War |
| 154–133 B.C.E. | Roman Wars in Spain |

The threat that a more powerful Macedon might pose to Rome's friends and, perhaps, even to Italy persuaded the Romans to intervene. Philip had already attempted to meddle in Roman affairs when he formed an alliance with Carthage during the Second Punic War, provoking a conflict known as the First Macedonian War (215–205 B.C.E.). In 200 B.C.E., in an action that began the Second Macedonian War, the Romans sent an ultimatum to Philip ordering him not to attack any Greek city and to pay reparations to Pergamum. These orders were meant to provoke, not avoid, war, and Philip refused to obey. Two years later the Romans sent out a talented young general, Flamininus, who demanded that Philip withdraw from Greece entirely. In 197 B.C.E., with Greek support, Flamininus defeated Philip at Cynoscephalae, ending the war. The Greek cities freed from Philip were made autonomous, and in 196 B.C.E., Flamininus proclaimed the freedom of the Greeks.

Soon after the Romans withdrew from Greece, they came into conflict with Antiochus, who was expanding his power in Asia and on the European side of the Hellespont. On the pretext of freeing the Greeks from Roman domination, he landed an army on the Greek mainland. The Romans routed Antiochus at Thermopylae and quickly drove him from Greece. In 189 B.C.E., they crushed his army at Magnesia in Asia Minor. Once again, the Romans took no territory for themselves and left several Greek cities in Asia free. They regarded Greece, and now Asia Minor, as a kind of protectorate in which they could intervene or not as they chose.

This relatively mild policy was destined to end as the stern and businesslike policies of the conservative censor Cato gained favor in Rome. A new harshness was to be applied to allies and bystanders, as well as to defeated opponents.

In 179 B.C.E., Perseus succeeded Philip V as king of Macedon. He tried to gain popularity in Greece by favoring the democratic and revolutionary forces in the cities. The Romans, troubled by his threat to stability, launched the Third Macedonian War (172–168 B.C.E.), and in 168 B.C.E. Aemilius Paulus defeated Perseus at Pydna. The peace that followed this war, reflecting the changed attitude at Rome, was harsh.

**The West**    Harsh as the Romans had become toward the Greeks, they treated the people of the Iberian Peninsula (Spain and Portugal), whom they considered barbarians, even worse. They committed dreadful atrocities, lied, cheated, and broke treaties to exploit and pacify the natives, who fought back fiercely in guerrilla style. From 154 to 133 B.C.E., the fighting waxed, and it became hard to recruit Roman soldiers to participate in the increasingly ugly war. At last, in 134 B.C.E., Scipio Aemilianus took the key city of Numantia by siege and burned it to the ground. This put an end to the war in Spain.

Roman treatment of Carthage was no better. Although Carthage lived up to its treaty with Rome faithfully and posed no threat, some Romans refused to abandon their hatred of the traditional enemy. At last the Romans took advantage of a technical breach of the peace to destroy Carthage. In 146 B.C.E., Scipio Aemilianus took the city, plowed up its land, and put salt in the furrows as a symbol of the permanent abandonment of the site. The Romans incorporated it as the province of Africa, one of six Roman provinces, including Sicily, Sardinia-Corsica, Macedonia, Hither Spain, and Further Spain.

# CIVILIZATION IN THE EARLY ROMAN REPUBLIC

Close and continued association with the Greeks of the Hellenistic world wrought important changes in the Roman style of life and thought. The Roman attitude toward the Greeks ranged from admiration for their culture and history to contempt for their constant squabbling, their commercial practices, and their weakness.

**HOW DID** contact with the Hellenistic world affect Rome?

## RELIGION

The Greeks influenced Roman religion almost from the beginning. The Romans identified their own gods with Greek equivalents and incorporated Greek mythology into their own. Mostly, however, Roman religious practice remained simple and Italian, until the third century B.C.E. brought important new influences from the East.

**Traditional Religion and Character**    In early Rome the family stood at the center of religious observance, and gods of the household and farm were most important. In the early days, before they were influenced by the Etruscans and Greeks, Roman religion knew little of mythology: Their gods were impersonal forces, *numina*, rather than deities in human or superhuman form. Their image of an afterlife was vague and insubstantial. Morality played little role in Roman religion but, since failure to perform the necessary rites correctly could bring harm on the entire state, everyone had to participate in religious observance as a civic duty and evidence of patriotism.

## ENCOUNTERING THE PAST

### ROMAN COMEDY

In Rome, as in Greece, religious festivals were public entertainments involving gladiatorial contests, chariot races, and dramas. Initially, Roman audiences sat on hillsides and watched performances staged on temporary wooden platforms. Toward the end of the republican period, however, wealthy Romans began to donate permanent amphitheaters to their communities, and theaters spread to all the lands Rome ruled.

Tragedies modeled on Greek examples were staged in Rome, but the works of the republic's best playwrights—Plautus (ca. 254–184 B.C.E.) and Terence (ca. 195–159 B.C.E.)—belong to the genre of Hellenistic New Comedy. The standard set for such plays was a city street where stock characters (clever slaves, dim-witted masters, young lovers, and shrewish women) enacted plots involving a tangle of mistaken identities, love affairs, and domestic disputes. The result was very similar to the situation comedies that are staples of modern television.

IS THERE any significance in the fact that the great plays that survive from the era of the Roman Republic are comedies, not tragedies?

**This mosaic shows** a scene from Roman comedy in which musicians played a significant role.

© Araldo de Luca/CORBIS

**Who made up the audience for Roman comedy?**

In 205 B.C.E., the Senate approved the public worship of Cybele, the Great Mother goddess from Phrygia in Asia Minor. Hers was a fertility cult accompanied by ecstatic, frenzied, and sensual rites that so outraged conservative Romans that they soon banned the cult. Similarly, the Senate banned the worship of Dionysus, or Bacchus, in 186 B.C.E. In the second century B.C.E., interest in Babylonian astrology also grew, and the Senate's attempt in 139 B.C.E. to expel the "Chaldaeans," as the astrologers were called, did not prevent the continued influence of their superstition.

## EDUCATION

Education in the early republic was entirely the responsibility of the family, the father teaching his own son at home. It is not clear whether in these early times girls received any education, though they certainly did later on. The boys learned to read, write, calculate, and how to farm. They memorized the laws of the Twelve Tables, learned how to perform religious rites, heard stories of the great deeds of early Roman history and particularly those of their ancestors, and engaged in the physical training appropriate for potential soldiers.

**Hellenized Education**    In the third century B.C.E., the Romans came into contact with the Greeks of southern Italy, and this contact changed Roman education. Greek teachers introduced the study of language, literature, and philosophy, as well as the idea of a liberal education, or what the Romans called **humanitas**, the root of our concept of the humanities. The aim of education changed from the mastery of practical, vocational skills to an emphasis on broad intellectual training, critical thinking, an interest in ideas, and the development of a well-rounded person. The new emphasis required students to learn Greek, for Rome did not yet have a literature of its own. Hereafter, educated Romans were expected to be bilingual.

In the late republic, Roman education, though still entirely private, became more formal and organized. From the ages of seven to twelve, boys went to elementary school. At school the boys learned to read and write, using a wax tablet and a stylus, and to do simple arithmetic with an abacus and pebbles (*calculi*). Discipline was harsh and corporal punishment frequent. From twelve to sixteen, boys went to a higher school, where instructors provided a liberal education, using Greek and Latin literature as their subject matter.

At sixteen, some boys went on to advanced study in rhetoric. The instructors were usually Greek. They trained their charges by studying models of fine speech of the past and by having them write, memorize, and declaim speeches suitable for different occasions.

This style of education broadened the Romans' understanding through the careful study of a foreign language and culture. It made them a part of the older and wider culture of the Hellenistic world, a world they had come to dominate and needed to understand.

**Education for Women**    Though the evidence is limited, we can be sure that girls of the upper classes received an education equivalent at least to the early stages of a boy's

*humanitas*    Wide-ranging intellectual curiosity and habits of critical thinking that are the goals of liberal education.

**This carved relief** from the second century C.E. shows a schoolmaster and his pupils. The pupil at the right is arriving late.

Rheinisches Landesmuseum, Trier, Germany. Alinari/Art Resource, NY

**Why was education so important to the future success of elite Roman boys?**

education. They were probably taught by tutors at home rather than going to school, as was increasingly the fashion among boys in the late republic. Young women did not study with philosophers and rhetoricians, for they were usually married by the age at which the men were pursuing their higher education. Still, some women continued their education and became prose writers or poets.

## SLAVERY

Like most other ancient peoples, the Romans had slaves from early in their history, but slavery became a basic element in the Roman economy and society only during the second century B.C.E., after the Romans had conquered most of the lands bordering the Mediterranean. In the time between the beginning of Rome's first war against Carthage (264 B.C.E.) and the conquest of Spain (133 B.C.E.), the Romans enslaved some 250,000 prisoners of war, greatly increasing the availability of slave labor and reducing its price. Many slaves worked as domestic servants, feeding the growing appetite for luxury of the Roman upper class; at the other end of the spectrum, many worked in the mines of Spain and Sardinia. Some worked as artisans in small factories and shops or as public clerks. Slaves were permitted to marry, and they produced sizable families. As in Greece, domestic slaves and those used in crafts and commerce could earn money, keep it, and, in some cases, use it to purchase their own freedom. *Manumission* (the freeing of slaves) was common among the Romans.

The unique development in the Roman world was the emergence of an agricultural system that employed and depended on a vast number of slaves. By the time of Jesus, there were between 2 and 3 million slaves in Italy, and about 35 to 40 percent of the total population, most of them part of great slave gangs that worked the vast plantations the Romans called **latifundia**. *Latifundia* owners sought maximum profits and treated their slaves simply as means to that end. The slaves often worked in chains, were oppressed by brutal foremen, and lived in underground prisons.

**latifundia** Great estates that produced capital-intensive cash crops for the international market.

Such harsh treatment led to serious slave rebellions of a kind we do not hear of in other ancient societies. A rebellion in Sicily in 134 B.C.E. kept the island in turmoil for more than two years, and the rebellion of the gladiators led by Spartacus in 73 B.C.E. produced an army of 70,000 slaves that repeatedly defeated the Roman legions and overran southern Italy before it was brutally crushed.

Slavery retained its economic and social importance in the first century of the imperial period, but its centrality began to decline in the second. The reasons for this decline are rather obscure. A rise in the cost of slaves and a consequent reduction in their economic value seem to have been factors. More important, it appears, was a general economic decline that permitted increasing pressure on the free lower classes. More and more they were employed as **coloni**—tenant farmers. Over centuries, these increasingly serflike *coloni* replaced most agricultural slave labor.

**coloni** Tenant farmers who were bound to the lands they worked.

# ROMAN IMPERIALISM: THE LATE REPUBLIC

Rome's expansion in Italy and overseas was accomplished without a grand general plan. Whether intended or not, Rome's expansion brought the Romans an empire and, with it, power, wealth, and responsibilities. The need to govern an empire beyond the seas would severely test the republican constitution, Roman society, and the Roman character.

**HOW DID** the expansion of Rome change the Republic?

## THE AFTERMATH OF CONQUEST

War and expansion changed the economic, social, and political life of Italy. Before the Punic Wars, most Italians owned their own farms, which provided the greater part of

**This wall painting** from the first century B.C.E. comes from the villa of Publius Fannius Synistor at Pompeii and shows a woman playing a cithera.

Roman. Paintings. Pompeian, Boscoreale. 1st Century B.C. *Lady Playing the Cithara*. Wall painting from the east wall of large room in the villa of Publius Fannius Synistor. Fresco on lime plaster. H. 6 ft. 1 1/2 in. W. 6 ft. 1 1/2 in. (18 × 187 cm.) The Metropolitan Museum of Art, Rogers Fund, 1903. (03.14.5) Photograph © 1986 The Metropolitan Museum of Art

**What social and political functions were played by the Roman villa?**

the family's needs. Fourteen years of fighting in the Second Punic War did terrible damage to Italian farmland. Many veterans returning from the wars found it impossible or unprofitable to go back to their farms. Some moved to Rome, where they could find work as laborers, but most stayed in the country as tenant farmers or hired hands. Often, the wealthy converted the abandoned land into *latifundia* for growing cash crops—grain, olives, and grapes for wine—or into cattle ranches.

The upper classes had plenty of capital to operate these estates because of profits from the war and from exploiting the provinces. Land was cheap, and so was slave labor. By fair means and foul, large landholders obtained great quantities of public land and forced small farmers from it. These changes separated the people of Rome and Italy more sharply into rich and poor, landed and landless, privileged and deprived. The result was political, social, and, ultimately, constitutional conflict that threatened the existence of the republic.

## THE GRACCHI

By the middle of the second century B.C.E., the problems caused by Rome's rapid expansion troubled perceptive Roman nobles. The fall in status of peasant farmers made it harder to recruit soldiers and came to present a political threat as well. The patron's traditional control over his clients was weakened when they fled from their land. Even those former landowners who worked on the land of their patrons as tenants or hired hands were less reliable. The introduction of the secret ballot in the 130s B.C.E. made them even more independent.

**Tiberius Gracchus** In 133 B.C.E., Tiberius Gracchus tried to solve these problems. He became tribune for 133 B.C.E. on a program of land reform; some of the most powerful members of the Roman aristocracy helped him draft the bill. They meant it to be a moderate attempt at solving Rome's problems. The bill's target was public land that had been acquired and held illegally, some of it for many years. The bill allowed holders of this land to retain as many as five hundred iugera (approximately 320 acres), but the state would reclaim anything over that and redistribute it in small lots to the poor, who would pay a small rent to the state and could not sell what they had received.

The bill aroused great hostility. Its passage would hurt many senators who held vast estates. Others thought it would be a bad precedent to allow any interference with property rights, even if they involved illegally held public land. Still others feared the political gains that Tiberius and his associates would make if the beneficiaries of their law were properly grateful to its drafters.

When Tiberius put the bill before the tribal assembly, one of the tribunes, M. Octavius, interposed his veto. Tiberius went to the Senate to discuss his proposal, but the senators continued their opposition. Unwilling to give up, he put his bill before the tribal assembly again. Again Octavius vetoed. So Tiberius, strongly supported by the people, had Octavius removed from office, violating the constitution. The assembly's removal of a magistrate implied a fundamental shift of power from the Senate to the people. If the assembly could pass laws the Senate opposed and a tribune vetoed, and if they could remove magistrates, then Rome would become a democracy like Athens instead of a traditional oligarchy.

Tiberius proposed a second bill, harsher than the first and more appealing to the people, for he had given up hope of conciliating the Senate. This bill, which passed the assembly, provided for a commission to carry it out. When King Attalus of Pergamum died and left his kingdom to Rome, Tiberius proposed using the Pergamene revenue to finance the commission. This proposal challenged the Senate's control both of finances and of foreign affairs. Hereafter there could be no compromise: Either Tiberius or the Roman constitution must go under.

Tiberius understood the danger he would face if he stepped down from the tribunate, so he announced his candidacy for a second successive term, striking another blow at tradition. His opponents feared he might go on to hold office indefinitely, to dominate Rome in what appeared to them a demagogic tyranny. At the elections a riot broke out, and a mob of senators and their clients killed Tiberius and some three hundred of his followers and threw their bodies into the Tiber River. The Senate had put down the threat to its rule, but at the price of the first internal bloodshed in Roman political history.

The tribunate of Tiberius Gracchus changed Roman politics. Heretofore Roman political struggles had generally been struggles for honor and reputation between great families or coalitions of such families. Fundamental issues were rarely at stake. The revolutionary proposals of Tiberius, however, and the senatorial resort to bloodshed created a new situation. From then on, Romans could pursue a political career that was not based solely on influence within the aristocracy; pressure from the people might be an effective substitute. In the last century of the republic, politicians who sought such backing were called *populares*, whereas those who supported the traditional role of the Senate were called *optimates*, or "the best men."

**Gaius Gracchus**   The tribunate of Gaius Gracchus (brother of Tiberius) was much more dangerous than that of Tiberius. All the tribunes of 123 B.C.E. were his supporters, so there could be no veto, and a recent law permitted the reelection of tribunes. Gaius's program appealed to a variety of groups. First, he revived the agrarian commission, which had been allowed to lapse. Because there was not enough good public land left to meet the demand, he proposed to establish new colonies: two in Italy and one on the old site of Carthage. Among other popular acts, he put through a law stabilizing the price of grain in Rome, which involved building granaries to guarantee an adequate supply. Finally, Gaius undercut his opponents by passing legislation to the advantage of the **equestrians** (men rich enough to qualify for cavalry service), effectively pitting the republic's two wealthiest classes, the senators and the equestrians, against each other.

Gaius easily won reelection as tribune for 122 B.C.E. He aimed at giving citizenship to the Italians, both to resolve their dissatisfaction and to add them to his political coalition. But the common people did not want to share the advantages of Roman citizenship. The Senate seized on this proposal to drive a wedge between Gaius and his supporters.

The Romans did not reelect Gaius for 121 B.C.E., leaving him vulnerable to his enemies. A hostile consul provoked an incident that led to violence. The Senate invented an extreme decree ordering the consuls to see to it that no harm came to the republic; in effect, this decree established martial law. Gaius was hunted down and killed, and a senatorial court condemned and put to death some 3,000 of his followers without any trial.

## MARIUS AND SULLA

For the moment, the senatorial oligarchy had fought off the challenge to its traditional position. Before long, it faced more serious dangers arising from troubles abroad. The first grew out of a dispute over the succession to the throne of Numidia, a client kingdom of Rome's near Carthage.

*populares*   Politicians who followed Tiberius's example of politics and governing.

*optimates*   ("the best men") Opponents of Tiberius and defenders of the traditional prerogatives of the Senate.

**equestrians**   Men rich enough to qualify for cavalry service.

**This statue of** an unknown member of the Roman nobility from late in the first century illustrates a fundamental custom. He carries the images of two of his ancestors, probably his father and grandfather.

Marble. Musei Capitolini, Rome, Italy. Photograph ©Scala/Art Resource, NY

**What role did illustrious ancestors play in the lives of elite Roman men?**

**Marius and the Jugurthine War**   The victory of Jugurtha, who became king of Numidia, and his massacre of Roman and Italian businessmen in the province, gained Roman attention. Although the Senate was reluctant to become involved, pressure from the equestrians and the people forced the declaration of what became known as the Jugurthine War in 111 B.C.E.

As the war dragged on, the people, sometimes with good reason, suspected the Senate of taking bribes from Jugurtha. They elected C. Marius (157–86 B.C.E.) to the consulship for 107 B.C.E. The assembly, usurping the role of the Senate, assigned him to Numidia.

Marius quickly defeated Jugurtha, but Jugurtha escaped, and guerrilla warfare continued. Finally, Marius's subordinate, L. Cornelius Sulla (138–78 B.C.E.), trapped Jugurtha and brought the war to an end. Marius celebrated the victory, but Sulla, an ambitious though impoverished descendant of an old Roman family, resented being cheated of the credit he thought he deserved. Rumors credited Sulla with the victory and diminished Marius's role. Thus were the seeds planted for a mutual hostility that would last until Marius's death.

While the Romans were fighting Jugurtha, a far greater danger threatened Rome from the north. In 105 B.C.E., two barbaric tribes, the Cimbri and the Teutones, had come down the Rhone Valley and crushed a Roman army at Arausio (Orange) in southern France. When these tribes threatened again, the Romans elected Marius to his second consulship to meet the danger. He served five consecutive terms until 100 B.C.E., when the crisis was over.

While the barbarians were occupied elsewhere, Marius used the time to make important changes in the army. He began using volunteers for the army, mostly the dispossessed farmers and rural proletarians whose problems the Gracchi had not solved. Volunteers were most likely to enlist with a man who was a capable soldier and influential enough to obtain what he needed for them. They looked to him rather than to the state for their rewards. He, however, had to obtain these favors from the Senate if he was to maintain his power and reputation. Marius's innovation created both the opportunity and the necessity for military leaders to gain enough power to challenge civilian authority. The promise of rewards won these leaders the personal loyalty of their troops, and that loyalty allowed them to frighten the Senate into granting their demands.

**The Wars against the Italians (90–88 B.C.E.)**   For a decade Rome avoided serious troubles, but in that time the Senate took no action to deal with Italian discontent. Frustrated, the Italians revolted in 90 B.C.E. and established a separate confederation with its own capital and coinage.

Employing the traditional device of divide and conquer, the Romans immediately offered citizenship to those cities that remained loyal and soon made the same offer to the rebels if they laid down their arms. Even then, hard fighting was needed to put down the uprising, but by 88 B.C.E., the war against the allies was over. All the Italians became Roman citizens with the protections that citizenship offered.

**Sulla's Dictatorship**   During the war against the allies, Sulla had performed well. He was elected consul for 88 B.C.E. and was given command of the war against Mithridates, who was leading a major rebellion in Asia. At this point, the seventy-year-old Marius emerged from obscurity and sought the command for himself. With popular and equestrian support, he got the assembly to transfer the command to him. Sulla, defending the rights of the Senate and his own interests, marched his army against Rome. This was the first time a Roman general had used his army against fellow citizens. Marius and his friends fled, and Sulla regained the command. No sooner had he left again for

Asia, than Marius joined with the consul Cinna and seized Rome. He outlawed Sulla and massacred the senatorial opposition. Marius died soon after his election to a seventh consulship, for 86 B.C.E.

Cinna now was the chief man at Rome. Supported by Marius's men, he held the consulship from 87 to 84 B.C.E. His future depended on Sulla's fortunes in the East.

By 85 B.C.E., Sulla had driven Mithridates from Greece and had crossed over to Asia Minor. Eager to regain control of Rome, he negotiated a compromise peace. In 83 B.C.E., he returned to Italy and fought a civil war that lasted for more than a year. Sulla won and drove the followers of Marius from Italy. He had himself appointed dictator, not in the traditional sense, but to remake the state.

Sulla's first step was to wipe out the opposition. The names of those proscribed were posted in public. As they were outlaws, anyone could kill them and receive a reward. Sulla proscribed not only political opponents, but also his personal enemies and men whose only crime was their wealth. With the proceeds from the confiscations, Sulla rewarded his veterans, perhaps as many as 100,000 men, and thereby built a solid base of support.

Sulla had enough power to make himself the permanent ruler of Rome. He was traditional enough to want to restore senatorial government but reformed so as to prevent the misfortunes of the past. To deal with the decimation of the Senate caused by the proscriptions and the civil war, he enrolled three hundred new members, many of them from the equestrian order and the upper classes of the Italian cities. The office of tribune, which the Gracchi had used to attack senatorial rule, was made into a political dead end.

Sulla's most valuable reforms improved the quality of the courts and the entire legal system. He created new courts to deal with specified crimes, bringing the number of courts to eight. Because both judge and jurors were senators, the courts, too, enhanced senatorial power. These actions were the most permanent of Sulla's reforms, laying the foundation for Roman criminal law.

Sulla retired to a life of ease and luxury in 79 B.C.E. He could not, however, undo the effect of his own example—that of a general using the loyalty of his own troops to take power and to massacre his opponents, as well as innocent men. These actions proved to be more significant than his constitutional arrangements.

# THE FALL OF THE REPUBLIC

Within a year of Sulla's death, his constitution came under assault. To deal with an armed threat to its powers, the Senate violated the very procedures meant to defend them.

**WHAT EVENTS** led to the fall of the Republic?

## POMPEY, CRASSUS, CAESAR, AND CICERO

The Senate gave the command of the army to Pompey (106–48 B.C.E.), who was only twenty-eight and had never been elected to a magistracy. Then, when Sertorius, a Marian general, resisted senatorial control, the Senate appointed Pompey proconsul in Spain in 77 B.C.E. In 71 B.C.E., Pompey returned to Rome with new glory, having put down the rebellion of Sertorius. In 73 B.C.E., the Senate made another extraordinary appointment to put down a great slave rebellion led by the gladiator Spartacus. Marcus Licinius Crassus, a rich and ambitious senator, received powers that gave him command of almost all of Italy. Together with the newly returned Pompey, he crushed the rebellion in 71 B.C.E. Extraordinary commands of this sort proved to be the ruin of the republic.

Crassus and Pompey were ambitious men whom the Senate feared. Both demanded special honors and election to the consulship for the year 70 B.C.E. They joined forces, though they disliked and were jealous of each other. They both won election and repealed most of Sulla's constitution. This opened the way for further attacks on senatorial control and for collaboration between ambitious generals and demagogic tribunes.

In 67 B.C.E., a special law gave Pompey *imperium* for three years over the entire Mediterranean and fifty miles in from the coast. It also gave him the power to raise troops and money to rid the area of pirates. The assembly passed the law over senatorial opposition, and in three months Pompey cleared the seas of piracy. Meanwhile, a new war had broken out with Mithridates. In 66 B.C.E., the assembly transferred the command to Pompey, giving him unprecedented powers. He held *imperium* over all Asia, with the right to make war and peace at will. His *imperium* was superior to that of any proconsul in the field.

Once again, Pompey justified his appointment. He defeated Mithridates and drove him to suicide. By 62 B.C.E., he had extended Rome's frontier to the Euphrates River and had organized the territories of Asia so well that his arrangements remained the basis of Roman rule well into the imperial period. When Pompey returned to Rome in 62 B.C.E., he had more power, prestige, and popular support than any other Roman in history.

Rome had not been quiet in Pompey's absence. Crassus was the foremost among those who had reason to fear Pompey's return. Although rich and influential, Crassus did not have the confidence of the Senate, a firm political base of his own, or the kind of military glory needed to rival Pompey. During the 60s B.C.E., therefore, he allied himself with various popular leaders.

The ablest of these men was Gaius Julius Caesar (100–44 B.C.E.). Caesar was an ambitious young politician whose daring and rhetorical skill made him a valuable ally in winning the discontented of every class to the cause of the *populares*. Though Crassus was the senior partner, each needed the other to achieve what both wanted: significant military commands with which to build a reputation, a political following, and a military force to compete with Pompey's.

The chief opposition to Crassus's candidates for the consulship for 63 B.C.E. came from Cicero (106–43 B.C.E.). Cicero, though he came from outside the senatorial aristocracy, was no *popularis*. His program was to preserve the republic against demagogues and ambitious generals by making the government more liberal. He wanted to unite the stable elements of the state—the Senate and the equestrians—in a harmony of the orders. This program did not appeal to the senatorial oligarchy, but the Senate preferred Cicero to Catiline, a dangerous and popular politician thought to be linked with Crassus. Cicero and Antonius were elected consuls for 63 B.C.E., with Catiline running third.

Cicero soon learned of a plot hatched by Catiline. Catiline had run in the previous election on a platform of cancellation of debts; this appealed to discontented elements in general, but especially to the heavily indebted nobles and their many clients. Made desperate by defeat, Catiline planned to stir up rebellions around Italy, to cause confusion in the city, and to take it by force. Quick action by Cicero defeated Catiline.

## THE FIRST TRIUMVIRATE

Toward the end of 62 B.C.E., Pompey landed at Brundisium. Surprisingly, he disbanded his army, celebrated a great triumph, and returned to private life. He had delayed his return in the hope of finding Italy in such a state as to justify his keeping the army and dominating the scene. Cicero's quick suppression of Catiline prevented his plan. Pompey, therefore, had either to act illegally or to lay down his arms.

Pompey had achieved amazing things for Rome and simply wanted the Senate to approve his excellent arrangements in the East and to make land allotments to his veterans. But the Senate was jealous and fearful of overmighty individuals and refused his requests. Pompey was driven to an alliance with his natural enemies, Crassus and Caesar. They formed the First Triumvirate, a private political arrangement that enabled them, by working together, to dominate the republic.

## JULIUS CAESAR AND HIS GOVERNMENT OF ROME

Caesar was elected to the consulship for 59 B.C.E. The triumvirs' program was quickly enacted. Caesar got the extraordinary command that would give him a chance to earn the glory and power with which to rival Pompey: the governorship of Illyricum and Gaul for five years. A land bill settled Pompey's veterans comfortably, and his eastern settlement was ratified. Crassus, much of whose influence came from his position as champion of the equestrians, won for them a great windfall by having the government renegotiate a tax contract in their favor. To guarantee themselves against any reversal of these actions, the triumvirs continued their informal but effective collaboration, arranging for the election of friendly consuls and the departure of potential opponents.

Caesar was now free to seek the military success he craved. His province included Cisalpine Gaul in the Po Valley (by now occupied by many Italian settlers as well as Gauls) and Narbonese Gaul beyond the Alps (modern Provence).

Relying first on the excellent quality of his army and the experience of his officers and then on his own growing military ability, Caesar made great progress. By 56 B.C.E., he had conquered most of Gaul, but he had not yet consolidated his victories firmly. He therefore sought an extension of his command, but quarrels between Crassus and Pompey so weakened the Triumvirate that the Senate was prepared to order Caesar's recall.

To prevent the dissolution of his base of power, Caesar persuaded Crassus and Pompey to meet with him at Luca in northern Italy to renew the coalition. They agreed that Caesar would get another five-year command in Gaul, and Crassus and Pompey would be consuls again in 55 B.C.E. After that, they would each receive an army and a five-year command. Caesar was free to return to Gaul and finish the job. The capture of Alesia in 51 B.C.E. marked the end of the serious Gallic resistance and of Gallic liberty. For Caesar, it brought the wealth, fame, and military power he wanted. He commanded thirteen loyal legions, a match for his enemies as well as for his allies.

By the time Caesar was ready to return to Rome, the Triumvirate had dissolved and a crisis was at hand. At Carrhae, in 53 B.C.E., Crassus died trying to conquer the Parthians, successors to the Persian Empire. His death broke one link between Pompey and Caesar. The death of Caesar's daughter Julia, who had been Pompey's wife, dissolved another.

As Caesar's star rose, Pompey became jealous and fearful. In the late 50s B.C.E., political rioting at Rome caused the Senate to appoint Pompey sole consul. This grant of unprecedented power and responsibility brought Pompey closer to the senatorial aristocracy in mutual fear of, and hostility to, Caesar. The Senate wanted to bring Caesar back to Rome as a private citizen after his proconsular command expired. He would then be open to attack for past illegalities. Caesar tried to avoid the trap by asking permission to stand for the consulship in absentia.

Early in January 49 B.C.E., the more extreme faction in the Senate had its way. It ordered Pompey to defend the state and Caesar to lay down his command by a specified day. For Caesar, this meant exile or death, so he ordered his legions to cross the Rubicon River, the boundary of his province. (See Map 4–3, page 112.) This action started a civil war. In 45 B.C.E., Caesar defeated the last forces of his enemies under Pompey's sons at Munda in Spain.

Caesar made few changes in the government of Rome. The Senate continued to play its role, in theory. But its increased size, its packing with supporters of Caesar, and his own monopoly of military power made the whole thing a sham. He treated the

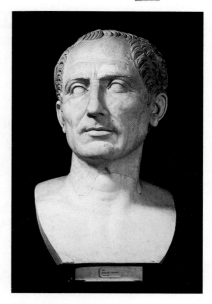

**A Bust of Julius Caesar.**

Bust of Julius Caesar (100–44 B.C.E.). Roman statesman. Museo Archeologico Nazionale, Naples, Italy. Photograph © Scala/Art Resource, NY

**What circumstances allowed for the rise of men like Caesar and Pompey to positions of unprecedented power?**

## MAP EXPLORATION

Interactive map: To explore this map further, go to **www.myhistorylab.com**

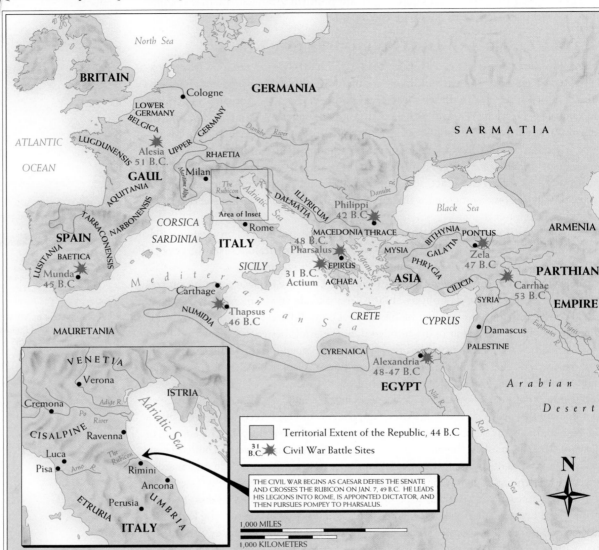

**MAP 4–3  The Civil Wars of the Late Roman Republic**   This map shows the extent of the territory controlled by Rome at the time of Caesar's death and the sites of the major battles of the civil wars of the late republic.

**What was** the principal goal of Roman foreign policy during the period of the Roman Republic? How did this goal contribute to Roman expansion?

Senate as his creature, sometimes with disdain. The enemies of Caesar were quick to accuse him of aiming at monarchy. (See "Compare & Connect: Did Caesar Want to Be King?," on pages 114–115.) A conspiracy under the leadership of Gaius Cassius Longinus and Marcus Junius Brutus included some sixty senators. On 15 March 44 B.C.E., Caesar entered the Senate, characteristically without a bodyguard, and was stabbed to death. The assassins regarded themselves as heroic tyrannicides but did not have a clear plan of action to follow the tyrant's death. No doubt they simply expected the republic to be restored in the old way, but things had gone too far for that. There followed instead thirteen more years of civil war, at the end of which the republic received its final burial.

## THE SECOND TRIUMVIRATE AND THE TRIUMPH OF OCTAVIAN

Caesar had had legions of followers, and he had a capable successor in Mark Antony. But the dictator had named his eighteen-year-old grandnephew, Gaius Octavius (63 B.C.E.–14 C.E.), as his heir and had left him three-quarters of his vast wealth. Octavius gathered an army, won the support of many of Caesar's veterans, and became a figure of importance—the future Augustus.

At first, the Senate tried to use Octavius against Antony, but when the conservatives rejected his request for the consulship, Octavius broke with them. Following Sulla's grim precedent, he took his army and marched on Rome. There he finally assumed his adopted name, C. Julius Caesar Octavianus. Modern historians refer to him at this stage in his career as Octavian, although he insisted on being called Caesar. In August 43 B.C.E., he became consul and declared the assassins of Caesar outlaws. Brutus and Cassius had an army of their own, so Octavian made a pact with Mark Antony and M. Aemilius Lepidus, a Caesarean governor of the western provinces. They took control of Rome and had themselves appointed "triumvirs to put the republic in order," with great powers. This was the Second Triumvirate, and unlike the first, it was legally empowered to rule almost dictatorially.

In 42 B.C.E., the triumviral army defeated Brutus and Cassius at Philippi in Macedonia, and the last hope of republican restoration died with the tyrannicides. Each of the triumvirs received a command. The junior partner, Lepidus, was given Africa, Antony took the rich and inviting East, and Octavian got the West and the many troubles that went with it. Octavian had to fight a war against Sextus, the son of Pompey, who held Sicily. He also had to settle 100,000 veterans in Italy, confiscating much property and making many enemies. Helped by his friend Agrippa, he defeated Sextus Pompey in 36 B.C.E.

Meanwhile Antony was in the East, chiefly at Alexandria with Cleopatra, the queen of Egypt. In 36 B.C.E., he attacked Parthia, with disastrous results. Octavian had promised to send troops to support Antony's Parthian campaign but never sent them. Antony was forced to depend on the East for support, and this meant reliance on Cleopatra. Octavian understood the advantage of representing himself as the champion of the West, Italy, and Rome. Meanwhile he represented Antony as the man of the East and the dupe of Cleopatra, her tool in establishing Alexandria as the center of an empire and herself as its ruler.

By 32 B.C.E., all pretense of cooperation ended. Octavian and Antony each tried to put the best face on what was essentially a struggle for power. Lepidus had been put aside some years earlier. Antony sought senatorial support and promised to restore the republican constitution. Octavian seized and published what was alleged to be the will of Antony, revealing his gifts of provinces to the children of Cleopatra. This caused the conflict to take the form of East against West, Rome against Alexandria.

In 31 B.C.E., the matter was settled at Actium in western Greece. Agrippa, Octavian's best general, cut off the enemy by land and sea, forcing and winning a naval battle. Octavian pursued Antony and Cleopatra to Alexandria, where both committed suicide. The civil wars were over, and at the age of thirty-two, Octavian was absolute master of the Mediterranean world. His power was enormous, but he had to restore peace, prosperity, and confidence. All of these required establishing a constitution that would reflect the new realities without offending unduly the traditional republican prejudices that still had so firm a grip on Rome and Italy.

# DID CAESAR WANT TO BE KING?

After the retirement and death of Sulla, his constitution was quickly destroyed, his attempt to restore the rule of the Senate proven a failure. The remaining years of the Roman Republic were occupied with a struggle among dynasts and senatorial factions to achieve dominance. From 49 to 46 B.C.E. Caesar and Pompey fought a great civil war that ended in total defeat for Pompey and the senatorial forces. Caesar was unchallenged master of the Roman world. His problem was to invent a system of government that would avoid the pitfalls of divided rule and yet rest upon widespread popular support. From antiquity to the present time, men have argued that his solution was nothing less than monarchy pure and simple. Others have denied that this was his goal. The question cannot be settled, for Caesar was assassinated before he could put his plans into practice, yet it is important to consider the problem both because of its intrinsic interest and because it represents a significant stage in the transition from republic to empire.

## QUESTIONS

1. What does Cassius Dio think Caesar wanted?

2. What is the opinion of Nicolaus of Damascus?

3. What is the significance of the debate?

## I. CASSIUS DIO

*Cassius Dio was a Greek of the third century* C.E. *who became a senator under the Roman Empire. He wrote an eighty-book history of Rome from the beginning to 229* C.E. *Here he tells the story of the growing suspicion among his enemies and the plots arising among them.*

When he had reached this point, the conduct of the men plotting against him became no longer doubtful, and in order to embitter even his best friends against him they did their best to traduce the man and finally called him "king,"—a name which was often heard in their consultations. When he refused the title and rebuked in a way those that so saluted him, yet did nothing by which he could be thought to be really displeased at it, they secretly adorned his statue, which stood on the rostra, with a diadem. And when Gaius Epidius Marullus and Lucius Cassetius Flavus, tribunes, took it down, he became thoroughly angry, although they uttered no insulting word and furthermore spoke well of him before the people as not desiring anything of the sort. At this time, though vexed, he remained quiet; subsequently, however, when he was riding in from Albanum, some men again called him king, and he said that his name was not king but Caesar: then when those tribunes brought suit against the first man that termed him king, he no longer restrained his wrath but showed evident irritation, as if these officials were actually aiming at the stability of his government. . . .

Something else that happened not long after these events proved still more clearly that while pretendedly he shunned the title, in reality he desired to assume it. When he had entered the Forum at the festival of the Lupercalia . . . Antony with his fellow priests saluted him as king and surrounding his brows with a diadem said: "The people gives this to you through my hands." He answered that Jupiter alone was king of the Romans and sent the diadem to him to the Capitol, yet he was not angry and caused it to he inscribed in the records that the royalty presented to him by the people through the consul he had refused to receive. It was accordingly suspected that this had been done by some prearranged plan and that he was anxious for the name but wished to be somehow compelled to take it, and the consequent hatred against him was intense.

Source: CassiusDio, 44.8–11, trans. by H.B. Foster, pp. 414–417.

## II. NICOLAUS OF DAMASCUS

*Nicolaus was born to a distinguished Greek family in the first century* B.C.E. *He served as adviser and court historian to Herod the Great of Judea. In addition to the biography of the young Augustus, from which the following selection is taken, he wrote dramas, philosophical works, and a multivolume history of the world.*

Such was the people's talk at that time. Later, in the course of the winter, a festival was held in Rome, called Lupercalia, in which old and young men together take part in a procession, naked except for a girdle, and anointed, railing at those whom they meet and striking them with pieces of goat's hide. When this festival came on Marcus Antonius was chosen director. He proceeded through the Forum, as was the custom, and the rest of the throng followed him. Caesar was sitting in a golden chair on the Rostra, wearing a purple toga. At first Licinius advanced toward him carrying a laurel wreath, though inside it a diadem was plainly visible. He mounted up, pushed up by his colleagues (for the place from which Caesar was accustomed to address the assembly was high), and set the diadem down before Caesar's feet. Amid the cheers of the crowd he placed it on Caesar's head. Thereupon Caesar called Lepidus, the master of horse, to ward him off, but Lepidus hesitated. In the meanwhile Cassius Longinus, one of the conspirators, pretending to be really well disposed toward Caesar so that he might the more readily escape suspicion, hurriedly removed the diadem and placed it in Caesar's lap. Publius Casca was also with him. While Caesar kept rejecting it, and among the shouts of the people, Antonius suddenly rushed up, naked and anointed, just as he was in the procession, and placed it on his head. But Caesar snatched it off, and threw it into the crowd. Those who were standing at some distance applauded this action, but those who were near at hand clamored that he should accept it and not repel the people's favor. Various individuals held different views of the matter. Some were angry, thinking it an indication of power out of place in a democracy; others, thinking to court favor, approved; still others spread the report that Antonius had acted as he did not without Caesar's connivance. There were many who were quite willing that Caesar be made king openly. All sorts of talk began to go through the crowd. When Antonius crowned Caesar a second time, the people shouted in chorus, 'Hail, King,' but Caesar still refusing the crown, ordered it to be taken to the temple of Capitolme Jupiter, saying that it was more appropriate there. Again the same people applauded as before. There is told another story, that Antonius acted thus wishing to ingratiate himself with Caesar, and at the same time was cherishing the hope of being adopted as his son. Finally, he embraced Caesar and gave the crown to some of the men standing near to place it on the head of the statue of Caesar which was near by. This they did. Of all the occurrences of that time this was not the least influential in hastening the action of the conspirators, for it proved to their very eyes the truth of the suspicions they entertained.

Source: Nicolaus of Damascus, *Life of Augustus*, 19–22, trans. by Clayton M. Hall (Menascha, WI: George Banta, 1923), p. 41. Reprinted by permission of Clayton M. Hall.

**A profile of Brutus,** one of Caesar's assassins, appeared on this silver coin. The reverse shows a cap of liberty between two daggers and reads "Ides of March."

Getty Images, Inc–Liaison

**What were the political goals of Caesar's assassins?**

# SUMMARY

**Prehistoric Italy** The Neolithic era came late to Italy, around 2500 B.C.E., followed by the Bronze Age starting around 1500 B.C.E. Bands of warring peoples speaking Italic languages invaded from across the Adriatic and along the northeastern coast starting around 1000 B.C.E.; within two centuries they had occupied the Appenines and were challenging the earlier settlers on the western plains. These peoples shaped Italy's history. *page 92*

## WHO WERE the Etruscans and how did they influence Rome?

**The Etruscans** Etruscan civilization emerged in Etruria around 800 B.C.E. The Etruscans formed a military ruling class that held power over the native Italians. Etruscan religion exerted a strong influence throughout the region. Etruscans expanded their domains and controlled large holdings in Italy, Corsica, and Elba. Etruscan power had peaked by 500 B.C.E., then declined rapidly under attack by the Gauls around 400 B.C.E. *page 92*

## HOW DID ideas about the family influence society and government in early Rome?

**Royal Rome** Rome's location on the Tiber River made it an important center for communication and trade. In the sixth century B.C.E., under the leadership of Etruscan kings, Rome developed political institutions that would endure through the Roman Republic, imperial Rome, and beyond. The kings of Rome held the power of *imperium*, but they were checked by the Senate and the curiate assembly. The family was the center of Roman life. Women and children had some protections. Upper-class women had positions of influence and respect greater than those available to Greek women. *Clientage* entailed mutual obligations between client and patron; the relationship was hereditary and sanctioned by religion. The two classes in royal Rome were *patricians*, a closed upper class that monopolized power, and the *plebeians*, who were originally poor but eventually came to include wealthy families unable to join the patrician class. *page 93*

## WHAT ROLE did consuls, the Senate, and the Assembly play in Republican government?

**The Republic** In 509 B.C.E., the noble families revolted successfully against the monarchy and created the Roman Republic. A limited form of the *imperium* was exercised by the consuls. Over the following centuries, the powers of the Senate increased substantially. Plebeians chafed against the limits on their political participation and other rights, leading to the Struggle of the Orders. By the middle of the third century B.C.E., Rome controlled the Italian peninsula. Conflict between Rome and Carthage in Sicily erupted in the First Punic War, through which Rome won control of Sicily. By mismanaging the peace, however, the Romans set the stage for the Second Punic War, in which Rome faced Hannibal. After winning every battle, Hannibal lost the war when the Roman general Scipio defeated the Carthaginians. Meanwhile, Rome had started meddling in Macedonian affairs, participating in the three Macedonian Wars. Rome's victory at the conclusion of the Third Macedonian War in 168 B.C.E. resulted in an uncharacteristically harsh peace. *page 95*

## HOW DID contact with the Hellenistic world affect Rome?

**Civilization in the Early Roman Republic** Educated Romans were bilingual, in Latin and Greek; Greek mythology was incorporated into Roman religion; education became Hellenized, and Greeks took on significant roles in the formal educational system. Girls did not attend school, but among the upper classes they were tutored at home. Slavery increased dramatically as the Romans enslaved prisoners of war. Manumission was common, and former slaves enjoyed social and economic mobility. The development of the *latifundia* system of agriculture—basically, cash-crop plantations that depended on slave labor—fueled the growth of a harsher and more oppressive form of slavery, with the result that significant slave rebellions occurred. Slavery declined gradually; in agriculture, tenant farmers called *coloni* slowly filled the economic niche of slavery. *page 103*

## HOW DID the expansion of Rome change the Republic?

**Roman Imperialism: The Late Republic** War, expansion, and the administration of an empire fundamentally altered Roman culture. The availability of cheap land and labor sharpened class differences throughout Italy. Tiberius Gracchus's unconstitutional tactics in attempting to pass land reform legislation in 133 B.C.E. led eventually to a riot in which Tiberius and three hundred of his supporters were killed. Roman politics was changed forever. Fundamental issues were now clearly at stake. Tiberius's brother Gaius Gracchus assumed the tribunate in 123 B.C.E. and passed some populist reforms, but he too was assassinated. Soon senatorial privilege was challenged from abroad, through the Jugurthine War that began in 111 B.C.E. Two ambitious generals, Marius and Sulla, gained power through their victories. Later, fighting barbarian tribes to the north, Marius introduced innovations into the army that made soldiers more loyal to their general than to the state. All Italians gained citizenship after a revolt. Between 88 and 83 B.C.E., Marius and Sulla dragged the Romans into civil war in their competition for power; Sulla won, assassinated his opponents, and attempted to reform the constitution and government institutions. *page 105*

**WHAT EVENTS** led to the fall of the Republic?

**The Fall of the Republic** Soon after Sulla's death, Crassus and Pompey intimidated the Senate into granting them extraordinary powers. By 60 B.C.E., when Crassus, Pompey, and Caesar all found their ambitions thwarted by the Senate, they formed the First Triumvirate, an informal political alliance to further their own private goals. Caesar was elected consul in 59 B.C.E. and enacted the triumvirs' program. Through impressive military conquest and intense diplomacy, Caesar held on to power until his assassination fifteen years later. Mark Antony and Gaius Octavius vied to succeed Caesar, although they joined with M. Aemilius Lepidus to form the Second Triumvirate to fight against Caesar's assassins in a civil war. After the triumvirate won, Octavian patronized the Roman arts and fostered the impression that Antony was a stooge of Cleopatra. When the power struggle between Octavian and Antony degenerated into battle, at Actium in 31 B.C.E., Octavian's forces won. *page 109*

# REVIEW QUESTIONS

1. How did the institutions of family and clientage and the establishment of patrician and plebeian classes contribute to the stability of the early Roman Republic? What was "the Struggle of the Orders"? What methods did plebeians use to get what they wanted?

2. Until 265 B.C.E., how and why did Rome expand its territory? How was Rome able to conquer and to control Italy? Why did Romans and Carthaginians clash in the First and Second Punic Wars? Could the wars have been avoided? What problems did the victory create for Rome?

3. What social, economic, and political problems faced Italy in the second century B.C.E.? How did Tiberius and Gaius Gracchus propose to solve them? What were the political implications of the Gracchan reform program? Why did reform fail?

4. What were the problems that plagued the Roman Republic in the last century B.C.E.? What caused these problems, and how did the Romans try to solve them? To what extent were ambitious, power-hungry generals responsible for the destruction of the republic?

## KEY TERMS

| | |
|---|---|
| **censors** (p. 96) | **Latium** (p. 93) |
| *coloni* (p. 105) | *optimates* (p. 107) |
| **consuls** (p. 96) | **patricians** (p. 95) |
| **equestrians** (p. 107) | **plebeians** (p. 95) |
| **Gaul** (p. 93) | *populares* (p. 107) |
| *humanitas* (p. 104) | **proconsulships** (p. 96) |
| *imperium* (p. 94) | **tribunes** (p. 97) |
| *latifundia* (p. 105) | |

For additional learning resources related to this chapter, please go to **www.myhistorylab.com**

myhistorylab

# 5

# The Roman Empire

**This statue of Emperor Augustus** (r. 27 B.C.E.–14 C.E.), now in the Vatican, stood in the villa of Augustus's wife, Livia. The figures on the elaborate breastplate are all of symbolic significance. At the top, for example, Dawn in her chariot brings in a new day under the protective mantle of the sky god; in the center, Tiberius, Augustus's future successor, accepts the return of captured Roman army standards from a barbarian prince; and at the bottom, Mother Earth offers a horn of plenty.

Vatican Museums & Galleries, Vatican City/Superstock

**What does this statue tell us about the Romans' vision of themselves and their empire?**

*ctavian's victory over Mark Antony in 31 B.C.E. ended a century of civil strife that had begun with the murder of Tiberius Gracchus. Octavian (subsequently known as Augustus) stabilized Rome by establishing a monarchy hidden behind a republican facade. The unification of the Mediterranean world promoted peace and economic expansion. The spread of Latin and Greek as the empire's official languages promoted growth of a common Classical tradition that had a great influence on the development of a new religion that appeared in the first century C.E.: Christianity.*

*In the third century C.E., Rome's institutions began to fail, and its emperors resorted to drastic measures to try to maintain order. The result was growing centralization and militarization of an increasingly authoritarian government. A wave of invasions in the second half of the fifth century finally initiated the empire's collapse.* ■

# THE AUGUSTAN PRINCIPATE

**HOW DID** Augustus transform Roman politics and government?

If the problems facing Octavian after the Battle of Actium in 31 B.C.E. were great, so were his resources for addressing them. He was the master of a vast military force, the only one in the Roman world, and he had loyal and capable assistants. Of enormous importance was the rich treasury of Egypt, which Octavian treated as his personal property. The people of Italy were eager for an end to civil war and a return to peace, order, and prosperity. The memory of Julius Caesar's fate, however, was still fresh in Octavian's mind. Its lesson was that it was dangerous to flaunt unprecedented powers and to disregard all republican traditions.

During the civil war Octavian's powers came from his triumviral status, whose dubious legality and unrepublican character were an embarrassment. From 31 B.C.E. on, he held the consulship each year, but this circumstance was neither strictly legal nor satisfactory. On 13 January 27 B.C.E., Octavian put forward a new plan in dramatic style, coming before the Senate to give up all his powers and provinces. In what was surely a rehearsed response, the Senate begged him to reconsider. At last he agreed to accept the provinces of Spain, Gaul, and Syria with proconsular power for military command and to retain the consulship in Rome. The other provinces would be governed by the Senate as before. Because the provinces he retained were border provinces that contained twenty of Rome's twenty-six legions, his true power was undiminished. The Senate, however, responded with almost hysterical gratitude, voting him many honors. Among them was the semireligious title **Augustus**, which implied veneration, majesty, and holiness. From this time on, historians speak of Rome's first emperor as Augustus and of his regime as the *Principate* (from *princeps*, or "first citizen"). This would have pleased him, for it helps conceal the novel, unrepublican nature of the regime and the naked power on which it rested.

**Augustus** ("revered") Name by which the Senate hailed Octavian for his restoration of the republic.

### ADMINISTRATION

Augustus made important changes in the government of Rome, Italy, and the provinces. Most of his reforms reduced inefficiency and corruption, ended the danger to peace and order from ambitious individuals, and lessened the distinction between Romans and Italians, senators and equestrians. The assemblies lost their significance as a working part of the constitution, and the Senate took on most of the functions of the assemblies. Augustus purged the old Senate of undesirable members and fixed its number at six hundred. He recruited its members from wealthy men of good character, who entered after serving as lesser magistrates. Augustus controlled the elections and en-

**This scene from** Augustus's *Ara Pacis*, the Altar of Peace, in Rome shows the general Marcus Agrippa (63–12 B.C.E.) in procession with the imperial family. Agrippa was a powerful deputy, close friend, and son-in-law of Augustus. He was chiefly responsible for the victory over Marc Antony at the Battle of Actium in 31 B.C.E.

Museum of the Ara Pacis, Rome, Italy

**How did ties of family and clientage shape Roman politics?**

sured that promising young men, whatever their origin, served the state as administrators and provincial governors. In this way, many equestrians and Italians who had no connection with the Roman aristocracy entered the Senate. For all his power, Augustus was always careful to treat the Senate with respect and honor.

Augustus divided Rome into regions and wards with elected local officials. He gave the city its first public fire department and police force. He carefully controlled grain distribution to the poor and created organizations to provide an adequate water supply. The Augustan period was one of great prosperity, based on the wealth brought in by the conquest of Egypt, on the great increase in commerce and industry made possible by general peace, on a vast program of public works, and on the revival of small farming by Augustus's resettled veterans.

The union of political and military power in the hands of the *princeps* enabled him to install rational, efficient, and stable government in the provinces for the first time. The emperor, in effect, chose the governors, removed the incompetent or rapacious, and allowed the effective ones to keep their provinces for longer periods. Also, he allowed much greater local autonomy, giving considerable responsibility to the upper classes in the provincial cities and towns and to the tribal leaders in less civilized areas.

## THE ARMY AND DEFENSE

The main external problem facing Augustus—and one that haunted all his successors—was the northern frontier. Rome needed to pacify the regions to the north and the northeast of Italy and to find defensible frontiers against the recurring waves of barbarians. Augustus's plan was to push forward into central Europe to create the shortest possible defensive line. The eastern part of the plan succeeded, and the campaign in the West started well. In 9 C.E., however, the German tribal leader Herrmann, or Arminius, as the Romans called him, ambushed and destroyed three Roman legions, and the aged Augustus abandoned the campaign, leaving a problem of border defense that bedeviled his successors.

Under Augustus, the armed forces achieved professional status. Together with the auxiliaries from the provinces, these forces formed a frontier army of about 300,000 men. The army permanently based in the provinces brought Roman culture to the natives. As time passed, the provincials on the frontiers became Roman citizens who helped strengthen Rome's defenses against the barbarians outside.

## RELIGION AND MORALITY

A century of political strife and civil war had undermined many of the foundations of traditional Roman society. To repair the damage, Augustus sought to preserve and restore the traditional values of the family and religion in Rome and Italy. He introduced laws curbing adultery and divorce and encouraging early marriage and the procreation of legitimate children. Augustus also worked at restoring the dignity of formal Roman religion, building many temples, reviving old cults, invigorating the priestly colleges, and banning the worship of newly introduced foreign gods.

# CIVILIZATION OF THE CICERONIAN AND AUGUSTAN AGES

**HOW DID** political developments shape the culture of the Ciceronian and Augustan ages?

The high point of Roman culture came in the last century of the republic and during the Principate of Augustus. Both periods reflected the dominant influence of Greek culture, especially its Hellenistic mode. Yet in spirit and sometimes in form, the art and writing of both periods show uniquely Roman qualities.

## THE LATE REPUBLIC

**Cicero**    The towering literary figure of the late republic was Cicero (106–43 B.C.E.). Cicero believed in a world governed by divine and natural law that human reason could perceive and human institutions reflect. He looked to law, custom, and tradition to produce both stability and liberty. His literary style, as well as his values and ideas, were an important legacy for the Middle Ages and, reinterpreted, for the Renaissance.

**History**    The last century of the republic produced some historical writing, much of which is lost to us. Sallust (86–35 B.C.E.) wrote a history of the years 78 to 67 B.C.E., but only a few fragments remain to remind us of his reputation as the greatest of republican historians. Julius Caesar wrote important treatises on the Gallic and civil wars. They are not fully rounded historical accounts, but chiefly military narratives written from Caesar's point of view and to enhance his repuation.

**Law**    The period from the Gracchi to the fall of the republic was important in the development of Roman law. Before that time, Roman law was essentially national and had developed chiefly by juridical decisions, case by case. Contact with foreign peoples and the influence of Greek ideas, however, forced a change. Quite early, the edicts of the magistrates who dealt with foreigners developed the idea of the **jus gentium**, or "law of peoples," as opposed to that arising strictly from the experience of the Romans. In the first century B.C.E., the influence of Greek thought made the idea of *jus gentium* identical with that of the **jus naturae**, or "natural law," taught by the Stoics.

**jus gentium**    Law of all peoples as opposed to the law that reflected only Roman practice.

**jus naturae**    Law of nature that enshrined the principles of divine reason that Cicero and the Stoics believed governed the universe.

# Overview   The Great Augustan Poets

| | |
|---|---|
| **VERGIL (70–19 B.C.E.)** | The most important of the Augustan poets, Vergil wrote somewhat artificial pastoral idylls. Vergil transformed the early Greek poet's praise of simple labor into a hymn to the human enterprise—the civilizing of the world of nature. His most important poem, the *Aeneid*, celebrated Italy's traditional religious cults and institutions. |
| **HORACE (65–8 B.C.E.)** | The son of a freedman, Horace was a highly skillful lyric poet. He produced a collection of genial, sometimes humorous, poems called *satires* and a number of *odes*, songs that glorify the Augustan order. He skillfully adapted Latin to the forms of Greek verse. |
| **PROPERTIUS (50–16 B.C.E.)** | Propertius joined Vergil and Horace as a member of the poetic circle favored by Augustus's wealthy friend Maecenas. He wrote elegies that were renowned for their grace and wit. |
| **OVID (43 B.C.E.–18 C.E.)** | Ovid was the only one of the great poets to run spectacularly afoul of Augustus. His poetic celebrations of the loose sexual mores of sophisticated Roman aristocrats did not serve the *princeps's* purpose. When Ovid published a poetic textbook on the art of seduction, *Ars Amatoria*, Augustus exiled him to a remote region of the empire. |

**Poetry**   The time of Cicero was also the period of two of Rome's greatest poets, Lucretius and Catullus, each representing a different aspect of Rome's poetic tradition. The Hellenistic poets and literary theorists saw two functions for the poet: entertainer and teacher. They thought the best poet combined both roles, and the Romans adopted the same view. Lucretius (ca. 99–55 B.C.E.) pursued a similar path in his epic poem *De Rerum Natura* (*On the Nature of the World*). In it, he set forth the scientific and philosophical ideas of Epicurus and Democritus with the zeal of a missionary trying to save society from fear and superstition.

Catullus (ca. 84–54 B.C.E.) was a thoroughly different kind of poet. He wrote poems that were personal—even autobiographical. He offered no moral lessons and was not interested in Rome's glorious history and in contemporary politics. In a sense, he is an example of the proud, independent, pleasure-seeking nobleman who characterized part of the aristocracy at the end of the republic.

## THE AGE OF AUGUSTUS

The spirit of the Augustan Age, the Golden Age of Roman literature, was different, reflecting the new conditions of society. Under Augustus, all patronage flowed from the *princeps*, usually through his chief cultural adviser, Maecenas.

The major poets of this time, Vergil and Horace, had lost their property during the civil wars. The patronage of the *princeps* allowed them the leisure and the security to write poetry, but it also made them dependent on him and limited their freedom of expression. These poets were not mere propagandists, however. It seems clear that mostly they believed in the virtues of Augustus and his reign and sang its praises with some degree of sincerity.

**Vergil**   Vergil (70–19 B.C.E.) was the most important of the Augustan poets. Vergil's greatest work is the *Aeneid*, a long national epic that placed the history of Rome in the great tradition of the Greeks and the Trojan War. Its hero, the Trojan warrior Aeneas,

**This mosaic found** in Tunisia shows the poet Vergil reading from his *Aeneid* to the Muses of Epic and Tragedy.

Roger Wood/CORBIS/Bettmann

**What does the mosaic imply about the relationship between Greek and Roman literature?**

personifies the ideal Roman qualities of duty, responsibility, serious purpose, and patriotism. As the Romans' equivalent of Homer, Vergil glorified not the personal honor and excellence of the Greek epic heroes, but the civic greatness, peace, and prosperity that Augustus and the Julian family had given to imperial Rome.

**Horace**   Horace (65–8 B.C.E.) was the son of a freedman. His *Odes*, which are ingenious in their adaptation of Greek meters to the requirements of Latin verse, best reveal his great skills as a lyric poet. Two of the odes are directly in praise of Augustus, and many of them glorify the new Augustan order, the imperial family, and the empire.

**Propertius**   Sextus Propertius lived in Rome in the second half of the first century B.C.E., a contemporary of Vergil and Horace. Like them, he was part of the poetic circle around Augustus's friend Maecenas. He wrote witty and graceful elegies.

**Ovid**   The career of Ovid (43 B.C.E.–18 C.E.) reveals the darker side of Augustan influence on the arts. He wrote light and entertaining love elegies that reveal the sophistication and the loose sexual code of a notorious sector of the Roman aristocracy whose values and amusements were contrary to the seriousness and family-centered life Augustus was trying to foster. Ovid's *Ars Amatoria*, a poetic textbook on the art of seduction, angered Augustus and was partly responsible for the poet's exile in 8 C.E. His most popular work is the *Metamorphoses*, a kind of mythological epic that turns Greek myths into charming stories in a graceful and lively style.

**History**   The achievements of Augustus, his emphasis on tradition, and the continuity of his regime with the glorious history of Rome encouraged both historical and antiquarian prose works. Livy's (59 B.C.E.–17 C.E.) *History of Rome* treated the period from the legendary origins of Rome until 9 B.C.E. Its purpose was moral, and he set up historical models as examples of good and bad behavior and, above all, patriotism. He glorified Rome's greatness and connected it with Rome's past, as Augustus tried to do.

**Architecture and Sculpture**   Augustus was as great a patron of the visual arts as he was of literature. His building program beautified Rome, glorified his reign, and contributed to the general prosperity and his own popularity. The Greek classical style, which aimed at serenity and the ideal type, influenced most of the building. The same features were visible in the portrait sculpture of Augustus and his family. The greatest monument of the age is the *Ara Pacis*, or "Altar of Peace," dedicated in 9 B.C.E. Part of it shows a procession in which Augustus and his family appear to move forward, followed in order by the magistrates, the Senate, and the people of Rome. There is no better symbol of the new order.

HOW WAS imperial Rome governed and what was life like for its people?

# IMPERIAL ROME, 14 TO 180 C.E.

## THE EMPERORS

Because Augustus was ostensibly only the "first citizen" of a restored republic and the Senate and the people theoretically voted him his powers, he could not legally name his successor. In fact, however, he plainly designated his heirs by lavishing favors on

them and by giving them a share in the imperial power and responsibility. Tiberius (r. 14–37 C.E.), his immediate successor, was
at first embarrassed by the ambiguity of his new role, but soon the
monarchical and hereditary nature of the regime became clear.
Gaius (Caligula, r. 37–41 C.E.), Claudius (r. 41–54 C.E.), and Nero
(r. 54–68 C.E.) were all descended from either Augustus or his
wife, Livia, and all were elevated because of that fact.

Gaius Caesar Germanicus succeeded Tiberius in 37 at the
age of twenty-five. He restored the use of trials for treason that
had darkened the reign of Tiberius and was vicious and cruel. He
claimed to be divine even while alive and was thought to aim at a
despotic monarchy like that of the Ptolemies in Egypt. Caligula
spent the large amount of money in the state treasury and tried to
get more by seizing the property of wealthy Romans. He was widely thought to be insane.

In 41 C.E., the naked military basis of imperial rule was revealed when the Praetorian Guard, having assassinated Caligula,
dragged the lame, stammering, and frightened Claudius from behind a curtain and made him emperor. Claudius left the throne to
his stepson Nero. Nero's incompetence and unpopularity, and especially his inability to control his armies, led to a serious rebellion in Gaul in 68 C.E. The year 69 saw four different emperors
assume power in quick succession as different Roman armies took
turns placing their commanders on the throne.

Vespasian (r. 69–79 C.E.) emerged victorious from the chaos,
and his sons, Titus (r. 79–81 C.E.) and Domitian (r. 81–96 C.E.),
carried forward his line, the Flavian dynasty. Vespasian, a tough soldier from the Italian middle class, was the first emperor who did not
come from the old Roman nobility.

The assassination of Domitian put an end to the Flavian dynasty. Because Domitian had no close relative who had been desig-
nated as successor, the Senate put Nerva (r. 96–98 C.E.) on the throne to avoid chaos. He
was the first of the five "good emperors," who included Trajan (r. 98–117 C.E.), Hadrian (r.
117–138 C.E.), Antoninus Pius (r. 138–161 C.E.), and Marcus Aurelius (r. 161–180 C.E.).

**Marcus Aurelius, emperor** of Rome from 161 to 180 C.E., was one
of the five "good emperors" who brought a period of relative peace
and prosperity to the empire. This is the only Roman bronze
equestrian statue that has survived.

Capitoline Museums, Rome, Italy/Canali PhotoBank, Milan/Superstock

**From the Roman point of view, what made Marcus Aurelius a "good
emperor"?**

## THE ADMINISTRATION OF THE EMPIRE

The provinces flourished economically and generally accepted Roman rule easily. (See
Map 5–1, page 126.) Imperial policy usually combined an attempt to unify the empire
and its various peoples with a respect for local customs and differences. Roman citizenship was spread ever more widely, and by 212 C.E., almost every free inhabitant of the
empire was a citizen. Latin became the language of the western provinces. Although
the East remained essentially Greek in language and culture, even it adopted many aspects of Roman life.

**Local Municipalities**   From an administrative and cultural standpoint, the empire was
a collection of cities and towns and had little to do with the countryside. Roman policy
during the Principate was to raise urban centers to the status of Roman municipalities,
with the rights and privileges attached to them. Therefore, the Romans enlisted the
upper classes of the provinces in their own government, spread Roman law and culture,
and won the loyalty of the influential people.

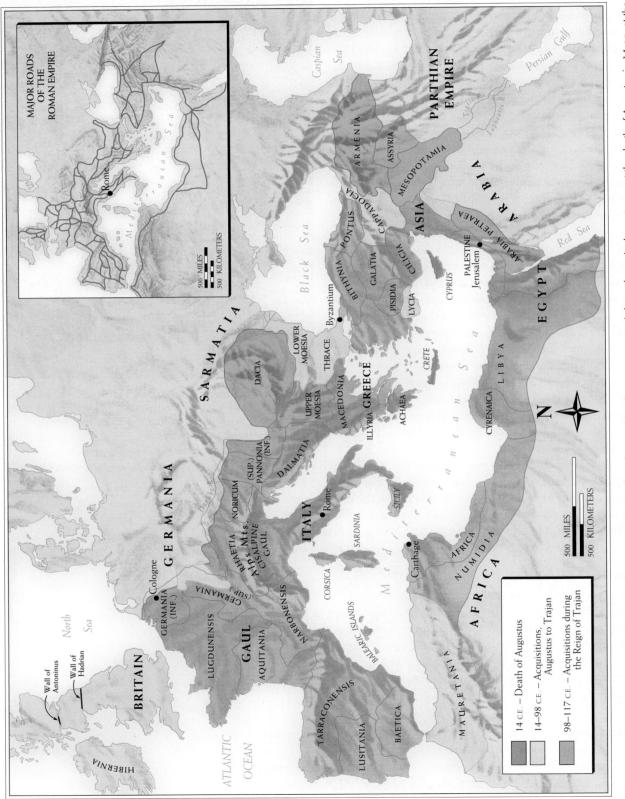

**MAP 5–1** **Provinces of the Roman Empire to 117 C.E.** The growth of the empire to its greatest extent is here shown in three stages—at the death of Augustus in 14 C.E., at the death of Nerva in 98, and at the death of Trajan in 117. The division into provinces is also shown. The insert shows the main roads that tied the far-flung empire together.

**What boundaries,** both manmade and natural, did the Roman Empire have at each stage of its expansion?

There were exceptions to this picture of success. The Jews found their religion incompatible with Roman demands and were savagely repressed when they rebelled in 66–70, 115–117, and 132–135 C.E. In Egypt, the Romans exploited the peasants with exceptional ruthlessness and did not pursue a policy of urbanization.

As the efficiency of the bureaucracy grew, so did the number and scope of its functions and therefore its size. The emperors came to take a broader view of their responsibilities for the welfare of their subjects than before. More and more the emperors intervened when municipalities got into difficulties, usually financial, sending imperial troubleshooters to deal with problems. The importance and autonomy of the municipalities shrank as the central administration took a greater part in local affairs. The price paid for the increased efficiency that centralized control offered was the loss of the vitality of the cities throughout the empire.

The success of Roman civilization also came at great cost to the farmers who lived outside of Italy. Taxes, rents, mandatory gifts, and military service drew capital away from the countryside to the cities on a scale not previously seen in the Graeco-Roman world. More and more the rich life of the urban elite came at the expense of millions of previously stable farmers.

**Foreign Policy**  Augustus's successors, for the most part, accepted his conservative and defensive foreign policy. Trajan was the first emperor to take the offensive in a sustained way. Between 101 and 106 C.E., he crossed the Danube and, after hard fighting, established the new province of Dacia between the Danube and the Carpathian Mountains. His intent was probably to defend the empire more aggressively by driving wedges into the territory of threatening barbarians. The same strategy dictated the invasion of the Parthian Empire in the East (113–117 C.E.). Trajan's early success was astonishing, and he established three new provinces in Armenia, Assyria, and Mesopotamia. But his lines were overextended. Rebellions sprang up, and the campaign crumbled. Trajan was forced to retreat, and he died before getting back to Rome.

Hadrian's reign marked an important shift in Rome's frontier policy. Heretofore, Rome had been on the offensive against the barbarians. Hadrian hardened the Roman defenses, building a stone wall in the south of Scotland and a wooden one across the Rhine-Danube triangle. The Roman defense became rigid, and initiative passed to the barbarians.

**Agriculture: The Decline of Slavery and the Rise of the *Coloni***  The defense of its frontiers put enormous pressure on the human and financial resources of the empire, but the effect of these pressures was not immediately felt. Internal peace and efficient

## SIGNIFICANT DATES FROM THE IMPERIAL PERIOD

### THE JULIO-CLAUDIAN DYNASTY

| | |
|---|---|
| 27 B.C.E.–14 C.E. | Augustus |
| ca. 4 B.C.E.–30 C.E. | Jesus of Nazareth |
| 14–37 C.E. | Tiberius |
| 37–41 C.E. | Gaius "Caligula" |
| 41–54 C.E. | Claudius |
| 54–68 C.E. | Nero |
| 69 C.E. | "Year of the Four Emperors" |

### THE FLAVIAN DYNASTY

| | |
|---|---|
| 69–79 C.E. | Vespasian |
| 79–81 C.E. | Titus |
| 81–96 C.E. | Domitian |
| ca. 70–100 C.E. | Composition of the Gospels |

### THE "GOOD EMPERORS"

| | |
|---|---|
| 96–98 C.E. | Nerva |
| 98–117 C.E. | Trajan |
| 117–138 C.E. | Hadrian |
| 138–161 C.E. | Antoninus Pius |
| 161–180 C.E. | Marcus Aurelius |

**Spoils from the** temple in Jerusalem were carried in triumphal procession by Roman troops. This relief from Titus's arch of victory in the Roman Forum celebrates his capture of Jerusalem after a two-year siege. The Jews found it difficult to reconcile their religion with Roman rule and frequently rebelled.

Scala/Art Resource, NY

**Why was the relationship between the Romans and the Jews so contentious?**

**Imperial Roman Cameo** of Livia and Tiberius.

©Burstein Collection/CORBIS

**What role did elite Roman women play in Roman politics?**

**QUICK REVIEW**

**Elite Women**

◆ Upper-class women were rich, educated, and influential

◆ Divorce was common and women used contraception

◆ Augustus's efforts to restore a more traditional model of the family failed

administration benefited agriculture as well as trade and industry. Farming and trade developed together as political conditions made it easier to sell farm products at a distance.

Small farms continued to exist, but the large estate, managed by an absentee owner and growing cash crops, dominated agriculture. At first, as in the republican period, slaves mostly worked these estates, but in the first century, this began to change. Economic pressures forced many of the free lower classes to become tenant farmers, or *coloni*, and eventually the *coloni* replaced slaves as the mainstay of agricultural labor. Eventually, they were tied to the land they worked, much as were the manorial serfs of the Middle Ages. Whatever its social costs, the system was economically efficient, however, and contributed to the general prosperity.

## WOMEN OF THE UPPER CLASSES

By the late years of the Roman republic, women of the upper classes had achieved a considerable independence and influence. Some of them had become wealthy through inheritance and were well educated. Women conducted literary salons and took part in literary groups. Marriage without the husband's right of *manus* became common, and some women conducted their sexual lives as freely as men. Such women were reluctant to have children and increasingly employed contraception and abortion to avoid childbirth.

Augustus tried to restore Rome to an earlier ideal of decency and family integrity that reduced the power and sexual freedom of women. He also introduced legislation to encourage the procreation of children, but the new laws seem to have had little effect. In the first imperial century, several powerful women played an important, if unofficial, political role. In later centuries, women were permitted to make wills and inherit from children. At the turn of the first century, the Emperor Domitian freed women from the need for guardianship.

## LIFE IN IMPERIAL ROME: THE APARTMENT HOUSE

The civilization of the Roman Empire depended on the vitality of its cities. The typical city had about 20,000 inhabitants, and perhaps only three or four had a population of more than 75,000. The population of Rome, however, was certainly greater than

**How did the Romans use buildings and monuments to establish their presence in conquered territories?**

500,000, perhaps more than a million. The rich lived in elegant homes called *domūs*. Though only a small portion of Rome's population lived in them, *domūs* took up as much as a third of the city's space. Public space for temples, markets, baths, gymnasiums, theaters, forums, and governmental buildings took up another quarter of Rome's territory.

This left less than half of Rome's area to house the mass of its inhabitants, who were squeezed into multiple dwellings that grew increasingly tall. Most Romans during the imperial period lived in apartment buildings called *insulae*, or "islands," that rose to a height of five or six stories and sometimes even more.

These buildings were divided into separate apartments (*cenicula*). The apartments were cramped and uncomfortable. They had neither central heating nor open fireplaces; heat and fire for cooking came from small portable stoves. The apartments were hot in summer, cold in winter, and stuffy and smoky when the stoves were lit. There was no plumbing, so tenants needed to go into the streets to wells or fountains for water and to public baths and latrines, or to less regulated places.

Despite these difficulties, the attractions of the city and the shortage of space caused rents to rise, making life in the *insulae* buildings expensive, uncomfortable, and dangerous. The houses were lightly built of concrete and brick and were far too high for the limited area of their foundations, and so they often collapsed. Laws limiting the height of buildings were not always obeyed and did not, in any case, always prevent disaster.

Even more serious was the threat of fire. Wooden beams supported the floors, and torches, candles, and oil lamps lit the rooms and braziers heated them. Fires broke out easily and, without running water, they usually led to disaster.

## THE CULTURE OF THE EARLY EMPIRE

The years from 14 to 180 C.E. were a time of general prosperity and a flourishing material and artistic culture, but one not as brilliant and original as in the Age of Augustus.

**Literature**    In Latin literature, the period between the death of Augustus and the time of Marcus Aurelius is known as the Silver Age. In contrast to the hopeful, positive optimists of the Augustans, the writers of the Silver Age were gloomy, negative, and pessimistic. In the works of the former period, praise of the emperor, his achievements, and the world abounds; in the latter, criticism and satire lurk everywhere.

The writers of the second century C.E. appear to have turned away from contemporary affairs and even recent history. Historical writing was about remote periods so there would be less danger of irritating imperial sensibilities. In the third century C.E., romances written in Greek became popular and offer further evidence of the tendency of writers of the time to seek and offer escape from contemporary realities.

**Architecture**    The main contribution of the Romans lay in two new kinds of buildings—the great public bath and a new freestanding kind of amphitheater—and in the advances in engineering that made these large structures possible. While keeping the basic post-and-lintel construction used by the Greeks, the Romans added to it the principle of the semicircular arch, borrowed from the Etruscans. The arch, combined with the post and lintel, produced the great Colosseum built by the Flavian emperors. When used internally in the form of vaults and domes, the arch permitted great buildings like the baths, of which the most famous and best preserved are those of the later emperors Caracalla (r. 211–217) and Diocletian (r. 284–305).

**Society**    One of the dark sides of Roman society, at least since the third century B.C.E., had been its increasing addiction to the brutal contests involving gladiators. By the end of the first century C.E., emperors regularly appealed to this barbaric entertainment as a way of winning the acclaim of their people. On broader fronts in Roman society, by the second century C.E., troubles were brewing that foreshadowed the difficult times ahead.

In the first century C.E., members of the upper classes vied with one another for election to municipal office and for the honor of doing service to their communities. By the second century C.E., the emperors had to intervene to correct abuses in local affairs and even to force unwilling members of the ruling classes to accept public office.

These difficulties reflected more basic problems. The prosperity that the end of civil war and the influx of wealth from the East brought could not sustain itself beyond the first half of the second century C.E. Population also appears to have declined for reasons that remain mysterious. The cost of government kept rising. The ever-increasing need for money compelled the emperors to raise taxes, to press hard on their subjects, and to bring on inflation by debasing the coinage. These elements brought about the desperate crises that ultimately destroyed the empire.

# THE RISE OF CHRISTIANITY

**WHO WAS** Jesus of Nazareth?

Christianity emerged, spread, survived, and ultimately conquered the Roman Empire despite its origin among poor people from an unimportant and remote province of the empire. Christianity faced the hostility of the established religious institutions of its native Judea. It also had to compete against the official cults of Rome and the highly sophisticated philosophies of the educated classes and against such other "mystery" religions as the cults of Mithra, Isis, and Osiris. The Christians also faced the opposition of the imperial government and formal persecution. Yet Christianity achieved toleration and finally exclusive command as the official religion of the empire.

# ENCOUNTERING THE PAST

## CHARIOT RACING

*Romans invested heavily in facilities for staging public entertainments, and among the earliest and most popular of these were race tracks. Romans were building race courses by the seventh and sixth centuries B.C.E. They called their tracks "circuses" ("circular") because of their curved layout. Rome's Circus Maximus ("Greatest Circus") was one of the earliest as well as the largest and most famous. It was used for a variety of events (riding exhibitions, wild animal hunts, etc.), but nothing rivaled the popularity of chariot racing.*

The races staged in the Circus Maximus involved seven laps around the track, a distance of about 2.7 miles. As many as twelve chariots might compete at one time. Various numbers of horses could be used to pull a chariot, but the most common arrangement was the *quadriga*, the four-horse team. Short straightaways, sharp turns, and a crowded field made for a dangerous and, therefore, crowd-pleasing race. Raw speed was often less important than strength, courage, and endurance. Racing companies called *factiones* were formed to sponsor stables and professional riders. They were known by their colors. The two first were the reds and the whites. They were eventually joined by the blues, greens, purples, and golds. Betting on the races was heavy, and factions went to extremes to win victories. Horses were drugged and drivers bribed—or murdered when they proved uncooperative.

**Romans bet heavily** on the kind of chariot races shown on this low relief and were fanatically attached to their favorite riders and stables.

© Araldo de Luca/CORBIS

WHY DID Roman politicians and emperors find it worth their while to spend lavishly on amusements like chariot races?

## JESUS OF NAZARETH

An attempt to understand this amazing outcome must begin with the story of Jesus of Nazareth. Jesus was born in the province of Judea in the time of Augustus. He was a most effective teacher in the tradition of the prophets. This tradition promised the coming of a Messiah (in Greek, *christos*—so Jesus Christ means "Jesus the Messiah"), the redeemer who would make Israel triumph over its enemies and establish the kingdom of God on earth. In fact, Jesus seems to have insisted the Messiah would not establish an earthly kingdom but would bring an end to the world as human beings knew it at the Day of Judgment. Until then (a day his followers believed would come soon), Jesus taught the faithful to abandon sin and worldly concerns; to follow him and his way; to follow the moral code described in the Sermon on the Mount, which preached love, charity, and humility; and to believe in him and his divine mission.

Jesus won a considerable following, especially among the poor, which caused great suspicion among the upper classes. His novel message and his criticism of the religious practices connected with the temple at Jerusalem and its priests provoked the hostility of the religious establishment. A misunderstanding of the movement made it easy to convince the Roman governor, Pontius Pilate, that Jesus and his followers might be dangerous revolutionaries. He was put to death in Jerusalem by the cruel and degrading device of crucifixion, probably in 30 C.E. His followers believed he was resurrected on the third day after his death, and that belief became a critical element in the religion they propagated throughout the Roman Empire and beyond.

**This second-century** statue in the Lateran Museum in Rome shows Jesus as the biblical Good Shepherd.

*The Good Shepherd*, marble, Height: as restored cm 99, as perserved cm 55, head cm 15.5. Late 3rd century A.D. Vatican Museums, Lateran Museums, Pio-Christian Museum, Inv. 28590. Courtesy of the Vatican Museums

**How did the image of Jesus evolve in the two centuries following his death?**

*agape* Common meal, or "love feast," that was the central ritual of the church in early Christianity.

**Eucharist** ("thanksgiving") Celebration of the Lord's Supper in which bread and wine were blessed and consumed.

The new belief spread quickly to the Jewish communities of Syria and Asia Minor. It might, however, have had only a short life as a despised Jewish heresy were it not for the conversion and career of Paul.

## PAUL OF TARSUS

Paul was born Saul, a citizen of the Cilician city of Tarsus in Asia Minor. He had been trained in Hellenistic culture and was a Roman citizen. But he was also a zealous member of the Jewish sect known as the Pharisees, the group that was most strict in its adherence to Jewish law. He took part in the persecution of the early Christians until his own conversion outside Damascus about 35 C.E., after which he changed his name from Saul to Paul.

The great problem facing the early Christians was to resolve their relationship to Judaism. If the new faith was a version of Judaism, then it must adhere to the Jewish law and seek converts only among Jews. James, called the brother of Jesus, was a conservative who held to that view, whereas the Hellenist Jews tended to see Christianity as a new and universal religion. Paul supported the position of the Hellenists and soon won many converts among the Gentiles. After some conflict within the sect, Paul won out.

Paul believed that the followers of Jesus should be *evangelists* (messengers) to spread the gospel, or "good news," of God's gracious gift. He taught that Jesus would soon return for the Day of Judgment, and that all who would, should believe in him and accept his way. Faith in Jesus as the Christ was necessary, but not sufficient, for salvation, nor could good deeds alone achieve it. That final blessing of salvation was a gift of God's grace that would be granted to all who asked for it.

## ORGANIZATION

Paul and the other apostles did their work well. The new religion spread throughout the Roman Empire and even beyond its borders. It had its greatest success in the cities and among the poor and uneducated. The rites of the early communities appear to have been simple and few. Baptism by water removed original sin and permitted participation in the community and its activities. The central ritual was a common meal called the **agape**, or "love feast," followed by the ceremony of the **Eucharist**, or "thanksgiving," a celebration of the Lord's Supper in which unleavened bread was eaten and unfermented wine was drunk. There were also prayers, hymns, or readings from the Gospels.

Not all the early Christians were poor, and the rich provided for the poor at the common meals. The sense of common love fostered in these ways focused the community's attention on the needs of the weak, the sick, the unfortunate, and the unprotected. This concern gave the early Christian communities a warmth and a human appeal that stood in marked contrast to the coldness and impersonality of the pagan cults. No less attractive were the promise of salvation, the importance to God of each human soul, and the spiritual equality of all in the new faith.

The future of Christianity depended on its communities finding an organization that would preserve unity within the group and help protect it against enemies outside. At first, the churches had little formal organization. By the second century C.E., as their numbers grew, the Christians of each city tended to accept the authority and leadership of bishops (*episkopoi*, or "overseers"). The congregations elected bishops to lead them in worship and to supervise funds. As time passed, the bishops extended their authority over the Christian communities in outlying towns and the countryside.

The bishops kept in touch with one another, maintained communications between different Christian communities, and prevented doctrinal and sectarian splintering, which would have destroyed Christian unity. They maintained internal discipline and dealt with the civil authorities. After a time they began the practice of coming together in councils to settle difficult questions, to establish orthodox opinion, and even to expel as heretics those who would not accept it. It is unlikely that Christianity could have survived the travails of its early years without such strong internal organization and government.

## THE PERSECUTION OF CHRISTIANS

The new faith soon incurred the distrust of the pagan world and of the imperial government. At first, Christians were thought of as a Jewish sect and were therefore protected by Roman law. It soon became clear, however, that they were different, both mysterious and dangerous. They denied the existence of the pagan gods and so were accused of atheism. Their refusal to worship the emperor was judged treasonous. Because they kept mostly to themselves, took no part in civic affairs, engaged in secret rites, and had an organized network of local associations, they were misunderstood and suspected. By the end of the first century, "the name alone"—that is, simple membership in the Christian community—was a crime.

But, for the most part, the Roman government did not take the initiative in attacking Christians in the first two centuries. (See "Compare & Connect: Christianity in the Roman Empire—Why Did the Romans Persecute the Christians?," on pages 134–135.) Mobs, not the government, started most persecutions in this period. Though they lived quiet, inoffensive lives, some Christians must have seemed unbearably smug and self-righteous. Unlike the tolerant, easygoing pagans, who were generally willing to accept the new gods of foreign people and add them to the pantheon, the Christians denied the reality of the pagan gods. They proclaimed the unique rightness of their own way and looked forward to their own salvation and the damnation of nonbelievers. It is not surprising, therefore, that pagans disliked these strange and unsocial people, tended to blame misfortunes on them, and, in extreme cases, turned to violence.

## THE EMERGENCE OF CATHOLICISM

Division within the Christian Church may have been an even greater threat to its existence than persecution from outside. Most Christians never accepted complex, intellectualized opinions but held to what even then were traditional, simple, conservative beliefs. This body of majority opinion, considered to be universal, or **catholic**, was enshrined by the church that came to be called Catholic. The Catholic Church's doctrines were deemed **orthodox**, that is, "holding the right opinions," whereas those holding contrary opinions were **heretics**.

The need to combat heretics, however, compelled the orthodox to formulate their own views more clearly and firmly. By the end of the second century C.E., an orthodox canon included the Old Testament, the Gospels, and the Epistles of Paul, among other writings. The orthodox declared the Catholic Church itself to be the depository of Christian teaching and the bishops to be its receivers. They also drew up a creed or brief statements of faith to which true Christians should adhere.

In the first century, all that was required of one to be a Christian was to be baptized, to partake of the Eucharist, and to call Jesus the Lord. By the end of the second century, an orthodox Christian—that is, a member of the Catholic Church—was required to accept its creed, its canon of holy writings, and the authority of the bishops. The loose structure of the apostolic church had given way to an organized body with recognized leaders able to define its faith and to exclude those who did not accept it.

**catholic** ("universal") As in "universal" majority of Christians.

**orthodox** ("correct") As in "correct" faith in Christianity.

**heretics** "Takers" of contrary positions, namely in Christianity.

# CHRISTIANITY IN THE ROMAN EMPIRE —

## Why Did the Romans Persecute the Christians?

The rise of Christianity and its spread throughout the Mediterranean presented a serious problem to the magistrates of the Roman Empire. Like most pagans, the Romans were tolerant of most religious beliefs. Persecution on religious grounds was unusual among the Romans. The Christians, however, were very different from votaries of Isis, Mithra, Magna Mater, even from the Jews. The Romans did, in fact, persecute the Christians with varying degrees of severity. The following passages shed light on the character of and reasons for these persecutions.

## QUESTIONS

1. Why did Nero blame the Christians?

2. On what grounds did Pliny punish the Christians?

3. What was the reaction of Trajan?

4. How did the approach of the two emperors compare?

**Thrown to the lions** in 275 C.E. by the Romans for refusing to recant his Christian beliefs, St. Mamai is an important martyr in the iconography of Georgia, a Caucasian kingdom that embraced Christianity early in the fourth century.

Courtesy of the Library of Congress

**How did persecution by the Romans shape Christians' image of themselves?**

## I. THE PERSECUTION BY NERO

*In 64 C.E., a terrible fire broke out in Rome that destroyed a good part of the city. Here the historian Tacitus tells us how the Emperor Nero dealt with its aftermath.*

The next thing was to seek means of propitiating the gods, and recourse was had to the Sibylline books, by the direction of which prayers were offered to Vulcanus, Ceres, and Proserpina. Juno, too, was entreated by the matrons, first, in the Capitol, then on the nearest part of the coast, whence water was procured to sprinkle the fane and image of the goddess. And there were sacred banquets and nightly vigils celebrated by married women. But all human efforts, all the lavish gifts of the emperor, and the propitiations of the gods, did not banish the sinister belief that the conflagration was the result of an order. Consequently, to get rid of the report, Nero fastened the guilt and inflicted the most exquisite tortures on a class hated for their abominations, called Christians by the populace. Christus, from whom the name had its origin, suffered the extreme penalty during the reign of Tiberius at the hands of one of our procurators, Pontius Pilatus, and a most mischievous superstition, thus checked for the moment, again broke out not only in Judaea, the first source of the evil, but even in Rome, where all things hideous and shameful from every part of the world find their centre and become popular. Accordingly, an arrest was first made of all who pleaded guilty; then, upon their information, an immense multitude was convicted, not so much of the crime of firing the city, as of hatred against mankind. Mockery of every sort was added to their deaths. Covered with the skins of beasts, they were torn by dogs and perished, or were nailed to crosses, or were doomed to the flames and burnt, to serve as a nightly illumination, when daylight had expired.

Nero offered his gardens for the spectacle, and was exhibiting a show in the circus, while he mingled with the people in the dress of a charioteer or stood aloft on a car. Hence, even for criminals who deserved extreme and exemplary punishment, there arose a feeling of compassion; for it was not, as it seemed, for the public good, but to glut one man's cruelty, that they were being destroyed.

Source: Tacitus, *Annals* 15.44, trans. by A. J. Church and W. J. Brodribb.

## II. THE EMPEROR TRAJAN AND THE CHRISTIANS

*Pliny the Younger was governor of the Roman province of Bithynia in Asia Minor about 112 B.C.E. Confronted by problems caused by Christians, he wrote to the Emperor Trajan to report his policies and to ask for advice. The following exchange between governor and emperor provides evidence of the challenge Christianity posed to Rome and the Roman response.*

### TO THE EMPEROR TRAJAN

Having never been present at any trials of the Christians, I am unacquainted with the method and limits to be observed either in examining or punishing them.

In the meanwhile, the method I have observed towards those who have been denounced to me as Christians is this: I interrogated them whether they were Christians; if they confessed it, I repeated the question twice again, adding the threat of capital punishment; if they still persevered, I ordered them to be executed. For whatever the nature of their creed might be, I could at least feel no doubt that contumacy and inflexible obstinacy deserved chastisement. There were others also possessed with the same infatuation, but being citizens of Rome, I directed them to be carried thither. . . .

### TRAJAN TO PLINY

The method you have pursued, my dear Pliny, in sifting the cases of those denounced to you as Christians is extremely proper. It is not possible to lay down any general rule which can be applied as the fixed standard in all cases of this nature. No search should be made for these people, when they are denounced and found guilty they must be punished; with the restriction, however, that when the party denies himself to be a Christian, and shall give proof that he is not (that is, by adoring our Gods he shall be pardoned on the ground of repentance even though he may have formerly incurred suspicion). Informations without the accuser's name subscribed must not be admitted in evidence against anyone, as it is introducing a very dangerous precedent, and by no means agreeable to the spirit of the age.

Source: From Pliny the Younger, *Letters*, trans. by W. Melmoth, rev. by W. M. Hutchinson (London: William Heinemann, Ltd; Cambridge, MA: Harvard University Press, 1925).

## ROME AS A CENTER OF THE EARLY CHURCH

During this same period, the church in Rome came to have special prominence. As the center of communications and the capital of the empire, Rome had natural advantages. After the Roman destruction of Jerusalem in 135 C.E., no other city had any convincing claim to primacy in the church. Besides having the largest single congregation of Christians, Rome also benefited from the tradition that Jesus' apostles Peter and Paul were martyred there.

Peter, moreover, was thought to be the first bishop of Rome. The Gospel of Matthew (16:18) reported Jesus' statement to Peter: "Thou art Peter [in Greek, *Petros*] and upon this rock [in Greek, *petra*] I will build my church." Because of the city's early influence and because of the Petrine doctrine derived from the Gospel of Matthew, later bishops of Rome claimed supremacy in the Catholic Church.

# THE CRISIS OF THE THIRD CENTURY

**HOW DID** economic developments lead to the political and military crisis of the third century?

Dio Cassius, a historian of the third century C.E., described the Roman Empire after the death of Marcus Aurelius as declining from "a kingdom of gold into one of iron and rust." Although we have seen that the gold contained more than a little impurity, there is no reason to quarrel with Dio's assessment of his own time.

## BARBARIAN INVASIONS

The pressure on Rome's frontiers reached massive proportions in the third century. In the East, a new power threatened the frontiers. In 224 C.E. a new Iranian dynasty, the Sassanians, seized control from the Parthians and brought new vitality to Persia. They soon recovered Mesopotamia and in 260 C.E. they humiliated the Romans by taking the emperor Valerian (r. 253–260) prisoner; he died in captivity.

On the western and northern frontiers, the pressure came not from a well-organized rival empire, but from an ever-increasing number of German tribes. Though the Germans had been in contact with the Romans at least since the second century B.C.E., civilization had not much affected them. Always eager for plunder, these tough barbarians were attracted by the civilized delights they knew existed beyond the frontier of the Rhine and Danube Rivers.

The most aggressive of the Germans in the third century C.E. were the Goths. Centuries earlier they had wandered from their ancestral home near the Baltic Sea into southern Russia. In the 220s and 230s C.E., they began to put pressure on the Danube frontier. By about 250 C.E., they were able to penetrate the empire and overrun the Balkans. The need to meet this threat and the one the Persian Sassanids posed in the East made the Romans weaken their western frontiers, and other Germanic peoples—the Franks and the Alemanni—broke through in those regions. There was danger that Rome would be unable to meet this challenge.

The unprecedentedly numerous and simultaneous attacks, no doubt, caused Rome's perils but its internal weakness encouraged these attacks. The Roman army was not what it had been in its best days. By the second century C.E., it was made up mostly of romanized provincials. The training and discipline with which the Romans had conquered the Mediterranean world had declined.

**QUICK REVIEW**

**Germanic Tribes**

- Germans had been in contact with Romans since second century B.C.E.
- Most aggressive of the Germans in the third century C.E. were the Goths
- Weakness of the Roman army heightened the danger posed by Germanic tribes

## ECONOMIC DIFFICULTIES

These changes were a response to the great financial needs the barbarian attacks caused. To raise money, the emperors invented new taxes, debased the coinage, and even sold the palace furniture. But it was still hard to recruit troops.

The same forces that caused problems for the army damaged society at large. The shortage of workers for the large farms, which had all but wiped out the independent family farm, reduced agricultural production. Distracted by external threats, the emperors were less able to preserve domestic peace. Piracy, brigandage, and the neglect of roads and harbors hampered trade. So, too, did the debasement of the coinage and the inflation in general. Imperial taxation and confiscations of the property of the rich removed badly needed capital from productive use.

More and more, the government had to demand services that had been given gladly in the past. Because the empire lived hand to mouth, with no significant reserve fund and no system of credit financing, the emperors had to compel the people to provide food, supplies, money, and labor. The upper classes in the cities were made to serve as administrators without pay and to meet deficits in revenue out of their own pockets. All these difficulties weakened Rome's economic strength when it was most needed.

## THE SOCIAL ORDER

The new conditions caused important changes in the social order. Hostile emperors and economic losses decimated the Senate and the traditional ruling class. Men coming up through the army took their places. The whole state began to take on an increasingly military appearance. Titles were assigned to ranks in society as to ranks in the army. The most important distinction was between the *honestiores* (senators, equestrians, the municipal aristocracy, and the soldiers) and the lower classes, or *humiliores*. *Honestiores* were given a privileged position before the law. They were given lighter punishments, could not be tortured, and alone had the right of appeal to the emperor.

As time passed, it became more difficult to move from the lower order to the higher, another example of the growing rigidity of the late Roman Empire. Peasants were tied to their lands, artisans to their crafts, soldiers to the army, merchants and shipowners to the needs of the state, and citizens of the municipal upper class to the collection and payment of increasingly burdensome taxes. Freedom and private initiative gave way before the needs of the state and its ever-expanding control of its citizens.

## CIVIL DISORDER

Marcus Aurelius' son and heir, Commodus, was killed on the last day of 192 C.E. The succeeding year was similar to the year 69. Three emperors ruled in swift succession, with Septimius Severus emerging to establish firm rule and a dynasty. The murder of Alexander Severus, the last of the dynasty, in 235 C.E., brought on a half century of internal anarchy and foreign invasion.

The empire seemed on the point of collapse. But the two conspirators who overthrew and succeeded the emperor Gallienus (r. 253–268) proved to be able soldiers. Claudius II Gothicus (268–270 C.E.) and Aurelian (270–275 C.E.) drove back the barbarians and stamped out internal disorder. The soldiers who followed Aurelian on the throne were good fighters who made significant changes in Rome's system of defense. Around Rome, Athens, and other cities, they built heavy walls that could resist barbarian attack. They drew back their best troops from the frontiers, relying chiefly on a newly organized heavy cavalry and a mobile army near the emperor's own residence.

Hereafter, mercenaries, who came from among the least civilized provincials and even from among the Germans, largely made up the army. The officers gave personal loyalty to the emperor rather than to the empire. These officers became a foreign,

**This porphyry sculpture** on the corner of the church of San Marco in Venice shows Emperor Diocletian (r. 284–305 C.E.) and his three imperial colleagues. Dressed for battle, they clasp one another to express their mutual solidarity.

John Heseltine © Dorling Kindersley

**Why did Diocletian find it necessary to divide the Roman Empire?**

hereditary caste of aristocrats that increasingly supplied high administrators and even emperors. In effect, the Roman people hired an army of mercenaries, who were only technically Roman, to protect them.

# THE LATE EMPIRE

**WHAT FACTORS** contributed to the decline and eventual fall of Rome?

During the fourth and fifth centuries, the Romans strove to meet the many challenges, internal and external, that threatened the survival of their empire. Growing pressure from barbarian tribes pushing against its frontier intensified the empire's tendency to smother individuality, freedom, and initiative, in favor of an intrusive and autocratic centralized monarchy. Economic and military weakness increased, and it became even harder to keep the vast empire together. Hard and dangerous times may well have helped the rise of Christianity, encouraging people to turn away from the troubles of this world to be concerned about the next.

## THE FOURTH CENTURY AND IMPERIAL REORGANIZATION

The period from Diocletian (r. 284–305 C.E.) to Constantine (r. 306–337 C.E.) was one of reconstruction and reorganization after a time of civil war and turmoil. Diocletian was from Illyria (the former Yugoslavia of the twentieth century). A man of undistinguished birth, he rose to the throne through the ranks of the army. He knew that the job of defending and governing the entire empire was too great for one individual.

**tetrarchy**    Coalition of four men, each of whom was responsible for a different part of the empire, established by Diocletian.

Diocletian therefore decreed the introduction of the **tetrarchy**, the rule of the empire by four men with power divided territorially. (See Map 5–2.) He allotted the provinces of Thrace, Asia, and Egypt to himself. His co-emperor, Maximian, shared with him the title of Augustus and governed Italy, Africa, and Spain. In addition, two

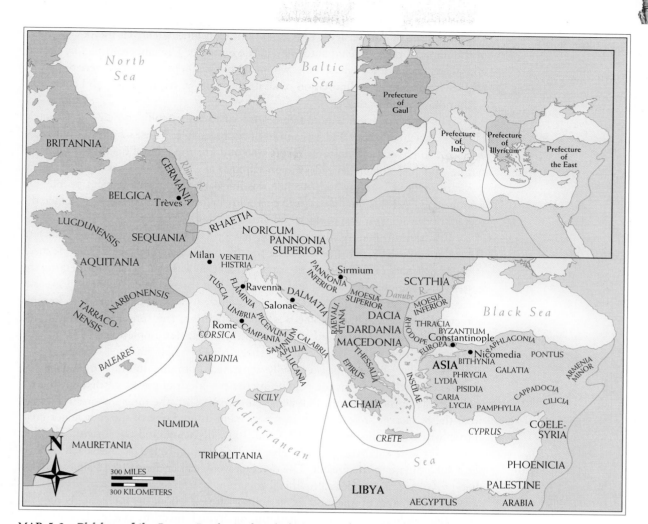

**MAP 5–2** **Divisions of the Roman Empire Under Diocletian** Diocletian divided the sprawling empire into four prefectures for more effective government and defense. The inset map shows their boundaries, and the larger map gives some details of regions and provinces. The major division between the East and the West was along the line running south between Pannonia and Moesia.

**Did Diocletian's** tetrarchy likely postpone or expedite the eventual fall of the Roman Empire?

men were given the subordinate title of Caesar: Galerius, who was in charge of the Danube frontier and the Balkans, and Constantius, who governed Britain and Gaul.

This arrangement not only afforded a good solution to the military problem but also provided for a peaceful succession. Diocletian was the senior Augustus, but each tetrarch was supreme in his own sphere. The Caesars were recognized as successors to each half of the empire, and marriages to daughters of the Augusti enhanced their loyalty.

In 305 C.E., Diocletian retired and compelled his co-emperor to do the same. But his plan for a smooth succession failed. In 310, there were five Augusti and no Caesars. Out of this chaos, Constantine, son of Constantius, produced order. In 324, he defeated his last opponent and made himself sole emperor, uniting the empire once again; he reigned until 337. Mostly, Constantine carried forward the policies of Diocletian. He supported Christianity, however, which Diocletian had tried to suppress.

**Development of Autocracy**   Diocletian and Constantine carried the development of the imperial office toward autocracy to the extreme. The emperor ruled by decree, consulting only a few high officials whom he himself appointed. The Senate had no role whatever, and the elimination of all distinctions between senator and equestrian further diminished its dignity.

The emperor was a remote figure surrounded by carefully chosen high officials. He lived in a great palace and was almost unapproachable. Those admitted to his presence had to prostrate themselves before him and kiss the hem of his robe, which was purple and had golden threads woven through it. The emperor was addressed as *dominus*, or "lord," and his right to rule was not derived from the Roman people, but from heaven. All this remoteness and ceremony had a double purpose: to enhance the dignity of the emperor and to safeguard him against assassination.

Constantine erected the new city of Constantinople on the site of ancient Byzantium on the Bosporus, which leads to both the Aegean and Black Seas. He made it the new capital of the empire. Its strategic location was excellent for protecting the eastern and Danubian frontiers, and, surrounded on three sides by water, it was easily defended. This location also made it easier to carry forward the policies that fostered autocracy and Christianity. Rome was full of tradition, the center of senatorial and even republican memories, and of pagan worship. Constantinople was free from both, and its dedication in 330 C.E. marked the beginning of a new era.

A civilian bureaucracy, carefully separated from the military to reduce the chances of rebellion by anyone combining the two kinds of power, carried out the autocratic rule of the emperors. Below the emperor's court, the most important officials were the *praetorian* prefects, each of whom administered one of the four major areas into which the empire was divided: Gaul, Italy, Illyricum, and the Orient. The four prefectures were subdivided into twelve territorial units called *dioceses*, each under a vicar subordinate to the prefect. The dioceses were further divided into almost a hundred provinces, each under a provincial governor.

A vast system of spies and secret police, without whom the increasingly rigid organization could not be trusted to perform, supervised the entire system. Despite these efforts, the system was corrupt and inefficient.

The cost of maintaining a 400,000-man army, as well as the vast civilian bureaucracy, the expensive imperial court, and the imperial taste for splendid buildings, strained an already weak economy. Diocletian's attempts to establish a reliable currency failed, leading instead to increased inflation. To deal with it, he resorted to price control with his Edict of Maximum Prices in 301 C.E. For each product and each kind of labor, a maximum price was set, and violations were punishable by death. The edict still failed.

Peasants unable to pay their taxes and officials unable to collect them tried to escape. Diocletian resorted to stern regimentation to keep all in their places and at the service of the government. The terror of the third century forced many peasants to seek protection in the *villa*, or "country estate," of a large and powerful landowner and to become tenant farmers. As social boundaries hardened, these *coloni* and their descendants became increasingly tied to their estates.

**Division of the Empire**   The peace and unity Constantine established did not last long. Constantius II (r. 337–361) won the struggle for succession after his death. Constantius's death, in turn, left the empire to his young cousin Julian (r. 361–363 C.E.), whom Christians called the Apostate because of his attempt to stamp out Christianity and restore paganism. Julian undertook a campaign against Persia to put a Roman on the throne of the Sassanids and end the Persian menace once and for all. He penetrated

**QUICK REVIEW**

**Constantinople**

- Dedicated by Constantine in 330 C.E.
- Situated on the Bosporus midway between eastern and Danube frontiers
- Marked the start of a new empire

deep into Persia but was killed in battle. His death ended the expedition and the pagan revival.

The Germans in the West took advantage of the eastern campaign to attack along the Rhine and upper Danube Rivers. In addition, even greater trouble was brewing along the middle and upper Danube. The eastern Goths, known as the Ostrogoths, occupied that territory. They were being pushed hard by their western cousins, the Visigoths, who in turn had been driven from their home in the Ukraine by the fierce Huns, a nomadic people from central Asia.

The emperor Valentinian I (r. 364–375 C.E.) saw he could not defend the empire alone and appointed his brother Valens (r. 364–378 C.E.) as co-ruler. Valentinian made his own headquarters at Milan and spent the rest of his life fighting and defeating the Franks and the Alemanni in the West. Valens was given control of the East. The empire was once again divided in two. The two emperors maintained their own courts, and the halves of the empire became increasingly separate and different. Latin was the language of the West and Greek of the East.

In 376, the Visigoths, pursued by the Huns, won rights of settlement and material assistance within the empire from the eastern emperor Valens (r. 364–378) in exchange for defending the eastern frontier as *foederati*, or special allies of the empire. The Visigoths, however, did not keep their bargain with the Romans and plundered the Balkan provinces. Nor did the Romans comply. They treated the Visigoths cruelly, even forcing them to trade their children for dogs to eat. Valens attacked the Goths and died, along with most of his army, at Adrianople in Thrace in 378. Theodosius I (r. 379–395 C.E.), an able and experienced general, was named co-ruler in the East. Theodosius tried to unify the empire again, but his death in 395 left it divided and weak.

**The Rural West**  The two parts of the empire went their different ways. The West became increasingly rural as barbarian invasions intensified. The *villa*, a fortified country estate, became the basic unit of life. There, *coloni* gave their services to the local magnate in return for economic assistance and protection from both barbarians and imperial officials. Many cities shrank to no more than tiny walled fortresses ruled by military commanders and bishops. The upper classes moved to the country and asserted an ever-greater independence from imperial authority. The new world emerging in the West by the fifth century and afterwards was increasingly made up of isolated units of rural aristocrats and their dependent laborers. The only institution providing a high degree of unity was the Christian Church. The pattern for the early Middle Ages in the West was already formed.

**The Byzantine East**  In the East the situation was different. Constantinople became the center of a vital and flourishing culture we call *Byzantine* that lasted until the fifteenth century. Because of its defensible location, the skill of its emperors, and the firmness and strength of its base in Asia Minor, it could deflect and repulse barbarian attacks. A strong navy allowed commerce to flourish in the eastern Mediterranean and, in good times, far beyond. Cities continued to prosper, and the emperors made their will good over the nobles in the countryside. The civilization of the Byzantine Empire was a unique combination of classical culture, the Christian religion, Roman law, and Eastern artistic influences. (See Chapter 6). Thus, when we contemplate the decline and fall of the Roman Empire in the fourth and fifth centuries, we are speaking only of the West. A form of classical culture persisted in the Byzantine East for a thousand years more.

## THE TRIUMPH OF CHRISTIANITY

The rise of Christianity to dominance in the empire was closely connected with the political and cultural experience of the third and fourth centuries. Political chaos and decentralization had religious and cultural consequences.

**Religious Currents in the Empire**   In some provinces, native languages replaced Latin and Greek, sometimes even for official purposes. The classical tradition that had been the basis of imperial life became the exclusive possession of a small, educated aristocracy. In religion, the public cults had grown up in an urban environment and were largely political in character. As the importance of the cities diminished, so did the significance of their gods. People might still take comfort in the worship of the friendly, intimate deities of family, field, hearth, storehouse, and craft, but these gods were too petty to serve their needs in a confused and frightening world. The only universal worship was of the emperor, but he was far off, and obeisance to his cult was more a political than a religious act.

In the troubled fourth and fifth centuries, people sought powerful, personal deities who would bring them safety and prosperity in this world and immortality in the next. Paganism was open and tolerant. Many people worshipped new deities alongside the old and even intertwined elements of several to form a new amalgam by the device called syncretism.

*Manichaeism* was an especially potent rival of Christianity. Named for its founder, Mani, a Persian who lived in the third century C.E., this movement contained aspects of various religious traditions, including Zoroastrianism from Persia and both Judaism and Christianity. The Manichaeans pictured a world in which light and darkness, good and evil, were constantly at war. Good was spiritual and evil was material. The movement reached its greatest strength in the fourth and fifth centuries, and some of its central ideas persisted into the Middle Ages.

Christianity had something in common with these cults and answered many of the same needs their devotees felt. None of them, however, attained Christianity's universality, and none appears to have given the early Christians as much competition as the ancient philosophies or the state religion.

**Imperial Persecution**   By the third century, Christianity had taken firm hold in the eastern provinces and in Italy. It had not made much headway in the West, however. (See Map 5–3.) As times became bad and the Christians became more numerous and visible, popular opinion came to blame disasters, natural and military, on the Christians.

About 250, the emperor Decius (r. 249–251 C.E.) invoked the aid of the gods in his war against the Goths and required all citizens to worship the state gods publicly. True Christians could not obey, and Decius started a major persecution. Many Christians—even some bishops—yielded to threats and torture, but others held out and were killed. Valerian (r. 253–260 C.E.) resumed the persecutions, partly to confiscate the wealth of rich Christians. His successors, however, found other matters more pressing, and the persecution lapsed until the end of the century.

By the time of Diocletian, the increasing number of Christians included high officials. But hostility to the Christians had also grown on every level. Diocletian's effort to bolster imperial power with the aura of divinity boded ill for the church, and in 303 he launched the most serious persecution inflicted on the Christians in the Roman Empire. He confiscated church property and destroyed churches and their sacred books. He deprived upper-class Christians of public office and judicial rights, imprisoned clergy, and enslaved Christians of the lower classes. He fined anyone refusing to sacrifice to the public gods. A final decree required public sacrifices and libations. The persecution horrified many pagans, and the plight and the demeanor of the martyrs aroused pity and sympathy.

Ancient states could not carry out a program of terror with the thoroughness of modern totalitarian governments, so the Christians and their church survived to enjoy what they must have considered a miraculous change of fortune. In 311, Galerius, who had been one of the most vigorous persecutors, was influenced, perhaps by his Christian wife, to issue the Edict of Toleration, permitting Christian worship.

The victory of Constantine and his emergence as sole ruler of the empire changed the condition of Christianity from a precariously tolerated sect to the religion the emperor favored. This put it on the path to becoming the official and only legal religion in the empire.

**Emergence of Christianity as the State Religion** The sons of Constantine continued to favor the new religion, but the succession of Julian the Apostate in 360 posed a new threat. Though he refrained from persecution, he tried to undo the work of Constantine by withdrawing the privileges of the church, removing Christians from high offices, and introducing a new form of pagan worship. His reign, however, was short, and his work did not last. In 394, Theodosius forbade the celebration of pagan cults and abolished the pagan religious calendar. At his death, Christianity was the official religion of the Roman Empire.

The establishment of Christianity as the state religion did not put an end to the troubles of the Christians and their church; instead, it created new ones and complicated some old ones. The favored position of the church attracted converts for the wrong reasons and diluted the moral excellence and spiritual fervor of its adherents. The problem of the relationship between church and state arose, presenting the possibility that religion would become subordinate to the state, as it had been in the classical world and in earlier civilizations. In the East, that largely happened.

In the West, the weakness of the emperors permitted church leaders to exercise remarkable independence. In 390, Ambrose, bishop of Milan, excommunicated Theodosius I for a massacre he had carried out, and the emperor did penance. This act provided an important precedent for future assertions of the church's autonomy and authority, but it did not end secular interference and influence in the church.

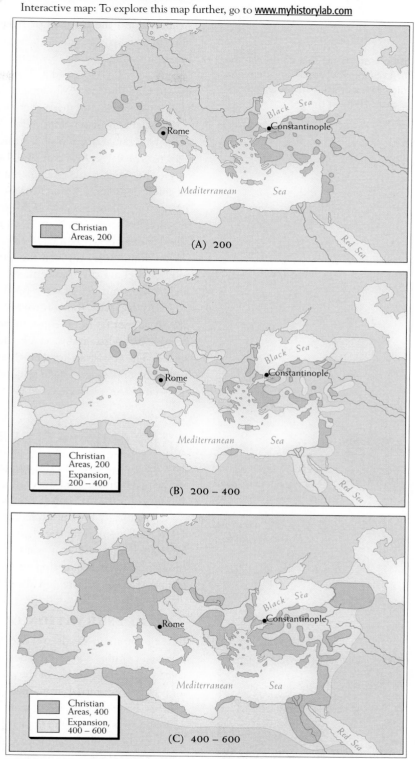

MAP 5–3    **The Spread of Christianity**    Christianity grew swiftly in the third, fourth, fifth, and sixth centuries—especially after the conversion of the emperors in the fourth century. By 600, on the eve of the birth of the new religion of Islam, Christianity was dominant throughout the Mediterranean world and most of Western Europe.

**How important** was state acceptance of Christianity to the religion's growth in the Roman Empire?

143

**Arianism**  Belief that Christ was the first of God the Father's creations and the being through whom the Father created all other things.

**Arianism and the Council of Nicea**    Internal divisions proved to be even more troubling as new heresies emerged. Among the many controversial views that arose, the most important and the most threatening was **Arianism**. A priest named Arius of Alexandria (ca. 280–336 C.E.) founded it. The issue creating difficulty was the relation of God the Father to God the Son. Arius argued that Jesus was a created being, unlike God the Father. He was, therefore, not made of the substance of God and was not eternal. For Arius, Jesus was neither fully man nor fully God, but something in between. Arius's view did away with the mysterious concept of the Trinity, the difficult doctrine that holds that God is three persons (the Father, the Son, and the Holy Spirit) and also one in substance and essence.

The Arian concept appeared simple, rational, and philosophically acceptable. To its ablest opponent, Athanasius, however, it had serious shortcomings. Athanasius (ca. 293–373 C.E.), later bishop of Alexandria, saw the Arian view as an impediment to any acceptable theory of salvation, to him the most important religious question. He adhered to the old Greek idea of salvation as involving the change of sinful mortality into divine immortality through the gift of "life." Only if Jesus were both fully human and fully God could the transformation of humanity to divinity have taken place in him and be transmitted by him to his disciples.

To deal with the controversy, Constantine called a council of Christian bishops at Nicaea, not far from Constantinople, in 325. At Nicaea, Athanasius's view won out, became orthodox, and was embodied in the Nicene Creed. But Arianism persisted and spread. The Christian emperors hoped to bring unity to their increasingly decentralized realms by imposing a single religion. Over time it did prove to be a unifying force, but it also introduced divisions where none had existed before.

# ARTS AND LETTERS IN THE LATE EMPIRE

**HOW DID** arts and letters in Late Rome reflect the developing relationship between pagan and Christian ideas?

The art and literature of the late empire reflect the confluence of pagan and Christian ideas and traditions and the conflict between them. Much of the literature is polemical and much of the art is propaganda.

A military revolution led by provincials whose origins were in the lower classes saved the empire from the chaos of the third century. Yet the new ruling class was not interested in leveling; it wanted instead to establish itself as a new aristocracy. It thought of itself as effecting a great restoration rather than a revolution and sought to restore classical culture and absorb it.

## THE PRESERVATION OF CLASSICAL CULTURE

One of the main needs and accomplishments of this period was the preservation of classical culture. Ways were discovered to make it available and useful to the newly arrived ruling class. Works of the great classical authors were reproduced in many copies and were transferred from perishable and inconvenient papyrus rolls to sturdier codices, bound volumes that were as easy to use as modern books. Scholars also digested long works like Livy's *History of Rome* into shorter versions, wrote learned commentaries, and compiled grammars. Original works by pagan writers of the late empire were neither numerous nor especially distinguished.

**Carving of the Crucifixion.**

c. 420 C.E. (ivory). British Museum, London, UK/Bridgeman Art Library

**What place did Christianity have in the Roman world at the time of the fall of the Western Roman Empire?**

## CHRISTIAN WRITERS

The late empire, however, did see a great outpouring of Christian writings, including many examples of Christian apologetics, in poetry and prose, and sermons, hymns, and biblical commentaries. Christianity could also boast important scholars. Jerome (348–420 C.E.), thoroughly trained in classical Latin literature and rhetoric, produced a revised version of the Bible in Latin. Commonly called the **Vulgate**, it became the Bible the Catholic Church used. Probably the most important eastern scholar was Eusebius of Caesarea (ca. 260–340 C.E.). His most important work, his *Ecclesiastical History*, was an attempt to set forth the Christian view of history.

The closeness and also the complexity of the relationship between classical pagan culture and that of the Christianity of the late empire are nowhere better displayed than in the career and writings of Augustine (354–430 C.E.), bishop of Hippo in North Africa. He was born at Carthage and was trained as a teacher of rhetoric. His training and skill in pagan rhetoric and philosophy made him peerless among his contemporaries as a defender of Christianity and as a theologian.

His greatest works are his *Confessions*, an autobiography describing the road to his conversion, and *The City of God*. The latter was a response to the pagan charge that the abandonment of the old gods and the advent of Christianity caused the Visigoths' sack of Rome in 410. The optimistic view some Christians held that God's will worked its way in history and was easily comprehensible needed further support in the face of this calamity. Augustine sought to separate the fate of Christianity from that of the Roman Empire. He contrasted the secular world, the City of Man, with the spiritual, the City of God. The former was selfish, the latter unselfish; the former evil, the latter good. All states, even a Christian Rome, were part of the City of Man and were therefore corrupt and mortal. Only the City of God was immortal, and it, consisting of all the saints on earth and in heaven, was untouched by earthly calamities.

Though the *Confessions* and *The City of God* are Augustine's most famous works, they emphasize only a part of his thought. His treatises *On the Trinity* and *On Christian Education* reveal the great skill with which he supported Christian belief with the learning, logic, and philosophy of the pagan classics. Augustine believed faith is essential and primary (a thoroughly Christian view), but it is not a substitute for reason (the foundation of classical thought). Instead, faith is the starting point for, and liberator of, human reason, which continues to be the means by which people can understand what faith reveals.

**Vulgate**   Latin translation of the Bible that became the standard text for the Catholic Church.

# THE PROBLEM OF THE DECLINE AND FALL OF THE EMPIRE IN THE WEST

The massive barbarian invasions of the fifth century put an end to effective imperial government in the West. For centuries people have speculated about the causes of the collapse of the ancient world. Some blame the slavery and a resulting failure to make advances in science and technology. Others blame excessive government interference in the economic life of the empire and still others the destruction of the urban middle class, the carrier of classical culture.

A simpler and more obvious explanation might begin with the observation that the growth of so mighty an empire as Rome's was by no means inevitable. Rome's greatness had come from conquests that provided the Romans with the means to expand still further, until there were not enough Romans to conquer and govern any more peoples and territory. When pressure from outsiders grew, the Romans lacked the resources to advance and defeat the enemy as in the past. The tenacity and success of their resistance for so long were remarkable. Without new conquests to provide the immense wealth needed to defend and maintain internal prosperity, the Romans finally yielded to unprecedented onslaughts by fierce and numerous attackers. Perhaps we would do well to think of the problem as did Edward Gibbon, the author of the great eighteenth-century study of Rome's collapse and transformation. Instead of asking why Rome fell, "we should rather be surprised that it had subsisted so long."

**WHY WERE** new conquests so important to the vitality of the Roman Empire?

# SUMMARY

## HOW DID Augustus transform Roman politics and government?

**The Augustan Principate** After defeating Mark Antony at Actium in 31 B.C.E., Octavian started transforming his rule into the functional equivalent of a monarchy. In 26 B.C.E., he made a show of giving up his powers, no doubt expecting the Senate to beg him to keep them, as it in fact did. From then on he was referred to as Augustus. He introduced administrative reforms, widened the talent pool from which senators were selected, and generally improved his subjects' standard of living. He professionalized the military and attempted to secure the northern frontier. He modeled austere morality and supported traditional Roman religion. *page 120*

## HOW DID political developments shape the culture of the Ciceronian and Augustan ages?

**Civilization of the Ciceronian and Augustan Ages** Roman culture flourished in the late republican period and in the Principate of Augustus. Hellenistic influences permeated the arts and literature, but the great works are clearly Roman in character. History, poetry, and law all found able practitioners in the late republic. Augustus simplified patronage for the arts. Augustan literature features some of the most recognizable names of the period: Vergil, Horace, Ovid, among others. Augustus also supported the visual arts; some of Rome's loveliest monuments were built under his reign. *page 122*

## HOW WAS imperial Rome governed and what was life like for its people?

**Imperial Rome, 14– to 180 C.E.** The monarchical, hereditary rule of Augustus's successors was based on undisguised military power. In 69 C.E., Vespasian, the first emperor who was not a descendant of Roman nobility, assumed the throne. His Flavian dynasty was followed by the five "good emperors." The provinces were generally peaceful during this period. Latin was spoken throughout the West; in the East, Greek was still the predominant language. Culturally, "Romanitas" spread throughout the cities and towns of the empire. The situation for Jews and for peasant farmers was not attractive. Border defenses, particularly in the north, were a recurring problem for the empire. Women's status improved. Many people lived in *insulae*, multistory apartment buildings that were cramped and uncomfortable. Latin literature experienced a Silver Age between 14 and 180 C.E., offering a more critical worldview than the works of the Augustan period. Archi-

tecture flourished. By the second century C.E., problems such as a decline in the vitality of local government, a stagnating economy, the expense of defense, and probably a mysterious decline in population were foreshadowing crises to come. *page 124*

## WHO WAS Jesus of Nazareth?

**The Rise of Christianity** Jesus of Nazareth was born in Judaea under the reign of Augustus. He gained a large following, particularly among the poor, with a message of a coming Day of Judgment and criticism of existing religious practices. Feared and misunderstood by the authorities, Jesus was crucified in Jerusalem, probably in 30 C.E. Written decades after his death, the Gospels present Jesus as the Son of God, a redeemer who was resurrected after death. The writings of Paul of Tarsus are especially important, since he makes the case that Christianity is a new and universal religion. The *agape* ("love feast") created a sense of solidarity across classes among early Christians, and it helped the religion spread throughout the Roman Empire and beyond. By the end of the second century C.E., the Catholic Church had been institutionalized as the definer of Christian orthodoxy. *page 130*

## HOW DID economic developments lead to the political and military crisis of the third century?

**The Crisis of the Third Century** External military threats and internal social weakness interacted in a vicious circle. Commodus came to power in 180 C.E. When he was assassinated in 192 C.E., civil war again erupted and military strongman Septimius Severus emerged victorious. In the third century C.E., others invaded the outskirts of the empire. Repelling these challenges required more resources than the society could spare; labor shortages, inflation, and neglect of infrastructure such as roads weakened Rome's economy. Social stratification increased. Invasions and anarchy characterized the middle of the third century C.E. *page 136*

## WHAT FACTORS contributed to the decline and eventual fall of Rome?

**The Late Empire** During the fourth and fifth centuries, the empire was reorganized and divided, and Christianity gained followers and power. Diocletian introduced the tetrarchy, but it did not lead to a smooth succession when he and his co-emperor retired in 305 C.E. Diocletian and Constantine both ruled autocratically from Eastern cities. Diocletian tried to suppress

Christianity, whereas Constantine supported it. Constantine's death was followed by yet another struggle for power. By the end of the fourth century, the empire had been divided permanently. Christianity's continued viability depended on its ability to cope with political interference and doctrinal disputes. *page 138*

**HOW DID** arts and letters in Late Rome reflect the developing relationship between pagan and Christian ideas?

**Arts and Letters in the Late Empire** Much of the art and literature of the late empire reflects the relationship between Christianity and pagan religions. The empire's new rulers came from the lower classes of the provinces; in their efforts to restore classical culture, they inevitably reshaped it. Christian writings were numerous, the most significant among them the works of Augustine in

which he combined Christian faith and pagan (Classical) reason. *page 144*

**WHY WERE** new conquests so important to the vitality of the Roman Empire?

**The Problem of the Decline and Fall of the Empire in the West** Imperial government fell in the West in the fifth century in the face of barbarian invasions. Ever since, historians and commentators have offered explanations, many of which seem specious. Like the early-twentieth-century historian Edward Gibbon, the authors believe the question should be more properly framed as, "How did the Roman Empire last as long as it did?" rather than, "Why did the Roman Empire decline and fall?" The Roman Empire could not expand forever; without the infusion of new people and new wealth that territorial conquest provided, the Roman Empire could not survive. *page 145*

# REVIEW QUESTIONS

1. How did Augustus alter Rome's constitution and government? How did his innovations solve the problems that had plagued the republic? Why were the Romans willing to accept him?

2. How did the literature of the Golden Age differ from that of the Silver Age? What did poets contribute to the success of Augustus's reforms?

3. Why were Christians persecuted by the Roman authorities? What enabled them to acquire such an enormous following by the fourth century C.E.?

4. What were the political, social, and economic problems that beset Rome in the third and fourth centuries C.E.? How did Diocletian and Constantine deal with them? Were these men able to halt Rome's decline? Were there problems they could not solve?

## KEY TERMS

*agape* (p. 132)
**Arianism** (p. 144)
**Augustus** (p. 120
**catholic** (p. 133)
**Eucharist** (p. 132)
**heretics** (p. 133

*jus gentium* (p. 122)
*jus naturale* (p. 122)
**orthodox** (p. 133)
**tetrarchy** (p. 138)
**Vulgate** (p. 145)

For additional learning resources related to this chapter, please go to **www.myhistorylab.com**

PEARSON
myhistorylab

# 6

# Late Antiquity and the Early Middle Ages:

## Creating a New European Society and Culture (476–1000)

**This illustration** from a fourteenth-century "Life of the Prophet" shows Muhammad's family—his daughter Fatima, her husband Ali, and Muhammad's father-in-law Abu Bakr—traveling together. Muhammad himself is not shown because like God he cannot be portrayed in Islamic art. Hence, whenever Muslims travel, Muhammad is in their midst but cannot be seen with the naked eye.

The New York Public Library/Art Resource, NY

**How do Muslims see the relationship between Muhammad, Jesus, and Moses?**

Scholars increasingly view the period between 250 C.E. and 800 C.E.—called *Late Antiquity*—as a single world, both cohesive and moving apart, bounded by the Roman and Sassanian (Persian) Empires. The Western and Eastern (Byzantine) empires of Rome never succumbed culturally to barbarian and Muslim invaders. In the East, the Sassanians created a powerful empire and deeply penetrated Rome's provinces. By the mid–eighth century, Arab conquests extended Muslim influence from the Middle East to North Africa and Spain. In Western Europe, Germanic heritage, Judeo-Christian religion, Roman language and law, and Greco-Byzantine administration and culture gradually combined to create a uniquely European way of life. ■

# ON THE EVE OF THE FRANKISH ASCENDANCY

**HOW DID** Germanic migrations contribute to the fall of the Roman Empire?

As we have already seen, by the late third century, the Roman Empire had become too large for a single emperor to govern and was beginning to fail. (See Chapter 5.) The emperor Diocletian (r. 284–305) tried to strengthen the empire by dividing it between himself and a co-emperor. The result was a dual empire with an eastern and a western half, each with its own emperor and, eventually, imperial bureaucracy and army. A critical shift of the empire's resources and orientation to the eastern half accompanied these changes. As imperial rule weakened in the West and strengthened in the East, it also became increasingly autocratic.

Diocletian's reign was followed by factional strife. His eventual successor, Constantine the Great (r. 306–337), briefly reunited the empire by conquest (his three sons and their successors would divide it again) and ruled as sole emperor of the eastern and western halves after 324. In that year, he moved the capital of the empire from Rome to Byzantium, an ancient Greek city that stood at the crossroads of the major sea and land routes between Europe and Asia Minor. Here, Constantine built the new city of Constantinople, which he dedicated in 330. As the imperial residence and the new administrative center of the empire, Constantinople gradually became a "new Rome." When the barbarian invasions of non-Roman Germanic and eastern peoples began in the late fourth century, the West was in political and economic disarray, and imperial power and prestige had shifted decisively to Constantinople and the East.

## GERMANIC MIGRATIONS

The German tribes did not burst in on the West all of a sudden. Before the massive migrations from the north and the east, Roman and Germanic cultures had commingled peacefully for centuries. Beginning in 376 with a great influx of Visigoths, or "west Goths," into the empire, this peaceful coexistence ended. The Visigoths, accomplished horsemen and fierce warriors, were themselves pushed into the empire by the emergence of a notoriously violent people, the Huns, from what is now Mongolia. The Visigoths ultimately reached southern Gaul and Spain. Soon to be Christianized, they won rights of settlement and material assistance within the empire from the Eastern emperor Valens (r. 364–378) in exchange for defending the eastern frontier as *foederati*, or the emperor's "special" allies. Instead of the promised assistance, however, the Visigoths received harsh treatment from their new allies. After repeated conflicts, the Visigoths rebelled and overwhelmed Valens at the Battle of Adrianople in 378. (See Chapter 5.)

Thereafter, the Romans passively permitted the settlement of barbarians within the heart of the Western empire. The Vandals crossed the Rhine in 406 and within three decades gained control of northwest Africa and much of the Mediterranean. The Burgundians, who came on the heels of the Vandals, settled in Gaul. Most important for subsequent Western history were the Franks, who settled northern and central

Gaul, some along the seacoast (the Salian Franks) and others along the Rhine, Seine, and Loire Rivers (the Ripuarian Franks).

Why was there so little Roman resistance to these Germanic tribes? The invaders were successful because they came in rapid succession upon a badly overextended Western empire divided politically by ambitious military commanders and weakened by decades of famine, pestilence, and over-taxation. The Eastern empire retained enough wealth and vitality to field new armies or to buy off the invaders. The Western empire, in contrast, succumbed not only because of moral decay and materialism, but also because of a combination of military rivalry, political mismanagement, disease, and sheer poverty.

## New Western Masters

In the early fifth century, Italy and the "eternal city" of Rome suffered devastating blows. In 410 the Visigoths, under Alaric (ca. 370–410), sacked Rome. In 452 the Huns, led by Attila—the "scourge of God"—invaded Italy. Rome was sacked still again, in 455—this time by the Vandals.

By the mid–fifth century, power in Western Europe had passed decisively from the hands of the Roman emperors to those of barbarian chieftains. In 476, the traditional date historians give for the fall of the Roman Empire, the barbarian Odovacer (ca. 434–493) deposed the last Western emperor Romulus Augustulus. The Eastern emperor Zeno (r. 474–491) recognized Odovacer's authority in the West, and Odovacer acknowledged Zeno as sole emperor, contenting himself to serve as Zeno's Western viceroy. In a later coup in 493, Theodoric (ca. 454–526), king of the Ostrogoths, or "east Goths," replaced Odovacer. Theodoric then governed with the full acceptance of the Roman people, the emperor in Constantinople, and the Christian church. By the end of the fifth century, the barbarians from west and east had saturated the Western empire. (See Map 6–1.)

## MAP EXPLORATION

Interactive map: To explore this map further, go to **www.myhistorylab.com**

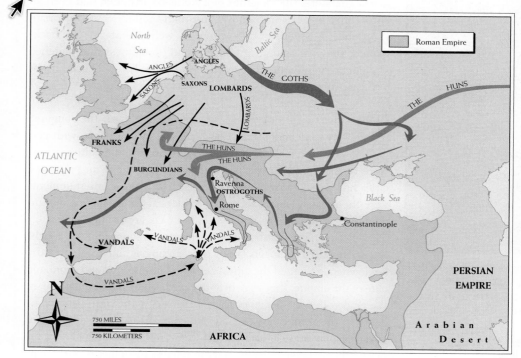

**MAP 6–1 Barbarian Migrations into the West in the Fourth and Fifth Centuries** The forceful intrusion of Germanic and non-Germanic barbarians into the Roman Empire from the last quarter of the fourth century through the fifth century made for a constantly changing pattern of movement and relations. The map shows the major routes taken by the usually unwelcome newcomers and the areas most deeply affected by the main groups.

**Which part** of the empire was least affected by barbarian migrations?

These barbarian military victories did not, however, obliterate Roman culture; Western Europe's new masters were willing to learn from the people they had conquered. They admired Roman culture and had no desire to destroy it. Except in Britain and northern Gaul, Roman law, Roman government, and Latin, the Roman language, coexisted with the new Germanic institutions.

All things considered, a gradual interpenetration of two strong cultures—a creative tension—marked the period of the Germanic migrations. The stronger culture was the Roman, and it became dominant in a later fusion. Despite Western military defeat, the Goths and the Franks became far more romanized than the Romans were germanized. Latin language, Nicene Catholic Christianity, and eventually Roman law and government were to triumph in the West during the Middle Ages.

# THE BYZANTINE EMPIRE

**HOW DID** the Byzantine Empire continue the legacy of Rome?

As the Roman Empire in the West succumbed to Germanic and other barbarian invasions, imperial power shifted to the eastern part of the Roman Empire, whose center was the city of Constantinople or Byzantium (modern-day Istanbul). It remained the sole imperial capital until the eighth century, when Charlemagne revived the Western empire and reclaimed its imperial title. In historical usage, the term *Byzantine* indicates the Hellenistic Greek, Roman, and Judaic monotheistic elements that distinguish the culture of the East from the Latin West.

## THE REIGN OF JUSTINIAN

The Byzantine Empire reached its pinnacle during the reign of Emperor Justinian (r. 527–565) and his like-minded wife, Empress Theodora (d. 548). A strongman ruler who expected all his subjects, clergy and laity, high and low, to submit absolutely to his hierarchical control, Justinian spent, built, and destroyed on a grand scale. Theodora, the daughter of a circus bear trainer, had been an entertainer in her youth and, if Justinian's tell-all court historian, Procopius, is believed, a prostitute as well. Whatever her background, she possessed an intelligence and toughness that matched and might even have exceeded that of her husband. Theodora was a true co-ruler.

**Cities** During Justinian's thirty-eight-year reign, the empire's strength lay in its more than 1,500 cities. Constantinople, with perhaps 350,000 inhabitants, was the largest city and the cultural crossroads of Asian and European civilizations. The dominant provincial cities had populations of 50,000. The most popular entertainments were the theater, where, according to clerical critics, nudity and immorality were on display, and the chariot races at the Hippodrome.

Between the fourth and fifth centuries, urban councils of roughly two hundred members, known as *Decurions*, all local, wealthy landowners, governed the cities. Being the intellectual and economic elite of the empire, they were heavily taxed, which did not make them the emperor's most docile or loyal servants. By the sixth century, fidelity to the throne had become the coin of the realm, and special governors, lay and clerical, chosen from the landholding classes, replaced the *decurion* councils as more reliable instruments of the em-

**Built during the** reign of Justinian, Hagia Sophia (Church of the Holy Wisdom) is a masterpiece of Byzantine and world architecture. After the Turkish conquest of Constantinople in 1453, Hagia Sophia was transformed into a mosque with four minarets, still visible today.

Turkish Tourism and Information Office

**What does Justinian's construction of the Hagia Sophia tell us about the relationship between church and state in the Byzantine Empire?**

peror's sovereign will. As the sixth and seventh centuries saw the beginning of new barbarian invasions of the empire from the north and the east, such political tightening was imperative.

**Law** The imperial goal—as reflected in Justinian's policy of "one God, one empire, one religion"—was to centralize government by imposing legal and doctrinal conformity throughout. To this end, the emperor ordered a collation and revision of Roman law. What Justinian wanted was loyal and docile subjects guided by clear and enforceable laws. The result was the *Corpus Juris Civilis*, or "body of civil law." This work laid the foundation for most subsequent European law. Because bringing subjects under the authority of a single sovereign was the fundamental feature of Roman law, rulers seeking to centralize their states especially benefited from Justinian's legal legacy.

**Reconquest in the West** Justinian sought to reconquer the imperial provinces lost to the barbarians in the West. Beginning in 533, his armies overran the Vandal kingdom in North Africa and Sicily, the Ostrogothic kingdom in Italy, and part of Spain. But the price paid in blood and treasure was enormous, particularly in Italy, where prolonged resistance by the Ostrogoths did not end until 554. By Justinian's death, his empire was financially exhausted, and plague had ravaged the population of Constantinople and much of the East. Although Byzantine rule survived in Sicily and parts of southern Italy until the eleventh century, most of Justinian's Western and North African conquests were soon lost to Lombard invaders from north of the Alps and to the Muslim Arabs. (See Map 6–2, page 154.)

**Empress Theodora and** Her Attendants. The union of political and spiritual authority in the person of the empress is shown by the depiction on Theodora's mantle of three magi carrying gifts to the Virgin and Jesus.

The Court of Empress Theodora. Byzantine early Christian mosaic. San Vitale, Ravenna, Italy Photograph © Scala/Art Resource, NY

**What role did the Empress Theodora play in Byzantine politics?**

**QUICK REVIEW**

**Theodora (d. 548)**

- Justinian's wife and his chief counselor
- Daughter of a circus performer who began her career as a prostitute
- A true co-ruler

## THE SPREAD OF BYZANTINE CHRISTIANITY

In the late sixth and seventh centuries, nomadic, pagan tribes of Avars, Slavs, and Bulgars invaded and occupied the Balkan provinces of the eastern empire, threatening a "dark age" there. More than once, these fierce raiders menaced Constantinople itself. Yet after almost two centuries of intermittent warfare, the Slavs and Bulgars eventually converted to Eastern Orthodoxy or Byzantine Christianity. Hoping to build a cultural-linguistic firewall against menacing Franks from the West who had conquered the Avars and were attempting to convert his people to Roman Catholicism in Latin, a language they did not understand, the Slav Duke Rastislav of Moravia turned in the ninth century to Constantinople for help. In response, the emperor sent two learned missionaries to convert the Moravians: the brothers, priests, and future saints Constantine, later known as Cyril, and Methodius. In Moravia, the two created a new, Greek-based alphabet, which permitted the Slavs to create their own written language. That language gave the Christian gospels and Byzantine theology a lasting Slavic home. Later, after the Bulgars conquered and absorbed many of the Slavs, that alphabet was elevated to a broader script known as Cyrillic after St. Cyril. Known today as Old Church Slavonic, it has ever since been the international Slavic language through which Byzantine Christianity penetrated eastern Europe.

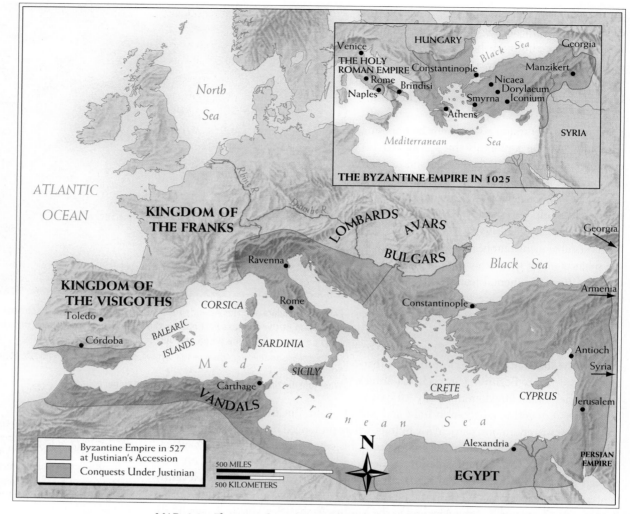

**MAP 6–2    The Byzantine Empire at the Time of Justinian's Death**    Justinian reconquered lands in the West that once belonged to the Roman Empire. From 500 to 1100, the Byzantine Empire was the center of Christian civilization. The inset shows the empire in 1025, before its losses to the Seljuk Turks.

**In the** second half of the first millennium C.E., how did the power and influence of Rome and Constantinople compare?

## PERSIANS AND MUSLIMS

During the reign of Emperor Heraclius (r. 610–641), the Byzantine Empire took a decidedly Eastern, as opposed to a Western Roman, direction. Heraclius spent his entire reign resisting Persian and Islamic invasions, the former successfully, the latter in vain. In 628 he defeated the Persian Sassanid king Chosroes and took back one of Western Christendom's great lost relics: a piece of Christ's Cross that Chosroes had carried off when he captured Jerusalem in 614. After 632, however, Islamic armies overran much of the empire, directly attacking Constantinople for the first time in the mid-670s. Not until Leo III of the Isaurian dynasty (r. 717–740) did the Byzantines succeed in repelling Arab armies and regaining most of Asia Minor, having lost forever Syria, Egypt, and North Africa. The setback was traumatic and forced a major restructuring of the diminished empire, creating a new system of provincial government under the direct authority of imperial generals. In the tenth century, a reinvigorated Byzantium went on the offensive, pushing back the Muslims in Armenia and northern Syria and conquering the Bulgar kingdom in the Balkans.

But like Justinian's conquests in the sixth century, these may have overtaxed the empire's strength; and in the eleventh century, Byzantine fortunes rapidly reversed. After inflicting a devastating defeat on the Byzantine army at Manzikert in Armenia in 1071, Muslim Seljuk Turks overran most of Asia Minor, from which the Byzantines had drawn most of their tax revenue and troops. The empire never fully recovered, yet its end—which came when the Seljuks' cousins, the Ottoman Turks, captured Constantinople in 1453—was still almost four centuries away. In 1092, after two decades of steady Turkish advance, the Eastern emperor Alexius I Comnenus (r. 1081–1118) called for Western aid, which helped spark the First Crusade. It also heightened tensions between Latin West and Greek East and exposed the riches of Constantinople to predatory Western eyes. A century later (1204), the Fourth Crusade was diverted from Jerusalem to Constantinople, not, however, to rescue the city, but rather to inflict more damage on it and on the Byzantine Empire than all previous non-Christian invaders had done before. (See Chapter 7.) When the Byzantines eventually recovered the city in 1261, Byzantine power was a shadow of its former self, the empire was impoverished, and the Turks had become a constant threat.

# ISLAM AND THE ISLAMIC WORLD

A new drama began to unfold in the sixth century with the awakening of a rival far more dangerous to the West than the German tribes: the new faith of **Islam**. By the time of Muhammad's death (632), Islamic armies were beginning to absorb the attention and the resources of the emperors in Constantinople and the rulers in the West.

## MUHAMMAD'S RELIGION

Muhammad (570–632), an orphan, was raised by a family of modest means. As a youth, he worked as a merchant's assistant, traveling the major trade routes. When he was twenty-five, he married a wealthy widow from the city of Mecca, the religious and commercial center of Arabia. Thereafter, himself a wealthy man, he became a kind of social activist, criticizing Meccan materialism, paganism, and unjust treatment of the poor and needy. At about age forty, a deep religious experience heightened his commitment to reform and it transformed his life. He began to receive revelations from the angel Gabriel, who recited God's word to him at irregular intervals. These revelations were collected after his death into the Islamic holy book, the **Qur'an** (literally, a "reciting"), which his followers compiled between 650 and 651. The basic message Muhammad received was a summons to all Arabs to submit to God's will. Followers of Muhammad's religion came to be called *Muslim* ("submissive" or "surrendering"); *Islam*, itself, means "submission."

The message was not a new one. A long line of Jewish prophets going back to Noah had reiterated it. According to Muslims, however, this line ended with Muhammad, who, as the last of God's chosen prophets, became "the Prophet." The Qur'an also recognized Jesus Christ as a prophet but denied that he was God's co-eternal and co-equal son. Like Judaism, Islam was a monotheistic and theocentric religion, not a trinitarian one like Christianity.

Mecca was a major pagan pilgrimage site (the **Ka'ba**, which became Islam's holiest shrine, housed a sacred black meteorite that was originally a pagan object of worship). Muhammad's condemnation of idolatry and immorality threatened the trade that flowed from the pilgrims, enraging the merchants of the city. Persecuted for their attacks on traditional religion, Muhammad and his followers fled Mecca in 622 for

**HOW DID** Islamic culture influence the West?

**Islam**   New religion appearing in Arabia in the sixth century in response to the work of the Prophet Muhammad.

**Qur'an**   Sacred book comprised of a collection of the revealed texts that God had chosen Muhammad to convey.

**Ka'ba**   One of Arabia's holiest shrines located in Mecca, the birthplace of Muhammad.

*Hegira* Forced flight of Muhammad and his followers to Medina, 240 miles north of Mecca. This event marks the beginning of the Islamic calendar.

Medina, 240 miles to the north. This event came to be known as the *Hegira* ("flight") and marks the beginning of the Islamic calendar.

In Medina, Muhammad organized his forces and drew throngs of devoted followers. He raided caravans going back and forth to Mecca. He also had his first conflicts with Medina's Jews, who were involved in trade with Mecca. By 624, he was able to conquer Mecca and make it the center of the new religion.

During these years the basic rules of Islamic practice evolved. True Muslims were expected (1) to be honest and modest in all their dealings and behavior; (2) to be unquestionably loyal to the Islamic community; (3) to abstain from pork and alcohol at all times; (4) to wash and pray facing Mecca five times a day; (5) to contribute to the support of the poor and needy; (6) to fast during daylight hours for one month each year; and (7) to make a pilgrimage to Mecca and visit the Ka'ba at least once in a lifetime. The last requirement reflects the degree to which Islam was an assimilationist religion: it "Islamicized" a major pagan religious practice.

Islam also permitted Muslim men to have up to four wives—provided they treated them all justly and gave each equal attention—and as many concubines as they wished. A husband could divorce a wife with a simple declaration, whereas, to divorce her husband, a wife had to show good cause before a religious judge. A wife was expected to be totally loyal and devoted to her husband and was allowed to show her face to no man but him. (See "Compare & Connect: The Battle of the Sexes in Christianity and Islam," pages 158–159.)

In contrast to Christianity, Islam drew no rigid distinction between the clergy and the laity. A lay scholarly elite developed, however, and held moral authority within Islamic society in domestic and religious matters. This elite, known as the *ulema*, or "persons with correct knowledge," served a social function similar to that of a professional priesthood or rabbinate. Its members were men of great piety and obvious learning whose opinions came to have the force of law in Muslim society. They also saw that Muslim rulers adhered to the letter of the Qur'an.

*ulema* ("Persons with correct knowledge") Scholarly elite leading Islam.

## ISLAMIC DIVERSITY

The success of Islam lay in its ability to unify and inspire tribal Arabs and other non-Jewish and non-Christian people. Islam also appealed to Arab pride, for it deemed Muhammad to be history's major religious figure and his followers to be God's chosen people.

As early as the seventh century, however, disputes arose among Muslims over the nature of Islamic society and authority within it that left permanent divisions. Disagreement over the true line of succession to Muhammad—the **caliphate**—was one source of discord. Another disagreement related to this was over doctrinal issues involving the extent to which Islam was an inclusive religion, open to sinners as well as to the virtuous. Several groups emerged from these disputes. The most radical was the Kharijites, whose leaders seceded from the camp of the caliph Ali (656–661) because Ali compromised with his enemies on a matter of principle. Righteous and judgmental, the Kharijites wanted all but the most rigorously virtuous Muslims excluded from the community of the faithful. In 661, a Kharijite assassinated Ali.

**caliphate** Office of the leader of the Muslim community.

Another, more influential group was the **Shi'a**, or "partisans of Ali" (*Shi'at Ali*). The Shi'a looked on Ali and his descendants as the rightful successors of Muhammad not only by virtue of kinship, but also by the expressed will of the Prophet himself. To the Shi'a, Ali's assassination revealed the most basic truth of a devout Muslim life: A true *imam*, or "ruler," must expect to suffer unjustly even unto death in the world, and so, too, must his followers. A distinctive theology of martyrdom has ever since been a mark of Shi'a teaching. And the Shi'a, until modern times, have been an embattled minority within mainstream Islamic society.

**Shi'a** The "party" of Ali. They believed Ali and his descendants were Muhammad's only rightful successors.

A third group, which has been dominant for most of Islamic history, was the majority centrist **Sunnis** (followers of *sunna*, or "tradition"). Sunnis have always put loyalty to the community of Islam above all else and have spurned the exclusivism and purism of the Kharijites and the Shi'a.

**Sunnis**   Followers of the *sunna*, "tradition." They emphasize loyalty to the fundamental principles of Islam.

## ISLAMIC EMPIRES

Under Muhammad's first three successors—the caliphs Abu Bakr (r. 632–634), Umar (r. 634–644), and Uthman (r. 644–655)—Islam expanded by conquest throughout the southern and eastern Mediterranean, into territories mostly still held today by Islamic states. In the eighth century, Muslim armies occupied parts of Spain in the West and of India in the East, producing a truly vast empire. (See Map 6–3.) The capital of this empire moved, first, from Mecca to Damascus in Syria, and then, in 750, to Baghdad in Iraq after the Abbasid dynasty replaced the Umayyads in a struggle for the caliphate. Thereafter, the huge Muslim Empire gradually broke up into separate states, some with their own line of caliphs claiming to be the true successors of Muhammad.

The early Muslim conquests would not have been so rapid and thorough had the contemporary Byzantine and Persian empires not been exhausted by decades of war. The Muslims struck at both empires in the 630s, completely overrunning the Persian Empire by 651. Most of the inhabitants in Byzantine Syria and Palestine, although Christian, were Semites like the Arabs. Any religious unity they felt with the Byzantine Greeks may have been offset by hatred of the Byzantine army of occupation and by resentment at Constantinople's efforts to impose Greek "orthodox" beliefs on the Monophysite churches

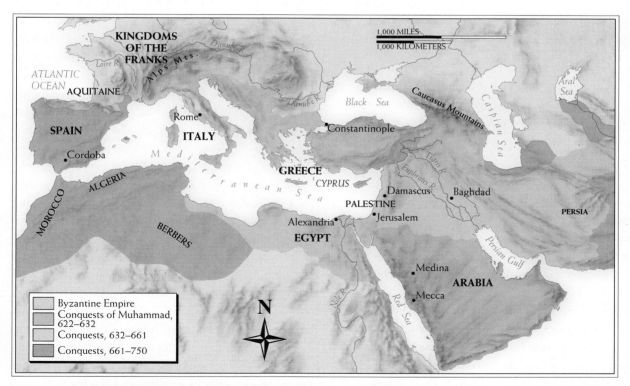

**MAP 6–3   Muslim Conquests and Domination of the Mediterranean to about 750 C.E.**   Within 125 years of Muhammad's rise, Muslims came to dominate Spain and all areas south and east of the Mediterranean.

**How were** Muslims able to dominate much of the area east and south of the Mediterranean within 125 years of Muhammad's rise?

# THE BATTLE OF THE SEXES IN CHRISTIANITY AND ISLAM

In early Christianity man and woman were viewed as one and the same offspring, Eve born of Adam, for which reason they were forever after drawn irresistibly to one another. What one did to the other, one also did to oneself, so tightly were they bound. And that bond between husband and wife made their relationship all the more caring and charitable.

Muhammad's role as a husband was by all accounts exemplary: a spouse who dealt shrewdly and fairly with his wives, a splendid model for his followers. In the teaching of the Qur'an, all conflict between husband and wife was to be resolved by talking and, that failing, by the husband's departure from the marital bed. Heeding the example of the Prophet and the teaching of the Qur'an, devout Muslim men viewed a husband's hitting a wife as a last resort in his disciplining of her. Yet, when a wife flagrantly disobeyed (*nashiz*) her husband, or, much worse, was unfaithful to him, hitting often became the husband's and society's first response.

## QUESTIONS

1. How does the marriage bond differ in the Christian and Muslim faiths? What does it mean to Christians to say that husband and wife are one flesh? Is that also the way spouses are perceived in Islam?

2. How successful is male discipline of self and of wife in Islam? Is Christian marriage too egalitarian and, hence, more vulnerable to failure?

3. If marriage is a mirror of a religion, what does it reveal Christianity and Islam to be?

## I. CHRISTIAN MARRIAGE

*St. John Chrysostom (347–407) elaborated the relationship between Christian spouses in his* Homily on Christian Spouses: *"Wives, be subject to your husbands, as to the Lord . . . Husbands, love your wives as Christ loved the Church." (Ephesians 5:22–25)*

There is no relationship between human beings so close as that of husband and wife, if they are united as they ought to be . . . God did not fashion woman independently from man . . . nor did He enable woman to bear children without man . . . He made the one man Adam to be the origin of all mankind, both male and female, and made it impossible for men and women to be self-sufficient [without one another] . . .

The love of husband and wife is [thus] the force that wields society together . . . Why else would [God] say, "Wives, be subject to your husbands?" Because when harmony prevails, the children are raised well, the household is kept in order . . . and great benefits, both for families and for states result . . .

Having seen the amount of obedience necessary, hear now about the amount of love that is needed. [If] you want your wife to be obedient to you . . . then be re-

sponsible for the same providential care of her as Christ has for the Church. Even if you see her belittling you, or despising and mocking you . . . subject her to yourself through affection, kindness, and your great regard for her . . . One's partner for life, the mother of one's children, the source of one's every joy, should never be fettered with fear and threats, but with love and patience . . . What sort of satisfaction could a husband have, if he lives with his wife as if she were a slave and not a woman [there] by her own free will. [So] suffer anything for her sake, but never disgrace her, for Christ never did this with the Church . . .

A wife should never nag her husband [saying] "You lazy coward, you have no ambition! Look at our relatives and neighbors; they have plenty of money. Their wives have far more than I do." Let no wife say any such thing; she is her husband's body, and it is not for her to dictate to her head, but rather to submit and obey . . . Likewise, if a husband has a wife who behaves this way, he must never exercise his authority by insulting and abusing her.

Source: Don S. Browning et al., *Sex, Marriage, and Family in World Religions* (New York: Columbia University Press), pp. 106–108.

قالَتْ بَلْ هُوَ وَمِنْ طَوْقِ الجُمَانَةِ النَّعَامَةَ أَكْذَبُ مِنْ أَبِي نُعَامَةَ حِينَ
مَخْرُوقِ الْيَمَامَةِ فَرَمَاهُنَّ زَيْدٌ رَفِيقَ السَّوَاطِ وَاسْتَنْشَاطَ لِاسْتِنْشَاطِهِ الْمُعْنَاظِ
وَقَالَ لَهَا وَيْلَكَ يَا دُفَانُ يَا فُجَارُ بِأَغِصَّةِ العُقَّار وَالجَارُ لَيَعْدِينَ فِي الخَلْوَةِ

لِيُعَدِّبَنِي وَبَدْرِبَنِي فِي الجِمَالَةِ نَكَدَنِي وَقَدْ عَلِمْتُ أَنْ جُنَّ بِنْتَ عَلَيْكَ وَدَنَوْنَ إِلَيْكَ
الفِتْنَةُ افْجَعْ مِنْ قِدَةٍ وَأَيْبَسُ مِنْ قِدَةٍ وَأَخْشَنُ مِنْ لِيفَةٍ وَأَنْزُ مِنْ حِفَّةٍ
وَأَقَلُ مِنْ مَضَةٍ وَآدُ رَامٍ مِنْ جَيْظَةٍ وَأَبْرُ مِنْ قَتَرَةٍ وَأَبُودُ مِنْ قَرَّةٍ وَأَحْرَنُ

**Muslims are enjoined** to live by the divine law, or Shari'a, and have a right to have disputes settled by an arbiter of the Shari'a. Here we see a husband complaining about his wife before the state-appointed judge, or *qadi*. The wife, backed up by two other women, points an accusing finger at the husband. In such cases, the first duty of the *qadi*, who should be a learned person of faith, is to try to effect a reconciliation before the husband divorces his wife, or the wife herself seeks a divorce.

Bibliothèque Nationale de France, Paris

**What role did clerics play in Islamic society?**

## II. MUSLIM MARRIAGE

*Chroniclers Abu Hamid Al-Ghazali (1058–1111), Ihya'Ulum, 2:34–35 (11th c. C.E.) elaborate the teaching of Qur'an 4:34: "Men are the protectors and maintainers of women because God has given [men] more strength . . . and because they support [women] from their means."*

Treating women well and bearing their ill treatment [is] required for marriage . . . God said, "keep them good company." [Among] the last things the Messenger [Muhammad] recommended was to take care of your slaves. Do not burden them with things beyond their capacity, and observe God's exhortations relating to your wives, for they are like slaves in your hands. You took them in trust from God and made them your wives by His words . . .

One should know that treating one's wife well does not only mean not harming her; it also means to endure ill treatment and be patient when she gets angry and loses her temper, a [method] the Messenger used to forgive his wives who argued with him and turned away from him for the whole day . . .

'A'ishah [a wife of the Prophet] once got angry and said to the Prophet . . . "You, who claims to be the Prophet of God!" The Messenger of God smiled and tolerated her in the spirit of forgiveness and generosity . . . It is believed that the first love story in Islam was that of Prophet Muhammad and 'A'ishah. The Prophet used to say to his other wives: "Do not upset me by saying bad things about 'A'ishah, for she is the only woman in whose company I have received the revelation [of God]! Anas [Ibn Malik, a ninth-century. chronicler] reported that the Prophet was the most compassionate person in matters concerning women and children . . .

Respond to [as he did to women's] harshness by teasing, joking, and kidding them, for it is certain this softens women's hearts. The Prophet said, "The people with the most perfect faith are those with the best ethics and those who are the kindest toward their families." Umar [a companion of the Prophet and the second caliph of Islam] once said: "One should always be like a child with his family, but when they need him they should find [in him] a man."

Source: Don S. Browning et al., *Sex, Marriage, and Family*, pp. 190–91, 194–95.

**A Muslim and a Christian** play the *ud*, or lute, together, from a thirteenth-century *Book of Chants* in the Escorial Monastery of Madrid. Medieval Europe was deeply influenced by Arab–Islamic culture, transmitted particularly through Spain. Some of the many works in Arabic on musical theory were translated into Latin and Hebrew, but the main influence on music came from the arts of singing and playing spread by minstrels.

A Moor and a Christian playing the lute, miniature in a book of music from the "Cantigas" of Alphonso X "the Wise" (1221–1284). Thirteenth century (manuscript). Monastero de El Excorial, El Escorial, Spain/Index/Bridgeman Art Library

**How would you characterize Muslim-Christian relations in medieval Spain?**

of Egypt and Syria. As a result, many Egyptian and Syrian Christians, hoping for deliverance from Byzantine oppression, appear to have welcomed the Islamic conquerors.

Although Islam gained converts from among the Christians in the Near East, North Africa, and Spain, its efforts to invade northern Europe were rebuffed. The ruler of the Franks, Charles Martel, defeated a raiding party of Arabs on the western frontier of Europe at Poitiers (today in central France) in 732. This victory and the failure to capture Constantinople ended any Arab effort to expand into Western or Central Europe.

## THE WESTERN DEBT TO ISLAM

Arab invasions and their presence in the Mediterranean area during the early Middle Ages contributed both directly and indirectly to the formation of Western Europe. They did so indirectly by driving Western Europeans back onto their native tribal and inherited Judeo-Christian, Greco-Roman, and Byzantine resources, from which they created a Western culture of their own. Also, by diverting the attention and energies of the Byzantine Empire during the formative centuries, the Arabs may have prevented it from expanding into and reconquering Western Europe. That allowed two Germanic peoples to gain ascendancy: first, the Franks and then the Lombards, who invaded Italy in the sixth century and settled in the Po valley around the city of Milan.

Despite the hostility of the Christian West to the Islamic world, there was nonetheless much creative interchange between these two different cultures, and the West profited greatly and directly from it. At this time, Arab civilizations were the more advanced, enjoying their golden age, and they had much to teach a toddling West. Between the eighth and tenth centuries, Cordoba, the capital of Muslim Spain, was a model multicultural city embracing Arabs, Berbers from North Africa, Christian converts to Islam, and Jews. Cordoba was a conduit for the finest Arabian tableware, leather, silks, dyes, aromatic ointments, and perfumes into the West. The Arabs taught Western farmers how to irrigate fields and Western artisans how to tan leather and refine silk. The West also gained from its contacts with Arabic scholars. Thanks to the skills of Islamic scholars, ancient Greek works on astronomy, mathematics, and medicine became available in Latin translation to Westerners. Down to the sixteenth century, the basic gynecological and child-care manuals guiding the work of Western midwives and physicians were compilations made by the Baghdad physician Al-Razi (Rhazes), the philosopher and physician Ibn-Sina (Avicenna) (980–1037), and Ibn Rushd (known in the West as Averröes, 1126–1198), who was also Islam's greatest authority on Aristotle. Jewish scholars also thrived amid the intellectual culture Islamic scholars created. The greatest of them all, Moses Maimonides (1135–1204), wrote in both Arabic and Hebrew.

# WESTERN SOCIETY AND THE DEVELOPING CHRISTIAN CHURCH

**HOW DID** the developing Christian church influence Western society during the early Middle Ages?

Facing barbarian invasions from the north and east and a strong Islamic presence in the Mediterranean, the West found itself in decline during the fifth and sixth centuries. As trade waned, cities rapidly fell on hard times, depriving the West of centers for the exchange of goods and ideas that might enable it to look and live beyond itself.

While these social changes were occurring, one institution remained firmly entrenched and increasingly powerful within the declining cities of the waning Roman Empire: the Christian church. As the Western empire crumbled, Roman governors withdrew and populations emigrated to the countryside, where the resulting vacuum of authority was filled by local bishops and cathedral chapters. The local cathedral became the center of urban life and the local bishop the highest authority for those who remained in the cities. In Rome, on a larger and more fateful scale, the pope took control of the city as the Western emperors gradually departed and died out. Left to its own devices, Western Europe soon discovered that the Christian church was its best repository of Roman administrative skills and classical culture. Alone in the West, the church retained an effective hierarchical administration, scattered throughout the old empire, staffed by the best educated minds in Europe and centered in emperor-less Rome.

## MONASTIC CULTURE

Throughout late antiquity the Christian church gained the services of growing numbers of monks, who were not only loyal to its mission, but also objects of great popular respect. Monastic culture proved again and again to be the peculiar strength of the church during the Middle Ages.

The popularity of monasticism began to grow as Roman persecution of Christians waned and Christianity became the favored religion of the empire during the fourth century. Christians came to view monastic life—embracing, as it did, the biblical "counsels of perfection" (chastity, poverty, and obedience)—as the purest form of religious practice, going beyond the baptism and creed that identified ordinary believers. This view evolved during the Middle Ages into a belief in the general superiority of the clergy and in the church's mission over the laity and the state. That belief served the papacy in later confrontations with secular rulers.

The first monks were hermits who had withdrawn from society to pursue a more perfect way of life. Anthony of Egypt (ca. 251–356), the father of hermit monasticism, went into the desert to pray and work, setting an example followed by hundreds in Egypt, Syria, and Palestine in the fourth and fifth centuries.

Hermit monasticism was soon joined by the development of communal monasticism. In the first quarter of the fourth century, Pachomius (ca. 286–346) organized monks in southern Egypt into a highly regimented community in which monks shared a life of labor, order, and discipline enforced by a strict penal code. Basil the Great (329–379) popularized communal monasticism throughout the East, providing a less severe rule than Pachomius, one that directed monks into such worldly services as caring for orphans, widows, and the infirm in surrounding communities.

Athanasius (ca. 293–373) and Martin of Tours (ca. 315–399) introduced monasticism to the West. The teachings of John Cassian (ca. 360–435) and Jerome (ca. 340–420) then helped shape the basic values and practices of Western monasticism. The great organizer of Western monasticism, however, was Benedict of Nursia (ca. 480–547). Benedict founded a monastery at Monte Cassino near Naples, Italy, in 529 and wrote *Rule for Monasteries*, a sophisticated and comprehensive plan for every activity of the monks, even detailing the manner in which they were to sleep. Periods of devotion (about four hours each day) were set aside for the "work of God." That is, regular prayers, liturgical activities, and study alternated with manual labor (farming). This program permitted not a moment's idleness and carefully nurtured the religious, intellectual, and physical well-being of the cloistered monks. The monastery was directed by an abbot, whose command the monks had to obey unquestioningly. During the early Middle Ages, Benedictine missionaries Christianized both England and Germany. Their disciplined organization and devotion to hard work made the Benedictines an economic and political power as well as a spiritual force wherever they settled.

## THE DOCTRINE OF PAPAL PRIMACY

Constantine and his successors, especially the Eastern emperors, ruled religious life with an iron hand and consistently looked on the church as little more than a department of the state. At first, state control of religion was also the rule in the West. Most of the early popes were mediocre and not very influential. To increase their influence, in the fifth and sixth centuries, they took advantage of imperial weakness and distraction to develop a new defense: the powerful weaponry of papal primacy. This doctrine raised the Roman pope, or pontiff, to unassailable supremacy within the church when it came to defining church doctrine. It also put him in a position to make important secular claims, paving the way to repeated conflicts between church and state, pope and emperor, throughout the Middle Ages.

Papal primacy was first asserted as a response to the decline of imperial Rome. It was also a response to the claims of the patriarchs of the Eastern church, who, after imperial power was transferred to Constantinople, looked on the bishop of Rome as an equal, but no superior. Roman pontiffs, understandably jealous of such claims and resentful of the political interference of Eastern emperors, launched a counteroffensive. Pope Damasus I (r. 366–384) took the first of several major steps in the rise of the Roman church when he declared a Roman "apostolic" primacy. Pointing to Jesus' words to Peter in the Gospel of Matthew (16:18) ("Thou art Peter, and upon this rock I will build my church"), he claimed himself and all other popes to be Peter's direct successors as the unique "rock" on which the Christian church was built. Pope Leo I (r. 440–461) took still another fateful step by assuming the title *pontifex maximus*, or "supreme priest." He further proclaimed himself to be endowed with a "plentitude of power," thereby establishing the supremacy of the bishop of Rome over all other bishops. During Leo's reign, an imperial decree recognized his exclusive jurisdiction over the Western church. At the end of the fifth century, Pope Gelasius I (r. 492–496) proclaimed the authority of the clergy to be "more weighty" than the power of kings, because priests had charge of divine affairs and the means of salvation.

Events as well as ideology favored the papacy. As barbarian and Islamic invasions isolated the West by diverting the attention of the Byzantine empire, they also prevented both emperors and the Eastern patriarchs from interfering in the affairs of the Western church. At the same time, the Franks became a new political ally of the church. The power of the exarch of Ravenna—the Byzantine emperor's viceroy in the West—was eclipsed in the late sixth century by invading Lombards who conquered most of Italy. Thanks to Frankish prodding, the Lombards became Nicene Christians loyal to Rome and a new counterweight to Eastern power and influence in the West. In an unprecedented act, Pope Gregory I, "the Great" (r. 590–604), instead of looking to the emperor in Constantinople for protection, negotiated an independent peace treaty with the Lombards.

## THE RELIGIOUS DIVISION OF CHRISTENDOM

In both East and West, religious belief alternately served and undermined imperial political unity. Since the fifth century, the patriarch of Constantinople had blessed Byzantine emperors in that city (the "second Rome"), attesting the close ties between rulers and the Eastern Church. While Orthodox Christianity was the religion that mattered most, it was not the only religion in the empire with a significant following. Nor did Byzantine rulers view religion as merely a political tool. From time to time, Christian heresies also received imperial support. Moreover, with imperial encouragement, Christianity absorbed pagan religious practices and beliefs that were too deeply rooted in rural and urban cultures to be eradicated, thus turning local gods and their shrines into Christian saints and holy places.

Over time, the differences between Eastern and Western Christianity grew. One issue even divided Justinian and his wife Theodora. Whereas Justinian remained strict-

**QUICK REVIEW**

**Papal Primacy**

◆ First asserted as a response to the decline of imperial Rome

◆ Pope Leo I (440–461) took the title *pontifex maximus*

◆ Constantinople lost influence over papacy as Byzantine control of Italy decreased

ly orthodox in his Christian beliefs, Theodora supported a divisive Eastern teaching that the Council of Chalcedon in 451 had condemned as a heresy, namely, that Christ had a single, immortal nature and was not both eternal God and mortal man in one and the same person. In reaction to the **Monophysite** controversy, orthodox Christianity became even more determined to protect the sovereignty of God.

A similar dispute appeared in Eastern debates over the relationship among the members of the Trinity, specifically whether the Holy Spirit proceeded only from the Father, as the Nicene-Constantinopolitan Creed taught, or from the Father and the Son (*filioque* in Latin), an idea that became increasingly popular in the West and was eventually adopted by the Western church and inserted into its creed. These disputes, which appear trivial and are almost unintelligible to many people today, seemed vitally important to many Christians at the time.

Another major rift between the Christian East and West was over the veneration of images in worship. In 726, Emperor Leo III (r. 717–741) forbade the use of images and icons that portrayed Christ, the Virgin Mary, and the saints throughout Christendom. As their veneration had been commonplace for centuries, the decree came as a shock, especially to the West where it was rejected as heresy. **Iconoclasm**, as the change in policy was called, drove the popes into the camp of the Franks, where they found in Charlemagne an effective protector against the Byzantine world. (See page 000.)

A third difference between East and West was the Eastern emperors' pretension to absolute sovereignty, both secular and religious. Expressing their sense of sacred mission, the emperors presented themselves in the trappings of holiness and directly interfered in matters of church and religion, what is called **Caesaropapism**, or the emperor acting as if he were pope as well as caesar. To a degree unknown in the West, Eastern emperors appointed and manipulated the clergy, convening church councils and enforcing church decrees. By comparison, the West nurtured a distinction between church and state that became visible in the eleventh century.

The Eastern church also rejected several disputed requirements of Roman Christianity. It denied the existence of Purgatory, permitted lay divorce and remarriage, allowed priests, but not bishops, to marry, and conducted religious services in the languages that people in a given locality actually spoke (the so-called "vernacular" languages) instead of Greek and Latin.

Having piled up over the centuries, these various differences ultimately resulted in a schism between the two churches in 1054. In that year a Western envoy of the pope, Cardinal Humbertus, visited the Patriarch of Constantinople, Michael Cerularius, in the hope of overcoming the differences that divided Christendom. The patriarch was not, however, welcoming. Relations between the two men quickly deteriorated, and cardinal and patriarch engaged in mutual recriminations and insults. Before leaving the city, Humbertus left a bull of excommunication on the altar of Hagia Sophia. In response, the patriarch proclaimed all Western popes to have been heretics since the sixth century! Nine hundred and eleven years would pass before this breach was repaired. In a belated ecumenical gesture in 1965, a Roman pope met with the patriarch of Constantinople to revoke the mutual condemnations of 1054.

**Monophysites**   Believers in a single, immortal nature of Christ; not both eternal God and mortal man in one and the same person.

**iconoclasm**   Opposition to the use of images in Christian worship.

**Caesaropapism**   Emperor acting as if he were pope as well as caesar.

**A ninth-century** Byzantine manuscript shows an iconoclast whiting out an image of Christ. The Iconoclastic Controversy was an important factor in the division of Christendom into separate Latin and Greek branches.

State Historical Museum, Moscow

**Why were religious and political disputes so often intertwined in the Byzantine Empire?**

## Overview    Major Political and Religious Developments of the Early Middle Ages

| | |
|---|---|
| **313** | Emperor Constantine issues the Edict of Milan |
| **325** | Council of Nicaea defines Christian doctrine |
| **410** | Rome invaded by Visigoths under Alaric |
| **413–426** | Saint Augustine writes *City of God* |
| **451** | Council of Chalcedon further defines Christian doctrine |
| **451–453** | Europe invaded by the Huns under Attila |
| **476** | Barbarian Odovacer deposes Western emperor and rules as king of the Romans |
| **489–493** | Theodoric establishes kingdom of Ostrogoths in Italy |
| **529** | Saint Benedict founds monastery at Monte Cassino |
| **533** | Justinian codifies Roman law |
| **622** | Muhammad's flight from Mecca (*Hegira*) |
| **711** | Muslim invasion of Spain |
| **732** | Charles Martel defeats Muslims between Poitiers and Tours |
| **754** | Pope Stephen II and Pepin III ally |

# THE KINGDOM OF THE FRANKS: FROM CLOVIS TO CHARLEMAGNE

**HOW DID** the reign of Clovis differ from that of Charlemagne?

A warrior chieftain, Clovis (ca. 466–511), who converted to Catholic Christianity around 496, founded the first Frankish dynasty, the Merovingians, named for Merovich, an early leader of one branch of the Franks. Clovis and his successors united the Salian and Ripuarian Franks, subdued the Arian Burgundians and Visigoths, and established the kingdom of the Franks within ancient Gaul, making the Franks and the Merovingian kings a significant force in Western Europe. The Franks themselves occupied a broad belt of territory that extended throughout modern France, Belgium, the Netherlands, and western Germany, and their loyalties remained strictly tribal and local.

## GOVERNING THE FRANKS

In attempting to govern this sprawling kingdom, the Merovingians encountered what proved to be the most persistent problem of medieval political history—the competing claims of the "one" and the "many." On the one hand, the king struggled for a centralized government and transregional loyalty, and on the other, powerful local magnates strove to preserve their regional autonomy and traditions.

The Merovingian kings addressed this problem by making pacts with the landed nobility and by creating the royal office of counts. The counts were men without possessions to whom the king gave great lands in the expectation that they would be, as the landed aristocrats often were not, loyal officers of the kingdom. Like local aristocrats, however, the Merovingian counts also let their immediate self-interest gain the upper hand. Once established in office for a period of time, they, too, became territorial rulers in their own right, so the Frankish kingdom progressively fragmented into independent regions and tiny principalities. The Frankish custom of dividing the kingdom equally among the king's legitimate male heirs furthered this tendency.

By the seventh century, the Frankish king was king in title only and had no effective executive power. Real power came to be concentrated in the office of the "mayor of the palace," spokesperson at the king's court for the great landowners of the three regions into which the Frankish kingdom was divided: Neustria, Austrasia, and Burgundy. Through this office, the Carolingian dynasty rose to power.

The Carolingians controlled the office of the mayor of the palace from the ascent to that post of Pepin I of Austrasia (d. 639) until 751, when, with the enterprising connivance of the pope, they simply seized the Frankish crown. Pepin II (d. 714) ruled in fact, if not in title, over the Frankish kingdom. His illegitimate son, Charles Martel ("the Hammer," d. 741), created a great cavalry by bestowing lands known as benefices, or **fiefs**, on powerful noblemen. In return, they agreed to be ready to serve as the king's army.

The fiefs so generously bestowed by Charles Martel to create his army came in large part from landed property he usurped from the church. The Carolingians created counts almost entirely from among the same landed nobility from which the Carolingians themselves had risen. The Merovingians, in contrast, had tried to compete directly with these great aristocrats by raising landless men to power. By playing to strength rather than challenging it, the Carolingians strengthened themselves, at least for the short term. The church, by this time dependent on the protection of the Franks against the Eastern emperor and the Lombards, could only suffer the loss of its lands in silence. Later, although they never returned them, the Franks partially compensated the church for these lands.

**The Frankish Church**    The church came to play a large and enterprising role in the Frankish government. By Carolingian times, monasteries were a dominant force. Their intellectual achievements made them respected centers of culture. Their religious teaching and example imposed order on surrounding populations. Their relics and rituals made them magical shrines to which pilgrims came in great numbers. Also, thanks to their many gifts and internal discipline and industry, many had become profitable farms and landed estates, their abbots rich and powerful magnates. Already in Merovingian times, the higher clergy were employed along with counts as royal agents.

It was the policy of the Carolingians, perfected by Charles Martel and his successor, Pepin III ("the Short," d. 768), to use the church to pacify conquered neighboring tribes—Frisians, Thüringians, Bavarians, and especially the Franks' archenemies, the Saxons. Conversion to Nicene Christianity became an integral part of the successful annexation of conquered lands and people. Christian bishops in missionary districts and elsewhere became lords, appointed by and subject to the king. In this ominous integration of secular and religious policy lay the seeds of the later investiture controversy of the eleventh and twelfth centuries. (See Chapter 7.)

The church served more than Carolingian territorial expansion. Pope Zacharias (r. 741–752) also sanctioned Pepin the Short's termination of the Merovingian dynasty and supported the Carolingian accession to outright kingship of the Franks. With the pope's public blessing, Pepin was proclaimed king by the nobility in council in 751. Zacharias's successor, Pope Stephen II (r. 752–757), did not let Pepin forget the favor of his predecessor. In 753, when the Lombards besieged Rome, Pope Stephen crossed the Alps and appealed directly to Pepin to cast out the invaders and to guarantee papal claims to central Italy, largely dominated at this time by the Eastern emperor. In 755, the Franks defeated the Lombards and gave the pope the lands surrounding Rome, creating what came to be known as the **Papal States**.

**fiefs**   ("Lands") Granted to cavalry men to fund their equipment and service.

**Papal States**   Central part of Italy where Pope Stephen II became the secular ruler when confirmed by the Franks in 755.

**Holy Roman Empire**   The domain of the German monarchs who revived the use of the Roman imperial title during the Middle Ages.

The papacy had looked to the Franks for an ally strong enough to protect it from the Eastern emperors. It is an irony of history that the church found in the Carolingian dynasty a Western imperial government that drew almost as slight a boundary between state and church and between secular and religious policy as did Eastern emperors. Although Carolingian patronage was eminently preferable to Eastern domination for the popes, it proved in its own way to be no less constraining.

## THE REIGN OF CHARLEMAGNE (768–814)

Charlemagne, the son of Pepin the Short, continued the role of his father as papal protector in Italy and his policy of territorial conquest in the north. By the time of his death on January 28, 814, Charlemagne's kingdom embraced modern France, Belgium, Holland, Switzerland, almost the whole of western Germany, much of Italy, a portion of Spain, and the island of Corsica. (See Map 6–4.)

**The New Empire**   Encouraged by his ambitious advisers, Charlemagne came to harbor imperial designs. He desired to be not only king of all the Franks but a universal emperor as well. Although he permitted the church its independence, he looked after it with a paternalism almost as great as that of any Eastern emperor. He used the church, above all, to promote social stability and hierarchical order throughout the kingdom—as an aid in the creation of a great Frankish Christian Empire. Charlemagne fulfilled his imperial pretensions on Christmas Day 800, when Pope Leo III (r. 795–816) crowned him emperor in Rome. This event began what would come to be known as the **Holy Roman Empire**, a revival of the old Roman Empire in the West, based in Germany after 870.

In 799, Pope Leo III had been imprisoned by the Roman aristocracy but escaped to the protection of Charlemagne, who restored him as pope. The fateful coronation of Charlemagne was thus, in part, an effort by the pope to enhance the church's stature and to gain some leverage over this powerful king. It was, however, no papal coup d'état; Charlemagne's control over the church remained as strong after the event as before. If the coronation benefited the church, as it certainly did, it also served Charlemagne's purposes.

**The New Emperor**   Charlemagne stood a majestic six feet three and a half inches tall. He was restless, ever ready for a hunt. Informal and gregarious, he insisted on the presence of friends even when he bathed. He was widely known for his practical jokes, lusty good humor, and warm hospitality. His capital, Aachen, was a festive palace city to which people and gifts came from all over the world. In 802, Charlemagne even received from the caliph of Baghdad, Harun-al-Rashid, a white elephant, whose transport across the Alps was as great a wonder as the creature itself.

**Problems of Government**   Charlemagne governed his kingdom through counts, of whom there were perhaps as many as 250, strategically located within the administrative districts into which the kingdom was divided. Carolingian counts tended to be local magnates who possessed the armed might and the self-interest to enforce the will of a generous king. Counts had three main duties: to maintain a local army loyal to the king, to collect tribute and dues, and to administer justice throughout their districts.

This last responsibility a count undertook through a district law court known as the *mallus*. The *mallus* received testimony from witnesses familiar with the parties involved in a dispute or criminal case, much as a modern court does. On occasion, in difficult cases where the testimony was insufficient to determine guilt or innocence, recourse would be taken to judicial duels or to a variety of "divine" tests or ordeals. Among these was the length of time it took a defendant's hand to heal after immersion in boiling water. In another, a defendant was thrown with his hands and feet bound into a river or pond that a priest had blessed. If he floated, he was pronounced guilty, because the pure water had obviously rejected him; if, however, the water received him and he sank, he was deemed innocent and quickly retrieved.

As in Merovingian times, many counts used their official position and new judicial powers to their own advantage and became little despots within their districts. As the strong became stronger, they also became more independent. They began to look on the land grants with which they were paid as hereditary possessions rather than generous royal donations—a development that began to fragment Charlemagne's kingdom. Charlemagne tried to oversee his overseers and improve local justice by creating special royal envoys. Known as *missi dominici*, these were lay and clerical agents (counts, archbishops, and bishops) who made annual visits to districts other than their own. Yet their impact was marginal. Permanent provincial governors, bearing the title of prefect, duke, or margrave, were created in what was still another attempt to supervise the counts and organize the outlying regions of the kingdom. Yet as these governors became established in their areas, they proved no less corruptible than the others.

Charlemagne never solved the problem of creating a loyal bureaucracy. Ecclesiastical agents proved no better than secular ones in this regard. Landowning bishops had not only the same responsibilities, but also the same secular lifestyles and aspirations as the royal counts. *Capitularies,* or royal decrees, discouraged the more outrageous behav-

**MAP 6-4 The Empire of Charlemagne to 814** Building on the successes of his predecessors, Charlemagne greatly increased the Frankish domains. Such traditional enemies as the Saxons and the Lombards fell under his sway.

**What reasons** might Charlemagne have had for expanding the Frankish domains into the regions in which he did?

**Carolingian Administration**

◆ 250 counts administred empire
◆ Counts tended to become despots in their own regions
◆ Charlemagne often appointed churchmen to government offices

ior of the clergy. However, Charlemagne also sensed, and rightly so as the Gregorian reform of the eleventh century would prove, that the emergence of a distinctive, reform-minded class of ecclesiastical landowners would be a danger to royal government. He purposefully treated his bishops as he treated his counts, that is, as vassals who served at the king's pleasure.

**Alcuin and the Carolingian Renaissance** Charlemagne accumulated great wealth in the form of loot and land from conquered tribes. He used part of this booty to attract Europe's best scholars to Aachen, where they developed court culture and education. By making scholarship materially as well as intellectually rewarding, Charlemagne attracted such scholars as Theodulf of Orleans, Angilbert, his own biographer Einhard, and the renowned Anglo-Saxon master Alcuin of York (735–804). In 782, at almost fifty years of age, Alcuin became director of the king's palace school. He brought classical and Christian learning to Aachen in schools run by the monasteries. Alcuin was handsomely rewarded for his efforts with several monastic estates, including that of Saint Martin of Tours, the wealthiest in the kingdom.

Although Charlemagne also appreciated learning for its own sake, his grand palace school was not created simply for the love of classical scholarship. Charlemagne wanted to upgrade the administrative skills of the clerics and officials who staffed the royal bureaucracy. By preparing the sons of the nobility to run the religious and secular offices of the realm, court scholarship served kingdom building.

The school provided basic instruction in the seven liberal arts, with special concentration on grammar, logic, rhetoric, and the basic mathematical arts. It therefore provided training in reading, writing, speaking, sound reasoning, and counting—the basic tools of bureaucracy.

Among the results of this intellectual activity was the appearance of a more accurate Latin in official documents and the development of a clear style of handwriting known as *Carolingian minuscule*. By making reading both easier and more pleasurable, Carolingian minuscule helped lay the foundations of subsequent Latin scholarship. It also increased lay literacy.

A modest renaissance of antiquity occurred in the palace school as scholars collected and preserved ancient manuscripts for a more curious posterity. These scholarly activities aimed at concrete reforms and helped bring uniformity to church law and liturgy, educate the clergy, and improve monastic morals. Through personal correspondence and visitations, Alcuin created a genuine, if limited, community of scholars and clerics at court. He did much to infuse the highest administrative levels with a sense of comradeship and common purpose.

**Interior of the palace** chapel of Charlemagne, Aachen.

French Government Tourist Office

**What were the most important achievements of the Carolingian Renaissance?**

## BREAKUP OF THE CAROLINGIAN KINGDOM

In his last years, an ailing Charlemagne knew his empire was ungovernable. The seeds of dissolution lay in regionalism, that is, the determination of each region, no matter how small, to look first—and often only—to its own self-interest. Despite his skill and resolve, Charlemagne's realm became too fragmented among powerful regional magnates. Charlemagne had been forced to recognize and even to enhance the power of regional magnates to gain needed financial and military support. But as in the Merovingian kingdom, the tail came increasingly also to wag the dog in the Carolingian.

**Louis the Pious** The Carolingian kings did not give up easily, however. Charlemagne's only surviving son and successor was Louis the Pious (r. 814–840). After Charlemagne's death, Louis no longer referred to himself as king of the Franks. He bore instead the single title of emperor. The assumption of this title reflected not only the Carolingian pretense to be an imperial dynasty, but also Louis's determination to unify his kingdom and raise its people above mere regional and tribal loyalties.

Unfortunately, Louis's own fertility joined with Salic, or Frankish, law and custom to prevent the attainment of this high goal. Louis had three sons by his first wife. According to Salic law, a ruler partitioned his kingdom equally among his surviving sons (Salic law forbade women to inherit the throne). Louis, who saw himself as an emperor and no mere king, recognized that a tripartite kingdom would hardly be an empire and acted early in his reign, in 817, to break this legal tradition. This he did by making his eldest son, Lothar (d. 855), co-regent and sole imperial heir by royal decree. To Lothar's brothers he gave important, but much lesser, *appanages*, or assigned hereditary lands; Pepin (d. 838) became king of Aquitaine, and Louis "the German" (d. 876) became king of Bavaria, over the eastern Franks.

In 823, Louis's second wife, Judith of Bavaria, bore him a fourth son, Charles, later called "the Bald" (d. 877). Mindful of Frankish law and custom and determined her son should receive more than just a nominal inheritance, the queen incited the brothers Pepin and Louis against Lothar, who fled for refuge to the pope. More important, Judith was instrumental in persuading Louis to adhere to tradition and divide the kingdom equally among his four living sons. As their stepmother and the young Charles rose in their father's favor, the three brothers, fearing still further reversals, decided to act against their father. Supported by the pope, they joined forces and defeated their father in a battle near Colmar in 833.

As the bestower of crowns on emperors, the pope had an important stake in the preservation of the revived Western empire and the imperial title. Louis's belated agreement to an equal partition of his kingdom threatened to weaken the pope as well as the royal family. Therefore, the pope condemned Louis and restored Lothar to his original inheritance. But Lothar's regained imperial dignity only stirred anew the resentments of his brothers, including his stepbrother, Charles, who joined in renewed warfare against him.

**The Treaty of Verdun and Its Aftermath** In 843, with the Treaty of Verdun, peace finally came to the surviving heirs of Louis the Pious. (Pepin had died in 838.) The great Carolingian Empire was divided into three equal parts. Lothar received a middle section, known as Lotharingia, which embraced roughly modern Holland, Belgium, Switzerland, Alsace-Lorraine, and Italy. Charles the Bald acquired the western part of the kingdom, or roughly modern France. And Louis the German took the eastern part, or roughly modern Germany.

The Treaty of Verdun proved to be only the beginning of Carolingian fragmentation. When Lothar died in 855, his middle kingdom was divided equally among his three surviving sons, the eldest of whom, Louis II, retained Italy and the imperial title. This partition of the partition sealed the dissolution of the great empire of Charlemagne.

## MAJOR DEVELOPMENTS OF THE EARLY MIDDLE AGES

| | |
|---|---|
| **313** | Emperor Constantine legalizes Christianity |
| **ca. 251–356** | Anthony of Egypt inspires the monastic movement |
| **410** | Visigoths sack the city of Rome |
| **476** | Deposition of Romulus Augustulus, last Western Roman emperor |
| **ca. 466–511** | Clovis founds the Franks' Merovingian dynasty |
| **527–565** | Reign of Byzantine emperor Justinian |
| **622** | Muhammad's *Hegira*, the foundation of Islam |
| **732** | Charles Martel stops the Muslim advance at Tours |
| **751** | Pepin III founds the Carolingian dynasty |
| **768–814** | Reign of Charlemagne |
| **ca. 875–950** | Invasions, feudal fragmentation, and the Dark Ages |

**This seventy-five-foot-long** Viking burial ship from the early ninth century is decorated with beastly figures. It bore a dead queen, her servant, and assorted sacrificed animals to the afterlife. The bodies of the passengers were confined within a burial cabin at midship surrounded with a treasure trove of jewels and tapestries.

Dorling Kindersley Media Library. Universitets Oldsaksamling © Dorling Kindersley

**How did the Viking invasions disrupt European life in the early Middle Ages?**

In Italy the demise of the Carolingian emperors enhanced for the moment the power of the popes, who had become adept at filling vacuums. The popes were now strong enough to excommunicate weak emperors and override their wishes. In a major church crackdown on the polygyny of the Germans, Pope Nicholas I (r. 858–867) excommunicated Lothar II for divorcing his wife. After the death of the childless emperor Louis II in 875, Pope John VIII (r. 872–882) installed Charles the Bald as emperor against the express last wishes of Louis II.

When Charles the Bald died in 877, both the papal and the imperial thrones suffered defeat. They became pawns in the hands of powerful Italian and German magnates, respectively. The last Carolingian emperor died in 911. This internal political breakdown of the empire and the papacy coincided with new barbarian attacks.

**Vikings, Magyars, and Muslims**   The late ninth and tenth centuries saw successive waves of Normans (North-men), better known as Vikings, from Scandinavia, Magyars, or Hungarians, the great horsemen from the eastern plains, and Muslims from the south. The political breakdown of the Carolingian Empire coincided with these new external threats, both probably set off by overpopulation and famine in northern and eastern Europe.

Taking to the sea in rugged longboats of doubled-hulled construction, the Vikings terrified their neighbors to the south, invading and occupying English and European coastal and river towns. In the 880s, the Vikings even penetrated to Aachen and besieged Paris. In the ninth century, the Vikings turned York in northern England into a major trading post for their woolens, jewelry, and ornamental wares. Erik the Red made it to Greenland, and his son, Leif Erikson wintered in Newfoundland and may even have reached New England five hundred years before Columbus. In the eleventh century, Christian conversions and the English defeat of the Danes and Norwegians effectively restricted the Vikings to their Scandinavian homelands.

Magyars, the ancestors of the modern Hungarians, swept into Western Europe from the eastern plains, while Muslims made incursions across the Mediterranean from North Africa. The Franks built fortified towns and castles in strategic locations, and when they could, they bought off the invaders with grants of land and payments of silver. In the resulting turmoil, local populations became more dependent than ever on local strongmen for life, limb, and livelihood—the essential precondition for the maturation of feudal society.

# FEUDAL SOCIETY

**WHAT WERE** the characteristics of a feudal society?

The Middle Ages were characterized by a chronic absence of effective central government and the constant threat of famine, disease, and foreign invasion. In this state of affairs, the weaker sought the protection of the stronger, and the true lords and masters became those who could guarantee immediate security from violence and starvation. The term *feudal society* refers to the social, political, military, and economic system that emerged from these conditions.

## ORIGINS

The origins of feudal government can be found in the divisions and conflicts of Merovingian society. In the sixth and seventh centuries, it became customary for individual freemen who did not already belong to families or groups that could protect them to place themselves under the protection of more powerful freemen. In this way the latter built up armies and became local magnates, and the former solved the problem of simple survival. Freemen who so entrusted themselves to others came to be described as **vassals**, *vassi* or

**vassal**   A person granted an estate or cash payments in return for rendering services to a lord.

"those who serve," from which evolved the term *vassalage*, meaning the placement of one-self in the personal service of another who promises protection in return.

Landed nobles, like kings, tried to acquire as many such vassals as they could, because military strength in the early Middle Ages lay in numbers. Because it proved impossible to maintain these growing armies within the lord's own household (as was the original custom) or to support them by special monetary payments, the practice evolved of simply granting them land as a "tenement." Vassals were expected to dwell on these *benefices*, or fiefs, and maintain horses, armor, and weapons in good order. Originally, vassals therefore were little more than gangs-in-waiting.

## VASSALAGE AND THE FIEF

Vassalage involved "fealty" to the lord. To swear fealty was to promise to refrain from any action that might in any way threaten the lord's well-being and to perform personal services for him on his request. Chief among the expected services was military duty as a mounted knight. This could involve a variety of activities: a short or long military expedition, escort duty, standing castle guard, or placing his own fortress at the lord's disposal, if the vassal had one. Limitations were placed on the number of days a lord could require services from a vassal. In France in the eleventh century, about forty days of service a year were considered sufficient. It also became possible for vassals to buy their way out of military service by a monetary payment, known as scutage. The lord, in turn, could use this payment to hire mercenaries, who often proved more efficient than contract-conscious vassals.

Beginning with the reign of Louis the Pious (r. 814–840), bishops and abbots swore fealty to the king and received their offices from him as a *benefice*. The king formally "invested" these clerics in their offices during a special ceremony in which he presented them with a ring and a staff, the symbols of high spiritual office. Long a sore point with the church, lay investiture of the clergy provoked a serious confrontation of church and state in the late tenth and eleventh centuries. At that time, reform-minded clergy rebelled against what they then believed to be a kind of involuntary clerical vassalage. Even reform-minded clerics, however, welcomed the king's grants of land and power to the clergy.

The lord's obligations to his vassals were specific. First, he was obligated to protect the vassal from physical harm and to stand as his advocate in public court. After fealty was sworn and homage paid, the lord provided for the vassal's physical maintenance by the bestowal of a *benefice*, or fief. The fief was simply the physical or material wherewithal to meet the vassal's military and other obligations. It could take the form of liquid wealth, as well as the more common grant of real property.

## DAILY LIFE AND RELIGION

**The Humble Carolingian Manor**   The agrarian economy of the early Middle Ages was organized and controlled through village farms known as manors. On these, peasants labored as tenants for a lord, that is, a more powerful landowner who allotted them land and tenements in exchange for their services and a portion of their crops. The part of the land tended for the lord was the *demesne*, on average about one-quarter to one-third of the arable land. All crops grown there were harvested for the lord. The manor also included common meadows for grazing animals and forests reserved exclusively for the lord to hunt in.

Peasants were treated according to their personal status and the size of their tenements. A freeman, that is, a peasant with his own modest *allodial*, or hereditary property (property free from the claims of an overlord), became a **serf** by surrendering his property to a greater landowner—a lord—in exchange for protection and assistance. The freeman received his land back from the lord with a clear definition of his economic and legal rights. Although the land was no longer his property, he had full

**serf** Peasant bound to the land he worked.

possession and use of it, and the number of services and amount of goods he was to supply to the lord were carefully spelled out.

Peasants who entered the service of a lord with little real property (perhaps only a few farm implements and animals) ended up as unfree serfs. Such serfs were far more vulnerable to the lord's demands, often spending up to three days a week working the lord's fields. Peasants who had nothing to offer a lord except their hands had the lowest status and were the least protected from excessive demands on their labor.

By the time of Charlemagne, the moldboard plow and the three-field system of land cultivation were coming into use. The moldboard plow cut deep into the soil, turning it to form a ridge, which provided a natural drainage system and permitted the deep planting of seeds. This made cultivation possible in the regions north of the Mediterranean, where soils were dense and waterlogged from heavy precipitation. The **three-field system** alternated fallow with planted fields each year, and this increased the amount of cultivated land by leaving only one-third fallow in a given year. It also better adjusted crops to seasons. In fall, one field was planted with winter crops of wheat or rye, to be harvested in early summer. In late spring, a second field was planted with summer crops of oats, barley, and beans. The third field was left fallow, to be planted in its turn with winter and summer crops. The new summer crops, especially beans, restored nitrogen to the soil and helped increase yields. (See "Encountering the Past: Medieval Cooking.")

These developments made possible what has been called the "expansion of Europe within Europe." They permitted the old lands formerly occupied by barbarians to be cultivated and filled with farms and towns. This, in turn, led to major population growth in the north and ultimately a shift of political power from the Mediterranean to northern Europe.

**The Cure of Carolingian Souls**   The lower clergy lived among, and were drawn from, peasant ranks. They fared hardly better than peasants in Carolingian times. As owners of the churches on their lands, the lords had the right to raise chosen serfs to the post of parish priest, placing them in charge of the churches on the lords' estates. Church law directed a lord to set a serf free before he entered the clergy. Lords, however, preferred a "serf priest," one who not only said the Mass on Sundays and holidays, but who also continued to serve his lord during the week.

The ordinary people looked to religion for comfort and consolation. They especially associated religion with the major Christian holidays and festivals, such as Christmas and Easter. They baptized their children, attended mass, tried to learn the Lord's Prayer and the Apostles' Creed, and received the last rites from the priest as death approached. Because local priests on the manors were no better educated than their congregations, religious instruction in the meaning of Christian doctrine and practice remained at a bare minimum.

## FRAGMENTATION AND DIVIDED LOYALTY

In addition to the fragmentation brought about by the multiplication of vassalage, effective occupation of land led gradually to claims of hereditary possession. Hereditary possession became a legally recognized principle in the ninth century and laid the basis for claims to real ownership. Fiefs given as royal donations became hereditary possessions and, over time, sometimes even the real property of the possessor.

Further, vassal obligations increased in still another way as enterprising freemen sought to accumulate as much land as possible. One man could become a vassal to several different lords. This development led in the ninth century to the "liege lord"—the one master the vassal must obey even against his other masters, should a direct conflict arise among them.

The problem of loyalty was reflected both in the literature of the period, with its praise of the virtues of honor and fidelity, and in the ceremonial development of the very

---

**three-field system**   Developed by medieval farmers, a system in which three fields were utilized during different growing seasons to limit the amount of nonproductive plowing and to restore soil fertility through crop rotation.

# ENCOUNTERING THE PAST

## MEDIEVAL COOKING

*Medieval cooks served things that modern diners would recognize: roasts, pastas, meat pies, and custards. But where modern chefs are preoccupied primarily with the taste of their fare, medieval cooks worried about the effect of their dishes on diners' health. Medieval physicians traced illness to imbalances among the so-called four humors: blood, black bile, yellow bile, and phlegm. Because the humors were generated by food, recipes had to be planned like medicines. Health depended on maintaining a balance between the poles of the opposites that the humors nurtured: wet–dry, cold–warm. If not moderated by cool, wet seasonings, a spicy dish might produce an excess of hot, dry humors that made one ill.*

Medieval people correctly intuited a link between diet and health, but from the modern point of view this did them little good. A fixation on meat as a prestige food meant vegetables were little appreciated. Most Europeans survived on a diet of mush or a porridge made by boiling bread in milk.

Medieval cooks were expected to be artists as well as scientists. Formal dining called for elaborately constructed dishes, such as castles executed in pastry or cooked birds stuffed back into their feathered skins. Dishes were sometimes tinted strange colors, modeled into odd shapes, or rendered otherwise amusing to the eye.

**[Top] The Lord of** the Manor Dining **[Bottom] Kitchen Scene, Chopping Meat**

From *The Luttrell Psalter*, by permission of The British Library (1000102.021)

**What was the relationship between the lord of the manor and the serfs and others who inhabited the manor?**

DID THE medieval understanding of the link between diet and health differ from the modern understanding— or was only the explanation different?

---

act of commendation by which a freeman became a vassal. In the mid–eighth century, an oath of fealty highlighted the ceremony. A vassal reinforced his promise of fidelity to the lord by swearing a special oath with his hand on a sacred relic or the Bible. In the tenth and eleventh centuries, paying homage to the lord involved not only swearing such an oath, but also placing the vassal's hands between the lord's and sealing the ceremony with a kiss.

As the centuries passed, personal loyalty and service became secondary to the acquisition of property. In developments that signaled the waning of feudal society in the tenth century, the fief came to overshadow fealty, the *benefice* became more important than vassalage, and freemen would swear allegiance to the highest bidder.

Feudal arrangements nonetheless provided stability throughout the early Middle Ages and aided the difficult process of political centralization during the High Middle Ages (c. 1000–1300). The genius of feudal government lay in its adaptability. Contracts of different kinds could be made with almost anybody, as circumstances required. The process embraced a wide spectrum of people, from the king at the top to the lowliest vassal in the remotest part of the kingdom. The foundations of the modern nation-state would emerge in France and England from the fine-tuning of essentially feudal arrangements as kings sought to adapt their goal of centralized government to the reality of local power and control.

# SUMMARY

## HOW DID Germanic migrations contribute to the fall of the Roman Empire?

**On the Eve of the Frankish Ascendancy** In the late fourth century, the Western empire was weakening, and the Visigoths were being forced out of their own home territories by invading Huns. The Visigoths defeated the Romans in the ensuing conflict. Soon other barbarians had established territories within the Western empire. By the mid–fifth century, Rome had been sacked repeatedly, and by the end of the century the Western empire was history. Roman culture endured, although it was transformed through its contact with the Germanic peoples. Christianity, too, endured and changed through cultural contact. *page 150*

## HOW DID the Byzantine Empire continue the legacy of Rome?

**The Byzantine Empire** The eastern portion of the Roman Empire endured as the Byzantine Empire. Although the empire lasted until Constantinople (the capital) fell to the Turks in 1453, it peaked under Justinian, in the mid–sixth century. Although Justinian and his wife, the empress Theodora, were both Christians, she was a believer in Monophysitism, a heresy that influenced the later course of the empire's history. Justinian codified Roman law, which was to prove influential in the West for centuries. Justinian supported Orthodox Christianity, although some of his successors supported other forms of Christianity. Constantinople and smaller urban centers formed the economic, administrative, and cultural backbone of the empire. The empire's eastern orientation increased under Heraclius in the early seventh century. In the early eighth century, Leo's Caesaropapism led him to attempt to ban the use of images in churches. *page 152*

## HOW DID Islamic culture influence the West?

**Islam and the Islamic World** In the seventh century, Muhammad founded a new religion on the Arabian peninsula. In 624, Muhammad's Medina-based army conquered Mecca, and in the following years the basic rules of Islamic life were articulated. Islam expanded substantially, until by 750 the Islamic Empire stretched from Spain through North Africa, the southern and eastern Mediterranean, and eastward into India. But this was the peak of Muslim territorial expansion, and Islam did not spread farther than Spain into the remnants of the Western Roman Empire. The West profited from its contact with Islam, since much of the Arab world's technology and scholarship was superior to Europe's in the early Middle Ages. *page 155*

## HOW DID the developing Christian church influence Western society during the early Middle Ages?

**Western Society and the Developing Christian Church** As trade declined throughout the West, people migrated from cities to farmlands. New types of relationships between landowners and peasants emerged, including serfdom, the manorial system, and the feudal system. The Christian church provided a strong element of continuity with the educational and administrative achievements of the Roman Empire. Monastic culture took shape. Christianity was a potent unifying and civilizing force within the West, although it was also the source of a fundamental rift with the Eastern Empire. By the middle of the eighth century, the papacy in Rome faced military threats from the north and doctrinal threats from the East; Pope Stephen boldly initiated an alliance with the Franks that influenced history for the next millennium or more. *page 160*

## HOW DID the reign of Clovis differ from that of Charlemagne?

**The Kingdom of the Franks: From Clovis to Charlemagne** Clovis founded the first Frankish dynasty, the Merovingians. Then the Carolingian dynasty made strategic alliances with the landed nobility and with the church. The most illustrious Carolingian ruler, Charlemagne, conquered additional lands and, on Christmas Day in 800 had himself crowned Holy Roman Emperor by Pope Leo III. His capital, Aachen, was a center of scholarship and intelligent administration. The social organization of the manor and innovations such as new plows improved agricultural productivity. Soon after Charlemagne's death in 814, his empire disintegrated as it was divided up, messily, among his grandsons. The late ninth and early tenth centuries were truly "dark ages" in Europe: Both secular and church-based organizations were weak, and at the same time invaders such as the Vikings were attacking. Peasants sought security at almost any price, so the institution of feudalism spread and matured. *page 164*

## WHAT WERE the characteristics of a feudal society?

**Feudal Society** The feudal system was built around the exchange of land, labor, and military protection. Vassals would swear fealty to a more powerful individual, in return for the promise of protection. Kings and nobles built their military strength by acquiring increasing numbers of vassals; as the system developed, benefices replaced residence in the lord's household, scutage replaced direct military service, and other innovations formalized and institutionalized the relationships of feudal society. All participants in the feudal system constantly negotiated and competed for advantage. Loyalties could become divided as vassals swore fealty to multiple lords to gain multiple landholdings. Eventually, vassals could claim hereditary possession of the lands they worked, reducing their sense of obligation to lords. Nonetheless, feudalism provided a first glimpse of many of the political and legal institutions that developed into the modern nation-state. *page 170*

# REVIEW QUESTIONS

1. What changes took place in the Frankish kingdom between its foundation and the end of Charlemagne's reign? What were the characteristics of Charlemagne's government? Why did Charlemagne encourage learning at his court? Why did his empire break apart?

2. How and why was the history of the eastern half of the former Roman Empire so different from that of its western half? Did Justinian strengthen or weaken the Byzantine Empire? How does his reign compare to Charlemagne's?

3. What were the tenets of Islam? How were the Muslims able to build an empire so quickly? What contributions did the Muslims make to the development of Western Europe?

4. How and why did feudal society begin? What were the essential features of feudalism? Do you think modern society could slip back into a feudal pattern?

## KEY TERMS

**Caesaropapism** (p. 163)
**caliphate** (p. 156)
**fiefs** (p. 165)
*Hegira* (p. 156)
**Holy Roman Empire** (p. 166)
**iconoclasm** (p. 163)
**Islam** (p. 155)
**Ka'ba** (p. 155)
**Monophysites** (p. 163)

**Papal States** (p. 165)
**Qur'an** (p. 155)
**serf** (p. 171)
**Shi'a** (p. 156)
**Sunnis** (p. 157)
**three-field system** (p. 172)
*ulema* (p. 156)
**vassal** (p. 170)

For additional learning resources related to this chapter, please go to **www.myhistorylab.com**

myhistorylab

# 7

# The High Middle Ages: The Rise of European Empires and States (1000–1300)

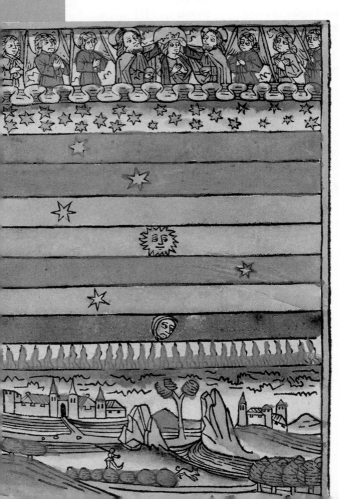

**In medieval Europe,** the traditional geocentric or earth-centered universe was usually depicted by concentric circles. In this popular German work on natural history, medicine, and science, Konrad von Megenberg (1309–1374) depicted the universe in a most unusual but effective manner. The seven known planets are contained within straight horizontal bands that separate the earth, below, from heaven, populated by the saints, above.

Konrad von Megenberg. *Buch der Natur* (Book of Nature). Augsburg: Johannes Bämler, 1481. Rosenwald Collection. Courtesy of the Library of Congress. Rare Book and Special Collections Division.

**How were medieval ideas of social and political hierarchy reflected in medieval models of the universe?**

E urope in the High Middle Ages (1000–1300) was characterized by political expansion and consolidation and by intellectual flowering and synthesis. This may indeed have been a more creative era than the Italian Renaissance or the German Reformation.

The borders of western Europe were secured against invaders, and Europeans, who had long been the prey of foreign powers, mounted a military and economic offensive against the East. By adapting feudal traditions, the rulers of England and France established nuclei for centrally governed nation-states. The parliaments and popular assemblies that emerged in some places enabled the propertied classes to exert some political influence. Germany and Italy, however, resisted the general trend toward political consolidation and remained fragmented until the nineteenth century.

The distinctive Western belief in the separation of church and state was established during the High Middle Ages. The popes acquired monarchical authority over the church and prevented it from being absorbed into Europe's emerging nation-states. Their methods, however, led to accusations that the papacy was diverting the church from its spiritual mission into the murky world of politics. ▪

# OTTO I AND THE REVIVAL OF THE EMPIRE

**HOW WAS** Otto able to secure the power of his Saxon dynasty?

The fortunes of both the old empire and the papacy began to revive after the dark period of the late ninth century and the early tenth century. In 918, the Saxon Henry I ("the Fowler," d. 936), the strongest of the German dukes, became the first non-Frankish king of Germany.

## UNIFYING GERMANY

Henry rebuilt royal power by forcibly combining the duchies of Swabia, Bavaria, Saxony, Franconia, and Lotharingia. He secured imperial borders by checking the invasions of the Hungarians and the Danes. Although much smaller than Charlemagne's empire, the German kingdom Henry created placed his son and successor Otto I (r. 936–973) in a strong territorial position.

The able Otto maneuvered his own kin into positions of power in Bavaria, Swabia, and Franconia. He refused to recognize each duchy as an independent hereditary entity, as the nobility increasingly expected, treating each instead as a subordinate member of a unified kingdom. In a truly imperial gesture in 951, he invaded Italy and proclaimed himself its king. In 955, he won his most magnificent victory by defeating the Hungarians at Lechfeld. That victory secured German borders against new barbarian attacks, further unified the German duchies, and earned Otto the well-deserved title "the Great."

## EMBRACING THE CHURCH

As part of a careful rebuilding program, Otto, following the example of his predecessors, enlisted the church. Bishops and abbots—men who possessed a sense of universal empire, yet because they did not marry, could not found competitive dynasties—were made princes and agents of the king.

In 961, Otto, who had long aspired to the imperial crown, responded to a call for help from Pope John XII (r. 955–964), who was then being bullied by an Italian enemy of the German king, Berengar of Friuli. In recompense for this rescue, Pope John crowned Otto emperor on February 2, 962. Otto, for his part, recognized the existence of the Papal States and proclaimed himself their special protector. Over time, such close cooperation between emperor and pope put the church more than ever under royal control.

Pope John belatedly recognized the royal web in which the church was becoming entangled and joined the Italian opposition to the new emperor. This turnabout brought Otto's swift revenge. An ecclesiastical synod over which Otto presided deposed Pope John and proclaimed that henceforth no pope could take office without first swearing an oath of allegiance to the emperor. Under Otto I, popes ruled at the emperor's pleasure.

Otto's successors—Otto II (r. 973–983) and Otto III (r. 983–1002)—became so preoccupied with running the affairs of Italy that their German base began to disintegrate, sacrificed to imperial dreams. The Ottonians reached far beyond their grasp when they tried to subdue Italy. As the briefly revived empire began to crumble in the first quarter of the eleventh century, the church, long unhappy with Carolingian and Ottonian domination, prepared to declare its independence and exact its own vengeance.

# THE REVIVING CATHOLIC CHURCH

During the late ninth and early tenth centuries, the clergy had become tools of kings and magnates, and the papacy a toy of Italian nobles. The church was about to gain renewed respect and authority, however, thanks not only to the failing fortunes of the overextended Ottonian empire, but also to a new, determined force for reform within the church itself.

**WHAT EXPLAINS** the popularity of the Cluniac reform movement?

## THE CLUNY REFORM MOVEMENT

The great monastery in Cluny in east-central France gave birth to a profoundly important monastic reform movement. The reformers of Cluny were aided by widespread popular respect for the church that found expression in lay religious fervor and generous baronial patronage of religious houses. Since the fall of the Roman Empire, popular support for the church had been especially inspired by the example set by monks. Monks remained the least secularized and most spiritual of the church's clergy. Their cultural achievements were widely admired, their relics and rituals were considered magical, and their high religious ideals and sacrifices were imitated by the laity.

William the Pious, duke of Aquitaine, founded Cluny in 910. Although the reformers who emerged at Cluny were loosely organized and their demands not always consistent, they shared a determination to maintain a spiritual church. They absolutely rejected the subservience of the clergy, especially that of the German bishops, to royal authority. They taught that the pope in Rome was sole ruler over all the clergy.

No local secular rulers, the Cluniacs asserted, could have any control over their monasteries. And they further denounced the sins of the flesh of the "secular" parish clergy, who maintained concubines in a relationship akin to marriage. The Cluny reformers thus resolved to free the clergy from both kings and "wives"—to create an independent and chaste clergy. Thus, the distinctive Western separation of church and state, and the celibacy of the Catholic clergy, both of which continue today, had their definitive origins in the Cluny reform movement.

Cluny rapidly became a center from which reformers were dispatched to other monasteries throughout France and Italy. Under its aggressive abbots, especially Saint Odo (r. 926–946), it grew to embrace almost fifteen hundred dependent cloisters, each devoted to monastic and church reform. In the latter half of the eleventh century, the Cluny reformers reached the summit of their influence when the papacy itself embraced their reform program.

**The monastery at Cluny.**
Kenneth J. Conant/French Embassy

In the late ninth and early tenth centuries the proclamation of a series of church decrees, called the Peace of God, reflected the influence of the Cluny movement. These decrees tried to lessen the endemic warfare of medieval society by threatening excommunication for all who, at any time, harmed members of such vulnerable groups as women, peasants, merchants, and the clergy. The Peace of God was subsequently reinforced by the Truce of God, a church order proclaiming that all men must abstain from violence and warfare during a certain part of each week (eventually from Wednesday night to Monday morning) and in all holy seasons.

Popes devoted to reforms like those urged by Cluny came to power during the reign of Emperor Henry III (r. 1039–1056). Pope Leo IX (r. 1049–1054) promoted regional synods to oppose *simony* (the selling of spiritual things, especially church offices) and clerical marriage (celibacy was not strictly enforced among the secular clergy until after the eleventh century). He also placed Cluniacs in key administrative posts in Rome.

During the turbulent minority of Henry III's successor, Henry IV (r. 1056–1106), reform popes began to assert themselves more openly. Pope Stephen IX (1057–1058) reigned without imperial ratification, contrary to the earlier declaration of Otto I. Pope Nicholas II (1059–1061) decreed in 1059 that a body of high church officials and advisers, known as the College of Cardinals, would henceforth choose the pope, establishing the procedures for papal succession that the Catholic Church still follows. With this action, the papacy declared its full independence from both local Italian and distant royal interference. Rulers continued nevertheless to have considerable indirect influence on the election of popes.

## THE INVESTITURE STRUGGLE: GREGORY VII AND HENRY IV

Alexander's successor was Pope Gregory VII (r. 1073–1085), a fierce advocate of Cluny's reforms who had entered the papal bureaucracy a quarter of a century earlier during the pontificate of Leo IX. It was he who put the church's declaration of independence to the test. Cardinal Humbert, a prominent reformer, argued that lay investiture of the clergy—that is, the appointment of bishops and other church officials by secular officials and rulers—was the worst form of simony. In 1075, Pope Gregory embraced these arguments and condemned, under penalty of excommunication, lay investiture of clergy at any level.

Gregory's prohibition came as a jolt to royal authority. Since the days of Charlemagne, emperors had routinely passed out bishoprics to favored clergy. Bishops, who received royal estates, were the emperors' appointees and servants of the state. Henry IV's Carolingian and Ottonian predecessors had carefully nurtured the theocratic character of the empire in both concept and administrative bureaucracy. The church and religion had become integral parts of government.

Now the emperor, Henry IV, suddenly found himself ordered to secularize the empire by drawing a distinct line between the spheres of temporal and spiritual—royal and ecclesiastical—authority and jurisdiction. Henry considered Gregory's action a direct challenge to his authority. The territorial princes, however, eager to see the emperor weakened, were quick to see the advantages of Gregory's ruling. If a weak emperor could not gain a bishop's ear, then a strong prince might, thus bringing the offices of the church into his orbit of power. In the hope of gaining an advantage over both the emperor and the clergy in their territory, the princes fully supported Gregory's edict.

The lines of battle were quickly drawn. Henry assembled his loyal German bishops at Worms in January 1076 and had them proclaim their independence from Gregory. Gregory promptly responded with the church's heavy artillery: He excommunicated Henry and absolved all Henry's subjects from loyalty to him. This turn of events delighted the German princes, and Henry found himself facing a general revolt led by the duchy of Saxony. He had no recourse but to come to terms with Gregory. In a famous scene, Henry prostrated himself outside Gregory's castle retreat at Canossa on January 25, 1077. There he reportedly stood barefoot in the snow off and on for three days before the pope agreed to absolve him.

Papal power had at this moment reached a pinnacle. But Gregory's power, as he must have known when he restored Henry to power, was soon to be challenged.

Henry regrouped his forces, regained much of his power within the empire, and soon acted as if the humiliation at Canossa had never occurred. In March 1080, Gregory excommunicated Henry once again, but this time the action was ineffectual. In 1084, Henry, absolutely dominant, installed his own antipope, Clement III, and forced Gregory into exile, where he died the following year. It appeared as if the old practice of kings controlling popes had been restored—with a vengeance. Clement, however, was never recognized within the church, and Gregory's followers, who retained wide popular support, later regained power.

The settlement of the investiture controversy came in 1122 with the Concordat of Worms. Emperor Henry V (r. 1106–1125) formally renounced his power to invest bishops with ring and staff. In exchange, Pope Calixtus II (r. 1119–1124) recognized the emperor's right to be present and to invest bishops with fiefs before and after their investment with ring and staff by the church. The old church-state back-scratching in this way continued, but now on different terms. The clergy received their offices and attendant religious powers solely from ecclesiastical authority and no longer from kings and emperors. Rulers continued to bestow lands and worldly goods on high clergy in the hope of influencing them. The Concordat of Worms thus made the clergy more independent, but not necessarily less worldly.

## THE CRUSADES

If an index of popular piety and support for the pope in the High Middle Ages is needed, the **Crusades** amply provide it. What the Cluny reform was to the clergy, the Crusades to the Holy Land were to the laity: an outlet for the heightened religious zeal, much of it fanatical, of the late eleventh and twelfth centuries.

Late in the eleventh century, the Byzantine Empire was under severe pressure from the Seljuk Turks, and the Eastern emperor, Alexius I Comnenus (r. 1081–1118), appealed for Western aid. At the Council of Clermont in 1095, Pope Urban II (r. 1088–1099) responded positively to that appeal, setting the First Crusade in motion. (See "Compare & Connect: Christian *Jihad*, Muslim *Jihad*," pages 184–185.) This event has puzzled some historians, because the First Crusade was a risky venture. Yet the pope, the nobility, and Western society at large had much to gain by removing large numbers of nobility temporarily from Europe. Too many idle, restless noble youths spent too great a part of their lives feuding with each other and raiding other people's lands. The nobility, in turn, saw that fortunes could be made in foreign wars. Pope Urban may well have believed that the Crusade would reconcile and reunite Western and Eastern Christianity.

The early Crusades were inspired by genuine religious piety and carefully orchestrated by a revived papacy. Popes promised the first Crusaders a plenary indulgence should they die in battle. That was a complete remission of the temporal punishment due them for unrepented mortal sins, and hence a release from suffering for them in purgatory. In addition to this spiritual reward, the prospect of a Holy War against the Muslim infidel also propelled the Crusaders.

**QUICK REVIEW**
**Investiture Struggle**

◆ Investiture struggle centered on authority to appoint and control clergy

◆ Pope Gregory excommunicated Henry IV when he proclaimed his independence from papacy

◆ Crisis settled in 1122 with Concordat of Worms

**Crusades** Campaigns authorized by the church to combat heresies and rival faiths.

En route the Crusaders also began a general cleansing of Christendom that would intensify during the thirteenth-century papacy of Pope Innocent III. Accompanied by the new mendicant orders of Dominicans and Franciscans, Christian knights attempted to rid Europe of Jews as well as Muslims. Along the Crusaders' routes, especially in the Rhineland, Jewish communities were subjected to pogroms.

**The First Victory** The Crusaders had not assembled merely to defend Europe's outermost borders against Muslim aggression. Their goal was to rescue the holy city of Jerusalem, which had been in the hands of the Muslims since the seventh century. To this end, three great armies—tens of thousands of Crusaders—gathered in France, Germany, and Italy and, taking different routes, reassembled in Constantinople in 1097. (See Map 7–1.) From there, they soundly defeated one Muslim army after another in a

## MAP EXPLORATION

Interactive map: To explore this map further, go to www.myhistorylab.com

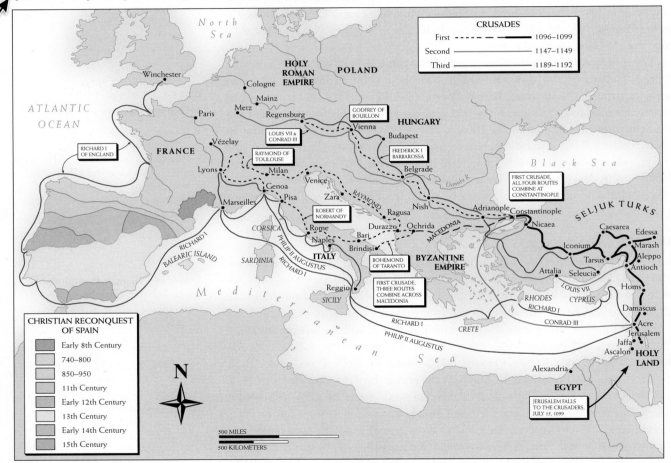

**MAP 7–1** **The Early Crusades** Routes and several leaders of the Crusades during the first century of the movement are shown. The names on this map do not exhaust the list of great nobles who went on the First Crusade. The even showier array of monarchs of the Second and Third Crusades still left the Crusades, on balance, ineffective in achieving their goals.

**Compare and** contrast the scope and result of each of the first three Crusades. Overall, how successful were these Crusades?

steady advance toward Jerusalem, which they captured on July 15, 1099. The Crusaders owed their victory to superior military discipline and weaponry and were also helped by the deep political divisions within the Islamic world that prevented a unified Muslim resistance.

The victorious Crusaders divided conquered territories into the feudal states of Jerusalem, Edessa, and Antioch, which were apportioned to them as fiefs from the pope. The Crusaders, however, remained small islands within a great sea of Muslims, who looked on the Western invaders as savages to be slain or driven out. Once settled in the Holy Land, the Crusaders found themselves increasingly on the defensive. Now an occupying rather than a conquering army, they became obsessed with fortification, building castles and forts throughout the Holy Land, the ruins of which can still be seen today.

Once secure within their new enclaves, the Crusaders ceased to live off the land, as they had done since departing Europe, and increasingly relied on imports from home. As they developed the economic resources of their new possessions, the once fierce warriors were transformed into international traders and businessmen.

**The Second and Third Crusades**   Native resistance broke the Crusaders' resolve around mid-century, and the forty-year-plus Latin presence in the East began to crumble. Edessa fell to Islamic armies in 1144. A Second Crusade, preached by Christendom's most eminent religious leader, the Cistercian monk Bernard of Clairvaux (1091–1153), attempted a rescue but met with dismal failure. In October 1187, Saladin (1138–1193), king of Egypt and Syria, reconquered Jerusalem. Save for a brief interlude in the thirteenth century, the holiest of cities remained thereafter in Islamic hands until the twentieth century.

A Third Crusade in the twelfth century (1189–1192) attempted yet another rescue, led by the most powerful Western rulers: Hohenstaufen emperor Frederick Barbarossa, Richard the Lion-Hearted, the king of England, and Philip Augustus, the king of France. It became instead a tragicomic commentary on the passing of the original crusading spirit. Frederick Barbarossa drowned while fording a small stream, the Saleph River, near the end of his journey across Asia Minor. Richard the Lion-Hearted and Philip Augustus reached Palestine, only to shatter the Crusaders' unity and chances of victory by their intense personal rivalry.

The long-term results of the first three Crusades had little to do with their original purpose. Politically and religiously they were a failure. The Holy Land reverted as firmly as ever to Muslim hands. The Crusades had, however, been a safety valve for violence-prone Europeans. More importantly, they stimulated Western trade with the East, as Venetian, Pisan, and Genoan merchants followed the Crusaders across Byzantium to lucrative new markets. The need to resupply the Christian settlements in the Near East also created new trade routes and reopened old ones long closed by Islamic supremacy over the Mediterranean.

**The Fourth Crusade**   It is a commentary on both the degeneration of the original crusading ideal and the Crusaders' true historical importance that a Fourth Crusade transformed itself into a piratical, commercial venture controlled by the Venetians. In 1202, 30,000 Crusaders arrived in Venice to set sail for Egypt. When they could not pay the price of transport, the Venetians negotiated an alternative venture: the conquest of Zara, a rival Christian port on the Adriatic. Zara, however, proved to be only their first digression; in 1204, they beseiged, captured, and sacked Constantinople itself.

This stunning event brought Venice new lands and maritime rights that assured its domination of the eastern Mediterranean. Constantinople was now the center for Western

**Thirteenth-century statue** of St. Maurice, patron saint of Magdeburg, Germany. An Egyptian Christian who commanded a Roman legion, St. Maurice was executed in 286 C.E. after refusing to worship the Roman gods. Portrayed as a white man for centuries, during the era of the Crusades, Maurice became a perfect talisman for Europeans venturing eastward.

Constantin Beyer

**What made St. Maurice so appealing to the Crusaders?**

# CHRISTIAN *JIHAD*, MUSLIM *JIHAD*

On November 26, 1095, Pope Urban II summoned the First Crusade to the Holy Land, its mission to take back Jerusalem from the Muslims. In a seeming propaganda and smear campaign, Urban depicted Muslims as savages. Roughly four years later, July 15, 1099, Western Crusaders captured the holy city with overwhelming force and untold carnage.

Eighty-eight years later, October 2, 1187, the fabled Sultan of Egypt and Syria, Saladin, returned Jerusalem to the Muslim fold by defeating the Third Crusade. During his march to Jerusalem, he massacred captured members of the Christian military religious orders of the Knights Templars and the Hospitallers, who were escorts and protectors of Christians journeying back and forth to the Holy Land.

## QUESTIONS

1. Were the Christian Crusades, as the pope argued, a legitimate reclamation of the Christian Holy Land, or a preemptive Christian *jihad*?

2. Did Saladin's counteroffensive have stronger legal and moral grounds?

3. What role did religion play in the behavior of both sides?

## I. POPE URBAN II (R. 1088–1099) PREACHES THE FIRST CRUSADE

*When Pope Urban II summoned the First Crusade in a sermon at the Council of Clermont on November 26, 1095, he painted at savage picture of the Muslims who controlled Jerusalem. Urban also promised the Crusaders, who responded by the tens of thousands, remission of their unrepented sins and assurance of heaven. Robert the Monk is one of four witnesses who has left us a summary of the sermon.*

From the confines of Jerusalem and the city of Constantinople a horrible tale has gone forth and very frequently has been brought to our ears, namely, that a race from the kingdom of the Persians [that is, the Seljuk Turks], an accursed race, a race utterly alienated from God, a generation forsooth which has not directed its heart and has not entrusted its spirit to God, has invaded the lands of those Christians and has depopulated them by the sword, pillage and fire; it has led away a part of the captives into its own country, and a part it has destroyed by cruel tortures; it has either entirely destroyed the churches of God or appropriated them for the rites of its own religion. They destroy the altars, after having defiled them with their uncleanness. They circumcise the Christians, and the blood of the circumcision they either spread upon the altars or pour into the vases of the baptismal font. When they wish to torture people by a base death, they perforate their navels, and dragging forth the extremity of the intestines, bind it to a stake; then with flogging they lead the victim around until the viscera having gushed forth, the victim falls prostrate upon the ground. Others they bind to a post and pierce with arrows. Others they compel to extend their necks and then, attacking them with naked swords, attempt to cut through the neck with a single blow. What shall I say of the abom-

**Krak des Chavaliers** served as the headquarters of the Knights of St. John (Hospitallers) during the Crusades. This fortress is among the most notable surviving examples of medieval military architecture.

Dorling Kindersley Media Library/Alistair Duncan © Dorling Kindersley

**What does the merger of military and religious values tell us about the Crusaders and their motives?**

inable rape of the women? The kingdom of the Greeks is now dismembered by them and deprived of territory so vast in extent that it can not be traversed in a march of two months. On whom therefore is the labor of avenging these wrongs and of recovering this territory incumbent, if not upon you? . . .

Jerusalem is the navel of the world; the land is fruitful above others, like another paradise of delights. This the Redeemer of the human race has made illustrious by His advent, has beautified by residence, has consecrated by suffering, has redeemed by death, has glorified by burial. This royal city, therefore, situated at the centre of the world, is now held captive by His enemies, and is in subjection to those who do not know God, to the worship of the heathens. She seeks therefore and desires to be liberated, and does not cease to implore you to come to her aid. From you especially she asks succor, because, as we have already said, God has conferred upon you above all nations great glory in arms.

Accordingly undertake this journey for the remission of your sins, with the assurance of the imperishable glory of the kingdom of heaven.

Source: Translations and reprints from *Original Sources of European History*, Vol. 1 (Philadelphia: Department of History, University of Pennsylvania, 1910), pp. 5–7.

## II. SALADIN ( R. 1174–1193) DEFEATS THE THIRD CRUSADE: THE REPORT OF AN EYEWITNESS

[En route to liberating Jerusalem] Saladin sought out the Templars and Hospitallers . . . saying: 'I shall purify the land of these two impure races.' He ordered them to be beheaded, choosing to have them dead rather than in prison. With him [were] scholars and sufis [mystics] . . . devout men and ascetics, each begging to kill one of them . . . Saladin, his face joyful, sat on his dais [while] the unbelievers [Christians] showed black despair . . . There were some who slashed and cut [the Christians] cleanly, and were thanked for it. Some refused and failed to act . . . I [the eye-witness] saw the man who laughed scornfully as he slaughtered [the Christians] . . . How much praise he won! [How great] the eternal rewards he secured by the blood he had shed . . . ! How many ills did he cure by the ills he brought upon a Templar . . . ! I saw how he killed unbelief to give life to Islam, and destroyed polytheism [i.e. Trinitarian Christianity] to build monotheism . . .

[Later, during the conquest of Jerusalem] the Franks [i.e. Crusaders] saw how violently the Muslims attacked [and] decided to ask for safe-conduct out of the city [agreeing to] hand Jerusalem over to Saladin . . . A deputation . . . asked for terms, but . . . Saladin refused to grant [them]. 'We shall deal with you,' he said, 'just as you dealt with the population of Jerusalem when you took it [from us] in 1099, with murder and enslavement and other such savageries . . . ! Despairing of this approach, [one of the city's Christian leaders] said: 'Know, O Sultan, that there are many of us in this city . . . At the moment we are fighting [against you] half-hearted in the hope to be spared by you as you have spared others—this because of our horror of death and our love of life. However, if we see that death is inevitable . . . we shall kill our children and our wives, burn our possessions, so as not to leave you with . . . a single man or woman to enslave [and we will also raze the city]. Saladin took counsel with his advisers [and] agreed to give the Franks assurances of safety on the understanding that each man, rich and poor alike [would pay] the appropriate ransom.

Source: From chronicles of Imad Ad-Din and Ibn Al-Athir, in Francesco Gabrieli, ed. and trans., *Arab Historians of the Crusades* (London: Routledge & Kegan Paul, 1957), pp. 138–140 and Carole Hillenbrand, *The Crusades: Islamic Perspectives* (Chicago: Fitzroy Dearborn Publishers, 1999), p. 554.

## SIGNIFICANT DATES FROM THE PERIOD OF THE HIGH MIDDLE AGES

| | |
|---|---|
| **910** | Cluniac reform begins |
| **955** | Otto I defeats Magyars |
| **1059** | College of Cardinals empowered to elect popes |
| **1066** | Norman conquest of England |
| **1075–1122** | Investiture Controversy |
| **1095–1099** | First Crusade |
| **1144** | Edessa falls; Second Crusade |
| **1152** | Hohenstaufen dynasty founded |
| **1154** | Plantagenet dynasty founded |
| **1187** | Jerusalem falls to Saladin |
| **1189–1192** | Third Crusade |
| **1202** | Fourth Crusade sacks Constantinople |
| **1209** | Albigensian Crusade |
| **1210** | Franciscan Order founded |
| **1215** | Fourth Lateran Council; Magna Carta |
| **1250** | Death of Frederick II |

**Albigensians**  Heretical sect that advocated a simple, pious way of life following the example set by Jesus and the Apostles, but rejecting key Christian doctrines.

trade throughout the Near East. Western control of Constantinople continued until 1261, when eastern emperor Michael Paleologus (r. 1261–1282) finally recaptured the city. This fifty-seven-year occupation of Contstantinople did nothing to heal the political and religious divisions between East and West.

## THE PONTIFICATE OF INNOCENT III (R. 1198–1216)

Pope Innocent III was a papal monarch in the Gregorian tradition of papal independence from secular domination. He proclaimed and practiced as none before him the doctrine of the plenitude of papal power. Although this pretentious theory greatly exceeded Innocent's ability to practice it, he and his successors did not hesitate to act on the ambitions it reflected. When Philip II, the king of France, tried unlawfully to annul his marriage, Innocent placed France under interdict, suspending all church services save baptism and the last rites. The same punishment befell England with even greater force when King John refused to accept Innocent's nominee for archbishop of Canterbury. Later in the chapter it will be shown how Innocent also intervened frequently and forcefully in the political affairs of the Holy Roman Empire.

**The New Papal Monarchy**  Innocent made the papacy a great secular power, with financial resources and a bureaucracy equal to those of contemporary monarchs. During his reign the papacy transformed itself, in effect, into an efficient ecclesio-commercial complex, which reformers would attack throughout the later Middle Ages. Innocent consolidated and expanded ecclesiastical taxes on the laity, the chief of which was "Peter's pence." Innocent also imposed an income tax of 2.5 percent on the clergy.

**Crusades in France and the East**  Innocent's predilection for power politics also expressed itself in his use of the Crusade, the traditional weapon of the church against Islam, to suppress internal dissent and heresy. Heresy had grown under the influence of native religious reform movements that tried, often naïvely, to disassociate the church from the growing materialism of the age and to keep it pure of political scheming. Heresy also stemmed from anticlericalism fed by real clerical abuses that the laity could see for themselves, such as immorality, greed, and poor pastoral service.

The idealism of these movements was too extreme for the papacy. In 1209, Innocent launched a Crusade against the **Albigensians**, also known as Cathars, or "pure ones." These advocates of an ascetic, dualist religion were concentrated in the area of Albi in Languedoc in southern France, but they also had adherents among the laity in Italy and Spain. The Albigensians generally sought a pure and simple religious life, claiming to follow the model of the apostles of Jesus in the New Testament. Yet they denied the Old Testament and its God of wrath, as well as God's incarnation in Jesus Christ; despite certain Christian influenced ideas, they were non-Christians. Their idea of a church was an invisible spiritual force, not a real-world institution.

The Crusades against the Albigensians were carried out by powerful noblemen from northern France and ended with a special Crusade led by King Louis VIII of France from 1225 to 1226, which destroyed the Albigensians as a political entity. Pope Gregory IX (r. 1227–1241) introduced the **Inquisition** into the region to complete the work of the Crusaders. This institution, a formal tribunal to detect and punish heresy, had been in use by the church since the mid–twelfth century as a way for bishops to maintain diocesan discipline. During Innocent's pontificate it became centralized in the papacy. Papal legates were dispatched to chosen regions to conduct interrogations, trials, and executions.

**The Fourth Lateran Council** Under Innocent's direction, the Fourth Lateran Council met in 1215 to formalize church discipline throughout the hierarchy, from pope to parish priest. The council enacted many important landmarks in ecclesiastical legislation. It gave full dogmatic sanction to the controversial doctrine of **transubstantiation**, according to which the bread and wine of the Lord's Supper become the true body and blood of Christ when consecrated by a priest in the sacrament of the Eucharist. It also enhanced the power and authority of the clergy, because it specified that only they could perform the miracle of the Eucharist.

In addition, the council made annual confession and Easter communion mandatory for every adult Christian. This legislation formalized the sacrament of penance as the church's key instrument of religious education and discipline in the later Middle Ages.

**Franciscans and Dominicans** During his reign, Pope Innocent gave official sanction to two new monastic orders: the Franciscans and the Dominicans. No other action of the pope had more of an effect on spiritual life. Unlike other regular clergy, the members of these mendicant orders, known as *friars*, did not confine themselves to the cloister. They went out into the world to preach the church's mission and to combat heresy, begging or working to support themselves (hence the term *mendicant*).

Lay interest in spiritual devotion, especially among urban women, was particularly intense at the turn of the twelfth century. In addition to the heretical Albigensians, there were movements of Waldensians, Beguines, and Beghards, each of which stressed biblical simplicity in religion and a life of poverty in imitation of Christ. Such movements were especially active in Italy and France. Their heterodox teachings—teachings that, although not necessarily heretical, nonetheless challenged church

**Inquisition** Formal ecclesiastical court dedicated to discovering and punishing heresy.

**transubstantiation** Christian doctrine which holds that, at the moment of priestly consecration, the bread and wine of the Lord's Supper become the body and blood of Christ.

**Dominicans** (left) **and Franciscans** (right). Unlike the other religious orders, the Dominicans and Franciscans did not live in cloisters but wandered about preaching and combating heresy. They depended for support on their own labor and the kindness of the laity.

Cliché Bibliothèque Nationale de France, Paris

**What was the relationship between the rise of the Dominicans and Franciscans and medieval urbanization?**

orthodoxy—and the critical frame of mind they promoted caused the pope deep concern. Innocent feared they would inspire lay piety to turn militantly against the church. The Franciscan and Dominican orders, however, emerged from the same background of intense religiosity. By sanctioning them and thus keeping their followers within the confines of church organization, the pope provided a response to heterodox piety as well as an answer to lay criticism of the worldliness of the papal monarchy.

The Franciscan order was founded by Saint Francis of Assisi (1182–1226), the son of a rich Italian cloth merchant, who became disaffected with wealth and urged his followers to live a life of extreme poverty. Pope Innocent recognized the order in 1210, and its official rule was approved in 1223. The Dominican order, the Order of Preachers, was founded by Saint Dominic (1170–1221), a well-educated Spanish cleric, and was sanctioned in 1216. Both orders received special privileges from the pope and were solely under his jurisdiction.

Pope Gregory IX (r. 1227–1241) canonized Saint Francis only two years after Francis's death. Two years after the canonization, however, Gregory canceled Saint Francis's own *Testament* as an authoritative rule for the Franciscan order. He did so because he found it to be an impractical guide for the order and because the unconventional nomadic life of strict poverty it advocated conflicted with papal plans to enlist the order as an arm of church policy. Most Franciscans themselves, under the leadership of moderates like Saint Bonaventure, general of the order between 1257 and 1274, also came to doubt the wisdom of extreme asceticism. In the fourteenth century, the pope condemned a radical branch, the Spiritual Franciscans, extreme followers of Saint Francis who considered him almost a new Messiah. In his condemnation, the pope declared absolute poverty a fictitious ideal that not even Christ endorsed.

**Beguines** Sisterhoods of pious, self-supporting single women.

The Dominicans, a less factious order, combated doctrinal error through visitations and preaching. They conformed new convents of **Beguines** (lay religious sisterhoods of single lay women in the Netherlands and Belgium; see Chapter 8) to the church's teaching, led the church's campaign against heretics in southern France, and staffed the offices of the Inquisition after Pope Gregory centralized it in 1223. The great Dominican theologian Thomas Aquinas (d. 1274) was canonized in 1322 for his efforts to synthesize faith and reason in an enduring definitive statement of Catholic belief. (See Chapter 8.)

The Dominicans and the Franciscans strengthened the church among the laity. Through the institution of so-called Third Orders, they provided ordinary men and women the opportunity to affiliate with the monastic life and pursue the high religious ideals of poverty, obedience, and chastity while remaining laypeople. Such organizations helped keep lay piety orthodox and within the church during a period of heightened religiosity.

# ENGLAND AND FRANCE: HASTINGS (1066) TO BOUVINES (1214)

**HOW DID** England and France develop strong monarchies?

In 1066, the death of the childless Anglo-Saxon ruler Edward the Confessor occasioned the most important change in English political life. Edward's mother was a Norman, giving the duke of Normandy a competitive, if not the best, hereditary claim to the English throne. Before his death, Edward, who was not a strong ruler, acknowledged that claim and even directed that his throne be given to William, the reigning duke of Normandy (d. 1087). Yet the Anglo-Saxon assembly, which customarily bestowed the royal power, had a mind of its own and vetoed Edward's last wishes, choosing instead Harold Godwinsson. This action triggered the swift conquest of

The *Battle of Hastings* Detail of the *Bayeux Tapestry*. c. 1073–1083. Wool embroidery on linen, height 200 (50.7 cm).

Centre Guillaume Le Conquerant. Detail of the *Bayeux Tapestry*—XIth century. By special permission of the City of Bayeux

**How did the Battle of Hastings alter the political landscape of England?**

England by the powerful Normans. William's forces defeated Harold's army at Hastings on October 14, 1066. Within weeks of the invasion William was crowned king of England in Westminster Abbey, both by right of heredity and by right of conquest.

## WILLIAM THE CONQUEROR

Thereafter, William embarked on a twenty-year conquest that eventually made all of England his domain. Every landholder, whether large or small, was henceforth his vassal, holding land legally as a fief from the king. William organized his new English nation shrewdly. He established a strong monarchy whose power was not fragmented by independent territorial princes. He kept the Anglo-Saxon tax system and the practice of court writs (legal warnings) as a flexible form of central control over localities. And he took care not to destroy the Anglo-Saxon quasi-democratic tradition of frequent "parleying"—that is, the holding of conferences between the king and lesser powers who had vested interests in royal decisions. The result was a unique blending of the "one" and the "many," a balance between monarchical and parliamentary elements that has ever since been a feature of English government—although the English Parliament as we know it today did not formally develop as an institution until the late thirteenth century.

For administration and taxation purposes William commissioned a county-by-county survey of his new realm, a detailed accounting known as the *Domesday Book* (1080–1086). The title of the book may reflect the thoroughness and finality of the survey. As none would escape the doomsday judgment of God, so no property was overlooked by William's assessors.

## HENRY II

William's son, Henry I (r. 1100–1135), died without a male heir, throwing England into virtual anarchy until the accession of Henry II (r. 1154–1189). Henry tried to recapture the efficiency and stability of his grandfather's regime, but in the process he steered the English monarchy rapidly toward an oppressive rule. Thanks to his inheritance from his father (the count of Anjou) and his marriage to Eleanor of Aquitaine (ca. 1122–1204), Henry brought to the throne virtually the entire west coast of France.

The union with Eleanor created the Angevin, or English-French, Empire. Eleanor married Henry while he was still the count of Anjou and not yet king of England. The marriage occurred eight weeks after the annulment of Eleanor's fifteen-year marriage to the ascetic French king Louis VII in March 1152. Although the annulment was granted on grounds of consanguinity (blood relationship), the true reason for the

**QUICK REVIEW**

**William the Conqueror (d. 1087)**

- ◆ October 14, 1066: Normans defeated Anglo-Saxons at the Battle of Hastings
- ◆ William's rule in England combined elements of continental feudalism and Anglo-Saxon tradition
- ◆ *Domesday Book* contained county-by-county survey of William's kingdom

# Overview A Comparison of Leaders in the High Middle Ages

| | ENGLAND | FRANCE | GERMANY |
|---|---|---|---|
| **LEADER** | Henry II | Louis IX | Frederick II |
| **REIGN** | (1154–1189) | (1226–1270) | (1212–1250) |
| **ACCOMPLISHMENTS** | Henry brought to the throne greatly expanded French holdings. The union with Eleanor created the Angevin (English–French) Empire. Henry conquered a part of Ireland and made the king of Scotland his vassal. | Louis IX embodied the medieval view of the perfect ruler. His greatest achievements lay at home. The French bureaucracy became an instrument of order and fair play in government under Louis. He abolished private wars and serfdom within his domain. Respected by the kings of Europe, Louis became an arbiter among the world's powers. | Within a year and a half of Frederick's crowning, the treacherous reign of Otto IV came to an end on the battlefields of Bouvines. |
| **FAILURES** | As Henry acquired new lands abroad, he became more autocratic at home. He tried to recapture the efficiency and stability of his grandfather's regime but in the process steered the English monarchy toward an oppressive rule. | Had Louis ruthlessly confiscated English territories on the French coast, he might have lessened, if not averted altogether, the conflict underlying the Hundred Years' War. | During his reign, Frederick effectively turned dreams of a unified Germany into a nightmare of disunity. Living mostly outside of Germany during his rule, he did little to secure the rights of the emperor in Germany. Frederick's relations with the pope were equally disastrous, leading to his excommunication on four different occasions. |

dissolution of the marriage was Louis's suspicion of her infidelity. According to rumor, Eleanor had been intimate with a cousin.

In addition to gaining control of most of the coast of France, Henry also conquered part of Ireland and made the king of Scotland his vassal. Louis VII saw a mortal threat to France in this English expansion. He responded by adopting what came to be a permanent French policy of containment and expulsion of the English from their continental holdings in France.

## ELEANOR OF AQUITAINE AND COURT CULTURE

Eleanor of Aquitaine was a powerful influence on both politics and culture in twelfth-century France and England. She accompanied her first husband, King Louis VII, on the Second Crusade, becoming an example for women of lesser stature, who were also then venturing in increasing numbers into war and business and other areas previously considered the province of men. After marrying Henry, she settled in Angers, the chief town of Anjou, where she sponsored troubadours and poets at her lively court. Eleanor spent the years 1154 to 1170 as Henry's queen in England. She separated from Henry in 1170, partly because of his public philandering and cruel treatment of her, and took revenge on him by joining ex-husband Louis VII in provoking Henry's three surviving sons, who were unhappy with their inheritance, into an unsuccessful rebellion against their father in 1173. From 1179 until his death in 1189, Henry kept Eleanor under mild house arrest to prevent any further such mischief from her.

After her separation from Henry in 1170 and until her confinement in England, Eleanor lived in Poitiers with her daughter Marie, the countess of Champagne, and the two made the court of Poitiers a famous center for the literature of courtly love. The most famous courtly literature was that of Chrétien de Troyes, whose stories of King Arthur and the Knights of the Round Table recounted the tragic story of Sir Lancelot's secret and illicit love for Arthur's wife, Guinevere.

## POPULAR REBELLION AND MAGNA CARTA

As Henry II acquired new lands abroad, he became more autocratic at home. He forced his will on the clergy in the Constitutions of Clarendon (1164). These measures limited judicial appeals to Rome, subjected the clergy to the civil courts, and gave the king control over the election of bishops. The result was strong political resistance from both the nobility and the clergy. The archbishop of Canterbury, Thomas à Becket (1118?–1170), once Henry's compliant chancellor, broke openly with the king and fled to Louis VII. Becket's subsequent assassination in 1170 and his canonization by Pope Alexander III in 1172 helped focus popular resentment against the king's heavy-handed tactics.

Under Henry's successors, the brothers Richard I, the Lion-Hearted (r. 1189–1199), and John (r. 1199–1216), new burdensome taxation in support of unnecessary foreign Crusades and a failing war with France turned resistance into outright rebellion. The last straw for the English was the defeat of the king's forces by the French at Bouvines in 1214. With the full support of the clergy and the townspeople, English barons revolted against John. The popular rebellion ended with the king's grudging recognition of **Magna Carta**, or "Great Charter," in 1215.

The Magna Carta put limits on autocratic behavior of the kind exhibited by the Norman kings and Plantagenet kings. It also secured the rights of the privileged against the monarchy. In Magna Carta the privileged preserved their right to be represented at the highest levels of government in important matters like taxation. The monarchy, however, was also preserved and kept strong. This balancing act, which gave power to both sides, had always been the ideal of feudal government.

Although King John continued to resist the Magna Carta in every way, and succeeding kings ignored it, Magna Carta nonetheless became a cornerstone of modern English law.

**Magna Carta**  ("Great Charter") Document spelling out limitations on royal authority agreed to by John in 1215. It created the foundation for modern English law.

## PHILIP II AUGUSTUS

The English struggle in the High Middle Ages had been to secure the rights of the privileged many, not the authority of the king. The French, by contrast, faced the opposite problem. In 987, noblemen chose Hugh Capet to succeed the last Carolingian ruler, replacing the Carolingian dynasty with the Capetian, a third Frankish dynasty that ruled France for twelve generations, until 1328. For two centuries thereafter, until the reign of Philip II Augustus (r. 1180–1223), powerful feudal princes contested Capetian rule, burying the principle of election.

During this period, after a rash attempt to challenge the more powerful French nobility before they had enough strength to do so, the Capetian kings concentrated their limited resources on securing the royal domain, their uncontested territory around Paris and the Île-de-France to the northeast. Aggressively exercising their feudal rights, French kings, especially after 1100, gained near absolute obedience from the noblemen in this area and established a solid base of power. By the reign of Philip II Augustus, Paris had become the center of French government and culture, and the Capetian dynasty a secure hereditary monarchy. Thereafter, the kings of France could impose their will on the French nobles, who were always in law, if not in political fact, the king's sworn vassals.

In an indirect way the Norman conquest of England helped stir France to unity and made it possible for the Capetian kings to establish a truly national monarchy. The duke of Normandy, who after 1066 was master of the whole of England, was also among the vassals of the French king in Paris. Capetian kings understandably watched with alarm as the power of their Norman vassal grew. Other powerful vassals of the king also watched with alarm. King Louis VI, the Fat (r. 1108–1137), entered an alliance with Flanders, traditionally a Norman enemy. King Louis VII (r. 1137–1180), assisted by a

## ENCOUNTERING THE PAST

### PILGRIMAGE

*Thomas à Becket's tomb at Canterbury quickly became one of the most frequented pilgrimage shrines in Europe. The perennially popular* Canterbury Tales *of Geoffrey Chaucer (ca. 1345–1400) provides a fictional account of one such trip. As Chaucer describes it, a medieval pilgrimage was both a spiritual and a social event. Because travel to distant shrines involved self-sacrifice (danger and expense), clergy often imposed pilgrimages as penances for sins. Pilgrims also set out on their own in the hope that contact with a saint's relics or the waters of a sacred well or spring would provide a miraculous cure for a bodily affliction. Parents even brought the corpses of dead infants to shrines to beg the saints to bring them back to life.*

The most prestigious pilgrimages were those to the Holy Lands and to the graves of St. Peter in Rome and St. James at Compostela in northern Spain. Pilgrim traffic was so great that businesses sprang up along these routes to assist travelers. Transportation, shelter, emergency services, and even guidebooks were available. Pilgrims, particularly to distant locales, often traveled in groups, and an opportunity to share stories and adventures with others made for diverting entertainment. Travel then, as now, was highly educational.

**A thirteenth-century** stained glass window depicts pilgrims traveling to Canterbury Cathedral.
© Archivo Iconografico, S.A./CORBIS

**How did pilgrimages stimulate the economic development of medieval Europe?**

WHY WERE pilgrimages so popular with medieval people?

brilliant minister, Suger, abbot of St. Denis and famous for his patronage of Gothic architecture, found allies in the great northern French cities and used their wealth to
build a royal army.

When he succeeded Louis VII as king, Philip II Augustus inherited financial resources and a skilled bureaucracy that put him in a strong position. He was able to resist the competition of the French nobility and the clergy and to focus on the contest
with the English king. Confronted at the same time with an internal and an international struggle, he proved successful in both. His armies occupied all the English king's
territories on the French coast except for Aquitaine. As a showdown with the English
neared on the continent, however, Holy Roman Emperor Otto IV (r. 1198–1215) entered the fray on the side of the English, and the French found themselves assailed from
both east and west. But when the international armies finally clashed at Bouvines in
Flanders on July 27, 1214, in what history records as the first great European battle, the
French won handily over the opposing Anglo-Flemish-German army. This victory unified France politically around the monarchy and thereby laid the foundation for
French ascendancy in the later Middle Ages.

# FRANCE IN THE THIRTEENTH CENTURY: THE REIGN OF LOUIS IX

Coming to power after the French victory at Bouvines (1214), Louis IX (r. 1226–1270)
inherited a unified and secure kingdom. Not beset by the problems of sheer survival,
and a reformer at heart, Louis found himself free to concentrate on what medieval people believed to be the business of civilization.

**IN WHAT** ways was
Louis IX of France the
"ideal" medieval
monarch?

## GENEROSITY ABROAD

Magnanimity in politics is not always a sign of strength, and Louis could be very magnanimous. Although in a strong position during negotiations for the Treaty of Paris
(1259), which momentarily settled the dispute between France and England, he refused
to take advantage of it to drive the English from their French possessions. Had he done
so and ruthlessly confiscated English territories on the French coast, he might have
lessened, if not averted altogether, the conflict underlying the Hundred Years' War,
which began in the fourteenth century. Instead he surrendered disputed territory on
the borders of Gascony to the English king, Henry III, and confirmed Henry's possession
of the duchy of Aquitaine.

Although he occasionally chastised popes for their crude political ambitions,
Louis remained neutral during the long struggle between the German Hohenstaufen
emperor Frederick II and the papacy and his neutrality worked to the pope's advantage.
Louis also remained neutral when his brother, Charles of Anjou, intervened in Italy
and Sicily against the Hohenstaufens, again to the pope's advantage. Urged on by the
pope and his noble supporters, Charles was crowned king of Sicily in Rome, and his
subsequent defeat of the son and grandson of Frederick II ended the Hohenstaufen dynasty. For such service to the church, both by action and by inaction, the Capetian
kings of the thirteenth century received many papal favors.

## ORDER AND EXCELLENCE AT HOME

Louis's greatest achievements lay at home. The efficient French bureaucracy, which his
predecessors had used to exploit their subjects, became under Louis an instrument of
order and fair play in local government. He sent forth royal commissioners (*enquêteurs*)

whose mission was to monitor the royal officials responsible for local governmental administration and to ensure that justice would truly be meted out to all. These royal ambassadors were received as genuine tribunes of the people. Louis further abolished private wars and serfdom within his royal domain. He gave his subjects the judicial right of appeal from local to higher courts and made the tax system, by medieval standards, more equitable. The French people came to associate their king with justice; consequently, national feeling, the glue of nationhood, grew strong during his reign.

Respected by the kings of Europe and possessed of far greater moral authority than the pope, Louis became an arbiter among the world's powers. During his reign French society and culture became an example to all of Europe, a pattern that would continue into the modern period. Northern France became the showcase of monastic reform, chivalry, and Gothic art and architecture. Louis's reign also coincided with the golden age of Scholasticism, which saw the convergence of Europe's greatest thinkers on Paris.

Louis's perfection remained, however, that of a medieval king. He sponsored the French Inquisition. He led two French Crusades against the Muslims, which, although inspired by the purest religious motives, proved to be personal disasters. During the first (1248–1254), Louis was captured and had to be ransomed out of Egypt. He died of a fever during the second in 1270. It was especially for this selfless, but also useless, service on behalf of the church that Louis later received the rare honor of sainthood.

# THE HOHENSTAUFEN EMPIRE (1152–1272)

**HOW DID** the policies of the Hohenstaufens lead to the fragmentation of Germany?

During the twelfth and thirteenth centuries, stable governments developed in both England and France. The story within the Holy Roman Empire, which embraced Germany, Burgundy, and northern Italy by the mid-thirteenth century, was different. (See Map 7–2.) There, primarily because of the efforts of the Hohenstaufen dynasty to extend imperial power into southern Italy, disunity and blood feuding remained the order of the day for two centuries. It left as a legacy the fragmentation of Germany until the nineteenth century.

## FREDERICK I BARBAROSSA

The investiture struggle had earlier weakened imperial authority. After the Concordat of Worms, the German princes were the supreme lay powers within the rich ecclesiastical territories and held a dominant influence over the appointment of the church's bishops.

The power of the emperor promised to return, however, with the accession to the throne of Frederick I Barbarossa (r. 1152–1190) of the Hohenstaufen dynasty, the strongest line of emperors yet to succeed the Ottonians. This new dynasty not only reestablished imperial authority but also started a new, deadlier phase in the contest between popes and emperors.

Frederick I confronted powerful feudal princes in Germany and Lombardy and a pope in Rome who still looked on the emperor as his creature. However, the incessant strife among the princes and the turmoil caused by the papacy's pretensions to great political power alienated many people. Such popular sentiment presented Frederick with an opportunity to recover imperial authority and he was shrewd enough to take advantage of it. Frederick especially took advantage of the contemporary revival of Roman law, which served him on two fronts. On one hand, it praised centralized authority, that of king or emperor, against the nobility; on the other, it stressed the secular origins of imperial power against the tradition of Roman election of the emperor and papal coronation of him, thus reducing papal involvement to a minimum.

**QUICK REVIEW**

**Frederick I Barbarossa (r. 1152–1190)**

- Founder of the Hohenstaufen dynasty
- From base in Switzerland waged war to control the German nobility
- Efforts to conquer Italy ended in defeat at Legnano in 1176

From his base in Switzerland, Frederick attempted to hold his empire together by invoking feudal bonds. He was relatively successful in Germany, thanks largely to the fall from power and exile in 1180 of his strongest German rival, Henry the Lion (d. 1195), the duke of Saxony. Although he could not defeat the many German duchies, Frederick never missed an opportunity to remind each German ruler of his prescribed duties as one who held his land legally as a fief of the emperor.

Italian popes proved to be the greatest obstacle to Frederick's plans to revive his empire. In 1155, he restored Pope Adrian IV (r. 1154–1159) to power in Rome after a religious revolutionary had taken control of the city. For his efforts, Frederick won a coveted papal coronation—and strictly on his terms, not on those of the pope. Despite fierce resistance to him in Italy, led by Milan, the door to Italy had opened, and an imperial assembly sanctioned his claims to Italian lands.

As this challenge to royal authority was occurring, Cardinal Roland, a skilled lawyer, became Pope Alexander III (r. 1159–1181). In a clever effort to strengthen the papacy against growing imperial influence, the new pope had, while still a cardinal, negotiated an alliance between the papacy and the Norman kingdom of Sicily. Thus, Frederick now found himself at war with the pope, Milan, and Sicily.

By 1167, the combined forces of the north Italian communes had driven Frederick back into Germany, and a decade later, in 1176, Italian forces soundly defeated his armies at Legnano. In the Peace of Constance in 1183, which ended the hostilities, Frederick recognized the claims of the Lombard cities to full rights of self-rule, a great blow to his imperial plans.

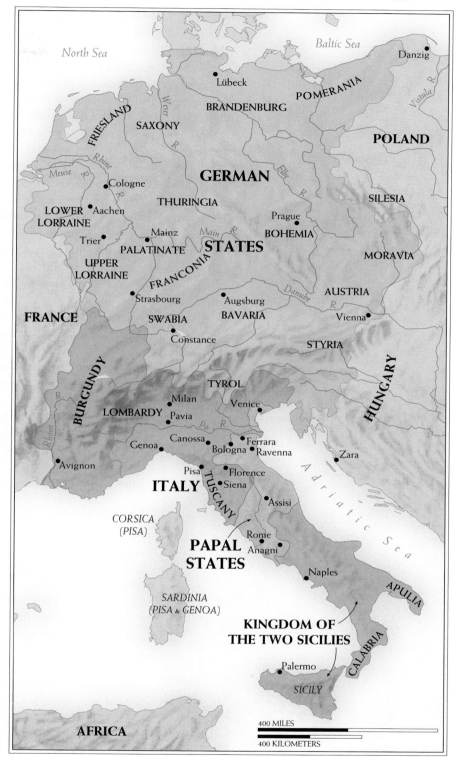

**MAP 7–2  Germany and Italy in the Middle Ages**  Medieval Germany and Italy were divided lands. The Holy Roman Empire (Germany) embraced hundreds of independent territories that the emperor ruled only in name. The papacy controlled the Rome area and tried to enforce its will on Romagna. Under the Hohenstaufens (mid–twelfth to mid–thirteenth centuries), internal German divisions and papal conflict reached new heights; German rulers sought to extend their power to southern Italy and Sicily.

**How did** Roman emperors, German rulers, and the papacy all vie for power in Germany and Italy in the Middle Ages?

## HENRY VI AND THE SICILIAN CONNECTION

Frederick's reign thus ended with stalemate in Germany and defeat in Italy. After the Peace of Constance, he seems to have accepted the reality of the empire's division among the feudal princes of Germany. However, in the last years of his reign he seized an opportunity to gain control of Sicily, then still a papal ally, and form a new territorial base of power for future emperors. The opportunity arose when the Norman ruler of the kingdom of Sicily, William II (r. 1166–1189), sought an alliance with Frederick that would free him to pursue a scheme to conquer Constantinople. In 1186, a fateful marriage occurred between Frederick's son, the future Henry VI (r. 1190–1197), and Constance, the eventual heiress to the kingdom of Sicily, which promised to change the balance of imperial-papal power.

It proved, however, to be but another well-laid plan that went astray. The Sicilian kingdom became a fatal distraction for succeeding Hohenstaufen kings, tempting them to sacrifice their traditional territorial base in northern Europe to dreams of imperialism. Equally disastrous for the Hohenstaufens, the union of the empire with Sicily left Rome encircled, ensuring even greater emmity from a papacy already thoroughly distrustful of the emperor.

When Henry VI became emperor in 1190, he thus faced a hostile papacy, German princes more defiant than ever of the emperor, and an England whose adventurous king, Richard the Lion-Hearted, plotted against Henry VI with the old Hohenstaufen enemy, the exiled duke of Saxony, Henry the Lion.

It was into these circumstances that the future Emperor Frederick II was born in 1194. Heretofore the German princes had not recognized birth alone as qualifying one for the imperial throne, although the offspring of the emperor did have the inside track. To ensure baby Frederick's succession and stabilize his monarchy, Henry campaigned vigorously for recognition of the principle of hereditary succession. He won many German princes to his side by granting them what he asked for himself and his son: full hereditary rights to their own fiefs. Not surprisingly, the encircled papacy strongly opposed hereditary succession and joined dissident German princes against Henry.

## OTTO IV AND THE WELF INTERREGNUM

Henry died in September 1197, leaving his son Frederick a ward of the pope. Henry's brother succeeded him as German king, but the Welf family, who were German rivals of the Hohenstaufens, put forth their own candidate, whom the English supported. The French, beginning a series of interventions in German affairs, stuck with the Hohenstaufens. The papacy supported first one side and then the other, depending on which seemed most to threaten it. The struggle for power threw Germany into anarchy and civil war.

The Welf candidate, Otto of Brunswick, outlasted his rival and was crowned Otto IV by his followers in Aachen in 1198, thereafter winning general recognition in Germany. In October 1209, Pope Innocent III (r. 1198–1216) boldly meddled in German politics by crowning Otto emperor in Rome. After his papal coronation, Otto proceeded to attack Sicily, an old imperial policy threatening to Rome. Four months after crowning Otto emperor, Pope Innocent excommunicated him.

## FREDERICK II

Casting about for a counterweight to the treacherous Otto, the pope joined with the French, who had remained loyal to the Hohenstaufens. In December 1212, with papal, French, and German support,

**Ekkehard and Uta, ca. 1240–1250** This famous noble pair founded Naumburg Cathedral in Germany in the middle of the thirteenth century and are exemplary studies of medieval nobility.

© Achim Bednorz Koln

**How was the importance of noble patronage reflected in the decoration and organization of medieval churches and cathedrals?**

Innocent's ward, Frederick of Sicily, son of the late Hohenstaufen emperor Henry VI, was crowned king of the Romans in the German city of Mainz. Within a year and a half, Philip Augustus ended the reign of Otto IV on the battlefield of Bouvines, and three years later (1215), Frederick II was crowned emperor again, this time in the sacred imperial city of Aachen.

During his reign, Frederick effectively turned dreams of a unified Germany into a nightmare of disunity, assuring German fragmentation into modern times. Frederick seemed to desire only the imperial title for himself and his sons and was willing to give the German princes whatever they wanted to secure it. It was this eager compliance with their demands that laid the foundation for six centuries of German division. In 1220, he recognized the jurisdictional claims of the ecclesiastical princes of Germany, and twelve years later (1232) he extended the same recognition to the secular princes. Frederick's concessions amounted to an abdication of imperial power in Germany.

Frederick's relations with the pope were equally disastrous, leading to his excommunication on four different occasions. He was also determined to control Lombardy and Sicily, a policy that was anathema to the pope. The papacy came to view Frederick as the Antichrist, the biblical beast of the Apocalypse, whose persecution of the faithful signaled the end of the world.

The papacy won the long struggle that ensued, although its victory was arguably a Pyrrhic one. During this bitter contest, Pope Innocent IV (r. 1243–1254) launched the church into European politics on a massive scale, a policy that left the church vulnerable to criticism from both religious reformers and royal apologists. Pope Innocent organized the German princes against Frederick, who—thanks to Frederick's grand concessions—were a superior force and able to gain full control of Germany by the 1240s.

When Frederick died in 1250, the German monarchy died with him. The princes established their own informal electoral college in 1257, which thereafter controlled the succession. The princes elected directly, and his offspring had no hereditary right to succeed him. The last male Hohenstaufen was executed in 1268.

## ROMANESQUE AND GOTHIC ARCHITECTURE

The High Middle Ages witnessed the peak of Romanesque art and the transition to the Gothic. Romanesque literally means "like Rome," and the art and architecture of the High Middle Ages embraced the classical style of ancient Rome. Romanesque churches are fortress-like. Rounded arches, thick stone walls, and heavy columns support their vaults or ceilings. In the early Middle Ages this architecture expressed the church's role as a refuge for the faithful and a new world power. Developed under the Carolingians and Ottonians, the Romanesque attained its perfection and predominated between 1050 and 1200.

Appearing first in mid-twelfth-century France, Gothic art and architecture evolved directly from the Romanesque. Gothic architecture's distinctive feature is a ribbed, crisscrossed ceiling, with pointed arches in place of rounded ones, a clever construction technique that allows Gothic churches to soar far above their Romanesque predecessors. The greater weight on the walls was off-loaded by exterior "flying" buttresses built directly into them. With the walls thus shored up, they could be filled with wide expanses of stained glass windows that flooded the churches with colored light.

**Transept, Cathedral of St. James,** Santiago de Compostela.

Achim Bednorz/© Achim Bednorz, Koln

**How did Gothic architecture embody the religious values of the High Middle Ages?**

# SUMMARY

**HOW WAS** Otto able to secure the power of his Saxon dynasty?

**Otto I and the Revival of the Empire** In 918, Henry I became the first Saxon king of Germany; eighteen years later his son Otto I took power, continuing his program of unification and expansion. He invaded Italy in 951 and proclaimed himself king. By the end of his reign, Otto the Great had even established authority over the Papal States and the pope himself. The Ottonian dynasty faltered in the early eleventh century, however, because Otto I's successors did not pay enough attention to events in Germany, and the church established an independent base of power for itself. By contrast, during this same period the Capetian kings in France focused on their home turf and built the basis for enduring royal power. *page 178*

**WHAT EXPLAINS** the popularity of the Cluniac reform movement?

**The Reviving Catholic Church** The Catholic Church shed the secular control of the ninth and tenth centuries to emerge as a powerful independent institution. The reform movement based at the French monastery in Cluny spread throughout Europe and was endorsed by the pope. In 1075, Pope Gregory VII outlawed lay investiture of the clergy; this led to a battle of wills between popes and emperors, until the 1122 Concordat of Worms formalized a new relationship between church and state. Meanwhile, the Crusades provided an outlet for popular religious zeal. Repeated Christian expeditions to the Holy Lands did not do much to encourage Muslim respect for Europeans, but the Crusades did stimulate trade and expose the West to the civilizations of the East. Around 1200, Pope Innocent III asserted increased papal power, suppressed internal dissent, clarified church doctrine, and sanctioned two new monastic orders: the Franciscans and the Dominicans. *page 179*

**HOW DID** England and France develop strong monarchies?

**England and France: Hastings (1066) to Bouvines (1214)** William, the duke of Normandy, won the Battle of Hastings in 1066 and soon was crowned king of England. Building on Anglo-Saxon traditions, he created a strong monarchy that used parleying to channel communications between the king and other leaders. William's grandson Henry married Eleanor of Aquitaine, creating the Angevin Empire. Later kings of England became more oppressive, raised taxes, and caused other problems, until English barons revolted and forced King John to recognize the Magna Carta in 1215. In roughly this same period in France, the Capetian kings first concentrated on securing their territory, then on exercising authority over the nobility. By 1214, in the battle at Bouvines against a combined English and German force, the French were able to defeat their opponents. *page 188*

**IN WHAT** ways was Louis IX of France the "ideal" medieval monarch?

**France in the Thirteenth Century: The Reign of Louis IX** In the middle of the thirteenth century, Louis IX enjoyed almost fifty years as the ruler of a unified and secure France. He was able to focus his energies on domestic reform and the cultivation of culture and religion. He improved the justice system and presided over the emergence of Paris as the intellectual capital of Europe. He was fiercely religious, sponsoring the French Inquisition and leading two Crusades. In his dealings with foreigners, especially the English, he might be accused of naïveté; he failed to press his advantage at the Treaty of Paris in 1259 and allowed the English to maintain their claims on various French lands, thereby setting the stage for the Hundred Years' War in the next century. *page 193*

**HOW DID** the policies of the Hohenstaufens lead to the fragmentation of Germany?

**The Hohenstaufen Empire (1152–1272)** While stable governments that balanced central authority with the local needs of the populace were developing in England and France, the leaders of the Holy Roman Empire were squandering their opportunities to develop a sustainable political structure, a failure that would have negative repercussions through centuries of German history. Throughout the Hohenstaufen dynasty, conflicts with the popes and imperial schemes to control Italian lands distracted Frederick I Barbarossa and his successors from the task of maintaining the allegiance of the nobility and keeping their territory unified. By the late thirteenth century, the Hohenstaufen dynasty had lost all meaningful power and Germany was fragmented. *page 194*

# REVIEW QUESTIONS

1. How did the Saxon king Otto I rebuild the German Empire and use the church to achieve his political goals? How did his program fit with the aspirations of the Cluny reform movement? What was at stake for each of the disputants in the investiture controversy? Who won?

2. What developments in western and eastern Europe led to the start of the crusading movement? How did the Crusades to the Holy Lands affect Europe and the Muslim world?

3. Why were France and England able to coalesce into reasonably strong states, but not Germany?

## KEY TERMS

**Albigensians** (p. 186)
**Beguines** (p. 188)
**Crusades** (p. 181)
**Inquisition** (p. 187)
**Magna Carta** (p. 191)
**transubstantiation** (p. 187)

For additional learning resources related to this chapter, please go to **www.myhistorylab.com**

PEARSON
**my**history**lab**

# 8

# Medieval Society:

## Hierarchies, Towns, Universities, and Families (1000–1300)

**The livelihood of towns** and castles depended on the labor of peasants in surrounding villages. Here a peasant family collects the September grape harvest from a vineyard outside a fortified castle in France in preparation for making wine.

The Granger Collection

**How did the labor of peasants make the lifestyle of medieval elites possible?**

F rom the tenth to the twelfth centuries, increasing political stability helped Europe advance on multiple fronts. Agricultural production increased, population exploded, and trade and urban life revived. Crusades multiplied contacts with foreign lands that stimulated both economic and cultural development. A new merchant class, the ancestors of modern capitalists, appeared to serve the West's growing markets, and an urban proletariat developed.

Muslim intellectuals guided Europe's scholars in the rediscovery of Classical literature, and an explosion of information led to the rise of the university. Literacy increased among the laity and a renaissance in art and thought blossomed in the twelfth century. The creative vigor that surged through Europe in the High Middle Ages became tangible in the awesome Gothic churches that were the supreme products of medieval art and science. ■

# THE TRADITIONAL ORDER OF LIFE

**WHAT WAS** the relationship between the three basic groups in medieval society?

In the art and literature of the Middle Ages, three basic social groups were represented: those who fought as mounted knights (the landed nobility), those who prayed (the clergy), and those who labored in fields and shops (the peasantry and village artisans). After the revival of towns in the eleventh century, a fourth social group emerged: long-distance traders and merchants.

## NOBLES

As a distinctive social group, not all nobles were originally great men with large hereditary lands. Many rose from the ranks of feudal vassals or warrior knights. The successful vassal attained a special social and legal status based on his landed wealth (accumulated fiefs), his exercise of authority over others, and his distinctive social customs—all of which set him apart from others in medieval society. By the late Middle Ages, a distinguishable higher and lower nobility living in both town and country had evolved. The higher were the great landowners and territorial magnates, who had long been the dominant powers in their regions, while the lower were comprised of petty landlords, descendants of minor knights, newly rich merchants able to buy country estates, and wealthy farmers patiently risen from ancestral serfdom.

**Warriors**   Arms were the nobleman's profession; to wage war was his sole occupation and reason for living. In the eighth century, the adoption of stirrups made mounted warriors, or cavalry, indispensable to a successful army (stirrups permitted the rider to strike a blow without falling off the horse). Good horses and the accompanying armor and weaponry of horse warfare were expensive. Thus only those with means could pursue the life of a cavalryman. The nobleman's fief gave him the means to acquire the expensive military equipment that his rank required. He maintained that enviable position as he had gained it, by fighting for his chief.

The nobility accordingly celebrated the physical strength, courage, and constant activity of warfare. Warring gave them both new riches and an opportunity to gain honor and glory. Knights were paid a share in the plunder of victory, and in war everything became fair game. They looked down on the peasantry as cowards who ran and hid during war. They held urban merchants, who amassed wealth by business methods strange to feudal society, in equal contempt. The nobility possessed as strong a sense of superiority over these "unwarlike" people as the clergy did over the general run of the laity.

**The Joys and Pains of the Medieval Joust** This scene from a manuscript from c. 1300–1349 idealizes medieval noblewomen and the medieval joust. Revived in the late Middle Ages, jousts were frequently held in peacetime. They kept the warring skills of noblemen sharp and became popular entertainment. Only the nobility were legally allowed to joust, but over time, uncommon wealth enabled a persistent commoner to qualify.

Universitatsbibliothek Heidelberg.

**What medieval values are reflected in this manuscript illustration? What significance do you attach to the fact that the spectators are women?**

**Knighthood**   The nobleman nurtured his sense of distinctiveness within medieval society by the chivalric ritual of dubbing to knighthood. This ceremonial entrance into the noble class became almost a religious sacrament. A bath of purification, confession, communion, and a prayer vigil preceded the ceremony. Thereafter, the priest blessed the knight's standard, lance, and sword. As prayers were chanted, the priest girded the knight with his sword and presented him his shield, enlisting him as much in the defense of the church as in the service of his lord. Dubbing raised the nobleman to a state as sacred in his sphere as clerical ordination made the priest in his.

In the twelfth century, knighthood was legally restricted to men of high birth. This circumscription of noble ranks came in reaction to the growing wealth, political power, and successful social climbing of newly rich townspeople (mostly merchants), who formed a new urban patriciate that was increasingly competitive with the lower nobility. Kings remained free, however, to raise up knights at will and did not shrink from increasing royal revenues by selling noble titles to wealthy merchants. But the law was building fences—fortunately, with gates—between town and countryside in the High Middle Ages.

**Sportsmen**   In peacetime, the nobility had two favorite amusements: hunting and tournaments. Where they could, noblemen progressively monopolized the rights to game, forbidding commoners from hunting in their "lord's" forests. This practice built resentment among common people to the level of revolt. Free game, fishing, and access to wood were basic demands in the petitions of grievance and the revolts of the peasantry throughout the High and later Middle Ages.

Tournaments also sowed seeds of social disruption, but more within the ranks of the nobility itself. As regions competed fiercely with one another for victory and glory, even mock battles with blunted weapons proved to be deadly. Often, tournaments got out of hand, ending with bloodshed and animosity among the combatants. The church came to oppose tournaments as occasions of pagan revelry and senseless violence. Kings and princes also turned against them as sources of division within their realms. (See "Encountering the Past: Warrior Games," page 204.)

**Courtly Love**   From the repeated assemblies in the courts of barons and kings, set codes of social conduct, or "courtesy," developed in noble circles. With the French leading the way, mannered behavior and court etiquette became almost as important as expertise on the battlefield. Knights became literate gentlemen, and lyric poets sang and moralized at court. The cultivation of a code of behavior and a special literature to eulogize it was not unrelated to problems within the social life of the nobility. Noblemen were notorious philanderers; their illegitimate children mingled openly with their legitimate offspring in their houses. The advent of courtesy was, in part, an effort to reform this situation.

Although the poetry of courtly love was sprinkled with frank eroticism and the beloved in these epics were married women pursued by those to whom they were not married, the poet usually recommended love at a distance, unconsummated by sexual intercourse. Court poets depicted those who succumbed to illicit carnal love as reaping at least as much suffering as joy.

**Social Divisions**   No medieval social group was absolutely uniform—not the nobility, the clergy, the townspeople, or even the peasantry. Noblemen formed a broad spectrum—from minor vassals without subordinate vassals to mighty barons, the principal vassals of a king or prince, who had many vassals of their own. Dignity and status within the nobility were directly related to the exercise of authority over others; a chief with many vassals obviously far excelled the small country nobleman who served another and was lord over none but himself.

**Lovers playing chess** on an ivory mirror back, ca. 1300.

The Bridgeman Art Library International

**What role did romantic love play in the relationships between elite men and women?**

# ENCOUNTERING THE PAST

## WARRIOR GAMES

*The cultural environment surrounding the medieval nobility—poetry, songs, arts, and entertainments— glorified war. This was consistent with the interests of a warrior class whose men spent their lives fighting and training for battle. A young nobleman might receive his first horse and dagger at the age of two. By the time he turned fourteen, he was ready to handle adult weapons.*

Tournaments (mock combats) provided him with both practical training and diversion. They proved so popular with all members of society that they survived as pastimes even after changes in warfare diminished the need for a knight's traditional skills.

The military preoccupations of the knights influenced the behavior of other members of medieval society. Aristocratic women hunted but were limited to the role of spectators at entertainments such as tournaments. Some clergy were famous sportsmen and warriors, but, like women, their taste for violence was usually satisfied vicariously by rooting for champions at tournaments and by playing chess, backgammon, and competitive games such as Tick, Tack, Toe. Commoners attended tournaments and developed similar warlike games and sports of their own. The equivalent of a tournament for men and boys of the lower classes was a rough ball game—an early version of rugby, soccer, or football. Medieval people were ingenious at inventing diversions for their idle hours, as Pieter Breughel's painting *Children's Games* (1560) documents. It depicts boys and girls engaged in seventy-eight different activities.

**Breughel, *Children's Games.***

Pieter the Elder Breughel (1525–1569), *Children's Games*, 1560. Oil on oakwood, 118 × 161 cm. Kunsthistoriches Museum, Vienna, Austria. Photo copyright Erich Lessing/Art Resource, NY

**What similarities and differences do you note between contemporary children's games and those depicted by Breughel?**

WHY DID the medieval nobility play warlike games? How did these influence the behavior of other members of society?

---

In the late Middle Ages, the landed nobility suffered a steep economic and political decline. Climatic changes and agricultural failures created large famines, and the great plague (see Chapter 9) brought unprecedented population loss. Changing military tactics occasioned by the use of infantry and heavy artillery during the Hundred Years' War made the noble cavalry nearly obsolete. Also, the alliance of wealthy towns with kings challenged the nobility within their own domains. A waning of the landed nobility occurred after the fourteenth century when the effective possession of land and wealth counted more than lineage for membership in the highest social class. Still a shrinking nobility continued to dominate society down to the nineteenth century, and they have been with us ever since.

## CLERGY

Unlike the nobility and the peasantry, the clergy was an open estate. Although the clerical hierarchy reflected the social classes from which the clergy came, one was still a cleric by religious training and ordination, not by the circumstances of birth or military prowess.

**Regular and Secular Clerics**   There were two basic types of clerical vocation: the regular clergy and the secular clergy. The **regular clergy** was made up of the orders of monks who lived according to a special ascetic rule (*regula*) in cloisters separated from the world. They were the spiritual elite among the clergy, and monks' personal sacrifices and high religious ideals made them much respected in high medieval society.

Many monks (and also nuns, who increasingly embraced the vows of poverty, obedience, and chastity without a clerical rank) secluded themselves altogether. The regular clergy, however, were never completely cut off from the secular world. They maintained frequent contact with the laity through such charitable activities as feeding the destitute and tending the sick, through liberal arts instruction in monastic schools, through special pastoral commissions from the pope, and as supplemental preachers and confessors in parish churches during Lent and other peak religious seasons. It became the mark of the Dominican and Franciscan friars to live a common life according to a special rule and still to be active in a worldly ministry. Some monks, because of their learning and rhetorical skills, even rose to prominence as secretaries and private confessors to kings and queens.

The **secular clergy**, those who lived and worked directly among the laity in the world (*saeculum*), formed a vast hierarchy. At the top were the high prelates—the wealthy cardinals, archbishops, and bishops, who were drawn almost exclusively from the nobility—and below them the urban priests, the cathedral canons, and the court clerks. Finally, there was the great mass of poor parish priests, who were neither financially nor intellectually far above the common people they served. Until the Gregorian reform in the eleventh century, parish priests lived with women in a relationship akin to marriage, and the communities they served accepted their concubines and children. Because of their relative poverty, priests often took second jobs as teachers, artisans, or farmers. Their parishioners also accepted and even admired this practice.

**New Orders**   One of the results of the Gregorian reform was the creation of new religious orders aspiring to a life of poverty and self-sacrifice in imitation of Christ and the first apostles. The more important were the Canons Regular (founded 1050–1100), the Carthusians (founded 1084), the Cistercians (founded 1098), and the Praemonstratensians (founded 1121). Carthusians, Cistercians, and Praemonstratensians practiced extreme austerity in their quest to recapture the pure religious life of the early church.

Strictest of them all were the Carthusians. Members lived in isolation and fasted three days a week. They also devoted themselves to long periods of silence and even self-flagellation in their quest for perfect self-denial and conformity to Christ.

The Cistercians (from Citeaux in Burgundy) were a reform wing of the Benedictine order. They hoped to avoid the materialistic influences of urban society and maintain uncorrupted the original *Rule* of Saint Benedict, which their leaders believed Cluny was compromising. The Cistercians accordingly stressed anew the inner life and spiritual goals of monasticism. They located their houses in remote areas and denied themselves worldly comforts and distractions.

The Canons Regular were independent groups of secular clergy (and also earnest laity) who, in addition to serving laity in the world, adopted the *Rule* of Saint Augustine (a monastic guide dating from around the year 500) and practiced the ascetic virtues of regular clerics. By merging the life of the cloister with traditional clerical duties, the Canons Regular foreshadowed the mendicant friars of the thirteenth century—the Dominicans and the Franciscans, who combined the ascetic ideals of the cloister with an active ministry in the world.

**regular clergy**   Monks and nuns who lived under the *regula* ("rule") of a cloister.

**secular clergy**   Clergy, such as bishops and priests, who lived and worked among the laity in the *saeculum* ("world").

**QUICK REVIEW**
**Clergy**

- Secular clergy worked and lived among the laity
- Regular clergy were monks and nuns who lived under the rule of a cloister
- Regular clergy maintained contact with the secular world

The monasteries and nunneries of the established orders recruited candidates from among wealthy social groups. Crowding in these convents and the absence of patronage gave rise in the thirteenth century to lay satellite convents known as Beguine houses. These convents housed religiously earnest single women from the upper and middle social strata. In the German city of Cologne, one hundred such houses were established between 1250 and 1350, each with eight to twelve "sisters."

**Prominence of the Clergy**    The clergy constituted a far greater proportion of medieval society than modern society. Estimates suggest that 1.5 percent of fourteenth-century Europe was in clerical garb. The clergy were concentrated in urban areas, especially in towns with universities and cathedrals, where, in addition to studying, they found work in a wide variety of religious services. In large university towns, the clergy might exceed 10 percent of the population.

Despite the moonlighting of poorer parish priests, the clergy as a whole, like the nobility, lived on the labor of others. Their income came from the regular collection of tithes and church taxes according to an elaborate system that evolved in the High and later Middle Ages. The church was, of course, a major landowner and regularly collected rents and fees. Monastic communities and high prelates amassed great fortunes. The immense secular power attached to high clerical posts can be seen in the intensity of the investiture struggle. (See Chapter 7.)

For most of the Middle Ages, the clergy were the "first estate," and theology was the queen of the sciences. Theologians elaborated the distinction between the clergy and the laity to the clergy's benefit. Secular rulers were not supposed to tax the clergy, who were holy persons, without special permission from the ecclesiastical authorities. Clerical crimes were under the jurisdiction of special ecclesiastical courts, not the secular courts. Because churches and monasteries were deemed holy places, they, too, were free from secular taxation and legal jurisdiction. By the late Middle Ages, townspeople increasingly resented the special immunities of the clergy. They complained that the clergy had greater privileges, yet fewer responsibilities, than all others who lived within the town walls.

## PEASANTS

The largest and lowest social group in medieval society was the one on whose labor the welfare of all the others depended: the agrarian peasantry. Many peasants lived on and worked the **manors** of the nobility. All were to one degree or another dependent on their lords and were considered to be their property. The manor in Frankish times was a plot of land within a village, ranging from twelve to seventy-five acres in size, assigned to a certain member by a settled tribe or clan. This member and his family became lords of the land, and those who came to dwell there formed a smaller, self-sufficient community within a larger village. In the early Middle Ages, such manors consisted of the dwellings of the lord and his family, the huts of the peasants, agricultural sheds, and fields.

**The Duties of Tenancy**    The landowner or lord of the manor required a certain amount of produce (grain, eggs, and the like) and a certain number of services from the peasant families that came to dwell on and farm his land. The tenants were free to divide the labor as they wished and could keep what goods remained after the lord's levies were met. A powerful lord might own many such manors.

There were both servile and free manors. The tenants of the latter had originally been freemen known as *coloni*. (See Chapter 5.) Original inhabitants of the territory and petty landowners, they swapped their small possessions for a guarantee of security from a more powerful lord, who came in this way to possess their land. Unlike the pure serfdom of the servile manors, whose tenants had no original claim to a part of the land,

**manor**   A self-sufficient rural community that was a fundamental institution of medieval life.

**QUICK REVIEW**

**Peasant Life**

- Peasants were the largest and lowest social group
- Many peasants worked on manors
- The lord was the supreme authority on his manor

the tenancy obligations on free manors tended to be limited, and the tenants' rights more carefully defined. It was a milder serfdom. Tenants of servile manors were, by comparison, far more vulnerable to the whims of their landlords. These two types of manors tended, however, to merge. The most common situation was the manor on which tenants of greater and lesser degrees of servitude dwelt together, their services to the lord defined by their personal status and local custom. In many regions free, self-governing peasant communities existed without any overlords and tenancy obligations.

The lord held both judicial and police powers. The lord also had the right to subject his tenants to exactions known as **banalities**. He could, for example, force them to breed their cows with his bull and to pay for the privilege, to grind their bread grains in his mill, to bake their bread in his oven, to make their wine in his wine press, to buy their beer from his brewery, and even to surrender to him the tongues or other choice parts of all animals slaughtered on his lands. The lord also collected a serf's best animal as an inheritance tax. Without the lord's permission, serfs could neither travel nor marry outside the manor in which they served.

In this **eleventh-century** manuscript, peasants harvest grain, trim vines, and plow fields behind yoked oxen.

The Labors of the 12 Months. Pietro de Crescenzi, Le Rustican. Ms.340/603. France, c. 1460. Location: Musée Condé, Chantilly, France. Giraudon/Art Resource, NY

**How did the changing seasons shape the activities of medieval serfs?**

**The Life of a Serf**   Exploited as the serfs may appear to have been from a modern point of view, their status was far from chattel slavery. It was to the lord's advantage to keep his serfs healthy and happy; his welfare, like theirs, depended on a successful harvest. Serfs had their own dwellings and modest strips of land and lived by the produce of their own labor and organization. They could market for their own profit what surpluses might remain after the harvest. They were free to choose their spouses within the local village, although they needed the lord's permission to marry a wife or husband from another village. Serfs could pass their property (their dwellings and field strips) and worldly goods on to their children.

Despite the social distinctions between free and servile serfs—and, within these groups, between those who owned plows and oxen and those who possessed only hoes—the common dependence on the soil forced close cooperation. The ratio of seed to grain yield was consistently poor. There was rarely an abundance of bread and ale, the staple peasant foods. Two important American crops, potatoes and corn (maize), were unknown in Europe until the sixteenth century. Pork was the major source of protein, and every peasant household had its pigs. At slaughter time a family might also receive a little tough beef. Basically, however, everyone depended on the grain crops. When they failed or fell short, peasants went hungry unless their lord had surplus stores he was willing to share.

**Changes in the Manor**   Two basic changes occurred in the evolution of the manor from the early to the later Middle Ages. The first was its fragmentation and the rise to dominance of the single-family holding. Such technological advances as the collar harness (ca. 800), the horseshoe (ca. 900), and the three-field system of crop rotation facilitated this development by making it easier for small family units to support themselves. As the lords parceled out their land to new tenants, their own plots became progressively smaller. This increase in tenants and decrease in the lord's fields brought about a corresponding reduction in the labor services exacted from the tenants. Also, the bringing of new fields into production increased individual holdings and modified labor services. In France, by the reign of Louis IX (r. 1226–1270), only a

**banalities**   Monopolies maintained by landowners giving them the right to demand that tenants pay to grind all their grain in the landowner's mill and bake all their bread in his oven.

few days of labor a year were required, whereas in the time of Charlemagne (r. 768–814) peasants had worked the lords' fields several days a week.

As the single-family unit replaced the clan as the basic nuclear group, assessments of goods and services fell on individual fields and households, no longer on manors as a whole. Family farms replaced manorial units. The peasants' carefully nurtured communal life made possible a family's retention of its land and dwelling after the death of the head of the household. In this way, land and property remained in the possession of a single family from generation to generation.

The second change in the evolution of the manor was the conversion of the serf's dues into money payments, a change brought about by the revival of trade and the rise of the towns. This development, completed by the thirteenth century, permitted serfs to hold their land as rent-paying tenants and to overcome their servile status. Although tenants thereby gained more freedom, they were not necessarily better off materially. Whereas servile workers could have counted on the benevolent assistance of their landlords in hard times, rent-paying workers were left, by and large, to their own devices. Their independence caused some landlords to treat them with indifference and even resentment.

By the mid-fourteenth century, a declining nobility in England and France, faced with the ravages of the great plague and the Hundred Years' War, tried to turn back the historical clock by increasing taxes on the peasantry and restricting their migration into the cities. The peasantry responded with armed revolts. They stand out at the end of the Middle Ages as violent testimony to the breakup of medieval society. As growing national sentiment would break its political unity and heretical movements would end its nominal religious unity, peasant revolts revealed the absence of medieval social unity.

# TOWNS AND TOWNSPEOPLE

**WHAT PROCESSES**
led to the rise of towns
and a merchant class?

In the eleventh and twelfth centuries, towns held only about 5 percent of Western Europe's population. Nonetheless, in the Middle Ages cities and towns were where the action was. There one might find the whole of medieval society, including its most creative segments.

## THE CHARTERING OF TOWNS

Feudal lords, both lay and clerical, originally dominated towns. The lords created the towns by granting charters to those who would agree to live and work within them. The charters guaranteed their safety and gave inhabitants a degree of independence unknown on the land. The purpose was originally to concentrate skilled laborers who could manufacture the finished goods lords and bishops wanted. By the eleventh century, skilled serfs began to pay their manorial dues in manufactured goods, rather than in field labor, eggs, chickens, and beans, as they had done earlier. In return for a fixed rent and proper subservience, serfs were also encouraged to move to the towns. There they gained special rights and privileges from the charters.

As towns grew and beckoned, serfs fled the countryside with their skills going directly to the new urban centers. There they found the freedom and profits that might lift an industrious craftsperson into higher social ranks. As this migration of serfs to the towns accelerated, the lords in the countryside offered them more favorable terms of tenure to keep them on the land. But serfs could not easily be kept down on the farms after they had discovered the opportunities of town life. In this way, the growth of towns improved the lot of serfs generally.

## THE RISE OF MERCHANTS

Not only did rural society give the towns their craftspeople and day laborers, the first merchants themselves may also have been enterprising serfs. Not a few long-distance traders were men who had nothing to lose and everything to gain by the enormous risks of foreign trade. They traveled together in armed caravans and convoys, buying goods and products as cheaply as possible at the source, and selling them for all they could get in Western ports. (See Map 8–1.) At first, traditional social groups—nobility, clergy, and peasantry—considered the merchants an oddity. Over time the powerful grew to respect the merchants, and the weak to imitate them, because wherever the merchants went, they left a trail of wealth behind.

## MAP EXPLORATION

Interactive map: To explore this map further, go to **www.myhistorylab.com**

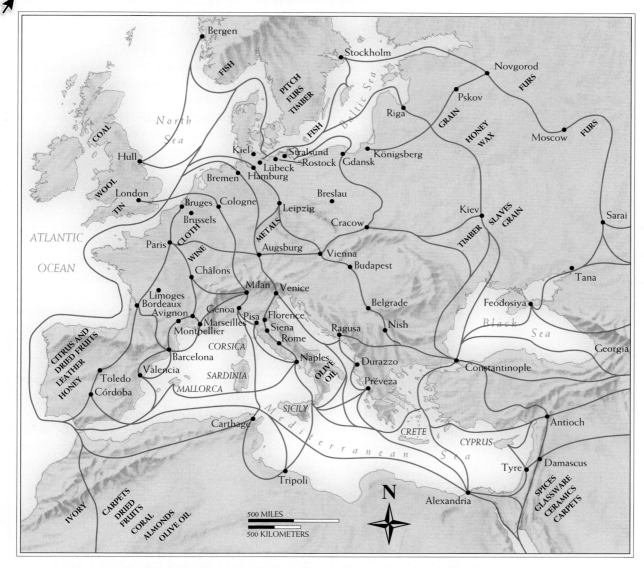

MAP 8–1 **Some Medieval Trade Routes and Regional Products**  The map shows some of the channels that came to be used in interregional commerce and what was traded in a particular region.

**Given the** kinds of items traded, was international trade essential or peripheral to the lives of medieval people?

## CHALLENGING THE OLD LORDS

As they grew in wealth and numbers, merchants formed their own protective associations and were soon challenging traditional seigneurial authority. They especially wanted to end the tolls and tariffs regional authorities imposed on the surrounding countryside. Such regulations hampered the flow of commerce on which both merchant and craftsperson in the growing urban export industries depended. Merchant guilds or protective associations also sprang up in the eleventh century and were followed in the twelfth century by those of craftspeople. Both quickly found themselves in conflict with the norms of a comparatively static agricultural society.

Merchants and craftspeople needed simple and uniform laws and a fluid government sympathetic to their new forms of business activity—not the fortress mentality of the lords of the countryside. The result was a struggle with the old nobility within and outside the towns. This conflict led towns in the High and later Middle Ages to form their own independent communes and to ally themselves with kings against the nobility in the countryside, a development that eventually rearranged the centers of power in medieval Europe and dissolved classic feudal government.

Because the merchants were so clearly the engine of the urban economy, small shopkeepers and artisans identified more with them than with the aloof royal lords and bishops who were the chartered town's original masters. The lesser nobility (the small knights) outside the towns also embraced the opportunities of the new mercantile economy. During the eleventh and twelfth centuries, the burgher upper class increased its economic strength and successfully challenged the old urban lords for control of the towns.

## NEW MODELS OF GOVERNMENT

With urban autonomy came new models of self-government. Around 1100, the old urban nobility and the new burgher upper class merged. From this new ruling class was born the aristocratic town council, which henceforth governed towns.

Enriching and complicating the situation, small artisans and craftspeople also slowly developed their own protective associations, or **guilds**, and began to gain a voice in government. Within town walls, people thought of themselves as citizens with basic rights, not subjects liable to their masters' whim. Economic hardship certainly continued to exist among the lower urban groups, despite their basic legal and political freedoms, but social mobility was at least a possibility in the towns.

**guild**  An association of merchants or craftsmen that offered protection to its members and set rules for their work and products.

**Keeping People in Their Places**    Traditional measures of success had great appeal within the towns. Despite their economic independence, the wealthiest urban groups admired and imitated the lifestyle of the old landed nobility. Although the latter treated the urban patriciate with disdain, successful merchants longed to live the noble, knightly life. When merchants became rich enough to do so, they took their fortunes to the countryside.

Such social climbing disturbed city councils, and when merchants departed for the countryside, towns often lost out economically. A need to be socially distinguished and distinct pervaded urban society. Towns tried to control this need by defining grades of luxury in dress and residence for the various social groups and vocations. Such sumptuary laws restricted the types and amount of clothing one might wear and how one might decorate one's dwelling architecturally. In this way, people were forced to dress and live according to their station in life. The intention of such laws was positive: to maintain social order and dampen social conflict by keeping everyone clearly and peacefully in their place.

**Social Conflict and Protective Associations (Guilds)**  Despite unified resistance to external domination, medieval towns were not internally harmonious social units. Conflict between haves and have-nots was inevitable, especially because medieval towns had little concept of social and economic equality. Only families of long standing in the town who owned property had full rights of citizenship and a direct say in the town's government at the highest levels. Government, in other words, was inbred and aristocratic.

Conflict also existed between the poorest workers in the export trades (usually the weavers and wool combers) and the economically better off and socially ascending independent workers and small shopkeepers. The better-off workers also had their differences with the merchants, whose export trade often brought competitive foreign goods into the city. So independent workers and small shopkeepers organized to restrict foreign trade to a minimum and corner the local market in certain items.

Over time, the formation of artisan guilds gave workers in the trades a direct voice in government. Ironically, the long-term effect of this gain limited the social mobility of the poorest artisans. The guilds gained representation on city councils, where, to discourage imports, they used their power to enforce quality standards and fair prices on local businesses. These actions tightly restricted guild membership, squeezing out poorer artisans and tradesmen. Unrepresented artisans and craftspeople constituted a true urban proletariat prevented by law from forming their own guilds or entering existing ones. The efforts by guild-dominated governments to protect local craftspeople and industries tended to narrow trade and depress the economy for all.

## TOWNS AND KINGS

By providing kings with the resources they needed to curb factious noblemen, towns became a major force in the transition from feudal societies to national governments. In many places kings and towns formally allied against the traditional lords of the land. Towns attracted kings and emperors for obvious reasons. They were a ready source of educated bureaucrats and lawyers who knew Roman law, the ultimate tool for running kingdoms and empires. Kings could also find money in the towns in great quantity, enabling them to hire their own armies instead of relying on the nobility. Towns had the human, financial, and technological resources to empower kings. By such alliances, towns won royal political recognition and guarantees for their constitutions.

It was also in the towns' interest to have a strong monarch as their protector against despotic local lords and princes, who were always eager to integrate or engulf the towns within their expanding territories. Unlike a local magnate, a king tended to remain at a distance, allowing towns to exercise their precious autonomy. A king was thus the more desirable overlord. It was also an advantage for a town to conduct its long-distance trade in the name of a powerful monarch.

## JEWS IN CHRISTIAN SOCIETY

The major urban centers, particularly in France and Germany, attracted many Jews during the late twelfth and thirteenth centuries. Jews gathered there both by choice and for safety in the increasingly hostile Christian world. Mutually wary of one another, Christians and Jews limited direct contact with one another to exchanges between their merchants and scholars. The church expressly forbade Jews from hiring Christians in their businesses and from holding any public authority over them. Jews freely conducted their own small businesses, catering to private clients, both Christian and Jewish. The wealthier Jews became bankers to kings and popes. Jewish intellectual and religious culture, always elaborate and sophisticated, both dazzled and threatened

**QUICK REVIEW**
**Town Society**

- Townspeople were very conscious of class distinctions
- Laws were enacted to limit competition among social classes
- Urban self-government tended to become progressively inbred and aristocratic

**QUICK REVIEW**
**Basis of the Alliance**

- Towns were a source of human, financial, and technological resources for kings
- Effective royal government created the best environment for commerce
- In many places, towns and kings allied against traditional lords

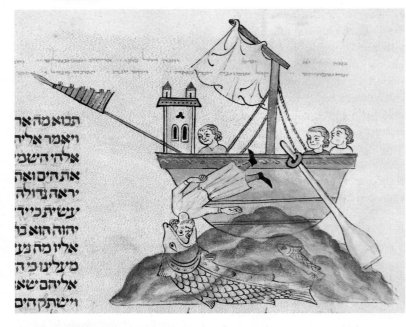

**Jonah is swallowed** by a great fish in a scene from a thirteenth-century Hebrew Torah from Portugal, an example of the rich Jewish heritage of medieval Iberia.

Instituto da Biblioteca Nacional, Lisbon, Portugal/Bridgeman Art Library

**What conditions in Spain allowed for the development of a wealthy and influential Jewish community?**

Christians who viewed it from outside. These various factors—the separateness of Jews, their exceptional economic power, and their rich cultural strength—contributed to envy, suspicion, and distrust among many Christians, whose religious teaching held Jews responsible for the death of Christ.

Between the late twelfth and fourteenth centuries, Jews were exiled from France and persecuted elsewhere. Two factors lay behind this unprecedented surge in anti-Jewish sentiment. The first was a desire by kings to confiscate Jewish wealth and property, and to eliminate the Jews as economic competitors with the monarchy. The church's increasing political vulnerability to the new dynastic monarchies also contributed to the surge in anti-Jewish sentiment. Faced with the loss of its political power, the church became more determined than ever to maintain its spiritual hegemony. Beginning with the Crusades and the creation of new mendicant orders, the church reasserted its claims to spiritual sovereignty over Europe, instigating campaigns against dissenters, heretics, witches, Jews, and infidels at home and abroad.

# SCHOOLS AND UNIVERSITIES

**WHAT INTELLECTUAL** trends accompanied the rise of universities?

In the twelfth century, Byzantine and Spanish Islamic scholars made it possible for the works of Aristotle on logic, the mathematical and astronomical writings of Euclid and Ptolemy, the basic works of Greek physicians and Arab mathematicians, and the larger texts of Roman law to circulate among Western scholars. Islamic scholars preserved these works and wrote extensive, thought-provoking commentaries on them, which were translated into Latin and made available to Western scholars and students. This renaissance of ancient knowledge produced an intellectual ferment that gave rise to Western universities.

## UNIVERSITY OF BOLOGNA

The first important Western university, established by Emperor Frederick I Barbarossa in 1158, was in Bologna. Originally, the term *university* meant simply a corporation of individuals (students and masters) who joined for their mutual protection from overarching episcopal authority (the local bishop oversaw the university) and from the local townspeople. Because townspeople then looked on students as foreigners without civil rights, such protective unions were necessary. They followed the model of an urban trade guild.

Bolognese students also "unionized" to guarantee fair rents and prices from their often reluctant hosts. And students demanded regular, high-quality teaching from their masters. In Italy, students actually hired their own teachers, set pay scales, and drew up desired lecture topics. Masters who did not keep their promises or live up to student expectations were boycotted. Price gouging by townspeople was met with the threat to move the university to another town.

Masters also formed their own protective associations and established procedures and standards for certification to teach within their ranks. The first academic degree was a certificate that licensed one to teach, a *licentia docendi*. It granted graduates in the liberal arts program—the program basic to all higher learning—as well as those in the higher professional sciences of medicine, theology, and law, "the right to teach anywhere" (*ius ibique docendi*).

Bologna was famous for the revival of Roman law. During the Frankish era and later, from the seventh to the eleventh centuries, only the most rudimentary manuals of Roman law had survived. With the growth of trade and towns in the late eleventh century, Western scholars had come into contact with the larger and more important parts of the *Corpus juris civilis* of Justinian, which had been lost during the intervening centuries. (See Chapter 6.) The study and dissemination of this recovered material was now undertaken in Bologna.

As Bologna was the model for southern European universities (those of Spain, Italy, and southern France) and the study of law, so Paris became the model for northern European universities and the study of theology. Oxford and Cambridge in England and (much later) Heidelberg in Germany were among its imitators. All these universities required a foundation in the liberal arts for advanced study in the higher sciences of medicine, theology, and law. The **liberal arts** program consisted of the *trivium* (grammar, rhetoric, and logic) and the *quadrivium* (arithmetic, geometry, astronomy, and music), the language arts and the mathematical arts.

**In this medieval school scene,** a teacher and his wife, with switches, teach children their music lessons.

German Information Center

**Why did elites send their sons to school? What skills did they hope they would acquire?**

## CATHEDRAL SCHOOLS

Before the emergence of universities, the liberal arts were taught in cathedral and monastery schools to train the clergy. By the late eleventh and twelfth centuries, cathedral schools also began to provide lectures for nonclerical students, broadening their curricula to include training for purely secular vocations.

After 1200, increasing numbers of future notaries and merchants who had no particular interest in becoming priests, but who needed Latin and related intellectual disciplines to fill their secular positions, studied side by side with aspiring priests in cathedral and monastery schools. By the thirteenth century, the demand for secretaries and notaries in growing urban and territorial governments and for literate personnel in the expanding merchant firms gave rise to schools for secular vocational preparation. With the appearance of these schools, the church began to lose its monopoly on higher education.

**liberal arts**  The medieval university program that consisted of the *trivium* (TRI-vee-um): grammar, rhetoric, and logic, and the *quadrivium* (qua-DRI-vee-um): arithmetic, geometry, astronomy, and music.

## UNIVERSITY OF PARIS

The University of Paris grew institutionally out of the cathedral school of Notre Dame, among others. King Philip Augustus and Pope Innocent III gave the new university its charter in 1200. At Paris the college, or house system, originated. In Paris, the most famous college was the Sorbonne, founded for theology students around 1257 by Robert de Sorbon, chaplain to the king. In Oxford and Cambridge, the colleges became the basic unit of student life and were indistinguishable from the university proper.

As a group, Parisian students had power and prestige. They enjoyed royal protections and privileges that were denied to ordinary citizens. Many Parisian students were well-to-do, many of whom were spoiled and petulant. They did not endear themselves to the townspeople, whom they considered inferior. Townspeople's resentments sometimes led to violence against students.

# Overview  Two Schools of the High Middle Ages

| **UNIVERSITY OF BOLOGNA** | • Chartered in 1158 |
| | • First of the great medieval schools to acquire recognition as a university |
| | • Students hired professors, set pay scales, and assigned lecture topics |
| | • Europe's premier center for advanced studies in law |

| **UNIVERSITY OF PARIS** | • Chartered in 1200 |
| | • Provided the model for the schools of northern Europe |
| | • Students given protections and privileges exceeding those of other citizens |
| | • Teachers were required to be examined thoroughly before being licensed |
| | • Twenty or more years were needed to earn a doctorate in theology |

**Scholasticism**   Method of study associated with the medieval university.

**In this engraving,** a teacher at the University of Paris leads fellow scholars in a discussion. As shown here, all of the students wore the scholar's cap and gown.

CORBIS/Bettmann

**How was the medieval understanding of knowledge reflected in medieval approaches to classroom instruction?**

## THE CURRICULUM

Before the "renaissance" of the twelfth century, when many Greek and Arabic texts became available to Western scholars and students in Latin translations, the education available within cathedral and monastery schools had been limited. Students learned grammar, rhetoric, and elementary geometry and astronomy. They had the classical Latin grammars of Donatus and Priscian, Saint Augustine's treatise *On Christian Doctrine* and Cassiodorus's treatise On *Divine and Secular Learning*. The writings of Boethius provided instruction in arithmetic and music and preserved the small body of Aristotle's works on logic then known in the West. After the textual finds of the early twelfth century, Western scholars possessed the whole of Aristotle's logic, the astronomy of Ptolemy, the writings of Euclid, and many Latin classics. By the mid–thirteenth century, almost all of Aristotle's works circulated in the West.

In the High Middle Ages, the learning process was basic. The assumption was that truth already existed; one did not have to go out and find it. Such conviction made logic and dialectic the focus of education. Students wrote commentaries on authoritative texts, especially those of Aristotle and the Church Fathers. This method of study, based on logic and dialectic, was known as **Scholasticism**. It reigned supreme in all the faculties—in law and medicine as well as in philosophy and theology. Students read the traditional authorities in their field, formed short summaries of their teaching, disputed them with their peers, and then drew conclusions.

Few books existed for students and those available were expensive hand-copied works. Students had to master a subject through lecture, discussion, and debate. This required memorization and the ability to think on one's feet. Rhetoric, or persuasive argument, was the ultimate goal, an ability to eloquently defend the knowledge one had gained by logic and dialectic.

## PHILOSOPHY AND THEOLOGY

Scholastics quarreled over the proper relationship between philosophy, by which they meant almost exclusively the writings of Aristotle, and theology, which they believed to be a "science" based on divine revelation. The problem between philosophy and theology arose because, in Christian eyes, Aristotle's writings contained heresy. Aristotle, for example, taught the eternality of the world, which called into question the Judeo-Christian teaching that God created the world in time, as the book of Genesis said. Church authorities wanted the works of Aristotle and other ancient authorities to be submissive handmaidens to Christian truth.

**Abelard**   When philosophers and theologians applied the logic and metaphysics of Aristotle to the interpretation of Christian revelation, many believed it posed a mortal threat to biblical truth and church authority. Few philosophers and theologians gained greater notoriety for such wrongful interpretation of the Scriptures than Peter Abelard (1079–1142). No one promoted the new Aristotelian learning more boldly than he, nor did any other pay more dearly for it. His bold subjection of church teaching to Aristotelian logic and dialectic made him many powerful enemies at a time when there was no tenure to protect genius and free speech in schools and universities. Accused of multiple transgressions of church doctrine, he recounted in an autobiography the "calamities" that had befallen him over a lifetime because of his boldness.

His critics especially condemned him for his subjective interpretations of Scripture. Rather than a God-begotten cosmic ransom of humankind from the Devil, Christ's crucifixion, he argued, redeemed Christians by virtue of its impact on their hearts and minds when they heard the story. Abelard's ethical teaching stressed intent over deed: The motives of the doer made an act good or evil, not the act itself. Inner feelings were thus more important for receiving divine forgiveness than the church's sacrament of penance administered by a priest.

Abelard's native genius and youthful disrespect for seniority and tradition gained him powerful enemies in high places. He gave those enemies the opportunity to strike him down when, in Paris, where he became Master of Students at Notre Dame, he seduced a bright, seventeen-year-old niece of a powerful canon, who hired him to be her tutor in his home. Her name was Héloïse and their passionate affair ended in public scandal, with Héloïse pregnant. Intent on punishing Abelard and ending his career, the enraged uncle exposed their secret marriage and hired men to castrate Abelard.

In the aftermath of those terrible events, the lovers entered cloisters nearby Paris: Héloïse at Argenteuil, Abelard at St. Denis. She continued to love Abelard and relive their passion in her mind, while Abelard became a self-condemning recluse, assuring Héloïse in his letters to her that his "love" had only been wretched desire. In 1121, a church synod ordered all his writings to be burned. Another synod in 1140 condemned nineteen propositions from his philosophical and theological works as heresy. Retracting his teaching, Abelard lived out the remaining two years of his life in an obscure priory near Chalons. As for Héloïse, she lived another twenty years and gained renown for her positive efforts to reform the rules for the cloistered life of women, under which she had suffered.

# WOMEN IN MEDIEVAL SOCIETY

**WHAT WAS** life like for women during the Middle Ages?

The image and the reality of medieval women are two different things. Male Christian clergy, whose ideal was a celibate life of chastity, poverty, and obedience, strongly influenced the image. Drawing on the Bible and classical medical, philosophical, and legal traditions predating Christianity, Christian thinkers depicted women as physically, mentally, and morally weaker than men.

## IMAGE AND STATUS

Both within and outside Christianity, this image of women was contradicted. In chivalric romances and courtly love literature of the twelfth and thirteenth centuries, as in the contemporaneous cult of the Virgin Mary, women were put on pedestals and treated as

# FAITH AND LOVE IN THE HIGH MIDDLE AGES

Separate and apart in their respective cloisters, Abelard and Héloïse performed a lengthy post-mortem on their tragic love affair in letters to one another. Therein, they showed their open wounds and shared completely different assessments of where their love had led them. Unhappy in the cloister, Héloïse had only regret for what they had lost, while Abelard, having found his true self in the cloister, looked back on their relationship only with shame.

## QUESTIONS

1. Did the expectations of contemporary religion and culture contribute to the tragedy of their love?

2. Did they have only themselves to blame?

3. Which of the two understood the situation better? Who, in the end, was the stronger?

## I. HÉLOÏSE TO ABELARD

Why, after our conversion [and entrance into the cloisters], which you alone decreed, am I fallen into such neglect and oblivion that I am neither refreshed by your presence, nor comforted by a letter in your absence . . . When I was enjoying carnal pleasures with you, many were uncertain whether I did so from love or from desire. Now the end [result] shows the spirit [in which I acted]. I have forbidden myself all pleasures so that I might obey your will. I have reserved nothing for myself, save this one thing: to be entirely yours . . .

When we enjoyed the delights of love . . . we were spared divine wrath. But when we corrected the unlawful with the lawful [by marriage] and covered the filth of fornication with the honesty of marriage, the wrath of the Lord vehemently fell upon us . . . For men taken in the most flagrant adultery what you suffered [castration] would have been a proper punishment. But what others might merit by adultery, you incurred by a [proper] marriage. What an adulteress brings to her lover, your own wife brought to you! And this did not happen when we were still indulging our old pleasures, but when we were separated and living chaste lives apart . . .

So sweet to me were those delights of lovers that they can neither displease me nor pass from my memory. Whatever I am doing, they always come to mind. Not even when I am asleep do they spare me . . . [At] Mass, when prayer ought to be pure, the memory of those delights thoroughly captivate my wretched soul rather than heed my prayers. And although I ought to lament what I have done, I sigh rather for what I now have to forego. Not only the things that we did, but the places and the times in which we did them are so fixed with you in my mind that I reenact them all . . . At times the thoughts of my mind

superior to men in purity. If the church harbored misogynist sentiments, it also condemned them, as in the case of the late-thirteenth-century *Romance of the Rose* and other popular bawdy literature.

The learned churchman Peter Lombard (1100–1169), whose *Four Books of the Sentences* every theological student annotated, asked why Eve had been created from Adam's rib rather than from his head or his feet? The answer: God took Eve from Adam's side because she was meant neither to rule over man, nor to be man's slave, but rather to stand squarely at his side, as his companion and partner in mutual aid and trust. By such insis-

**Adam and Eve** were not cast out of the Garden of Eden because of their sexual lust for one another but rather for their disobedience to God in eating the forbidden fruit from the Tree of Knowledge of Good and Evil. St. Augustine who, like Abelard, was known to exhibit a certain weakness for the charms of the opposite sex, taught that before their Fall, Adam and Eve had complete control over their libidos as opposed to their libidos having complete control over them. Their minds and hearts filled only with thoughts of God when, without any shame or self-indulgence, they engaged in sexual intercourse. Abelard and Héloïse's sexual lust and shame serve as a commentary on fallen humankind, tracing back to Adam and Eve.

Courtesy of the Library of Congress, Rare book and Special Collections Division

**How would you explain the fact that so many medieval books were highly ornate and richly decorated?**

are betrayed by the very motions of my body . . . 'O wretched person that I am, who shall deliver me from this body of death?' Would that I might truthfully add what follows: 'I thank God through Jesus Christ our Lord.'

## II. ABELARD TO HÉLOÏSE

Heloise, my lust sacrificed our bodies to such great infamy that no reverence for honor, nor for God, or for the days of our Lord's passion, or for any solemn thing whatsoever could I be stopped from wallowing in that filth . . . [and although you resisted] I made you consent. Wherefore most justly . . . of that part of my body have I been diminished wherein was the seat of my lust . . . God truly loved you [Heloise], not I. My love . . . was lust, not love. I satisfied my wretched desires in you . . . So weep for your Savior, not for your seducer, for your Redeemer, not for your defiler, for the Lord who died for you, not for me, his servant, who is now truly free for the first time . . .

O how detestable a loss [it would have been] if, given over to carnal pleasure, you were to bring forth a few children . . . for the world, when you are now delivered of a numerous progeny [i.e. the young nuns who are Heloise's wards in the cloister]. Nor would you then be more than a woman, you who now transcend even men, and have turned the curse of Eve into the blessing of Mary [by your chastity in the cloister]. O how indecent it would be for those holy hands of yours, which now turn the pages of sacred books, to serve the obscenities of womanly cares.

Source: *Letters of Abelard and Héloïse*, trans. by Charles Moncrieff (New York: Alfred A. Knopf, 1942), pp. 59–61, 78, 81, 97–98, 100, 103.

tence on the spiritual equality of men and women and their shared responsibility in marriage, the church to this extent also helped protect the dignity of women.

Germanic law treated women better than Roman law had done, recognizing basic rights that forbade their treatment as chattel. All major Germanic law codes recognized the economic freedom of women: their right to inherit, administer, dispose of, and confer property and wealth on their children. They could also press charges in court against men for bodily injury and rape, whose punishment, depending on the circumstances, ranged from fines, flogging, and banishment to blinding, castration, and death.

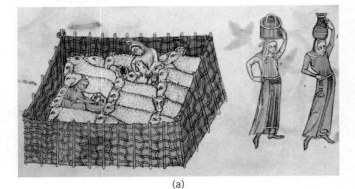
(a)

(b)

(c)

**A fourteenth-century** English manuscript shows women at their daily tasks: carrying jugs of milk from the sheep pen, feeding the chickens, carding and spinning wool.

By permission of The British Library

**What role did ordinary women play in the economic life of medieval Europe?**

## LIFE CHOICES

The nunnery was an option for single women from the higher social classes. Entrance required a dowry and could be almost as expensive as a wedding, although usually cheaper. Within the nunnery, a woman could rise to a position of leadership as an abbess or a mother superior, exercising authority denied her in much of secular life. The nunneries of the established religious orders remained under male supervision, however, so that even abbesses had to answer to higher male authority.

In the ninth century, under the influence of Christianity, the Carolingians made monogamous marriage official policy. Heretofore they had practiced polygamy and concubinage and permitted divorce. The result was both a boon and a burden to women. On one hand, wives gained greater dignity and legal security. On the other hand, a wife's labor as household manager and bearer of children greatly increased.

## WORKING WOMEN

Most medieval women were neither housewives nor nuns, but workers like their husbands. Between the ages of ten and fifteen, girls were apprenticed and gained trade skills much as did boys. If they married, they often continued their trade, operating their bake or dress shops next to their husbands' businesses, or becoming assistants and partners in the shops of their husbands. Women appeared in virtually every "blue-collar" trade, from butcher to goldsmith, but mostly worked in the food and clothing industries. Women belonged to guilds, just like men, and they became craft masters. By the fifteenth century, townswomen increasingly had the opportunity to go to school and gain at least vernacular literacy.

Women's gender, however, excluded them from the learned professions of scholarship, medicine, and law. Women's freedom of movement within a profession was more often regulated than a man's and their wages for the same work were not as great. Still, women remained as prominent and as creative a part of workaday medieval society as men. Rare was the medieval woman who considered herself merely a wife.

## THE LIVES OF CHILDREN

**WHAT WERE** the characteristics of childhood in the Middle Ages?

The image of medieval children and the reality of their lives were also two different things. Until recently, historians were inclined to believe that parents were emotionally distant from their children during the Middle Ages. Evidence of low esteem for children comes from a variety of sources.

## CHILDREN AS "LITTLE ADULTS"

Some historians maintain that medieval art and sculpture rarely portray children as being different from adults. If, pictorially, children and adults look alike, does that mean that people in the Middle Ages were unaware that childhood was a separate period of life requiring special care and treatment? High infant and child mortality also existed, which, one theorizes, could only have discouraged parents from making a deep emotional investment in their children.

During the Middle Ages, children also assumed adult responsibilities early in life. The children of peasants labored in the fields alongside their parents as soon as they could physically manage the work. Urban artisans and burghers sent their children out of their homes into apprenticeships in various crafts and trades between the ages of eight and twelve. Could loving parents remove a child from the home at so tender an age?

The practice of infanticide is another striking suggestion of low esteem for children in ancient and early medieval times. According to the Roman historian Tacitus (ca. 55–120), the Romans exposed unwanted children, especially girls, at birth to regulate family size. Infanticide, particularly of girls, continued to be practiced in the early Middle Ages, if its condemnation in penance books and by church synods is any measure.

## CHILDHOOD AS A SPECIAL STAGE

Despite such evidence of parental distance and neglect, there is another side to the story. Since the early Middle Ages, physicians and theologians had understood childhood to be a distinct and special stage of life. Isidore (560–636), bishop of Seville and a leading intellectual authority throughout the Middle Ages, distinguished six ages of life, the first four of which were infancy, childhood, adolescence, and youth.

According to the medical authorities, infancy proper extended from birth to anywhere between six months and two years and covered the period of speechlessness and suckling. The period thereafter, until age seven, was considered a higher level of infancy, marked by the beginning of a child's ability to speak and his or her weaning. At seven, when a child could think, act decisively, and speak clearly, childhood proper began. At this point a child could be reasoned with, profit from regular discipline, and begin to learn vocational skills. At seven a child was ready for schooling, private tutoring, or apprenticeship in a chosen craft or trade. Until physical growth was complete, which could extend to twenty-one years of age, the child or youth remained legally under the guardianship of parents or a surrogate authority.

There is evidence that high infant and child mortality, rather than distancing parents from their children, actually made them all the more precious to them. Both in learned and in popular medicine, sensible as well as fanciful cures existed for the leading killers of children (diarrhea, worms, pneumonia, and fever). When infants and children died, medieval parents can be found grieving as pitiably as modern parents do. In the art and literature of the Middle Ages, we find mothers baptizing dead infants and children, even carrying them to pilgrim shrines in the hope of miraculous revival.

Clear evidence of special attention being paid to children may be seen in children's toys and aids (walkers and potty chairs). Medieval authorities on child rearing widely condemned child abuse and urged moderation in disciplining and punishing children. In church art and drama, parents were urged to love their children as Mary loved Jesus. Early apprenticeships may also be seen as an expression of parental love and concern. In the Middle Ages, no parental responsibility was greater than that of equipping a child for useful and gainful work. Certainly, by the High Middle Ages if not earlier, children were widely viewed as special creatures with their own needs and rights.

# SUMMARY

**WHAT WAS** the relationship between the three basic groups in medieval society?

**The Traditional Order of Life** The nobility were warriors who lived off the labor of others and resided in mansions or castles in the countryside. The clergy constituted a noticeable portion of the medieval population. The "regular" clergy, who lived separately from the world, and the "secular" clergy, who lived among the laity, had their own hierarchies and responsibilities. The agrarian peasantry were the largest and most significant group. During the Middle Ages, families were the basic socioeconomic unit. *page 202*

**WHAT PROCESSES** led to the rise of towns and a merchant class?

**Towns and Townspeople** Towns grew in size and significance. The nobility and upper clergy's newfound taste for fancy manufactured goods was an early impetus for the growth of towns. Ironically, as towns grew and artisans and traders gained status, it was generally the nobility that suffered. Throughout Europe, it was common for townspeople and kings to form alliances that impinged on the traditional powers of the nobility. Cities, especially in France and Germany, also attracted large numbers of Jews. *page 208*

**WHAT INTELLECTUAL** trends accompanied the rise of universities?

**Schools and Universities** Starting in Bologna in 1158, Western universities taught the *trivium* (language arts) and the *quadrivium* (math). Scholasticism, the favored method of study, relied on logic, memorization, argumentation, and recitation. Most of the content of the instruction came from Latin translations of Greek and Arabic texts. Scholastics quarreled over the proper relationship of philosophy and theology. The life of Peter Abelard illustrates the danger of overly independent thinking in the Middle Ages. *page 212*

**WHAT WAS** life like for women during the Middle Ages?

**Women in Medieval Society** The male Christian clergy portrayed women in the Middle Ages as having two options: subjugated housewife or confined nun. The vast majority of them, in fact, worked in a range of trades, although they were concentrated in the food and clothing industries. Nuns avoided the problems associated with pregnancy and could attain some power. Aristocratic women could manage large households. *page 215*

**WHAT WERE** the characteristics of childhood in the Middle Ages?

**The Lives of Children** Most historians have probably misunderstood the lives of children in the Middle Ages. Children had a 30 to 50 percent chance of dying before they turned five, so some historians have suggested that parents would not risk making a big emotional investment in young children. Children worked as soon as they were able and are depicted in medieval art as "little adults," so some historians have wondered whether people in the Middle Ages had an understanding of childhood as a distinct phase of life, with its own needs. But medieval medical and clerical authorities did, in fact, write about childhood as a special stage in life, and evidence indicates that parents and society at large cherished their babies and children. *page 218*

# REVIEW QUESTIONS

1. How did the responsibilities of the nobility differ from those of the clergy and peasantry during the High Middle Ages? What led to the revival of trade and the growth of towns in the twelfth century? How did towns change medieval society?

2. What were the strengths and weaknesses of the educations provided by medieval universities? How would you evaluate the standard curriculum?

3. How would you define Scholasticism? What was the Scholastic program and method of study? Who were the main critics of Scholasticism, and what were their complaints?

4. Do Germanic law and Roman law reflect different understandings of the position of women in society? How did options and responsibilities differ for women in each of the social classes? What are the theories concerning the concept of childhood in the Middle Ages?

## KEY TERMS

**banalities** (p. 207)
**guild** (p. 210)
**liberal arts** (p. 213)
**manor** (p. 206)

**regular clergy** (p. 205)
**Scholasticism** (p. 214)
**secular clergy** (p. 205)

For additional learning resources related to this chapter, please go to **www.myhistorylab.com**

PEARSON
**my**history**lab**

# 9

# The Late Middle Ages:

## Social and Political Breakdown (1300–1453)

**A procession of flagellants** at Tournai in Flanders in 1349, marching with the crucified Christ and scourging themselves in imitation of his suffering.

© ARPL/HIP/The Image Works

**What was the psychological impact of the Black Death on medieval Europe?**

T he West endured so many calamities as the Middle Ages drew to a close that European civilization seemed in imminent danger of collapse. From 1337 to 1453, France and England were locked in a bloody conflict called the Hundred Years' War. Between 1347 and 1350, a devastating plague swept through Europe and carried off a third of its population. In 1378, a quarrel between competing candidates for the papacy began a schism that kept the church divided for thirty-nine years. In 1453, the Turks overran Constantinople and charged up the Danube valley toward the heart of Europe.

These crises were accompanied by intellectual developments that undercut many of the assumptions about faith, life, and the social order that had comforted earlier generations. Some philosophers concluded that human reason is much more limited in scope than the Scholastics had realized. Feudal institutions, which had been assumed to be divinely ordained, were assaulted by kings who aspired to absolute monarchy. Competing claims to authority were made by kings and popes, and both of these leaders were challenged by political theorists who argued that subjects had the right to hold rulers accountable for how they used their power. ▪

# THE BLACK DEATH

**WHAT WERE** the social and economic consequences of the "Black Death"?

The virulent plague known as the Black Death struck fourteenth-century Europe when it was already suffering from overpopulation and malnutrition.

## PRECONDITIONS AND CAUSES OF THE PLAGUE

In the fourteenth century, nine-tenths of the population worked the land. The three-field system of crop production increased the amount of arable land and with it the food supply. As that supply grew, however, so did the population. It is estimated that Europe's population doubled between the years 1000 and 1300 and began thereafter to outstrip food production.

Between 1315 and 1317, crop failures produced the greatest famine of the Middle Ages. Densely populated urban areas such as the industrial towns of the Netherlands suffered greatly. Decades of overpopulation, economic depression, famine, and bad health progressively weakened Europe's population and made it highly vulnerable to a virulent bubonic plague that struck with full force in 1348.

The **Black Death** followed the trade routes from Asia into Europe. Rats, or more precisely, the fleas the rats bore, on ships from the Black Sea area most likely brought it to Western Europe. Appearing in Constantinople in 1346 and Sicily in late 1347, it entered Europe through the ports of Venice, Genoa, and Pisa in 1348. From there it swept rapidly through Spain and southern France and into northern Europe. Areas that lay outside the major trade routes, like Bohemia, appear to have remained virtually unaffected. Bubonic plague made numerous reappearances in succeeding decades. (See Map 9–1.)

**Black Death**   Virulent plague that struck in Sicily in 1347 and spread through Europe. It discolored the bodies of its victims. By the early fifteenth century, the plague may have reduced the population of western Europe by two-fifths.

## POPULAR REMEDIES

Contemporaries could neither explain the plague nor defend themselves against it. To them, the Black Death was a catastrophe with no apparent explanation and against which there was no known defense. (See "Encountering the Past: Medieval Medicine," page 227.) Throughout much of Western Europe, it inspired an obsession with death and dying and a deep pessimism that endured long after the plague years.

Popular wisdom held that a corruption in the atmosphere caused the disease. Some blamed poisonous fumes released by earthquakes. Many wore aromatic amulets

## MAP EXPLORATION

Interactive map: To explore this map further, go to **www.myhistorylab.com**

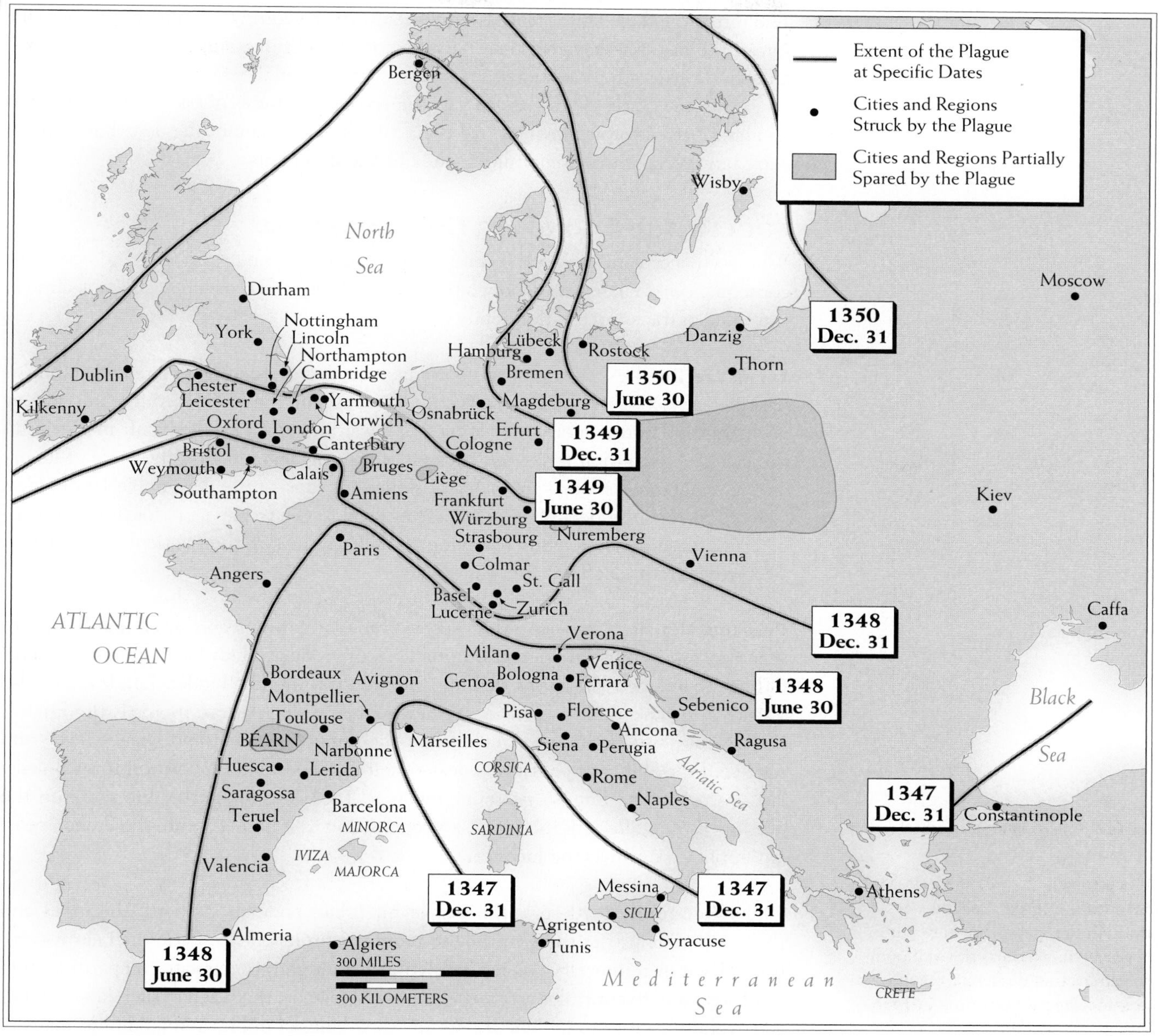

Extent of the Plague at Specific Dates
Cities and Regions Struck by the Plague
Cities and Regions Partially Spared by the Plague
North Sea
ATLANTIC OCEAN
Black Sea
Adriatic Sea
Mediterranean Sea
Bergen
Wisby
Moscow
Kiev
Caffa
Constantinople
Athens
Durham
York
Nottingham
Lincoln
Northampton
Cambridge
Dublin
Kilkenny
Chester
Leicester
Oxford
London
Yarmouth
Norwich
Canterbury
Bristol
Weymouth
Southampton
Calais
Bruges
Amiens
Liège
Osnabrück
Cologne
Hamburg
Lübeck
Rostock
Bremen
Magdeburg
Erfurt
Danzig
Thorn
Frankfurt
Würzburg
Strasbourg
Nuremberg
Colmar
St. Gall
Basel
Lucerne
Zurich
Vienna
Paris
Angers
Verona
Milan
Venice
Ferrara
Bologna
Genoa
Bordeaux
Avignon
Montpellier
Toulouse
BÉARN
Narbonne
Marseilles
Pisa
Florence
Ancona
Siena
Perugia
Sebenico
Ragusa
Rome
Naples
Huesca
Lerida
Saragossa
Teruel
Barcelona
MINORCA
IVIZA
MAJORCA
Valencia
CORSICA
SARDINIA
Messina
SICILY
Agrigento
Syracuse
Tunis
Algiers
Almeria
CRETE
1350 Dec. 31
1350 June 30
1349 Dec. 31
1349 June 30
1348 Dec. 31
1348 June 30
1347 Dec. 31
1347 Dec. 31
1347 Dec. 31
1348 June 30
300 MILES
300 KILOMETERS


MAP 9–1 **Spread of the Black Death** Apparently introduced by seaborne rats from Black Sea areas where plague-infested rodents had long been known, the Black Death brought huge human, social, and economic consequences. One of the lower estimates of Europeans dying is 25 million. The map charts the plague's spread in the mid–fourteenth century. Generally following trade routes, the plague reached Scandinavia by 1350, and some believe it then went on to Iceland and even Greenland. Areas off the main trade routes were largely spared.

**What does** the spread of the plague indicate about the networks of trade routes and economic development in Europe in the mid-fourteenth century?

as a remedy. There was a wide range of psychological and emotional responses to the crisis. One extreme reaction was processions of flagellants, religious fanatics who beat themselves in ritual penance, believing such action would bring divine intervention. The terror the flagellants created—and their dirty, bleeding bodies may have actually spread the disease—became so socially disruptive and threatening that the church finally outlawed such processions.

In some places, Jews were cast as scapegoats. Centuries of Christian propaganda had bred hatred toward Jews, as had their role as society's moneylenders. Pogroms occurred in several cities, sometimes incited by the flagellants.

## SOCIAL AND ECONOMIC CONSEQUENCES

Whole villages vanished in the wake of the plague. Among the social and economic consequences of such high depopulation were a shrunken labor supply and a decline in the value of the estates of the nobility.

**Farms Decline**    As the number of farm laborers decreased, wages increased and those of skilled artisans soared. Many serfs chose to commute their labor services into money payments and pursue more interesting and rewarding jobs in skilled craft industries in the cities. Agricultural prices fell because of waning demand, and the price of luxury and manufactured goods—the work of skilled artisans—rose. The noble landholders suffered the greatest decline in power. They were forced to pay more for finished products and for farm labor, while receiving a smaller return on their agricultural produce. Everywhere rents declined after the plague.

**Peasants Revolt**    To recoup their losses, some landowners converted arable land to sheep pasture, substituting more profitable wool production for labor-intensive grains. Others abandoned the farms, leasing them to the highest bidder. Landowners also sought to reverse their misfortune by new repressive legislation. In 1351, the English Parliament passed a Statute of Laborers, which limited wages to pre-plague levels and restricted the ability of peasants to leave their masters' land. Opposition to such legislation sparked the English peasants' revolt in 1381. In France the direct tax on the peasantry, the *taille*, was increased, and opposition to it helped ignite the French peasant uprising known as the **Jacquerie**.

**Cities Rebound**    Although the plague hit urban populations hard, the cities and their skilled industries came in time to prosper from its effects. Cities had always protected their own interests, passing legislation as they grew to regulate competition from rural areas and to control immigration. After the plague, the reach of such laws extended beyond the cities to include the surrounding lands of nobles and landlords, many of whom now peacefully integrated into urban life.

Expensive clothes and jewelry, furs from the north, and silks from the south were in great demand in the decades after the plague. The prices of manufactured and luxury items rose to new heights, which, in turn, encouraged workers to migrate from the countryside to the city and learn the skills of artisans. Townspeople profited coming and going. As wealth poured into the cities and per capita income rose, the prices of agricultural products from the countryside, now less in demand, declined.

The church also gained and lost. It suffered as a landholder and was politically weakened, yet it also received new revenues from the vastly increased demand for religious services for the dead and the dying, along with new gifts and bequests.

*taille*    The direct tax on the French peasantry.

**Jacquerie**    (From "Jacques Bonhomme," a peasant caricature) Name given to the series of bloody rebellions that desperate French peasants waged beginning in 1358.

# ENCOUNTERING THE PAST

## MEDIEVAL MEDICINE

*Medieval medicine was a mix of practices ranging from diet, exercise regimens, and medicines to prayer, magical amulets, and incantations. Celestial forces (the stars and planets) were assumed to influence human physical and mental states, and physicians turned to astrology for help in explaining illnesses and devising treatments. In a world where lives tended to be short and suffering difficult to ease, people were desperate for cures and willing to take advice from any source. The wealthy sought help from university-trained physicians. These men were the most prestigious, if not inevitably the most effective, healers. They relied on diet and medication to treat internal illnesses. Apothecaries supplied their patients with medicinal herbs, and surgeons performed any physical operations they prescribed. Some surgeons had university educations, but many were humble barbers who learned their trade as apprentices.*

Bloodletting was prescribed as a treatment for illness and a preservative of health, for medical theory held that illness was a result of an imbalance of humors (fluids) in the body. Greek science maintained there were four elements (earth, air, fire, and water), each associated with a quality (hot, cold, moist, and dry). The mix of these in the body determined its condition, and treatment called for draining off excesses or shifting humors to different locations in the body. Physicians commonly diagnosed problems by examining urine and blood and checking pulses. The urine flask was the medieval equivalent of the stethoscope—the badge of the physician.

**A Caricature of Physicians** (Early Sixteenth Century). A physician carries a uroscope (for collecting and examining urine); discolored urine signaled an immediate need for bleeding. The physician/surgeon wears surgical shoes and his assistant carries a flail—a comment on the risks of medical services.

Hacker Art Books Inc.

**How did medieval doctors respond to the challenges the plague presented?**

WHAT KIND of medical help was available to medieval people?

## NEW CONFLICTS AND OPPORTUNITIES

The economic and political power of local artisans and trade guilds grew steadily in the late Middle Ages, along with the demand for their goods and services. The merchant and patrician classes found it increasingly difficult to maintain their traditional dominance and grudgingly gave guild masters a voice in city government. As the guilds won political power, they encouraged restrictive legislation to protect local industries. The restrictions, in turn, caused conflict between master artisans, who wanted to keep their numbers low and expand their industries at a snail's pace, and the many journeymen, who were eager to rise to the rank of master. To the long-existing conflict between the guilds and the ruling urban patriciate was now added one within the guilds themselves.

Also, after 1350, the results of the plague put two traditional "containers" of monarchy—the landed nobility and the church—on the defensive. Kings now exploited growing national sentiment in an effort to centralize their governments and

## Overview    **Effects of the Black Death**

| | |
|---|---|
| **SOCIAL** | Rumors abounded that unpopular minorities were spreading the disease. Serfs began to abandon farming for more lucrative jobs in towns. |
| **ECONOMIC** | Agricultural profits diminished because consumers were fewer. Prices rose for luxury and manufactured goods as artisans became scarce. |
| **CULTURAL** | Churches saw increased demand for masses for the dead. Deep pessimism, superstition, and obsession with death were inspired. |
| **POLITICAL** | Nobles used their monopoly of political power to reverse declining fortunes. Laws passed freezing low wages and ordering peasants to stay on the land. |

economies. At the same time, the battles of the Hundred Years' War demonstrated the military superiority of paid professional armies over the traditional noble cavalry, thus bringing the latter's future role into question. The plague also killed many members of the clergy—perhaps one-third of the German clergy fell victim as they dutifully ministered to the sick and dying. This reduction in clerical ranks occurred in the same century that saw the pope move from Rome to Avignon in southeast France (1309–1377) and the Great Schism (1378–1417) divide the Church into warring factions.

# THE HUNDRED YEARS' WAR AND THE RISE OF NATIONAL SENTIMENT

**HOW DID** the Hundred Years' War contribute to a growing sense of national identity in France and England?

To field the armies and collect the revenues that made their existence possible, late medieval rulers depended on carefully negotiated alliances among a wide range of lesser powers. To maintain the order they required, the Norman kings of England and the Capetian kings of France fine-tuned traditional feudal relationships by stressing the duties of lesser to higher powers and the unquestioning loyalty noble vassals owed to the king. The result was a degree of centralized royal power unseen before in these lands and a growing national consciousness that together equipped both France and England for international warfare.

### THE CAUSES OF THE WAR

The conflict that came to be known as the Hundred Years' War began in May 1337 and lasted until October 1453. The English king Edward III (r. 1327–1377), the grandson of Philip the Fair of France (r. 1285–1314), may have started the war by asserting a claim to the French throne after the French king Charles IV (r. 1322–1328), the last of Philip the Fair's surviving sons, died without a male heir. The French barons had no intention of placing the then fifteen-year-old Edward on the French throne. They chose instead the first cousin of Charles IV, Philip VI of Valois (r. 1328–1350), the first of a new French dynasty that would rule into the sixteenth century.

But there was, of course, more to the war than just an English king's assertion of a claim to the French throne. England and France were then emergent territorial powers in too close proximity to one another. Edward was actually a vassal of Philip VI, holding several sizable French territories as fiefs from the king of France. English possession of any French land was repugnant to the French because it threatened the royal policy of centralization. England and France also quarreled over control of Flanders, which, although a French fief, was subject to political influence from England because its principal industry, the manufacture of cloth, depended on supplies of imported English wool. Compounding these frictions was a long history of prejudice and animosity between the French and English people, who constantly confronted one another on the high seas and in ports. Taken together, these various factors made the Hundred Years' War a struggle for national identity as well as for control of territory.

**Edward III pays** homage to his feudal lord Philip VI of France. Legally, Edward was a vassal of the king of France.

Archives Snark International/Art Resource, NY

**What tensions were there between ties of vassalage and national identity?**

**French Weakness**　For most of the conflict, until after 1415, the major battles ended in often stunning English victories. (See Map 9–2, page 230.) The primary reason for these French failures was internal disunity caused by endemic social conflicts. Unlike England, fourteenth-century France was still struggling to make the transition from a splintered feudal society to a centralized "modern" state.

Desperate to raise money for the war, French kings resorted to such financial policies as depreciating the currency and borrowing heavily from Italian bankers, which aggravated internal conflicts. In 1355, in a bid to secure funds, the king turned to the **Estates General**, a representative council of townspeople, clergy, and nobles. Although it levied taxes at the king's request, its independent members also exploited the king's plight to broaden their own regional sovereignty, thereby deepening territorial divisions.

**Estates General**　Assembly of representatives from France's propertied classes.

France's defeats also reflected English military superiority. The English infantry was more disciplined than the French, and English archers carried a formidable weapon, the longbow, capable of firing six arrows a minute with enough force to pierce an inch of wood or the armor of a knight at two hundred yards.

Finally, French weakness during the Hundred Years' War was due, in no small degree, to the comparative mediocrity of its royal leadership. English kings were far shrewder.

## PROGRESS OF THE WAR

The war had three major stages of development, each ending with a seemingly decisive victory by one or the other side.

**The Conflict During the Reign of Edward III**　In the first stage of the war, Edward embargoed English wool to Flanders, sparking urban rebellions by merchants and the trade guilds. The Flemish cities revolted against the French and in 1340 signed an alliance with England acknowledging Edward as king of France. On June 23 of that same year, in the first great battle of the war, Edward defeated the French fleet in the Bay of Sluys, but his subsequent effort to invade France by way of Flanders failed.

In 1346, Edward attacked Normandy and, after a series of easy victories that culminated at the Battle of Crécy, seized the port of Calais. Exhaustion of both sides and the onset of the Black Death forced a truce in late 1347, as the war entered a brief lull. In 1356, near Poitiers, the English won their greatest victory, routing France's noble cavalry and taking the French king, John II the Good (r. 1350–1364), captive back to England. A complete breakdown of political order in France followed.

## MAP EXPLORATION

Interactive map: To explore this map further, go to www.myhistorylab.com

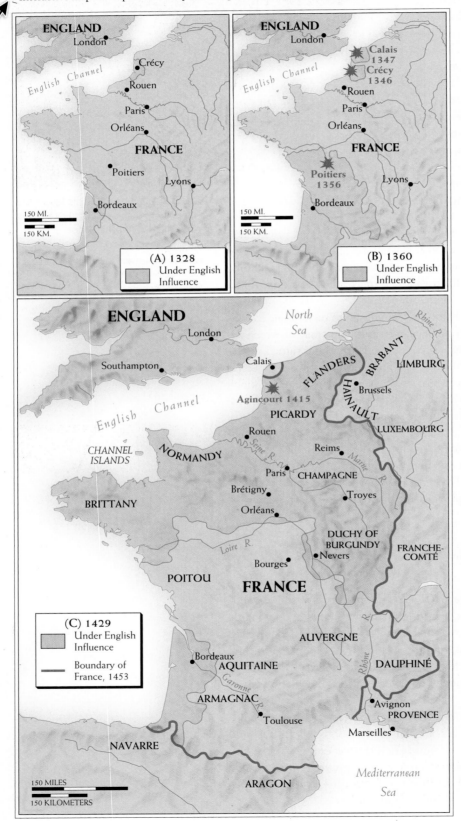

**(A) 1328** Under English Influence

**(B) 1360** Under English Influence

**(C) 1429** Under English Influence — Boundary of France, 1453

Power in France now lay with the Estates General. Led by the powerful merchants of Paris, that body took advantage of royal weakness, demanding and receiving rights similar to those the Magna Carta had granted to the English privileged classes. Yet, unlike the English Parliament, which represented the interests of a comparatively unified English nobility, the French Estates General was too divided to be an instrument for effective government.

To secure their rights, the French privileged classes forced the peasantry to pay ever-increasing taxes and to repair their war-damaged properties without compensation. This bullying became more than the peasants could bear, and they rose up in several regions in a series of bloody rebellions known as the Jacquerie in 1358. The nobility quickly put down the revolt, matching the rebels atrocity for atrocity.

On May 9, 1360, another milestone of the war was reached when England forced the Peace of Brétigny-Calais on the French. This agreement declared an end to Edward's vassalage to the king of France and affirmed his sovereignty over English territories in France (including Gascony, Guyenne, Poitou, and Calais). France also agreed to pay a ransom of 3 million gold crowns to win King John the Good's release. In return, Edward simply renounced his claim to the French throne.

Such a partition was unrealistic, and sober observers on both sides knew it could not last. France struck back in the late 1360s and, by the time of Edward's death in 1377, had beaten the English back to coastal enclaves and the territory around Bordeaux.

**MAP 9–2  The Hundred Years' War**  The Hundred Years' War went on intermittently from the late 1330s until 1453. These maps show the remarkable English territorial gains up to the sudden and decisive turning of the tide of battle in favor of the French by the forces of Joan of Arc in 1429.

**Using the** map as a reference, what were the major English victories or French weaknesses that led to England's significant influence in France by 1429?

**French Defeat and the Treaty of Troyes** After Edward's death the English war effort lessened, partly because of domestic problems within England. During the reign of Richard II (r. 1377–1399), England had its own version of the Jacquerie. In June 1381, long-oppressed peasants and artisans joined in a great revolt of the underprivileged classes under the leadership of John Ball, a secular priest, and Wat Tyler, a journeyman. As in France, the revolt was brutally crushed within the year, but it left the country divided for decades.

England recommenced the war under Henry V (r. 1413–1422), who took advantage of internal French turmoil created by the rise to power of the duchy of Burgundy. With France deeply divided, Henry V struck hard in Normandy, routing the French at Agincourt on October 25, 1415. In the years thereafter, belatedly recognizing that the defeat of France would leave them easy prey for the English, the Burgundians closed ranks with French royal forces. The renewed French unity was shattered in September 1419 when the duke of Burgundy was assassinated. The duke's son and heir, determined to avenge his father's death, joined forces with the English.

France now became Henry V's for the taking—at least in the short run. The Treaty of Troyes in 1420 disinherited the legitimate heir to the French throne and proclaimed Henry V the successor to the French king, Charles VI. When Henry and Charles died within months of one another in 1422, the infant Henry VI of England was proclaimed in Paris to be king of both France and England.

The son of Charles VI went into retreat in Bourges, where, on the death of his father, he became Charles VII to most of the French people, who ignored the Treaty of Troyes. Displaying unprecedented national feeling inspired by the remarkable Joan of Arc, they soon rallied to his cause and united in an ultimately victorious coalition.

**Joan of Arc and the War's Conclusion** Joan of Arc (1412–1431), a peasant from Domrémy in Lorraine in eastern France, presented herself to Charles VII in March 1429, declaring that the King of Heaven had called her to deliver besieged Orléans from the English. Charles's desperation overcame his skepticism, and he gave Joan his leave. Circumstances worked perfectly to her advantage. The English force, already exhausted by a six-month siege, was at the point of withdrawal when Joan arrived with fresh French troops. After repulsing the English from Orléans, the French enjoyed a succession of victories they popularly attributed to Joan. She rather had given the French something military experts could not: an enraged sense of national identity and destiny.

Within a few months of the liberation of Orléans, Charles VII received his crown in Rheims, ending the nine-year "disinheritance" prescribed by the Treaty of Troyes. The king now forgot his liberator as quickly as he had embraced her. When the Burgundians captured Joan in May 1430, he might have secured her release, but did little to help her. She was turned over to the Inquisition in English-held Rouen. She was executed as a relapsed heretic on May 30, 1431.

In 1435, the duke of Burgundy made peace with Charles, allowing France to force the English back. By 1453, when the war ended, the English held only their coastal enclave of Calais.

**A contemporary portrait** of Joan of Arc (1412–1431) in the National Archives in Paris.

Anonymous, 15th century. Joan of Arc. Franco-Flemish miniature. Archives Nationales, Paris, France. Photograph copyright Bridgeman-Giraudon/Art Resource, NY

**Who felt threatened by Joan of Arc? Why?**

## SIGNIFICANT DATES FROM THE PERIOD OF THE LATE MIDDLE AGES

| | |
|---|---|
| 1309–1377 | Avignon Papacy |
| 1340 | Sluys, first major battle of Hundred Years' War |
| 1346 | Battle of Crécy and seizure of Calais |
| 1347 | Black Death strikes |
| 1356 | Battle of Poitiers |
| 1358 | Jacquerie disrupts France |
| 1360 | Peace of Brétigny-Calais |
| 1378–1417 | Great Schism |
| 1381 | English Peasants' Revolt |
| 1414–1417 | Council of Constance |
| 1415 | Battle of Agincourt |
| 1420 | Treaty of Troyes |
| 1431 | Joan of Arc executed as a heretic |
| 1431–1449 | Council of Basel |
| 1453 | End of Hundred Years' War |

**HOW DID** secular rulers challenge papal authority in the fourteenth and fifteenth centuries?

The Hundred Years' War devastated France, but it also awakened French nationalism and hastened the transition there from a feudal monarchy to a centralized state. It saw Burgundy become a major European political power. It also encouraged the English, in response to the seesawing allegiance of the Netherlands throughout the conflict, to develop their own clothing industry and foreign markets. In both France and England, the burden of the on-again, off-again war fell most heavily on the peasantry, who were forced to support it with taxes and services.

# ECCLESIASTICAL BREAKDOWN AND REVIVAL: THE LATE MEDIEVAL CHURCH

## THE THIRTEENTH-CENTURY PAPACY

The late Middle Ages was a time of turmoil for the Catholic Church. As early as the reign of Pope Innocent III (r. 1198–1216), when papal power reached its height, there were ominous developments. Innocent's transformation of the papacy into a great secular power weakened the church spiritually even as it strengthened it politically. Thereafter, the church as a papal monarchy increasingly parted company with the church as the "body of the faithful." It was against this perceived "papal church" and in the name of the "true Christian church" that both reformers and heretics protested until the Protestant Reformation.

What Innocent began, his successors perfected. Under Urban IV (r. 1261–1264), the papacy established its own law court, the *Rota Romana*, which tightened and centralized the church's legal proceedings. The latter half of the thirteenth century saw an elaboration of the system of clerical taxation. In the same period, papal power to determine appointments to many major and minor church offices was greatly broadened. The thirteenth-century papacy became a powerful political institution governed by its own law and courts, serviced by an efficient international bureaucracy, and preoccupied with secular goals.

Papal centralization of the church undermined both diocesan authority and popular support. Rome's interests, not local needs, came to control church appointments, policies, and discipline. To its critics, the church in Rome was hardly more than a legalized, "fiscalized," bureaucratic institution.

**Political Fragmentation**    More than internal religious disunity was undermining the thirteenth-century church. The demise of imperial power meant the papacy in Rome was no longer the leader of anti-imperial sentiment in Italy. Instead of being the center of Italian resistance to the emperor, popes now found themselves on the defensive against their old allies.

Rulers with a stake in Italian politics now directed the intrigue formerly aimed at the emperor toward the College of Cardinals. Such efforts to control the decisions of the college led Pope Gregory X (r. 1271–1276) to establish the practice of sequestering the cardinals immediately upon the death of the pope. The purpose of this so-called conclave of cardinals was to minimize political influence on the election of new popes, but the college became so politicized that it proved to be of little avail.

In 1294, such a conclave, in frustration after a deadlock of more than two years, chose a saintly, but inept, hermit as Pope Celestine V. Celestine abdicated under suspicious circumstances after only a few weeks in office. Celestine's tragicomic reign shocked the Cardinals into electing his opposite, Pope Boniface VIII (r. 1294–1303), a nobleman and a skilled politician. His pontificate, however, would mark the beginning of the end of papal pretensions to great-power status.

# Boniface VIII and Philip the Fair

Boniface came to rule when England and France were maturing as nation-states. Boniface had the further misfortune of bringing to the papal throne memories of the way earlier popes had brought kings and emperors to their knees. Painfully he was to discover that the papal monarchy of the early thirteenth century was no match for the new political powers of the late thirteenth century.

**The Royal Challenge to Papal Authority** France and England were on the brink of all-out war when Boniface became pope in 1294. As both countries mobilized for war, they used the pretext of preparing for a Crusade to tax the clergy heavily. Viewing English and French taxation of the clergy as an assault on traditional clerical rights, Boniface took a strong stand against it. On February 5, 1296, he issued a bull, *Clericis laicos*, which forbade lay taxation of the clergy without papal approval and revoked all previous papal dispensations in this regard.

In England, Edward I retaliated by denying the clergy the right to be heard in royal court, in effect removing from them the protection of the king. But France's Philip IV "the fair" (r. 1285–1314) struck back with a vengeance: In August 1296, he forbade the exportation of money from France to Rome, thereby denying the papacy the revenues it needed to operate. Boniface had no choice but to come to terms quickly with Philip. He conceded Philip the right to tax the French clergy "during an emergency."

Boniface's fortunes appeared to revive in 1300, a "Jubilee year." During such a year, all Catholics who visited Rome and fulfilled certain conditions had the penalties for their unrepented sins remitted. Tens of thousands of pilgrims flocked to Rome, and Boniface, heady with this display of popular religiosity, reinserted himself into international politics. He championed Scottish resistance to England, for which he received a firm rebuke from an outraged Edward I and from Parliament.

But once again a confrontation with the king of France proved the more costly. Philip seemed to be eager for another fight with the pope. He arrested Boniface's Parisian legate, Bernard Saisset. Accused of heresy and treason, Saisset was tried and convicted in the king's court. Thereafter, Philip demanded that Boniface recognize the process against Saisset, something Boniface could do only if he was prepared to surrender his jurisdiction over the French episcopate. Boniface could not sidestep this challenge, and he acted swiftly to champion Saisset as a defender of clerical political independence within France. A bull, *Ausculta fili*, or "Listen, My Son," was sent to Philip in December 1301, pointedly informing him that "God has set popes over kings and kingdoms."

**Unam Sanctam (1302)** Philip unleashed a ruthless antipapal campaign. Increasingly placed on the defensive, Boniface made a last-ditch stand against state control of national churches. On November 18, 1302, he issued the bull *Unam Sanctam*. This famous statement of papal power declared that temporal authority was "subject" to the spiritual power of the church. On its face a bold assertion, *Unam Sanctam* was, in truth, the desperate act of a besieged papacy. (See "Compare & Connect: Who Runs the World: Priests or Princes?" pages 234–235.)

After *Unam Sanctam*, the French and their Italian allies moved against Boniface with force. Philip's chief minister, Guillaume de Nogaret, denounced Boniface to the French clergy as a heretic and common criminal. In mid-August 1303, his army surprised the pope at his retreat in Anagni, beat him up, and almost executed him before an aroused populace returned him safely to Rome. The ordeal, however, proved to be too much, and Boniface died in October 1303.

Boniface's immediate successor, Benedict XI (r. 1303–1304), excommunicated Nogaret for his deed, but there was to be no lasting papal retaliation. Benedict's successor, Clement V (r. 1305–1314), was forced into French subservience.

**Pope Boniface VIII** (r. 1294–1303), depicted here, opposed the taxation of the clergy by the kings of France and England and issued one of the strongest declarations of papal authority over rulers, the bull *Unam Sanctam*. This statue is in the Museo Civico, Bologna, Italy.

Statue of Pope Boniface VIII. Museo Civico, Bologna. Scala/Art Resource, NY

**What tools did the papacy have to ensure the implementation of its policies?**

# WHO RUNS THE WORLD: PRIESTS OR PRINCES?

In one of the boldest papal bulls in the history of Christianity, Pope Boniface VIII declared the temporal authority of rulers to be subject to papal authority. Behind that ideology lay a long, bitter dispute between the papacy and the kings of France and England. Despite the strained scholastic arguments from each side's apologists, the issue was paramount and kingdoms were at stake. The debaters were Giles of Rome and John of Paris, the former a philosopher and papal adviser, the latter a French Dominican and Aristotle expert. Quoting ecclesiastical authorities, Giles defended a papal theocracy, while John made the royal case for secular authority.

## QUESTIONS

1. Are the arguments pro and con logical and transparent?

2. How is history invoked to support their positions?

3. Which of the two seems to have the better authorities behind his arguments?

**Papal ring:** gold with an engraving on each side and set with a square stone.

Dorling Kindersley Media Library. Geoff Dann © The British Museum

**What were the most important sources of the papacy's wealth and power?**

## I. GILES OF ROME, *ON ECCLESIASTICAL POWER* (1301)

Hugh of St. Victor . . . declares that the spiritual power has to institute the earthly power and to judge it if it has not been good . . . We can clearly prove from the order of the universe that the church is set above nations and kingdoms [Jeremias 1:10] . . . It is the law of divinity that the lowest are led to the highest through intermediaries . . . At Romans 13 . . . the Apostle, having said that there is no power except from God, immediately added: "And those that are, are ordained of God." If then there are two swords [governments], one spiritual, the other temporal, as can be gathered from the words of the Gospel, "Behold, here are two swords" (Luke 22:38), [to which] the Lord at once added, "It is enough" because these two swords suffice for the church, [then] it follows that these two swords, these two powers and authorities, are [both] from God, since there is no power except from God. But, therefore they must be rightly ordered since, what is from God must be ordered. [And] they would not be so

In 1309, Clement moved the papal court to Avignon, an imperial city on the southeastern border of France. Situated on land that belonged to the pope, the city maintained its independence from the French king. In 1311, Clement made it his permanent residence. There the papacy would remain until 1377.

ordered unless one sword was led by the other and one was under the other since, as Dionysius said, the law of divinity which God gave to all created things requires this . . . Therefore the temporal sword, as being inferior, is led by the spiritual sword, as being superior, and the one is set below the other as an inferior below a superior.

It may be said that kings and princes ought to be subject spiritually but not temporally . . . But those who speak thus have not grasped the force of the argument. For if kings and princes were only spiritually subject to the church, one sword would not be below the other, nor temporalities below spiritualities; there would be no order in the powers, the lowest would not be led to the highest through intermediaries. If they are ordered, the temporal sword must be below the spiritual, and [royal] kingdoms below the vicar of Christ, and that by law . . . [then] the vicar of Christ must hold dominion over temporal affairs.

## II. JOHN OF PARIS, *TREATISE ON ROYAL AND PAPAL POWER* (1302–1303)

It is easy to see which is first in dignity, the kingship or the priesthood . . . A kingdom is ordered to this end, that an assembled multitude may live virtuously . . . and it is further ordered to a higher end which is the enjoyment of God; and responsibility for this end belongs to Christ, whose ministers and vicars are the priests. Therefore, the priestly power is of greater dignity than the secular and this is commonly conceded . . .

But if the priest is greater in himself than the prince and is greater in dignity, it does not follow that he is greater in all respects. For the lesser secular power is not related to the greater spiritual power as having its origin from it or being derived from it as the power of a proconsul is related to that of the emperor, which is greater in all respects since the power of the former is derived from the latter. The relationship is rather like that of a head of a household to a general of armies, since one is not derived from the other but both from a superior power. And so the secular power is greater than the spiritual in some things, namely in temporal affairs, and in such affairs it is not subject to the spiritual power in any way because it does not have its origin from it, but rather both have their origin immediately from the one supreme power, namely, the divine. Accordingly the inferior power is not subject to the superior in all things, but only in those where the supreme power has subordinated it to the greater. [For example] a teacher of literature or an instructor in morals directs the members of a household to a very noble end: the knowledge of truth. [That] end is more noble than [that] of a doctor who is concerned with a lower end, namely, the health of bodies. But who would say therefore that the doctor should be subjected to the teacher in preparing his medicines . . . ? Therefore, the priest is greater than the prince in spiritual affairs and, on the other hand, the prince is greater in temporal affairs.

Source: Brian Tierney, *The Crisis of Church and State 1050–1300* (Toronto: Toronto University Press, 1996), pp. 198–199, 209–209.

After Boniface's humiliation, popes never again seriously threatened kings and emperors, despite continuing papal excommunications and political intrigue. The relationship between church and state now tilted in favor of the state, and the control of religion fell into the hands of powerful monarchies. Ecclesiastical authority would become subordinate to larger secular political policies.

**Avignon papacy** Period from 1309 to 1377 when the papal court was situated in Avignon, France, and gained a reputation for greed and worldly corruption.

# THE AVIGNON PAPACY (1309–1377)

The **Avignon papacy** was in appearance, although not always in fact, under strong French influence. Under Clement V, the French dominated the College of Cardinals, testing the papacy's agility both politically and economically.

**Pope John XXII** Pope John XXII (r. 1316–1334), the most powerful Avignon pope, tried to restore papal independence and to return to Italy. This goal led him into war with the Visconti, the powerful ruling family of Milan, and a costly contest with Emperor Louis IV (r. 1314–1347). John had challenged Louis's election as emperor in 1314 in favor of the rival Habsburg candidate. When John obstinately and without legal justification refused to recognize Louis's election, the emperor declared him deposed and put in his place an antipope. Two outstanding pamphleteers wrote lasting tracts for the royal cause: William of Ockham, whom John excommunicated in 1328, and Marsilius of Padua (ca. 1290–1342), whose teaching John declared heretical in 1327.

In his *Defender of Peace* (1324), Marsilius of Padua stressed the independent origins and autonomy of secular government. Clergy were subjected to the strictest apostolic ideals and confined to purely spiritual functions, and all power of coercive judgment was denied the pope. Marsilius argued that spiritual crimes must await an eternal punishment. This assertion directly challenged the power of the pope to excommunicate rulers and place countries under interdict. The *Defender of Peace* depicted the pope as a subordinate member of a society over which the emperor ruled supreme and in which temporal peace was the highest good.

John XXII made the papacy a sophisticated international agency and adroitly adjusted it to the growing European money economy. The more the Curia, or papal court, mastered the latter, however, the more vulnerable it became to criticism. Under John's successor, Benedict XII (r. 1334–1342), the papacy became entrenched in Avignon. His high-living French successor, Clement VI (r. 1342–1352), placed papal policy in lockstep with the French. In this period the cardinals became barely more than lobbyists for policies their secular patrons favored.

**National Opposition to the Avignon Papacy** As Avignon's fiscal tentacles probed new areas, monarchies took strong action to protect their interests. The latter half of the fourteenth century saw legislation restricting papal jurisdiction and taxation in France, England, and Germany. In England, where the Avignon papacy was identified with the French enemy after the outbreak of the Hundred Years' War, Parliament passed statutes that restricted payments and appeals to Rome and the pope's power to make high ecclesiastical appointments several times between 1351 and 1393.

In France, the so-called Gallican, or French, liberties regulated ecclesiastical appointments and taxation. These national rights over religion had long been exercised in fact, and the church legally acknowledged them in the *Pragmatic Sanction of Bourges* in 1438. In German and Swiss cities in the fourteenth and fifteenth centuries, local governments also limited and even overturned traditional clerical privileges and immunities.

# JOHN WYCLIFFE AND JOHN HUSS

The popular lay religious movements that most successfully assailed the late medieval church were the Lollards in England and the Hussites in Bohemia. The Lollards looked to the writings of John Wycliffe (d. 1384) to justify their demands, while moderate and extreme Hussites turned to those of John Huss (d. 1415), although both Wycliffe and Huss would have disclaimed the extremists who revolted in their names.

Wycliffe was an Oxford theologian and a philosopher of high standing. His work initially served the anticlerical policies of the English government. After 1350, English kings greatly reduced the power of the Avignon papacy to make ecclesiastical appointments and to collect taxes within England, a position that Wycliffe strongly supported. His views on clerical poverty followed original Franciscan ideals and, more by accident than by design, gave justification to government restriction and even confiscation of church properties within England.

Wycliffe also maintained that personal merit, not rank and office, was the true basis of religious authority. This was a dangerous teaching, because it raised allegedly pious laypeople above allegedly corrupt ecclesiastics, regardless of the latter's official stature. It thus threatened secular as well as ecclesiastical dominion and jurisdiction. At his posthumous condemnation by the pope, Wycliffe was accused of the ancient heresy of Donatism—the teaching that the efficacy of the church's sacraments did not only lie in their true performance, but also depended on the moral character of the clergy who administered them. Wycliffe also anticipated certain Protestant criticisms of the medieval church by challenging papal infallibility, the sale of indulgences (pardons for unrepented sins), the authority of Scripture, and the dogma of transubstantiation.

The Lollards, English advocates of Wycliffe's teaching, preached in the vernacular, disseminated translations of Holy Scripture, and championed clerical poverty. After the English peasants' revolt in 1381, an uprising filled with egalitarian notions that could find support in Wycliffe's teaching, Lollardy was officially viewed as subversive. Opposed by an alliance of church and crown, it became a capital offense in England by 1401.

Heresy was less easily brought to heel in Bohemia, where it coalesced with a strong national movement. The University of Prague, founded in 1348, became the center for both Czech nationalism and a religious reform movement. The latter began within the bounds of orthodoxy. It was led by local intellectuals and preachers, the most famous of whom was John Huss, the rector of the university after 1403. The Czech reformers supported vernacular translations of the Bible and were critical of traditional ceremonies and allegedly superstitious practices, particularly those relating to the sacrament of the Eucharist.

Wycliffe's teaching appears early to have influenced the movement. Regular traffic between England and Bohemia had existed since the marriage in 1381 of Anne of Bohemia to King Richard II. Czech students studied at Oxford and returned with Wycliffe's writings.

Huss became the leader of the pro-Wycliffe faction at the University of Prague. In 1410, his activities brought about his excommunication, and Prague was placed under papal interdict. In 1414, Huss won an audience with the newly assembled Council of Constance. Within weeks of his arrival in early November 1414, he was accused of heresy and imprisoned. He died at the stake on July 6, 1415, and was followed there less than a year later by his colleague Jerome of Prague.

The reaction in Bohemia to the execution of these national heroes was fierce revolt. Militant Hussites, the Taborites, set out to transform Bohemia by force into a religious and social paradise under the military leadership of John Ziska. After a decade of belligerent protest, the Hussites won significant religious reforms and control over the Bohemian church from the Council of Basel.

## THE GREAT SCHISM (1378–1417) AND THE CONCILIAR MOVEMENT TO 1449

Pope Gregory XI (r. 1370–1378) reestablished the papacy in Rome in January 1377, ending what had come to be known as the "Babylonian Captivity" of the church in Avignon, a reference to the biblical bondage of the Israelites. The return to Rome proved to be short-lived, however.

**Urban VI and Clement VII** On Gregory's death, the cardinals, in Rome, elected an Italian archbishop as Pope Urban VI (r. 1378–1389), who immediately announced his

**A portrayal of** John Huss as he was led to the stake at Constance. After his execution, his bones and ashes were scattered in the Rhine River to prevent his followers from claiming them as relics. This pen-and-ink drawing is from Ulrich von Richenthal's *Chronicle of the Council of Constance* (ca. 1450).

CORBIS/Bettmann

**How did Czech nationalism and a desire for religious reform combine in the movement centered on John Huss?**

### QUICK REVIEW
**John Huss**

◆ 1403: Huss becomes rector of the University of Prague and begins religious reform movement

◆ Reformers used vernacular translations of the Bible and rejected practices they saw as superstitious

◆ Huss was burned at the stake as a heretic in 1415

intention to reform the Curia. The cardinals, most of whom were French, responded by calling for the return of the papacy to Avignon. The French king, Charles V (r. 1364–1380), wanting to keep the papacy within the sphere of French influence, lent his support to what came to be known as the Great Schism.

On September 20, 1378, five months after Urban's election, thirteen cardinals, all but one of whom was French, formed their own conclave and elected Pope Clement VII (r. 1378–1397), a cousin of the French king. Allegiance to the two papal courts divided along political lines. England and its allies (the Holy Roman Empire, Hungary, Bohemia, and Poland) acknowledged Urban VI, whereas France and those in its orbit (Naples, Scotland, Castile, and Aragon) supported Clement VII.

Two approaches were initially taken to end the schism. One tried to win the mutual cession of both popes, thereby clearing the way for the election of a new pope. The other sought to secure the resignation of the one in favor of the other. Both approaches proved fruitless. Each pope considered himself fully legitimate, and too much was at stake for either to make a magnanimous concession. One way remained: the deposition of both popes by a special council of the church.

**Conciliar Theory of Church Government**　The correctness of a conciliar deposition of a pope was debated a full thirty years before any direct action was taken. Advocates of conciliar theory sought to fashion a church in which a representative council could effectively regulate the actions of the pope. The conciliarists defined the church as the whole body of the faithful, of which the elected head, the pope, was only one part. The conciliarists further argued that a council of the church acted with greater authority than the pope alone.

**Justice in the** late Middle Ages. Depicted are the most common forms of corporal and capital punishment in Europe in the late Middle Ages and the Renaissance. At top: burning, hanging, drowning. At center: blinding, quartering, the wheel, cutting of hair (a mark of great shame for a freeman). At bottom: thrashing, decapitation, amputation of hand (for thieves).

Herzog August Bibliothek Wolfenbuttel

**Why were medieval punishments so often carried out in public?**

**The Council of Pisa (1409–1410)**　On the basis of the arguments of the conciliarists, cardinals representing both popes convened a council on their own authority in Pisa in 1409, deposed both the Roman and the Avignon popes, and elected a new pope, Alexander V. To the council's consternation, neither pope accepted its action, and Christendom suddenly faced the spectacle of three contending popes. Although most of Latin Christendom accepted Alexander and his Pisan successor John XXIII (r. 1410–1415), the popes of Rome and Avignon refused to step down.

**The Council of Constance (1414–1417)**　The intolerable situation ended when Emperor Sigismund prevailed on John XXIII to summon a new council in Constance in 1414, which the Roman pope Gregory XII also recognized. In a famous declaration entitled *Sacrosancta*, the council asserted its supremacy and elected a new pope, Martin V (r. 1417–1431), after the three contending popes had either resigned or been deposed.

**The Council of Basel (r. 1431–1449)**　Conciliar government of the church peaked at the Council of Basel, when the council directly negotiated church doctrine with heretics. In 1432, the Hussites of Bohemia entered into negotiations with the council and, in November 1433, an agreement among the emperor, the council, and the Hussites gave the Bohemians jurisdiction over their church similar to what the French and the English held.

The end of the Hussite wars and the new reform legislation curtailing the pope's powers of appointment and taxation were the high points of the Council of Basel and ominous signs of what lay ahead for the church. The exercise of such power by a council did not please the pope, and in 1438, he upstaged the Council of Basel by negotiating a reunion with the Eastern church. Although the agreement, signed in Florence in 1439, was short-lived, it restored papal prestige and signaled the demise of the conciliar movement. Having overreached itself, the

Council of Basel collapsed in 1449. A decade later, Pope Pius II (r. 1458–1464) issued the papal bull *Execrabilis* (1460) condemning appeals to councils as "erroneous and abominable" and "completely null and void."

**Consequences**  A major consequence of the conciliar movement was the devolving of greater religious responsibility onto the laity and secular governments. Without effective papal authority and leadership, secular control of national or territorial churches increased. Kings asserted their power over the church in England and France. In German, Swiss, and Italian cities, magistrates and city councils reformed and regulated religious life.

# MEDIEVAL RUSSIA

In the late tenth century, Prince Vladimir of Kiev (r. 980–1015), then Russia's dominant city, received delegations of Muslims, Roman Catholics, Jews, and Greek Orthodox Christians, each of which hoped to persuade the Russians to embrace their religion. Vladimir chose Greek Orthodoxy, which became the religion of Russia, adding strong cultural bonds to the close commercial ties that had long linked Russia to the Byzantine Empire.

**HOW DID** Mongol rule shape Russia's development?

## POLITICS AND SOCIETY

Vladimir's successor, Yaroslav the Wise (r. 1016–1054), developed Kiev into a magnificent political and cultural center, with architecture rivaling that of Constantinople. He also pursued contacts with the West in an unsuccessful effort to counter the political influence of the Byzantine emperors. After his death, rivalry among their princes slowly divided Russians into three cultural groups: the Great Russians, the White Russians, and the Little Russians (Ukrainians). Autonomous principalities also challenged Kiev's dominance, and it became just one of several national centers. Government in the principalities combined monarchy (the prince), aristocracy (the prince's council of noblemen), and democracy (a popular assembly of all free adult males). The broadest social division was between freemen and slaves. Freemen included the clergy, army officers, **boyars** (wealthy landowners), townspeople, and peasants.

**boyars**  Wealthy landowners among the freemen in late medieval Russia.

## MONGOL RULE (1243–1480)

In the thirteenth century, Mongol, or Tatar, armies swept through China, much of the Islamic world, and Russia. Ghengis Khan (1155–1227) invaded Russia in 1223, and Kiev fell to his grandson Batu Khan in 1240. Russian cities became dependent, tribute-paying principalities of the segment of the Mongol Empire known as the *Golden Horde*. The conquerors stationed their own officials in all the principal Russian towns to oversee taxation and the conscription of Russians into Tatar armies.

The Mongols, however, left Russian political and religious institutions largely intact and, thanks to their far-flung trade, brought most Russians greater prosperity. Princes of Moscow collected tribute for their overlords and grew wealthy under Mongol rule. As that rule weakened, the Moscow princes took control of the territory surrounding the city. Gradually the principality of Moscow expanded through land purchases, colonization, and conquest. In 1380, Grand Duke Dimitri of Moscow (r. 1350–1389) defeated Tatar forces at Kulikov Meadow, a victory that marked the beginning of the decline of the Mongol hegemony. Another century would pass, however, before Ivan III, the Great (d. 1505), would bring all of northern Russia under Moscow's control and end Mongol rule (1480). Moscow replaced Kiev as the political and religious center of Russia. After Constantinople fell to the Turks in 1453, the city became, in Russian eyes, the "third Rome."

**Genghis Khan Holding an Audience.** This Persian miniature shows the great conqueror and founder of the Mongol empire with members of his army and entourage as well as an apparent supplicant (lower right).

The Art Archive/Picture Desk, Inc./Kobal Collection

**What threat did the Mongols pose to medieval Europe?**

# SUMMARY

## WHAT WERE the social and economic consequences of the "Black Death"?

**The Black Death** Between 1347 and the early fifteenth century, close to 40 percent of the population of western Europe was killed by the Black Death. People had no idea what the bubonic plague was, how it was transmitted, or how to treat the sick. The fear inspired by the disease itself, and by the responses to it, influenced European attitudes and religious beliefs for centuries. The sharp reduction in population changed fundamental social, economic, and political patterns. Increased demand and reduced supply of luxury goods brought more power and wealth to cities and to skilled artisans; the landed nobility suffered economically as demand for food diminished. *page 224*

## HOW DID the Hundred Years' War contribute to a growing sense of national identity in France and England?

**The Hundred Years' War and the Rise of National Sentiment** The so-called Hundred Years' War between England and France actually lasted for more than a century, from 1337 to 1453, although there were long intervals of peace during this period. The direct cause of the war was controversy over the succession to the French throne. Despite a smaller population, less wealth, and fighting on enemy soil, England got the better of France in most of the significant early battles. England began the conflict as a more cohesive state than France. Eventually, however, the French began to see past regional rivalries, and Joan of Arc inspired an emergent national pride. *page 228*

## HOW DID secular rulers challenge papal authority in the fourteenth and fifteenth centuries?

**Ecclesiastical Breakdown and Revival: The Late Medieval Church** Through the thirteenth century, popes had worked to centralize church power. As nation-states gained cohesiveness, kings started to challenge papal authority. Throughout most of the fourteenth century, the papacy was based in Avignon, France, rather than Rome. The conciliar theory proposed that the pope just oversee a church that should rightfully be dominated by the faithful as a group. The Council of Basel in the fifteenth century provided a model of lay rights and responsibilities for other church and national organizations. *page 232*

## HOW DID Mongol rule shape Russia's development?

**Medieval Russia** Kiev was the most important city in Russia around the turn of the millennium, so Prince Vladimir of Kiev's selection of Greek Orthodoxy as the state religion had ramifications that endure to the present. Starting in the eleventh century, Kiev lost its preeminence, and Russians split into three geographic and cultural groupings: the Great Russians, the White Russians, and the Little Russians or Ukrainians. In 1223, Ghengis Khan sent a Mongol (or Tatar) army into Russia. The Golden Horde brought much of Russia into the Mongol Empire. Mongol rule ended in 1480, by which time Moscow was the dominant city within Russia. *page 239*

# REVIEW QUESTIONS

1. What were the causes of the Black Death? Why did it spread so quickly? What were its effects on European society? How important do you think disease is in changing the course of history?

2. What were the causes of the Hundred Years' War? What advantages did each side have? Why were the French ultimately victorious?

3. What changes took place in the church and in its relationship to secular society between 1200 and 1450? How did it respond to political threats from increasingly powerful monarchs? How great an influence did the church have on secular events?

4. What is meant by the term "Avignon papacy"? What caused the Great Schism? How was it resolved? Why did kings in the late thirteenth and early fourteenth centuries have more power over the church than it had over them? What did kings hope to achieve through their struggles with the church?

5. How did the Kievan and medieval Russian states develop in terms of religion, politics, and social structure? What effect did Mongol rule have on Russian lands?

## KEY TERMS

**Avignon papacy** (p. 236)
**Black Death** (p. 224)
**boyars** (p. 239)
**Estates General** (p. 229)
**Jacquerie** (p. 226)
*taille* (p. 226)

For additional learning resources related to this chapter, please go to **www.myhistorylab.com**

PEARSON
myhistorylab

# 10

# Renaissance and Discovery

**The Renaissance celebrated** human beauty and dignity. Here the Flemish painter Rogier van der Weyden (1400–1464) portrays an ordinary woman more perfectly on canvas than she could ever have appeared in life.

Rogier van der Weyden (Netherlandish, 1399.1400–1464), *Portrait of a Lady*. 1460. .370 × .270 (14 1/16 X 10 5/8) framed: .609 × .533 × .114 (24 X 21 X 4 1/2). Photo: Bob Grove. Andrew W. Mellon Collection. Photograph © Board of Trustees, National Gallery of Art, Washington, DC

**What personal qualities might the painter have wanted viewers to see in his subject?**

T he late medieval period was an era of creative disruption. The social order that had persisted in Europe for a thousand years failed, but Europe did not decline. It merely changed direction. By the late fifteenth century, its population had nearly recovered from the losses inflicted by the plagues, famines, and wars of the fourteenth century. Able rulers were establishing stable, centralized governments, and Italy's city-states were doing especially well. Italy's strategic location enabled it to dominate world trade, which still centered on the Mediterranean. Italy's commercial wealth gave its leaders means to provide patronage for education and the arts and fund the famous Italian Renaissance.

Renaissance scholars, the humanists, revived the study of classical Greek and Latin languages and literature. They reformed education and, thanks to the invention of the printing press, became the first scholars able to reach out to the general public. In their eagerness to educate ordinary men and women, they championed the use of vernacular languages as vehicles for art and serious thought.

During the late fifteenth and the sixteenth centuries, powerful nations arose in Western Europe and sponsored voyages of exploration that spread Europe's influence around the globe. The colonies they planted and empires they built yielded a flood of gold, information, and new materials that transformed the Western way of life. ■

# THE RENAISSANCE IN ITALY (1375–1527)

**HOW DID** humanism affect culture and the arts in fourteenth- and fifteenth-century Italy?

The Renaissance (which means "rebirth" in French) was a time of transition from medieval to modern times. Medieval Europe, especially before the twelfth century, had been a fragmented feudal society with an agricultural economy, and the church largely dominated its thought and culture. Renaissance Europe, especially after the fourteenth century, was characterized by growing national consciousness and political centralization, an urban economy based on organized commerce and capitalism, and growing lay and secular control of thought and culture, including religion. Italy between 1375 and 1527, a century and a half of cultural creativity, most strikingly reveals the distinctive features of the Renaissance.

## THE ITALIAN CITY-STATE

Renaissance society first took shape within the merchant cities of late medieval Italy. Italy had always had a cultural advantage over the rest of Europe because its geography made it the natural gateway between East and West. Venice, Genoa, and Pisa had traded uninterruptedly with the Near East throughout the Middle Ages, maintaining vibrant urban societies by virtue of such trade. When commerce revived on a large scale in the eleventh century, Italian merchants had quickly mastered the business skills of organization, bookkeeping, scouting new markets, and securing monopolies. During the thirteenth and fourteenth centuries, trade-rich cities became powerful city-states, dominating the political and economic life of the surrounding countryside. By the fifteenth century, the great Italian cities were the bankers for much of Europe.

**Florentine women doing** needlework, spinning, and weaving. These activities took up much of a woman's time and contributed to the elegance of dress for which Florentine men and women were famed.

Palazzo Schifanoia, Ferrara. Alinari/Art Resource, NY

**How important was the textile industry to the cultural development of Renaissance Florence?**

**Growth of City-States**    The endemic warfare between pope and emperor and the Guelf (propapal) and Ghibelline (proimperial) factions this warfare spawned assisted the growth of Italian cities and urban culture. Either of these factions might successfully have subdued the cities had they permitted each other to concentrate on doing so. Instead, they chose to weaken one another, which strengthened the merchant oligarchies of the cities.

Unlike the great cities of northern Europe, which kings and territorial princes dominated, the great Italian cities remained free to expand on their own. Becoming independent states, they absorbed the surrounding countryside, assimilating the local nobility in a unique urban meld of old and new rich. Five such major, competitive states evolved: the duchy of Milan, the republics of Florence and Venice, the Papal States, and the kingdom of Naples. (See Map 10–1.)

**Social Class and Conflict**   Social strife and competition for political power became so intense within the cities that most evolved into despotisms just to survive. Florence was the most striking example of social division and anarchy. Four distinguishable social groups existed within the city. There was the old rich, or *grandi*, the nobles and merchants who traditionally ruled the city. The emergent newly rich merchant class, capitalists and bankers known as the *popolo grosso*, or "fat people," formed a second group. In the late thirteenth and early fourteenth centuries, they began to challenge the old rich for political powers. Then there were the middle-burgher ranks of guild masters, shop owners, and professionals, the smaller businesspeople who, in Florence, as elsewhere, tended to side with the new rich against the conservative policies of the old rich. Finally, there was the *popolo minuto*, or the "little people," the lower economic classes. In 1457, one-third of the population of Florence, about 30,000 people, was officially listed as paupers, that is, as having no wealth at all.

These social divisions produced conflict at every level of society, to which was added the ever-present fear of foreign intrigue. In 1378, a great uprising of the poor, known as the Ciompi Revolt, occurred. It resulted from a combination of three factors that made life unbearable for those at the bottom of society: the feuding between the old rich and the new rich; the social anarchy created when the Black Death cut the city's population almost in half; and the collapse of the great banking houses of Bardi and Peruzzi, which left the poor more vulnerable than ever. The Ciompi Revolt established a chaotic four-year reign of power by the lower Florentine classes. True stability did not return to Florence until the ascent to power of the Florentine banker and statesman, Cosimo de' Medici (1389–1464) in 1434.

**Despotism and Diplomacy**   Cosimo de' Medici was the wealthiest Florentine and a natural statesman. He controlled the city internally from behind the scenes, manipulating the constitution and influencing elections. His grandson, Lorenzo the Magnificent (1449–1492; r. 1478–1492), ruled Florence in almost totalitarian fashion during the last, chaotic quarter of the fifteenth century. The assassination of his brother in

## MAP EXPLORATION

Interactive map: To explore this map further, go to **www.myhistorylab.com**

**MAP 10–1   Renaissance Italy**   The city-states of Renaissance Italy were self-contained principalities whose internal strife was monitored by their despots and whose external aggression was long successfully controlled by treaty.

**How did** city-states help shape the political climate of Renaissance Italy?

1478 by a rival family, the Pazzi, who had long plotted with the pope against the Medicis, made Lorenzo a cautious and determined ruler.

Despotism elsewhere was even less subtle. To prevent internal social conflict and foreign intrigue from paralyzing their cities, the dominant groups cooperated to install hired strongmen, or despots. Known as a *podestà*, the despot's sole purpose was to maintain law and order. He held executive, military, and judicial authority, and his mandate was direct and simple: to permit, by whatever means required, the normal flow of business activity without which neither the old rich and new rich, nor the poor of a city, could long survive, much less prosper. Because despots could not count on the loyalty of the divided populace, they operated through mercenary armies obtained through military brokers known as **condottieri**.

Mercifully, the political turbulence and warfare of the times also gave birth to the art of diplomacy. Through their diplomats, the various city-states stayed abreast of foreign military developments and, when shrewd enough, gained power and advantage over their enemies without actually going to war. Most city-states established resident embassies in the fifteenth century for that very purpose. Their ambassadors not only represented them in ceremonies and at negotiations, but they also became their watchful eyes and ears at rival courts.

The Italian city proved a congenial climate for an unprecedented flowering of thought and culture. Italian Renaissance culture was promoted vigorously in all the major city-states. Such widespread support occurred because the main requirement for patronage of the arts and letters was the one thing that Italian cities of the High Renaissance had in abundance: great wealth.

## HUMANISM

The most important Renaissance intellectual movement, humanism, was the scholarly study of the Latin and Greek classics and of the ancient Church Fathers, both for its own sake and in the hope of reviving respected ancient norms and values. Humanists advocated the **studia humanitatis**, a liberal arts program of study embracing grammar, rhetoric, poetry, history, politics, and moral philosophy. Not only were these subjects considered a joy in themselves, but they also celebrated the dignity of humankind and prepared people for a life of virtuous action.

The first humanists were orators and poets. They wrote original literature in both classical and vernacular languages, inspired by and modeled on the newly discovered works of the ancients. They also taught rhetoric within the universities. When humanists were not employed as teachers of rhetoric, princely and papal courts sought their talents as secretaries, speechwriters, and diplomats.

The study of classical and Christian antiquity had existed before the Italian Renaissance. There were memorable recoveries of ancient civilization during the Carolingian renaissance of the ninth century, within the cathedral school of Chartres in the twelfth century, during the great Aristotelian revival in Paris in the thirteenth century, and among the Augustinians in the early fourteenth century. These precedents, however, only partially compare with the achievements of the Italian Renaissance of the fourteenth and fifteenth centuries. The latter was far more secular and lay-dominated, had much broader interests, was blessed with many more recovered manuscripts, and its scholars possessed far superior technical skills than those who had delivered the earlier "rebirths" of antiquity.

Unlike their Scholastic rivals, humanists were less bound to recent tradition; nor did they focus all their attention on summarizing and comparing the views of recognized authorities. Their most respected sources were classical and biblical, not medieval philoso-

---

**condottieri**  Military brokers from whom one could hire a mercenary army.

**studia humanitatis (humanism)**  Scholarship of the Renaissance that championed the study of Latin and Greek classics and Christian church fathers as an end in itself and as a guide to reforming society. Some claim it is an un-Christian philosophy emphasizing human dignity, individualism, and secular values.

# ENCOUNTERING THE PAST

## THE GARDEN

*Gardens were sources of both necessities and pleasures for the people of the Middle Ages and the Renaissance, and every household from the grandest to the humblest had one. In addition to their practical functions, gardens had religious and social associations. They were enclosed behind walls, fences, or hedges to protect their contents, and they served as private retreats in a world that offered little shelter for privacy. They called to mind the Garden of Eden and the more sensuous pleasures of the garden described in the Bible's Song of Songs (4:12). They were symbols of paradise and reminders of the temptations that led to Adam's fall.*

Wealthy people had gardens (adorned with grottoes and fountains) that were designed primarily for pleasure. They provided ideal settings for the romantic trysts of courtly lovers. Even great houses, however, like the cottages of the poor, also had gardens devoted to much more utilitarian purposes. A medieval/Renaissance household depended on its garden for much of its food and medicine. The fruit it produced was mainly used to concoct sweet drinks, and it was the source of the limited range of vegetables medieval people consumed: cabbage, lentils, peas, beans, onions, leeks, beets, and parsnips. The herbs and flowers from gardens were highly prized as flavorings for a diet heavy on bland, starchy foods. They were also the era's most effective medicines.

**A wealthy man** oversees apple picking at harvest time in a fifteenth-century French orchard. In the town below, individual house gardens can be seen. Protective fences, made of woven sticks, keep out predatory animals.

By permission of the British Library

WHAT WERE some of the purposes that gardens served during the Middle Ages and early Renaissance?

Teresa McClean, *Medieval English Gardens* (New York: Viking Press, 1980), pp. 64, 133; Marilyn Stokstad and Jerry Stannard, *Gardens of the Middle Ages* (Lawrence, KS: Spencer Museum, 1983), pp. 19–21, 61.

---

phers and theologians. Avidly searching out manuscript collections, Italian humanists made the full riches of Greek and Latin antiquity available to contemporary scholars.

**Petrarch, Dante, and Boccaccio** Francesco Petrarch (1304–1374) was the "father of humanism." Petrarch celebrated ancient Rome in his *Letters to the Ancient Dead,* fancied personal letters to Cicero, Livy, Vergil, and Horace. He also wrote a Latin epic poem (*Africa,* a poetic historical tribute to the Roman general Scipio Africanus) and biographies of famous Roman men (*Lives of Illustrious Men*). His most famous contemporary work was a collection of highly introspective love sonnets to a certain Laura, a married woman he admired romantically from a safe distance. His critical textual studies, elitism, and contempt for the learning of the Scholastics were features many later humanists also shared. As with many later humanists, Classical and Christian values coexist uneasily in his work.

Petrarch was, however, far more secular in orientation than his famous near-contemporary Dante Alighieri (1265–1321), whose *Vita Nuova* and *Divine Comedy* form, with Petrarch's sonnets, the cornerstones of Italian vernacular literature. Petrarch's student and friend Giovanni Boccaccio (1313–1375) was also a pioneer of humanist studies. His *Decameron*—one hundred often bawdy tales told by three men and seven women in a safe country retreat away from the plague that ravaged Florence in 1348 (see Chapter 9)—is both a stinging social commentary (it exposes sexual and economic misconduct) and a sympathetic look at human behavior.

**Educational Reforms and Goals**    Humanists delighted in taking their mastery of ancient languages directly to the past, refusing to be slaves to later tradition. Such an attitude not only made them innovative educators, but also kept them constantly in search of new sources of information. In the search, they assembled magnificent manuscript collections, treating them as potent medicines for the ills of contemporary society, and capable of enlightening the minds of any who would immerse themselves in them.

The goal of humanist studies was wisdom eloquently spoken, both knowledge of the good and the ability to move others to desire it. Learning was not meant to remain abstract and unpracticed. "It is better to will the good than to know the truth," Petrarch taught, and it became a motto of many later humanists, who, like Petrarch, believed learning ennobled people.

The ideal of a useful education and well-rounded people inspired far-reaching reforms in traditional education. Vittorino da Feltre (d. 1446) exemplified the ideals of humanist teaching. Not only did he have his students read the difficult works of Pliny, Ptolemy, Terence, Plautus, Livy, and Plutarch, but he also subjected them to vigorous physical exercise and games.

Despite the grinding scholarly process of acquiring ancient knowledge, humanistic studies were not confined to the classroom. As Baldassare Castiglione's (1478–1529) *Book of the Courtier* illustrates, the rediscovered knowledge of the past was both a model and a challenge to the present. Written as a practical guide for the nobility at the court of Urbino, a small duchy in central Italy, it embodies the highest ideals of Italian humanism. The successful courtier is said to be one who knows how to integrate knowledge of ancient languages and history with athletic, military, and musical skills, while at the same time practicing good manners and exhibiting a high moral character.

Privileged, educated noblewomen also promoted the new education and culture at royal courts. Among them was Christine de Pisan (1363?–1434), the Italian-born daughter of the physician and astrologer of French king Charles V. She became an expert in classical, French, and Italian languages and literature. Married at fifteen and the widowed mother of three at twenty-seven, she wrote lyric poetry to support herself and was much read throughout the courts of Europe. Her most famous work, *The Treasure of the City of Ladies*, is a chronicle of the accomplishments of the great women of history.

**Christine de Pisan,** who has the modern reputation of being the first European feminist, presents her internationally famous book *The Treasure of the City of Ladies*, also known as *The Book of Three Virtues*, to Isabella of Bavaria amid her ladies in waiting.

Historical Picture Archive/CORBIS/Bettmann

**How does Pisan's widowhood help explain her intellectual career?**

## QUICK REVIEW
### Humanist Education

- Humanists sought reform of education to serve humanist values
- *Book of the Courtier*: Provided practical advice for conduct at court
- Women profited from education reform and helped guide it

**The Florentine "Academy" and the Revival of Platonism**    Of all the important recoveries of the past made during the Italian Renaissance, none stands out more than the revival of Greek studies in fifteenth-century Florence. Renaissance thinkers were especially attracted to the Platonic tradition and to those Church Fathers who tried to synthesize Platonic philosophy with Christian teaching. The Florentine Platonic Academy evolved under the patronage of Cosimo de' Medici and the supervision of Marsilio Ficino (1433–1499) and Pico della Mirandola (1463–1494). The Academy was actually not a formal school, but an informal gathering of influential Florentine humanists devoted to the revival of the works of Plato and the Neoplatonists: Plotinus, Proclus, Porphyry, and Dionysius the Areopagite. To this end, Ficino edited and published the complete works of Plato.

The appeal of Platonism lay in its flattering view of human nature. It distinguished between an eternal sphere of being and the perishable world in which humans actually lived. Human reason was believed to belong to the former—to have preexisted in this pristine world and still to commune with it, to which human knowledge of eternal mathematical and moral truth bore direct witness.

Strong Platonic influence is evident in Pico's *Oration on the Dignity of Man*, perhaps the most famous Renaissance statement on the nature of humankind. (See "Compare & Connect: Is the 'Renaissance Man' a Myth?" pages 250–251.) The *Oration* drew on Platonic teaching to depict humans as the only creatures in the world who possessed the freedom to be whatever they chose, able at will to rise to the height of angels or just as quickly to wallow with pigs.

**Critical Work of the Humanists: Lorenzo Valla**   Because they were guided by scholarly ideals of philological accuracy and historical truth, the humanists could become critics of tradition even when that was not their intention. Dispassionate critical scholarship shook long-standing foundations, not the least of which were those of the medieval church.

The work of Lorenzo Valla (1406–1457), author of the standard Renaissance text on Latin philology, *Elegances of the Latin Language* (1444), reveals the explosive character of the new learning. Although a good Catholic, Valla became a hero to later Protestant reformers. His popularity among them stemmed from his exposé of the *Donation of Constantine* and his defense of predestination against the advocates of free will.

The fraudulent *Donation*, written in the eighth century, purported to be a grant of vast territories that the Roman emperor Constantine (r. 307–337) donated to the pope. Using textual analysis and historical logic, Valla demonstrated that the document was filled with anachronistic terms, such as *fief*, and contained information that could not have existed in a fourth-century document. In the same dispassionate way, he also pointed out errors in the Latin Vulgate, still the authorized version of the Bible for the Western church.

Such discoveries did not make Valla any less loyal to the church, nor did they prevent his faithful fulfillment of the office of apostolic secretary in Rome under Pope Nicholas V (r. 1447–1455). Nonetheless, historical humanistic criticism of this type also served those less loyal to the medieval church. Young humanists formed the first identifiable group of Martin Luther's supporters.

**Civic Humanism**   Education, humanists believed, should promote individual virtue and public service, hence the designation, civic humanism. The most striking examples of this were found in Florence, where three humanists served as chancellors of the city: Coluccio Salutati (1331–1406), Leonardo Bruni (ca. 1370–1444), and Poggio Bracciolini (1380–1459). Each used his rhetorical skills to rally the Florentines against the aggression of Naples and Milan. Bruni and Poggio wrote adulatory histories of the city. Another accomplished humanist scholar, Leon Battista Alberti (1402–1472), was a noted Florentine architect and builder. However, many modern scholars doubt that humanistic scholarship really accounted for such civic activity and rather view the three famous humanist chancellors of Florence as men who simply wanted to exercise power.

Toward the end of the Renaissance, many humanists became cliquish and snobbish, an intellectual elite more concerned with narrow scholarly interests and writing

**QUICK REVIEW**
**Humanists and Plato**

♦ Humanists led revival of Greek studies
♦ Humanists were particularly attracted to Platonic tradition
♦ Plato's appeal lay in his view of human nature

# IS THE "RENAISSANCE MAN" A MYTH?

As several illustrations in this chapter attest, the great artists of the Renaissance (Raphael, Leonardo da Vinci, Albrecht Dürer) romanticized their human subjects and made them larger than life. Not only was the iconic "Renaissance man" perfectly proportioned physically, but he was also effective in what he undertook, endowed with the divine freedom and power to be and to do whatever he chose.

## QUESTIONS

1. Who or what are Pico's and Dürer's glorified humans? Is the vaunted "Renaissance Man" real or fictional?

2. What is one to make of an era fixated on the perfect body and mind?

3. Is Martin Luther's rejoinder (the bondage of the will) a breath of fresh air or religious misanthropy?

## I. PICO DELLA MIRANDOLA, *ORATION ON THE DIGNITY OF MAN* (CA. 1486)

*One of the most eloquent descriptions of the Renaissance image of human beings comes from the Italian humanist Pico della Mirandola (1463–1494). In his famed* Oration on the Dignity of Man *(ca. 1486), Pico describes humans as free to become whatever they choose.*

*Pico's "Renaissance Man" stands in stark contrast to the devout Christian pilgrim of the Middle Ages. The latter found himself always at the crossroads of heaven and hell, in constant fear of sin, death, and the devil, regularly confessing his sins and receiving forgiveness in an unending penitential cycle. Had the Middle Ages misjudged human nature? Was there a great transformation in human nature between the Middle Ages and the Renaissance?*

The best of artisans [God] ordained that that creature (man) to whom He had been able to give nothing proper to himself should have joint possession of whatever had been peculiar to each of the different kinds of being. He therefore took man as a creature of indeterminate nature and, assigning him a place in the middle of the world, addressed him thus: "Neither a fixed abode nor a form that is thine alone nor any function peculiar to thyself have we given thee, Adam, to the end that according to thy longing and according to thy judgment thou mayest have and possess what abode, what form, and what functions thou thyself shalt desire. The nature of all other beings is limited and constrained within the bounds of laws prescribed by Us. Thou, constrained by no limits, in accordance with thine own free will, in whose hand We have placed thee, shalt ordain for thyself the limits of thy nature. We have set thee at the world's center that thou mayest from thence more easily observe whatever is in the world. We have made thee neither of heaven nor of earth, neither mortal nor immortal, so that with freedom of choice and with honor, as though the maker and molder of thyself, thou mayest fashion thyself in whatever shape thou shalt prefer. Thou shalt have the power to degenerate into the lower forms of life, which are brutish. Thou shalt have the power, out of thy soul's judgment, to be reborn into the higher forms, which are divine." O supreme generosity of God the Father, O highest and most marvelous felicity of man! To him it is granted to have whatever he chooses, to be whatever he wills.

Source: Giovanni Pico della Mirandola, *Oration on the Dignity of Man*, in *The Renaissance Philosophy of Man*, ed. by E. Cassirer et al. (Chicago: Phoenix Books, 1961), pp. 224–225.

## II. ALBRECHT DÜRER

*In 1500, Albrecht Dürer, then twenty-eight, painted the most famous self-portrait of the European Renaissance and Reformation, one that celebrated his own beauty and genius by imposing his face on a portrayal of Christ, a work of art that has been called "the birth of the modern artist."*

**Albrecht Dürer (1471–1528), *Self-portrait at Age 28 with Fur Coat*.**

1500. Oil on wood, 67 × 49 cm. Alte Pinakothek, Munich, Germany. Photograph © Scala/Art Resource, NY

**What might Dürer be saying about himself in this self-portrait?**

*Fourteen years later (1514), on the occasion of his mother's death, Dürer engraved another famous image of himself, only now as a man in deep depression, or melancholy, his mind darkened and his creativity throttled.*

*In this self-portrait he is neither effective nor handsome, much less heroic and divine, not a self-portrait of a Renaissance man.*

## III. MARTIN LUTHER, *ON THE BONDAGE OF THE WILL* (1525)

*The greater challenge to the Renaissance man came from Martin Luther, who met his "Pico" in the northern humanist Desiderius Erasmus. Like Pico, Erasmus, flying in the face of Reformation theology, conceived free will to be "a power of the human will by which a man may apply himself to those things that lead to eternal salvation, or turn away from the same." Of such thinking, Luther made short-shift.*

It is in the highest degree wholesome and necessary for a Christian to know whether or not his will has anything to do in matters pertaining to salvation . . . We need to have in mind a clear-cut distinction between God's power and ours and God's work and ours, if we would live a godly life . . . The will, be it God's or man's, does what it does, good or bad, under no compulsion, but just as it wants or pleases, as if totally free . . . Wise men know what experience of life proves, that no man's purposes ever go forward as planned, but events overtake all men contrary to their expectation. . . . Who among us always lives and behaves as he should? But duty and doctrine are not therefore condemned, rather they condemn us.

God has promised His grace to the humbled, that is, to those who mourn over and despair of themselves. But a man cannot be thoroughly humbled till he realizes that his salvation is utterly beyond his own powers, counsels, efforts, will and works, and depends absolutely on the will, counsel, pleasure, and work of Another: GOD ALONE. As long as he is persuaded that he can make even the smallest contribution to his salvation, he . . . does not utterly despair of himself, and so is not humbled before God, but plans for himself a position, an occasion, a work, which shall bring him final salvation. But he who [no longer] doubts that his destiny depends entirely only on the will of God . . . waits for God to work in him, and such a man is very near to grace for his salvation. So if we want to drop this term ("free will") altogether, which would be the safest and most Christian thing to do, we may, still in good faith, teach people to use it to credit man with 'free will' in respect not of what is above him, but of what is below him . . . However, with regard to God and in all that bears on salvation or damnation, he has no 'free will' but is a captive, prisoner and bond-slave, either to the will of God, or to the will of Satan.

Source: Martin Luther, *On the Bondage of the Will*, ed. by J. I Packer & O. R. Johnston (Westwood, NJ: Fleming H. Fevell Co., 1957), pp. 79, 81, 83, 87, 100, 104, 107, 137.

**Albrecht Dürer, *Melencolia I* (1514).**

Engraving. 23.8 X 18.9 cm. Courtesy of the Library of Congress.

**What symbols did Dürer employ to suggest the effects of melancholy?**

pure, classical Latin than with revitalizing civic and social life. In reaction to this elitist trend, the humanist historians Niccolò Machiavelli (1469–1527) and Francesco Guicciardini (1483–1540) wrote in Italian and made contemporary history their primary source and subject matter. Here, arguably, we can see the two sides of humanism: deep scholarship and practical politics.

## RENAISSANCE ART

In Renaissance Italy, as in Reformation Europe, the values and interests of the laity were no longer subordinated to those of the clergy. In education, culture, and religion, the laity assumed a leading role and established models for the clergy to emulate. This development was due in part to the church's loss of international power during the great crises of the late Middle Ages. The rise of national sentiment and the emergence of national bureaucracies staffed by laymen, not clerics, and the rapid growth of lay education over the fourteenth and fifteenth centuries also encouraged it. Medieval Christian values were adjusted to a more this-worldly spirit.

This new perspective on life is prominent in the painting and sculpture of the High Renaissance (1450–1527), when art and sculpture reached their full maturity. Whereas medieval art tended to be abstract and formulaic, Renaissance art emphatically embraced the natural world and human emotions. Renaissance artists gave their works a rational, even mathematical, order—perfect symmetry and proportionality reflecting a belief in the harmony of the universe.

Renaissance artists were helped by the development of new technical skills during the fifteenth century. In addition to the availability of oil paints, two special techniques gave them an edge: the use of shading to enhance naturalness (*chiaroscuro*) and the adjustment of the size of figures to give the viewer a feeling of continuity with the painting (*linear perspective*). These techniques enabled the artist to portray space realistically and to paint a more natural world. The result, compared to their flat Byzantine and Gothic counterparts, was a three-dimensional canvas filled with energy and life.

Giotto (1266–1336), the father of Renaissance painting, signaled the new direction. An admirer of Saint Francis of Assisi, whose love of nature he shared, Giotto painted a more natural world. Though still filled with religious seriousness, his work was no longer an abstract and unnatural depiction of the world. The painter Masaccio (1401–1428) and the sculptor Donatello (1386–1466) also portrayed the world around them literally and naturally. The great masters of the High Renaissance—Leonardo da Vinci (1452–1519), Raphael (1483–1520), and Michelangelo Buonarroti (1475–1564)—reached the heights of such painting.

**Leonardo da Vinci**    A true master of many skills, Leonardo exhibited the Renaissance ideal of the universal person. One of the greatest painters of all time, he also advised Italian princes and the French king Francis I (r. 1515–1547) on military engineering. He advocated scientific experimentation, dissected corpses to learn anatomy, and was a self-taught botanist. His inventive mind foresaw such modern machines as airplanes and submarines. His great skill in conveying inner moods through complex facial expression is apparent not only in his most famous painting, the *Mona Lisa*, but in his self-portrait as well.

**Raphael**    A man of great kindness and a painter of great sensitivity, his contemporaries loved Raphael as much for his person as for his work. He is most famous for his tender madonnas and the great fresco in the Vatican, *The School of Athens,* a virtually perfect example of Renaissance technique. It depicts Plato and Aristotle surrounded by other great philosophers and scientists of antiquity who bear the features of Raphael's famous contemporaries.

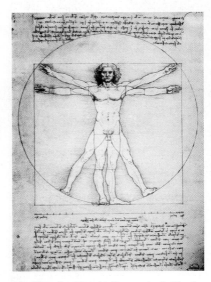

**The Vitruvian Man,** by Leonardo da Vinci, c. 1490. Like most other Renaissance artists, Leonardo sought to portray human beauty and perfection. This sketch is named after the first-century c.e. Roman architect Marcus Pollio Vitruvius, who used squares and circles to demonstrate the human body's symmetry and proportionality.

Corbis/Bettmann

**Why did da Vinci use geometry to demonstrate man's perfection?**

**mannerism**    Reaction against the simplicity, symmetry, and idealism of High Renaissance art. It made room for the strange, even the abnormal, and gave free reign to the subjectivity of the artist. The name reflects a tendency by artists to employ "mannered" ("affected") techniques—distortions that expressed individual perceptions and feelings.

**Michelangelo**   The melancholy genius Michelangelo also excelled in a variety of arts and crafts. His eighteen-foot sculpture of David, which long stood majestically in the great square of Florence, is a perfect example of Renaissance devotion to harmony, symmetry, and proportion, all serving the glorification of the human form. Four different popes commissioned works by Michelangelo. The frescoes in the Vatican's Sistine Chapel are the most famous, painted during the pontificate of Pope Julius II (r. 1503–1513), who also set Michelangelo to work on his own magnificent tomb.

His later works mark, artistically and philosophically, the passing of High Renaissance painting and the advent of a new style known as **mannerism**, which reached its peak in the late sixteenth and early seventeenth centuries. A reaction to the simplicity and symmetry of High Renaissance art, which also had a parallel in contemporary music and literature, mannerism made room for the strange and the abnormal, giving freer reign to the individual perceptions and feelings of the artist, who now felt free to paint, compose, or write in a "mannered," or "affected," way. Tintoretto (d. 1594) and El Greco (d. 1614) are mannerism's supreme representatives.

**Combining the painterly** qualities of all the other Renaissance masters; Raphael created scenes of tender beauty and subjects sublime in both flesh and spirit.

Musée du Louvre, Paris/Giraudon, Paris/SuperStock

**How did Raphael use the depiction of human emotion to comment on the nature of divine truth?**

## SLAVERY IN THE RENAISSANCE

Throughout Renaissance Italy, slavery flourished as extravagantly as art and culture. A thriving Western slave market existed as early as the twelfth century, when the Spanish sold Muslim slaves captured in raids and war to wealthy Italians and other buyers. In addition to widespread household or domestic slavery, collective plantation slavery, following East Asian models, also developed in the eastern Mediterranean during the High Middle Ages. In the savannas of Sudan and the Venetian estates on the islands of Cyprus and Crete, gangs of slaves cut sugarcane, setting the model for later slave plantations in the Mediterranean and the New World.

After the Black Death (1348–1350) reduced the supply of laborers everywhere in Western Europe, the demand for slaves soared. Slaves were imported from Africa, the Balkans, Constantinople, Cyprus, Crete, and the lands surrounding the Black Sea.

Tatars and Africans appear to have been the worst treated, but as in ancient Greece and Rome, slaves at this time were generally accepted as family members and integrated into households. Not a few women slaves became mothers of their masters' children. Fathers often adopted children of such unions and raised them as their legitimate heirs. It was also in the interest of their owners to keep slaves healthy and happy; otherwise they would be of little use and even become a threat. Slaves nonetheless remained a foreign and suspected presence in Italian society; they were, as all knew, uprooted and resentful people.

| SIGNIFICANT DATES FROM THE ITALIAN RENAISSANCE (1375–1527) | |
|---|---|
| **1434** | Medici rule established in Florence |
| **1454–1455** | Treaty of Lodi |
| **1494** | Charles VIII of France invades Italy |
| **1495** | League of Venice |
| **1499** | Louis XII invades Italy |
| **1500** | The Borgias conquer Romagna |
| **1512–1513** | The Holy League defeats the French |
| **1515** | Francis I invades Italy |
| **1527** | Sack of Rome by imperial soldiers |

# ITALY'S POLITICAL DECLINE: THE FRENCH INVASIONS (1494–1527)

As a land of autonomous city-states, Italy had always relied on internal cooperation for its peace and safety from foreign invasion—especially by the Turks. Such cooperation was maintained during the second half of the fifteenth century, thanks to a political alliance known as the Treaty of Lodi (1454–1455). Its terms brought Milan and Naples,

**WHAT WERE** the causes of Italy's political decline?

long traditional enemies, into the alliance with Florence. These three stood together for decades against Venice, which frequently joined the Papal States to maintain an internal balance of power. However, when a foreign enemy threatened Italy, the five states could also present a united front.

Around 1490, after the rise to power of the Milanese despot Ludovico il Moro, hostilities between Milan and Naples resumed. The peace that the Treaty of Lodi made possible ended in 1494 when Naples, supported by Florence and the Borgia Pope Alexander VI (r. 1492–1503), threatened Milan. Ludovico made a fatal response to these new political alignments: He appealed to the French for aid. French kings had ruled Naples from 1266 to 1442 before being driven out by Duke Alfonso of Sicily. Breaking a wise Italian rule, Ludovico invited the French to reenter Italy and revive their dynastic claim to Naples. In his haste to check rival Naples, Ludovico did not recognize sufficiently that France also had dynastic claims to Milan. Nor did he foresee how insatiable the French appetite for new territory would become once French armies had crossed the Alps and encamped in Italy.

## CHARLES VIII'S MARCH THROUGH ITALY

The French king Louis XI had resisted the temptation to invade Italy while nonetheless keeping French dynastic claims in Italy alive. His successor, Charles VIII (r. 1483–1498), an eager youth in his twenties, responded to Ludovico's call with lightning speed. Within five months, he had crossed the Alps (August 1494) and raced as conqueror through Florence and the Papal States into Naples. As Charles approached Florence, its Florentine ruler, Piero de' Medici, who was allied with Naples against Milan, tried to placate the French king by handing over Pisa and other Florentine possessions. Such appeasement only brought about Piero's exile by a citizenry that was being revolutionized by a radical Dominican preacher named Girolamo Savonarola (1452–1498). Savonarola convinced the fearful Florentines that the French king's arrival was a long-delayed and fully justified divine vengeance on their immorality.

That allowed Charles to enter Florence without resistance. Between Savonarola's fatal flattery and the payment of a large ransom, the city escaped destruction. After Charles's departure, Savonarola exercised virtual rule over Florence for four years, but the Florentines eventually tired of his puritanical tyranny and executed him (May 1498).

Charles's lightning march through Italy also struck terror in non-Italian hearts. Ferdinand of Aragon (r. 1479–1516), who had hoped to expand his own possessions in Italy from his base in Sicily, now found himself vulnerable to a French-Italian axis. In response he created a new counteralliance—the League of Venice. Formed in March 1495, the League brought Venice, the Papal States, and Emperor Maximilian I (r. 1493–1519) together with Ferdinand against the French. When Milan, which had come to regret inviting the French into Italy, joined the League, Charles was forced to retreat.

## POPE ALEXANDER VI AND THE BORGIA FAMILY

The French returned to Italy under Charles's successor, Louis XII (r. 1498–1515). This time a new Italian ally, the Borgia pope, Alexander VI, assisted them. He placed papal policy in tandem with the efforts of his powerful family to secure a political base in Romagna in north central Italy.

In Romagna, several principalities had fallen away from the church during the Avignon papacy. Venice, the pope's ally within the League of Venice, continued to contest the Papal States for their loyalty. Seeing that a French alliance would allow him to reestablish control over the region, Alexander worked hard to secure French favor and to make it possible for both the French king and the pope to realize their ambitions within Italy. Louis invaded Milan in August 1499. In 1500, Louis and Ferdinand of Aragon divided Naples between them, and the pope and his illegitimate son, Cesare Borgia, conquered the cities of Romagna without opposition. Alexander's victorious son was given the title "duke of Romagna."

## POPE JULIUS II

Cardinal Giuliano della Rovere, a strong opponent of the Borgia family, succeeded Alexander VI as Pope Julius II (r. 1503–1513). He suppressed the Borgias and placed their newly conquered lands in Romagna under papal jurisdiction. Julius raised the Renaissance papacy to its peak of military prowess and diplomatic intrigue, gaining him the title of "warrior pope."

Assisted by his powerful allies, Pope Julius drove the Venetians out of Romagna in 1509 and fully secured the Papal States. Having realized this long-sought papal goal, Julius turned to the second major undertaking of his pontificate: ridding Italy of his former ally, the French invader. Julius, Ferdinand of Aragon, and Venice formed a second Holy League in October 1511 and were joined by Emperor Maximilian I and the Swiss. In 1512, the league had the French in full retreat, and the Swiss defeated them in 1513 at Novara.

The French were nothing if not persistent. They invaded Italy a third time under Louis's successor, Francis I (r. 1515–1547). French victory won the Concordat of Bologna from the pope in August 1516, an agreement that gave the French king control over the French clergy in exchange for French recognition of the pope's superiority over church councils and his right to collect annates in France. This concordat helped keep France Catholic after the outbreak of the Protestant Reformation, but the new French entry into Italy set the stage for the first of four major wars with Spain in the first half of the sixteenth century: the Habsburg-Valois wars, none of which France won.

## NICCOLÒ MACHIAVELLI

The foreign invasions made a shambles of Italy. One who watched as French, Spanish, and German armies wreaked havoc on Italy was Niccolò Machiavelli (1469–1527). The more he saw, the more convinced he became that Italian political unity and independence were ends that justified any means.

A humanist and a careful student of ancient Rome, Machiavelli was impressed by the way Roman rulers and citizens had then defended their homeland. They possessed *virtù*, the ability to act decisively and heroically for the good of their country. Stories of ancient Roman patriotism and self-sacrifice were Machiavelli's favorites, and he lamented the absence of such traits among his compatriots.

Machiavelli also held republican ideals, which he did not want to see vanish from Italy. He believed a strong and determined people could struggle successfully with fortune. He scolded the Italian people for the self-destruction their own internal feuding was causing. He wanted an end to that behavior above all, so a reunited Italy could drive all foreign armies out.

His fellow citizens were not up to such a challenge. The juxtaposition of what Machiavelli believed the ancient Romans had been, with the failure of his contemporaries to attain such high ideals, made him the famous cynic whose name—in the epithet "Machiavellian"—has become synonymous with ruthless political expediency. Only a strongman, he concluded, could impose order on so divided and selfish a people; the salvation of Italy required, for the present, cunning dictators.

It has been argued that Machiavelli wrote *The Prince* in 1513 as a cynical satire on the way rulers actually do behave and not as a serious recommendation of unprincipled despotic rule. But Machiavelli seems to have been in earnest when he advised rulers to discover the advantages of fraud and brutality, at least as a temporary means to

**Santi di Tito's** portrait of Machiavelli, perhaps the most famous Italian political theorist, who advised Renaissance princes to practice artful deception and inspire fear in their subjects if they wished to be successful.

Scala/Art Resource, NY

**Should we consider Machiavelli a humanist? Why or why not?**

the higher end of a unified Italy. He apparently hoped to see a strong ruler emerge from the Medici family, which had captured the papacy in 1513 with the pontificate of Leo X (r. 1513–1521). At the same time, the Medici family retained control over the powerful territorial state of Florence. *The Prince* was pointedly dedicated to Lorenzo de' Medici, duke of Urbino and grandson of Lorenzo the Magnificent.

Whatever Machiavelli's hopes may have been, the Medicis were not destined to be Italy's deliverers. The second Medici pope, Clement VII (r. 1523–1534), watched helplessly as the army of Emperor Charles V sacked Rome in 1527, also the year of Machiavelli's death.

# REVIVAL OF MONARCHY IN NORTHERN EUROPE

**HOW WERE** the powerful monarchies of northern Europe different from their predecessors?

After 1450, the emergence of truly sovereign rulers set in motion a shift from divided feudal monarchy to unified national monarchies. Dynastic and chivalric ideals of feudal monarchy did not, however, vanish. Territorial princes remained on the scene and representative bodies persisted and even grew in influence. Still, in the late fifteenth and early sixteenth centuries, the old problem of the one and the many was now progressively decided in favor of national monarchs.

The feudal monarchy of the High Middle Ages was characterized by the division of the basic powers of government between the king and his semiautonomous vassals. The nobility and the towns then acted with varying degrees of unity and success through evolving representative assemblies, such as the English Parliament, the French Estates General, and the Spanish *Cortés*, to thwart the centralization of royal power into a united nation. But after the Hundred Years' War and the Great Schism in the church, the nobility and the clergy were in decline and less able to block growing national monarchies.

The increasingly important towns now began to ally with the king. Loyal, business-wise townspeople, not the nobility and the clergy, increasingly staffed royal offices and became the king's lawyers, bookkeepers, military tacticians, and foreign diplomats. This new alliance between king and town broke the bonds of feudal society and made possible the rise of sovereign states.

In a sovereign state, the powers of taxation, war making, and law enforcement no longer belong to semiautonomous vassals, but are concentrated in the monarch and exercised by his or her chosen agents. Taxes, wars, and laws become national, rather than merely regional, matters. Only as monarchs became able to act independently of the nobility and representative assemblies could they overcome the decentralization that impeded nation building.

The many were, of course, never totally subjugated to the one. But in the last half of the fifteenth century, rulers demonstrated that the law was their creature. They appointed civil servants whose vision was no longer merely local or regional. These royal ministers and agents could become closely attached to the localities they administered in the ruler's name, and regions were able to secure congenial royal appointments. Nonetheless, these new executives remained royal executives, bureaucrats whose outlook was now "national" and whose loyalty was to the "state."

Monarchies also began to create standing national armies in the fifteenth century. The noble cavalry receded as the infantry and the artillery became the backbone of royal armies. Mercenary soldiers were recruited from Switzerland and Germany to form the major part of the "king's army." Professional soldiers who fought for pay and booty proved far more efficient than feudal vassals who fought simply for honor's sake. Monarchs who failed to meet their payrolls, however, now faced a new danger of mutiny and banditry by foreign troops.

The growing cost of warfare in the fifteenth and sixteenth centuries increased the monarch's need for new national sources of income. The great obstacle was the stubborn belief of the highest social classes that they were immune from government taxation. The nobility guarded their properties and traditional rights and despised taxation as an insult and a humiliation. Royal revenues accordingly had to grow at the expense of those least able to resist and least able to pay.

The monarchs had several options when it came to raising money. As feudal lords, they could collect rents from their royal domains. They could also levy national taxes on basic food and clothing. The rulers could also levy direct taxes on the peasantry, which they did through agreeable representative assemblies of the privileged classes in which the peasantry did not sit. Innovative fund-raising devices in the fifteenth century included the sale of public offices and the issuance of high-interest government bonds. Rulers still did not levy taxes on the powerful nobility, but instead, they borrowed from rich nobles and the great bankers of Italy and Germany. In money matters, the privileged classes remained as much the kings' creditors and competitors as their subjects.

## FRANCE

Charles VII (r. 1422–1461) was a king made great by those who served him. His ministers and advisors created a permanent professional army and helped develop a strong economy, diplomatic corps, and national administration during Charles's reign. These sturdy tools in turn enabled Charles's son and successor, the ruthless Louis XI (r. 1461–1483), to make France a great power.

French nation building had two political cornerstones in the fifteenth century. The first was the collapse of the English Empire in France following the Hundred Years' War. The second was the defeat of Charles the Bold (r. 1467–1477) and his duchy of Burgundy. Louis XI and Habsburg emperor Maximilian I divided the conquered Burgundian lands between them, with the treaty-wise Habsburgs getting the better part. The dissolution of Burgundy ended its constant intrigue against the French king and left Louis XI free to secure the monarchy. Between the newly acquired Burgundian lands and his own inheritance, the king was able to end his reign with a kingdom almost twice the size of that he had inherited.

A strong nation is a two-edged sword. Because Louis's successors inherited a secure and efficient government, they felt free to pursue what proved ultimately to be a bad foreign policy. Conquests in Italy in the 1490s and a long series of losing wars with the Habsburgs in the first half of the sixteenth century left France, by the mid-sixteenth century, once again a defeated nation almost as divided as it had been during the Hundred Years' War.

## SPAIN

Both Castile and Aragon had been poorly ruled and divided kingdoms in the mid–fifteenth century, but the union of Isabella of Castile (r. 1474–1504) and Ferdinand of Aragon (r. 1479–1516) in 1469 changed that situation. Although the marriage of Ferdinand and Isabella dynastically united the two kingdoms, they remained constitutionally separated. Each retained its respective government agencies—separate laws, armies, coinage, and taxation—and cultural traditions.

Ferdinand and Isabella could do together what neither was able to accomplish alone: subdue their realms, secure their borders, venture abroad militarily, and Christianize the whole of Spain. Between 1482 and 1492 they conquered the Moors in Granada. Naples became a Spanish possession in 1504. By 1512, Ferdinand had secured his northern borders by conquering the kingdom of Navarre. Internally, the Spanish king and queen won the allegiance of the *Hermandad*, a powerful league of cities and towns that served them against stubborn noble landowners. The crown also extended its authority over the wealthy chivalric orders, further limiting the power of the nobility.

Spain had long been remarkable among European lands as a place where three religions—Islam, Judaism, and Christianity—coexisted with a certain degree of toleration. That toleration was to end dramatically under Ferdinand and Isabella, who made Spain the prime exemplar of state-controlled religion.

Ferdinand and Isabella exercised almost total control over the Spanish church as they placed religion in the service of national unity. They appointed the higher clergy and the officers of the Inquisition. The latter, run by Tomás de Torquemada (d. 1498), Isabella's confessor, was a key national agency established in 1479 to monitor the activity of converted Jews (*conversos*) and Muslims (*Moriscos*) in Spain. In 1492, the Jews were exiled and their properties confiscated. In 1502, nonconverting Moors in Granada were driven into exile by Cardinal Francisco Jiménez de Cisneros (1437–1517).

Despite a certain internal narrowness, Ferdinand and Isabella were rulers with wide horizons. They contracted anti-French marriage alliances that came to determine a large part of European history in the sixteenth century. In 1496, their eldest daughter, Joanna, later known as "the Mad," married Archduke Philip, the son of Emperor Maximilian I. The fruit of this union, Charles I, was the first to rule over a united Spain; by his inheritance and election as emperor in 1519, his empire almost equaled in size that of Charlemagne. A second daughter, Catherine of Aragon, wed Arthur, the son of the English king Henry VII. After Arthur's premature death, she was betrothed to his brother, the future King Henry VIII (r. 1509–1547), whom she married eight years later, in 1509. The failure of this marriage became the key factor in the emergence of the Anglican church and the English Reformation.

The new power of Spain was also revealed in Ferdinand and Isabella's promotion of overseas exploration. They sponsored the Genoese adventurer Christopher Columbus (1451–1506), who arrived at the islands of the Caribbean while sailing west in search of a shorter route to the spice markets of the Far East. This patronage led to the creation of the Spanish Empire in Mexico and Peru, whose gold and silver mines helped make Spain Europe's dominant power in the sixteenth century.

## ENGLAND

The latter half of the fifteenth century was a period of especially difficult political trial for the English. Following the Hundred Years' War, civil warfare broke out between two rival branches of the royal family: the House of York and the House of Lancaster. The roots of the war lay in succession irregularities after the forced deposition of the erratic king Richard II (r. 1377–1399). This conflict, known to us today as the Wars of the Roses (because York's symbol, according to legend, was a white rose and Lancaster's a red rose), kept England in turmoil from 1455 to 1485.

The duke of York and his supporters in the prosperous southern towns challenged the Lancastrian monarchy of Henry VI (r. 1422–1461). In 1461, Edward IV (r. 1461–1483), son of the duke of York, seized power and instituted a strong-arm rule that lasted more than twenty years; it was only briefly interrupted, in 1470–1471, by Henry VI's short-lived restoration. Assisted by able ministers, Edward effectively increased the power and finances of the monarchy. His brother, Richard III (r. 1483–1485), usurped the throne from Edward's son. Richard's reign saw the growth of support for the exiled Lancastrian Henry Tudor, who returned to England to defeat Richard on Bosworth Field in August 1485.

Henry Tudor ruled as Henry VII (r. 1485–1509), the first of the new Tudor dynasty that would dominate England throughout the sixteenth century. He succeeded in disciplining the English nobility through a special instrument of the royal will known as the

**QUICK REVIEW**

**Unification of Spain**

- Aragon and Castile unified by marriage of Ferdinand and Isabella
- 1492: The last Muslim state in the Iberian peninsula, Granada, falls
- Ferdinand and Isabella sought to create religious uniformity in their lands by force

**Early British** pound coin, 1545, showing Henry VII on throne.

Dorling Kindersley Media Library/Chas Howson © The British Museum

Court of Star Chamber. Created with the sanction of Parliament in 1487, the court was intended to end the perversion of English justice by "over-mighty subjects," that is, powerful nobles who used intimidation and bribery to win favorable verdicts in court cases.

Henry shrewdly used English law to further the ends of the monarchy. He managed to confiscate lands and fortunes of nobles with such success that he was able to govern without dependence on Parliament for royal funds, always a cornerstone of a strong monarchy. In these ways, Henry began to shape a monarchy that would develop into one of early modern Europe's most exemplary governments during the reign of his granddaughter, Elizabeth I (r. 1558–1603).

## THE HOLY ROMAN EMPIRE

Germany and Italy were the striking exceptions to the steady development of politically centralized lands in the last half of the fifteenth century. In Germany, territorial rulers and cities resisted every effort at national consolidation and unity. By the late fifteenth century, Germany was hopelessly divided into some three hundred autonomous political entities.

The princes and the cities did work together to create the machinery of law and order, if not of union, within the divided empire. Emperor Charles IV (r. 1346–1378) and the major German territorial rulers reached an agreement in 1356 known as the **Golden Bull**. It established a seven-member electoral college consisting of the archbishops of Mainz, Trier, and Cologne; the duke of Saxony; the margrave of Brandenburg; the count Palatine; and the king of Bohemia. This group also functioned as an administrative body. They elected the emperor and, in cooperation with him, provided what transregional unity and administration existed.

In the fifteenth century, an effort was made to control incessant feuding by the creation of an imperial diet known as the *Reichstag*. This was a national assembly of the seven electors, the nonelectoral princes, and representatives from the sixty-five imperial free cities. The cities were the weakest of the three bodies represented in the diet. During such an assembly in Worms in 1495, the members won from Emperor Maximilian I an imperial ban on private warfare, the creation of a Supreme Court of Justice to enforce internal peace, and an imperial Council of Regency to coordinate imperial and internal German policy. The emperor only grudgingly conceded the latter because it gave the princes a share in executive power.

These reforms were still a poor substitute for true national unity. In the sixteenth and seventeenth centuries, the territorial princes became virtually sovereign rulers in their various domains. Such disunity aided religious dissent and conflict. It was in the cities and territories of still feudal, fractionalized, backward Germany that the Protestant Reformation broke out in the sixteenth century.

**Golden Bull** Arrangements agreed to by the Holy Roman Emperor and the major German territorial rulers in 1356 that helped stabilize Germany.

# THE NORTHERN RENAISSANCE

The scholarly works of northern humanists created a climate favorable to religious and educational reforms on the eve of the Reformation. Northern humanism was initially stimulated by the importation of Italian learning through such varied intermediaries as students who had studied in Italy, merchants who traded there, and the Brothers of the Common Life. This last was an influential lay religious movement that began in the Netherlands and permitted men and women to live a shared religious life without making formal vows of poverty, chastity, and obedience.

The northern humanists, however, developed their own distinctive culture. They tended to come from more diverse social backgrounds and to be more devoted to religious reforms than their Italian counterparts. They were also more willing to write for lay

HOW DID the northern Renaissance affect culture in Germany, England, France, and Spain?

audiences as well as for a narrow intelligentsia. Thanks to the invention of printing with movable type, it became possible for humanists to convey their educational ideals to laypeople and clerics alike. Printing gave new power and influence to elites in both church and state, who now could popularize their viewpoints freely and widely.

**The printing press** made possible the diffusion of Renaissance learning. No book stimulated more at this time than did the Bible. With Gutenberg's publication of a printed Bible in 1454, scholars gained access to a dependable, standardized text, so Scripture could be discussed and debated as never before.

This item is reproduced by permission of The Huntington Library, San Marino, California

**How did the advent of printing change the nature of the Renaissance?**

## THE PRINTING PRESS

A variety of forces converged in the fourteenth and fifteenth centuries to give rise to the invention of the printing press. Since the days of Charlemagne, kings and princes had encouraged schools and literacy to help provide educated bureaucrats to staff the offices of their kingdoms. By the fifteenth century, a new literate lay public had been created, thanks to the enormous expansion of schools and universities during the late Middle Ages. The invention of a cheap way to manufacture paper also helped make books economical and broaden their content.

In response to the demand for books that the expansion of lay education and literacy created, Johann Gutenberg (d. 1468) invented printing with movable type in the mid–fifteenth century in the German city of Mainz, the center of printing for the whole of Western Europe. Thereafter, books were rapidly and handsomely produced on topics both profound and practical and were intended for ordinary lay readers, scholars, and clerics alike.

Literacy deeply affected people everywhere, nurturing self-esteem and a critical frame of mind. By standardizing texts, the print revolution made anyone who could read an instant authority. Rulers in church and state now had to deal with a less credulous and less docile laity. Print was also a powerful tool for political and religious propaganda. Kings could now indoctrinate people as never before, and clergymen found themselves able to mass-produce both indulgences and pamphlets.

## ERASMUS

The far-reaching influence of Desiderius Erasmus (1466?–1536), the most famous northern humanist, illustrates the impact of the printing press. Through his printed works, Erasmus gained fame both as an educational and as a religious reformer. A lifelong Catholic, his life and work make clear that many loyal Catholics wanted major reforms in the church long before the Reformation made them a reality.

Erasmus aspired to unite classical ideals of humanity and civic virtue with the Christian ideals of love and piety. He believed disciplined study of the classics and the Bible, if begun early enough, was the best way to reform individuals and society. He summarized his own beliefs with the phrase *philosophia Christi*, a simple, ethical piety in imitation of Christ. He set this ideal in stark contrast to what he believed to be the dogmatic, ceremonial, and bullying religious practices of the later Middle Ages.

Erasmus was a true idealist, who expected more from people than the age's theologians believed them capable of doing. To promote what he deemed to be the essence of Christianity, he made ancient Christian sources available in their original versions, believing that if people would only imbibe the pure sources of the faith, they would recover the moral and religious health the New Testament promises. To this end, Erasmus edited the works of the Church Fathers and produced a Greek edition of the New Testament (1516), later adding a new Latin translation of the latter (1519). Martin Luther used both of those works when he translated the New Testament into German in 1522.

These various enterprises did not please the church authorities. They remained unhappy with Erasmus's "improvements" on the Vulgate, Christendom's Bible for over a thousand years, and his popular anticlerical writings. At one point in the mid–sixteenth century, all of Erasmus's works were on the church's *Index of Forbidden Books*. Luther also condemned Erasmus for his views on the freedom of human will. Still, Erasmus's works put sturdy tools of reform in the hands of both Protestant and Catholic reformers.

## HUMANISM AND REFORM

In Germany, England, France, and Spain, humanism stirred both educational and religious reform.

**Germany**   Rudolf Agricola (1443–1485), the "father of German humanism," spent ten years in Italy and introduced Italian learning to Germany when he returned. Conrad Celtis (d. 1508), the first German poet laureate, and Ulrich von Hutten (1488–1523), a fiery knight, gave German humanism a nationalist coloring hostile to non-German cultures, particularly Roman culture.

The controversy that brought von Hutten onto the historical stage and unified reform-minded German humanists was the Reuchlin affair. Johann Reuchlin (1455–1522) was Europe's foremost Christian authority on Hebrew and Jewish learning. Around 1506, supported by the Dominican order in Cologne, a Christian who had converted from Judaism began a movement to suppress Jewish writings. When this man, whose name was Pfefferkorn, attacked Reuchlin, many German humanists, in the name of academic freedom and good scholarship—not for any pro-Jewish sentiment—rushed to Reuchlin's defense. When Martin Luther came under attack in 1517 for his famous ninety-five theses against indulgences, many German humanists saw a repetition of the Scholastic attack on Reuchlin and rushed to his side.

**England**   Thomas More (1478–1535), a close friend of Erasmus, is the best known English humanist. His *Utopia* (1516), a conservative criticism of contemporary society, rivals the plays of Shakespeare as the most read sixteenth-century English work. *Utopia* depicted an imaginary society based on reason and tolerance that overcame social and political injustice by holding all property and goods in common and requiring everyone to earn their bread by their own work.

More became one of Henry VIII's most trusted diplomats. His repudiation of the Act of Supremacy (1534), which made the king of England head of the English church in place of the pope (see Chapter 11), and his refusal to recognize the king's marriage to Anne Boleyn, however, led to his execution in July 1535. Although More remained Catholic, humanism in England, as also in Germany, helped prepare the way for the English Reformation.

**France**   The French invasions of Italy made it possible for Italian learning to penetrate France, stirring both educational and religious reform. Guillaume Budé (1468–1540), an accomplished Greek scholar, and Jacques Lefèvre d'Etaples (1454–1536), a biblical authority, were the leaders of French humanism. Lefèvre's scholarly works exemplified the new critical scholarship and influenced Martin Luther. Guillaume Briçonnet (1470–1533), the bishop of Meaux, and Marguerite d'Angoulême (1492–1549), sister of King Francis I, the future queen of Navarre, and a successful spiritual writer in her own right, cultivated a generation of young reform-minded humanists. The future Protestant reformer John Calvin was a product of this native reform circle.

**Spain**   Whereas in England, France, and Germany, humanism prepared the way for Protestant reforms, in Spain it entered the service of the Catholic Church. Here the key figure was Francisco Jiménez de Cisneros (1437–1517), a confessor to Queen Isabella and, after 1508, the "Grand Inquisitor"—a position that allowed him to enforce

**Albrecht Dürer (1471–1528),** *Portrait of the Moorish Woman Katharina*, drawing.

Uffizi Florence, Italy. Albrecht Dürer (1471–1528), *Portrait of the Moorish Woman Katharina*. Drawing. Uffizi Florence, Italy. Photograph © Foto Marburg/Art Resource, NY

**What might explain the interest of early modern artists in ordinary people as subjects?**

# Overview  Humanism and Reform

| | |
|---|---|
| **GERMANY** | • Rudolf Agricola, the father of German humanism, brought Italian learning to Germany. |
| | • German humanism was given a nationalist coloring hostile to non-German cultures. |
| | • The Reuchlin affair caused the unification of reform-minded German humanists. |
| | • When Martin Luther came under attack in 1517, many German humanists rushed to his side. |
| **ENGLAND** | • Thomas More is the best known English humanist. |
| | • More's *Utopia* depicted a tolerant, just society that held property and goods in common. |
| | • Humanism in England played a key role in preparing the way for the English Reformation. |
| **FRANCE** | • Guillaume Budé and Jacques Lefèvre d'Etaples were the leaders of French humanism. |
| | • Lefèvre's works exemplified the new critical scholarship and influenced Martin Luther. |
| | • A new generation was cultivated by Marguerite d'Angoulême. |
| | • The future Protestant reformer John Calvin was a product of this native reform circle. |
| **SPAIN** | • Unlike the other countries, in Spain humanism entered the service of the Catholic Church. |
| | • Francisco Jiménez de Cisneros was the key figure in Spanish humanism. |
| | • In Jiménez's *Complutensian Polygot Bible*, Hebrew, Greek, and Latin appeared together. |
| | • This with church reform helped keep Spain strictly Catholic in the Age of Reformation. |

the strictest religious orthodoxy. His great achievement, taking fifteen years to complete, was the *Complutensian Polyglot Bible*, a six-volume work that placed the Hebrew, Greek, and Latin versions of the Bible in parallel columns. Such scholarly projects and internal church reforms joined with the repressive measures of Ferdinand and Isabella to keep Spain strictly Catholic throughout the Age of Reformation.

# VOYAGES OF DISCOVERY AND THE NEW EMPIRES IN THE WEST AND EAST

**WHAT WERE** the motives for European voyages of discovery, and what were the consequences?

The discovery of the Americas dramatically expanded the horizons of Europeans, both geographically and intellectually. Knowledge of the New World's inhabitants and the exploitation of its mineral and human wealth set new cultural and economic forces in motion throughout Western Europe.

Beginning with the voyages of the Portuguese and Spanish in the fifteenth century, commercial supremacy progressively shifted from the Mediterranean and Baltic seas to the Atlantic seaboard, setting the stage for global expansion. (See Map 10–2.)

## THE PORTUGUESE CHART THE COURSE

Seventy-seven years before Columbus, who sailed under the flag of Spain, set foot in the Americas, Prince Henry "the Navigator" (1394–1460), brother of the king of Portugal, captured the North African Muslim city of Ceuta. His motives were mercenary and religious, both a quest for gold and spices and the pious work of saving the souls of Muslims and pagans who had no knowledge of Christ. Thus began the Portuguese exploration of the African coast, first in search of gold and slaves, and then by century's end, of a sea route around Africa to Asia's spice markets.

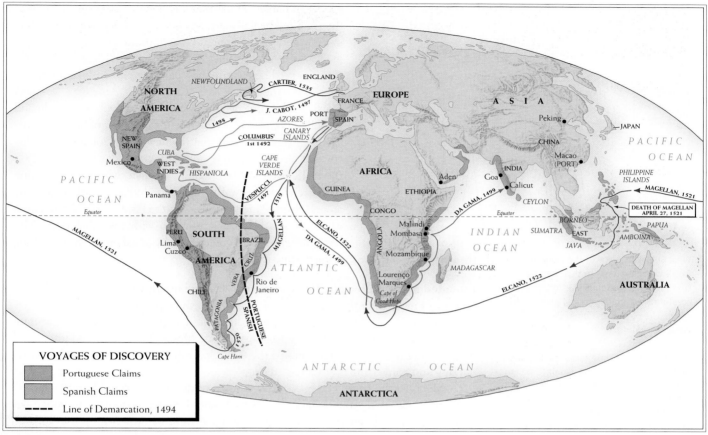

MAP 10–2 **European Voyages of Discovery and the Colonial Claims of Spain and Portugal in the Fifteenth and Sixteenth Centuries**

The map depicts Europe's global expansion in the fifteenth and sixteenth centuries.

**What reasons** did European explorers have for their many voyages of discovery?

Before there was a sea route to the East, Europeans could only get spices through the Venetians, who bought or bartered them from Muslim merchants in Egypt and the Ottoman Empire. The Portuguese resolved to beat this powerful Venetian-Muslim monopoly by sailing directly to the source.

Bartholomew Dias (ca. 1450–1500) pioneered the eastern Portuguese Empire after safely rounding the Cape of Good Hope at the tip of Africa in 1487. A decade later, in 1498, Vasco da Gama (1469–1525) stood on the shores of India. When he returned to Portugal, he carried a cargo of spices worth sixty times the cost of the voyage. Later, the Portuguese established colonies in Goa and Calcutta on the coast of India, whence they challenged the Arabs and the Venetians for control of the spice trade.

The Portuguese had concentrated their explorations on the Indian Ocean. The Spanish turned west, believing they could find a shorter route to the East Indies by sailing across the Atlantic. Instead, Christopher Columbus (1451–1506) discovered the Americas.

## THE SPANISH VOYAGES OF COLUMBUS

Thirty-three days after departing the Canary Islands, on October 12, 1492, Columbus landed in San Salvador (Watlings Island) in the eastern Bahamas. Thinking he was in the East Indies, he mistook his first landfall as an outer island of Japan. Not until his third voyage to the Caribbean in 1498 did Columbus realize that Cuba was not Japan and South America was not China.

Naked, friendly natives met Columbus and his crew on the beaches of the New World. They were Taino Indians, who spoke a variant of a language known as Arawak. Believing the island on which he landed to be the East Indies, Columbus called these

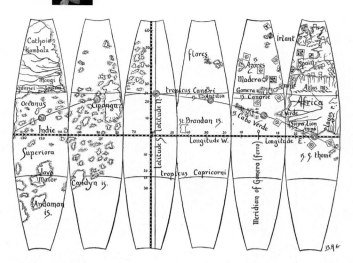

**What Columbus knew** of the world in 1492 was contained in this map by the Nuremberg geographer Martin Behaim, creator of the first spherical globe of the earth. The ocean section of Behaim's globe is reproduced here. Departing the Canary Islands (in the second section from the right), Columbus expected his first major landfall to be Japan (Cipangu, in the second section from the left). When he landed at San Salvador, he thought he was on the outer island of Japan. Thus, when he arrived in Cuba, he thought he was in Japan.

From *Admiral of the Ocean Sea* by Samuel Eliot Morison. Copyright © 1942 by Samuel Eliot Morison; Copyright © renewed 1970 by Samuel Eliot Morison. By permission of Curtis Brown Ltd.

**What errors in his understanding of geography led Columbus to conclude he could reach Japan by sailing west?**

people Indians, a name that stuck with Europeans even after they realized he had actually discovered a new continent. The natives' generosity amazed Columbus, as they freely gave his men all the corn, yams, and sexual favors they desired. He also observed how easily the Spanish could enslave them.

On the heels of Columbus, Amerigo Vespucci (1451–1512), after whom America is named, and Ferdinand Magellan (1480–1521) explored the coastline of South America. Their travels proved that the new lands Columbus had discovered were an entirely unknown continent that opened on the still greater Pacific Ocean. Magellan, who was continuing the search for a westward route to the Indies, made it all the way around South America and across the Pacific to the Philippines, where he was killed in a skirmish with the inhabitants. The remnants of his squadron eventually sailed on to Spain, making them the first sailors to circumnavigate the globe.

**Intended and Unintended Consequences**   Columbus's first voyage marked the beginning of more than three centuries of a vast Spanish empire in the Americas. What began as voyages of discovery became expeditions of conquest, not unlike the warfare Christian Aragon and Castile waged against Islamic Moors. Those wars had just ended in 1492, and their conclusion imbued the early Spanish explorers with a zeal for conquering and converting non-Christian peoples.

Much to the benefit of Spain, the voyages of discovery created Europe's largest and longest surviving trading bloc and spurred other European countries to undertake their own colonial ventures. The wealth extracted from its American possessions financed Spain's commanding role in the religious and political wars of the sixteenth and seventeenth centuries, while fueling a Europe-wide economic expansion.

European expansion also had a profound biological impact. Europeans introduced numerous new species of fruits, vegetables, and animals into the Americas and brought American species back to Europe. European expansion also spread European diseases. Vast numbers of Native Americans died from measles and smallpox epidemics, while Europeans died from a virulent form of syphilis that may have originated in the Americas.

For the Native Americans, the voyages of discovery were the beginning of a long history of conquest, disease, and slave labor they could neither evade nor survive. In both South and North America, Spanish rule left a lasting imprint of Roman Catholicism, economic dependency, and hierarchical social structure, all still visible today. (See Chapter 18.)

## THE SPANISH EMPIRE IN THE NEW WORLD

When the first Spanish explorers arrived, the Aztec Empire dominated Mesoamerica, which stretches from Central Mexico to Guatemala, and the Inca Empire dominated Andean South America. Both were rich, and their conquest promised the Spanish the possibility of acquiring large quantities of gold.

**The Aztecs in Mexico**   The forebears of the Aztecs had arrived in the Valley of Mexico early in the twelfth century, where they lived as a subservient people. In 1428, however, they began a period of imperial expansion. By the time of Spanish conquest, the Aztecs ruled almost all of central Mexico from their capital Tenochtitlán (modern-day Mexico City). The Aztecs' brutal rule bred resentment and fear among their subject peoples.

In 1519, Hernán Cortés (1485–1547) landed in Mexico with about five hundred men and a few horses. He opened communication with Moctezuma II (1466–1520), the Aztec emperor. Moctezuma may initially have believed Cortés to be the god Quetzalcoatl, who, according to legend, had been driven away centuries earlier but had promised to return. Whatever the reason, Moctezuma hesitated to confront Cortés, attempting at first to appease him with gold, which only whetted Spanish appetites. Cortés forged alliances with the Aztecs' subject peoples, most importantly, with Tlaxcala, an independent state and traditional enemy of the Aztecs. His forces then marched on Tenochtitlán, where Moctezuma welcomed him. Cortés soon seized Moctezuma, who died in unexplained circumstances. The Aztecs' wary acceptance of the Spaniards turned to open hostility. The Spaniards were driven from Tenochtitlán and were nearly wiped out, but they returned and laid siege to the city. The Aztecs, under their last ruler, Cuauhtemoc (ca. 1495–1525), resisted fiercely, but were finally defeated in 1521.

**Armored Spanish soldiers,** under the command of Pedro de Alvarado (d. 1541) and bearing crossbows, engage unprotected and crudely armed Aztecs, who are nonetheless portrayed as larger than life by Spanish artist Diego Duran (sixteenth century).

Codex Duran: Pedro de Alvarado (c. 1485–1541), companion-at-arms of Hernando Cortés (1485–1547) besieged by Aztec warriors (vellum) by Diego Duran (16th century), Codex Duran, Historia De Las Indias (16th century). Biblioteca Nacional, Madrid, Spain. The Bridgeman Art Library International Ltd.

**How accurate are the depictions of Spanish _conquistadors_ and Aztec warriors in this image?**

**The Incas in Peru** The second great Native American civilization the Spanish conquered was that of the Incas in the highlands of Peru. Like the Aztecs, the Incas also began to expand rapidly in the fifteenth century and, by the time of the Spanish conquest, controlled an enormous empire.

In 1532, largely inspired by Cortés's example in Mexico, Francisco Pizarro (c. 1478–1541) landed on the western coast of South America with about two hundred men to take on the Inca Empire. Pizarro lured Atahualpa (ca. 1500–1533), the Inca ruler, into a conference and then seized him, killing hundreds of Atahualpa's followers in the process. The imprisoned Atahualpa tried to ransom himself with a hoard of gold, but instead of releasing him, Pizarro executed him in 1533. The Spaniards then captured Cuzco, the Inca capital, but Inca resistance did not end until the 1570s.

The conquests of Mexico and Peru are among the most dramatic and brutal events in modern history. Small military forces armed with advanced weapons subdued, in a remarkably brief time, two powerful peoples. The spread of European diseases, especially smallpox, among the Native Americans, also aided the conquest. But beyond the drama and bloodshed, these conquests, as well as those of other Native American peoples, marked a fundamental turning point. Native American cultures endured, accommodating themselves to European dominance, but the Spanish conquests of the early sixteenth century marked the beginning of the transformation of South America into Latin America.

## THE CHURCH IN SPANISH AMERICA

Roman Catholic priests had accompanied the earliest explorers and the conquerors of the Native Americans. They were filled with zeal not only to convert the inhabitants to Christianity, but also to bring to them European learning and civilization.

Tension, however, existed between the early Spanish conquerors and the mendicant friars who sought to minister to the Native Americans. Without conquest, the church could not convert the Native Americans, but the priests often deplored the harsh conditions imposed on the native peoples. By far the most effective and outspoken clerical critic of the Spanish conquerors was Bartolomé de Las Casas (1474–1566), a Dominican. He contended that conquest was not necessary for conversion.

Despite such protests, by the end of the sixteenth century, the Church in Spanish America had become largely an institution upholding the colonial status quo. Although individual priests defended the communal rights of Indian peoples, the colonial Church prospered as the Spanish elite prospered by exploiting the resources and peoples of the New World. The Church became a great landowner through crown grants and bequests from Catholics who died in the New World. The monasteries took on an economic as well as a spiritual life of their own. Whatever its concern for the spiritual welfare of the Native Americans, the Church remained one of the indications that Spanish America was a conquered world. By the end of the colonial era in the late eighteenth century, the Roman Catholic Church had become one of the most conservative forces in Latin America.

## THE ECONOMY OF EXPLOITATION

From the beginning, both the Native Americans and their lands were drawn into the Atlantic economy and the world of competitive European commercialism. For the Indians of Latin America and, somewhat later, the black peoples of Africa, that drive for gain meant forced labor.

The colonial economy of Latin America had three major components: mining, agriculture, and shipping. Each involved labor, servitude, and the intertwining of the New World economy with that of Spain.

***conquistadores*** "Conquerors."

**Mining**    The early ***conquistadores***, or "conquerors," were primarily interested in gold, but by the mid–sixteenth century, silver mining provided the chief source of metallic wealth. The great mining centers were Potosí in Peru and somewhat smaller sites in northern Mexico. Exploring for silver continued throughout the colonial era. Its production by forced labor for the benefit of Spaniards and the Spanish crown epitomized the wholly extractive economy that stood at the foundation of colonial life.

**Agriculture**    The major rural and agricultural institution of the Spanish colonies was the ***hacienda***, a large landed estate owned by persons originally born in Spain (*peninsulares*) or persons of Spanish descent born in America (*creoles*). Laborers on the *hacienda* were usually subject in some legal way to the owner and were rarely free to move from working for one landowner to another.

***hacienda***    Large landed estate that characterized most Spanish colonies.

The *hacienda* economy produced two major products: foodstuffs for mining areas and urban centers and leather goods used in mining machinery. Both farming and ranching were subordinate to the mining economy.

In the West Indies, the basic agricultural unit was the plantation. In Cuba, Hispaniola, Puerto Rico, and other islands, the labor of black slaves from Africa produced sugar to supply an almost insatiable demand for the product in Europe.

A final major area of economic activity in the Spanish colonies was urban service occupations, including government offices, the legal profession, and shipping. Those who worked in these occupations were either *peninsulares* or *creoles*, with the former dominating more often than not.

**Labor Servitude**    All this extractive and exploitive economic activity required labor, and the Spanish in the New World decided early that the native population would supply it. A series of social devices was used to draw them into the new economic life the Spanish imposed.

***encomienda***    Legal grant of the right to the labor of a specific number of Indians for a particular period of time. This was used as a Spanish strategy for exploiting the labor of the natives.

The first of these was the ***encomienda***, a formal grant of the right to the labor of a specific number of Indians, usually a few hundred, but sometimes thousands, for a particular period of time. The *encomienda* was in decline by the mid–sixteenth century because the Spanish monarchs feared its holders might become too powerful. There were also humanitarian objections to this particular kind of exploitation of the Indians.

The passing of the *encomienda* led to a new arrangement of labor servitude: the *repartimiento*. This device required adult male Indians to devote a certain number of days of labor annually to Spanish economic enterprises. *Repartimiento* service was often harsh, and some Indians did not survive their stint. The limitation on labor time led some Spanish managers to abuse their workers on the assumption that fresh workers would soon replace them.

The eventual shortage of workers and the crown's pressure against extreme versions of forced labor led to the use of free labor. The freedom, however, was more in appearance than reality. Free Indian laborers were required to purchase goods from the landowner or mine owner, to whom they became forever indebted. This form of exploitation, known as *debt peonage*, continued in Latin America long after the nineteenth-century wars of liberation.

Black slavery was the final mode of forced or subservient labor in the New World. Both the Spanish and the Portuguese had earlier used African slaves in Europe. The sugar plantations of the West Indies and Brazil now became the major center of black slavery.

The conquest, the forced labor of the economy of exploitation, and the introduction of European diseases had devastating demographic consequences for the Native Americans. Within a generation, the native population of New Spain (Mexico) was reduced to an estimated 8 percent of its numbers, from 25 million to 2 million.

## THE IMPACT ON EUROPE

Among contemporary European intellectuals, Columbus's discovery increased skepticism about the wisdom of the ancients. If traditional knowledge about the world had been so wrong geographically, how trustworthy was it on other matters? For many, Columbus's discovery demonstrated the folly of relying on any fixed body of presumed authoritative knowledge. Both in Europe and in the New World, there were those who condemned the explorers' treatment of American natives, as more was learned about their cruelty. Three centuries later, however, on the third centenary of Columbus's discovery (1792), the great thinkers of the age lionized Columbus for having opened up new possibilities for civilization and morality.

On the material side, the influx of spices and precious metals into Europe from the new Portuguese and Spanish Empires was a mixed blessing. It contributed to a steady rise in prices during the sixteenth century that created an inflation rate estimated at 2 percent a year. The new supply of bullion from the Americas joined with enlarged European production to increase greatly the amount of coinage in circulation, and this increase, in turn, fed inflation. Prices doubled in Spain by 1550, quadrupled by 1600. In Luther's Wittenberg in Germany, the cost of basic food and clothing increased almost 100 percent between 1519 and 1540.

The new wealth enabled governments and private entrepreneurs to sponsor basic research and expansion in the printing, shipping, mining, textile, and weapons industries. There is also evidence of large-scale government planning in such ventures as the French silk industry and the Habsburg-Fugger development of mines in Austria and Hungary.

In the thirteenth and fourteenth centuries, capitalist institutions and practices had already begun to develop in the rich Italian cities. Those who owned the means of production, either privately or corporately, were clearly distinguished from the workers who operated them. Wherever possible, entrepreneurs created monopolies in basic goods. High interest was charged on loans—actual, if not legal, usury. The "capitalist" virtues of thrift, industry, and orderly planning were everywhere in evidence—all intended to permit the free and efficient accumulation of wealth.

The late fifteenth and the sixteenth centuries saw the maturation of this type of capitalism together with its attendant social problems. The new wealth and industrial expansion raised the expectations of the poor and the ambitious and heightened the reactionary tendencies of the wealthy. This effect, in turn, aggravated the traditional social divisions between the clergy and the laity, the urban patriciate and the guilds, and the landed nobility and the agrarian peasantry.

These divisions indirectly prepared the way for the Reformation as well, by making many people critical of traditional institutions and open to new ideas—especially those that seemed to promise greater freedom and a chance at a better life.

## HOW DID humanism affect culture and the arts in fourteenth- and fifteenth-century Italy?

**The Renaissance in Italy (1375–1527)** The Renaissance first appeared in Italy and thrived from 1375 to 1527. This period, a transition between the medieval and modern worlds, was a time of unprecedented cultural creativity. Italian city-states, with their extensive trade networks and their competition with one another, were great incubators for artistic expression, political innovation, and humanistic studies. The significance of "humanism" is debated by scholars today, but for Renaissance Italians humanism implied studies of Classical languages and arts that offered moral preparation for a life of virtuous action. Authors and artists, including Petrarch, Dante, Boccaccio, Leonardo da Vinci, Raphael, and Michelangelo, exemplify the values of Renaissance humanism. *page 244*

## WHAT WERE the causes of Italy's political decline?

**Italy's Political Decline: The French Invasions (1494–1527)** In the late fifteenth century, the balance of power among Italian city-states that had been enforced by the Treaty of Lodi started to unravel. In 1495, at the invitation of the Milanese leader Ludovico il Moro, French king Charles VIII invaded Italy and conquered Florence. This invasion triggered several rounds of diplomacy, alliance making, and strategic marriages involving families of popes, the leaders of Italian city-states, French kings, and the rulers of Aragon and Brittany, among others. A quarter century of military conflicts led to political fragmentation and military weakness in Italy. In 1513, Niccolò Machiavelli wrote *The Prince*, in which he argued that only a strong and cunning dictator could unify Italy. *page 253*

## HOW WERE the powerful monarchies of northern Europe different from their predecessors?

**Revival of Monarchy in Northern Europe** Sovereign monarchies, in which kings and their appointed agents—usually townspeople, not nobility—control national policies on taxation, warfare, and law enforcement, emerged in France, Spain, and England in the late fifteenth century. In France, Charles VII and, later, Louis XI were able to capitalize on the French victories over England and Burgundy, to expand French territory, build trade and industry, and suspend the Estates General. In Spain, Isabella of Castile and Ferdinand of Aragon married in 1469, and they proceeded to impose state control on religion, arrange marriages for their children that would shape future European history, and sponsor global exploration. In England, Henry VII founded the Tudor dynasty and found ways to govern without consulting Parliament. The Holy Roman Empire (Germany) was northern Europe's chief example of a country that failed to develop a strong centralized monarchy. *page 256*

## HOW DID the northern Renaissance affect culture in Germany, England, France, and Spain?

**The Northern Renaissance** The Renaissance spread from Italy to northern Europe through traders and merchants, students, religious practitioners, and others. Northern humanists, however, were more interested in religious reforms and in spreading humanism to a broad audience than Italian humanists had been. Gutenberg's invention of the moveable-type printing press facilitated the wide dissemination of texts. Erasmus exemplified northern humanists' interest in reform of the Catholic Church. In Germany, England, and France, humanism laid the groundwork for the Reformation, but in Spain, the humanist movement, like most other aspects of culture, was controlled by Ferdinand and Isabella and therefore did not challenge the church. *page 259*

## WHAT WERE the motives for European voyages of discovery, and what were the consequences?

**Voyages of Discovery and the New Empire in the West and East** In the fifteenth century, Europeans began the process of expansion that eventually led to European control over huge regions of the globe. Searching for gold, spices, and later, slaves, the Portuguese, Spanish, and others established maritime trade routes to the coasts of Africa, India, and the Americas. Spain established an empire in what became Latin America, introducing Catholicism, new forms of social, political, and economic organization—including servitude—and diseases to which the indigenous peoples had no resistance. Mexico lost approximately 92 percent of its population within a generation after the Spanish conquest. Spain's empire brought new ideas and products to Europe and led to inflation. *page 262*

# Review Questions

1. How would you define Renaissance humanism? In what ways was the Renaissance a break with the Middle Ages? Who were the leading literary and artistic figures of the Italian Renaissance? What defined them as people of the Renaissance?

2. What was the purpose and outcome of the French invasion of Italy in 1494? Given the cultural productivity of Renaissance Italy, is it a valid assumption that creative work thrives best in periods of calm and peace?

3. How did the northern Renaissance differ from the Italian Renaissance? In what ways was Erasmus the embodiment of the northern Renaissance?

4. What prompted the voyages of discovery? How did the Spanish establish their empire in the Americas? What did native peoples experience during and after the conquest?

## KEY TERMS

*condottieri* (p. 246)
*conquistadores* (p. 266)
*encomienda* (p. 266)
**Golden Bull** (p. 259)

*hacienda* (p. 266)
**mannerism** (p. 252)
*studia humanitas* **(humanism)** (p. 246)

For additional learning resources related to this chapter, please go to **www.myhistorylab.com**

PEARSON
myhistorylab

# 11

# The Age of Reformation

**Painted on the eve** of the Reformation, Matthias Grunewald's (ca. 1480–1528) *Crucifixion* shows a Christ who takes all the sins of the world into his own body, as his mother, Mary Magdalene, and John the Baptist share the pain of his afflictions.

Musée Unterlinden, Colmar, France/SuperStock

**How did images such as this one convey the teachings of Christianity to worshippers?**

I n the second decade of the sixteenth century, a powerful religious movement began in northern Germany. Reformers, attacking what they believed to be superstitions and abuses of authority, rebelled against the medieval church. The Protestant Reformation that resulted from their efforts opposed aspects of the Renaissance—especially the optimistic view of human nature that humanist scholars derived from classical literature. The reformers did, however, embrace some Renaissance ideas, particularly educational reforms and training in ancient languages that equipped scholars to go to the original sources of important texts. Protestant challenges to Catholic practices were based on appeals to the Hebrew and Greek Scriptures. ■

# SOCIETY AND RELIGION

**WHAT WAS** the social and religious background of the Reformation?

The Protestant Reformation occurred at a time of sharp conflict between the emerging nation-states of Europe bent on conformity and centralization within their realms, and the self-governing towns and villages long accustomed to running their own affairs. Many townspeople and village folk perceived in the religious revolt an ally in their struggle to remain politically free and independent.

## SOCIAL AND POLITICAL CONFLICT

The Reformation broke out first in the free imperial cities of Germany and Switzerland, and the basic tenets of Lutheran and Zwinglian Protestantism remained visible in subsequent Protestant movements. There were about sixty-five free imperial cities, each a small kingdom unto itself. Most had Protestant movements, but with mixed success and duration. Some quickly turned Protestant and remained so. Some were Protestant only for a short time. Still others developed mixed confessions.

A seeming life-and-death struggle with higher princely or royal authority was not the only conflict late medieval cities were experiencing. They also coped with deep social and political divisions. Certain groups favored the Reformation more than others. In many places, guilds whose members were economically prospering and socially rising were in the forefront of the Reformation. Evidence also suggests that people who felt pushed around and bullied by either local or distant authority—a guild by an autocratic local government, or a city or region by a powerful prince or king—often perceived an ally in the Protestant movement.

Social and political experience naturally influenced religious change in town and countryside. A Protestant sermon or pamphlet praising religious freedom seemed directly relevant, for example, to the townspeople of German and Swiss cities who faced incorporation into the territory of a powerful local prince, who looked on them as his subjects rather than as free citizens. Like city dwellers, the peasants on the land also heard in the Protestant message a promise of political liberation, even a degree of social betterment. More than the townspeople, the peasants found their traditional liberties—from fishing and hunting rights to representation at local diets—progressively being chipped away by the secular and ecclesiastical landlords of the age.

## POPULAR RELIGIOUS MOVEMENTS AND CRITICISM OF THE CHURCH

The Protestant Reformation could also not have occurred without the monumental challenges to the medieval church during its "exile" in Avignon, the Great Schism, the Conciliar period, and the Renaissance papacy. For sizable numbers of people in future Protestant lands, the medieval church had ceased to provide a viable foundation for

religious piety. Many intellectuals and laypeople felt a sense of spiritual crisis. Between the secular pretensions of the papacy and the dry teaching of Scholastic theologians, laity and clerics alike began to seek a more heartfelt, idealistic, and—often, in the eyes of the pope—heretical religious piety. The late Middle Ages were marked by independent lay and clerical efforts to reform local religious practice and by widespread experimentation with new religious forms.

A variety of factors contributed to the growing lay criticism of the church. Urban laypeople were increasingly knowledgeable about the world around them and about the rulers who controlled their lives. They traveled widely—as soldiers, pilgrims, explorers, and traders. New postal systems and the printing press increased the information at their disposal. A new age of books and libraries raised literacy and heightened curiosity. Laypeople were able to shape the cultural life of their communities.

For many participants in lay religious movements, a simple religion of love and self-sacrifice like that of Jesus and the first disciples seemed to be the ideal. To that end, the laity sought a more egalitarian church—one that gave the members as well as the head of the church a voice—and also a more spiritual church—one that lived manifestly according to its New Testament model.

**The Modern Devotion**   One of the more constructive lay religious movements in northern Europe on the eve of the Reformation was that of the Brothers of the Common Life, also known as the Modern Devotion, a kind of boarding school for reform-minded laity. The brothers fostered religious life outside formal church offices and apart from formal religious vows—a lay religious life of prayer and study without surrendering the world. Centered at Zwolle and Deventer in the Netherlands, the brother and (less numerous) sister houses of the Modern Devotion spread rapidly throughout northern Europe and influenced parts of southern Europe as well. In these houses clerics and laity shared a common life, stressing individual piety and practical religion. Lay members were not expected to take special religious vows or to wear a special religious dress, nor did they abandon their ordinary secular vocations.

The brothers were also educators. They worked as copyists, sponsored many religious and some classical publications, ran hospices for poor students, and conducted schools for the young—especially boys preparing for the priesthood or a monastic vocation. Thomas à Kempis (d. 1471) summarized the philosophy of the brothers in what became the most popular religious book of the period, the *Imitation of Christ*. This semi-mystical guide to the inner life was intended primarily for monks and nuns but was also widely read by laity who wanted to pursue the ascetic life.

**Lay Control over Religious Life**   On the eve of the Reformation, Rome's international network of church offices, which had unified Europe religiously during the Middle Ages, was falling apart in many areas. This collapse was hurried along by a growing sense of regional identity, an increasingly competent local secular administration, and a newly emerging nationalism. The long-entrenched *benefice* system of the medieval church had permitted important ecclesiastical posts to be sold to the highest bidders and had often failed to enforce the requirement that priests and bishops had to live in their parishes and dioceses. Such a system threatened a vibrant, lay spiritual life. Rare was the late medieval German town that did not have complaints about the maladministration, concubinage, or financial greed of its clergy—especially the higher clergy (bishops, abbots, and prelates).

The sale of indulgences, in particular, had been repeatedly attacked before Luther came on the scene. On the eve of the Reformation, this practice had expanded to permit people to buy release from time in purgatory for both themselves and their deceased loved ones. Rulers and magistrates had little objection to their sale and might even encourage it, as long as a generous portion of the income the sales generated

**Martin Schongauer** (c. 1430–1491), a German engraver, portrays the devil's temptation of St. Anthony in the wilderness as a robust physical attack by demons rather than the traditional melancholic introspection.

National Gallery of Art, Washington DC

**How did sixteenth-century people imagine the devil and his place in everyday life?**

remained in the local coffers. Yet when an indulgence was offered primarily for the benefit of distant interests, as with the sale of indulgences to raise money for a new Saint Peter's basilica in Rome that Luther protested, resistance arose also for strictly financial reasons: Their sale drained away local revenues.

City governments also undertook to improve local religious life on the eve of the Reformation by endowing preacherships. These positions, supported by *benefices*, made possible the hiring of well-trained pastors who provided regular preaching and pastoral care beyond the performance of the Mass. These preacherships often became platforms for Protestants.

Magistrates also carefully restricted the growth of ecclesiastical properties and clerical privileges. During the Middle Ages, canon and civil law had recognized special clerical rights in both property and person. Churches and monasteries were exempted from the taxes and laws that affected others. Law also deemed it inappropriate for holy persons (clergy) to burden themselves with such "dirty jobs" as military service, compulsory labor, standing watch at city gates, and other ordinary civic obligations. Moreover, the clergy came to enjoy an immunity from the jurisdiction of civil courts.

Already on the eve of the Reformation, measures were passed to restrict these clerical privileges and to end their abuses. Governments grew tired of church interference in what to them were strictly secular political spheres of competence and authority. Secular authorities accordingly began to scrutinize the church's acquisition of new properties, finding ways to get around its right of asylum when it interrupted the administration of justice, and generally bringing the clergy under local tax codes.

# MARTIN LUTHER AND THE GERMAN REFORMATION TO 1525

**WHY DID** Martin Luther challenge the church?

Unlike England and France, late medieval Germany lacked the political unity to enforce "national" religious reforms during the late Middle Ages. As popular resentment of clerical immunities and ecclesiastical abuses spread among German cities and towns, an unorganized "national" opposition to Rome formed. German humanists had long given voice to such criticism, and by 1517 it was pervasive enough to provide a solid foundation for Martin Luther's protest of indulgences and the theology that legitimated them.

The son of a successful Thüringian miner, Luther (1483–1546) was educated in Mansfeld, Magdeburg (where the Brothers of the Common Life had been his teachers), and Eisenach. Between 1501 and 1505, he attended the University of Erfurt, where the nominalist teachings of William of Ockham and Gabriel Biel (d. 1495) prevailed. (See Chapter 8.) After receiving his master-of-arts degree in 1505, Luther registered with the law faculty in accordance with his parents' wishes. But he never began the study of law. To the disappointment of his family, he instead entered the Order of the Hermits of Saint Augustine in Erfurt on July 17, 1505.

Ordained in 1507, Luther pursued a traditional course of study. In 1510, he journeyed to Rome on the business of his order, finding there justification for the many criticisms of the church he had heard in Germany. In 1511, he moved to the Augustinian monastery in Wittenberg, where he earned his doctorate in theology in 1512, thereafter to become a leader within the monastery, the new university, and the spiritual life of the city.

## JUSTIFICATION BY FAITH ALONE

Luther was especially plagued by the disproportion between his own sense of sinfulness and the perfect righteousness God required for salvation, according to traditional church teaching. His insight into the meaning of "justification by faith alone" (*sola fide*) was a gradual process between 1513 and 1518. The righteousness that God demands, he concluded, did not result from charitable acts and religious ceremonies but was given in full measure to any and all who believe in and trust Jesus Christ as their perfect righteousness satisfying to God.

The medieval church had always taught that salvation was a joint venture, a combination of divine mercy and human good works, what God alone could do and what man was expected to do in return. Luther also believed that faith without charitable service to one's neighbor was dead. The issue was not whether good works should be done, but how those works should be regarded. It was unbiblical, Luther argued, to treat works as contributing to one's eternal salvation, something only an almighty God could bestow.

Good works were expected over a lifetime, Luther taught, but not because they earned salvation. The believer who is bound to Christ by faith already possesses God's perfect righteousness. It is this knowledge of faith that sets narcissistic souls free to serve their neighbors selflessly. Such service is ethical, not soteriological—a good work, not a saving work. God is pleased when those who believe in him do good works, and he expects his people always to do them, but he does not take those works into account when he is merciful and bestows eternal life, which would make God a puppet of man.

## THE ATTACK ON INDULGENCES

Luther's doctrine of justification by faith was incompatible with the church's practice of issuing indulgences, for an **indulgence** was a remission of the obligation to perform a "work of satisfaction" for a sin. The medieval church taught that after priests absolved penitents of guilt, penitents still had to pay penalties for their sins. They could discharge their penalties in this life by prayers, fasting, almsgiving, retreats, and pilgrimages. If their works of satisfaction were insufficient at the time of their deaths, they would continue to suffer for them in purgatory.

Indulgences were originally given to Crusaders who could not complete their penances because they had fallen in battle. By the late Middle Ages, indulgences had become an aid to laypeople made genuinely anxious by their fear of a future suffering in purgatory for neglected penances or unrepented sins. In 1343, Pope Clement VI (r. 1342–1352) proclaimed the existence of a "treasury of merit," an infinite reservoir of good works in the church's possession that could be dispensed at the pope's discretion. In 1476, Pope Sixtus IV (r. 1471–1484) extended indulgences to the unrepented sins of all Christians in purgatory.

By Luther's time, indulgences were regularly dispensed for small cash payments, modest sums that were regarded as a good work of almsgiving. Indulgence preachers presented them to the laity as remitting not only their own future punishments, but also those of dead relatives presumed still to be suffering in purgatory.

In 1517, Pope Leo X (r. 1513–1521) revived a plenary Jubilee Indulgence that had first been issued by Pope Julius II (r. 1503–1513), the proceeds of which were to rebuild St. Peter's Basilica in Rome. Such an indulgence promised forgiveness of all outstanding unrepented sins upon the completion of certain acts. That indulgence was subsequently preached on the borders of Saxony in the territories of the future Archbishop Albrecht of Mainz. The famous indulgence preacher John Tetzel (d. 1519) was enlisted to preach the indulgence in Albrecht's territories.

When Luther posted his ninety-five theses against indulgences on the door of Castle Church in Wittenberg (October 31, 1517), he protested especially the impression Tetzel created that indulgences remitted sins and released unrepentant sinners from punishment in purgatory. Luther believed these claims went far beyond the traditional practice and seemed to make salvation something that could be bought and sold.

**indulgence** Remission of the obligation to perform a "work of satisfaction" for a sin.

**A contemporary caricature** depicts John Tetzel, the famous indulgence preacher. The last lines of the jingle read: "As soon as gold in the basin rings, right then the soul to Heaven springs." It was Tetzel's preaching that spurred Luther to publish his ninety-five theses.

Courtesy Stiftung Luthergedenkstaten in Sachsen-Anhalt/Lutherhalle, Wittenberg

**Why did Luther find the practice of indulgences particularly offensive?**

MAP 11–1 **The Empire of Charles V**
Dynastic marriages and simple chance concentrated into Charles's hands rule over the lands shown here, plus Spain's overseas possessions. Crowns and titles rained down on him; his election in 1519 as emperor gave him new distractions and responsibilities.

**Were the** acquisitions of large portions of Europe more of a burden than a privilege for Charles V?

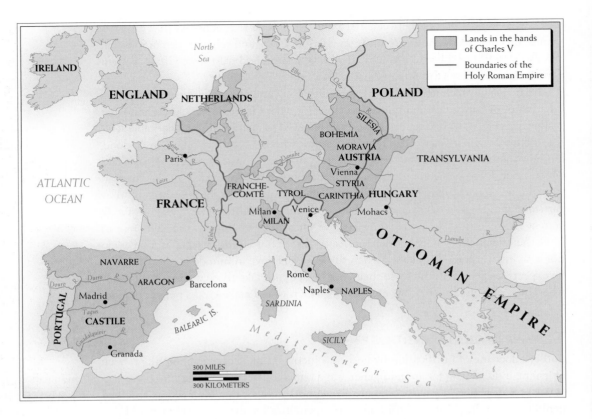

## ELECTION OF CHARLES V

The ninety-five theses were embraced by Nuremberg humanists, who translated and widely circulated them. This made Luther a central figure in an already organized national German cultural movement against foreign influence and competition, particularly on the part of the Italians. In October, he was summoned before the general of the Dominican order in Augsburg to answer for his criticism of the church. Yet as sanctions were being prepared against him, Emperor Maximilian I died (January 12, 1519)—a fortunate event for the budding Reformation, because it turned attention away from heresy in Saxony to the contest for a new emperor.

In that contest, the pope backed the French king, Francis I. However, Charles I of Spain, a youth of nineteen, successfully succeeded his grandfather as Emperor Charles V. (See Map 11–1.) Charles was blessed by both the long tradition of the Habsburg imperial rule and a massive campaign chest that secured the votes of the seven imperial electors. The most prominent among the seven was Frederick the Wise, Luther's lord and protector. Frederick took great pride in his new University of Wittenberg, and he was not about to let any harm come to his famous court preacher.

## LUTHER'S EXCOMMUNICATION AND THE DIET OF WORMS

In the same month in which Charles was elected emperor, Luther debated the Ingolstadt professor John Eck in Leipzig (June 27, 1519). During this contest, Luther challenged the infallibility of the pope and the inerrancy of church councils, appealing, for the first time, to the sovereign authority of Scripture alone. He burned all his bridges to the old church when he further defended certain teachings of John Huss, who had been condemned to death for heresy at the Council of Constance.

In 1520, Luther signaled his new direction with three famous pamphlets. The *Address to the Christian Nobility of the German Nation* urged the German princes to force reforms on

### QUICK REVIEW

**The Condemnation of Luther**

- June 15, 1520: Papal bull condemns Luther as a heretic
- April 1521: Luther refuses to recant before the imperial diet in Worms
- May 26, 1521: Luther placed under imperial ban, making his heresy a crime punishable by the state

the Roman church, especially to curtail its political and economic power in Germany. The *Babylonian Captivity of the Church* attacked the traditional seven sacraments, arguing that only two, baptism and the Eucharist, were unquestionably biblical, and it exalted the authority of Scripture, church councils, and secular princes over that of the pope. The eloquent *Freedom of a Christian* summarized the new teaching of salvation by faith alone.

On June 15, 1520, Leo's papal bull *Exsurge Domine* ("Arise, O Lord") condemned Luther for heresy and gave him sixty days to retract. The final bull of excommunication was issued on January 3, 1521.

In April 1521, Luther presented his views before the Diet of Worms, over which the newly elected Emperor Charles V presided. Ordered to recant, Luther declared that to do so would be to act against Scripture, reason, and his conscience. On May 26, 1521, he was placed under the imperial ban, which made him an "outlaw" to secular as well as religious authority. For his own protection, friends disguised and hid him in Wartburg Castle at the instruction of Elector Frederick. There, he spent almost a year, from April 1521 to March 1522. During his stay, he translated the New Testament into German using Erasmus's new Greek text and Latin translation, while overseeing by correspondence the first steps of the Reformation in Wittenberg.

## IMPERIAL DISTRACTIONS: WAR WITH FRANCE AND THE TURKS

The Reformation was greatly helped in these early years by the emperor's war with France and the advance of the Ottoman Turks into eastern Europe. Against both adversaries Charles V, who remained a Spanish king with dynastic responsibilities in Spain and Austria, needed loyal German troops, to which end he sought friendly relations with the German princes. Between 1521 and 1559, Spain (the Habsburg dynasty) and France (the Valois dynasty) fought four major wars over disputed territories within Italy and along their respective borders.

Thus preoccupied, the emperor agreed through his representatives at the German Diet of Speyer (1526) that each German territory was free to enforce the Edict of Worms (1521) against Luther "so as to be able to answer in good conscience to God and the emperor." That concession in effect gave the German princes, who five years earlier had refused to publish the emperor's condemnation of Luther, territorial sovereignty in religious matters. It also bought the Reformation time to put down deep roots in Germany and Switzerland.

## HOW THE REFORMATION SPREAD

In the late 1520s and 1530s, the Reformation passed from the free hands of the theologians and pamphleteers into the firmer ones of the magistrates and princes. In many cities, the latter quickly mandated new religious reforms. The elector of Saxony and the prince of Hesse, the two most powerful German Protestant rulers, led the politicization of religious reform within their territories. Like the urban magistrates, the German princes recognized the political and economic opportunities offered them by the demise of the Roman Catholic Church in their lands. In the 1530s, German Protestant lands formed a powerful defensive alliance, the Schmaldkaldic League, and prepared for war with the Catholic emperor.

## THE PEASANTS' REVOLT

In its first decade, the Reformation suffered more from internal division than from imperial interference. By 1525, Luther had become almost as much an object of protest within Germany as was the pope. Original allies, sympathizers, and fellow travelers increasingly declared their independence from Wittenberg.

**In 1520, Luther's** first portrait, shown here, depicted him as a tough, steely eyed monk. Afraid that this portrayal might convey defiance rather than reform to Emperor Charles V, Elector Frederick the Wise of Saxony, Luther's protector, ordered court painter Lucas Cranach to soften the image. The result was a Luther placed within a traditional monk's niche reading an open Bible, a reformer, unlike the one depicted here, who was prepared to listen as well as to instruct.

Martin Luther as a monk 1521. © Foto Marburg/Art Resource, NY

**Why was Luther so concerned about his public image?**

**A handwritten manuscript** depicts the execution of Jaklein Rohrbach. The sixteenth-century German radical burns at a stake inside a ring of fire.

Courtesy of the Library of Congress

**Why were heretics seen as such a threat to established authority and order?**

# A RAW DEAL FOR THE COMMON MAN, OR HIS JUST DESSERTS?

Beginning in the late fifteenth century, German feudal lords, both secular and ecclesiastical, increased labor and crop quotas on their peasant tenants, while restricting their freedoms and overriding their customary laws as well. In 1525, massive revolts occurred in southern Germany, in what became the largest social uprising before the French Revolution. Among those responding directly to the revolt were two highly respected authorities: Wittenberg theologian Martin Luther and Nuremberg artist Albrecht Dürer.

## QUESTIONS

1. What is there in Luther's religious teaching that might have led the peasants to think he would support their revolt? What personal interest might he have had in turning them his way? What does he advise them to do to address their grievances properly?

2. Does Dürer's 1527 sketch *Memorial to the Peasants' Revolt*, depicting a peasant sitting atop a chicken coop with a sword thrust through his back, suggest a greater sympathy for the peasants on his part? Or is it possible that both Luther and Dürer agreed that the peasants received their just desserts for rebelling against lawful authority?

## I. MARTIN LUTHER, *AN ADMONITION TO PEACE* (1525)

### ON STOPPING THE WAR

We have no one on earth to thank for this mischievous rebellion, except you lords and princes, especially you blind bishops and mad priests and monks . . . In your government you do nothing but flay and rob your subjects in order that you may lead a life of splendor and pride, until the poor common folk can bear it no longer . . .

[As for] the peasants, they must take the name and title of a people who fight because they will not and ought not endure wrong or evil, according to the teaching of nature. You should have *that* name, and let the name of Christ alone . . . [As for your so-called 'Christian' demands for] freedom of game, birds, fish, wood, forests, labor services, tithes, imposts, excises, and release from the death tax, these I leave to the lawyers, for they are things that do not concern a Christian who is a martyr on this earth . . . Let the name of Christian alone and act in some other name, as men and women who want human and natural rights.

Source: Cited by Steven Ozment, *The Age of Reform* (New Haven, CT: Yale University Press, 1980), pp. 280–282.

## II. MARTIN LUTHER, *AGAINST THE ROBBING AND MURDERING PEASANTS* (1525)

### FINAL WORDS

[The princes] should have no mercy on obstinate, hardened, blinded peasants who refuse to listen to reason. Let everyone, as he is able, strike, hew, stab, and slay, as though among mad dogs, so that by doing so he may show mercy to those [non-rebelling peasants] who have been ruined, put to flight, and led astray by these rebelling peasants [so that] peace and safety may return . . .

Source: Ozment, *The Age of Reform*, p. 284.

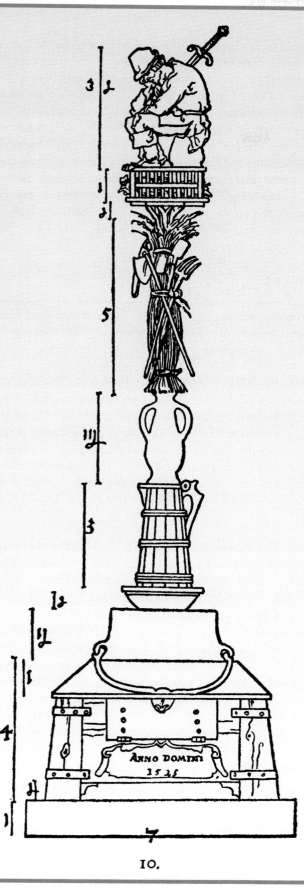

10.

## III. *AN OPEN LETTER CONCERNING THE HARD BOOK AGAINST THE PEASANTS* (1525)

### FINAL WORDS

From the start I had two fears. If the peasants became lords, the devil would become abbot; if these tyrants became lords, the devil's dam would become abbess. Therefore I wanted to do two things: quiet the peasants and instruct the lords. The peasants were unwilling, and now they have their reward. The lords will not hear, and they shall have their reward also.

Source: Ozment, *The Age of Reform*, p. 287.

## IV. ALBRECHT DÜRER, *MEMORIAL TO THE PEASANTS' REVOLT* (1527)

Dürer's "Memorial to the Peasants," drawn in 1527, the year before his death, appeared in a book devoted to "phrase perspectives in art." Fearing that Protestant iconoclasm (destruction of icons) and the coming of religious wars would remove decorative art from the churches, his book was to be a primer for artists who in the aftermath of such destruction would have to learn the art of painting all over again. The sketch shows a peasant sitting atop a chicken coop with a sword thrust through his back, the classic iconography of betrayal.

At this time Dürer's peers, friends, and associates condemned the Peasants' Revolt as strongly as Luther. During the war Dürer painted portraits of the Fuggers, the great merchant family the peasants despised, and also Margrave Casimir of Brandenburg-Ansbach, a brutal slayer of peasants and Anabaptists. Within this context might Dürer's slain rebellious peasant, like Luther's, have gotten his just due?

Source: Joseph Leo Koerner, *The Moment of Self-Portraiture in Renaissance Art* (Chicago: Chicago University Press, 1993), p. 235.

**The caption reads:** "He who wants to commemorate his victory over the rebellious peasants might use to that end a structure such as I portray here."

Illustration from Jane Campbell Hutchinson, *Albrecht Dürer: A Biography* (Princeton, NJ: Princeton University Press, 1990)

**What was this monument meant to say about the Peasants' War?**

Like the German humanists, the German peasantry also had at first believed Luther to be an ally. Peasant leaders, several of whom had been Lutherans, saw in Luther's teaching about Christian freedom and his criticism of monastic landowners a point of view close to their own. They openly solicited Luther's support of their alleged "Christian" political and economic rights, including a revolutionary demand of release from serfdom.

Luther had initially sympathized with the peasants, condemning the tyranny of the princes and urging them to meet the just demands of the peasants. The Lutherans, however, were not social revolutionaries and they saw no hope for their movement if it became intertwined with a peasant revolution. When the peasants revolted against their landlords in 1524–1525, invoking Luther's name, Luther predictably condemned them as "un-Christian" and urged the princes to crush the revolt mercilessly. Tens of thousands of peasants (estimates run between 70,000 and 100,000) died by the time the revolt was suppressed.

# THE REFORMATION ELSEWHERE

**WHERE DID** other reform movements develop and how were they different from Luther's?

Although the German Reformation was the first, Switzerland and France had their own independent church reform movements almost simultaneously with Germany's. From them developed new churches as prominent and lasting as the Lutheran.

## ZWINGLI AND THE SWISS REFORMATION

Switzerland was a loose confederacy of thirteen autonomous *cantons*, or states, and their allied areas. Some cantons became Protestant, some remained Catholic, and a few others managed to effect a compromise. There were two main preconditions of the Swiss Reformation. First was the growth of national sentiment occasioned by popular opposition to foreign mercenary service. (Providing mercenaries for Europe's warring nations was a major source of Switzerland's livelihood.) Second was a desire for church reform that had persisted in Switzerland since the councils of Constance (1414–1417) and Basel (1431–1449).

**The Reformation in Zurich**   Ulrich Zwingli (1484–1531), the leader of the Swiss Reformation, had been humanistically educated. He credited Erasmus over Luther with having set him on the path to reform. By 1518, Zwingli was also widely known for his opposition to the sale of indulgences and to religious superstition.

In 1519, he won the post of people's priest in the main church of Zurich. From his new position, Zwingli engineered the Swiss Reformation. Zwingli's reform guideline was simple and effective: Whatever lacked literal support in Scripture was to be neither believed nor practiced. As had also happened with Luther, that test soon raised questions about such honored traditional teachings and practices as fasting, transubstantiation, the worship of saints, pilgrimages, purgatory, clerical celibacy, and certain sacraments. A disputation held on January 29, 1523, concluded with the city government's sanction of Zwingli's Scripture test. Thereafter Zurich became the center of the Swiss Reformation. The new regime imposed a harsh discipline that made the city one of the first examples of puritanical Protestantism.

**The Marburg Colloquy**   Landgrave Philip of Hesse (1504–1567) sought to unite Swiss and German Protestants in a mutual defense pact. However, Luther's and Zwingli's bitter theological differences, especially over the nature of Christ's presence in the Eucharist, spoiled his efforts.

Philip of Hesse brought the two Protestant leaders together in his castle in Marburg in early October 1529, to work out their differences. However, the effort proved to be in vain. Although cooperation between the two Protestant sides did not cease altogether, the disagreement splintered the Protestant movement theologically and politically.

**Swiss Civil Wars**   As the Swiss cantons divided themselves between Protestantism and Catholicism, civil wars erupted. There were two major battles, both at Kappel, one in June 1529 and a second in October 1531. The first ended in a Protestant victory, which forced the Catholic cantons to break their foreign alliances and to recognize the rights of Swiss Protestants. After the second battle, Zwingli lay wounded on the battlefield, and when discovered, he was unceremoniously executed. The subsequent treaty confirmed the right of each canton to determine its own religion.

## ANABAPTISTS AND RADICAL PROTESTANTS

The moderate pace and seemingly low ethical results of the Lutheran and Zwinglian reformations discontented many people, among them some of the original followers of Luther and Zwingli. These were devout fundamentalist Protestants who desired a more rapid and thorough implementation of Apostolic Christianity. They accused the reform movements that went before them of having gone only halfway. The most important of these radical groups were the **Anabaptists**, the sixteenth-century ancestors of the modern Mennonites and Amish. The Anabaptists were especially distinguished by their rejection of infant baptism and their insistence on only adult baptism, as was the case with Jesus, who was baptized as an adult. Only a thoughtful consenting adult, able to understand the Scriptures and what the biblical way of life required, could enter the covenant of faith.

**Anabaptists** ("rebaptizers") The most important of several groups of Protestants forming more radical organizations that sought a more rapid and thorough restoration of the "primitive Christianity" described in the New Testament.

**Conrad Grebel and the Swiss Brethren**   Conrad Grebel (1498–1526), with whom Anabaptism originated, performed the first adult rebaptism in Zurich in January 1525. Initially a co-worker of Zwingli's and an even greater biblical literalist, Grebel broke openly with him. In a religious disputation in October 1523, Zwingli supported the city government's plea for a peaceful, gradual removal of resented traditional religious practices—not the rush to perfection the Anabaptists demand.

The alternative of the Swiss Brethren, as Grebel's group came to be called, was embodied in the *Schleitheim Confession* of 1527. This document distinguished Anabaptists not only by their practice of adult baptism, but also by their pacifism, refusal to swear oaths, and nonparticipation in the offices of secular government. By both choice and coercion, Anabaptists physically separated from established society to form a more perfect communion modeled on the first Christians. Because of the close connection between religious and civic life in the sixteenth century, the political authorities also viewed such separatism as a threat to basic social bonds, even as a form of sedition.

**The Anabaptist Reign in Münster**   Brutal measures were universally applied against nonconformists after Anabaptist extremists came to power in the German city of Münster in 1534–1535. Led by two Dutch emigrants, a baker, Jan Matthys of Haarlem, and a tailor, Jan Beukelsz of Leiden, the Anabaptists in Münster forced Lutherans and Catholics in the city either to convert or to emigrate. After their departure, the city was blockaded by besieging armies. Under such pressures, Münster was transformed into an Old Testament theocracy, replete with charismatic leaders and the practice of polygamy.

These developments shocked the outside world, and Protestant and Catholic armies united to crush the radicals. After this episode, moderate, pacifistic Anabaptism became the norm among most nonconformists. Menno Simons (1496–1561), the founder of the Mennonites, set an example of nonprovocative separatist Anabaptism, which became the historical form in which Anabaptist sects survived down to the present.

**Spiritualists and Antrinitarians**    Another diverse and highly individualistic group of Protestant dissenters was the Spiritualists. These were mostly isolated individuals distinguished by their disdain for external, institutional religion. They believed the only religious authority was the Spirit of God, which spoke not in some past revelation, but here and now in the heart and mind of every listening individual.

A final group of persecuted radical Protestants also destined for prominence in the modern world was the Antitrinitarians. These were exponents of a commonsense, rational, and ethical religion. These thinkers were the strongest opponents of Calvinism, especially its belief in original sin and predestination, and have a deserved reputation as defenders of religious toleration.

## JOHN CALVIN AND THE GENEVAN REFORMATION

In the second half of the sixteenth century, Calvinism replaced Lutheranism as the dominant Protestant force in Europe. Calvinists believed strongly in both divine predestination and the individual's responsibility to reorder society according to God's plan. They were determined to transform society so men and women lived their lives externally as they professed to believe internally, and were presumably destined to live eternally.

The namesake of Calvinism and its perfect embodiment, John Calvin (1509–1564), was born into a well-to-do French family, the son of the secretary to the bishop of Noyon. It was probably in the spring of 1534 that Calvin experienced that conversion to Protestantism by which he said his "long stubborn heart" was "made teachable" by God. His own hard experience became a personal model of reform by which he would measure the recalcitrant citizenry of Geneva. His mature theology stressed the sovereignty of God's will over all creation and the necessity of humankind's conformity to it.

**Portrait of John Calvin.**
Library of Congress

**Political Revolt and Religious Reform in Geneva**    Whereas in Saxony religious reform paved the way for a political revolution against the emperor, in Geneva a political revolution against the local prince-bishop laid the foundation for the religious change. Genevans revolted against their resident prince-bishop in the late 1520s, and the city council assumed his legal and political powers in 1527.

In late 1533, the Protestant city of Bern dispatched two reformers to Geneva: Guillaume Farel (1489–1565) and Antoine Froment (1508–1581). In the summer of 1535, after much internal turmoil, the Protestants triumphed, and the traditional Mass and other religious practices were removed. On May 21, 1536, Geneva voted officially to adopt the Reformation.

Calvin, an exile from France, arrived in Geneva after these events, in July 1536, and was persuaded by Ferel to stay and assist the Reformation. He agreed and drew up articles for the governance of the new church, as well as a catechism to guide and discipline the people. Both were presented for approval to the city councils in early 1537.' Opponents feared Calvin and Farel were going too far too fast. Geneva's powerful Protestant ally, Bern, which had adopted a more moderate Protestant reform, pressured Geneva's magistrates to restore traditional religious ceremonies and holidays that Calvin and Farel had abolished. When the reformers opposed these actions, they were exiled from the city.

Calvin went to Strasbourg, a model Protestant city, where he became pastor to French exiles and wrote biblical commentaries. He also produced a second edition of his masterful *Institutes of the Christian Religion*, which many consider the definitive theological statement of the Protestant faith. Most importantly, he learned from the Strasbourg reformer Martin Bucer how to achieve his goals.

**Calvin's Geneva**    In 1540, Geneva elected officials both favorable to Calvin and determined to establish full Genevan political and religious independence from Bern.

They knew Calvin would be a valuable ally in that undertaking and invited him to return. This he did in September 1540, never to leave the city again. Within months of his return, the city implemented new ecclesiastical ordinances that provided for cooperation between the magistrates and the clergy in matters of internal discipline.

The controversial doctrine of predestination was at the center of Calvin's theology as justification by faith was at Luther's. Calvin did not discuss predestination until the end of his great theological work *Institutes of the Christian Religion*. Explaining why he delayed its discussion, he described predestination as a doctrine only for mature Christians. For true believers, predestination recognized that the world and all who dwell in it are in God's hands from eternity to eternity, regardless of all else. By believing that, and living as the Bible instructed them to do, Calvinists found consoling, presumptive evidence that they were among God's elect.

Possessed of such assurance, Calvinists turned their energies to transforming society spiritually and morally. The consistory, or Geneva's regulatory court, became his instrument of power. Composed of the elders and the pastors and presided over by one of the city's chief magistrates, that body implemented the strictest moral discipline.

After 1555, Geneva became home to thousands of exiled Protestants who had been driven out of France, England, and Scotland. Refugees numbering more than 5,000, most of them utterly loyal to Calvin, made up more than one-third of Geneva's population. All of Geneva's magistrates were now devout Calvinists, greatly strengthening Calvin's position in the city.

> **QUICK REVIEW**
> **Theocracy in Geneva**
>
> ◆ Magistrates and clergy cooperated to enforce Calvin's vision
> ◆ Consistory handed out punishments for moral and religious transgressions
> ◆ Calvin and his followers showed little mercy to their opponents

# POLITICAL CONSOLIDATION OF THE LUTHERAN REFORMATION

**WHAT WERE** the political ramifications of the Reformation?

By 1530, the Reformation was in Europe to stay. It would, however, take several decades and major attempts to eradicate it, before all would recognize this fact. With the political triumph of Lutheranism in the empire by the 1550s, Protestant movements elsewhere gained a new lease on life.

## THE DIET OF AUGSBURG

Charles V devoted most of his first decade as emperor to the pursuit of politics and military campaigns outside the empire, particularly in Spain and Italy. In 1530, he returned to the empire to direct the Diet of Augsburg. This assembly of Protestant and Catholic representatives had been called to address the growing religious division within the empire in the wake of the Reformation's success. With its terms dictated by the Catholic emperor, the diet adjourned with a blunt and unrealistic order to all Lutherans to revert to Catholicism.

The Reformation was by this time too firmly established for that to occur. In February 1531, the Lutherans responded with the formation of their own defensive alliance, the Schmalkaldic League. The league took as its banner the **Augsburg Confession**, a moderate statement of Protestant beliefs that had been spurned by the emperor at the Diet of Augsburg. Under the leadership of Landgrave Philip of Hesse and Elector John Frederick of Saxony, the league achieved a stalemate with the emperor, who was again distracted by renewed war with France and the ever-resilient Turks.

**Augsburg Confession** Moderate Protestant creed endorsed by the Schmalkaldic League (a defensive alliance of Lutherans).

## THE EXPANSION OF THE REFORMATION

In the 1530s, German Lutherans formed regional consistories, judicial bodies composed of theologians and lawyers, which oversaw and administered the new Protestant churches and replaced the old Catholic episcopates. Educational reforms provided for compulsory primary education, schools for girls, a humanist revision of the traditional curriculum, and instruction of the laity in the new religion.

The Reformation also entrenched itself elsewhere. Introduced into Denmark by King Christian II (r. 1513–1523), Lutheranism thrived there under Frederick I (r. 1523–1533), who joined the Schmalkaldic League. Under Christian III (r. 1536–1559), Lutheranism became the official state religion.

In Sweden, King Gustavus Vasa (r. 1523–1560), supported by a Swedish nobility greedy for church lands, embraced Lutheranism, confiscated church property, and subjected the clergy to royal authority at the Diet of Vesteras (1527).

In politically splintered Poland, Lutherans, Anabaptists, Calvinists, and even Antitrinitarians found room to practice their beliefs. Primarily because of the absence of a central political authority, Poland became a model of religious pluralism and toleration in the second half of the sixteenth century.

### REACTION AGAINST PROTESTANTS

Charles V made abortive efforts in 1540–1541 to enforce a compromise between Protestants and Catholics. As these and other conciliar efforts failed, he turned to a military solution. In 1547, imperial armies crushed the Protestant Schmalkaldic League, defeating and capturing John Frederick of Saxony and Philip of Hesse. The emperor established puppet rulers in Saxony and Hesse and issued an imperial law mandating that Protestants everywhere readopt old Catholic beliefs and practices.

### THE PEACE OF AUGSBURG

The Reformation was too entrenched by 1547 to be ended even by brute force. Confronted by fierce resistance and weary from three decades of war, the emperor was forced to relent. After a defeat by Protestant armies in 1552, Charles reinstated the Protestant leaders and guaranteed Lutherans religious freedoms in the Peace of Passau (August 1552). With this declaration, he effectively surrendered his lifelong quest for European religious unity.

The Peace of Augsburg in September 1555 made the division of Christendom permanent. This agreement recognized in law what had already been well established in practice: *Cuius regio, eius religio,* meaning the ruler of a land would determine its religion. People discontented with the religion of their region were permitted to migrate to another.

The Peace of Augsburg did not extend official recognition to Calvinism and Anabaptism as legal forms of Christian belief and practice. Anabaptists had long adjusted to such exclusion by forming their own separatist communities. Calvinists, however, were not separatists. They remained determined to secure the right to worship publicly as they pleased, and to shape society according to their own religious convictions. While Anabaptists retreated and Lutherans enjoyed the security of an established religion, Calvinists organized to lead national revolutions throughout northern Europe in the second half of the sixteenth century.

## THE ENGLISH REFORMATION TO 1553

**HOW DID** royal dynastic concerns shape the Reformation in England?

Lollardy, humanism, and widespread anticlerical sentiments prepared the way for Protestant ideas, which entered England in the early sixteenth century.

### THE PRECONDITIONS OF REFORM

In the early 1520s, future English reformers met in Cambridge to discuss Lutheran writings smuggled into England by merchants and scholars. One of these future reformers was William Tyndale (ca. 1492–1536), who translated the New Testament into English in 1524–1525 while in Germany. Printed in Cologne and Worms, Tyndale's New Testament began to circulate in England in 1526.

Cardinal Thomas Wolsey (ca. 1475–1530), the chief minister of King Henry VIII (r. 1509–1547), and Sir Thomas More (1478–1535), Wolsey's successor, guided royal opposition to incipient English Protestantism. The king himself defended the seven sacraments against Luther, receiving as a reward the title "Defender of the Faith" from Pope Leo X.

## THE KING'S AFFAIR

Lollardy and humanism may have provided some native seeds for religious reform, but it was Henry's unhappy marriage to Catherine of Aragon (d. 1536) and obsession to get a male heir that broke the soil and allowed the seeds to take root. In 1509, Henry had married Catherine, the daughter of Ferdinand and Isabella of Spain and the aunt of Emperor Charles V. By 1527, the union had produced only one surviving child, a daughter, Mary. Although women could inherit the throne, Henry fretted over the political consequences of leaving only a female heir.

Henry came even to believe that God had cursed his union with Catherine, who had many miscarriages and stillbirths. The reason lay in Catherine's previous marriage to Henry's brother Arthur. After Arthur's premature death, Henry's father, Henry VII, betrothed her to Henry to keep the English alliance with Spain intact. The two were wed in 1509, a few days before Henry VIII received his crown. Because marriage to the wife of one's brother was prohibited by both canon and biblical law (see Leviticus 18:16, 20:21), the marriage had required a special dispensation from Pope Julius II.

By 1527, Henry was also thoroughly enamored of Anne Boleyn, one of Catherine's ladies-in-waiting. He determined to put Catherine aside and take Anne as his wife. This he could not do in Catholic England, however, without a papal annulment of the marriage to Catherine. Therein lay a special problem. Pope Clement VII was then a prisoner of Emperor Charles V, who also happened to be Catherine's nephew, and he was not about to encourage the pope to annul the royal marriage. Even if such coercion had not existed, it would have been virtually impossible for the pope to grant an annulment of a marriage that not only had survived for eighteen years but had also been made possible in the first place by a special papal dispensation.

Cardinal Wolsey, who aspired to become pope, was placed in charge of securing the royal annulment. When he failed to secure the annulment through no fault of his own, he was dismissed in disgrace in 1529. Thomas Cranmer (1489–1556) and Thomas Cromwell (1485–1540), both of whom harbored Lutheran sympathies, thereafter became the king's closest advisers. Finding the way to a papal annulment closed, Henry's new advisers struck a different course: Why not simply declare the king supreme in English spiritual affairs as he was in English temporal affairs? Then the king could settle the king's affair himself.

## THE "REFORMATION PARLIAMENT"

In 1529, Parliament convened for what would be a seven-year session that earned it the title of the "Reformation Parliament." During this period, it passed a flood of legislation that harassed, and finally placed royal reins on, the clergy. In so doing, it established a precedent that would remain a feature of English government: Whenever fundamental changes are made in religion, the monarch must consult with and work through Parliament. In January 1531, the Convocation (a legislative assembly representing the English clergy) publicly recognized Henry as head of the church in England "as far as the law of Christ allows." In 1532, Parliament published official grievances against the church, ranging from alleged indifference to the needs of the laity to an

**Hans Holbein the Younger** (1497–1543) was the most famous portrait painter of the Reformation. Here he portrays a seemingly almighty Henry VIII.

© Scala / Art Resource

**What qualities did Holbein intend the viewer to see in Henry VIII?**

**Act of Supremacy**   Act of 1534 proclaiming Henry VIII "the only supreme head on earth of the Church of England."

excessive number of religious holidays. In the same year, Parliament passed the Submission of the Clergy, which effectively placed canon law under royal control and thereby the clergy under royal jurisdiction.

In January 1533, Henry wed the pregnant Anne Boleyn, with Thomas Cranmer officiating. In February 1533, Parliament made the king the highest court of appeal for all English subjects. In March 1533, Cranmer became archbishop of Canterbury and led the Convocation in invalidating the king's marriage to Catherine. In 1534, Parliament ended all payments by the English clergy and laity to Rome and gave Henry sole jurisdiction over high ecclesiastical appointments. The Act of Succession in the same year made Anne Boleyn's children legitimate heirs to the throne, and the **Act of Supremacy** declared Henry "the only supreme head in earth of the Church of England."

When Thomas More and John Fisher, bishop of Rochester, refused to recognize the Act of Succession and the Act of Supremacy, Henry had them executed, making clear his determination to have his way regardless of the cost. In 1536 and 1538, Parliament dissolved England's monasteries and nunneries.

## WIVES OF HENRY VIII

Henry's domestic life lacked the consistency of his political life. In 1536, Anne Boleyn was executed for alleged treason and adultery, and her daughter Elizabeth, like Elizabeth's half-sister Mary before her, was declared illegitimate by her father. His third wife, Jane Seymour, died in 1537 shortly after giving birth to the future Edward VI. Henry wed Anne of Cleves sight unseen on the advice of Cromwell, the purpose being to create by the marriage an alliance with the Protestant princes of Germany. Neither the alliance nor the marriage proved worth the trouble; the marriage was annulled by Parliament, and Cromwell was dismissed and executed. Catherine Howard, Henry's fifth wife, was beheaded for adultery in 1542. His last wife, Catherine Parr, a patron of humanists and reformers, for whom Henry was the third husband, survived him to marry still a fourth time—obviously she was a match for the English king.

## THE KING'S RELIGIOUS CONSERVATISM

Henry's boldness in politics and domestic affairs did not extend to religion. Despite the break with Rome, Henry remained decidedly conservative in his religious beliefs. With the Ten Articles of 1536, he made only mild concessions to Protestant tenets. Otherwise Catholic doctrine was maintained in a country filled with Protestant sentiment.

Angered by the growing popularity of Protestant views, even among his chief advisers, Henry struck directly at them in the Six Articles of 1539. These reaffirmed transubstantiation, denied the Eucharistic cup to the laity, declared celibate vows inviolable, provided for private Masses, and ordered the continuation of oral confession. England had to await Henry's death before it could become a genuinely Protestant country.

## THE PROTESTANT REFORMATION UNDER EDWARD VI

When Henry died in 1547, his son and successor, Edward VI (d. 1553), was only ten years old. Edward reigned under the successive regencies of Edward Seymour, who became the duke of Somerset (1547–1550), and the earl of Warwick, who became known as the duke of Northumberland (1550–1553). During this time, England enacted the Protestant Reformation. The new king and Somerset corresponded directly with John Calvin.

In 1547, the chantries, places where endowed Masses had traditionally been said for the dead, were dissolved. In 1549, the Act of Uniformity imposed Thomas Cranmer's *Book of Common Prayer* on all English churches. Images and altars were removed from the churches in 1550. The Second Act of Uniformity, passed in 1552, imposed a revised *Book of Common Prayer* on all English churches. A forty-two-article confession of faith, also written by Thomas Cranmer, set forth a moderate Protestant doctrine. It taught justification by faith and the supremacy of Holy Scripture, denied transubstantiation (although not the real presence), and recognized only two sacraments.

All these changes were short-lived, however. In 1553, Catherine of Aragon's daughter succeeded Edward (who had died in his teens) to the throne as Mary I (d. 1558) and restored Catholic doctrine and practice with a single-mindedness rivaling that of her father. It was not until the reign of Anne Boleyn's daughter, Elizabeth I (r. 1558–1603), that England worked out a lasting religious settlement.

# CATHOLIC REFORM AND COUNTER-REFORMATION

The Protestant Reformation did not take the medieval church completely by surprise. There were many internal criticisms and efforts at reform before there was a Counter-Reformation in reaction to Protestant successes.

**WHAT WAS** the Counter-Reformation and how successful was it?

## SOURCES OF CATHOLIC REFORM

Before the Reformation began, ambitious proposals had been made for church reform. But sixteenth-century popes, ever mindful of how the councils of Constance and Basel had stripped the pope of his traditional powers, squelched such efforts to change the laws and institutions of the church.

Despite such papal foot-dragging, the old church was not without its reformers. Many new religious orders also sprang up in the sixteenth century to lead a broad revival of piety within the church. The first of these orders was the Theatines, founded in 1524, to groom devout and reform-minded leaders at the higher levels of the church hierarchy. Another new order, whose mission pointed in the opposite direction, was the Capuchins. Recognized by the pope in 1528, they sought to return to the original ideals of Saint Francis and became popular among the ordinary people to whom they directed their ministry. The Somaschi, who became active in the mid-1520s, and the Barnabites, founded in 1530, worked to repair the moral, spiritual, and physical damage done to people in war-torn Italy. For women, there was the influential new order of Ursulines. Founded in 1535, it established convents in Italy and France for the religious education of girls from all social classes.

## IGNATIUS OF LOYOLA AND THE JESUITS

Of the various reform groups, none was more instrumental in the success of the Counter-Reformation than the Society of Jesus, the new order of Jesuits. Organized by Ignatius of Loyola in the 1530s, the church recognized it in 1540. The society grew within a century from its original 10 members to more than 15,000 members scattered throughout the world, with thriving missions in India, Japan, and the Americas.

The founder of the Jesuits, Ignatius of Loyola (1491–1556), developed a program of religious and moral self-discipline that came to be embodied in the *Spiritual Exercises*. This psychologically perceptive devotional guide contained mental and emotional exercises designed to teach one absolute spiritual self-mastery over one's feelings. It taught that a person could shape his or her own behavior—even create a new religious self—through disciplined study and regular practice.

The exercises of Ignatius were intended to teach good Catholics to deny themselves and submit without question to higher church authority and spiritual direction. Perfect discipline and self-control were the essential conditions of such obedience. To these were added the enthusiasm of traditional spirituality and mysticism and uncompromising loyalty to the church's cause. This potent combination helped counter the

**MAP EXPLORATION**

⌖Interactive map: To explore this map further, go to www.myhistorylab.com

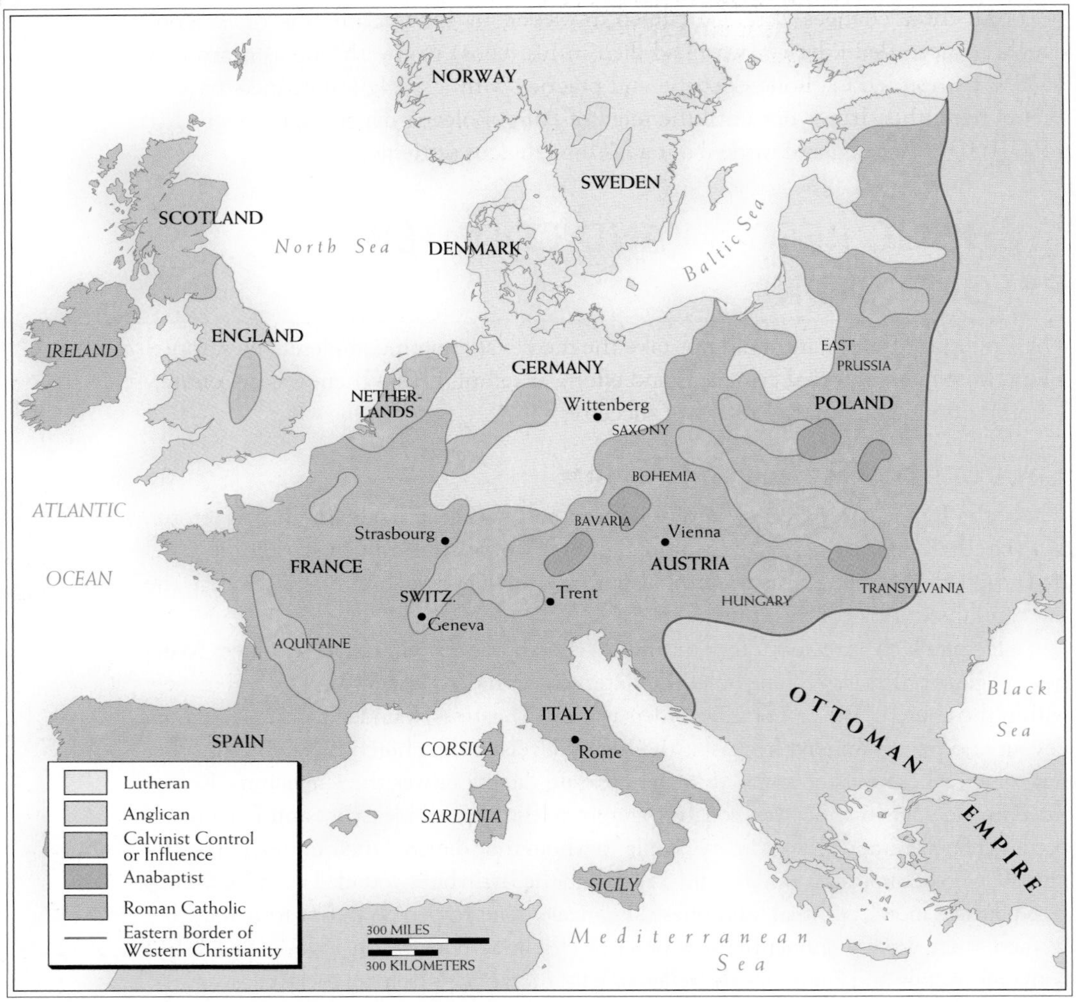

MAP 11–2   **The Religious Situation about 1560**   By 1560, Luther, Zwingli, and Loyola were dead, Calvin was near the end of his life, the English break from Rome was complete, and the last session of the Council of Trent was about to assemble. This map shows the "religious geography" of western Europe at the time.

**How would** you characterize Christianity in western Europe at this time? Which reform movements seem to have had the most success?

*Map showing the religious situation in Europe about 1560, with labels for NORWAY, SWEDEN, SCOTLAND, DENMARK, IRELAND, ENGLAND, GERMANY, NETHERLANDS, Wittenberg, SAXONY, EAST PRUSSIA, POLAND, BOHEMIA, BAVARIA, Strasbourg, Vienna, AUSTRIA, FRANCE, SWITZ., Geneva, Trent, HUNGARY, TRANSYLVANIA, AQUITAINE, SPAIN, CORSICA, SARDINIA, ITALY, Rome, SICILY, OTTOMAN EMPIRE, North Sea, Baltic Sea, ATLANTIC OCEAN, Black Sea, Mediterranean Sea.*

Legend:
- Lutheran
- Anglican
- Calvinist Control or Influence
- Anabaptist
- Roman Catholic
- Eastern Border of Western Christianity

300 MILES
300 KILOMETERS

Reformation and win many Protestants back to the Catholic fold, especially in Austria and parts of Germany. (See Map 11–2.)

## THE COUNCIL OF TRENT (1545–1563)

The broad success of the Reformation and the insistence of the Emperor Charles V forced Pope Paul III (r. 1534–1549) to call a general council of the church to reassert church doctrine. The council met in 1545 in the imperial city of Trent in northern Italy. There were three sessions, spread over eighteen years, with long interruptions due to war, plague, and imperial and papal politics. The council met from 1545 to 1547, from 1551 to 1552, and from 1562 to 1563, a period that spanned the reigns of four different popes.

The council's most important reforms concerned internal church discipline. Steps were taken to curtail the selling of church offices and other religious goods. Many bishops who resided in Rome were forced to move to their dioceses. Trent strengthened the authority of local bishops so they could effectively discipline popular religious practices. The bishops were also subjected to new rules that required them to be highly visible by preaching regularly and conducting annual visitations of their diocesan parishes. Parish priests were required to be neatly dressed, better educated, strictly celibate, and active among their parishioners. To train priests, Trent also called for a seminary in every diocese.

Not a single doctrinal concession was made to the Protestants, however. Instead, the Council of Trent reaffirmed the traditional Scholastic education of the clergy; the role of good works in salvation; the authority of tradition; the seven sacraments; transubstantiation; the withholding of the Eucharistic from the laity; clerical celibacy; purgatory; the veneration of saints, relics, and sacred images; and indulgences. The council resolved medieval Scholastic quarrels in favor of the theology of Saint Thomas Aquinas, further enhancing his authority within the church. Thereafter, the church offered its strongest resistance to groups like the Jansenists, who endorsed the medieval Augustinian tradition, a source of alternative Catholic, as well as many Protestant, doctrines.

Rulers initially resisted Trent's reform decrees, fearing a revival of papal political power and new confessional conflicts within their lands. Over time, however, and with the pope's assurances that religious reforms were his sole intent, the new legislation took hold, and parish life revived under a devout and better trained clergy.

# THE SOCIAL SIGNIFICANCE OF THE REFORMATION IN WESTERN EUROPE

The Lutheran, Zwinglian, and Calvinist reformers all sought to work within the framework of reigning political power. Luther, Zwingli, and Calvin saw themselves and their followers as subject to definite civic responsibilities and obligations. They wanted reform to take shape within reigning laws and institutions. They thus remained highly sensitive to what was politically and socially possible in their age.

**WHAT WAS** the social significance of the Reformation and how did it affect family life?

## THE REVOLUTION IN RELIGIOUS PRACTICES AND INSTITUTIONS

The Reformation may have been politically conservative, but by the end of the sixteenth century, it had brought about radical changes in traditional religious practices and institutions in those lands where it succeeded.

**Religion in Fifteenth-Century Life** In the fifteenth century, on the streets of the great cities of Europe that later turned Protestant, the clergy and the religious were everywhere. They made up 6 to 8 percent of the urban population, and they exercised considerable political as well as spiritual power. They legislated and taxed, they tried cases in special church courts, and they enforced their laws with threats of excommunication. The church calendar regulated daily life. About one-third of the year was given over to some kind of religious observance or celebration.

Monasteries, and especially nunneries, were prominent and influential institutions. The children of society's most powerful citizens resided there. Local aristocrats identified with particular churches and chapels, whose walls recorded their lineage and proclaimed their generosity. On the streets, friars begged alms from passersby. In the churches, the Mass and liturgy were read entirely in Latin. Images of saints were regularly displayed, and on certain holidays their relics were paraded about and venerated.

## SIGNIFICANT DATES FROM THE PERIOD OF THE PROTESTANT REFORMATION

| | |
|---|---|
| 1517 | Luther posts ninety-five theses against indulgences |
| 1519 | Charles V becomes Holy Roman Emperor |
| 1521 | Diet of Worms condemns Luther |
| 1524–1525 | Peasants' Revolt in Germany |
| 1527 | The Schleitheim Confession of the Anabaptists |
| 1529 | Marburg Colloquy between Luther and Zwingli |
| 1529 | England's Reformation Parliament convenes |
| 1531 | Formation of Protestant Schmalkaldic League |
| 1533 | Henry VIII weds Anne Boleyn |
| 1534 | England's Act of Supremacy |
| 1534–1535 | Anabaptists take over Münster |
| 1536 | Calvin arrives in Geneva |
| 1540 | Jesuits, founded by Ignatius of Loyola, recognized as order by pope |
| 1546 | Luther dies |
| 1547 | Armies of Charles V crush Schmalkaldic League |
| 1547–1553 | Edward VI, king of England |
| 1555 | Peace of Augsburg |
| 1553–1558 | Mary Tudor, queen of England |
| 1545–1563 | Council of Trent |
| 1558–1603 | Elizabeth I, queen of England; the Anglican settlement |

Local religious shrines enjoyed a booming business. Pilgrims gathered there by the hundreds—even thousands—many sick and dying, all in search of a cure or a miracle, but also for diversion and entertainment. Several times during the year, special preachers arrived in the city to sell letters of indulgence.

People everywhere complained about the clergy's exemption from taxation and also often from the civil criminal code. People also grumbled about having to support church offices whose occupants actually lived and worked elsewhere, turning the cure of souls over to poorly trained and paid substitutes. Townspeople expressed concern that the church had too much influence over education and culture.

**Religion in Sixteenth-Century Life**   In these same cities, after the Reformation had firmly established itself, few changes in politics and society were evident. The same aristocratic families governed as before, and the rich generally got richer and the poor poorer. Overall numbers of clergy fell by two-thirds, and religious holidays shrank by one-third. Cloisters were nearly gone, and many that remained were transformed into hospices for the sick and poor or into educational institutions, their endowments turned over to these new purposes.

The churches were reduced in number by at least one-third, and worship was conducted almost completely in the vernacular. Indulgence preachers no longer appeared. Local shrines were closed down, and anyone found openly venerating saints, relics, and images was subject to fine and punishment.

Copies of Luther's translation of the New Testament (1522) or, more often, excerpts from it could be found in private homes, and the new clergy encouraged meditation on the Bible. The clergy could marry, and most did. They paid taxes and were punished for their crimes in civil courts. Committees composed of roughly equal numbers of laity and clergy, over whose decisions secular magistrates had the last word, regulated domestic moral life.

Not all Protestant clergy remained enthusiastic about this new lay authority in religion. And the laity was also ambivalent about certain aspects of the Reformation. Over half of the original converts returned to the Catholic fold before the end of the sixteenth century.

## THE REFORMATION AND EDUCATION

Another major cultural achievement of the Reformation was its implementation of many of the educational reforms of humanism in new Protestant schools and universities. Many Protestant reformers in Germany, France, and England were humanists. And even when their views on church doctrine and human nature separated them from the humanist movement, the Protestant reformers continued to share a common opposition to Scholasticism and a belief in the unity of wisdom, eloquence, and action. The humanist program of studies, providing the language skills to deal authoritatively with original sources, proved to be a more appropriate tool for the elaboration of Protestant doctrine than it did for Scholastic dialectic, which remained ascendant in the Counter-Reformation.

When, in August 1518, Philip Melanchthon (1497–1560), "the praeceptor of Germany," a young humanist and professor of Greek, arrived at the University of Wittenberg, his first act was to reform the curriculum on the humanist model. Together, Luther and Melanchthon restructured the University of Wittenberg's curriculum. Commentaries on Lombard's *Sentences* were dropped, as was canon law. Straightforward historical study replaced old Scholastic lectures on Aristotle. Students read primary sources directly, rather than by way of accepted Scholastic commentators. Candidates for theological degrees defended the new doctrine on the basis of their own study of the Bible. New chairs of Greek and Hebrew were created.

In Geneva, John Calvin and his successor, Theodore Beza, founded the Genevan Academy, which later evolved into the University of Geneva. That institution, created primarily to train Calvinist ministers, pursued ideals similar to those set forth by

Luther and Melanchthon. Calvinist refugees who studied there later carried Protestant educational reforms to France, Scotland, England, and the New World.

Some famous contemporaries decried what they saw as a narrowing of the original humanist program as Protestants took it over. Humanist culture and learning nonetheless remained indebted to the Reformation. The Protestant endorsement of the humanist program of studies remained as significant for the humanist movement as the latter had been for the Reformation. Protestant schools and universities consolidated and preserved for the modern world many of the basic pedagogical achievements of humanism. There, the *studia humanitatis*, although often as little more than a handmaiden to theological doctrine, found a permanent home, one that remained hospitable even in the heyday of conservative Protestantism.

## THE REFORMATION AND THE CHANGING ROLE OF WOMEN

The Protestant reformers favored clerical marriage and opposed monasticism and the celibate life. From this position, they challenged the medieval tendency alternately to degrade women as temptresses (following the model of Eve) and to exalt them as virgins (following the model of Mary). Protestants opposed the popular antiwoman and antimarriage literature of the Middle Ages. They praised woman in her own right, but especially in her biblical vocation as mother and housewife. Although wives remained subject to their husbands, new laws gave them greater security and protection.

Protestants placed a high value on marriage and family life. In opposition to the celibate ideal of the Middle Ages, Protestants stressed, as no religious movement before them had ever done, the sacredness of home and family. The ideal of the companionate marriage—that is, of husband and wife as co-workers in a special God-ordained community of the family, sharing authority equally within the household—led to an expansion of the grounds for divorce in Protestant lands as early as the 1520s. Women gained an equal right with men to divorce and remarry in good conscience—unlike the situation in Catholicism, where only a separation from bed and table, not divorce and remarriage, was permitted a couple in a failed marriage. The reformers were more willing to permit divorce and remarriage on grounds of adultery and abandonment than were secular magistrates, who feared liberal divorce laws would lead to social upheaval.

Typical of reforms and revolutions in their early stages, Protestant doctrines emboldened women as well as men. Renegade nuns wrote exposés of the nunnery in the name of Christian freedom and justification by faith, declaring the nunnery was no special woman's place at all and that supervisory male clergy made their lives as unpleasant and burdensome as any abusive husband. Women in the higher classes, who enjoyed new social and political freedoms during the Renaissance, found in Protestant theology a religious complement to their greater independence in other walks of life. Some cloistered noblewomen, however, protested the closing of nunneries, arguing that the cloister provided them a more interesting and independent way of life than they would have known in the secular world.

Because Protestants wanted women to become pious housewives, they encouraged the education of girls to literacy in the vernacular, with the expectation that they would thereafter model their lives on the Bible. However, women also found biblical passages that made clear their equality to men in the presence of God. Education also gave some women roles as independent authors on behalf of the Reformation. Although small advances from a modern perspective, these were also steps toward the emancipation of women.

# FAMILY LIFE IN EARLY MODERN EUROPE

Changes in the timing and duration of marriage, family size, and infant and child care suggest that family life was under a variety of social and economic pressures in the sixteenth and seventeenth centuries.

**WHAT WAS** family life like in early modern Europe?

# ENCOUNTERING THE PAST

## TABLE MANNERS

*Humanists believed that education ought to mix pleasure with discipline. The family meal was, therefore, a suitable occasion for instructing the young in the lessons of life. Learning required neatness, order, respect, and attentiveness—traits that Hans Sachs, a sixteenth-century father, wanted his children to learn at his table.*

Listen you children who are going to table.
Wash your hands and cut your nails.
Do not sit at the head of the table;
This is reserved for the father of the house.
Do not commence eating until a blessing has been said.
. . .permit the eldest to begin first.
Proceed in a disciplined manner.
Do not snort or smack like a pig.
Do not reach violently for bread. . . .
Do not stir food around on your plate or linger over it. . . .
Rushing through your meal is bad manners.
Do not reach for more food while your mouth is still full,
Nor talk with your mouth full. . . .
Chew your food with your mouth closed.
Do not lick the corners of your mouth like a dog. . . .
Do not belch or cry out. . . .
Do not stare at a person as if you were watching him eat.
Do not elbow the person sitting next to you. . . .
Do not rock back and forth on the bench, lest you let loose a stink. . . .
If sexual play occurs at table, pretend you do not see it. . . .

Do not pick your nose. . . .
Let no one wipe his mouth on the table cloth. . . .
Silently praise and thank God for the food he has graciously provided.

Source: From Steven Ozment, *When Fathers Ruled: Family Life in Reformation Europe,* trans. by Steven Ozment (Cambridge, MA: Harvard University Press, 1983), pp. 142–143.

**A Family Meal**

In Max Geisberg, *The German Single-Leaf Woodcuts,* ill: *1500–1550,* rev. and ed. by W. L. Strauss (New York: Hacker Art Books, 1974). Used by permission of Hacker Art Books

**What role did the family play in early modern religious life?**

HOW DO table manners prepare a child for life?

## LATER MARRIAGES

Between 1500 and 1800, men and women in Western Europe married at later ages than they had in previous centuries: men in their mid- to late-twenties, and women in their early- to mid-twenties. Late marriage in the West reflected the difficulty couples had supporting themselves independently. It simply took the average couple a longer time than before to prepare themselves materially for marriage. In the sixteenth century, one in five women never married, and these, combined with the estimated 15 percent who were unmarried widows, constituted a large unmarried female population. A later marriage was also a shorter marriage; in an age when few people lived into their sixties couples who married in their thirties spent less time together than couples who married in their twenties. Also, because women who bore children for the first time at advanced ages had higher mortality rates, late marriage meant more frequent remarriage for men. As the rapid growth of orphanages and foundling homes between 1600 and 1800 makes clear, delayed marriage increased premarital sex and the number of illegitimate children.

## ARRANGED MARRIAGES

Marriage tended to be "arranged" in the sense that the parents met and discussed the terms of the marriage before the prospective bride and bridegroom became direct parties to the preparations. The wealth and social standing of the bride and the bridegroom, however, were not the only things considered when youth married. By the fifteenth century, it was usual for the future bride and bridegroom to have known each other and to have had some prior relationship. Parents did not force total strangers to live together, and children had a legal right to resist a coerced marriage, which was by definition invalid. The best marriage was one desired by both the bride and groom and their families.

## FAMILY SIZE AND BIRTH CONTROL

The West European family was conjugal, or nuclear, consisting of a father and a mother and two to four children who survived into adulthood. This nuclear family lived within a larger household, including in-laws, servants, laborers, and boarders. The average husband and wife had six to seven children, a new birth about every two years. Of these, an estimated one-third died by age five, and one-half by their teens. Rare was the family, at any social level, that did not experience child death.

Artificial birth control (sponges, acidic ointments) has existed since antiquity. The church's condemnation of *coitus interruptus* (male withdrawal before ejaculation) during the thirteenth and fourteenth centuries suggests the existence of a contraceptive mentality, that is, a conscious, regular effort at birth control. Early birth control measures, when applied, were not very effective, and for both historical and moral reasons, the church opposed them.

## WET NURSING

The church allied with the physicians of early modern Europe on another intimate family matter. Both condemned women who hired wet nurses to suckle their newborn children. The practice was popular among upper-class women and reflected their social standing. It appears to have increased the risk of infant mortality by exposing infants to a strange and shared milk supply from women who were often not as healthy as the infants' own mothers and lived under less sanitary conditions. Nursing was distasteful to some upper-class women, whose husbands also preferred that they not do it. Because the church forbade lactating women from indulging in sexual intercourse, a nursing wife

## Overview  The Reformation and the Changing Role of Women

| | |
|---|---|
| **EDUCATION** | • Encouraged female literacy in the vernacular<br>• Women found biblical passages that suggested they were equal to men<br>• Women became independent authors |
| **LATER MARRIAGES** | • Men and women tended to wait until their mid- to late twenties to marry<br>• Later marriages meant marriages of shorter duration<br>• Remarriage was now more common for men who lost wives in childbearing |
| **ARRANGED MARRIAGES** | • Bride and groom often knew each other in advance of marriage<br>• Emotional feeling for one another was increasingly respected by parents<br>• Forced marriages were, by definition, invalid and often failed |
| **FAMILY SIZE** | • Large households consisted of in-laws, servants, laborers, and boarders<br>• The average husband and wife had seven or eight children but most families experienced infant mortality and child death |
| **WET NURSING** | • Church and physicians condemned the use of wet nurses<br>• Upper-class women viewed the use of wet nurses as a symbol of high rank<br>• The practice increased the rate of infant mortality |

could become a reluctant lover. Nursing also had a contraceptive effect. Some women prolonged nursing their children to delay a new pregnancy, and some husbands cooperated in this form of family planning. For other husbands, however, especially noblemen and royalty who desired an abundance of male heirs, nursing seemed to rob them of offspring and jeopardize their patrimony—hence their support of hired wet nurses.

### Loving Families?

The traditional Western European family had features that seem cold and distant. Children between the ages of eight and thirteen were routinely sent from their homes into apprenticeships, school, or employment in the homes and businesses of relatives, friends, and occasionally strangers. The emotional ties between spouses also seem to have been as tenuous as those between parents and children. Widowers and widows often married again within a few months of their spouses' deaths, and marriages with extreme difference in age between partners suggest limited affection.

In response to modern-day criticism, an early modern parent might well have asked, "What greater love can parents have for their children than to equip them well for a worldly vocation?" A well-apprenticed child was a self-supporting child, and hence a child with a future. In light of the comparatively primitive living conditions, contemporaries also appreciated the purely utilitarian and humane side of marriage and understood when widowers and widows quickly remarried. Marriages with extreme disparity in age, however, were no more the norm in early modern Europe than the practice of wet nursing, and they received just as much criticism and ridicule.

## LITERARY IMAGINATION IN TRANSITION

**HOW WAS** the transition from medieval to modern reflected in the works of the great literary figures of the era?

As Europe approached the seventeenth century, it was no longer medieval but neither was it yet modern. The great literary figures of the era produced transitional works that combined traditional values and fresh perspectives on human life.

### Miguel de Cervantes Saavedra: Rejection of Idealism

Spanish literature of the sixteenth and seventeenth centuries reflects the peculiar religious and political history of Spain in this period. Traditional Catholic teaching was a major influence on Spanish life. Since the joint reign of Ferdinand and Isabella (1479–1504), the church had received the unqualified support of the reigning political power.

A second influence on Spanish literature was the aggressive piety of Spanish rulers. Their intertwining of Catholic piety and political power underlay a third influence: preoccupation with medieval chivalric virtues, in particular, questions of honor and loyalty. The novels and plays of the period almost invariably focus on a special test of character, bordering on the heroic, that threatens honor and reputation. In this regard, Spanish literature remained more Catholic and medieval than that of England and France, where major Protestant movements had occurred. The writer generally acknowledged to be Spain's greatest, Cervantes, was preoccupied in his work with the strengths and weaknesses of traditional religious idealism.

Cervantes (1547–1616) had only a smattering of formal education. He educated himself by wide reading in popular literature and immersion in the "school of life." As a young man, he worked in Rome for a Spanish cardinal. As a soldier, he was decorated for gallantry in the Battle of Lepanto against the Turks (1571). He also spent five years as a slave in Algiers after his ship was pirated in 1575. Later, while working as a tax collector, he was imprisoned several times for padding his accounts, and it was in prison that he began, in 1603, to write his most famous work, *Don Quixote*.

The first part of *Don Quixote* appeared in 1605. The intent of this work seems to have been to satirize the chivalric romances then popular in Spain. But Cervantes could not conceal his deep affection for the character he created as an object of ridicule. Cervantes presented Don Quixote as a none-too stable middle-aged man. Driven mad by reading too many chivalric romances, he had come to believe he was an aspiring knight who had to prove his worthiness by brave deeds. To this end, he donned a rusty suit of armor and chose for his inspiration an unworthy peasant girl (Dulcinea), whom he fancied to be a noble lady to whom he could, with honor, dedicate his life.

Don Quixote's foil—Sancho Panza, a clever, worldly wise peasant who serves as Quixote's squire—watches with bemused skepticism as his lord repeatedly makes a fool of himself as he gallops across the countryside. The story ends tragically with Don Quixote's humiliating defeat at the hand of a well-meaning friend who, disguised as a knight, bested Quixote in combat and forced him to renounce his quest for knighthood. Don Quixote did not, however, come to his senses but rather returned to his village to die a brokenhearted old man.

Throughout the novel, Cervantes juxtaposes the down-to-earth realism of Sancho Panza with the old-fashioned religious idealism of Don Quixote. The reader perceives that Cervantes admired the one as much as the other and meant to portray both as representing attitudes necessary for a happy life.

## WILLIAM SHAKESPEARE: DRAMATIST OF THE AGE

There is much less factual knowledge about Shakespeare (1564–1616) than we would expect of the greatest playwright in the English language. He apparently worked as a schoolteacher for a time and in this capacity gained his broad knowledge of Renaissance literature. His own reading and enthusiasm for the learning of his day are manifest in the many literary allusions that appear in his plays.

Shakespeare lived the life of a country gentleman. There is none of the Puritan distress over worldliness in his work. He took the new commercialism and the bawdy pleasures of the Elizabethan Age in stride and with amusement. He was a radical neither in politics nor religion. The few allusions in his works to the Puritans seem more critical than complimentary.

That Shakespeare was interested in politics is apparent from his historical plays and the references to contemporary political events that fill all his plays. He viewed government through the character of the individual ruler, whether Richard III or Elizabeth Tudor, rather than in terms of ideal systems or social goals. By modern standards, he was a political conservative, accepting the social rankings and the power structure of his day and demonstrating unquestioned patriotism.

Elizabethan drama was already a distinctive form when Shakespeare began writing. Unlike French drama of the seventeenth century, which was dominated by classical models, English drama developed in the sixteenth and seventeenth centuries as a blending of many forms: classical comedies and tragedies, medieval morality plays, and contemporary Italian short stories.

Shakespeare wrote histories, comedies, and tragedies. *Richard III* (1593), an early play, stands out among the histories, although some scholars view the picture it presents of Richard as an unprincipled villain as "Tudor propaganda." Shakespeare's comedies, although not attaining the heights of his tragedies, surpass his history plays in originality.

Shakespeare's tragedies are considered his unique achievement. Four of these were written within a three-year period: *Hamlet* (1603), *Othello* (1604), *King Lear* (1605), and *Macbeth* (1606). The most original of the tragedies, *Romeo and Juliet* (1597), transformed an old popular story into a moving drama of "star-cross'd lovers."

Shakespeare's works struck universal human themes, many of which were deeply rooted in contemporary religious traditions. His plays were immensely popular with both the playgoers and the play readers of Elizabethan England. Still today, the works of no other dramatist from his age are performed in theaters or on film more regularly than his.

**William Shakespeare.**
Library of Congress

# SUMMARY

## WHAT WAS the social and religious background of the Reformation?

**Society and Religion** The Protestant Reformation had roots in political, social, and economic concerns. The emergence of centralizing national governments was challenging local custom and authority through much of Europe; in Germany and Switzerland, the free imperial cities were important early hotbeds of Protestantism. Often, groups (such as guilds) or regions in which people felt controlled by authority figures were particularly receptive to Protestantism. Laypeople were gaining power to criticize, and attempt to reform, the church, both because they were gaining cultural authority in general and because the church's crises had cost it so much credibility. *page 272*

## WHY DID Martin Luther challenge the church?

**Martin Luther and the German Reformation to 1525** Martin Luther, like many other Germans, was concerned about the church's sale of indulgences and other financial and political arrangements. An ordained priest with a doctorate in theology, he developed the doctrine of justification by faith alone, which offers salvation to believers in Christ. In 1517, Luther posted ninety-five theses against indulgence on the door of a church in Wittenberg. This sparked the Reformation. In the following years, Luther developed and publicized his theology; he was excommunicated in 1521. German humanists, peasants, and others supported Luther and his ideas, although Luther urged princes to suppress the peasants' revolt of 1524–1525. *page 274*

## WHERE DID other reform movements develop and how were they different from Luther's?

**The Reformation Elsewhere** In Switzerland, France, and elsewhere in Europe, variations of Protestantism developed. In the 1520s, Ulrich Zwingli orchestrated the Swiss Reformation, from his post as the people's priest in the main church of Zurich. Zwingli believed a literal reading of Scripture should guide Christian beliefs and practices. More radical groups emerged, including Anabaptists, who believed baptism should only be performed on adults, who were capable of choosing their religion. John Calvin and his followers wanted to transform society morally, starting in Geneva in 1540. In the second half of the sixteenth century, Calvinism displaced Lutheranism as Europe's dominant form of Protestantism. *page 280*

## WHAT WERE the political ramifications of the Reformation?

**Political Consolidation of the Lutheran Reformation** Between 1530 and 1552, the emperor Charles V made repeated attempts to persuade or force Protestants to revert to Catholicism. The 1555 Peace of Augsburg formalized Lutheranism's official status in the empire. Lutheranism also became the official state religion in Denmark and Sweden. Calvinists and Anabaptists, among others, were still excluded from official recognition throughout Europe. *page 283*

## HOW DID royal dynastic concerns shape the Reformation in England?

**The English Reformation to 1553** King Henry VIII's marital history had dramatic consequences for England's religion: Because Henry wanted to marry Anne Boleyn, and because Pope Clement VII would not annul Henry's marriage to Catherine of Aragon, Parliament decreed that the king, not the pope, was the "supreme head on earth of the Church of England." But, by the 1530s, many of Henry's subjects were far more sympathetic to Protestantism than the king himself was; Henry's Church of England differed little from the Catholic Church. Only under the reign of his son, Edward VI, was Protestantism really instituted in England. *page 284*

## WHAT WAS the Counter-Reformation and how successful was it?

**Catholic Reform and Counter-Reformation** Protestants were not the only critics of the Catholic Church. Although the popes resisted reform, many new reform-oriented orders were established in the sixteenth century. Ignatius of Loyola founded what became one of the most significant of these orders, the Jesuits, who stressed a powerful combination of discipline and traditional spirituality. Between 1545 and 1563, a council of the church met at Trent to reassert Catholic doctrine. As a result of the Council of Trent, internal church discipline was reformed, but doctrine became even more strongly traditional and scholastic in orientation. Improvements in the education and behavior of local clergy helped revive parish life. *page 287*

## WHAT WAS the social significance of the Reformation and how did it affect family life?

**The Social Significance of the Reformation in Western Europe** Although the Reformation was politically conservative, it revolutionized religious practice and institutions in part of Europe. In cities that became Protestant, many aspects of life were transformed. The numbers of clergy in these cities declined by two-thirds, one-third of all churches were closed, there were one-third fewer religious holidays, and most cloisters were closed. Some changes did not endure: More than half the original converts to Protestantism returned to the Catholic Church by the end of the sixteenth century. Protestant reformers helped disseminate humanist learning and culture. The ideal of the companionate marriage and other Protestant views helped improve the status of women. *page 289*

## WHAT WAS family life like in early modern Europe?

**Family Life in Early Modern Europe** Marriage occurred at a later age in the sixteenth through eighteenth centuries than it had previously in Europe and England. One reason for this shift was that, in a time of population growth, it took couples longer to accumulate the capital needed to raise a family. Parents were involved in arranging their children's marriages, although the couple's own wishes also carried significant weight. Generally, two to four children survived to adulthood in the European nuclear family. Birth control was not very effective; wet nursing was controversial. Although they sometimes exhibited it in ways that may seem strange to us, early modern parents almost certainly loved their children, and probably also each other. *page 291*

## HOW WAS the transition from medieval to modern reflected in the works of the great literary figures of the era?

**Literary Imagination in Transition** Miguel de Cervantes Saavedra and William Shakespeare are among the most renowned authors of this period. Cervantes lived and worked in Catholic Spain; Shakespeare was a product of Protestant England. Their writings reflect their very different situations and interests. Cervantes's most famous work, *Don Quixote*, pays homage to the tradition of chivalric romance. Shakespeare's dramas cover a wide range of topics, including history; his universal themes and brilliant technique explain his enduring popularity. *page 294*

# REVIEW QUESTIONS

1. What were the main problems of the church that contributed to the Protestant Reformation? On what did Luther and Zwingli agree? On what did they disagree? What about Luther and Calvin?

2. What was the Catholic Reformation? What were the major reforms instituted by the Council of Trent? Did the Protestant Reformation have a healthy effect on the Catholic Church?

3. Why did Henry VIII break with the Catholic Church? Did he establish a truly Protestant religion in England? What problems did his successors face as a result of his religious policies?

4. What impact did the Reformation have on women in the sixteenth and seventeenth centuries? What new factors and pressures affected relations between men and women, family size, and child care during this period?

## KEY TERMS

**Act of Supremacy** (p. 286)　　**Augsburg Confession** (p. 283)
**Anabaptists** (p. 281)　　**indulgence** (p. 275)

For additional learning resources related to this chapter, please go to **www.myhistorylab.com**

myhistorylab

# 12

# The Age of Religious Wars

**The massacre of worshipping Protestants** at Vassy, France (March 1, 1562), which began the French wars of religion. An engraving by an unidentified seventeenth-century artist.

The Granger Collection

**How did politics and religion combine to produce civil war in sixteenth-century France?**

*Political rivalries and religious conflicts combined to make the late sixteenth and the early seventeenth centuries an "age of religious wars." The era was plagued by civil conflicts within nations and by battles among nations. Catholic and Protestant factions contended within France, the Netherlands, and England. The Catholic monarchies of France and Spain attacked the Protestant regimes in England and the Netherlands. Ultimately, every major nation in Europe was drawn into a conflict that devastated Germany: the Thirty Years' War (1618–1648).* ∎

# RENEWED RELIGIOUS STRUGGLE

**HOW DID** religious conflict in Europe evolve over the course of the second half of the sixteenth century?

**Counter-Reformation** A reorganization of the Catholic Church that equipped it to meet the challenges posed by the Protestant Reformation.

**Contrast between** an eighteenth-century Catholic baroque church in Ottobeuren, Bavaria, and a seventeenth-century Calvinist plain church in the Palatinate. The ornamental Catholic church (left) inspires worshippers to self-transcendence, while the undecorated Protestant church (right) focuses attention on God's word.

(Left) Vanni/Art Resource, NY (Right) German National Museum, Nuremberg, Germany

**How did the baroque style reflect early modern Catholicism?**

**Why did Protestant churches such as this one avoid ornament and decoration?**

During the first half of the sixteenth century, religious conflict had been confined to central Europe and was primarily a struggle by Lutherans and Zwinglians to secure rights and freedoms for themselves. In the second half of the century, the focus shifted to Western Europe—to France, the Netherlands, England, and Scotland—and became a struggle by Calvinists for recognition. After the Peace of Augsburg (1555) and acceptance of the principle that a region's ruler determined its religion (*cuius regio, eius religio*), Lutheranism became a legal religion in the Holy Roman Empire. The Peace of Augsburg did not, however, extend recognition to non-Lutheran Protestants. Anabaptists and other sectarians continued to be scorned as heretics and anarchists, and Calvinists were not strong enough to gain legal standing.

Outside the empire, the struggle for religious freedom had intensified in most countries. After the Council of Trent adjourned in 1563, Catholics began a Jesuit-led international counteroffensive against Protestants. At the time of John Calvin's death in 1564, Geneva had become both a refuge for Europe's persecuted Protestants and an international school for Protestant resistance, producing leaders equal to the new Catholic challenge.

Genevan Calvinism and Catholicism as revived by the Council of Trent were two equally dogmatic, aggressive, and irreconcilable church systems. Calvinism adopted an organization that magnified regional and local religious authority. Boards of presbyters, or elders, represented the individual congregations of Calvinists, directly shaping policy. By contrast, the **Counter-Reformation** sponsored a centralized episcopal church system hierarchically arranged from pope to parish priest and stressing unquestioning obedience to the person at the top. Calvinism proved attractive to proponents of political decentralization who opposed such hierarchical rule, in principle, whereas the Roman Catholic Church, an institution also devoted to one head and one law, found absolute monarchy congenial.

## Overview  Main Events of French Wars of Religion

| | |
|---|---|
| **1559** | Treaty of Cateau-Cambrésis ends Habsburg-Valois wars |
| **1559** | Francis II succeeds to French throne under regency of his mother, Catherine de Médicis |
| **1562** | Protestant worshippers massacred at Vassy in Champagne by the duke of Guise |
| **1572** | The Saint Bartholomew's Day Massacre leaves thousands of Protestants dead |
| **1589** | Assassination of Henry III brings the Huguenot Henry of Navarre to throne as Henry IV |
| **1593** | Henry IV embraces Catholicism |
| **1598** | Henry IV grants Huguenots religious and civil freedoms in the Edict of Nantes |
| **1610** | Henry IV assassinated |

As religious wars engulfed Europe, the intellectuals perceived the wisdom of religious pluralism and toleration more quickly than did the politicians. A new skepticism, relativism, and individualism in religion became respectable in the sixteenth and seventeenth centuries. (See Chapter 14.) The French essayist Michel de Montaigne (1533–1592) asked in scorn of the dogmatic mind, "What do I know?" The Lutheran Valentin Weigel (1533–1588), surveying a half century of religious strife in Germany, advised people to look within themselves for religious truth and no longer to churches and creeds.

Such skeptical views gained currency in larger political circles only at the cost of painful experience. Religious strife and civil war were best held in check where rulers tended to subordinate theological doctrine to political unity, urging tolerance, moderation, and compromise—even indifference—in religious matters. Rulers of this kind came to be known as *politiques*, and the most successful among them was Elizabeth I of England. By contrast, Mary I of England, Philip II of Spain, and Oliver Cromwell, all of whom took their religion with the utmost seriousness and refused any compromise, did not, in the end, achieve their political goals.

***politiques***    Rulers who tended to subordinate theological doctrine to political unity.

**Huguenots**    French Protestants.

## THE FRENCH WARS OF RELIGION (1562–1598)

French Protestants, known as **Huguenots**, were already under surveillance in France in the early 1520s when Lutheran writings and doctrines began to circulate in Paris. The capture of the French king Francis I by the forces of Emperor Charles V at the Battle of Pavia in 1525 provided a motive for the first wave of Protestant persecution in France. The French government hoped thereby to pacify the Habsburg victor, a fierce opponent of German Protestants, and to win their king's swift release.

**WHAT CAUSED** the civil war between the Huguenots and the Catholics in France and what was the outcome?

A second major crackdown came a decade later. When Protestants plastered Paris and other cities with anti-Catholic placards on October 18, 1534, mass arrests of suspected Protestants followed. The government retaliation drove John Calvin and other members of the French reform party into exile. Save for a few brief interludes, the French monarchy remained a staunch foe of the Protestants until the ascension to the throne of Henry IV of Navarre in 1589.

The Habsburg-Valois wars (see Chapter 11) had ended with the Treaty of Cateau-Cambrésis in 1559, after which Europe experienced a moment of peace. The same year, however, marked the beginning of internal French conflict and a shift of the European balance of power away from France to Spain. The premature death of the

French king, Henry II, brought to the throne his sickly fifteen-year-old son, Francis II, who died after reigning only a year (1559–1560). With the monarchy weakened, three powerful families saw their chance to control France and began to compete for the young king's ear: the Bourbons, whose power lay in the south and west; the Montmorency-Chatillons, who controlled the center of France; and the strongest among them, the Guises, who were dominant in eastern France.

The Guises had little trouble establishing firm control over the young king. Throughout the latter half of the sixteenth century, the name "Guise" remained interchangeable with militant, reactionary Catholicism. The Bourbon and Montmorency-Chatillon families, in contrast, developed strong Huguenot sympathies, largely for political reasons. The Bourbon Louis I, prince of Condé (d. 1569), and the Montmorency-Chatillon admiral Gaspard de Coligny (1519–1572) became the political leaders of the French Protestant resistance.

## APPEAL OF CALVINISM

Often for different reasons, ambitious aristocrats and discontented townspeople joined Calvinist churches in opposing the Guise-dominated French monarchy. Although they made up only about one-fifteenth of the population, Huguenots held important geographic areas and were heavily represented among the more powerful segments of French society. A good two-fifths of the French aristocracy became Huguenots. Many apparently hoped to establish within France a principle of territorial sovereignty akin to what the Peace of Augsburg had secured within the Holy Roman Empire. Calvinism thus served the forces of political decentralization.

John Calvin and Theodore Beza sought to advance their cause by currying favor with powerful aristocrats. Beza converted Jeanne d'Albert, the mother of the future Henry IV. The prince of Condé was apparently converted in 1558 under the influence of his Calvinist wife. For many aristocrats—Condé probably among them—Calvinist religious convictions proved useful to their political goals.

The military organization of Condé and Coligny progressively merged with the religious organization of the French Huguenot churches, creating a potent combination that benefited both political and religious dissidents. Calvinism justified and inspired political resistance, while the resistance made Calvinism a viable religion in Catholic France. Each side had much to gain from the other.

## CATHERINE DE MÉDICIS AND THE GUISES

Following Francis II's death in 1560, the queen mother, Catherine de Médicis (1519–1589) became regent for her minor son, Charles IX (r. 1560–1574). At a meeting in Poissy, she tried unsuccessfully to reconcile the Protestant and Catholic factions. Fearing the power and guile of the Guises, Catherine, whose first concern was always to preserve the monarchy, sought allies among the Protestants. In 1562, after conversations with Beza and Coligny, she issued the January Edict, which granted Protestants freedom to worship publicly outside towns—although only privately within them—and to hold synods. In March 1562, this royal toleration came to an abrupt end when the duke of Guise surprised a Protestant congregation at Vassy in Champagne and massacred many worshippers. That event marked the beginning of the French wars of religion.

Had Condé and the Huguenot armies rushed immediately to the queen's side after this attack, Protestants might well have secured an alliance with the crown. The queen mother's fear of Guise power was great. Condé's hesitation, however, placed the young king and the queen mother, against their deepest wishes, under firm Guise control. Cooperation with the Guises became the only alternative to capitulation to the Protestants.

**Catherine de Médicis** (1519–1589) exercised power in France during the reigns of her three sons Francis II (r. 1559–1560), Charles IX (r. 1560–1574), and Henry III (r. 1574–1589).

Getty Images, Inc.—Liaison

**What role did Catherine de Médicis play in France's wars of religion?**

**The Peace of Saint-Germain-en-Laye**   During the first French war of religion, fought between April 1562 and March 1563, the duke of Guise was assassinated. A brief resumption of hostilities in 1567–1568 was followed by the bloodiest of all the conflicts, between September 1568 and August 1570. In this period, Condé was killed, and Huguenot leadership passed to Coligny. In the peace of Saint-Germain-en-Laye (1570), which ended the third war, the crown, acknowledging the power of the Protestant nobility, granted the Huguenots religious freedoms within their territories and the right to fortify their cities.

Perpetually caught between fanatical Huguenot and Guise extremes, Queen Catherine had always sought to balance one side against the other. After the Peace of Saint-Germain-en-Laye, the crown tilted manifestly toward the Bourbon faction and the Huguenots, and Coligny became Charles IX's most trusted adviser. Unknown to the king, Catherine began to plot with the Guises against the ascendant Protestants. As she had earlier sought Protestant support when Guise power threatened to subdue the monarchy, she now sought Guise support as Protestant influence grew.

There was reason for Catherine to fear Coligny's hold on the king. Louis of Nassau, the leader of Protestant resistance to Philip II in the Netherlands, had gained Coligny's ear. Coligny used his influence to win the king of France over to a planned French invasion of the Netherlands to support the Dutch Protestants. This would have placed France squarely on a collision course with mighty Spain. Catherine recognized far better than her son that France stood little chance in such a contest.

**The Saint Bartholomew's Day Massacre**   When Catherine lent her support to the infamous Saint Bartholomew's Day Massacre of Protestants, she did so out of a far less reasoned judgment. Her decision appears to have been made in near panic. On August 22, 1572, Coligny was struck down, although not killed, by an assassin's bullet. Catherine had apparently been party to this Guise plot to eliminate Coligny. After its failure, she feared both the king's reaction to her complicity with the Guises and the Coligny's response. Catherine convinced Charles that a Huguenot coup was afoot, inspired by Coligny, and that only the swift execution of Protestant leaders could save the crown from a Protestant attack on Paris.

On Saint Bartholomew's Day, August 24, 1572, Coligny and 3,000 fellow Huguenots were butchered in Paris. Within three days coordinated attacks across France killed an estimated 20,000 Huguenots. It is a date that has ever since lived in infamy for Protestants.

The event changed the nature of the struggle between Protestants and Catholics both within and beyond the borders of France. It was thereafter no longer an internal contest between Guise and Bourbon factions for French political influence, nor was it simply a Huguenot campaign to win basic religious freedoms. Henceforth, in Protestant eyes, it became an international struggle for sheer survival against an adversary whose cruelty justified any means of resistance.

**Protestant Resistance Theory**   Only as Protestants faced suppression and sure defeat did they begin to sanction active political resistance. At first, they tried to practice the biblical precept of obedient subjection to worldly authority (Romans 13:1).

The exiled Scots reformer John Knox (1513–1572), who had seen Mary of Guise, the Regent of Scotland, and Mary I of England crush his cause, laid the groundwork for later Calvinist resistance. In his famous *First Blast of the Trumpet against the Terrible Regiment of Women* (1558), he declared that the removal of a heathen tyrant was not only permissible, but also a Christian duty. He had the Catholic queen of England in mind.

After the great massacre of French Protestants on Saint Bartholomew's Day 1572, Calvinists everywhere came to appreciate the need for an active defense of their religious

**QUICK REVIEW**

**Saint Bartholomew's Day Massacre**

- August 24, 1572: 3,000 Huguenots ambushed in Paris and killed
- Within three days, some 20,000 Huguenots were killed throughout France
- Massacre changed the nature of the conflict between Protestants and Catholics throughout Europe

rights. Classical Huguenot theories of resistance appeared in three major works of the 1570s. The first was the *Franco-Gallia* of François Hotman (1573), a humanist argument that the representative Estates General of France historically held higher authority than the French king. The second was Theodore Beza's *On the Right of Magistrates over Their Subjects* (1574), which justified the correction and even the overthrow of tyrannical rulers by lower authorities. Finally, Philippe du Plessis Mornay's *Defense of Liberty against Tyrants* (1579) admonished princes, nobles, and magistrates beneath the king, as guardians of the rights of the body politic, to take up arms against tyranny in other lands.

## THE RISE TO POWER OF HENRY OF NAVARRE

Henry III (r. 1574–1589) was the last of Henry II's sons to wear the French crown. He found the monarchy wedged between a radical Catholic League, formed in 1576 by Henry of Guise, and vengeful Huguenots. Like the queen mother, Henry sought to steer a middle course. In this effort, he received support from a growing body of neutral Catholics and Huguenots, who put the political survival of France above its religious unity. Such *politiques* were prepared to compromise religious creeds to save the nation.

The Peace of Beaulieu in May 1576 granted the Huguenots almost complete religious and civil freedom. France, however, was not ready then for such sweeping toleration. Within seven months of the Peace, the Catholic League forced Henry to return to the illusory quest for absolute religious unity in France. In October 1577, the king truncated the Peace of Beaulieu and once again limited areas of permitted Huguenot worship. Thereafter, Huguenot and Catholic factions returned to their accustomed anarchical military solutions. The Protestants were led by Henry of Navarre, a legal heir to the French throne by virtue of his descent in a direct male line from St. Louis IX (d. 1270).

In the mid-1580s, the Catholic League, with Spanish support, became dominant in Paris. In what came to be known as the Day of the Barricades, Henry III attempted to rout the league with a surprise attack in 1588. The effort failed, and the king had to flee Paris. Forced by his weakened position into unkingly guerrilla tactics, and also emboldened by news of the English victory over the Spanish Armada in 1588, Henry had both the duke and the cardinal of Guise assassinated. Led by still another Guise brother, the Catholic League reacted with a fury that matched the earlier Huguenot response to the Massacre of Saint Bartholomew's Day. The king was now forced to strike an alliance with the Protestant Henry of Navarre in April 1589.

As the two Henrys prepared to attack the Guise stronghold of Paris, however, an enraged Dominican friar killed Henry III. Thereupon, the Bourbon Huguenot Henry of Navarre succeeded the childless Valois king to the French throne as Henry IV (r. 1589–1610). Pope Sixtus V and Philip II were aghast at the sudden prospect of a Protestant France. They had always wanted France to be religiously Catholic and politically weak, and they now acted to achieve that end. Spain rushed troops to support the besieged Catholic League.

Henry came to the throne as a *politique*, long weary with religious strife and fully prepared to place political peace above absolute religious unity. He believed a royal policy of tolerant Catholicism would be the best way to achieve such peace. On July 25, 1593, he publicly abandoned the Protestant faith and embraced the traditional and majority religion of his country. "Paris is worth a Mass," he is reported to have said. Most of the French church and people, having known internal strife too long, rallied to his side. By 1596, the Catholic League was dispersed, its ties with Spain were broken, and the wars of religion in France, to all intents, had ground to a close.

**Henry IV of France** (r. 1589–1610) on horseback, painted in 1594.

Réunion des Musées Nationaux/Art Resource, NY

**What did Henry IV hope to accomplish with the Edict of Nantes?**

## THE EDICT OF NANTES

On April 13, 1598, Henry IV's famous Edict of Nantes proclaimed a formal religious settlement. The following month, on May 2, 1598, the Treaty of Vervins ended hostilities between France and Spain.

In 1591, Henry IV had already assured the Huguenots of at least qualified religious freedoms. The Edict of Nantes made good that promise. It recognized minority religious rights within what was to remain an officially Catholic country. This religious truce—and it was never more than that—granted the Huguenots, who by this time numbered well over a million, freedom of public worship, the right of assembly, admission to public offices and universities, and permission to maintain fortified towns. They were to exercise most of the new freedoms, however, within their own towns and territories. Concession of the right to fortify their towns revealed the continuing distrust between French Protestants and Catholics. As significant as it was, the edict only transformed a long hot war between irreconcilable enemies into a long cold war.

A Catholic fanatic assassinated Henry IV in May 1610. Although he is best remembered for the Edict of Nantes, Henry IV's political and economic policies were equally important. They laid the foundations for the transformation of France into the absolute state it would become under Cardinal Richelieu and Louis XIV. (See Chapter 13.)

# IMPERIAL SPAIN AND PHILIP II (R. 1556–1598)

## PILLARS OF SPANISH POWER

**HOW WAS** Philip II able to dominate international politics for much of the latter half of the sixteenth century?

Until the English defeated the mighty Spanish Armada in 1588, no one person stood larger in the second half of the sixteenth century than Philip II of Spain. Philip was heir to the intensely Catholic and militarily supreme western Habsburg kingdom.

**New World Riches and Population Growth**   Populous and wealthy Castile gave Philip a solid home base. The regular arrival in Seville of bullion from the Spanish colonies in the New World provided additional wealth. He nonetheless never managed to erase the debts his father left or to finance his own foreign adventures fully.

The new American wealth brought dramatic social change to the peoples of Europe during the second half of the sixteenth century. As Europe became richer, it was also becoming more populous. In the economically and politically active towns of France, England, and the Netherlands, populations had tripled and quadrupled by the early seventeenth century. Europe's population exceeded 70 million by 1600.

The combination of increased wealth and population triggered inflation. A steady 2 percent a year rise in prices in much of Europe had serious cumulative effects by the mid–sixteenth century. There were more people and more coinage in circulation than before, but less food and fewer jobs; wages stagnated while prices doubled and tripled in much of Europe.

This was especially the case in Spain. Because the new wealth was concentrated in the hands of a few, the traditional gap between the haves—the propertied, privileged, and educated classes—and the have-nots widened. Nowhere did the unprivileged suffer more than in Spain, where the Castilian peasantry, the backbone of Philip II's great empire, became the most heavily taxed people of Europe.

**Efficient Bureaucracy and Military**   Philip II shrewdly organized the lesser nobility into a loyal and efficient national bureaucracy. A reclusive man, he managed his kingdom by pen and paper rather than by personal presence. He was also a learned and pious Catholic, although some popes suspected he used religion as much for political as for devotional purposes. That he was a generous patron of the arts and culture can be seen in his unique retreat outside Madrid, the Escorial, a combination palace, church, tomb, and monastery.

**Supremacy in the Mediterranean**    During the first half of Philip's reign, attention focused almost exclusively on the Mediterranean and the Turkish threat. By history, geography, and choice, Spain had traditionally been Catholic Europe's champion against Islam. During the 1560s, the Turks advanced deep into Austria, and their fleets dominated the Mediterranean. Between 1568 and 1570, armies under Philip's half brother, Don John of Austria (1547–1578), the illegitimate son of Charles V, suppressed and dispersed the Moors in Granada.

In May 1571, a Holy League of Spain, Venice, Genoa, and the pope, again under Don John's command, formed to check Turkish belligerence in the Mediterranean. In the largest naval battle of the sixteenth century, Don John's fleet engaged the Ottoman navy under Ali Pasha off Lepanto in the Gulf of Corinth on October 7, 1571. Before the engagement ended, over a third of the Turkish fleet had been sunk or captured, and 30,000 Turks had died. The resilient Ottomans would rebuild and regroup, but, for the moment, the Mediterranean belonged to Spain, and the Europeans were left to fight each other. Philip's armies also suppressed resistance in neighboring Portugal, when Philip inherited the throne of that kingdom in 1580. The union with Portugal not only enhanced Spanish sea power, but it also brought Portugal's overseas empire in Africa, India, and Brazil into the Spanish orbit.

## THE REVOLT IN THE NETHERLANDS

The spectacular Spanish military success in southern Europe was not repeated in northern Europe. When Philip attempted to impose his will within the Netherlands and on England and France, he learned the lessons of defeat.

**Cardinal Granvelle**    The Netherlands was the richest area not only of Philip's Habsburg kingdom, but of Europe as well. In 1559, Philip departed the Netherlands for Spain, never again to return. His half sister, Margaret of Parma, assisted by a special council of state, became regent in his place. The council was headed by the extremely able Antoine Perrenot (1517–1586), known after 1561 as Cardinal Granvelle, who hoped to break down the traditional local autonomy of the seventeen Netherlands provinces by stages and establish in its place a centralized royal government directed from Madrid.

The merchant towns of the Netherlands were, however, Europe's most independent; many, like magnificent Antwerp, were also Calvinist strongholds. Two members of the council of state led a stubborn opposition to the Spanish overlords, who now attempted to reimpose their traditional rule with a vengeance. They were the Count of Egmont (1522–1568) and William of Nassau, the Prince of Orange (1533–1584), known as "the Silent" because of his small circle of confidants.

In 1561, Cardinal Granvelle proceeded with his plans for the ecclesiastical reorganization of the Netherlands. It was intended to tighten the control of the Catholic hierarchy over the country and to accelerate its consolidation as a Spanish ward. Organizing the Dutch nobility in opposition, Orange and Egmont succeeded in gaining Granvelle's removal from office in 1564. Aristocratic control of the country after Granvelle's departure, however, proved woefully inefficient. Popular unrest grew, especially among urban artisans, who joined the congregations of radical Calvinist preachers in large numbers.

**The Compromise**    The year 1564 also saw the first fusion of political and religious opposition to Regent Margaret's government. This opposition resulted from Philip II's unwise insistence on trying to enforce the decrees of the Council of Trent throughout the Netherlands. William of Orange's younger brother, Louis of Nassau, who had been raised a Lutheran, led the opposition with support from the Calvinist-inclined lesser nobility and townspeople. A national covenant called the *Compromise* was drawn up, a solemn pledge to resist the decrees of Trent and the Inquisition. When Regent Margaret's government spurned the protesters as "beggars" in 1566, Calvinists rioted throughout the country. Louis called for aid from French Huguenots and German Lutherans, and a full-scale rebellion against the Spanish regency appeared imminent.

**The Duke of Alba**   The rebellion failed to materialize, however, because the higher nobility of the Netherlands would not support it. Their shock at Calvinist iconoclasm and anarchy was as great as their resentment of Granvelle's more subtle repression. Philip, determined to make an example of the Protestant rebels, dispatched the duke of Alba to suppress the revolt. His army of 10,000 journeyed northward from Milan in 1567 in a show of combined Spanish and papal might. Before Alba's reign of terror ended, the counts of Egmont and Horn and several thousand suspected heretics were publicly executed.

**Resistance and Unification**   William of Orange was an exile in Germany during these turbulent years. He now emerged as the leader of a broad movement for the independence of the Netherlands from Spain. The northern, Calvinist-inclined provinces of Holland, Zeeland, and Utrecht, of which Orange was the *Stadholder*, or governor, became his base. As in France, political resistance in the Netherlands gained both organization and inspiration by merging with Calvinism.

The early victories of the resistance attest to the popular character of the revolt. A case in point is the capture of the port city of Brill by the "Sea Beggars," an international group of anti-Spanish exiles and criminals, among them many Englishmen. In 1572, the Beggars captured Brill and other seaports in Zeeland and Holland. Mixing with the native population, they quickly sparked rebellions against Alba in town after town and spread the resistance southward. In 1574, the people of Leiden heroically resisted a long Spanish siege. The Dutch opened the dikes and flooded their country to repulse the hated Spanish. The faltering Alba had by that time ceded power to Don Luis de Requesens, who replaced him as commander of the Spanish forces in the Netherlands in November 1573.

**The Pacification of Ghent**   The greatest atrocity of the war came after Requesens's death in 1576. Spanish mercenaries, leaderless and unpaid, ran amok in Antwerp on November 4, 1576, leaving 7,000 people dead in the streets. The event came to be known as the Spanish Fury.

These atrocities accomplished in just four days what neither religion nor patriotism had previously been able to do. The ten largely Catholic southern provinces (what is roughly modern Belgium) now came together with the seven largely Protestant northern provinces (what is roughly the modern Netherlands) in unified opposition to Spain. This union, known as the Pacification of Ghent, was accomplished on November 8, 1576. It declared internal regional sovereignty in matters of religion, a key clause that permitted political cooperation among the signatories, who were not agreed over religion. Four provinces initially held out, but they soon made the resistance unanimous by joining the all-embracing Union of Brussels in January 1577. For the next two years, the Spanish faced a unified and determined Netherlands.

Confronted by unified Netherlands' resistance, Spain signed the humiliating Perpetual Edict in February 1577, which provided for the removal of all Spanish troops from the Netherlands within twenty days. The withdrawal gave the country to William of Orange and effectively ended, for the time being, whatever plans Philip may have had for using the Netherlands as a staging area for an invasion of England.

**The Union of Arras and the Union of Utrecht**   The Spanish, however, were nothing if not persistent. Don John and Alexander Farnese of Parma, the Regent Margaret's son, revived Spanish power in the southern provinces, where fear of Calvinist extremism had moved the leaders to break the Union of Brussels. In January 1579, the southern provinces formed the Union of Arras and soon made peace with Spain. The northern provinces responded by forming the Union of Utrecht.

**The Milch Cow,** a sixteenth-century satirical painting depicting the Netherlands as a cow in whom all the great powers of Europe have an interest. Elizabeth of England is feeding her (England had long-standing commercial ties with Flanders); Philip II of Spain is attempting to ride her (Spain was trying to reassert its control over the entire area); William of Orange is trying to milk her (he was the leader of the anti-Spanish rebellion); and the king of France holds her tail (France hoped to profit from the rebellion at Spain's expense).

The *Milch Cow.* Rijksmuseum, Amsterdam

**What made the Netherlands a focal point for international conflict in the sixteenth century?**

**Netherlands Independence**    Seizing what now appeared to be a last opportunity to break the back of Netherlands' resistance, Philip II declared William of Orange an outlaw and placed a bounty of 25,000 crowns on his head. The act predictably stiffened the resistance of the northern provinces.

Spanish efforts to reconquer the Netherlands continued into the 1580s. William of Orange, assassinated in July 1584, was succeeded by his seventeen-year-old son, Maurice (1567–1625), who, with the assistance of England and France, continued the Dutch resistance. Fortunately for the Netherlands, Philip II began now to meddle directly in French and English affairs. He signed a secret treaty with the Guises (the Treaty of Joinville in December 1584) and sent armies under Alexander Farnese into France in 1590. Hostilities with the English, who openly aided the Dutch rebels, also increased. Gradually, they built to a climax in 1588, when Philip's great Armada was defeated in the English Channel.

These new fronts overextended Spain's resources, thus strengthening the Netherlands. Spanish preoccupation with France and England now permitted the northern provinces to drive out all Spanish soldiers by 1593. In 1596, France and England formally recognized their independence. Peace was not, however, concluded with Spain until 1609, when the Twelve Years' Truce gave the northern provinces virtual independence. Full recognition came with the Peace of Westphalia in 1648.

# ENGLAND AND SPAIN (1553–1603)

**WHAT ROLE** did Catholic and Protestant extremism play in the struggle for supremacy between England and Spain?

Before Edward VI died in 1553, he agreed to a device to make the Protestant Lady Jane Grey his successor in place of the Catholic Mary Tudor (r. 1553–1558). Yet popular support for the principle of hereditary monarchy was too strong to deprive Mary of her rightful rule. Uprisings in London and elsewhere led to Jane Grey's removal from the throne within days of her crowning, and she was eventually beheaded.

## MARY I (R. 1553–1558)

Once enthroned, Mary proceeded to act even beyond the worst fears of the Protestants. In 1554, she entered a highly unpopular political marriage with Philip (later Philip II) of Spain, a symbol of militant Catholicism to English Protestants. Mary's domestic measures were equally shocking to the English people and even more divisive. During her reign, Parliament repealed the Protestant statutes of Edward and reverted to the Catholic religious practice of her father, Henry VIII. The great Protestant leaders of the Edwardian Age—John Hooper, Hugh Latimer, and Thomas Cranmer—were executed for heresy. Hundreds of Protestants either joined them in martyrdom or fled to the Continent.

## ELIZABETH I (R. 1558–1603)

Mary's successor was her half sister, Elizabeth I, the daughter of Henry VIII and Anne Boleyn. Elizabeth had remarkable and enduring successes in both domestic and foreign policy. Between 1559 and 1603, she guided a religious settlement through Parliament that prevented religious differences from tearing England apart in the sixteenth century. A ruler who subordinated religious to political unity, Elizabeth merged a centralized episcopal system that she firmly controlled with broadly defined Protestant doctrine and traditional Catholic ritual.

**Portrait of Mary I** (r. 1553–1558), Queen of England.

Queen Mary I, 1554 (oil on panel) by Sir Anthonis Mor (Antonio Moro) (1517/20–76/7). Prado, Madrid, Spain/Bridgeman Art Library

**Why did Mary I's policies toward Spain spark so much resentment among her subjects?**

In 1559, an Act of Supremacy passed Parliament, repealing all the anti-Protestant legislation of Mary Tudor and asserting Elizabeth's right as "supreme governor" over both spiritual and temporal affairs. In the same year, the Act of Uniformity mandated for every English parish a revised version of the second *Book of Common Prayer* (1552). In 1563, the issuance of the Thirty-Nine Articles, a revision of Thomas Cranmer's original forty-two, made a moderate Protestantism the official religion within the Church of England.

**Catholic and Protestant Extremists**    Elizabeth hoped to avoid both Catholic and Protestant extremism by pursuing a middle way. Elizabeth could not prevent the emergence of subversive Catholic and Protestant zealots, however. When she ascended the throne, Catholics were in the majority in England. The extremists among them, encouraged by the Jesuits and aided by the Spanish, plotted against her.

Catholic extremists hoped eventually to replace Elizabeth with Mary Stuart, Queen of Scots. Elizabeth acted swiftly against Catholic assassination plots, rarely letting her emotions override her political instincts. Despite proven cases of Catholic treason and even attempted regicide, she executed fewer Catholics during her forty-five years on the throne than Mary Tudor had executed Protestants during her brief five-year reign.

Elizabeth showed little mercy, however, to any who threatened the unity of her rule. She dealt cautiously with the Puritans, who were Protestants working within the national church to "purify" it of every vestige of "popery" and to make its Protestant doctrine more precise. Sixteenth-century Puritans were not true separatists. They enjoyed popular support and were led by widely respected men like Thomas Cartwright (d. 1603). They worked through Parliament to create an alternative national church of semiautonomous congregations governed by representative presbyteries (hence, **Presbyterians**), following the model of Calvin and Geneva. Elizabeth dealt firmly, but subtly, with them, conceding nothing that lessened the hierarchical unity of the Church of England and her control over it.

The more extreme Puritans wanted every congregation to be autonomous, a law unto itself, with neither higher episcopal nor presbyterian control. They came to be known as **Congregationalists**. Elizabeth and her second archbishop of Canterbury, John Whitgift (d. 1604), refused to tolerate this group, whose views on independence they found patently subversive. The Conventicle Act of 1593 gave such separatists the option either to conform to the practices of the Church of England or face exile or death.

**Deterioration of Relations with Spain**    A series of events led inexorably to war between England and Spain, despite the sincere desires of both Philip II and Elizabeth to avoid a confrontation. In 1567, the Spanish duke of Alba marched his mighty army into the Netherlands, which was, from the English point of view, simply a convenient staging area for a Spanish invasion of England. Pope Pius V (r. 1566–1572), who favored a military conquest of Protestant England, "excommunicated" Elizabeth for heresy in 1570. This mischievous act encouraged both internal resistance and international intrigue against the queen. Two years later, as noted earlier, the piratical sea beggars, many of whom were Englishmen, occupied the port of Brill in the Netherlands and aroused the surrounding countryside against the Spanish.

In 1571, England signed a mutual defense pact with France. Also in the 1570s, Elizabeth's famous seamen John Hawkins (1532–1595) and Sir Francis Drake (1545?–1596) began to prey regularly on Spanish shipping in the Americas.

After the Saint Bartholomew's Day Massacre, Elizabeth was the only protector of Protestants in France and the Netherlands. In 1585, she signed the Treaty of Nonsuch, which provided English soldiers and cavalry to the Netherlands. Funds that had previously been funneled covertly to support Henry of Navarre's army in France now flowed openly.

**Mary, Queen of Scots**    These events made a tinderbox of English–Spanish relations. The spark that finally touched it off was Elizabeth's execution of Mary, Queen of Scots (1542–1587).

**Presbyterians**    Puritans who favored a national church of semiautonomous congregations governed by representative presbyteries.

**Congregationalists**    The more extreme Puritans who believed every congregation ought to be autonomous, a law unto itself controlled by neither bishops nor presbyterian assemblies.

**An idealized likeness** of Elizabeth Tudor when she was a princess, attributed to Flemish court painter L. B. Teerling, ca. 1551. The painting shows her blazing red hair and alludes to her learning by the addition of books.

Unknown. Formerly attributed to William Scrots. Elizabeth I, when princess (1533–1603). The Royal Collection © 2002, Her Majesty Queen Elizabeth II

**What qualities did Teerling intend the viewer to see in the young Elizabeth?**

# A GREAT DEBATE OVER RELIGIOUS TOLERANCE

On October 27, 1553, the Spanish physician and amateur theologian Michael Servetus died at the stake in Geneva for alleged "blasphemies against the Holy Trinity." A bold and confident man, he had also incurred the wrath of Rome before badgering John Calvin in Geneva on theological issues. In the wake of Servetus's execution, Calvin was much criticized for fighting heresy with capital punishment. In 1544, he came to his own defense in a tract entitled *Defense of the Orthodox Faith in the Holy Trinity Against the Monstrous Errors of Michael Servetus of Spain*. Thereafter, Sebastian Castellio, an accomplished humanist and former rector of the college in Geneva, whom Calvin had driven out of the city years earlier, began a series of writings against Calvin. One of his titles, *Whether Heretics Should Be Punished By the Sword of the Magistrates*, was an anonymous anthology on religious toleration that included a supporting excerpt from John Calvin himself! Writing over the years under several pseudonyms for safety's sake, Castellio excerpted statements from Calvin's works and put them in a sustained "debate" with his own more liberal point of view.

## QUESTIONS

1. Why does Calvin believe that heresy deserves capital punishment?

2. What are Castellio's best rebuttal arguments?

3. Why does Castellio write under pseudonyms?

## I. *WHETHER HERETICS SHOULD BE PUNISHED BY THE SWORD OF THE MAGISTRATES*

CALVIN: Kings are duty bound to defend the doctrine of piety.

CASTELLIO: [Yes, but] to kill a man is not to defend doctrine, but rather to kill a man . . .

CALVIN: What of today? The majority of people have lost all sense of shame and openly mock God. They burst as boldly into God's awesome mysteries as pigs poke their snouts into costly storehouses.

CASTELLIO: Calvin appears to be criticizing himself. For truly the awesome mysteries of God are the Trinity, predestination, and election. But this man [Calvin] speaks so assuredly about these matters that one would think he was in Paradise. So thorny is his own teaching about the Trinity . . . that by his own curiosity he weakens and makes doubtful the consciences of the simple. He has taught so crudely about predestination that innumerable men have been seduced into a security as great as that which existed before the Flood . . .

Tell me, in brief, what you think about predestination.

CALVIN: I have been taught the following about predestination: All men are not created in an equal state. Rather in eternity, God, by inevitable decree, determined in advance those whom he would save and those whom he would damn to destruction. Those whom he has deemed worthy of salvation have been chosen by his mercy without consideration of their worthiness. And those given damnation, he shuts off from life by a just and irreprehensible, albeit incomprehensible, judgment.

CASTELLIO: So you maintain that certain men are created by God already marked for damnation so that they cannot be saved?

CALVIN: Precisely.

CASTELLIO: But what if they *should* obey God? Would they not then be saved?

CALVIN: They would then be saved. However, they are not able to obey God, because God excludes them from the knowledge of his name and the spirit of his justification so that they can and will do only evil and are inclined only to every kind of sin.

CASTELLIO: Hence, they have that inclination [to sin] from God's creation and predestination?

CALVIN: They have it so, just as surely as God has created the wolf with the inclination to eat sheep!

CASTELLIO: Therefore they have been damned and rejected by God even before they existed?

CALVIN: Exactly.

CASTELLIO: But are they not damned for their sins?

CALVIN: Indeed so. Those who were destined to that [damned] lot are completely worthy of it.

CASTELLIO: When were they worthy of it?

CALVIN: When they were destined to it?

CASTELLIO: Then they have 'been' before they 'are'. Do you see what you are saying?!

CALVIN: I don't understand.

CASTELLIO: If they were worthy, then they 'were.' For to be worthy is to be. And if you concede that they have been damned before they are, then they have 'been' before they were.

CALVIN: God elects the foolish things of the world to confound the wise.

CASTELLIO: Calvin and his kind reject the foolish things of the world so that they may exalt the wise [themselves]. Hence, they admit hardly anyone into . . . their circle who is not accomplished in sciences and languages . . . If Christ himself came to them, he would certainly be turned away if he spoke no Latin . . .

[But] Christ wishes to be judged by common sense and refers the matters of the gospel to human judgment . . . He would never have employed such analogies had he wished to deprive us of our common sense. And who would have believed him had he taught things repugnant to nature and contradictory to human experience . . .? What kind of master would he have been, had he said to the woman who cried out to him and washed his feet with her hair: "O woman, whatever your sin, it was done by God's decree!

Source: Steven Ozment, *Mysticism and Dissent: Religious Ideology and Social Protest in the Sixteenth Century* (New Haven, CT: Yale University Press, 1973), pp. 171–179.

**Despite her Protestant sympathies,** Queen Elizabeth I of England (r. 1558–1603) steered clear of both Catholic and Protestant extremism. Despite proven cases of Catholic treason and even attempted regicide, she executed fewer Catholics during her forty-five years on the throne than Mary Tudor had executed Protestants during her brief five-year reign.

Courtesy of the Library of Congress, Rare Book and Special Collections Division

**How did Elizabeth I want to be seen by her people?**

# ENCOUNTERING THE PAST

## GOING TO THE THEATER

*The Elizabethan era was a Golden Age for English the-ater. During the late Middle Ages, troupes of players had toured the countryside performing morality plays. The church often sponsored these companies, for plays offered religious education and moral instruction as well as entertainment. The rural theater was nothing more than a circular field ringed with mounds of earth on which spectators sat. Four tents were pitched at the points of the compass to give actors opportunities to enter and exit the action as the plot required.*

During the fifteenth century, players began to stage their productions in the courtyards of urban inns. Inns were renovated to provide permanent stages and more complex sets. The enclosed space also made it possible to limit the audience to paying customers and to turn theater into a profitable busi-ness enterprise. The urban setting altered the content as well as the staging of plays. The allegorical moraliz-ing of the medieval country theater was replaced by a more ribald, worldly entertainment, and the inn set-ting provided the workmen and young women who comprised much of the audience with rooms to which to retreat for performances of their own.

London's theater world matured in the late six-teenth and early seventeenth centuries in the work of Shakespeare and his contemporaries. Special the-aters (notably the Rose and the Globe, for which Shakespeare wrote) were built in the 1590s on the south bank of the river Thames. Plays were hugely popular with Londoners. Women were excluded from the stage, so all parts were acted by men and boys. Audiences (particularly in "the pit," the ground floor) were rowdy. They responded to the witty repartee and bawdy action on stage and overindulged in the food and drink sold during the performance.

**A seventeenth-century** sketch of the Swan Theatre, which stood near Shakespeare's Globe Theatre on the south bank of the Thames.

The Bridgeman Art Library

**Who went to the theater in the seventeenth century? What kinds of plays did they see?**

HOW DID medieval theater differ from the theater of Elizabeth's era?

Mary Stuart was the daughter of King James V of Scotland and Mary of Guise and had resided in France from the time she was six years old. This thoroughly French and Catholic queen had returned to Scotland after the death of her husband, the French king Francis II, in 1561. There she found a successful, fervent Protestant Refor-mation legally sanctioned the year before by the Treaty of Edinburgh (1560).

In 1568, a public scandal forced Mary's abdication and flight to her cousin Elizabeth in England. Mary's reputed lover, the earl of Bothwell, was, with cause, suspected of hav-ing killed her legal husband, Lord Darnley. When a packed court acquitted Bothwell, he subsequently married Mary. The outraged reaction from Protestant nobles forced Mary to surrender the throne to her one-year-old son, the future James VI of Scotland and, later, Elizabeth's successor as King James I of England. Because of Mary's clear claim to the English throne, she was an international symbol of a possible Catholic England and consumed by the desire to be England's queen. For this reason, her presence in England, where she resided under house arrest for nineteen years, was a constant discomfort to Elizabeth.

In 1583, Elizabeth's vigilant secretary, Sir Francis Walsingham, uncovered a plot against Elizabeth involving the Spanish ambassador Bernardino de Mendoza. After Mendoza's deportation in January 1584, popular antipathy toward Spain and support for Protestant resistance in France and the Netherlands became massive throughout England.

In 1586, Walsingham uncovered still another plot against Elizabeth, the so-called Babington plot, after Anthony Babington, who was caught seeking Spanish support for an attempt on the queen's life. This time he had uncontestable proof of Mary's complicity. Mary was executed on February 18, 1587. This event dashed all Catholic hopes for a bloodless reconversion of Protestant England. Philip II ordered his Armada to make ready for the invasion of England.

**The Armada**   On May 30, 1588, 130 ships bearing 25,000 sailors and soldiers under the command of the duke of Medina-Sidonia set sail for England. In the end, however, the English won a stunning victory. The invasion barges that were to transport Spanish soldiers from the galleons onto English shores were prevented from leaving Calais and Dunkirk. The swifter English and Netherlands' ships, helped by what came to be known as an "English wind," dispersed the waiting Spanish fleet, over one-third of which never returned to Spain.

The news of the Armada's defeat gave heart to Protestant resistance everywhere. Although Spain continued to win impressive victories in the 1590s, it never fully recovered. By the time of Philip's death on September 13, 1598, his forces had been rebuffed on all fronts. His seventeenth-century successors were all inferior leaders who never knew responsibilities equal to his, nor did Spain ever again know such imperial grandeur. The French soon dominated the Continent, and in the New World the Dutch and the English whittled away at Spain's overseas empire.

Elizabeth died on March 23, 1603, leaving behind her a strong nation poised to expand into a global empire.

**QUICK REVIEW**

**The Spanish Armada**

- Assembled for invasion of Protestant England
- Comprised of 130 ships bearing 25,000 sailors and soldiers
- Failure of Armada in May 1588 dealt a severe blow to Spain's military power

# THE THIRTY YEARS' WAR (1618–1648)

The Thirty Years' War in the Holy Roman Empire was the last and most destructive of the wars of religion. What made the Thirty Years' War so devastating was the entrenched hatred of the various sides and their seeming determination to sacrifice all for their religious beliefs. When the hostilities ended in 1648, the peace terms shaped the map of northern Europe much as we know it today.

**WHAT TOLL** did the Thirty Years' War take on Germany?

## PRECONDITIONS FOR WAR

**Fragmented Germany**   In the second half of the sixteenth century, Germany was an almost ungovernable land of about 360 autonomous political entities. The Peace of Augsburg (1555) had given each of them significant sovereignty within its own borders. Many of these little lands also had great-power pretensions.

Because of its central location, Germany had always been Europe's highway for merchants and traders going north, south, east, and west. Europe's rulers pressed in on Germany both because of trade and because some held lands or legal privileges within certain German principalities. German princes, in their turn, looked to import and export markets beyond German borders and opposed efforts to consolidate the Holy Roman Empire, lest their territorial rights, confirmed by the Peace of Augsburg, be overturned. German princes were not loath to turn to Catholic France or to the kings of Denmark and Sweden for allies against the Habsburg emperor.

After the Council of Trent, Protestants in the empire suspected the existence of an imperial and papal conspiracy to re-create the Catholic Europe of pre-Reformation times. The imperial diet, which the German princes controlled, demanded strict observance of the constitutional rights of Germans, as set forth in agreements with the emperor since the mid–fourteenth century. In the late sixteenth century, the emperor ruled only to the degree to which he was prepared to use force of arms against his subjects.

**Religious Division**   Religious conflict accentuated the international and internal political divisions. (See Map 12–1.) During this period, the population within the Holy Roman Empire was about equally divided between Catholics and Protestants, the latter having perhaps a slight numerical edge by 1600. The terms of the Peace of Augsburg had attempted to freeze the territorial holdings of the Lutherans and the Catholics (the so-called *ecclesiastical reservation*). In the intervening years, however, the Lutherans had gained and kept political control in some Catholic areas, as had the Catholics in a few previously Lutheran areas. Such territorial reversals, or the threat of them, only increased the suspicion and antipathy between the two sides.

The Lutherans had been far more successful in securing their rights to worship in Catholic lands than the Catholics had been in securing such rights in Lutheran lands. The Catholic rulers, who were in a weakened position after the Reformation, had made, but resented, concessions to Protestant communities within their territories. With the passage of time, they demanded that all ecclesiastical princes, electors, archbishops, bishops, and abbots who had deserted the Catholic for the Protestant side be immediately deprived of their religious offices and that their ecclesiastical holdings be promptly returned to Catholic control in accordance with the ecclesiastical reservation. However, the Lutherans and, even more so, the Calvinists in the Palatinate ignored this stipulation at every opportunity.

**Calvinism and the Palatinate**   As elsewhere in Europe, Calvinism was the political and religious leaven within the Holy Roman Empire on the eve of the Thirty Years' War. Unrecognized as a legal religion by the Peace of Augsburg, it gained a strong foothold within the empire when Frederick III (r. 1559–1576), a devout convert to Calvinism, became Elector Palatine (ruler within the Palatinate; see Map 12–1) and made it the official religion of his domain. By 1609, Palatine Calvinists headed a Protestant defensive alliance that received support from Spain's sixteenth-century enemies: England, France, and the Netherlands.

The Lutherans came to fear the Calvinists almost as much as they did the Catholics. By their bold missionary forays into the empire, Palatine Calvinists seemed to the Lutherans to threaten the Peace of Augsburg—and hence the legal foundation of the Lutheran states. Also, outspoken Calvinist criticism of the doctrine of Christ's real presence in the Eucharist shocked the more religiously conservative Lutherans.

**Maximilian of Bavaria and the Catholic League**   If the Calvinists were active within the Holy Roman Empire, so also were their Catholic counterparts, the Jesuits. From staunchly Catholic Bavaria, the Jesuits launched successful missions throughout the empire, winning such major cities as Strasbourg and Osnabrück back to the Catholic fold by 1600. In 1609, Maximilian I, duke of Bavaria (r. 1597–1651), organized a Catholic league to counter a new Protestant alliance that had been formed in the same year under the leadership of Calvinist Elector Palatine, Frederick IV (r. 1583–1610). When the league fielded a great army under the command of Count Johann von Tilly, the stage was set, both internally and internationally, for the worst of the religious wars, the Thirty Years' War.

## FOUR PERIODS OF WAR

The war went through four distinguishable periods. During its course, it drew in every major Western European nation—at least diplomatically and financially, if not by direct

**QUICK REVIEW**

**Religious Divisions in the Holy Roman Empire**

◆ By 1600 slightly more Protestants than Catholics in Holy Roman Empire
◆ Peace of Augsburg (1555) did not succeed in freezing religion of territories
◆ Divisions within Protestant camp complicated situation

## MAP EXPLORATION

Interactive map: To explore this map further, go to **www.myhistorylab.com**

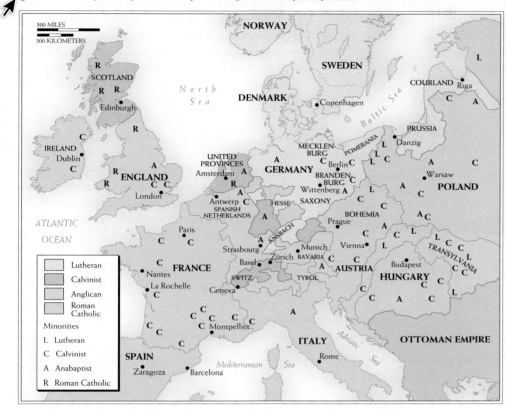

MAP 12–1  **Religious Divisions about 1600**  By 1600, few could seriously expect Christians to return to a uniform religious allegiance. In Spain and southern Italy, Catholicism remained relatively unchallenged, but note the existence elsewhere of large religious minorities, both Catholic and Protestant.

**How would** you explain the division between Catholic and Protestant regions in Europe?

military intervention. The four periods were the Bohemian (1618–1625); the Danish (1625–1629); the Swedish (1630–1635); and the Swedish-French (1635–1648).

**The Bohemian Period**   The war broke out in Bohemia after the ascent to the Bohemian throne in 1618 Habsburg Ferdinand, archduke of Styria, who was also heir to the imperial throne and a fervent Catholic. No sooner had Ferdinand become king of Bohemia than he revoked the religious freedoms of Bohemian Protestants. The Protestant nobility in Prague responded to Ferdinand's act in May 1618 by throwing his regents out the window of the royal palace. The event has ever since been known as the "defenestration of Prague." In the following year Ferdinand became Holy Roman Emperor as Ferdinand II (r. 1619–1637), by the unanimous vote of the seven electors. The Bohemians, however, defiantly deposed him in Prague and declared the Calvinist elector Palatine, Frederick V (r. 1616–1623), their king.

What had begun as a revolt of the Protestant nobility against an unpopular king of Bohemia escalated into an international war. Spain sent troops to Ferdinand, who found more motivated allies in Maximilian of Bavaria and the Lutheran elector John George I of Saxony (r. 1611–1656).

Ferdinand's army routed Frederick V's troops at the Battle of White Mountain in 1620. By 1622, Ferdinand had not only subdued and re-Catholicized Bohemia, but conquered the Palatinate as well. Meanwhile, Maximilian of Bavaria pressed the conflict into northwestern Germany, laying claim to land as he went.

**The Danish Period**   These events raised new fears that a reconquest and re-Catholicization of the empire now loomed, which was precisely Ferdinand II's design. The Lutheran king Christian IV (r. 1588–1648) of Denmark, who already

**Bohemian protesters throw** three of Emperor Ferdinand II's agents out of windows at Hradschin Castle in Prague to protest his revocation of Protestant freedoms.

Bildarchiv Preussischer Kulturbesitz/Art Resource, NY

**How did this event lead to the outbreak of the Thirty Years' War?**

held territory within the empire as the duke of Holstein, was eager to extend Danish influence over the coastal towns of the North Sea. With English, French, and Dutch encouragement, he picked up the Protestant banner of resistance, opening the Danish period of the conflict (1625–1629). Entering Germany with his army in 1626, he was, however, quickly humiliated by Maximilian and forced to retreat into Denmark.

As military success made Maximilian stronger and an untrustworthy ally, Emperor Ferdinand sought a more pliant tool for his policies in Albrecht of Wallenstein (1583–1634), a powerful mercenary. A brilliant and ruthless military strategist, Wallenstein carried Ferdinand's campaign into Denmark. By 1628, he commanded a crack army of more than 100,000 men and also became a law unto himself, completely outside of the emperor's control.

Wallenstein, however, had so broken Protestant resistance that Ferdinand could issue the Edict of Restitution in 1629, reasserting the Catholic safeguards of the Peace of Augsburg (1555). It reaffirmed the illegality of Calvinism and it ordered the return of all church lands the Lutherans had acquired since 1552. The new edict struck panic in the hearts of Protestants and Habsburg opponents everywhere.

**The Swedish Period**   Gustavus Adolphus II of Sweden (r. 1611–1632), a deeply pious king of a unified Lutheran nation, became the new leader of Protestant forces within the empire, opening the Swedish period of the war (1630–1635). He was controlled by two interested bystanders: (1) the French minister Cardinal Richelieu (1585–1642), whose foreign policy was to protect French interests by keeping the Habsburg armies tied down in Germany, and (2) the Dutch, who had not forgotten Spanish Habsburg rule in the sixteenth century. In alliance with the electors of Brandenburg and Saxony and led by their great general Gustavus Adolphus, the Swedes won a smashing victory at Breitenfeld in 1630—one that reversed the course of the war so dramatically that it has been regarded as the most decisive engagement of the long conflict.

Gustavus Adolphus died at the hands of Wallenstein's forces during the Battle of Lützen (November 1632)—a costly engagement for both sides that created a brief standstill. Ferdinand had long resented Wallenstein's independence, although he was the major factor in imperial success. In 1634, Ferdinand had Wallenstein assassinated. The episode is a telling commentary on this war without honor. Despite the deep religious motivations, greed and political gain were the real forces at work in the Thirty Years' War.

In the Peace of Prague in 1635, the German Protestant states, led by Saxony, reached a compromise with Ferdinand. France and the Netherlands, however, continued to support Sweden. Desiring to maximize their investment in the war, they refused to join the agreement. Their resistance to settlement plunged the war into its fourth and most devastating phase.

**The Swedish-French Period**   The French openly entered the war in 1635, sending men and munitions as well as financial subsidies. Thereafter, the war dragged on for thirteen years, with French, Swedish, and Spanish soldiers looting the length and breadth of Germany. By the time peace talks began at Münster and Osnabrück in Westphalia in 1644, the war had killed an estimated one-third of the German population. It has been called the worst European catastrophe since the Black Death of the fourteenth century.

## THE TREATY OF WESTPHALIA

The Treaty of Westphalia in 1648 ended all hostilities within the Holy Roman Empire. It was the first general peace in Europe after a war unprecedented for its number of warring parties. (See Map 12–2.) The treaty rescinded Ferdinand's Edict of Restitution and reasserted the major feature of the religious settlement of the Peace of Augsburg ninety-three years earlier: The ruler of a land determines the official religion of that land. The treaty also gave the Calvinists their long-sought legal recognition. The independence of the Swiss Confederacy and the United Provinces of the Netherlands, long recognized in fact, was now proclaimed in law. Bavaria became an elector state, Brandenburg-Prussia emerged as the most powerful northern German state, and the other German princes became supreme over their principalities.

By confirming the territorial sovereignty of Germany's many political entities, the Treaty of Westphalia perpetuated German division and political weakness into the modern period. The petty regionalism within the empire also reflected on a small scale the drift of larger European politics. In the seventeenth century, distinctive nation-states, each with their own political, cultural, and religious identity, reached maturity and firmly established the competitive nationalism of the modern world.

### MAP EXPLORATION

Interactive map: To explore this map further, go to www.myhistorylab.com

MAP 12–2 **Europe in 1648** At the end of the Thirty Years' War, Spain still had extensive possessions. Austria and Brandenburg-Prussia were rising powers, the independence of the United Provinces and Switzerland was recognized, and Sweden had footholds in northern Germany.

**What does** this map indicate about the German lands and the Holy Roman Empire in 1648?

# SUMMARY

**HOW DID** religious conflict in Europe evolve over the course of the second half of the sixteenth century?

**Renewed Religious Struggle** The Peace of Augsburg recognized Lutheranism as a legal religion in the Holy Roman Empire in 1555. For the remainder of the sixteenth century, religious strife centered on the conflict between Calvinism and Catholicism. Calvinism and Catholicism both were dogmatic, aggressive, and irreconcilable. Slowly some intellectuals—and a very few political leaders—came to adopt a more skeptical, tolerant view of religion, but in the meantime the Thirty Years' War between 1618 and 1648 drew every nation of Europe into some degree of religious conflict. *page 300*

**WHAT CAUSED** the civil war between the Huguenots and the Catholics in France and what was the outcome?

**The French Wars of Religion (1562–1598)** The rulers of France repeatedly cracked down on France's Protestant Huguenots. After the death of King Henry II, the French monarchy was weak. Although Calvinists made up only a small part of the population, France's Calvinists included much of the aristocracy. Catherine de Médicis attempted with some success to play Catholics and Huguenots off against each other. In 1593, a few years after the Bourbon Huguenot Henry of Navarre took the French throne, Henry renounced his Protestantism in favor of Catholicism; his 1598 Edict of Nantes sanctioned minority religious rights within Catholic France. *page 301*

**HOW WAS** Philip II able to dominate international politics for much of the latter half of the sixteenth century?

**Imperial Spain and the Reign of Philip II (r. 1556–1598)** Philip II, who ruled Spain through most of the second half of the sixteenth century, controlled vast territories, many people, and much wealth. For the first twenty-five years or so of Philip's reign, his attention was focused on the demographic and economic changes within his kingdom, defense against the Turks in the Mediterranean, and the annexation of Portugal (which led to control over Portugal's wealthy colonies). The second half of his reign was overshadowed by unrest and, eventually, defeat in the Netherlands. *page 305*

**WHAT ROLE** did Catholic and Protestant extremism play in the struggle for supremacy between England and Spain?

**England and Spain (1553–1603)** Catholic Mary I ruled England for five bloody years. Many Protestants were martyred or exiled during her reign. She married Spain's Prince Philip. Her half sister, Elizabeth I, succeeded her and ruled for most of the second half of the sixteenth century (r. 1558–1603). Elizabeth was probably the most successful European leader of her time. She steered a middle course between extremes in all areas, most notably religion, where she created the moderate Anglican church. She took firm measures against extremist Puritans (with the Conventicle Act), against would-be assassins (she executed Mary Queen of Scots for plotting against her), and Spain (the English navy defeated Spain's Armada in 1588). *page 308*

**WHAT TOLL** did the Thirty Years' War take on Germany?

**The Thirty Years' War (1618–1648)** Germany's political fragmentation, and conflict throughout Europe among Lutherans, Catholics, and Calvinists, set the stage for the Thirty Years' War. This devastating conflict drew in all the major lands of Europe before it was over; it has shaped the map of Europe up to the present. There were four distinct phases to the war, named after the region that was most actively involved in fighting at that time: the Bohemian period (1618–1625), the Danish period (1625–1629), the Swedish period (1630–1635), and the Swedish-French period (1635–1648). Finally, the 1648 Treaty of Westphalia put an end to hostilities and, among other provisions, reasserted the right of each ruler to determine the religion in his or her land. *page 313*

# REVIEW QUESTIONS

1. What part did politics play in the religious positions adopted by France's leaders? How did the French monarchy decide which side to favor? What led to the infamous Saint Bartholomew's Day Massacre? What resulted from it?

2. How did Spain acquire the dominant position in Europe in the sixteenth century? What were its strengths and weaknesses as a nation? What were Philip II's goals? Which did he fail to achieve? Why?

3. What changes occurred in the religious policies of England's government in the process of establishing the Anglican church? What were Mary I's political objectives? What was Elizabeth I's "settlement"? How was it imposed on England? Who were her opponents? What were their criticisms of her?

4. Why was the Thirty Years' War fought? Could matters have been resolved without war? To what extent did politics determine the outcome of the war? What were the terms and objectives of the Treaty of Westphalia?

## KEY TERMS

**Congregationalists** (p. 309)    *politiques* (p. 301)
**Counter-Reformation** (p. 300)    **Presbyterians** (p. 309)
**Huguenots** (p. 301)

For additional learning resources related to this chapter, please go to **www.myhistorylab.com**

PEARSON
myhistorylab

# 13

# European State Consolidation in the Seventeenth and Eighteenth Centuries

**Peter the Great** (r. 1682–1725), seeking to make Russia a military power, reorganized the country's political and economic structures. His reign saw Russia enter fully into European power politics.

*The Apotheosis of Tsar Peter the Great 1672–1725* by unknown artist, 1710. Historical Museum, Moscow, Russia/E.T. Archive

**How would you reconcile this image of Peter the Great with his reputation as a modernizer and reformer?**

B etween the early seventeenth and mid–twentieth centuries, no region so dominated other parts of the world politically, militarily, and economically as Europe. Such had not been the case before this period, nor would it be so after World War II. This era of European dominance coincided with a shift of power with Europe itself from the Mediterranean—in particular, Spain and Portugal—to the states of northern Europe.

By the mid–1700s, five states—Great Britain, France, Austria, Prussia, and Russia—organized themselves politically and came to dominate Europe, and later, large areas of the world through military might and economic strength. These states arose at the expense of Spain, Portugal, the United Provinces of the Netherlands, Poland, Sweden, the Ottoman Empire, and the Holy Roman Empire. ■

# THE NETHERLANDS: GOLDEN AGE TO DECLINE

**WHAT WAS** the Dutch Golden Age and what led to its decline?

The seven provinces that became the United Provinces of the Netherlands emerged as a nation after revolting against Spain in 1572. During the seventeenth century, the Dutch engaged in a series of naval wars with England. Then, in 1672, the armies of Louis XIV invaded the Netherlands. Prince William III of Orange (1650–1702), the grandson of William the Silent (1533–1584) and the hereditary chief executive, or *stadtholder*, of Holland, the most important of the provinces, rallied the Dutch and eventually led the entire European coalition against France. As a part of that strategy, he answered the invitation of Protestant English aristocrats in 1688 to assume, along with his wife Mary, the English throne.

During both the seventeenth and eighteenth centuries, the political and economic life of the Netherlands differed from that of the rest of Europe. The other major nations pursued paths toward strong central government. By contrast, the Netherlands was formally a republic. Each of the provinces retained considerable authority. The Dutch deeply distrusted monarchy and the ambitions of the House of Orange. Nonetheless, when confronted with major military challenges, the Dutch would permit the House of Orange and, most notably, William III to assume dominant leadership. When William died in 1702 and the wars with France ended in 1714, the Dutch reverted to their republican structures.

Although the provinces making up the Netherlands were traditionally identified with the Protestant cause in Europe, toleration marked Dutch religious life. While governments in other European states attempted to impose a single religion on their people or tore themselves apart in religious conflict, in the Netherlands peoples of differing religious faiths lived together peacefully.

## URBAN PROSPERITY

Beyond the climate of religious toleration, what most amazed seventeenth-century contemporaries about the Dutch Republic was its economic prosperity. Its remarkable economic achievement was built on the foundations of high urban consolidation, transformed agriculture, extensive trade and finance, and an overseas commercial empire.

In the Netherlands, more people lived in cities than in any other area of Europe. Key transformations in Dutch farming that served as the model for the rest of Europe made this urban transformation possible. During the seventeenth century, the Dutch drained and reclaimed land from the sea, which they used for highly profitable farming.

**The technologically advanced** fleet of the Dutch East India Company, shown here at anchor in Amsterdam, linked the Netherlands' economy with that of Southeast Asia.

Andries van Eertvelt (1590–1652), *The Return to Amsterdam of the Fleet of the Dutch East India Company in 1599*. Oil on copper. Johnny van Haeften Gallery, London, UK. The Bridgeman Art Library

**What role did naval power play in producing the Golden Age of the Netherlands?**

Dutch fishermen dominated the market for herring and supplied much of the continent's dried fish. The Dutch also supplied textiles to many parts of Europe. The overseas trades also supported a vast shipbuilding and ship supply industry. The most advanced financial system of the day supported all of this trade, commerce, and manufacturing.

The final foundation of Dutch prosperity was a seaborne empire. Dutch traders established a major presence in East Asia, particularly in spice-producing areas of Java, the Moluccas, and Sri Lanka. The vehicle for this penetration was the Dutch East Indies Company (chartered in 1602). The company eventually displaced Portuguese dominance in the spice trade of East Asia and for many years prevented English traders from establishing a major presence there.

## ECONOMIC DECLINE

The decline in political influence of the United Provinces of the Netherlands occurred in the eighteenth century. After the death of William III of Britain in 1702, unified political leadership vanished. Naval supremacy slowly but steadily passed to the British. The fishing industry declined, and the Dutch lost their technological superiority in shipbuilding. Similar stagnation overtook the Dutch domestic industries.

What saved the United Provinces from becoming completely insignificant in European affairs was its continued financial dominance. Well past the middle of the eighteenth century, Dutch banks continued to finance European trade, and the Amsterdam stock exchange remained an important financial institution.

# TWO MODELS OF EUROPEAN POLITICAL DEVELOPMENT

The United Netherlands, like Venice and the Swiss cantons, was a republic governed without a monarch. Elsewhere in Europe, monarchy of two fundamentally different patterns predominated in response to the military challenges of international conflict.

The two models became known as *parliamentary monarchy* and *political absolutism*. England embodied the first, and France, the second. The political forces that led to the creation of these two models had arisen from military concerns. During the second half of the sixteenth century, changes in military organization, weapons, and tactics sharply increased the cost of warfare. Because their traditional sources of income could not finance these growing expenses, in addition to the other costs of government, monarchs sought new revenues. Only monarchies that succeeded in building a secure financial base that was not deeply dependent on the support of noble estates, diets, or assemblies achieved absolute rule. The French monarchy succeeded in this effort, whereas the English monarchy failed. That success and failure led to the two models of government—*absolutism* in France and *parliamentary monarchy* in England—that shaped subsequent political development in Europe.

**WHAT FACTORS** led to the different political paths taken by England and France in the seventeenth century?

**political absolutism**   Government by a ruler with absolute authority.

**parliamentary monarchy**   Rule by a monarch with some parliamentary guidance or input.

# CONSTITUTIONAL CRISIS AND SETTLEMENT IN STUART ENGLAND

## JAMES I

In 1603 James VI, the son of Mary Stuart, Queen of Scots, who had been King of Scotland since 1567 succeeded without opposition or incident the childless Elizabeth I as James I of England. He also inherited a large royal debt and a fiercely divided church. A strong believer in the divine right of kings, he expected to rule with a minimum of consultation beyond his own royal court.

**HOW DID** conflicts over taxation and religion lead to civil war in Stuart England?

Parliament met only when the monarch summoned it, which James hoped to do rarely. In place of parliamentarily approved revenues, James developed other sources of income, largely by levying new custom duties known as *impositions*. Members of Parliament regarded this as an affront to their authority over the royal purse, but they did not seek a serious confrontation. Rather, throughout James's reign they wrangled and negotiated.

The religious problem also festered under James. Since the days of Elizabeth, **Puritans** within the Church of England had sought to eliminate elaborate religious ceremonies and replace the hierarchical episcopal system of church governance under bishops appointed by the king with a more representative Presbyterian form like that of the Calvinist churches in Scotland and on the Continent. At the Hampton Court Conference of January 1604, James rebuffed the Puritans and firmly declared his intention to maintain and even enhance the Anglican episcopacy.

Religious dissenters began to leave England. In 1620, Puritan separatists founded Plymouth Colony on Cape Cod Bay in North America, preferring flight from England to Anglican conformity. Later in the 1620s, a larger, better financed group of Puritans left England to found the Massachusetts Bay Colony.

James's court became a center of scandal and corruption. He governed by favorites, of whom the most influential was the duke of Buckingham, whom rumor made the king's homosexual lover. Buckingham controlled royal patronage and openly sold peerages and titles to the highest bidders—a practice that angered the nobility because it cheapened their rank.

James's foreign policy roused further opposition and doubt about his Protestant loyalty. In 1604, he concluded a much needed peace with Spain, England's longtime adversary. The war had been ruinously expensive, but his subjects considered the peace a sign of pro-Catholic sentiment. James's unsuccessful attempt to relax penal laws against Catholics further increased suspicions, as did his wise hesitancy in 1618 to rush English troops to the aid of German Protestants at the outbreak of the Thirty Years' War. In 1624, shortly before James's death, England again went to war against Spain, largely in response to parliamentary pressures.

**Puritans** English Protestants who advocated the "further reformation" of the Anglican Church.

# Overview　Two Models of Government

|  | FRANCE'S ABSOLUTISM | ENGLAND'S PARLIAMENTARY MONARCHY |
|---|---|---|
| **RELIGIOUS FACTORS** | Louis XIV, with the support of Catholics, crushed Protestantism for religious uniformity. | A strong Protestant religious movement known as Puritanism limited the monarchy. |
| **INSTITUTIONAL DIFFERENCES** | Opposition to the monarchy lacked a tradition of liberties, representation, or bargaining tools. | Parliament was to be consulted, and it appealed to concepts of liberty when conflicts arose. |
| **ECONOMIC POLICIES** | Louis XIV made French nobility dependent on his good will by supporting their status. | Political groups invoked traditional liberties to resist the monarchy's economic intrusions. |
| **ROLE OF PERSONALITIES** | Louis XIV had guidance from Cardinals Mazarin and Richelieu, training him to be hardworking. | The four Stuart monarchs, acting on whims, had trouble simply making people trust them. |

## ENCOUNTERING THE PAST

### EARLY CONTROVERSY OVER TOBACCO AND SMOKING

*King James defended sports from the Puritan charge that all amusements were sinful when enjoyed on the Sabbath, but the king did not favor all popular pleasures. He was ardently opposed to tobacco, one of the novelties that Europeans discovered in the Americas. Tobacco smoking excited opposition almost from the start. Spanish missionaries associated it with pagan religious practices. Sir Francis Bacon (1561–1626) noted it was addictive, and it was condemned by both Christian and Muslim clerics. None of this, however, impeded the spreading use of the pipe.*

In 1604, James published a work that left smokers in no doubt as to his opinion of them and their practice. In *A Counterblast to Tobacco* he wrote, "Have you not reason then to be ashamed, and to forbear this filthy novelty . . . ? In your abuse thereof sinning against God, harming yourselves in person . . . [with a] custom loathsome to the eye, hateful to the nose, harmful to the brain, dangerous to the lungs, and the black stinking fume thereof, nearest resembling the horrible Stygian smoke of the pit that is bottomless." [*A Counterblast to Tobacco* (1604), reprinted by the Rodale Press, London, 1954, p. 36.] James tried to stem the use of tobacco by heavily taxing it. When this had the result of encouraging smugglers, James lowered the tax. That, however, produced a

stream of revenue that became increasingly important to his government. In 1614, he made the importation of tobacco a royal monopoly, and by 1619, Virginia was shipping 40,000 pounds of tobacco to England annually. James's government, like modern ones, put itself in the odd position of depending on taxes imposed to stop the practice that produced those taxes.

**Practically from the** moment of its introduction into Europe tobacco smoking was controversial. Here a court jester is portrayed as exhaling rabbits from a pipe as three pipe-smoking gentlemen look on.
© Christel Gerstenberg/Corbis

**What activities did early modern writers associate with tobacco smoking?**

## CHARLES I

Parliament had favored the war with Spain but would not adequately finance it because its members distrusted the monarchy. Unable to gain adequate funds from Parliament, Charles I (r. 1625–1649), like his father, resorted to extra-parliamentary measures. These included levying new tariffs and duties, attempting to collect discontinued taxes, and subjecting English property owners to a so-called forced loan (a tax theoretically to be repaid) and then imprisoning those who refused to pay.

When Parliament met in 1628, its members would grant new funds only if Charles recognized the Petition of Right. This document required that henceforth there should be no forced loans or taxation without the consent of Parliament, that no freeman should be imprisoned without due cause, and that troops should not be billeted in private homes. Charles agreed to the petition, but whether he would keep his word was doubtful. The next year after further disputes, Charles dissolved Parliament and did not recall it until l640.

**Years of Personal Rule**   Charles might have ruled indefinitely without Parliament had not his religious policies provoked war with Scotland. James I had allowed a wide variety of religious observances in England, Scotland, and Ireland; by contrast, Charles hoped to impose religious conformity at least within England and Scotland. In 1637, Charles and his

**QUICK REVIEW**

**Charles I (r. 1625–1649)**

- 1629: Charles dissolves Parliament in face of criticism of his policies
- Unable to wage foreign wars without funds granted by Parliament
- 1640: Efforts to enforce religious conformity within England and Scotland force Charles to reconvene Parliament

high-church Archbishop William Laud (1573–1645), against the opposition of both the English Puritans and the Presbyterian Scots, tried to impose on Scotland the English episcopal system and a prayer book almost identical to the Anglican Book of Common Prayer.

The Scots rebelled, and Charles, with insufficient resources for war, was forced in 1640 to call Parliament. It refused even to consider funds for war until the king agreed to redress a long list of political and religious grievances. The king, in response, immediately dissolved that Parliament—hence its name, the Short Parliament (April–May 1640). When the Scots defeated an English army at the Battle of Newburn in the summer of 1640, Charles reconvened Parliament—this time on its terms—for a long and fateful duration.

## THE LONG PARLIAMENT AND CIVIL WAR

The landowners and the merchant classes represented in Parliament had long resented the king's financial measures and paternalistic rule. The Puritans in Parliament resented his religious policies and distrusted the influence of his Roman Catholic wife. What became known as the Long Parliament (1640–1660) thus acted with widespread support and general unanimity when it convened in November 1640.

Parliament abolished the courts that had enforced royal policy and prohibited the levying of new taxes without its consent. In addition, Parliament resolved that no more than three years should elapse between its meetings and that the king could not dissolve it without its own consent.

In January 1642, Charles invaded Parliament, intending to arrest certain of his opponents, but they escaped. The king then left London and began to raise an army. Shocked, a majority of the House of Commons passed the Militia Ordinance, which gave Parliament authority to raise an army of its own. The die was now cast. For the next four years (1642–1646), civil war engulfed England with the king's supporters known as Cavaliers and the parliamentary opposition as Roundheads.

## OLIVER CROMWELL AND THE PURITAN REPUBLIC

Two factors led finally to Parliament's victory. The first was an alliance with Scotland in 1643 that committed Parliament to a Presbyterian system of church government. The second was the reorganization of the parliamentary army under Oliver Cromwell (1599–1658), a country squire of iron discipline and strong, independent religious sentiment.

Defeated militarily by June 1645, Charles for the next several years tried to take advantage of divisions within Parliament, but Cromwell and his army foiled him. Members who might have been sympathetic to the monarch were expelled from Parliament in December 1648. After a trial by a special court, Charles was executed on January 30, 1649, as a public criminal. Parliament then abolished the monarchy, the House of Lords, and the Anglican Church.

From 1649 to 1660, England became officially a Puritan republic, although Cromwell dominated it. When in 1653, the House of Commons wanted to disband his expensive army of 50,000 men, Cromwell instead disbanded Parliament. He ruled thereafter as Lord Protector.

Cromwell's military dictatorship, however, proved no more effective than Charles's rule and became just as harsh and hated. People deeply resented his Puritan prohibitions of drunkenness, theatergoing, and dancing. Political liberty vanished in the name of religious conformity. When Cromwell died in 1658, the English were ready by 1660 to restore both the Anglican Church and the monarchy.

## CHARLES II AND THE RESTORATION OF THE MONARCHY

After negotiations with the army, Charles II (r. 1660–1685) returned to England amid great rejoicing. England returned to the status quo of 1642, with a hereditary monarch,

*King CHARLES the FIRST in the HOUSE of COMMONS, demanding the FIVE impeached MEMBERS to be delivered up to his AUTHORITY.*

**One of the** key moments in the conflict between Charles I and Parliament occurred in January 1642 when Charles personally arrived at the House of Commons intent on arresting five members who had been responsible for opposing him. They had already escaped. Thereafter Charles departed London to raise his army. The event was subsequently often portrayed in English art. The present illustration is from an eighteenth-century engraving.

The Granger Collection, New York

**How did Charles I see the relationship between himself and Parliament?**

**Oliver Cromwell's New** Model Army defeated the royalists in the English Civil War. After the execution of Charles I in 1649, Cromwell dominated the short-lived English republic, conquered Ireland and Scotland, and ruled as Lord Protector from 1653 until his death in 1658.

Dorling Kindersley Media Library

**What kind of government did Cromwell think was best for England?**

a Parliament of Lords and Commons that met only when the king summoned it, and the Anglican Church, with its bishops and prayer book, supreme in religion.

The king, however, had secret Catholic sympathies and favored religious toleration. He wanted to allow loyal Catholics and Puritans to worship freely. Yet ultra-royalists in Parliament between 1661 and 1665, through a series of laws known as the Clarendon Code, excluded Roman Catholics, Presbyterians, and Independents from the official religious and political life of the nation.

In 1670 by the Treaty of Dover, England and France formally allied against the Dutch, their chief commercial competitor. In a secret portion of this treaty, Charles pledged to announce his conversion to Catholicism as soon as conditions in England permitted this to happen. In return for this announcement (which Charles never made), Louis XIV promised to pay Charles a substantial subsidy. In an attempt to unite the English people behind the war with Holland, and as a sign of good faith to Louis XIV, Charles issued a Declaration of Indulgence in 1672, suspending all laws against Roman Catholics and non-Anglican Protestants. Parliament refused to fund the war, however, until Charles rescinded the measure. After he did so, Parliament passed the Test Act requiring all civil and military officials of the crown to swear an oath against the doctrine of transubstantiation—which no loyal Roman Catholic could honestly do. Parliament had aimed the Test Act largely at the king's brother, James, duke of York, heir to the throne and a recent, devout convert to Catholicism.

In 1678, a notorious liar named Titus Oates swore before a magistrate that Charles's Catholic wife, through her physician, was plotting with Jesuits and Irishmen to kill the king so James could assume the throne. Parliament believed Oates. In the ensuing hysteria, known as the Popish Plot, several innocent people were tried and executed.

More suspicious than ever of Parliament, Charles II turned again to increased customs duties and the assistance of Louis XIV for extra income. By these means, he was able to rule from 1681 to 1685 without recalling Parliament.

## THE "GLORIOUS REVOLUTION"

When James II (r. 1685–1688) became king, he immediately demanded the repeal of the Test Act. When Parliament balked, he dissolved it and proceeded to appoint Catholics to high positions in both his court and the army. In 1687, he issued another Declaration of Indulgence suspending all religious tests and permitting free worship. In June 1688, James imprisoned seven Anglican bishops who had refused to publicize his suspension of laws against the Catholics. Each of these actions represented a direct royal attack on the local authority of nobles, landowners, the church, and other corporate bodies whose members believed they possessed particular legal privileges.

The English had hoped that James would be succeeded by Mary (r. 1689–1694), his Protestant eldest daughter. She was the wife of William III of Orange, the leader of European opposition to Louis XIV. But on June 20, James II's Catholic second wife gave birth to a son. There was now a Catholic male heir to the throne. The Parliamentary opposition invited William to invade England to preserve its "traditional liberties," that is, the Anglican Church and parliamentary government.

William of Orange arrived with his army in November 1688 and was received with considerable popular support. James fled to France, and Parliament, in 1689, proclaimed William III and Mary II the new monarchs, thus completing the "**Glorious Revolution**." William and Mary, in turn, recognized a Bill of Rights that limited the powers of the monarchy and guaranteed the civil liberties of the English privileged classes. The Bill of Rights also prohibited Roman Catholics from occupying the English throne. The Toleration Act of 1689 permitted worship by all Protestants and outlawed only Roman Catholics and those who denied the Christian doctrine of the Trinity.

The parliamentary measure closing this century of strife was the Act of Settlement (1701), which provided for the English crown to go to the Protestant House of Hanover in Germany if Queen Anne (r. 1702–1714), the second daughter of James II and the heir to the childless William III, died without issue. Thus, at Anne's death in 1714, the Elector of Hanover became King George I of Great Britain (r. 1714–1727) since England and Scotland had been combined in an Act of Union in 1707.

### THE AGE OF WALPOLE

George I almost immediately confronted a challenge to his title. James Edward Stuart (1688–1766), the Catholic son of James II, landed in Scotland in December 1715 but met defeat less than two months later.

Despite the victory over the Stuart pretender, the political situation after 1715 remained in flux until Sir Robert Walpole (1676–1745) took over the helm of government. Walpole maintained peace abroad and promoted the status quo at home. Britain's foreign trade spread from New England to India. Because the central government refrained from interfering with the local political influence of nobles and other landowners, they were willing to serve as local government administrators, judges, and military commanders, and to collect and pay the taxes to support a powerful military force, particularly a strong navy. As a result, Great Britain became not only a European power of the first order but eventually a world power as well.

The power of the British monarchs and their ministers had real limits. Parliament could not wholly ignore popular pressure. Newspapers and public debate flourished. Free speech could be exercised, as could freedom of association. There was no large standing army. There existed significant religious toleration. Walpole's enemies could and did openly oppose his policies, which would not have been possible on the Continent. Consequently, the English state combined considerable military power with both religious and political liberty. British political life became the model for all progressive Europeans who questioned the absolutist political developments of the Continent.

## RISE OF ABSOLUTE MONARCHY IN FRANCE: THE WORLD OF LOUIS XIV

**WHY WERE** efforts to establish absolute monarchy successful in France but unsuccessful in England?

*Fronde* Widespread rebellions in France between 1649 and 1652 (named after a slingshot used by street ruffians) aimed at reversing the drift toward absolute monarchy and preserving local autonomy.

The French monarchy, which had faced numerous challenges from strong, well-armed nobles and discontented Protestants during the first half of the seventeenth century, only gradually achieved the firm authority for which it became renowned later in the century. The groundwork for Louis XIV's (r. 1643–1715) absolutism had been laid by two powerful chief ministers, Cardinal Richelieu (1585–1642) under Louis XIII (r. 1610–1643), and then by Cardinal Mazarin (1602–1661). Both Richelieu and Mazarin attempted to impose direct royal administration on France. The centralizing policies of Richelieu and then of Mazarin, however, finally provoked a series of widespread rebellions among French nobles between 1649 and 1652 known as the *Fronde* (after the slingshots used by street boys).

Though unsuccessful, these rebellions convinced Louis XIV and his advisors that heavy-handed policies could endanger the throne. Thereafter Louis would concentrate unprecedented authority in the monarchy, but he would be more subtle than his predecessors. His genius was to make the monarchy the most important and powerful political institution in France while also assuring the nobles and other wealthy groups of their social standing and influence on the local level.

## YEARS OF PERSONAL RULE

On the death of Mazarin in 1661, Louis XIV assumed personal control of the government at the age of twenty-three. Louis devoted enormous personal energy to his political tasks. He ruled through councils that controlled foreign affairs, the army, domestic administration, and economic regulations. Each day he spent hours with the ministers of these councils, whom he chose from families long in royal service or from among people just beginning to rise in the social structure. Unlike the more ancient noble families, the latter had no real or potential power bases in the provinces and depended solely on the king for their standing in both government and society.

Louis made sure, however, that the nobility and other major social groups would benefit from the growth of his own authority. Although he controlled foreign affairs and limited the influence of noble institutions on the monarchy, he never tried to abolish those institutions or limit their local authority. The crown, for example, usually conferred informally with regional judicial bodies, called *parlements*, before making rulings that would affect them. Likewise, the crown would rarely enact economic regulations without consulting local opinion.

**Gold Fleur-de-Lis** with Gold Crown.

Neil Lukas © Dorling Kindersley, Courtesy of l'Etablissement Public du Musée et du Domaine National de Versailles

**Why was it so important to Louis XIV to look like a king at all times?**

## VERSAILLES

Louis and his advisors became masters of propaganda and political image creation. Louis never missed an opportunity to impress the grandeur of his crown on the French people, but most especially on the French nobility. The central element of the image of the monarchy was the palace of Versailles, which, when completed, was the largest secular structure in Europe. More than any other monarch of the day, Louis XIV used the physical setting of his court to exert political control. Versailles was a temple to royalty, designed and decorated to proclaim the glory of the Sun King, as Louis was known. A spectacular estate with magnificent fountains and gardens, it housed thousands of the more important nobles, royal officials, and servants. Some nobles paid for their own residence at the palace, thus depleting their resources; others required royal patronage to remain in residence. In either case they became dependent on the monarch. Although it consumed over half Louis's annual revenues, Versailles paid significant political dividends.

Because Louis ruled personally, he was himself the chief source of favors and patronage in France. To emphasize his prominence, he organized life at court around every aspect of his own daily routine. Elaborate etiquette governed every detail of life at Versailles. Moments near the king were important to most court nobles because they were effectively excluded from the real business of government. The king's rising and dressing were times of rare intimacy, when nobles could whisper their special requests in his ear. Fortunate nobles held his night candle when he went to his bed.

**Palace of Versailles,** garden facade. The terrace later became part of the Hall of Mirrors.

Chateau de Versailles, France/The Bridgeman Art Library

**What political motives were behind the transformation of Versailles into the seat of the French monarchy?**

## KING BY DIVINE RIGHT

An important source for Louis's concept of royal authority was his devout tutor, the political theorist Bishop Jacques-Bénigne Bossuet (1627–1704). Bossuet defended what he called the "**divine right of kings**" and cited examples of Old Testament rulers divinely appointed by and answerable only to God. Although kings might be duty bound to reflect God's will in their rule, yet as God's regents on earth they could not be bound to the dictates of mere nobles and parliaments. Such assumptions lay behind Louis XIV's alleged declaration: "*L'état, c'est moi*" ("I am the state"). (See "Compare & Connect: The Debate over the Origin and Character of Political Authority," pages 330–331.)

**divine right of kings** The belief that God appoints kings and that kings are accountable only to God for how they use their power.

# THE DEBATE OVER THE ORIGIN AND CHARACTER OF POLITICAL AUTHORITY

During the second half of the seventeenth century a profound dispute occurred among European political philosophers over the origin and character of political authority. Some political philosophers, here illustrated by the French bishop Jacques-Bénigne Bossuet, contended that monarchs governed absolutely by virtue of authority derived from God. Other philosophers, here illustrated by the English writer John Locke, contended that political authority originated in the consent of the governed and that such authority was inherently limited in its scope.

## QUESTIONS

1. Why might Bossuet have wished to make such extravagant claims for absolute royal power? How might these claims be transferred to any form of government?

2. How does Bossuet's argument for absolute royal authority lead also to the need for a single uniform religion in France?

3. Why does Locke find an absolute monarch in conflict with his subjects and they with him?

4. How do Locke's views serve to provide a foundation for parliamentary government?

5. How might subjects governed according to Bossuet's and Locke's principles relate differently to their monarchs and to the officials of monarchs administering their local communities?

## I. BISHOP BOSSUET DEFENDS THE DIVINE RIGHT OF KINGS

*The revolutions of the seventeenth century caused many to fear anarchy far more than tyranny, among them the influential French bishop Jacques-Bénigne Bossuet (1627–1704), the leader of French Catholicism in the second half of the seventeenth century. Louis XIV made him court preacher and tutor to his son, for whom Bossuet wrote a celebrated universal history. In the following excerpt, Bossuet defends the divine right and absolute power of kings. He depicts kings as embracing in their person the whole body of the state and the will of the people they govern and, as such, as being immune from judgment by any mere mortal.*

The royal power is absolute. . . . The prince need render account of his acts to no one. "I counsel thee to keep the king's commandment, and that in regard of the oath of God. Be not hasty to go out of his sight; stand not on an evil thing for he doeth whatsoever pleaseth him. Where the word of a king is, there is power; and who may say unto him, What doest thou? Whoso keepeth the commandment shall feel no evil thing" [Eccles. 8:2–5]. Without this absolute authority the king could neither do good nor repress evil. It is necessary that his power be such that no one can hope to escape him, and finally, the only protection of individuals against the public authority should be their innocence. This confirms the teaching of St. Paul: "Wilt thou then not be afraid of the power? Do that which is good" [Rom. 13:3].

God is infinite, God is all. The prince, as prince, is not regarded as a private person: he is a public personage, all the state is in him; the will of all the people is included in his. As all perfection and all strength are united in God, so all the power of individuals is united in the person of the prince. What grandeur that a single man should embody so much! . . .

Behold an immense people united in a single person; behold this holy power, paternal and absolute; behold the secret cause which governs the whole body of the state, contained in a single head: you see the image of God in the king, and you have the idea of royal majesty. God is holiness itself, goodness itself, and power itself. In these things lies the majesty of God. In the image of these things lies the majesty of the prince.

Source: From *Politics Drawn from the Very Words of Holy Scripture*, as quoted in James Harvey Robinson, ed., *Readings in European History*, vol. 2 (Boston: Athenaeum, 1906), pp. 275–276.

## II. JOHN LOCKE DENOUNCES THE IDEA OF ABSOLUTE MONARCHY

**Title Page from** *Two Treatises of Government* by John Locke, London, 1690.

Courtesy of the Library of Congress (Rosenwald Collection, Rare Book and Special Collections Division)

**How did Locke challenge traditional notions of European monarchy?**

*John Locke (1632–1704) was the most important English philosopher of the late seventeenth century. As will be seen in Chapter 14, he wrote on a wide variety of subjects including both political philosophy and religious toleration. In 1690 he published his second Treatise of Civil Government. In this work he defended limitations on government and rooted political authority in the consent of the governed. He drafted the treatise in the late 1670s in response to Tory assertions of absolute monarchy set forth by supporters of Charles II. The treatise was published in the wake of the Revolution of 1688 and was read at the time as a justification of that event. Locke's thought would almost a century later influence the American Declaration of Independence. In the passages below Locke explains that under absolute monarchy citizens must submit to an authority from which they can make no appeal. Consequently, there is a necessary conflict between citizens and the absolute monarchy. It was to escape such conflict and to secure property and liberty that human beings had left the state of nature to found civil society.*

Man being born . . . with a title to perfect freedom, and an uncontrolled enjoyment of all the rights and privileges of the law of nature, equally with any other man, or number of men in the world, hath by nature a power, not only to preserve his property, that is, his life, liberty and estate, against the injuries and attempts of other men; but to judge of, and punish the breaches of that law in others, as he is persuaded the offence deserve . . . [T]here and there only is political society, where every one of the members hath quitted this natural power, resigned it up into the hands of the community in all cases that excludes him not from appealing for protection to the law established by it. And thus all private judgment of every particular member being excluded, the community comes to be umpire, by settled standing rules, indifferent, and the same to all parties; and by men having authority from the community, for the execution of those rules, decides all the differences that may happen between any members of that society concerning any matter of right . . .

Whenever therefore any number of men are so united into one society, as to quit every one his executive power of the law of nature, and to resign it to the public, there and there only is a political, or civil society. . . .

Hence it is evident, that absolute monarchy, which by some men is counted the only government in the world, is indeed inconsistent with civil society, and so can be no form of civil government at all; for the end of civil society, being to avoid, and remedy those inconveniencies of the state of nature, which necessarily follow from every man's being judge in his own case, by setting up a known authority, to which every one of that society may appeal upon any injury received, or controversy that may arise, and which every one of the society ought to obey; whereever any persons are, who have not such an authority to appeal to, for the decision of any difference between them, there those persons are still in the state of nature; and so is every absolute prince, in respect of those who are under his dominion.

For he being supposed to have all, both legislative and executive power in himself alone, there is no judge to be found, no appeal lies open to any one, who may fairly, and indifferently, and with authority decide, and from whose decision relief and redress may be expected of any injury, or inconveniency, that may be suffered from the prince, or by his order: so that such a man, however intitled, czar, or grand seignior, or how you please, is as much in the state of nature, with all under his dominion, as he is with the rest of mankind: for where-ever any two men are, who have no standing rule, and common judge to appeal to on earth, for the determination of controversies of right betwixt them, there they are still in the state of nature, and under all the inconveniencies of it. . .

Source: John Locke, *Of Civil Government*, paragraphs 87, 89, 90, 91 in *Two Treatises of Government*, a new ed. (London: C. and J. Rivington et al., 1824), pp. 179–183.

**Louis XIV of France** came to symbolize absolute monarchy though such government was not as absolute as the term implied. This state portrait was intended to convey the grandeur of the king and of his authority. The portrait was brought into royal council meetings when the king himself was absent.

Hyacinthe Rigaud (1659–1743), *Portrait of Louis XIV*. Louvre, Paris, France. Dorling Kindersley Media Library/Max Alexander. © Dorling Kindersley, courtesy of l'Etablissement public du musée et du domaine national de Versailles

**What does this portrait tell us about Louis XIV's ideas about kingship?**

**Gallican Liberties** The French Roman Catholic Church's ecclesiastical independence of papal authority in Rome.

**Jansenism** Appearing in the 1630s, it followed the teachings of St. Augustine, who stressed the role divine grace played in human salvation.

Despite these claims, Louis's rule did not exert the oppressive control over the daily lives of his subjects that police states would do in the nineteenth and twentieth centuries. His absolutism functioned primarily in the classic areas of European state action—the making of war and peace, the regulation of religion, and the oversight of economic activity.

## LOUIS'S EARLY WARS

By the late 1660s, France was superior to any other European nation in population, administrative bureaucracy, army, and national unity. Because of the economic policies of Jean-Baptiste Colbert (1619–1683), his most brilliant minister, Louis could afford to raise and maintain a large and powerful army. Louis was particularly concerned to secure France's northern borders along the Spanish Netherlands, the Franche-Comté, Alsace, and Lorraine from which foreign armies had invaded France and could easily do so again. Louis was also determined to frustrate Habsburg ambitions that endangered France and, as part of that goal, sought to secure his southern borders toward Spain. Whether reacting to external events or pursuing his own ambitions, Louis's pursuit of French interests threatened and terrified neighboring states and led them to form coalitions against France.

The early wars of Louis XIV included conflicts with Spain and the United Netherlands. The first was the War of the Devolution in which Louis supported the alleged right of his first wife, Marie Thérèse, to inherit the Spanish Netherlands. In 1667, Louis's armies invaded Flanders and the Franche-Comté. He was repulsed by the Triple Alliance of England, Sweden, and the United Provinces. By the Treaty of Aix-la-Chapelle (1668), he gained control of certain towns bordering the Spanish Netherlands.

In 1670, with the secret Treaty of Dover, England and France became allies against the Dutch. Louis invaded the Netherlands again in 1672. The Prince of Orange, the future William III of England, forged an alliance with the Holy Roman Emperor, Spain, Lorraine, and Brandenburg against Louis, now regarded as a menace to the whole of Western Europe, Catholic and Protestant alike. The war ended inconclusively with the Peace of Nijmwegen, signed with different parties in successive years (1678, 1679). France gained more territory, including the Franche-Comté.

## LOUIS'S REPRESSIVE RELIGIOUS POLICIES

Louis believed that political unity and stability required religious conformity. To that end he carried out repressive actions against both Roman Catholics and Protestants.

**Suppression of the Jansenists** The French crown and the French Roman Catholic church had long jealously guarded their ecclesiastical independence or "**Gallican Liberties**" from papal authority in Rome. However, after the conversion to Roman Catholicism of Henry IV in 1593, the Jesuits, fiercely loyal to the authority of the pope, had monopolized the education of French upper-class men, and their devout students promoted the religious reforms and doctrines of the Council of Trent.

A Roman Catholic religious movement known as **Jansenism** arose in the 1630s in opposition to the theology and the political influence of the Jesuits. Jansenists adhered to the teachings of St. Augustine (354–430) that had also influenced many Protestant doctrines. Serious and uncompromising, they particularly opposed Jesuit teachings about free will. They believed with Augustine that original sin had so corrupted humankind that individuals could by their own effort do nothing good nor contribute anything to their own salvation.

On May 31, 1653, Pope Innocent X declared heretical five Jansenist theological propositions on grace and salvation. In 1660, Louis permitted the papal bull banning Jansenism to be enforced in France. Thereafter, Jansenists either retracted their views or went underground.

By persecuting the Jansenists, Louis XIV turned his back on the long tradition of protecting the Gallican Liberties of the French Church and fostered within the French Church a core of opposition to royal authority. This had long-term political significance. During the eighteenth century after the death of Louis XIV, the Parlement of Paris and other French judicial bodies would reassert their authority in opposition to the monarchy. These courts were sympathetic to the Jansenists because of their common resistance to royal authority. Jansenism, because of its austere morality, then also came to embody a set of religious and moral values that contrasted with what eighteenth-century public opinion saw as the corruption of the mid-eighteenth-century French royal court.

**Revocation of the Edict of Nantes**    After the Edict of Nantes in 1598, relations between the Catholic majority (nine-tenths of the French population) and the Protestant minority had remained hostile. After the Peace of Nijmwegen, Louis launched a methodical campaign against the Huguenots in an effort to unify France religiously. Louis hounded Huguenots out of public life, banning them from government office and excluding them from such professions as printing and medicine. He used financial incentives to encourage them to convert to Catholicism. In 1681, he bullied them by quartering troops in their towns. Finally, in October 1685, Louis revoked the Edict of Nantes, and extensive religious repression followed. Protestant churches and schools were closed, Protestant ministers exiled, nonconverting laity were condemned to be galley slaves, and Protestant children were baptized by Catholic priests.

The revocation was a major blunder. Henceforth, Protestants across Europe considered Louis a fanatic who must be resisted at all costs. More than a quarter million people, many of whom were highly skilled, left France. They formed new communities abroad and joined the resistance to Louis in England, Germany, Holland, and the New World. As a result of the revocation of the Edict of Nantes and the ongoing persecution of Jansenists, France became a symbol of religious repression in contrast to England's reputation for moderate, if not complete, religious toleration.

**Portrait of Françoise d'Aubigne,** Marquise de Maíntenon (1635–1719), Mistress and Second Wife of Louis XIV, by Pierre Mignard (1612–1695).

*Portrait of Françoise d'Aubigne, Marquise de Maintenon (1635–1719), Mistress and Second Wife of Louis XIV,* c. 1694. Oil on canvas, 128 &infin; 97 cm. Inv.: MV 3637. Chateaux de Versailles et de Trianon, Versailles. Bridgeman-Giraudon/Art Resource, NY

**What role did elite women play in the court of Louis XIV?**

## LOUIS'S LATER WARS

**The League of Augsburg and the Nine Years' War**    After the Treaty of Nijmwegen in 1678–1679, Louis maintained his army at full strength and restlessly probed beyond his borders. In 1681 his forces occupied the free city of Strasbourg on the Rhine River, prompting new defensive coalitions to form against him. One of these, the League of Augsburg, grew to include England, Spain, Sweden, the United Provinces, and the major German states. Between 1689 and 1697, the League and France battled each other in the Nine Years' War, while England and France struggled to control North America. The Peace of Ryswick, signed in September 1697, which ended the war, secured Holland's borders and thwarted Louis's expansion into Germany.

**War of the Spanish Succession**    On November 1, 1700, the last Habsburg king of Spain, Charles II (r. 1665–1700), died without direct heirs. He left his entire inheritance to Louis's grandson Philip of Anjou, who became Philip V of Spain (r. 1700–1746). Spain and the vast trade with its American empire appeared to have fallen to France. In September 1701, England, Holland, and the Holy Roman Empire formed the Grand Alliance to preserve the balance of power by once and for all securing Flanders as a neutral barrier between Holland and France and by gaining for the emperor, who was also a Habsburg, his fair share of the Spanish inheritance. Louis soon increased the political stakes by recognizing the Stuart claim to the English throne.

In 1701 the War of the Spanish Succession (1701–1714) began, and it soon enveloped Western Europe. John Churchill, the Duke of Marlborough (1650–1722) bested Louis's soldiers in every major engagement, although French arms triumphed in Spain. After 1709 the war became a bloody stalemate.

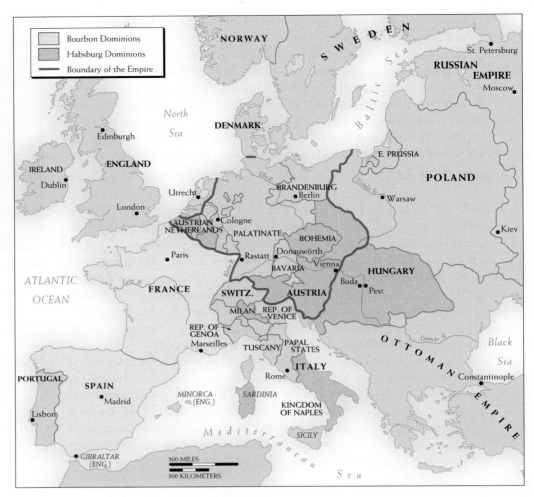

France finally made peace with England at Utrecht in July 1713, and with Holland and the emperor at Rastatt in March 1714. Philip V remained king of Spain, but England got Gibraltar and the island of Minorca, making it a Mediterranean power. (See Map 13–1.) Louis also recognized the right of the House of Hanover to the English throne.

## FRANCE AFTER LOUIS XIV

Despite its military reverses in the War of the Spanish Succession, France remained a great power. It was less strong in 1715 than in 1680, but it still possessed the largest European population, an advanced, if troubled, economy, and the administrative structure bequeathed it by Louis XIV. Moreover, even if France and its resources had been drained by the last of Louis's wars, the other major states of Europe were similarly debilitated. Louis XIV was succeeded by his five-year-old great-grandson Louis XV (r. 1715–1774). The young boy's uncle, the duke of Orléans, became regent and remained so until his death in 1720. The regency, marked by financial and moral scandals, further undermined the faltering prestige of the monarchy.

**John Law and the Mississippi Bubble**  The duke of Orléans was a gambler, and for a time he turned over the financial management of the kingdom to John Law (1671–1729), a Scottish mathematician and fellow gambler. Law believed an increase in the paper-money supply would stimulate France's economic recovery. With the permission of the regent, he established a bank in Paris that issued paper money. Law then

Despite these internal difficulties, Leopold I (r. 1658–1705) managed to resist the advances of the Ottoman Empire into central Europe, which included a siege of Vienna in 1683, and to thwart the aggression of Louis XIV. He achieved Ottoman recognition of his sovereignty over Hungary in 1699 and extended his territorial holdings over much of the Balkan peninsula and western Romania. These conquests allowed the Habsburgs to hope to develop Mediterranean trade through the port of Trieste on the northern coast of the Adriatic Sea and helped compensate for their loss of effective power over the Holy Roman Empire. Strength in the East gave them greater political leverage in Germany. Joseph I (r. 1705–1711) continued Leopold's policies.

When Charles VI (r. 1711–1740) succeeded Joseph, a new problem was added to the chronic one of territorial diversity. He had no male heir, and there was only the weakest of precedents for a female ruler of the Habsburg domains. Charles feared that on his death the Austrian Habsburg lands might fall prey to the surrounding powers, as had those of the Spanish Habsburgs in 1700. He was determined to prevent that disaster and to provide his domains with the semblance of legal unity. To those ends, he devoted most of his reign to seeking the approval of his family, the estates of his realms, and the major foreign powers for a document called the ***Pragmatic Sanction***.

**Pragmatic Sanction**   Document recognizing Charles VI's daughter Maria Theresa as his heir.

This instrument provided the legal basis for a single line of inheritance within the Habsburg dynasty through Charles VI's daughter Maria Theresa (r. 1740–1780). When Charles VI died in October 1740, he believed that he had secured legal unity for the Habsburg Empire and a safe succession for his daughter. Despite the Pragmatic Sanction, however, his failure to provide his daughter with a strong army or a full treasury left her inheritance open to foreign aggression. In December 1740, Frederick II of Prussia invaded the Habsburg province of Silesia in eastern Germany. Maria Theresa had to fight for her inheritance.

## PRUSSIA AND THE HOHENZOLLERNS

The rise of Prussia occurred within the German power vacuum created by the Peace of Westphalia. It is the story of the extraordinary Hohenzollern family, which had ruled Brandenburg since 1417. Through inheritance the family had acquired the duchy of Cleves, and the counties of Mark and Ravensburg in 1614, East Prussia in 1618, and Pomerania in 1648. Except for Pomerania, none of these lands shared a border with Brandenburg. Still, by the late seventeenth century, the geographically scattered Hohenzollern holdings represented a block of territory within the Holy Roman Empire, second in size only to that of the Habsburgs.

The person who began to forge these areas into a modern state was Frederick William (r. 1640–1688), who became known as the Great Elector. He established himself and his successors as the central uniting power by breaking the local noble estates, organizing a royal bureaucracy, and building a strong army.

Between 1655 and 1660, Sweden and Poland fought each other across the Great Elector's holdings in Pomerania and East Prussia. Frederick William had neither an adequate army nor the tax revenues to confront this threat. In 1655, the Brandenburg estates refused to grant him new taxes; however, he proceeded to collect them by military force. In 1659, a different grant of taxes, originally made in 1653, elapsed; Frederick William continued to collect them as well as those he had imposed by his own authority. He used the money to build an army, which allowed him to continue to enforce his will without the approval of the nobility. Similar coercion took place against the nobles in his other territories.

There was, however, a political and social trade-off between the Elector and his various nobles. In exchange for their obedience to the Hohenzollerns, the **Junkers**, or German noble landlords, received the right to demand obedience from their serfs. Frederick William also tended to choose as the local administrators of the tax structure

**Junkers**   (Prussian nobles) They were allowed to demand absolute obedience from the serfs on their estates in exchange for their support of the Hohenzollerns.

men who would normally have been members of the noble branch of the old parliament. As the years passed, Junkers increasingly dominated the army officer corps, and this situation became even more pronounced during the eighteenth century. All officials and army officers took an oath of loyalty directly to the Elector. The army and the Elector thus came to embody the otherwise absent unity of the state.

The achievement of a royal title was one of the few state-building accomplishments of the Elector's heir, Frederick I (r. 1688–1713). In the War of the Spanish Succession, he put his army at the disposal of the Habsburg Holy Roman Emperor Leopold I. In exchange, the emperor permitted Frederick to assume the title of "King in Prussia" in 1701.

His successor, Frederick William I (r. 1713–1740), was both the most eccentric monarch to rule the Hohenzollern domains and one of the most effective. He organized the bureaucracy along military lines. The Prussian military grew from about 39,000 in 1713 to over 80,000 in 1740, making it the third or fourth largest army in Europe. Separate laws applied to the army and to civilians. Laws, customs, and royal attention made the officer corps the highest social class of the state. Military service thus attracted the sons of Junkers. In this fashion the army, the Junker nobility, and the monarchy became forged into a single political entity.

Although Frederick William I built the best army in Europe, he avoided conflict. His army was a symbol of Prussian power and unity, not an instrument for foreign adventures or aggression. At his death in 1740, he passed to his son Frederick II, later known as Frederick the Great (r. 1740–1786), this superb military machine but not the wisdom to refrain from using it. Almost immediately on coming to the throne, Frederick II upset the Pragmatic Sanction and invaded Silesia. He thus crystallized the Austrian-Prussian rivalry for the control of Germany that would dominate central European affairs for over a century.

## QUICK REVIEW

### Frederick William's Army

- Grew from 39,000 in 1713 to over 80,000 in 1740
- Separate laws applied to the army and civilians
- The officer corps became the highest social class of the state

# RUSSIA ENTERS THE EUROPEAN POLITICAL ARENA

**HOW DID** Peter the Great transform Russia into a powerful, centralized nation?

The emergence of Russia in the late seventeenth century as an active European power was a wholly new factor in European politics.

## THE ROMANOV DYNASTY

The reign of Ivan IV (r. 1533–1584), later known as Ivan the Terrible, had commenced well but ended badly. About midway in his reign he underwent a personality change that led him to move from a program of sensible reform of law, government, and the army toward violent personal tyranny. A period known as the "Time of Troubles" followed upon his death. In 1613, hoping to end the uncertainty, an assembly of nobles elected as tsar a seventeen-year-old boy named Michael Romanov (r. 1613–1645). Thus began the dynasty that ruled Russia until 1917.

Michael Romanov and his two successors, Aleksei (r. 1654–1676) and Theodore II (r. 1676–1682), brought stability and modest bureaucratic centralization to Russia. The country remained, however, weak and impoverished. After years of turmoil, the *boyars*, the old nobility, still largely controlled the bureaucracy. Furthermore, the government and the tsars faced the danger of mutiny from the *streltsy*, or guards of the Moscow garrison.

## PETER THE GREAT

In 1682, Peter (r. 1682–1725)—ten years old at the time—ascended the fragile Russian throne as co-ruler with his half brother. He and the sickly Ivan V had come to power on the shoulders of the *streltsy*, who expected to be rewarded for their support. Violence and bloodshed had surrounded the disputed succession. Matters became even more confused

when the boys' sister, Sophia, was named regent. Peter's followers overthrew her in 1689. From that date onward, Peter ruled personally, although in theory he shared the crown until Ivan died in 1696. The dangers and turmoil of his youth convinced Peter of two things: First, the power of the tsar must be made secure from the jealousy of the *boyars* and the greed of the *streltsy*; second, Russian military power must be increased.

Northwestern Europe, particularly the military resources of the maritime powers, fascinated Peter I, who eventually became known as Peter the Great. In 1697, he made a famous visit in transparent disguise to western Europe. An imitator of the first order, Peter returned to Moscow determined to copy what he had seen abroad, for he knew warfare would be necessary to make Russia a great power. Yet he understood his goal would require him to confront the long-standing power and traditions of the Russian nobles.

**Taming the *Streltsy* and *Boyars***    In 1698, while Peter was abroad, the *streltsy* had rebelled. On his return, Peter brutally suppressed the revolt. Approximately a thousand of the rebels were put to death, and their corpses remained on public display to discourage disloyalty. Peter then set about building a new military. He drafted an unprecedented 130,000 soldiers, and by the end of his reign he had a well-disciplined army of 300,000.

Peter also made a sustained attack on the *boyars* and their attachment to traditional Russian culture. After his European journey, he personally shaved the long beards of the court *boyars* and sheared off the customary long hand-covering sleeves of their shirts and coats, which had made them the butt of jokes among other European courts. Peter became highly skilled at balancing one group off against another while never completely excluding any as he set about to organize Russian government and military forces along the lines of the more powerful European states.

**Developing a Navy**    In the mid-1690s, Peter oversaw the construction of ships to protect his interests in the Black Sea against the Ottoman Empire. In 1695, he began a war with the Ottomans and captured Azov on the Black Sea in 1696. Part of the reason for Peter's trip to western Europe in 1697 was to learn how to build still better warships, this time for combat on the Baltic. The construction of a Baltic fleet was essential in Peter's struggles with Sweden that over the years accounted for many of his major steps toward westernizing his realm.

**Russian Expansion in the Baltic: The Great Northern War**    Following the end of the Thirty Years' War in 1648, Sweden had consolidated its control of the Baltic, thus preventing Russian possession of a port on that sea and permitting Polish and German access to the sea only on Swedish terms.

In 1697, Charles XII (r. 1697–1718) came to the Swedish throne. He was headstrong, to say the least, and perhaps insane. In 1700, Peter the Great began a drive to the west against Swedish territory to gain a foothold on the Baltic. The result was the Great Northern War (1700–1721). By 1709, Peter had decisively defeated the Swedes at the Battle of Poltava in Ukraine. Thereafter, the Swedes could maintain only a holding action against their enemies. When the Great Northern War came to a close in 1721, the Peace of Nystad confirmed the Russian conquest of Estonia, Livonia, and part of Finland. Henceforth, Russia possessed ice-free ports and a permanent influence on European affairs.

**Founding St. Petersburg**    At one point, the domestic and foreign policies of Peter the Great intersected. This was at the site on the Gulf of Finland where he founded his new capital city of St. Petersburg in 1703. There he built government structures and compelled the *boyars* to construct town houses. He thus imitated those European monarchs who had copied Louis XIV by constructing smaller versions of Versailles. The

**Table of Ranks**    Issued by Peter the Great to draw nobles into state service, it made rank in the bureaucracy or military, not lineage, the determinant of an individual's social status.

## EVENTS AND REIGNS

| | |
|---|---|
| 1533–1584 | Ivan the Terrible |
| 1584–1613 | Time of Troubles |
| 1613 | Michael Romanov becomes tsar |
| 1640–1688 | Frederick William, the Great Elector |
| 1643–1715 | Louis XIV, the Sun King |
| 1648 | Independence of the Netherlands recognized |
| 1682–1725 | Peter the Great |
| 1683 | Turkish siege of Vienna |
| 1688–1713 | Frederick I of Prussia |
| 1697 | Peter the Great's European tour |
| 1700–1721 | The Great Northern War |
| 1703 | Saint Petersburg founded |
| 1711–1740 | The Great Northern War |
| 1703 | Saint Petersburg founded |
| 1711–1740 | Charles VI, the Pragmatic Sanction |
| 1713 | War of the Spanish Succession ends |
| 1713–1740 | Frederick William I of Prussia |
| 1714 | George I founds England's Hanoverian dynasty |
| 1715 | Louis XV becomes king of France |
| 1720–1741 | Robert Walpole dominates British politics |
| 1726–1743 | Cardinal Fleury |
| 1727 | George II |
| 1740 | Maria Theresa succeeds to the Habsburg throne |
| 1740 | Frederick II invades Silesia |

founding of St. Petersburg went beyond establishing a central imperial court, however; it symbolized a new Western orientation of Russia and Peter's determination to hold his position on the Baltic coast.

**The Case of Peter's Son Aleksei**    Peter's son Aleksei had been born to his first wife whom he had divorced in 1698. By 1716, Peter was becoming convinced that his opponents looked to Aleksei as a focus for their possible sedition while Russia remained at war with Sweden. There was some truth to these concerns because the next year Aleksei went to Vienna where he attempted to enter into a vague conspiracy with the Habsburg emperor Charles VI.

Peter, who was investigating official corruption, realized his son might become a rallying point for those he accused. Early in 1718, when Aleksei reappeared in St. Petersburg, the tsar began to look into his son's relationships with Charles VI. During this six-month investigation, Peter personally interrogated Aleksei, who was eventually condemned to death and died under mysterious circumstances on June 26, 1718.

**Reforms of Peter the Great's Final Years**    The interrogations surrounding Aleksei had revealed greater degrees of court opposition than Peter had suspected. Recognizing he could not eliminate his opponents the way he had attacked the *streltsy* in 1698, Peter undertook radical administrative reforms designed to bring the nobility and the Russian Orthodox Church more closely under the authority of persons loyal to the tsar.

**Administrative Colleges**    In December 1717, Peter reorganized his domestic administration to sustain his own personal authority and to fight rampant corruption. To achieve this goal, Peter looked to Swedish institutions called *colleges*—bureaus of several persons operating according to written instructions rather than departments headed by a single minister. He created eight of these colleges to oversee matters such as the collection of taxes, foreign relations, war, and economic affairs. Each college was to receive advice from a foreigner. Peter divided the members of these colleges between nobles and persons he was certain would be personally loyal to himself.

**Table of Ranks**    Peter made another major administrative reform with important consequences when in 1722 he published a **Table of Ranks**, which was intended to draw the nobility into state service. That table equated a person's social position and privileges with his rank in the bureaucracy or the military, rather than with his lineage among the traditional landed nobility. Peter thus made the social standing of individual *boyars* a function of their willingness to serve the central state.

**Achieving Secular Control of the Church**    Peter also moved to suppress the independence of the Russian Orthodox Church. In 1721, Peter simply abolished the position of *patriarch*, the bishop who had been head of the church. In its place he established a government department called the *Holy Synod*, which consisted of several bishops headed by a layman, called the *procurator general*. This body would govern the church in accordance with the tsar's secular requirements.

For all the numerous decisive actions Peter had taken since 1718, he still had not settled on a successor. Consequently, when he died in 1725, there was no clear line of succession to the throne. For more than thirty years, soldiers and nobles again determined who ruled Russia. Peter had laid the foundations of a modern Russia, but not the foundations of a stable state.

**Ottoman Empire** The authority Instanbul's Ottoman Turkish sultan exercised over the Balkans, the Middle East, and North Africa from the end of the Middle Ages to World War I.

# THE OTTOMAN EMPIRE

Governing a remarkably diverse collection of peoples that ranged from Baghdad westward across the Arabian peninsula, Anatolia, the Balkan peninsula, and across North Africa from Egypt to Algiers, the **Ottoman Empire** was the largest and most stable political entity to arise in or near Europe following the collapse of the Roman Empire. (See Map 13–3.) It had achieved this power between the eleventh and early sixteenth centuries as Ottoman tribes migrated westward from the steppes of Asia.

**WHAT WAS** the attitude of the Ottoman rulers toward religion in their empire and how was this reflected in their policies?

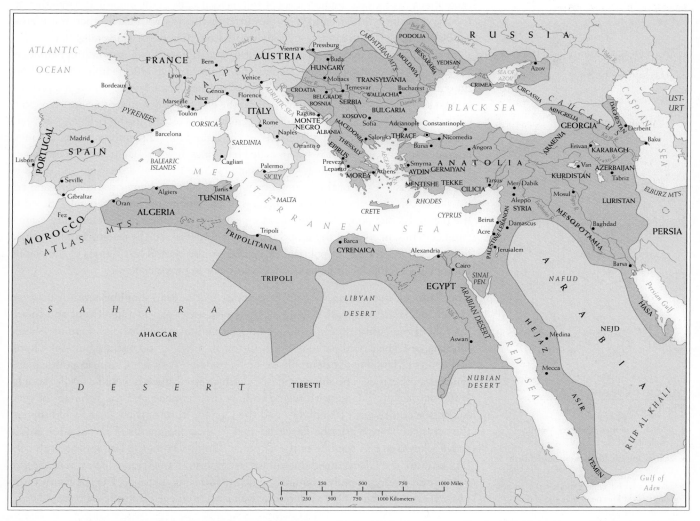

**MAP 13–3** **The Ottoman Empire in the Late Seventeenth Century** By the 1680s, the Ottoman Empire had reached its maximum extent, but the Ottoman failure to capture Vienna in 1683 marked the beginning of a long and inexorable decline that ended with the empire's collapse after World War I.

**From the** late 1600s until 1918, which non-Turkish peoples would rise up against Turkish rule in the Ottoman Empire?

**millets**   Communities of the officially recognized religions that governed portions of the Ottoman Empire.

## RELIGIOUS TOLERATION AND OTTOMAN GOVERNMENT

The Ottoman Empire was the dominant political power in the Muslim world after 1516, when it administered the holy cities of Mecca and Medina as well as Jerusalem, and arranged the safety of Muslim pilgrimages to Mecca. Yet its population was exceedingly diverse ethnically, linguistically, and religiously with significant numbers of Orthodox and Roman Catholic Christians and, after the late fifteenth century, thousands of Jews from Spain.

The Ottomans extended far more religious toleration to their subjects than existed anywhere in Europe. The Ottoman sultans governed their empire through units, called **millets**, of officially recognized religious communities. Various laws and regulations applied to the persons who belonged to a particular millet rather than to a particular administrative territory. Non-Islamic persons in the empire, known as *dhimmis*, or followers of religions tolerated by law, could practice their religion and manage their internal community affairs through their own religious officials. They were, however, also second-class citizens generally unable to rise in the service of the empire, subject to certain restrictions, and required to pay special taxes. Nonetheless, they often attained economic success because they possessed the highest level of commercial skills in the empire. Because the Ottomans discouraged their various peoples from interacting with each other, the Islamic population rarely acquired these and other skills from their non-Islamic neighbors.

The Ottoman dynasty also kept itself separated from the most powerful families of the empire by recruiting military leaders and administrative officers from groups whom the sultans believed would be personally loyal to them. For example, through a practice known as the *devshirme*, the Ottomans, until the end of the seventeenth century, recruited their most elite troops from Christian communities usually in the Balkans. Christian boys so recruited were raised as Muslims and organized into elite military units, the most famous of which were infantry troops called *Janissaries*. It was thought these troops would be extremely loyal to the sultan and the state because they owed their life and status to the sultan. As a result of this policy, entry into the elite military organizations and advancement in the administrative structures of the empire remained generally closed to the native Islamic population and most especially to members of the most elite Islamic families. Thus, in contrast to Europe, few people from the socially leading families gained military, administrative, or political experience in the central institutions of the empire but remained primarily linked to local government in provincial cities.

**The Role of the *Ulama***   Again in contrast to the long-standing tension between church and state in Europe, Islamic religious authorities played a significant and enduring role in the political, legal, and administrative life of the Ottoman Empire. Islamic scholars, or *Ulama*, dominated not only Ottoman religious institutions but also schools and courts of law. There essentially existed a trade-off between Ottoman political and religious authorities. The sultan and his administrative officials would consult these Islamic scholars for advice with regard to how their policies and the behavior of their subjects accorded with Islamic law and the Qur'an. In turn, the *Ulama* would support the Ottoman state while the latter deferred to their judgments. This situation would prove a key factor in the fate of the Ottoman Empire. From the late seventeenth century onward, the *Ulama* urged the sultans to conform to traditional life even as the empire confronted a rapidly changing and modernizing Europe. The Janissaries also resisted changes that might undermine their own privileged status.

## THE END OF OTTOMAN EXPANSION

From the fifteenth century onward, the Ottoman Empire had tried to push further westward into Europe. The Ottomans made their deepest military invasion into Europe in 1683, when they unsuccessfully besieged Vienna. Although that defeat proved to be

**QUICK REVIEW**

**The *Ulama***

- *Ulama*: Dominant group of Muslim scholars
- Sultan and his advisors consulted with *Ulama*
- *Ulama* advised against modernization and adoption of European ideas

decisive, many observers at the time thought it the result only of an overreach of power by the Ottomans rather than as a symptom of a deeper decline, which was actually the case.

Gradually, from the seventeenth century onward, the authority of the grand vizier, the major political figure after the sultan, began to grow. This development meant that more and more authority lay with the administrative and military bureaucracy. Rivalries for power among army leaders and nobles, as well as their flagrant efforts to enrich themselves, weakened the effectiveness of the government. About the same time local elites in the various provincial cities of the empire began to assert their own influence.

External factors also accounted for both the blocking of Ottoman expansion in the late seventeenth century and then its slow decline thereafter. During the European Middle Ages, the Islamic world had far outdistanced Europe in learning, science, and military prowess. From the fifteenth century onward, however, Europeans had begun to make rapid advances in technology, wealth, and scientific knowledge. For example, they designed ships for the difficult waters of the Atlantic and thus eventually opened trade routes to the East around Africa and reached the Americas. As trade expanded, Europeans achieved new commercial skills, founded trading posts in South Asia, established the plantation economies and precious metal mines of the Americas, and became much wealthier. By the seventeenth century, Europeans, particularly the Dutch and Portuguese, imported directly from Asia or America commodities such as spices, sugar, and coffee that they had previously acquired through the Ottoman Empire. During the same decades, Europeans developed greater military and naval power and new weapons.

During the 1690s, the Ottomans unsuccessfully fought a league of European states including Austria, Venice, Malta, Poland, and Tuscany, joined by Russia, which, as we have already seen, was emerging as a new aggressive power to the north. In early 1699, the defeated Ottomans negotiated the Treaty of Carlowitz, which required them to surrender significant territory lying not at the edges, but at the heart of their empire in Europe, including most of Hungary, to the Habsburgs. This treaty meant not only the loss of territory, but also of the revenue the Ottomans had long drawn from those regions. From this time onward, Russia and the Ottomans would duel for control of regions around the Black Sea with Russia achieving ever greater success by the close of the eighteenth century.

Despite these defeats, the Ottomans remained deeply inward looking, continuing to regard themselves as superior to the once underdeveloped European West. The Ottoman leaders, isolated from both their own leading Muslim subjects and from Europe, failed to understand what was occurring far beyond their immediate borders, especially European advances in military technology. When during the eighteenth century the Ottoman Empire began to recognize the new situation, it tended to borrow European technology and import foreign advisers, thus failing to develop its own infrastructure. Moreover, the powerful influence of the *Ulama* worked against imitation of Christian Europe. This influence by Muslim religious teachers occurred just as governments, such as that of Peter the Great, and secular intellectuals across Europe, through the influence of the Enlightenment (see Chapter 17), were increasingly diminishing the influence of the Christian churches in political and economic affairs. Consequently, European intellectuals began to view the once feared Ottoman Empire as a declining power and Islam as a backward-looking religion.

***Devshirme.*** An Ottoman portrayal of the *Devshirme*. This miniature painting from about 1558 depicts the recruiting of young Christian children for the Sultan's elite Janissary corps.

British Library, London, UK/Bridgeman Art Library

**What was the relationship between the Ottoman government and its Christian subjects?**

# SUMMARY

**WHAT WAS** the Dutch Golden Age and what led to its decline?

**The Netherlands: Golden Age to Decline** By the mid–eighteenth century, Britain and France had emerged as the dominant powers in Western Europe and Spain had lost influence. The United Netherlands had enjoyed a Golden Age in the seventeenth century, and it was more urbanized than any other area of Europe. Dutch agriculture and financial systems were models for the rest of Europe, and the Dutch were the leading traders of Europe. After the death of William of Orange in 1702, the loose republican system that had given the Netherlands valuable flexibility turned into a handicap in the absence of leadership. *page 322*

**WHAT FACTORS** led to the different political paths taken by England and France in the seventeenth century?

**Two Models of European Political Development** In the seventeenth century, England and France developed two different forms of government that served as models for other European countries in the eighteenth century. In England, nobles and the wealthy were politically active and had a tradition of broad liberties, representation, and bargaining with the monarch through Parliament. The English nobility felt little admiration or affection for the Stuart monarchs. In France, members of the French nobility believed the strength of Louis XIV served their personal interests as well as those of the king. This led to the so-called absolutism of the French monarchy, which became the country's sole significant national institution. *page 323*

**HOW DID** conflicts over taxation and religion lead to civil war in Stuart England?

**Constitutional Crisis and Settlement in Stuart England** In the first half of the seventeenth century, many of the English suspected that their leaders were Catholic sympathizers. Oliver Cromwell led opposition in a civil war from 1642 to 1646, and then ruled until 1658. In 1660, the Stuart monarchy was restored under Charles II. His relationship with Parliament was testy. His brother and successor, the Catholic James II, was not as astute as Charles II. In 1688, members of Parliament invited William III of Orange to invade England and take the throne. After the success of the "Glorious Revolu-

tion," in 1689, William and Mary recognized a Bill of Rights, limiting the monarchy's powers, guaranteeing civil liberties to some, formalizing Parliament's role, and barring Catholics from the throne. The 1689 Toleration Act allowed Protestants freedom to worship but denied Catholics similar privileges. The monarchy in Great Britain passed to the house of Hanover, and George I sought support from the Whigs. Robert Walpole functioned as George's prime minister. Parliament checked royal influence and provided strong central political authority. Britain's economy was strong, and political life was remarkably free. *page 323*

**WHY WERE** efforts to establish absolute monarchy successful in France but unsuccessful in England?

**Rise of Absolute Monarchy in France: The World of Louis XIV** Louis XIV's monarchy gathered unprecedented power on the national level in the area of foreign and military affairs, domestic administration, and economic regulation. At the same time, Louis was careful to allow nobles to retain their local power and privileges. He ensured loyalty to the crown by employing nobles in his administration and crafted a political image as the "Sun King" based at Versailles. At this palace, Louis built a system of patronage that effectively excluded many nobles from government, even as it occupied them in ritual and ceremony all designed to promote Louis's personal rule and divine right monarchy. Louis's armies instilled fear in France's neighbors, prompting several alliances to be formed against France throughout his reign. He repressed the anti-Jesuit Jansenists and revoked the Edict of Nantes, which had ensured toleration of French Protestants. These policies reinforced Europe's image of Louis as a repressive fanatic and sowed the seeds of domestic opposition to the monarchy, not only among Jansenist sympathizers, but also in noble and judicial bodies. *page 328*

**WHAT WERE** the main characteristics that defined the Polish, Austrian, and Prussian states in the seventeenth and eighteenth centuries?

**Central and Eastern Europe** The economies and political structures of central and eastern Europe were weaker than those of the West. Late in the seventeenth century, Poland could not develop a strong central authority, while Austria, Prussia, and Russia emerged as political and military powers. The Habsburg Empire expanded so much that by the eighteenth and nineteenth centuries, Habsburg power and influence were based more on territories outside of Germany than within. Political unity was in short supply. The Hohenzollerns created a Prussian army that, according to an axiom, possessed the nation, rather than the other way around. *page 335*

ably successful in most of his efforts. His critical failure was that, when he died in 1725, he had not appointed a successor; for decades after his death, power reverted to nobles and soldiers. *page 338*

**HOW DID** Peter the Great transform Russia into a powerful, centralized nation?

**Russia Enters the European Political Arena** In the seventeenth century, Russia became one of the nations of Europe, and the Romanov dynasty was founded. Russia's old nobility, the *boyars*, retained considerable authority until Peter (later Peter the Great) assumed personal rule in 1689. Peter was zealous in his efforts to westernize Russia, to curb the power of the *boyars* and Moscow garrison guards (the *streltsy*), and to increase the nation's military strength. He was remark-

**WHAT WAS** the attitude of the Ottoman rulers toward religion in their empire and how was this reflected in their policies?

**The Ottoman Empire** The Ottoman Empire was diverse ethnically, linguistically, and religiously and offered more religious freedom than could be found anywhere in Europe. Social and political structures prevented leading families from interacting meaningfully with the ruling elite, which limited the infusion of new ideas and personalities into government. Military defeats in the late seventeenth century marked the beginning of the end for the Ottoman Empire. *page 341*

# REVIEW QUESTIONS

1. Why did Britain and France remain leading powers while the United Netherlands declined? How did the structure of British government change under the political leadership of Walpole?

2. What similarities and differences do you see between the systems of government and religious policies in place in England and France at the end of the seventeenth century? What accounts for the path each nation took?

3. Why did the English king and Parliament come into conflict in the 1640s? What was the "Glorious Revolution"? How did England in 1700 differ from England in 1600?

4. How did Louis XIV consolidate his monarchy? How successful was his foreign policy? What were the domestic and international consequences of his religious policies?

5. How did Peter the Great's plan for building a greater Russia compare with the conduct of the Ottoman leaders who allowed their empire to decline?

6. How was the Hohenzollern family able to forge a conglomerate of diverse landholdings into the state of Prussia? How do the Hohenzollerns and the Habsburgs compare in the ways they dealt with the problems that confronted their domains?

7. What sorts of political and diplomatic problems did questions about successions to thrones create for various states between 1685 and 1740?

## KEY TERMS

**divine right of kings** (p. 329)
*Fronde* (p. 328)
**Gallican Liberties** (p. 332)
**Glorious Revolution** (p. 327)
**Jansenism** (p. 332)
**Junkers** (p. 337)
**millets** (p. 342)
**Ottoman Empire** (p. 341)

*parlements*(p. 335)
**parliamentary monarchy** (p. 323)
**political absolutism** (p. 323)
**Pragmatic Sanction** (p. 337)
**Puritans** (p. 324)
*Sejm* (p. 336)
**Table of Ranks** (p. 340)

For additional learning resources related to this chapter, please go to **www.myhistorylab.com**

myhistorylab

# 14

# New Directions in Thought and Culture in the Sixteenth and Seventeenth Centuries

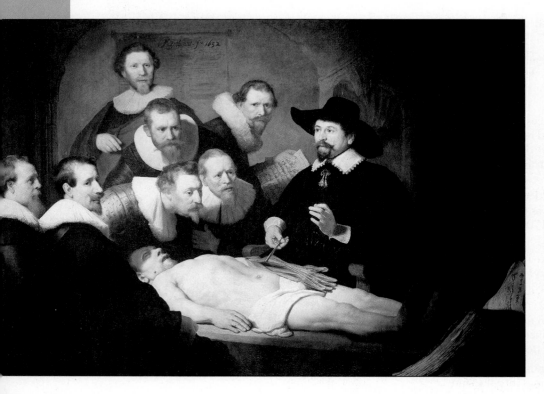

**The great Dutch artist** Rembrandt van Rijn (1606–1669) recorded the contemporary life of the United Provinces of the Netherlands during its Golden Age. The new sciences including medicine made much progress in the Netherlands, which was a center for publishing and instrument making and known for its religious toleration. *The Anatomy Lesson of Dr. Tulp* (1632) presents the dissection of a cadaver of an executed criminal by the noted Dutch physician Dr. Nicolass Tulp who stands on the right surrounded by other members of the Amsterdam Guild of Surgeons. Such dissections were a controversial part of new emerging medical education with only one a year permitted in Amsterdam. The dramatic use of light and darkness is characteristic of the painting of the baroque style.

Rembrandt van Rijn (1606–1669). *The Anatomy Lesson of Dr. Tulp.* Mauritshuis, The Hague, The Netherlands. SCALA/Art Resource, NY

**What does this painting tell us about the development of medical education in the seventeenth century?**

THE SCIENTIFIC REVOLUTION *page 348*

**WHAT WAS** the scientific revolution?

PHILOSOPHY RESPONDS TO CHANGING SCIENCE *page 351*

**WHAT IMPACT** did the new science have on philosophy?

THE NEW INSTITUTIONS OF EXPANDING NATURAL KNOWLEDGE *page 358*

**WHAT WAS** the social and political context for scientific inquiry in the seventeenth century?

WOMEN IN THE WORLD OF THE SCIENTIFIC REVOLUTION *page 359*

**WHAT ROLE** did women play in the scientific revolution?

THE NEW SCIENCE AND RELIGIOUS FAITH *page 361*

**WHAT EFFORTS** were made to reconcile the new science and religion?

CONTINUING SUPERSTITION *page 363*

**WHAT EXPLAINS** the witch hunts and panics of the sixteenth and seventeenth centuries?

BAROQUE ART *page 364*

**HOW DID** baroque art serve both religious and secular ends?

D uring the sixteenth and seventeenth centuries, science created a new view of the universe that challenged many previously held beliefs. Earth moved from the center of the universe and became only one of several planets orbiting a sun that was only one of countless stars. This new cosmology forced people to re-think humanity's place in the larger scheme of things. The new scientific ideas came into apparent conflict with traditional religion and raised doubts about the grounds for faith and morality. Europeans discovered the world was a much more complex place than their ancestors had imagined. The telescope opened the heavens to them while the microscope disclosed the existence of a realm of microorganisms. A spate of scientific discoveries added to the intellectual dislocation already created by the Reformation and contact with the New World. ■

# THE SCIENTIFIC REVOLUTION

**WHAT WAS** the scientific revolution?

**scientific revolution**   The emergence in the sixteenth century of rational and empirical methods of research that challenged traditional thought and promoted the rise of science and technology.

The process that established the new view of the universe is normally termed the *scientific revolution*. The revolution-in-science metaphor must be used carefully, however. Not everything associated with the "new" science was necessarily new. Sixteenth- and seventeenth-century natural philosophers were often reexamining and rethinking theories and data from the ancient world and the late Middle Ages. Moreover, the word *revolution* normally denotes rapid, collective political change involving many people. The scientific revolution was not rapid. It was a complex movement with many false starts and brilliant people suggesting wrong as well as useful ideas. Nor did it involve more than a few hundred people who labored in widely separated studies and crude laboratories located in Poland, Italy, Denmark, Bohemia, France, and Great Britain. Furthermore, the achievements of the new science were not simply the function of isolated brilliant scientific minds. The leading figures of the scientific revolution often drew on the aid of artisans and craftspeople to help them construct new instruments for experimentation and to carry out those experiments. Finally, because the practice of science involves social activity as well as knowledge, the revolution also saw the establishment of new social institutions to support the emerging scientific enterprise.

Natural knowledge was only in the process of becoming science as we know it today during the era of the scientific revolution. In fact the word *scientist*, which was only coined in the 1830s, did not yet exist in the seventeenth century, nor did anything resembling the modern scientific career. Individuals devoted to natural philosophy might work in universities or in the court of a prince or even in their own homes and workshops. Only in the second half of the seventeenth century did formal societies and academies devoted to the pursuit of natural philosophy come into existence.

Although new knowledge emerged in many areas during the sixteenth and seventeenth centuries, including medicine, chemistry, and natural history, the scientific achievements that most captured the learned imagination and persuaded people of the cultural power of natural knowledge were those that occurred in astronomy.

## NICOLAUS COPERNICUS REJECTS AN EARTH-CENTERED UNIVERSE

Nicolaus Copernicus (1473–1543) was a Polish priest and an astronomer. In 1543, the year of his death, Copernicus published *On the Revolutions of the Heavenly Spheres*. What Copernicus's work did was to provide an intellectual springboard for a complete criticism of the then-dominant view of the position of Earth in the universe. He had undertaken this task to help the papacy reform the calendar, so that it could correctly calculate the date for Easter based on a more accurate understanding of astronomy.

**The Ptolemaic System**  In Copernicus's time, the standard explanation of the place of Earth in the heavens combined the mathematical astronomy of Ptolemy, contained in his work entitled the *Almagest* (150 C.E.), with the physical cosmology of Aristotle. Over the centuries, commentators on Ptolemy's work had developed several alternative **Ptolemaic systems**, on the basis of which they made mathematical calculations relating to astronomy. Most of these writers assumed Earth was the center of the universe, an outlook known as *geocentrism*. Drawing on Aristotle, these commentators assumed that above Earth lay a series of concentric spheres, one of which contained the moon, another the sun, and still others the planets and the stars. At the outer regions of these spheres lay the realm of God and the angels. Earth had to be the center because of its heaviness. The stars and the other heavenly bodies had to be enclosed in the spheres so they could move, since nothing could move unless something was actually moving it. The state of rest was presumed to be natural; motion required explanation.

The Ptolemaic model gave rise to many problems, which had long been recognized. For example, at certain times the planets appeared to be going backwards. Complex mathematical models were developed to account for this phenomenon. Other intellectual, but nonobservational, difficulties related to the immense speed at which the spheres had to move around Earth. To say the least, the Ptolemaic systems were cluttered. They were effective, however, as long as one assumed Aristotelian physics to be correct.

**Copernicus's Universe**  Copernicus's *On the Revolutions of the Heavenly Spheres* challenged the Ptolemaic picture in the most conservative manner possible. He adopted many elements of the Ptolemaic model but transferred them to a *heliocentric* (sun-centered) model, which assumed Earth moved about the sun in a circle. The repositioning of the Earth had not been Copernicus's goal. Rather, he appears to have set out to achieve new intelligibility and mathematical elegance in astronomy by rejecting Aristotle's cosmology and by removing the earth from the center of the universe. His system was no more accurate than the existing ones for predicting the location of the planets. He had used no new evidence. The major impact of his work was to provide another way of confronting some of the difficulties inherent in Ptolemaic astronomy. The Copernican system did not immediately replace the old astronomy, but it allowed other people who were also discontented with the Ptolemaic view to think in new directions. Indeed, for at least a century, only a minority of natural philosophers and astronomers embraced the Copernican system.

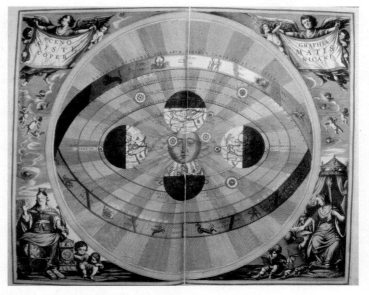

**Scenographia: Systematis Copernicani** Astrological Chart, ca. 1543.

British Library, London, UK/Bridgeman Art Library

**What was the relationship between astronomy and astrology in the sixteenth century?**

**Ptolemaic system**  Astronomical theory, named after Greek astronomer Ptolemy, that assumed Earth was the center point of a ball-shaped universe composed of concentric layers of rotating crystalline spheres to which the heavenly bodies were attached.

**QUICK REVIEW**

*On the Revolutions of the Heavenly Spheres*

◆ Copernicus's work meant as a revision of Ptolemy's model

◆ If Earth was assumed to rotate around the sun, the model would be vastly simplified

◆ Model slow to attract adherents

# TYCHO BRAHE AND JOHANNES KEPLER MAKE NEW SCIENTIFIC OBSERVATIONS

The Danish astronomer Tycho Brahe (1546–1601) took the next major step toward the conception of a sun-centered system. He did not embrace Copernicus's view of the universe and actually spent most of his life advocating an Earth-centered system. Brahe's contribution was the construction of scientific instruments with which he made more extensive naked-eye observations of the planets than anyone else had ever done. His labors produced a vast body of astronomical data from which his successors could work.

When Brahe died, his assistant, Johannes Kepler (1571–1630), a German astronomer, took possession of these tables. Kepler was a convinced Copernican and a more consistently rigorous advocate of a heliocentric model than Copernicus himself had been. Like Copernicus, Kepler was deeply influenced by Renaissance Neoplatonism, which held the sun in special honor. In keeping with this outlook, Kepler was determined to find in Brahe's numbers mathematical harmonies that would support a sun-centered universe. Based on the mathematical relationships that emerged from his study of Brahe's observations, Kepler set forth the first astronomical model that actually portrayed motion—that is, the path of the planets—and those orbits were elliptical, not circular. Kepler published his findings in his 1609 book entitled *The New Astronomy*. He had used Copernicus's sun-centered universe and Brahe's empirical data to solve the problem of planetary motion.

Kepler had also defined a new problem. None of the available theories could explain why the planetary orbits were elliptical or, for that matter, why planetary motion was orbital at all rather than simply moving off along a tangent. That solution awaited the work of Sir Isaac Newton.

## Galileo Galilei Argues for a Universe of Mathematical Laws

From Copernicus to Brahe to Kepler, there had been little new information about the heavens that might not have been known to Ptolemy. In 1609, however, the same year that Kepler published *The New Astronomy*, an Italian mathematician and natural philosopher named Galileo Galilei (1564–1642) first turned a telescope on the heavens. Using that recently invented Dutch instrument, he saw stars where none had been known to exist, mountains on the moon, spots moving across the sun, and moons orbiting Jupiter. The heavens were far more complex than anyone had suspected. In the *Starry Messenger* (1610) and *Letters on Sunspots* (1613), he used his considerable rhetorical skills to argue that his newly observed physical evidence, particularly the phases of Venus, required a Copernican interpretation of the heavens.

Galileo's career illustrates that the forging of the new science involved more than just presenting arguments and evidence. In 1610, he had left the University of Padua for Florence, where he became the philosopher and mathematician to the Grand Duke of Tuscany, who was a Medici. Galileo was now pursuing natural philosophy in a princely court and had become dependent on princely patronage. To win such support both for his continued work and for his theories, he named the moons of Jupiter after the Medicis. As a natural philosopher working with the new telescope, he had literally presented recently discovered heavenly bodies to his patron. By his political skills and his excellent prose, he had transformed himself into a high-profile advocate of Copernicanism. Galileo's problems with the Roman Catholic Church (see page 000) arose from both his ideas and his flair for self-advertisement.

Galileo not only popularized the Copernican system but also articulated the concept of a universe subject to mathematical laws. More than any other writer of the century, he argued that nature displayed mathematical regularity in its most minute details. For Galileo, the universe was rational; however, its rationality was not that of medieval scholastic logic, but of mathematics. Copernicus had thought that the heavens conformed to mathematical regularity; Galileo saw this regularity throughout physical nature.

A world of quantities was replacing one of qualities. The new natural philosophy portrayed nature as cold, rational, mathematical, and mechanistic. What was real and lasting was what was mathematically measurable. For many people, the power of the mathematical arguments that appeared irrefutable proved more persuasive than the new information from physical observation that produced so much controversy. Few intellectual shifts have wrought such momentous changes for Western civilization.

## ISAAC NEWTON DISCOVERS THE LAWS OF GRAVITATION

The question that continued to perplex seventeenth-century scientists who accepted the theories of Copernicus, Kepler, and Galileo was how the planets and other heavenly bodies moved in an orderly fashion. It was this issue of planetary motion that the Englishman Isaac Newton (1642–1727) addressed and, in so doing, established a basis for physics that endured for more than two centuries.

In 1687, Newton published *The Mathematical Principles of Natural Philosophy*, better known by its Latin title of *Principia Mathematica*. Galileo's mathematical bias permeated Newton's thought, as did his view that inertia applied to bodies both at rest and in motion. Newton reasoned that the planets and all other physical objects in the universe moved through mutual attraction, or gravity. Every object in the universe affected every other object through gravity. The attraction of gravity explained why the planets moved in an orderly, rather than a chaotic, manner. Newton demonstrated this relationship mathematically; he made no attempt to explain the nature of gravity itself.

Newton was a mathematical genius, but he also upheld the importance of empirical data and observation. Like Francis Bacon, he believed in empiricism—that one must observe phenomena before attempting to explain them. The final test of any theory or hypothesis for him was whether it described what was actually observed. Newton was a great opponent of the rationalism of the French philosopher René Descartes (see page 000), which he believed included insufficient guards against error. Consequently, as Newton's own theory of universal gravitation became increasingly accepted, so, too, was Baconian empiricism.

**Sir Isaac Newton's** experiments dealing with light passing through a prism became a model for writers praising the experimental method.

CORBIS/Bettmann

**In what sense was Newton's work the culmination of the scientific revolution?**

# PHILOSOPHY RESPONDS TO CHANGING SCIENCE

The revolution in scientific thought contributed directly to a major reexamination of Western philosophy. Several of the most important figures in the scientific revolution, such as Bacon and Descartes, were also philosophers discontented with the scholastic heritage. Newton's interests likewise extended to philosophy; he wrote broadly on many topics, including scientific method and theology.

**WHAT IMPACT** did the new science have on philosophy?

## NATURE AS MECHANISM

If a single idea informed all of these philosophers, though in different ways, it was the idea of *mechanism*. The proponents of the new science sought to explain the world in terms of mechanical metaphors, or the language of machinery. Nature conceived as machinery removed much of the mystery of the world and the previous assumption of the presence of divine purpose in nature. The qualities that seemed to inhere in matter came to be understood as the result of mechanical arrangement. Some writers came to understand God as a kind of divine watchmaker or mechanic who had arranged the world as a machine that would thereafter function automatically. The drive to a mechanical understanding of

**Published in 1620,** *Novum Organum* ("new organ or instrument") by Francis Bacon is one of the most important works of the scientific revolution. In this and other works Bacon attacked the long-held belief that most truth had already been discovered. This allegorical image, from the frontispiece of *Novum Organum,* shows a ship striking out for unknown territories, seeking, as did Bacon, for a new understanding of the natural world. The ship is flanked by the mythical pillars of Hercules that stand at the point where the Mediterranean meets the Atlantic—the realm of the unknown and unexplored.

Courtesy of the Library of Congress

**What sort of future did Bacon imagine for the human race?**

**empiricism**   The use of experiment and observation derived from sensory evidence to construct scientific theory or philosophy of knowledge.

nature also meant that the language of science and of natural philosophy would become largely that of mathematics.

This new mode of thinking transformed physical nature from a realm in which Europeans looked for symbolic or sacramental meaning related to the divine into a realm where they looked for utility or usefulness. Natural knowledge became the path toward the physical improvement of human beings through their ability to command and manipulate the processes of nature. Many people associated with the new science also believed such knowledge would strengthen the power of their monarchs.

## FRANCIS BACON: THE EMPIRICAL METHOD

Bacon (1561–1626) was an Englishman of almost universal accomplishment. He was a lawyer, a high royal official, and the author of histories, moral essays, and philosophical discourses. Traditionally, he has been regarded as the father of **empiricism** and of experimentation in science. Much of this reputation was actually unearned. Bacon was not a natural philosopher, except in the most amateur fashion. His real accomplishment was setting an intellectual tone and helping create a climate conducive to scientific work.

In books such as *The Advancement of Learning* (1605), the *Novum Organum* (1620), and *The New Atlantis* (1627), Bacon attacked the scholastic belief that most truth had already been discovered and only required explanation, as well as the scholastic reverence for authority in intellectual life. He urged contemporaries to strike out on their own in search of a new understanding of nature. Bacon was one of the first major European writers to champion innovation and change.

Bacon believed that human knowledge should produce useful results—deeds rather than words. In particular, knowledge of nature should be enlisted to improve the human condition. These goals required modifying or abandoning scholastic modes of learning and thinking. Scholastic philosophers could not escape from their syllogisms to examine the foundations of their thought and intellectual presuppositions. Bacon urged that philosophers and investigators of nature examine the evidence of their senses before constructing logical speculations. By directing natural philosophy toward an examination of empirical evidence, Bacon hoped it would achieve new knowledge and thus new capabilities for humankind.

Bacon boldly compared himself with Columbus, plotting a new route to intellectual discovery. The comparison is significant, because it displays the consciousness of a changing world that appears so often in writers of the late sixteenth and early seventeenth centuries. They were rejecting the past not from simple contempt or arrogance, but rather from a firm understanding that the world was much more complicated than their medieval forebearers had thought. Neither Europe nor European thought could remain self-contained. Like the new worlds on the globe, new worlds of the mind were also emerging.

Most of the people in Bacon's day, including the intellectuals influenced by humanism, thought that the best era of human history lay in antiquity. Bacon dissented vigorously from that view. He looked to a future of material improvement achieved through the empirical examination of nature. His own theory of induction from empirical evidence was unsystematic, but his insistence on appealing to experience influenced others whose methods were more productive. He and others of his outlook received almost daily support from the reports not only of European explorers, but also of ordinary seamen who now sailed all over the world and could describe wondrous cultures, as well as plants and animals, unknown to the European ancients.

Bacon believed that expanding natural knowledge had a practical purpose and its goal was human improvement. Some scientific investigation does have this character. Much pure research does not. Bacon, however, linked science and material progress in the public mind. This was a powerful idea that still influences Western civilization. It has made science and those who can appeal to the authority of science major forces for change and innovation. As a person actively associated with politics, Bacon also believed the pursuit of new knowledge would increase the power of governments and monarchies. Again, his thought in this area opened the way for the eventual strong links between governments and the scientific enterprise.

**QUICK REVIEW**

**The Empirical Method**

♦ Francis Bacon believed Scholasticism did nothing more than arrange old ideas

♦ Thinkers should reexamine the foundations of their thought

♦ Reliance on empirical evidence would yield the best results

## RENÉ DESCARTES: THE METHOD OF RATIONAL DEDUCTION

Descartes (1596–1650) was a gifted mathematician who invented analytic geometry. His most important contribution, however, was to develop a scientific method that relied more on deduction—reasoning from general principle to arrive at specific facts—than empirical observation and induction.

In 1637, he published his *Discourse on Method*, in which he rejected scholastic philosophy and education and advocated thought founded on a mathematical model. (See "Compare & Connect: Descartes and Swift Debate the Scientific Enterprise," pages 354–355.) In the *Discourse*, he began by saying he would doubt everything except those propositions about which he could have clear and distinct ideas. This approach rejected all forms of intellectual authority, except the conviction of his own reason. Descartes concluded that he could not doubt his own act of thinking and his own existence. From this base, he proceeded to deduce the existence of God. The presence of God was important to Descartes because God guaranteed the correctness of clear and distinct ideas. Since God was not a deceiver, the ideas of God-given reason could not be false.

On the basis of such an analysis, Descartes concluded that human reason could fully comprehend the world. He divided existing things into two basic categories: thinking things and things occupying space—mind and body, respectively. Thinking was the defining quality of the mind, and extension (the property by which things occupy space) was the defining quality of material bodies. Human reason could grasp and understand the world of extension, which became the realm of the natural philosopher. That world had no place for spirits, divinity, or anything nonmaterial.

Descartes's emphasis on deduction, rational speculation, and internal reflection by the mind, all of which he explored more fully in his *Meditations* of 1641, has influenced philosophers from his time to the present. His deductive methodology, however, eventually lost favor to scientific induction, whereby scientists draw generalizations derived from and test hypotheses against empirical observations.

**Queen Christina of** Sweden (r. 1632–1654), shown here with the French philosopher and scientist René Descartes, was one of many women from the elite classes interested in the new science. In 1649 she invited Descartes to live at her court in Stockholm, but he died a few months after moving to Sweden.

Pierre-Louis the Younger Dumesnil (1698–1781), *Christina of Sweden (1626–89) and Her Court: Detail of the Queen and René Descartes (1596–1650) at the Table.* Oil on canvas. Chateau de Versailles, France/Bridgeman Art Library

**What role did monarchs like Christina play in promoting scientific research?**

# DESCARTES AND SWIFT DEBATE THE SCIENTIFIC ENTERPRISE

Throughout the seventeenth and eighteenth century, various writers asserted that the growth of natural knowledge held the promise of improving the human situation. Others, who did not dispute the truth or correctness of the new natural knowledge, nonetheless questioned whether it could actually improve the human situation. In these two documents the French philosopher René Descartes upholds the former position while many decades later the English satirist Jonathan Swift questions the usefulness of the new natural knowledge pursued by the Royal Society of London and by implication by other European scientific academies.

## QUESTIONS

1. How does Descartes compare the usefulness of science with previous speculative philosophy?

2. What, if any, limits does he place on the extension of scientific knowledge?

3. Why might Swift have so emphasized what he saw as the impracticality of science?

4. How might Swift's presentation be seen as manifesting jealousy of a literary figure toward the growing influence of science?

5. How does Swift's passage serve as an effort to refute the promise of science championed by Bacon and Descartes?

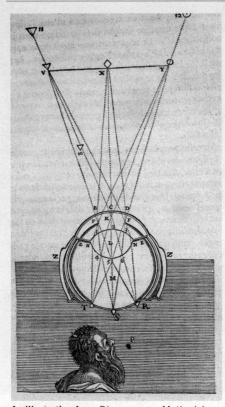

**An Illustration from** *Discourse on Method*, by René Descartes (1637).

Courtesy of the Library of Congress

**What place did mathematics have in Descartes's vision of the universe?**

## I. DESCARTES EXPLORES THE PROMISE OF EXPANDING NATURAL KNOWLEDGE

*In 1637, Descartes published his* Discourse on Method. *He wrote against what he believed to be the useless speculations of scholastic philosophy. He championed the careful investigation of physical nature on the grounds that it would expand the scope of human knowledge beyond anything previously achieved and, in doing so, make human beings the masters of nature. This passage contains much of the broad intellectual and cultural argument that led to the ever-growing influence and authority of science from the seventeenth century onward.*

My speculations were indeed truly pleasing to me; but I recognize that other men have theirs, which perhaps please them even more. As soon, however, as I had acquired some general notions regarding physics, and on beginning to make trial of them in various special difficulties had observed how far they can carry us and how much they differ from the principles hitherto employed, I believed that I could not keep them hidden without grievously sinning against the law which lays us under obligation to promote, as far as in us lies, the general good of all mankind. For they led me to see that it is possible to obtain knowledge highly useful in life, and that in place of the speculative philosophy taught in the Schools we can have a practical philosophy, by means of which, knowing the force and the actions of fire, water, air, and of the stars, of the heavens, and of all the bodies that surround us—knowing them as distinctly as we know the various crafts of the artisans—we may in the same fashion employ them in all the uses for which they are suited, thus rendering ourselves the masters and possessors of nature. This is to be desired, not only with a view to the invention of an infinity of arts by which we would be enabled to enjoy without heavy labor the fruits of the earth and all its conveniences, but above all for the preservation of health, which is, without doubt, of all blessings in this life, the first of all goods and the foundation on which the others rest. For the mind is so dependent on the temper and disposition of the bodily organisms that if any means can ever be found to render men wiser and more capable than they have hitherto been, I believe that it is in the science of medicine that the means must be sought. . . . With no wish to depreciate it, I am yet sure there is no one, even of those engaged in the profession, who does not admit that all we know is almost nothing in comparison with what remains to be discovered; and that we could be freed from innumerable maladies, both of body and of mind, and even perhaps from the infirmities of age, if we had sufficient knowledge of their causes and of the remedies provided by nature.

Source: From René Descartes, *Discourse on Method*, in *Descartes's Philosophical Writings*, ed. by Norman Kemp Smith (New York: The Modern Library, 1958), pp. 130–131. Reprinted by permission of Macmillan Press Ltd.

## II. JONATHAN SWIFT SATIRIZES SCIENTIFIC SOCIETIES

*Swift, the greatest author of English satire in the eighteenth century, was a deeply pessimistic person who thought much of the promise held forth for scientific enterprise would never be realized. In the third voyage of Gulliver's Travels, published in 1726, Swift portrays Gulliver as visiting the land of Lagardo where he encounters a learned academy filled with scholars pursuing outlandish projects. Swift lists the efforts of a whole series of Projectors, each of which is more impractical than the next. This passage in which Swift pillories the various people who hoped to receive patronage for projects from persons associated with the Royal Society of London remains one of the most famous satires of science in the English language. That Swift wrote it is a testimony to the cultural authority that science had achieved by the early eighteenth century.*

Gulliver reports a conversation he encountered while visiting Lagardo:

"The Sum of his Discourse was to this Effect. That about Forty Years ago, certain Persons went up to *Laputa*, either upon Business or Diversion; and after five Months Continuance, came back with a very little Smattering in Mathematics, but full of Volatile Spirits acquired in that Airy Region. That these Persons upon their Return, began to dislike the Management of every Thing below; and fell into Schemes of putting all Arts, Sciences, Languages, and Mechanics upon a new Foot. To this End they procured a Royal Patent for erecting an Academy of *Projectors* in *Lagado*; And the Humour prevailed so strongly among the People, that there is not a Town of any Consequence in the Kingdom without such an Academy. In these Colleges, the Professors contrive new Rules and Methods of Agriculture and Building, and new Instruments and Tools for all Trades and Manufactures, whereby, as they undertake, one Man shall do the Work of Ten; a Palace may be built in a Week, of Materials so durable as to last for ever without repairing. All the Fruits of the Earth shall come to Maturity at whatever Season we think fit to chuse; and increase an Hundred Fold more than they do at present; with innumerable other happy Proposals. The only Inconvenience is, that none of these Projects are yet brought to Perfection; and in the mean time, the whole Country lies miserably waste, the Houses in Ruins, and the People without Food or Cloaths. By all which, instead of being discouraged they are Fifty Times more violently bent upon prosecuting their Schemes, driven equally on by Hope and Depair. . . ."

Gulliver then reports what he found occurring in the rooms of an academy in Lagardo:

"The first Man I saw . . . had been Eight Years upon a Project for extracting Sun-Beams out of Cucumbers, which were to be put into Vials hermetically sealed, and let out to warm the Air in raw inclement Summers. . . .

"I saw another at work to calcine ice into Gunpowder . . .

"There was another most ingenius Architect who had contrived a new Method for building Houses, by beginning at the Roof, and working downwards to the Foundation. . . .

In another Apartment I was highly pleased with a Projector, who had found a Device of plowing the Ground with Hogs, to save the Charges of Plows, Cattle, and Labour. The Method is this: In an Acre of Ground you bury at six Inches Distance, and eight deep, a quantity of Acorns, Dates, Chesnuts, and other Masts or Vegetables whereof these Animals are fondest; then you drive six Hundred or more of them into the Field, where in a few Days they will root up the whole Ground in search of their Food, and make it fit for sowing, at the same time manuring it with their Dung. It is true, upon Experiment they found the Charge and Trouble very great, and they had little or no Crop. However, it is not doubted that this Invention may be capable of great Improvement."

Source: Jonathan Swift, *Gulliver's Travels*, Part III, chaps. iv and v (New York: The Heritage Press, 1960), pp. 193–194, 197–199.

## THOMAS HOBBES: APOLOGIST FOR ABSOLUTE GOVERNMENT

Nowhere did the impact of the methods of the new science so deeply affect political thought as in the thought of Thomas Hobbes (1588–1679), the most original political philosopher of the seventeenth century.

An urbane and much-traveled man, Hobbes enthusiastically supported the new scientific movement. During the 1630s, he visited Paris, where he came to know Descartes, and Italy, where he spent time with Galileo. He took special interest in the works of William Harvey (1578–1657), who was famous for his discovery of the circulation of blood through the body.

Hobbes had written works of political philosophy before the English Civil War, but the turmoil of that struggle led him in 1651 to publish his influential work *Leviathan*. His aim was to provide a rigorous philosophical justification for a strong central political authority. Hobbes portrayed human beings and society in a thoroughly materialistic and mechanical way. He traced all psychological processes to bare sensation and regarded all human motivations as egoistical, intended to increase pleasure and minimize pain.

According to Hobbes, human beings in their natural state are inclined to a "perpetual and restless desire" for power. Because all people want and, in their natural state, possess a natural right to everything, their equality breeds enmity, competition, diffidence, and perpetual quarreling—"a war of every man against every man." Hobbes, contrary to Aristotle and Christian thinkers like Thomas Aquinas (1225–1274), rejected the view that human beings are naturally sociable. Rather, they are self-centered creatures who lack a master. Thus, whereas earlier and later philosophers saw the original human state as a paradise from which humankind had fallen, Hobbes saw it as a state of natural, inevitable conflict in which neither safety, security, nor any final authority existed. Human beings in this state of nature were constantly haunted by fear of destruction and death.

Human beings escaped this terrible state of nature, according to Hobbes, only by entering into a particular kind of political contract according to which they agreed to live in a commonwealth tightly ruled by a recognized sovereign. This contract obliged every person, for the sake of peace and self-defense, to agree to set aside personal rights to all things and to be content with as much liberty against others as he or she would allow others against himself or herself.

Because, however, words and promises are insufficient to guarantee this agreement, the contract also established the coercive use of force by the sovereign to compel compliance. Believing the dangers of anarchy to be always greater than those of tyranny, Hobbes thought that rulers should be absolute and unlimited in their power, once established as authority. Hobbes's political philosophy has no room for protest in the name of individual conscience or for individual appeal to some other legitimate authority beyond the sovereign.

The specific structure of this absolute government was not of enormous concern to Hobbes. He believed absolute authority might be lodged in either a monarch or a legislative body, but once that person or body had been granted authority, there existed no argument for appeal. For all practical purposes, obedience to the Hobbesian sovereign was absolute.

Hobbes's argument for an absolute political authority that could assure order aroused sharp opposition. Monarchists objected to his willingness to assign sovereign authority to a legislature.

**The Famous Title Page** Illustration for Hobbes's *Leviathan*. The ruler is pictured as absolute lord of his lands, but note that the ruler incorporates the mass of individuals whose self-interests are best served by their willing consent to accept him and cooperate with him.

Courtesy of the Library of Congress

**How did Hobbes see the relationship between a monarch and his or her subjects?**

Republicans rejected his willingness to accept a monarchical authority. Many Christian writers, including those who supported the divine right of kings, furiously criticized his materialist arguments for an absolute political authority. Other Christian writers attacked his refusal to recognize the authority of either God or the church as standing beside or above his secular sovereign. The religious critique of Hobbes meant that his thought had little immediate practical impact, but his ideas influenced philosophical literature from the late seventeenth century onward.

## JOHN LOCKE: DEFENDER OF MODERATE LIBERTY AND TOLERATION

Locke (1632–1704) proved to be the most influential philosophical and political thinker of the seventeenth century. Although he was less original than Hobbes, his political writings became a major source of criticism of absolutism and provided a foundation for later liberal political philosophy in both Europe and America. His philosophical works dealing with human knowledge became the most important work of psychology for the eighteenth century.

Locke wrote two treatises on government that were eventually published in 1690. In the first of these, he rejected arguments for absolute government that based political authority on the patriarchal model of fathers ruling over a family. After the publication of this treatise, no major political philosopher again appealed to the patriarchal model. In that regard, though not widely read today, Locke's *First Treatise of Government* proved enormously important by clearing the philosophical decks, so to speak, of a long-standing traditional argument that could not stand up to rigorous analysis.

In his *Second Treatise of Government*, Locke presented an extended argument for a government that must necessarily be both responsible for and responsive to the concerns of the governed. Locke portrayed the natural human state as one of perfect freedom and equality in which everyone enjoyed, in an unregulated fashion, the natural rights of life, liberty, and property. Locke, contrary to Hobbes, regarded human beings in their natural state as creatures of reason and basic goodwill rather than of uncontrolled passion and selfishness. For Locke, human beings possess a strong capacity for dwelling more or less peacefully in society before they enter a political contract. What they experience in the state of nature is not a state of war, but a condition of competition and modest conflict that requires a political authority to sort out problems rather than to impose sovereign authority. They enter into the contract to form political society to secure and preserve the rights, liberty, and property that they already possess prior to the existence of political authority. In this respect, government exists to protect the best achievements and liberty of the state of nature, not to overcome them. Thus, by its very foundation, Locke's government is one of limited authority.

The conflict that Hobbes believed characterized the state of nature emerged for Locke only when rulers failed to preserve people's natural freedom and attempted to enslave them by absolute rule. The relationship between rulers and the governed is that of trust, and if the rulers betray that trust, the governed have the right to replace them.

In his *Letter Concerning Toleration* (1689), Locke used the premises of the as yet unpublished *Second Treatise* to defend extensive religious toleration among Christians, which he saw as an answer to the destructive religious conflict of the past two centuries. To make his case for toleration, Locke claimed that each individual was required to work out his or her own religious salvation and these efforts might lead various people to join different religious groups. For its part, government existed by its very nature to preserve property, not to make religious decisions for its citizens. Consequently, Locke urged a wide degree of religious toleration among differing voluntary Christian groups. He did not, however, extend toleration to Roman Catholics, whom he believed to have given allegiance to a foreign prince (i.e., the pope), to non-Christians, or to atheists, whom he believed could not be trusted to keep their word. Despite these limitations, Locke's *Letter Concerning Toleration* established a powerful foundation for the future extension of toleration, religious liberty, and the separation of church and state.

Finally, just as Newton had set forth laws of astronomy and gravitation, Locke hoped to elucidate the basic structures of human thought. He did so in the most immediately influential of his books, his *Essay Concerning Human Understanding* (1690), which became the major work of European psychology during the eighteenth century. There, Locke portrayed a person's mind at birth as a blank tablet whose content would be determined by sense experience. It was a reformer's psychology, which contended that the human condition could be improved by changing the environment.

Locke's view of psychology rejected the Christian understanding of original sin, yet he believed his psychology had preserved religious knowledge. He thought such knowledge came through divine revelation in Scripture and also from the conclusions that human reason could draw from observing nature. He hoped this interpretation of religious knowledge would prevent human beings from falling into what he regarded as fanaticism arising from the claims of alleged private revelations and irrationality arising from superstition. For Locke, reason and revelation were compatible and together could sustain a moderate religious faith that would avoid religious conflict.

# THE NEW INSTITUTIONS OF EXPANDING NATURAL KNOWLEDGE

**WHAT WAS** the social and political context for scientific inquiry in the seventeenth century?

One of the most fundamental features of the expansion of science was the emerging idea that *genuinely new knowledge* about nature and humankind could be discovered. The proponents of the new natural knowledge and the new philosophy sought to pursue what Bacon called the advancement of learning. New knowledge would be continuously created. This outlook required new institutions.

The expansion of natural knowledge had powerful social implications. Both the new science and the philosophical outlook associated with it opposed Scholasticism and Aristotelianism. These were not simply disembodied philosophical outlooks, but ways of approaching the world of knowledge most scholars in the universities of the day still believed in.

Not surprisingly, the advanced thinkers of the seventeenth century often criticized the universities. Some of the criticism of universities was exaggerated. Medical faculties, on the whole, welcomed the advancement of learning in their fields of study. Most of the natural philosophers had themselves received their education at universities. Moreover, however slowly new ideas might penetrate universities, the expanding world of natural knowledge would be taught to future generations. With that diffusion of science into the universities came new supporters of scientific knowledge beyond the small group of natural

**Colbert was Louis XIV's** most influential minister. He sought to expand the economic life of France and to associate the monarchy with the emerging new science from which he hoped might flow new inventions and productive technology. Here he is portrayed presenting members of the French Academy of Science to the monarch on the founding of the French Academy.

Henri Testelin (1616–1695) (after Le Brun). Minister of Finance Colbert presenting the members of the Royal Academy of Science (founded in 1667) to Louis XIV. Study for a tapestry. Photo: Gerard Blot. Chateaux de Versailles et de Triaanon, Versailles, France. Reunion des Musées Nationaux/Art Resource, NY

**What role did Colbert believe science could play in the development of the French economy?**

philosophers themselves. Universities also provided much of the physical and financial support for teaching and investigating natural philosophy and employed many scientists, the most important of whom was Newton himself.

Yet because of the reluctance of universities to rapidly assimilate the new science, its pioneers quickly understood that they required a framework for cooperating and sharing information that went beyond existing intellectual institutions. Consequently, they and their supporters established what have been termed "institutions of sharing" that allowed information and ideas associated with the new science to be gathered, exchanged, and debated. The most famous of these institutions was the Royal Society of London, founded in 1660, whose members consciously saw themselves as following the path Bacon had laid out almost a half century earlier. In addition to these major institutions, the new science was discussed and experiments were carried out in many local societies and academies.

These societies met regularly to hear papers and observe experiments. These groups also published information relating to natural philosophy and often organized libraries for their members. Perhaps most important, they attempted to separate the discussion and exploration of natural philosophy from the religious and political conflicts of the day. They intended science to exemplify an arena for the polite exchange of ideas and for civil disagreement and debate.

The activities of the societies also constituted a kind of crossroads between their own members always drawn from the literate classes, and people outside the elite classes, whose skills and practical knowledge might be important for advancing the new science. The latter included craftspeople who could manufacture scientific instruments, sailors whose travels had taken them to foreign parts and who might report on the plants and animals they had seen there, and workers who had practical knowledge of problems in the countryside.

The work, publications, and interaction of the scientific societies with both the government and private business established a distinct role and presence for scientific knowledge in European social life. By 1700, that presence was relatively modest, but it would grow steadily during the coming decades. The groups associated with the new science saw themselves as championing modern practical achievements of applied knowledge and urging religious toleration, mutual forbearance, and political liberty. Such people would form the social base for the eighteenth-century movement known as the **Enlightenment**.

**Enlightenment**   The eighteenth-century movement led by the *philosophes* that held that change and reform were both desirable through the application of reason and science.

# WOMEN IN THE WORLD OF THE SCIENTIFIC REVOLUTION

The same factors that had long excluded women from participating in most intellectual life continued to exclude them from working in the emerging natural philosophy. Traditionally, the institutions of European intellectual life had all but excluded women. Women could and did exercise influence over princely courts where natural philosophers, such as Galileo, sought patronage, but they usually did not determine those patronage decisions or benefit from them. Queen Christina of Sweden (r. 1632–1654), who brought René Descartes to Stockholm to provide the regulations for a new science academy, was an exception. When various scientific societies were founded, women were not admitted to membership. In that regard, there were virtually no social spaces that might have permitted women to pursue science easily.

**WHAT ROLE** did women play in the scientific revolution?

**Margaret Cavendish, who** wrote widely on scientific subjects, was the most accomplished woman associated with the new science in seventeenth-century England.

ImageWorks/Mary Evans Picture Library Ltd.

**What role did women play in the scientific revolution?**

Yet a few isolated women from two different social settings did manage to engage in the new scientific activity—noblewomen and women from the artisan class. In both cases, they could do so only through their husbands or male relatives.

The social standing of certain noblewomen allowed them to command the attention of ambitious natural philosophers who were part of their husband's social circle. Margaret Cavendish (1623–1673) actually made significant contributions to the scientific literature of the day. As a girl she had been privately tutored and become widely read. Her marriage to the duke of Newcastle introduced her into a circle of natural philosophers. She understood the new science, quarreled with the ideas of Descartes and Hobbes, and criticized the Royal Society for being more interested in novel scientific instruments than in solving practical problems. She was the only woman in the seventeenth century to be allowed to visit a meeting of the Royal Society of London.

Women associated with artisan crafts actually achieved greater freedom to pursue the new sciences than did noblewomen. Traditionally, women had worked in artisan workshops, often with their husbands, and might take over the business when their spouse died. In Germany, much study of astronomy occurred in these settings, with women assisting their fathers or husbands. One German female astronomer, Maria Cunitz, published a book on astronomy that many people thought her husband had written until he added a preface supporting her sole authorship. Elisabetha and Johannes Hevelius constituted a wife-and-husband astronomical team, as did Maria Winkelmann and her husband Gottfried Kirch. Winkelmann had worked jointly with her husband who was the official astronomer of the Berlin Academy of Sciences and was responsible for an official calendar the academy published. When her husband died in 1710, Winkelmann applied for permission to continue the work, basing her application for the post on the guild's tradition of allowing women to continue their husbands' work, in this case the completion of observations required to create an accurate calendar. After much debate, the academy formally rejected her application on the grounds of her gender, although its members knew of her ability and previous accomplishments. Years later, she returned to the Berlin Academy as an assistant to her son, who had been appointed astronomer. Again, the academy insisted that she leave, forcing her to abandon astronomy. She died in 1720.

Such policies of exclusion, however, did not altogether prevent women from acquiring knowledge about scientific endeavors. Margaret Cavendish had composed a *Description of a New World, Called the Blazing World* (1666) to introduce women to the new science. Other examples of scientific writings for a female audience were Bernard de Fontenelle's *Conversations on the Plurality of Worlds* and Francesco Algarotti's *Newtonianism for Ladies* (1737). During the 1730s, Emilie du Châtelet (1706–1749) aided Voltaire in his composition of an important French popularization of Newton's science. Her knowledge of mathematics was more extensive than his and crucial to his completing his book. She also translated Newton's *Principia* into French, an accomplishment made possible only by her exceptional understanding of advanced mathematics.

Still, with few exceptions, women were barred from science and medicine until the late nineteenth century, and not until the twentieth century did they enter these fields in significant numbers.

**QUICK REVIEW**

**Women and Science**

◆ Significant obstacles stood in the way of women doing scientific work

◆ A few elite women, notably Margaret Cavendish, were allowed to make contributions

◆ Women from the artisan classes had more opportunities than other women

# THE NEW SCIENCE AND RELIGIOUS FAITH

For many contemporaries, the new science posed a potential challenge to religion. Three major issues were at stake. First, certain theories and discoveries did not agree with biblical statements about the heavens. Second, who would decide conflicts between religion and science—church authorities or the natural philosophers? Finally, for many religious thinkers, the new science seemed to replace a universe of spiritual meaning and significance with a purely materialistic one.

**WHAT EFFORTS** were made to reconcile the new science and religion?

## THE CASE OF GALILEO

The condemnation of Galileo by Roman Catholic authorities in 1633 is the single most famous incident of conflict between modern science and religious institutions. The condemnation of Copernicanism and of Galileo occurred at a particularly difficult moment in the history of the Roman Catholic Church. In response to Protestant emphasis on private interpretation of Scripture, the Council of Trent (1545–1563) had stated that only the church itself possessed the authority to interpret the Bible. Furthermore, after the Council, the Roman Catholic Church had adopted a more literalist mode of reading the Bible in response to the Protestant emphasis on the authority of Scripture. Galileo's championing of Copernicanism took place in this particular climate of opinion and practice when the Roman Catholic Church, on the one hand, could not surrender the interpretation of the Bible to a layman and, on the other, had difficulty moving beyond a literal reading of the Bible, lest the Protestants accuse it of abandoning Scripture.

In a *Letter to the Grand Duchess Christina* (1615), Galileo, as a layman, had published his own views about how Scripture should be interpreted to accommodate the new science. To certain Roman Catholic authorities, his actions resembled those of a Protestant who looked to himself rather than the church to understand the Bible. In early 1616, the Roman Catholic Inquisition formally censured Copernicus's views, placing *On the Revolutions of the Heavenly Spheres* in the Index of Prohibited Books. The ground for the condemnation was Copernicus's disagreement with the literal word of the Bible and the biblical interpretations of the Church Fathers.

Galileo, who was not on trial in 1616, was formally informed of the condemnation of Copernicanism. Exactly what agreement he and the Roman Catholic authorities reached as to what he would be permitted to write about Copernicanism remains unclear. It appears that he agreed not to advocate that Copernican astronomy was actually physically true, but only to suggest that it could be true in theory.

In 1623, however, a Florentine acquaintance of Galileo's was elected as Pope Urban VIII. He gave Galileo permission to resume discussing the Copernican system, which he did in *Dialogue on the Two Chief World Systems* (1632). The book clearly was designed to defend the physical truthfulness of Copernicanism. Moreover, the voices in the dialogue favoring the older system appeared slow-witted—and those voices presented the views of Pope Urban. Feeling humiliated and betrayed, the pope ordered an investigation of Galileo's book. The actual issue in Galileo's trial of 1633 was whether he had disobeyed the mandate of 1616, and he was held to have done so even though the exact nature of that mandate was less than certain. Galileo was condemned, required to renounce his views, and placed under the equivalent of house arrest in his home near Florence for the last nine years of his life.

**Galileo Galilei.**
© Bettmann/CORBIS

## BLAISE PASCAL: REASON AND FAITH

Blaise Pascal (1623–1662), a French mathematician and a physical scientist who surrendered his wealth to pursue an austere, self-disciplined life, made one of the most influential efforts to reconcile faith and the new science. He aspired to write a work that would refute both dogmatism and skepticism. He never produced a definitive

# Overview    **Major Works of the Scientific Revolution**

| YEAR | WORK | AUTHOR |
|------|------|--------|
| **1543** | *On the Revolutions of the Heavenly Spheres* | Copernicus |
| **1605** | *The Advancement of Learning* | Bacon |
| **1609** | *The New Astronomy* | Kepler |
| **1610** | *The Starry Messenger* | Galileo |
| **1620** | *Novum Organum* | Bacon |
| **1632** | *Dialogue on the Two Chief World Systems* | Galileo |
| **1637** | *Discourse on Method* | Descartes |
| **1651** | *Leviathan* | Hobbes |
| **1687** | *Principia Mathematica* | Newton |
| **1689** | *Letter Concerning Toleration* | Locke |
| **1690** | *An Essay Concerning Human Understanding* | Locke |
| **1690** | *Treatises of Government* | Locke |

refutation of the two sides. Rather, he formulated his views on these matters in piece-meal fashion in a provocative collection of reflections on humankind and religion published posthumously under the title *Pensées (Thoughts)*.

Pascal believed that in religious matters, only the reasons of the heart and a "leap of faith" could prevail. For him, religion was not the domain of reason and science. He saw two essential truths in the Christian religion: A loving God exists, and human beings, because they are corrupt by nature, are utterly unworthy of God. He believed the atheists and the deists of his age had overestimated reason. To Pascal, reason itself was too weak to resolve the problems of human nature and destiny. Ultimately, reason should drive those who truly heeded it to faith in God and reliance on divine grace.

Pascal made a famous wager with the skeptics. It is a better bet, he argued, to believe God exists and to stake everything on his promised mercy than not to do so. This is because, if God does exist, the believer will gain everything, whereas, should God prove not to exist, comparatively little will have been lost by having believed in him.

Convinced that belief in God improved life psychologically and disciplined it morally (regardless of whether God proved in the end to exist), Pascal worked to strengthen traditional religious belief. He urged his contemporaries to seek self-understanding by "learned ignorance" and to discover humankind's greatness by recognizing its misery. He hoped thereby to counter what he believed to be the false optimism of the new rationalism and science.

## THE ENGLISH APPROACH TO SCIENCE AND RELIGION

Francis Bacon established a key framework for reconciling science and religion that long influenced the English-speaking world. He argued there were two books of divine revelation: the Bible and nature. Because both books of revelation shared the same author, they must be compatible. Whatever discord might first appear between science and religion must eventually be reconciled.

Later in the seventeenth century, with the work of Newton, the natural universe became a realm of law and regularity. Most natural philosophers were devout people who saw in the new picture of physical nature a new picture of God. The Creator of

**QUICK REVIEW**

**Blaise Pascal (1623–1662)**

- French mathematician and physical scientist
- His *Pensées (Thoughts)* was meant to refute both dogmatism and skepticism
- Believed reason could lead humans to religion, but that religion operated beyond reason

this rational, lawful nature must also be rational. To study nature was to come to a better understanding of that Creator. Science and religious faith were not only compatible, but also mutually supportive.

Finally, the new science and the technological and economic innovations associated with its culture came again, especially among English thinkers, to be interpreted as part of a divine plan. By the late seventeenth century, natural philosophy and its practical achievements had become associated in the public mind with consumption and the market economy. Scientific advance and economic enterprise came to be interpreted in the public mind as the fulfillment of God's plan: Human beings were meant to improve the world. This outlook provided a religious justification for the processes of economic improvement that would characterize much of eighteenth-century Western Europe.

# CONTINUING SUPERSTITION

Despite the great optimism among certain European thinkers associated with the new ideas in science and philosophy, traditional beliefs and fears long retained their hold on Western culture.

**WHAT EXPLAINS**
the witch hunts and panics of the sixteenth and seventeenth centuries?

## WITCH HUNTS AND PANIC

Nowhere is the dark side of early modern thought and culture more strikingly visible than in the witch hunts and panics that erupted in almost every Western land. Between 1400 and 1700, courts sentenced an estimated 70,000 to 100,000 people to death for harmful magic (*maleficium*) and diabolical witchcraft.

Why did witch panics occur in the sixteenth and early seventeenth centuries? The disruptions created by religious division and warfare were major factors. (The peak years of the religious wars were also those of the witch hunts.) Some argue that the Reformation spurred the panics by taking away the traditional defenses against the devil and demons, thus compelling societies to protect themselves preemptively by searching out and executing witches. Political consolidation by secular governments and the papacy played an even greater role, as both aggressively conformed their respective realms in an attempt to eliminate competition for the loyalty of their subjects.

## VILLAGE ORIGINS

The roots of belief in witches are found in both popular and elite culture. In village societies, feared and respected "cunning folk" helped people cope with natural disasters and disabilities by magical means. Those who were most in need of security and influence, particularly old, impoverished single or widowed women, often made claims to such magical powers. In village society witch beliefs may also have been a way to defy urban Christian society's attempts to impose its orthodox beliefs, laws, and institutions on the countryside. Under church persecution local fertility cults, whose semipagan practices were intended to ensure good harvests, acquired the features of diabolical witchcraft.

## INFLUENCE OF THE CLERGY

Popular belief in magical power was the essential foundation of the witch hunts. Had ordinary people not believed that "gifted persons" could help or harm by magical means, and had they not been willing to accuse them, the hunts would never have occurred. However, the contribution of Christian theologians was equally great. In the late thirteenth century, the Church declared its magic to be the only true magic. Since such powers were not innate to humans, the theologians reasoned, they must come either from God or from the devil. Those from God were properly exercised within and by the church. Any who practiced magic outside and against the Church did so on behalf of the devil. From such rea-

**Three witches charged** with practicing harmful magic are burned alive in Baden in southwest Germany. On the left, two of them are feasting with demons at a sabbat

Bildarchiv Preussicher Kulturbesitz

soning grew allegations of "pacts" between nonpriestly magicians and Satan. Attacking accused witches became a way for the church to extend its spiritual hegemony.

### WHO WERE THE WITCHES?

Roughly 80 percent of the victims of witch hunts were women, most single and aged over forty. Three groups of women appear especially to have drawn the witch-hunter's attention. The first was widows, who, living alone in the world after the deaths of their husbands, were often dependent on help from others, unhappy, and known to strike out. A second group was midwives, whose work made them unpopular when mothers and newborns died during childbirth. (See "Encountering the Past: Midwives.") Finally, there were women healers and herbalists, who were targeted because their work gave them a moral and spiritual authority over people whom the church wished to reserve for its priests.

### END OF THE WITCH HUNTS

Several factors helped end the witch hunts. One was the emergence of a more scientific point of view. In the seventeenth century, mind and matter came to be viewed as two independent realities, making it harder to believe that thoughts in the mind or words on the lips could alter physical things. With advances in medicine, the rise of insurance companies, and the availability of lawyers, people gained greater physical security against the physical afflictions and natural calamities that drove the witch panics. Finally, the witch hunts began to get out of hand. Tortured witches, when asked whom they saw at witches' sabbats, sometimes alleged having seen leading townspeople there, and even the judges themselves! At this point the trials ceased to serve the interests of those conducting them, becoming dysfunctional and threatening anarchy as well.

**baroque**   Naturalistic style associated with seventeenth-century painting, sculpture, and architecture that emphasized the emotional connection between art and the observer.

## BAROQUE ART

**HOW DID** baroque art serve both religious and secular ends?

Art historians use the term **baroque** to denote the style associated with seventeenth-century painting, sculpture, and architecture. Baroque painters depicted their subjects in a thoroughly naturalistic, rather than an idealized, manner. This faithfulness to nature paralleled the interest in natural knowledge associated with the rise of the new science and the deeper understanding of human anatomy that was achieved during this period. These painters, the most famous of whom was Michelangelo Caravaggio (1573–1610), also were devoted to picturing sharp contrasts between light and darkness, which created dramatic scenes in their painting. Consequently, both baroque painting and sculpture have been seen as theatrical and intending to draw the observer into an emotional involvement with the subject that is being portrayed.

The work of baroque artists served both religious and secular ends. Baroque painters, especially in Roman Catholic countries, often portrayed scenes from the Bible and from the lives of saints intended to instruct the observer in religious truths. Artists used the same style of painting, however, to present objects and scenes of everyday life in new realistic detail. Such was the case with Dutch painters of still lifes who portrayed all manner of elaborate foodstuffs as well as with artists such Louis LeNain (1593–1648) who painted scenes of French peasant life.

Baroque art became associated, rightly or wrongly, with both Roman Catholicism and absolutist politics. The style first emerged in papal Rome, where Gian Lorenzo Bernini's great Tabernacle—situated under the dome of St. Peter's basilica, above the space where St. Peter is said to be buried—is the most famous example, along with the two vast colonnades outside the church. Bernini also created the dramatic sculpture of the Spanish mystic St. Teresa of Avila (1515–1582), depicting her in religious ecstasy.

The association of baroque art with Roman Catholicism had its counterpart in the secular world. Charles I (r. 1625–1649) of England employed the Roman Catholic

**Bernini designed the** elaborate Baldacchino that stands under the dome of St. Peter's Basilica. It is one of the major examples of baroque interior decoration.

Scala/Art Resource, NY

**In what ways did baroque art reflect the values of seventeenth-century Catholicism?**

## ENCOUNTERING THE PAST

### MIDWIVES

*Although women were excluded from formal medical training until well into the nineteenth century, the delivery of children was largely left to professional women called midwives. Midwifery was a trade often pursued by elderly or widowed women of the lower social classes. They underwent years of apprenticeship but were not permitted to organize themselves into guilds. They were licensed by civil and church authorities who were invariably men. Sometimes upperclass women were appointed to supervise them.*

A reputation for respectability and discretion was essential for a midwife, for she witnessed some of life's most private moments and was privy to the intimate affairs of families. Her character was also assumed to have an effect on the outcome of a birth. A bad character was said to produce stillbirths and imperfectly formed infants. Carelessness or incompetence could, of course, void her license.

Midwives had religious and civic duties associated with births. In emergencies they could baptize failing infants. They registered births, and they were required to report to the authorities any suspicion of abortion or infanticide. A trusted midwife might also be called on to testify to a child's legitimacy.

Male physicians began to replace midwives in the eighteenth century, and civil authorities increasingly required persons who assisted at births to have a formal medical training that was not available to women. Midwives, however, never ceased to serve the poor and rural populations of Europe.

**Until well into** the eighteenth century, midwives oversaw the delivery of most children in Europe.
CORBIS

**Why were midwives viewed with suspicion by many physicians?**

WHY WAS midwifery long considered a female activity? Why did men eventually take charge of supervising the birthing process?

---

Flemish artist Peter Paul Rubens (1577–1640) to decorate the ceiling of the Banqueting Hall at his palace in London with paintings commemorating his father James I (r. 1603–1625). Charles's employment of him fed Puritan suspicions that the king harbored Roman Catholic sympathies. Consequently, it was not by coincidence that Charles I was led to his execution in 1649 through the Rubens-decorated Banqueting Hall to his death on the scaffold erected outside.

The most elaborate baroque monument to political absolutism was Louis XIV's palace at Versailles. (See Chapter 13.) Room after room was decorated with vast, dramatic paintings and murals presenting Louis as the Sun King. Monarchs across Europe, Protestant as well as Catholic, who hoped to imitate Louis's absolutism in their own domains, erected similar, if smaller, palaces filled with elaborate decoration.

# SUMMARY

## WHAT WAS the scientific revolution?

**The Scientific Revolution** What we now call "science" emerged as a field of inquiry in the seventeenth century as "natural philosophy." Copernicus, hoping to simplify Ptolemy's geocentric system, had tentatively proposed in the sixteenth century that the sun might be the center of circular planetary motion. Brahe disagreed and performed extensive observations attempting to support the geocentric model. Brahe's assistant Kepler used Brahe's data to propose, in a 1609 book, that the sun was at the center of elliptical planetary orbits. Also in 1609, Galileo was the first to study astronomy through a telescope. Galileo became a strong advocate for the heliocentric universe and popularized the idea that the universe is rational and subject to the laws of mathematics. Finally, Newton combined mathematical modeling and scientific observation to derive his famous laws of motion and theory of universal gravitation. *page 348*

## WHAT IMPACT did the new science have on philosophy?

**Philosophy Responds to Changing Science** Scientists of the seventeenth century were called natural philosophers, and there was some overlap between philosophers and natural philosophers. For this reason, and because of the challenges to traditional thinking posed by scientific work in this period, philosophers were profoundly influenced by the scientific revolution. Galileo's mathematical modeling of the physical world translated into a mechanistic worldview that was widespread among philosophers. Bacon, Descartes, Hobbes, and Locke all articulated philosophies that took aspects of the new science into account and also had implications for social and political organization. *page 351*

## WHAT WAS the social and political context for scientific inquiry in the seventeenth century?

**The New Institutions of Expanding Natural Knowledge** Through the Reformation, most intellectuals had believed their task was to recover and elaborate on knowledge from the Classical/biblical period. The expansion of natural knowledge changed universities and existing centers of learning, and it led to the creation of new "institutions of sharing."

Scientific societies encouraged new kinds of social mingling and the cross-fertilization of ideas. *page 358*

## WHAT ROLE did women play in the scientific revolution?

**Women in the World of the Scientific Revolution** European universities had offered little room for scholarship by women; the institutions of science soon turned out to be even more exclusionary. Two categories of women were occasionally able to work around these constraints: noblewomen and female artisans. Women did write important scientific works and popularizations. *page 359*

## WHAT EFFORTS were made to reconcile the new science and religion?

**The New Science and Religious Faith** The new science challenged religion in three ways: Some scientific observations contradicted biblical descriptions (e.g., of the heavens); it was unclear who should resolve any potential conflicts between science and religion, natural philosophers or church authorities; and the new philosophy's materialism seemed to some to preclude spirituality. Most natural philosophers worked hard to reconcile their work with religious views, and they were generally successful. Galileo's condemnation by the church, however, was a dramatic exception to the general rule of accommodation between science and religion. *page 361*

## WHAT EXPLAINS the witch hunts and panics of the sixteenth and seventeenth centuries?

**Continuing Superstition** Through the seventeenth century, most Europeans believed in some form of magic and in the power of demons. "Magic," in the form of transubstantiation, was indeed at the heart of Christian ritual. Although such beliefs had been present for centuries, witch hunts and panics soared in the late sixteenth and early seventeenth centuries. Possible explanations for this phenomenon include the impact of wars and upheaval, spiritual insecurity in the aftermath of the Reformation, and villagers' sublimated hostility toward urban leaders. There is also a variety of possible explanations for why witch hunts died out in the seventeenth century. *page 363*

**HOW DID** baroque art serve both religious and secular ends?

**Baroque Art** In the seventeenth century, styles of painting, sculpture, and architecture collectively known as *baroque* came to prominence across Europe. Baroque depictions were naturalistic rather than idealized and sought to involve the observer on an emotional level through dramatic portrayals and contrasts of light and darkness. Catholic baroque art and architecture aimed to instruct and impress. Secular artists depicted everyday life but also created grandiose monuments to political absolutism, such as Louis XIV's palace at Versailles. *page 364*

# REVIEW QUESTIONS

1. What contributions to the scientific revolution were made by Copernicus, Brahe, Kepler, Galileo, and Newton? Was the scientific revolution truly a revolution? Which has a greater impact on history, political or intellectual revolution?

2. How do the political philosophies of Hobbes and Locke compare? How did each view human nature? Would you rather live under a government designed by Hobbes or by Locke? Why?

3. What prevented women from playing a greater role in the development of the new science? How did family connections enable some women to contribute to the advance of natural philosophy?

4. What things account for the Church's condemnation of Galileo? How did Pascal try to reconcile faith and reason? How do you explain the fact that witchcraft and witch hunts flourished during an age of scientific enlightenment?

5. What purposes and goals did baroque painting, sculpture, and architecture serve in the religious and secular spheres?

## KEY TERMS

**baroque** (p. 364)
**empiricism** (p. 352)
**Enlightenment** (p. 359)

**Ptolemaic system** (p. 349)
**scientific revolution** (p. 348)

For additional learning resources related to this chapter, please go to **www.myhistorylab.com**

PEARSON
**myhistorylab**

# 15

# Society and Economy Under the Old Regime in the Eighteenth Century

**During the eighteenth** century farm women normally worked in the home and performed such tasks as churning butter as well as caring for children. As time passed, tasks such as making butter were mechanized and women were displaced from such work.

Francis Wheatley (RA) (1747–1801), *Morning*, signed and dated 1799, oil on canvas, 17½ × 21½ in. (44.5 × 54.5 cm), Yale Center for British Art, Paul Mellon Collection, USA/Bridgeman Art Library (B1977.14.120)

**What role did women play in the family economy?**

**Academy**   School founded by Plato in Athens to train statesmen and citizens.

**Acropolis**   At the center of the city of Athens, the most famous example of a citadel.

**Act of Supremacy**   Act of 1534 proclaiming Henry VIII "the only supreme head on earth of the Church of England."

*agape*   Common meal, or "love feast," that was the central ritual of the church in early Christianity.

*agora*   Place for markets and political assemblies.

**Ahura Mazda**   The chief deity of Zoroastrianism, the native religion of Persia. Ahura Mazda is the creator of the world, the source of light, and the embodiment of good.

**Albigensians**   Heretical sect that advocated a simple, pious way of life following the example set by Jesus and the Apostles, but rejecting key Christian doctrines.

**Anabaptists**   ("rebaptizers") The most important of several groups of Protestants forming more radical organizations that sought a more rapid and thorough restoration of the "primitive Christianity" described in the New Testament.

**anarchists**   Those who opposed any cooperation with industry or government.

*Anschluss*   Union of Germany and Austria.

**anti-Semitism**   Prejudice against Jews often displayed through hostility.

**apartheid**   (a-PAR-tid) An official policy of segregation, assignment of peoples to distinct regions, and other forms of social, political, and economic discrimination based on race associated primarily with South Africa.

**appeasement**   Allied policy of making concessions to Germany based on the belief that Germany's grievances were real and Hitler's goals limited.

**Aramaic**   Semitic language spoken widely throughout the Middle East in antiquity.

**Areopagus**   Council heading Athens's government comprised of a group of nobles that annually chose the city's nine *archons*, the magistrates who administered the *polis*.

*arete*   The highest virtue in Homeric society: the manliness, courage, and excellence that equipped a hero to acquire and defend honor.

**Arianism**   Belief that Christ was the first of God the Father's creations and the being through whom the Father created all other things.

**aristocratic resurgence**   Eighteenth-century resurgence of nobles that mantained the exclusiveness of noble rank, made it difficult to obtain, reserved powerful posts to nobles, and protected nobles from taxation.

**Attica**   Region (about 1,000 square miles) that Athens dominated.

**Augsburg Confession**   Moderate Protestant creed endorsed by the Schmalkaldic League (a defensive alliance of Lutherans).

**Augustus**   ("revered") Name by which the Senate hailed Octavian for his restoration of the republic.

**Avignon Papacy**   Period from 1309 to 1377 when the papal court was situated in Avignon, France, and gained a reputation for greed and worldly corruption.

**Axis**   Forces (opposed to the Allies) joined together in Europe, including Germany and Italy, before and during World War II.

**banalities**   Monopolies maintained by landowners giving them the right to demand that tenants pay to grind all their grain in the landowner's mill and bake all their bread in his oven.

**baroque**   Artistic and architectural styles that were naturalistic rather than idealized to involve observer on an emotional level through dramatic portrayals.

**Beguines**   Sisterhoods of pious, self-supporting single women.

**Black Death**   Virulent plague that struck in Sicily in 1347 and spread through Europe. It discolored the bodies of its victims. By the early fifteenth century, the plague may have reduced the population of Western Europe by two-fifths.

**Bolsheviks**   ("majority") Lenin's turn-of-the-century Russian faction favoring a party of elite professionals who would provide the working class with centralized leadership.

**boyars**   Wealthy landowners among the freemen in late medieval Russia.

**Brezhnev Doctrine**   Asserted the right of the Soviet Union to intervene in domestic politics of communist countries.

**Bronze Age**   (3100–1200 B.C.E.) Began with the increasing importance of metal that also ended the Stone Ages.

**Caesaropapism**   Emperor acting as if he were pope as well as caesar.

**caliphate**   Office of the leader of the Muslim community.

**categorical imperative**   Kant's view that all human beings possess an innate sense of moral duty, an inner command to act in every situation as one would have other people act in that same situation.

**catholic**   ("universal") As in "universal" majority of Christians.

**censors**   Men of unimpeachable reputation, chosen to carry the responsibility for enrolling, keeping track of, and determining the status and tax liability of each citizen.

**Chartism**   The London Working Men's Association's 1838 proposal for political reform featuring the Six Points.

**Christian democratic parties**   Post–World War II parties that welcomed non-Catholic members and fought for democracy, social reform, and economic growth.

**civilization**   Stage in the evolution of organized society that has among its characteristics urbanism, long-distance trade, writing systems, and accelerated technological and social development.

**civilizing mission**   The concept that Western nations could bring advanced science and economic development to non-Western parts of the world that justified imperial administration.

**clientage**   The custom in ancient Rome whereby men became supporters of more powerful men in return for legal and physical protection and economic benefits.

**Cold War**   Period between the end of World War II (1945) and the collapse of the Soviet Union (1991) in which U.S. and Soviet relations were tense, seemingly moments away from actual war at any time during these years.

**collectivization**   The bedrock of Stalinist agriculture, which forced Russian peasants to give up their private farms and work as members of collectives, large agricultural units controlled by the state.

*coloni*   Tenant farmers who were bound to the lands they worked.

**concentration camps** Camps first established by Great Britain in South Africa during the Boer War to incarcerate noncombatant civilians; later, camps established for political prisoners and other persons deemed dangerous to the state in the Soviet Union and Nazi Germany. The term is now primarily associated with the camps established by the Nazis during the Holocaust.

*condottieri* Military brokers from whom one could hire a mercenary army.

**Congregationalists** The more extreme Puritans who believed every congregation ought to be autonomous, a law unto itself controlled by neither bishops nor presbyterian assemblies.

*conquistadores* "Conquerors."

**conservatism** Form of political thought that, in mid-nineteenth-century Europe, promoted legitimate monarchies, landed aristocracies, and established churches.

**Consulate** A republican facade for one-man government by Napoleon.

**consuls** Elected magistrates from patrician families chosen annually to lead the army, oversee the state religion, and sit as judges.

**containment** American foreign policy strategy (beginning in 1947) for countering the communist threat and resisting the spread of Soviet influence.

**Convention** The newly elected French body that met on September 21, 1792, whose first act was to declare France a republic—a nation governed by an elected assembly without a king.

**Counter-Reformation** A reorganization of the Catholic Church that equipped it to meet the challenges posed by the Protestant Reformation.

**Creole** Merchants, landowners, and professional people of Spanish descent.

**Crusades** Campaigns authorized by the church to combat heresies and rival faiths.

**cubism** Autonomous realm of art with no purpose beyond itself. Includes as many different perspectives, angles, or views of the object as possible.

**culture** Way of life invented by a group and passed on by teaching.

**cuneiform** Developed by the Sumerians as the very first writing system ever used, it used several thousand characters, some of which stood for words and some for sounds.

**deism** The *philosophes'* theology. A rational religion, a faith without fanaticism and intolerance that acknowledged the sovereign authority of reason.

**Delian League** Pact joined in 478 B.C.E. by Athenians and other Greeks to continue the war with Persia.

*détente* Relaxation of tensions between the United States and Soviet Union that involved increased trade and reduced deployment of strategic arms.

**"divine right of kings"** The belief that God appoints kings and that kings are accountable only to God for how they use their power.

**domestic system of textile production** Means by which urban merchants obtained their wares. They bought wool or other unfinished fiber for distribution to peasant workers who took it home, spun it into thread, wove it into cloth, and returned the finished product to the merchants for sale.

*Duce* (DO-chay) Meaning "leader." Mussolini's title as head of the Fascist Party.

**ego** Among Freud's three entities of the mind, the *ego* mediates between the impulsive id and the self-denying superego.

*émigrés* French aristocrats and enemies of the revolution who fled to countries on France's borders and set up bases for counterrevolutionary activities.

**empiricism** The use of experiment and observation derived from sensory evidence to construct scientific theory or philosophy of knowledge.

*encomienda* Legal grant of the right to the labor of a specific number of Indians for a particular period of time. This was used as a Spanish strategy for exploiting the labor of the natives.

**Enlightenment** The eighteenth-century movement led by the *philosophes* that held that change and reform were both desirable through the application of reason and science.

**Epicureans** People who believed the proper pursuit of humankind is undisturbed withdrawal from the world.

**equestrians** Men rich enough to qualify for cavalry service.

**Estates General** Assembly of representatives from France's propertied classes.

**Etruscans** A people of central Italy who exerted the most powerful external influence on the early Romans. Etruscan kings ruled Rome until 509 B.C.E.

**Eucharist** ("thanksgiving") Celebration of the Lord's Supper in which bread and wine were blessed and consumed.

**euro** Launched in 1999 by the EU, a single currency circulating in most of Western Europe.

**European Constitution** Treaty that would transfer considerable decision-making authority from governments of the individual states to the European Union's central institutions.

**European Economic Community (EEC)** European nations as members of the "Common Market" pledging to eliminate tariffs, guarantee unimpeded flow of capital and labor, and establish uniform wage scales and social benefits.

**European Union (EU)** Formerly the European Economic Community (EEC), renamed in 1993.

**existentialism** Maintains that the human condition is greater than the sum of its parts and can only be grouped as whole.

**fascism** System of extreme right-wing dictatorial government.

**fiefs** ("lands") Granted to cavalry men to fund their equipment and service.

**Fourteen Points** President Woodrow Wilson's idealistic principles articulated as America's goals in World War I, including self-determination for nationalities, open diplomacy, freedom of the seas, disarmament, and establishment of a league of nations to keep the peace.

*Fronde* Widespread rebellions in France between 1649 and 1652 (named after a slingshot used by street ruffians) aimed at reversing the drift toward absolute monarchy and preserving local autonomy.

*Führer* (FYOOR-er) Meaning "leader." The title taken by Hitler when he became dictator of Germany.

**Gallican Liberties** The French Roman Catholic Church's ecclesiastical independence of papal authority in Rome.

**Gaul** Area that is now modern France.

**ghettos** Separate districts in cities and entire villages in the countryside where Jews lived apart from Christians in eighteenth-century Europe.

*glasnost* ("openness") Gorbachev's policy of opening the way for unprecedented public discussion and criticism of Soviet history and the Communist Party. Censorship was relaxed and dissidents were released from prison.

**"Glorious Revolution"** Parliament's bloodless 1688 declaration of a vacant throne and proclamation that William and Mary were its heirs.

**Golden Bull** Arrangements agreed to by the Holy Roman Emperor and the major German territorial rulers in 1356 that helped stabilize Germany.

**Great Depression** A prolonged worldwide economic downturn that began in 1929 with the collapse of the New York Stock Exchange.

**Great Purges** The arrests, trials, Communist Party expulsions, and executions—beginning with the assassination of Politburo member Sergei Kirov in December 1934—that mainly targeted Party officials and reached its climax from 1936 to 1938.

**Great Trek** The migration by Boer (Dutch) farmers during the 1830s and 1840s from regions around Cape Town into the eastern and northeastern regions of South Africa that ultimately resulted in the founding of the Orange Free State and Transvaal.

**Green movement** Made up, in part, of members from the radical student groups of the 1960s, this movement was anticapitalistic, peace oriented, in opposition of nuclear arms, and condemned business for producing pollution. Unlike earlier student groups, though, the Greens opted to compete in the electoral process.

**guild** An association of merchants or craftsmen that offered protection to its members and set rules for their work and products.

*hacienda* Large landed estate that characterized most Spanish colonies.

*Hegira* Forced flight of Muhammad and his followers to Medina, 240 miles north of Mecca. This event marks the beginning of the Islamic calendar.

**Hellenistic** Term that describes the cosmopolitan civilization, established under the Macedonians, that combined aspects of Greek and Middle Eastern cultures.

**Helots** Slaves to the Spartans that revolted and nearly destroyed Sparta in 650 B.C.E.

**heretics** "Takers" of contrary positions, namely in Christianity.

**hieroglyphs** ("sacred carving") Greek name for Egyptian writing. The writing was often used to engrave holy texts on monuments.

**Holocaust** The Nazi extermination of millions of European Jews between 1940 and 1945. Also called the "final solution to the Jewish problem."

**Holy Roman Empire** The domain of the German monarchs who revived the use of the Roman imperial title during the Middle Ages.

**home rule** Government of a country or locality by its own citizens.

*hoplite* A true infantry soldier who began to dominate the battlefield in the late eighth century B.C.E.

*Homo sapiens* Our own species, which dates back roughly 200,000 years.

*hubris* Arrogance produced by excessive wealth or good fortune.

**Huguenots** French Protestants, named after Besançon Hugues, the leader of the revolt that won Geneva its freedom at that time.

*humanitas* Wide-ranging intellectual curiosity and habits of critical thinking that are the goals of liberal education.

**iconoclasm** Opposition to the use of images in Christian worship.

**id** Among Freud's three entities of the mind, the *id* consists of innate, amoral, irrational drives for sexual gratification, aggression, and sensual pleasure.

*Iliad* Homer's poem narrates a dispute between Agamemnon the king and his warrior Achilles, whose honor is wounded and then avenged.

*imperator* "Commander in chief."

**imperialism** The extension of a nation's authority over other nations or areas through conquest or political or economic hegemony.

**Imperialism of Free Trade** The advance of European economic and political interests in the nineteenth century by demanding that non-European nations allow European nations, most particularly Great Britain, to introduce their manufactured goods freely into all nations or to introduce other goods, such as opium into China, that allowed these nations to establish economic influence and to determine the terms of trade.

*imperium* Right held by a Roman king to enforce commands by fines, arrests, and corporal and capital punishment.

**impressionism** Focuses on social life and leisured activities of the urban middle and lower-middle classes; a fascination with light, color, and representation of momentary experience of social life or of landscape.

**indulgence** Remission of the obligation to perform a "work of satisfaction" for a sin.

**Industrial Revolution** Term coined by early-nineteenth-century observers to describe the changes that the spreading use of powered machinery made in society and economics.

**Inquisition** Formal ecclesiastical court dedicated to discovering and punishing heresy.

**Intolerable Acts** Series of laws passed by Parliament in 1774 that closed the port of Boston, reorganized the government of Massachusetts, quartered soldiers in private homes, and transferred trials of customs officials accused of crimes to England.

**Ionia** Western coast of Asia Minor.

**Islam** New religion appearing in Arabia in the sixth century in response to the work of the Prophet Muhammad.

**Jacobins** The best organized of the political clubs, they embraced the most radical of the Enlightenment's political theories, and they wanted a republic, not a constitutional monarchy.

**Jacquerie** (From "Jacques Bonhomme," a peasant caricature) Name given to the series of bloody rebellions that desperate French peasants waged beginning in 1358.

**Jansenism** Appearing in the 1630s, it followed the teachings of St. Augustine, who stressed the role divine grace played in human salvation.

*jihad* A struggle; interpreted as a call for religious war.

**Junkers** (Prussian nobles) They were allowed to demand absolute obedience from the serfs on their estates in exchange for their support of the Hohenzollerns.

*jus gentium* Law of all peoples as opposed to the law that reflected only Roman practice.

*jus naturale* Law of nature that enshrined the principles of divine reason that Cicero and the Stoics believed governed the universe.

**Ka'ba** One of Arabia's holiest shrines located in Mecca, the birthplace of Muhammad.

**Keynesian economics** Economic theories and programs ascribed to John M. Keynes and his followers advocating government monetary and fiscal policies that increase employment and spending.

*Kristallnacht* (KRIS-tahl-NAHKT) Meaning "crystal night" because of the broken glass that littered German streets after the looting and destruction of Jewish homes, businesses, and synagogues across Germany on the orders of the Nazi Party in November 1938.

*Kulturkampf* ("cultural struggle") An extreme church-state conflict waged by Bismarck in Germany during the 1870s in response to a perceived threat to German political unity from the Roman Catholic Church.

**laissez-faire** Policy of noninterference, especially the policy of government noninterference in economic affairs or business.

*latifundia* Great estates that produced capital-intensive cash crops for the international market.

**Latium** Region located in present-day Italy that included the small town of Rome.

*Lebensraum* German for "living space."

*levée en masse* Order for total military mobilization of both men and property.

**liberal arts** The medieval university program that consisted of the *trivium* (TRI-vee-um): grammar, rhetoric, and logic, and the *quadrivium* (qua-DRI-vee-um): arithmetic, geometry, astronomy, and music.

**Lower Egypt** The Nile's one-hundred-mile deep, triangularly shaped delta.

**Luftwaffe** The German air force.

**Lyceum** School founded by Aristotle in Athens that focused on the gathering and analysis of data from all fields of knowledge.

**Magna Carta** ("Great Charter") Document spelling out limitations on royal authority agreed to by John in 1215. It created foundation for modern English law.

**mandate** Territory under the aegis of the League of Nations but actually ruled as a colony.

**mannerism** Reaction against the simplicity, symmetry, and idealism of High Renaissance art. It made room for the strange, even the abnormal, and gave free reign to the subjectivity of the artist. The name reflects a tendency by artists to employ "mannered" ("affected") techniques—distortions that expressed individual perceptions and feelings.

**manor** A self-sufficient rural community that was a fundamental institution of medieval life.

**Marshall Plan** The U.S. European Recovery Program introduced by George C. Marshall, American secretary of state, whereby America provided extensive economic aid to the European states, conditional only on their working together for their mutual benefit.

**Marxism** Socialist movement begun by Karl Marx in the mid–nineteenth century that differed from competing socialist views primarily in its claim to a scientific foundation and in its insistence on reform through revolution.

*Mein Kampf* (*My Struggle*) Strategy dictated by Adolf Hitler during his period of imprisonment in 1923 outlining his political views.

**Mensheviks** ("minority") Turn-of-the-century Russian faction that wanted to create a party with a large mass membership (like Germany's SPD).

**mercantilism** Economic theory in which governments heavily regulated trade and promoted empires in order to increase national wealth.

**Methodism** Movement begun in England by John Wesley, an Oxford-educated Anglican priest, the first major religion to embody romanticism. It emphasized religion as a "method" for living more than a set of doctrines.

**millets** Communities of the officially recognized religions that governed portions of the Ottoman Empire.

**Minoan** Civilization of Crete (2100–1150 B.C.E.), and the Aegean's first civilization, named for a legendary king on the island.

**modernism** Movement of the 1870s criticizing middle-class society and traditional morality.

**Monophysites** Believers in a single, immortal nature of Christ; not both eternal God and mortal man in one and the same person.

**monotheism** Having faith in a single God.

**Mycenaean** Civilization occupying mainland Greece during the Late Helladic era (1580–1150 B.C.E.).

**nationalism** The belief that the people who share an ethnic identity (language, culture, and history) should also be recognized as having a right to a government and political identity of their own.

**NATO** North Atlantic Treaty Organization, a mutual defense pact.

**natural selection** Darwin and Wallace's theory that those species with a unique trait that gives them a marginal advantage in the struggle for existence change the nature of their species by reproducing more successfully than their competitors; the fittest survive to pass on their unique characteristics.

**naturalists** Authors who tried to portray nature and human life without sentimentality.

**Nazis** Members of the National Socialist German Workers' Party that formed in 1920 and supported a mythical Aryan race alleged to be the source of the purest German lineage.

**neo-Gothic** Style that idealized nature and portrayed it in all its power.

**neoclassicism** Style that embodied a return to figurative and architectural models drawn from the Renaissance and the ancient world.

**Neolithic** "New Stone" Age, dating back 10,000 years to when people living in some parts of the Middle East made advances in the production of stone tools and shifted from hunting and gathering to agriculture.

**New Economic Policy (NEP)** A limited revival of capitalism, especially in light industry and agriculture, introduced by Lenin in 1921 to repair the damage inflicted on the Russian economy by the Civil War and war communism.

**New Imperialism** The extension in the late nineteenth and early twentieth centuries of Western political and economic dominance to Asia, the Middle East, and Africa.

**nomes** Egyptian districts ruled by regional governors who were called nomarchs.

*Odyssey* Homer's epic poem that tells of the wanderings of the hero Odysseus.

*oikos* The Greek household, always headed by a male.

**Old Regime** Eighteenth-century era marked by absolutist monarchies, agrarian economies, tradition, hierarchy, corporateness, and privilege.

*optimates* ("the best men") Opponents of Tiberius and defenders of the traditional prerogatives of the Senate.

**orthodox** ("correct") As in "correct" faith in Christianity.

**Ottoman Empire** The authority Istanbul's Ottoman Turkish sultan exercised over the Balkans, the Middle East, and North Africa from the end of the Middle Ages to World War I.

**Paleolithic** Greek for "old stone"; the earliest period in cultural development that began with the first use of stone tools about a million years ago and continued until about 10,000 B.C.E.

**Panhellenic (All Greek)** Sense of cultural identity that all Greeks felt in common with one other.

**papal infallibility** Assertion that the pope's pronouncements on matters of faith and morals could not be questioned.

**Papal States** Central part of Italy where Pope Stephen II became the secular ruler when confirmed by the Franks in 755.

*parlements* Regional courts allowed considerable latitude by Louis XIV to deal with local issues.

**parliamentary monarchy** English rule by a monarch with some parliamentary guidance or input.

**patricians** Upper class of Roman families that originally monopolized all political authority. Only they could serve as priests, senators, and magistrates.

**Peloponnesian Wars** Series of wars between Athens and Sparta beginning in 460 B.C.E.

**Peloponnesus** Southern half of the Greek peninsula.

*perestroika* ("restructuring") Means by which Gorbachev wished to raise his country's standard of living.

*petite bourgeoisie* New lower-middle class made up of white-collar workers such as secretaries, retail clerks, and lower-level bureaucrats.

**phalanx** Tight military formation of men eight or more ranks deep.

**pharaoh** The god-kings of ancient Egypt.

**Pharisee** Member of a Jewish sect known for strict adherence to the Jewish law.

**Phoenicians** Seafaring people (Canaanites and Syrians) who scattered trading colonies from one end of the Mediterranean to the other.

**plebeians** Commoner class of Roman families, usually families of small farmers, laborers, and artisans who were early clients of the patricians.

**political absolutism** Government by a ruler with absolute authority.

*politique* Ruler or person in a position of power who puts the success and well-being of his or her state above all else.

**polytheists** Name given those who workship many gods and/or goddesses.

**Popular Front** A government of all left-wing parties that took power in France in 1936 to enact social and economic reforms.

*populares* Politicians who followed Tiberius's example of politics and governing.

**positivism** Comte's philosophy that all knowledge should be the kind of knowledge common to the physical sciences.

**postimpressionism** Focuses more on form and structure to bring painting of modern life back in touch with earlier artistic traditions.

**Pragmatic Sanction** Document recognizing Charles VI's daughter Maria Theresa as his heir.

**Presbyterians** Puritans who favored a national church of semiautonomous congregations governed by representative presbyteries.

**proconsulships** Extension of terms for consuls who had important work to finish.

**protectorate** A non-Western territory administered by a Western nation without formal conquest or annexation, usually a de facto colony.

**Ptolemaic system** Astronomical theory, named after Greek astronomer Ptolemy, that assumed Earth was the center point of a ball-shaped universe composed of concentric layers of rotating crystalline spheres to which the heavenly bodies were attached.

**Puritans** English Protestants who wanted simpler forms of church ceremony and strictness and gravity in personal behavior.

**Qur'an** Sacred book comprised of a collection of the revealed texts that God had chosen Muhammad to convey.

**racism** Belief that some peoples are innately superior to others.

**realists** Authors who tried to describe human behavior with scientific objectivity, rejecting the Romantic idealization of nature, poverty, love, and polite society, and portraying the hypocrisy, physical and psychic brutality, and the dullness that underlay bourgeois life.

**regular clergy** Those clergy living under a *regula*, the rule of a monastic order.

*Reichstag* (RIKES-stahg) The German parliament, which existed in various forms, until 1945.

**Reign of Terror** Extreme measures employed by the French government in an effort to protect the revolution.

**rococo** Style that embraced lavish, often lighthearted decoration with an emphasis on pastel colors and the play of light.

**romanticism** Reaction against the rationalism and scientism of the Enlightenment, insisting on the importance of human feelings, intuition, and imagination as supplements for reason in the human quest to understand the world.

**SA** The Nazi parliamentary forces, or storm troopers.

*sans-culottes* Parisians (shopkeepers, artisans, wage earners, and factory workers who had been ignored by the Old Regime) who, along with radical Jacobins, began the second revolution in France.

**Scholasticism** Method of study associated with the medieval university.

**scientific revolution** The emergence in the sixteenth century of rational and empirical methods of research that challenged traditional thought and promoted the rise of science and technology.

**second Industrial Revolution**   Started after 1850, it expanded the production of steel, chemicals, electricity, and oil.

**secular clergy**   Clergy, such as bishops and priests, who lived and worked among the laity in the *saeculum* ("world").

**Sejm**   Central legislative body to which the Polish nobles belonged.

**September Massacres**   The execution ordered by the Paris Commune of approximately 1,200 aristocrats, priests, and common criminals who, because they were being held in city jails, were assumed to be counterrevolutionaries.

**serf**   Peasant bound to the land he worked.

**Shi'a**   The "party" of Ali. They believed Ali and his descendants were Muhammad's only rightful successors.

**social Darwinism**   Spencer's argument (coming close to claiming that might makes right) used to justify neglect of the poor and the working class, exploitation of colonial peoples, and aggressive competition among nations.

**socialist realism**   Doctrine of Soviet art and literature that sought to create figurative, traditional, optimistic, and easily intelligible scenes of a bold socialist future of prosperity and solidarity.

**Sophists**   Professional teachers who emerged in Greece in the mid–fifth century B.C.E. who were paid to teach techniques of rhetoric, dialectic, and argumentation.

**spheres of influence**   A region, city, or territory where a non-Western nation exercised informal administrative influence through economic, diplomatic, or military advisers.

**spinning jenny**   Invented by James Hargreaves in 1765, this machine spun sixteen spindles of thread simultaneously.

**SS**   The chief security units of the Nazi state.

**Stoics**   People who sought freedom from passion and harmony with nature.

*studia humanitas* **(humanism)**   Scholarship of the Renaissance that championed the study of Latin and Greek classics and Christian church fathers as an end in itself and as a guide to reforming society. Some claim it is an un-Christian philosophy emphasizing human dignity, individualism, and secular values.

*Sturm und Drang*   ("Storm and Stress") Movement in German romantic literature that emphasized feeling and emotion.

**suffragettes**   Derisive name for members of the Women's Social and Political Union, who lobbied for votes for women.

*Sunnis*   Followers of the *sunna*, "tradition." They emphasize loyalty to the fundamental principles of Islam.

**superego**   Among Freud's three entities of the mind, the *superego* internalizes the moral imperatives that society and culture impose on the personality.

*symposium*   A men's drinking party at the center of aristocratic social life in archaic Greece.

**Table of Ranks**   Issued by Peter the Great to draw nobles into state service, it made rank in the bureaucracy or military, not lineage, the determinant of an individual's social status.

**tabula rasa**   (a blank page) John Locke's *An Essay Concerning Human Understanding* (1690) theorized that at birth the human mind is a tabula rasa.

*taille*   The direct tax on the French peasantry.

**ten lost tribes**   Israelites who were scattered and lost to history when the northern kingdom of Israel fell to the Assyrians in 722 B.C.E.

**tetrarchy**   Coalition of four men, each of whom was responsible for a different part of the empire, established by Diocletian.

**Thermidorian Reaction**   Tempering of revolutionary fervor that led to the establishment of a new constitutional regime.

**Third Estate**   Members of the commercial and professional middle classes, or everyone but the clergy (the First Estate) and the nobility (the Second Estate).

**Third Reich**   Hitler's regime of Nazis.

**three-field system**   Developed by medieval farmers, a system in which three fields were utilized during different growing seasons to limit the amount of nonproductive plowing and to restore soil fertility through crop rotation.

**transistor**   Miniaturized electronics circuitry making the vacuum tube obsolete.

**transubstantiation**   Christian doctrine which holds that, at the moment of priestly consecration, the bread and wine of the Lord's Supper become the body and blood of Christ.

**tribunes**   Officials elected by the plebeian tribal assembly given the power to protect plebeians from abuse by patrician magistrates.

*ulema*   ("Persons with correct knowledge") Scholarly elite leading Islam.

**Upper Egypt**   Narrow valley extending 650 miles from Aswan to the border of Lower Egypt.

**utilitarianism**   Maintained that people should always pursue the course that promotes the greatest happiness for the greatest number.

**utopian socialists**   Early critics of industrialism whose visionary programs often involved plans to establish ideal societies based on noncapitalistic values.

**vassal**   A person granted an estate or cash payments in return for rendering services to a lord.

**Vulgate**   Latin translation of the Bible that became the standard text for the Catholic Church.

**War Communism**   The economic policy adopted by the Bolsheviks during the Russian Civil War to seize the banks, heavy industry, railroads, and grain.

**Warsaw Pact**   Mutual defense agreement among Albania, Bulgaria, Czechoslovakia, East Germany, Hungary, Poland, Romania, and the Soviet Union.

**water frame**   Invented in 1769 by Richard Arkwright, this water-powered device produced a 100 percent cotton fabric rather than the standard earlier blend of cotton and linen.

**Weimar Republic**   German republic that came to power in 1918 embodying the hopes of German liberals.

**Zionism**   Movement based on the theory that if Jews were unacceptable as citizens of European nations, their only safety lay in establishing a nation of their own.

## Chapter 1

C. ALDRED, *The Egyptians* (1998). Probably the best one-volume history of the subject.

P. BRIANT, *From Cyrus to Alexander: A History of the Persian Empire* (2002). A scholarly account of ancient Persia with greater knowledge of the Persian evidence than is usual.

T. BRYCE, *The Kingdom of the Hittites* (1998). A fine new account.

M. EHRENBERG, *Women in Prehistory* (1989). Discusses the role of women in early times.

B. M. FAGAN, *People of the Earth: An Introduction to World Prehistory*, 11th ed. (2003). A narrative account of human prehistory up to the earliest civilizations.

W. W. HALLO AND W. K. SIMPSON, *The Ancient Near East: A History*, rev. ed. (1998). A fine survey of Egyptian and Mesopotamian history.

A. KAMM, *The Israelites: An Introduction* (1999). A brief, excellent, and accessible account.

R. MATTHEWS, *Archaeology of Mesopotamia: Theories and Approaches* (2003). A fascinating investigation of the theories, methods, approaches, and history of Mesopotamian archaeology from its origins in the nineteenth century up to the present day.

J. B. PRITCHARD, ED., *Ancient Near Eastern Texts Relating to the Old Testament* (1969). A good collection of documents in translation with useful introductory material.

R. RUDGLEY, *The Lost Civilizations of the Stone Age* (1999). A bold new interpretation that claims that many elements of civilization were already present in the Stone Age.

H. W. F. SAGGS, *Babylonians* (1995). A general account of ancient Mesopotamia by an expert scholar.

I. SHAW, ED., *The Oxford History of Ancient Egypt* (2000). An up-to-date survey by leading scholars.

W. K. SIMPSON ET AL., *The Literature of Ancient Egypt: An Anthology of Stories, Instructions, Stelae, Autobiographies, and Poetry* (2003). A fine collection of writings from ancient Egypt.

D. C. SNELL, *Life in the Ancient Near East, 3100–332 B.C.E.* (1997). A social history with emphasis on culture and daily life.

## Chapter 2

E. K. ANHALT, *Solon the Singer* (1993). A fine study of the Athenian poet-politician.

W. BURKERT, *The Orientalizing Revolution: Near Eastern Influence on Greek Culture in the Early Archaic Age* (1992). A study of the Eastern impact on Greek literature and religion from 750 to 650 B.C.E.

J. CHADWICK, *The Mycenaean World* (1976). A readable account by an author who helped decipher Mycenaean writing.

R. DREWS, *The Coming of the Greeks* (1988). A fine study of the arrival of the Greeks as part of the movement of Indo-European peoples.

J. V. A. FINE, *The Ancient Greeks* (1983). An excellent survey that discusses historical problems and the evidence that gives rise to them.

M. I. FINLEY, *World of Odysseus*, rev. ed. (1965). A fascinating attempt to reconstruct Homeric society.

V. D. HANSON, *The Other Greeks* (1995). A revolutionary account of the invention of the family farm by the Greeks and the central role of agrarianism in shaping the Greek city-state.

V. D. HANSON, *The Western Way of War* (1989). A brilliant and lively discussion of the rise and character of the *hoplite* phalanx and its influence on Greek society.

J. M. HURWIT, *The Art and Culture of Early Greece* (1985). A fascinating study of the art of early Greece in its literary and cultural context.

W. K. LACEY, *The Family in Ancient Greece* (1984). A valuable survey of family life in ancient Greece.

P. B. MANVILLE, *The Origins of Citizenship in Ancient Athens* (1990). An examination of the origins of citizenship in the time of Solon of Athens.

J. F. McGLEW, *Tyranny and Political Culture in Ancient Greece* (1993). A study of tyranny and its effect on Greek political tradition.

S. G. MILLER, *Ancient Greek Athletics* (2004). The best available account.

R. OSBORNE, *Greece in the Making, 1200–479 B.C.* (1996). An up-to-date, well-illustrated account of early Greek history.

S. PRICE, *Religions of the Ancient Greeks* (1999). A valuable survey from early times through the fifth century B.C.E.

R. SALLARES, *The Ecology of the Ancient Greek World* (1991). A valuable study of the Greeks and their environment.

D. M. SCHAPS, *Economic Rights of Women in Ancient Greece* (1981). Exploration of the economic conditions of ordinary free Greek women.

B. STRAUSS, *The Battle of Salamis: The Naval Encounter That Saved Greece—and Western Civilization* (2004). A lively account of the great Persian invasion of Greece.

C. G. THOMAS AND C. CONANT, *Citadel to City-State: The Transformation of Greece, 1200–700 B.C.E.* (1999). A good account of Greece's emergence from the Dark Ages into the world of the *polis*.

H. VAN WEES, *Greek Warfare: Myths and Realities* (2004). An account of Greek fighting that challenges traditional understandings.

## Chapter 3

J. BUCKLER, *Aegean Greece in the Fourth Century BC* (2003). A political, diplomatic, and military history of the Aegean Greeks of the fourth century B.C.E.

W. BURKERT, *Greek Religion* (1985). A fine general study.

P. CARTLEDGE, *Alexander the Great: The Hunt for a New Past* (2004). A learned and lively biography.

P. CARTLEDGE, *Spartan Reflections* (2001). A collection of valuable essays by a leading scholar of ancient Sparta.

G. CAWKWELL, *Philip of Macedon* (1978). A brief but learned account of Philip's career.

Y. GARLAN, *Slavery in Ancient Greece* (1988). An up-to-date survey.

R. GARLAND, *Daily Life of the Ancient Greeks* (1998). A good account of the way the Greeks lived.

P. GREEN, *From Alexander to Actium* (1990). A brilliant synthesis of the Hellenistic period.

P. GREEN, *The Greco-Persian War* (1996). A lively account by a fine scholar with a keen feeling for the terrain.

E. S. GRUEN, *Heritage and Hellenism: The Reinvention of Jewish Tradition* (1998). A fine account of the interaction between Jews and Greeks in Hellenistic times.

C. D. HAMILTON, *Agesilaus and the Failure of Spartan Hegemony* (1991). An excellent biography of the king who was the central figure in Sparta during its domination in the fourth century B.C.E.

R. JUST, *Women in Athenian Law and Life* (1988). A good study of the place of women in Athenian life.

D. KAGAN, *The Peloponnesian War* (2003). An analytic narrative of the great war between Athens and Sparta.

D. KAGAN, *Pericles of Athens and the Birth of Athenian Democracy* (1991). An account of the life and times of the great Athenian statesman.

B. M. W. KNOX, *The Heroic Temper: Studies in Sophoclean Tragedy* (1964). A brilliant analysis of tragic heroism.

D. M. LEWIS, *Sparta and Persia* (1977). A valuable discussion of relations between Sparta and Persia in the fifth and fourth centuries B.C.E.

C. B. PATTERSON, *The Family in Greek History* (1998). An interesting interpretation of the relationship between family and state in ancient Greece.

J. J. POLLITT, *Art and Experience in Classical Greece* (1972). A scholarly and entertaining study of the relationship between art and history in Classical Greece, with excellent illustrations.

J. J. POLLITT, *Art in the Hellenistic Age* (1986). An extraordinary analysis that places the art in its historical and intellectual context.

R. W. SHARPLES, *Stoics, Epicureans, and Sceptics. An Introduction to Hellenistic Philosophy* (1996). A brief and useful introduction.

B. S. STRAUSS, *Athens after the Peloponnesian War* (1987). An excellent discussion of Athens's recovery and of the nature of Athenian society and politics in the fourth century B.C.E.

I. WORTHINGTON, *Demosthenes, Statesman and Orator* (2000). A useful collection of essays on the career and importance of the Athenian political leader.

## Chapter 4

G. BARKER AND T. RASMUSSEN, *The Etruscans* (2000). A valuable new study of a mysterious people.

R. BAUMANN, *Women and Politics in Ancient Rome* (1995). A study of the role of women in Roman public life.

A. H. BERNSTEIN, *Tiberius Sempronius Gracchus: Tradition and Apostasy* (1978). An interpretation of Tiberius's place in Roman politics.

T. J. CORNELL, *The Beginnings of Rome: Italy and Rome from the Bronze Age to the Punic Wars* (1995). A fine new study of early Rome.

T. CORNELL AND J. MATTHEWS, *Atlas of the Roman World* (1982). Presents a comprehensive view of the Roman world in its physical and cultural setting.

J-M. DAVID, *The Roman Conquest of Italy* (1997). A good analysis of how Rome united Italy.

E. S. GRUEN, *The Hellenistic World and the Coming of Rome* (1984). A new interpretation of Rome's conquest of the eastern Mediterranean.

W. V. HARRIS, *War and Imperialism in Republican Rome, 327–70 B.C.E.* (1975). An analysis of Roman attitudes and intentions concerning imperial expansion and war.

T. HOLLAND, *Rubicon: The Last Years of the Roman Republic* (2004). A lively account of the fall of the republic.

S. LANCEL, *Carthage, A History* (1995). A good account of Rome's great competitor.

H. MOURITSEN, *Plebs and Politics in the Late Roman Republic* (2001). A new study of Roman republican politics and the place of the common people in them.

J. POWELL AND J. PATTERSON, *Cicero the Advocate* (2004). A careful study of the Roman statesman's legal career.

H. H. SCULLARD, *A History of the Roman World 753–146 B.C.E.*, 4th ed. (1980). An unusually fine narrative history with useful critical notes.

## Chapter 5

W. BALL, *Rome in the East* (2000). A study of the eastern parts of the empire and how they interacted with the West.

A. A. BARRETT, *Livia: First Lady of Imperial Rome* (2004). Biography of Augustus's powerful and controversial wife.

P. BROWN, *The Rise of Western Christendom: Triumph and Diversity, 200–1000*, 2nd ed. (2003). A vivid picture of the spread of Christianity by a master of the field.

A. FERRILL, *The Fall of the Roman Empire, The Military Explanation* (1986). An interpretation that emphasizes the decline in the quality of the Roman army.

K. GALINSKY, *Augustan Culture* (1996). A work that integrates art, literature, and politics.

E. GIBBON, *The History of the Decline and Fall of the Roman Empire*, 2nd ed. 7 vols., ed. by J. B. Bury (1909–1914). A masterwork of the English language.

D. JOHNSTON, *Roman Law in Context* (2000). Places Rome's law in the context of its economy and society.

D. KAGAN, ED., *The End of the Roman Empire: Decline or Transformation?*, 3rd ed. (1992). A collection of essays on the problems of the decline and fall of the Roman Empire.

C. KELLY, *Ruling the Later Roman Empire* (2004). A study of the complexities of Roman government in the last centuries of the empire.

J. LENDON, *Empire of Honour: The Art of Government in the Roman World* (1997). A brilliant study that reveals how an aristocratic code of honor led the upper classes to cooperate in Roman rule.

R. W. MATHISON, *Roman Aristocrats in Barbarian Gaul: Strategies for Survival* (1993). An unusual slant on the late empire.

S. MATTERN, *Rome and the Enemy: Imperial Strategy in the Principate* (1999). A study of Rome's foreign and imperial policy under the Principate.

F. G. B. MILLAR, *The Emperor in the Roman World, 31 B.C.–A.D. 337* (1977). A study of Roman imperial government.

H. M. D. PARKER, *A History of the Roman World from A.D. 138 to 337* (1969). A good survey.

D. S. POTTER, *The Roman Empire at Bay: A.D. 180–395* (2004). An account of the challenges to Rome in the third and fourth centuries and how the Romans tried to meet them.

M. I. ROSTOVTZEFF, *Social and Economic History of the Roman Empire*, 2nd ed. (1957). A masterpiece whose main thesis is much disputed.

V. RUDICH, *Political Dissidence under Nero, The Price of Dissimulation* (1993). A brilliant exposition of the lives and thoughts of political dissidents in the early empire.

G. E. M. DE STE. CROIX, *The Class Struggle in the Ancient World* (1981). An ambitious interpretation of all of classical civilization from a Marxist perspective.

R. SYME, *The Roman Revolution* (1960). A brilliant study of Augustus, his supporters, and their rise to power.

**Chapter 6**

K. ARMSTRONG, *Muhammad: A Biography of the Prophet* (1992). Substantial popular biography.

G. BARRACLOUGH, *The Origins of Modern Germany* (1963). Originally published in 1946 and still the best survey of medieval Germany.

R. BARTLETT, *The Making of Europe* (1993). How migration and colonization created Europe.

G. W. BOWERSOCK ET AL., *Interpreting Late Antiquity: Essays on the Postclassical World* (2001). Introductory essays presenting a unified interpretation of the centuries between 250 C.E. and 800 C.E.

P. BROWN, *Augustine of Hippo: A Biography* (1967). Late antiquity seen through the biography of its greatest Christian thinker.

P. BROWN ET AL., EDS., *The Rise of Western Christendom: Triumph and Diversity* (1997). Sweeping, detailed summary.

VIRGINIA BURRUS, ED., *A Peoples' History of Christianity, II* (2005). Substantial and accessible.

R. COLLINS, *Charlemagne* (1998). Latest biography.

J. W. CURRIER, *Clovis, King of the Franks* (1997). Biography of founder of first Frankish dynasty.

F. L. GANSHOF, *Feudalism* (1964). The most profound brief analysis of the subject.

P. GODMAN ET AL., EDS., *Charlemagne's Heir: New Perspectives on Louis the Pious (814–40)* (1990). Latest research on the king whose divided kingdom set the boundaries of modern Europe.

S. GUTHRIE, *Arab Social Life in the Middle Ages* (1995). How Arab society holds itself together.

A. HOURANI, *A History of the Arab Peoples* (1991). Comprehensive with overviews of the origins and early history of Islam.

B. LEWIS, *The Middle East: A Brief History of the Last 2,000 Years* (1995). An authoritative overview.

R. MCKITTERICK, ED., *Carolingian Culture: Emulation and Innovation* (1994). The culture from which Western Europe was born.

R. J. MORRISSEY, *Charlemagne and France: A 1000 Years of Mythology* (2002). The European argument over who owns Charlemagne.

J. J. NORRIS, *Byzantium: The Decline and Fall* (1995). The final volume in an essential three-volume history of Byzantium.

P. RICHE, *The Carolingians: A Family Who Forged Europe* (1993). Readable account of the dynasty from start to finish.

P. SAWYER, *Kings and Vikings: Scandinavia and Europe A.D. 700–1100* (1994). Raiding Vikings and their impact on Europe.

W. WALTHER, *Woman in Islam* (1981). One hour spent with this book teaches more about the social import of Islam than days spent with others.

**Chapter 7**

J. W. BALDWIN, *The Government of Philip Augustus* (1986). The standard work.

S. FLANAGAN, *Hildegard of Bingen, 1098–1179: A Visionary Life* (1998). Latest biography of a powerful religious woman.

S. D. GOITEIN, *Letters of Medieval Jewish Traders* (1973). Rare first-person accounts.

E. M. HALLAM, *Capetian France 987–1328* (1980). Good on politics and heretics.

J. C. HOLT, *Magna Carta*, 2nd ed. (1992). Succeeding generations interpret the famous document.

K. LEYSER, *Medieval Germany and Its Neighbors, 900–1250* (1982). Basic and authoritative.

H. E. MAYER, *The Crusades*, trans. by John Gilligham (1972). The best one-volume account.

W. MELCZER, *The Pilgrim's Guide to Santiago de Compostela* (1993). Do's and dont's, and what the medieval pilgrim might expect along the way.

C. MORIARITY, ED., *The Voice of the Middle Ages: In Personal Letters, 1100–1500* (1989). Rare first-person accounts.

J. B. MORRALL, *Political Thought in Medieval Times* (1962). Readable, elucidating account.

J. RICHARD, *Saint Louis: Crusader King of France* (1992). Biography of Louis IX and an exploration of the mental, political, and religious world of the thirteenth century.

J. RILEY-SMITH, *The Oxford Illustrated History of the Crusades* (1995). Sweeping account.

C. TYERMAN, *Fighting for Christendom* (2004). Brief and accessible.

**Chapter 8**

E. AMT, ED., *Women's Lives in Medieval Europe: A Sourcebook* (1993). Outstanding collection of sources.

P. ARIES, *Centuries of Childhood: A Social History of Family Life* (1962). Influential pioneer effort on the subject.

J. W. BALDWIN, *The Scholastic Culture of the Middle Ages: 1000–1300* (1971). Good brief synthesis.

M. BLACK, *The Medieval Cookbook* (1992). Dishing it up in the Middle Ages.

M. T. Clanchy, *Abelard: A Medieval Life* (1998). The biography of the famous philosopher and seducer of Héloïse.

L. Grane, *Peter Abelard: Philosophy and Christianity in the Middle Ages* (1970). Places Abelard in his philosophieal and theological context.

B. A. Hanawalt, *Growing Up in Medieval London* (1993). Positive portrayal of parental and societal treatment of children.

D. Herlihy, *Women, Family, and Society in Medieval Europe: Historical Essays, 1978–91* (1995). A major historian's collected essays.

A. Hopkins, *Knights* (1990). Europe's warriors and models.

D. Krueger, ed., *Byzantine Christianity* (2006).

E. Male, *The Gothic Image: Religious Art in France in the Thirteenth Century* (1913). An enduring classic.

L. De Mause, ed., *The History of Childhood* (1974). Substantial essays on the inner as well as the material lives of children.

R. I. Moore, *The Formation of a Persecuting Society: Power and Deviance in Western Europe, 950–1250* (1987). A sympathetic look at heresy and dissent.

J. T. Noonan, *Contraception: A History of Its Treatment by the Catholic Theologians and Canonists* (1967). Fascinating account of medieval theologians' take on sex.

S. Ozment, *Ancestors: The Loving Family in Old Europe* (2001). A sympathetic look at families past.

S. Shahar, *The Fourth Estate: A History of Women in the Middle Ages* (1983). A comprehensive survey, making clear the great variety of women's work.

## Chapter 9

C. Allmand, *The Hundred Years' War: England and France at War, c. 1300–c. 1450* (1988). Overview of the war's development and consequences.

P. R. Backscheider et al., eds., *A Journal of the Plague Year* (1992). The Black Death at ground level.

R. Barber, ed., *The Pastons: Letters of a Family in the War of the Roses* (1984). Rare revelations of English family life in an age of crisis.

E. H. Gillett et al., *Life and Times of John Huss: The Bohemian Reformation of the Fifteenth Century* (2001). The latest biography.

J. Huizinga, *The Waning of the Middle Ages: A Study of the Forms of Life, Thought, and Art in France and the Netherlands in the Dawn of the Renaissance* (1924). Exaggerated, but engrossing study of mentality at the end of the Middle Ages.

P. Kahn et al., *Secret History of the Mongols: The Origins of Ghingis Kahn* (1998). Introduction to the greatest Mongol ruler.

S. Ozment, *The Age of Reform, 1250–1550* (1980). Highlights of late medieval intellectual and religious history.

E. Perroy, *The Hundred Years' War*, trans. by W. B. Wells (1965). Still the most comprehensive one-volume account.

M. Spinka, *John Huss's Concept of the Church* (1966). Lucid account of Hussite theology.

W. R. Trask, ed./trans., *Joan of Arc in Her Own Words* (1996). Joan's interrogation and self-defense.

P. Ziegler, *The Black Death* (1969). Highly readable account.

## Chapter 10

D. Abulafia, *The Discovery of Mankind: Atlantic Encounters in the Age of Columbus* (2008). Emphasizes contact between peoples in its exploration of European colonization of the Americas.

L. B. Alberti, *The Family in Renaissance Florence,* trans. by R. N. Watkins (1962). A contemporary humanist, who never married, explains how a family should behave.

K. Atchity, ed., *The Renaissance Reader* (1996). The Renaissance in its own words.

H. Baron, *The Crisis of the Early Italian Renaissance,* vols. 1 and 2 (1966). A major work on the civic dimension of Italian humanism.

G. A. Brucker, *Giovanni and Lusanna: Love and Marriage in Renaissance Florence* (1986). Love in the Renaissance shown to be more Bergman than Fellini.

J. Burckhardt, *The Civilization of the Renaissance in Italy* (1958). Modern edition of an old nineteenth-century classic that still has as many defenders as detractors.

R. E. Conrad, *Children of God's Fire: A Documentary History of Black Slavery in Brazil* (1983). Not for the squeamish.

L. Hanke, *Bartholomé de Las Casas: An Interpretation of His Life and Writings* (1951). Biography of the great Dominican critic of Spanish exploitation of Native Americans.

J. Hankins, *Plato in the Renaissance* (1992). A magisterial study of how Plato was read and interpreted by Renaissance scholars.

D. Herlihy and C. Klapisch-Zuber, *Tuscans and Their Families* (1985). Important work based on unique demographic data that give the reader a new appreciation of quantitative history.

J. C. Hutchison, *Albrecht Dürer: A Biography* (1990). A solid biography of the German artist.

L. Martines, *Power and Imagination: City States in Renaissance Italy* (1980). Stimulating account of cultural and political history.

S. E. Morrison, *Admiral of the Ocean Sea: A Life of Christopher Columbus* (1946). Still the best Columbus read.

E. Panofsky, *Meaning in the Visual Arts* (1955). Eloquent treatment of Renaissance art.

J. H. Parry, *The Age of Reconnaissance* (1964). A comprehensive account of exploration in the years 1450 to 1650.

I. A. Richter, ed., *The Notebooks of Leonardo da Vinci* (1985). The master in his own words.

A. Wheatcroft, *The Habsburgs* (1995). The dynasty that ruled the center of late medieval and early modern Europe.

C. C. Willard, *Christine de Pizan* (1984). Demonstration of what an educated woman could accomplish in the Renaissance.

## Chapter 11

H. Bloom, *Shakespeare: The Invention of the Human* (1998). An analysis of the greatest writer in the English language.

T. A. BRADY, JR., ED., *Handbook of European History: Late Middle Ages, Renaissance, Reformation* (1995). Essays summarizing recent research on aspects of the Reformation.

P. COLLINSON, *The Reformation* (2004). Portrays the Reformation as creating religious pluralism and civil liberty despite itself.

E. DUFFY, *The Stripping of the Altars: Traditional Religion in England, 1400–1580* (1992). Strongest of recent arguments that popular piety survived the Reformation in England.

M. DURAN, *Cervantes* (1974). Detailed biography.

B. S. GREGORY, *Salvation at Stake: Christian Martyrdom in Early Modern Europe* (1999). Massive, enthralling study of religion.

R. HOULBROOKE, *English Family Life, 1450–1716. An Anthology from Diaries* (1988). A rich collection of documents illustrating family relationships.

J. C. HUTCHISON, *Albrecht Dürer: A Biography* (1990). An art historian chronicles both the life and work of the artist.

H. JEDIN, *A History of the Council of Trent,* vols. 1 and 2 (1957–1961). Still the gold standard.

P. JOHNSTON AND R. W. SCRIBNER, *The Reformation in Germany and Switzerland* (1993). Reformation from the bottom up.

D. MACCOLLOCH, *The Reformation* (2004). Finds old Catholics and non-Protestant Evangelicals to be the forerunners of modern religion.

H. A. OBERMAN, *Luther: Man between God and the Devil* (1989). Perhaps the best account of Luther's life, by a Dutch master.

J. O'MALLEY, *The First Jesuits* (1993). Detailed account of the creation of the Society of Jesus and its original purposes.

S. OZMENT, *The Age of Reform, 1250–1550: An Intellectual and Religious History of Late Medieval and Reformation Europe* (1980). A broad survey of major religious ideas and beliefs.

B. ROBERTS, *Through the Keyhole: Dutch Child-Rearing Practices in the 17th and 18th Centuries* (1998). A study of three elite families.

Q. SKINNER, *The Foundations of Modern Political Thought II: The Age of Reformation* (1978). A comprehensive survey that treats every political thinker and tract.

D. STARKEY, *Elizabeth: The Struggle for the Throne* (2000). Details the early years of Elizabeth's life.

L. STONE, *The Family, Sex, and Marriage in England 1500–1800* (1977). Controversial, but enduring in many respects.

G. STRAUSS, ED. AND TRANS., *Manifestations of Discontent in Germany on the Eve of the Reformation* (1971). Rich collection of both rural and urban sources.

F. WENDEL, *Calvin: The Origins and Development of His Religious Thought,* trans. by P. Mairet (1963). The best treatment of Calvin's theology.

H. WUNDER, *He Is the Sun, She Is the Moon: A History of Women in Early Modern Germany* (1998). A model of gender history.

## Chapter 12

F. BRAUDEL, *The Mediterranean and the Mediterranean World in the Age of Philip the Second,* vols. 1 and 2 (1976). Widely acclaimed "big picture" by a master historian.

N. Z. DAVIS, *Society and Culture in Early Modern France* (1975). Essays on popular culture.

R. DUNN, *The Age of Religious Wars, 1559–1689* (1979). Excellent brief survey of every major conflict.

J. H. FRANKLIN, ED. AND TRANS., *Constitutionalism and Resistance in the Sixteenth Century: Three Treatises by Hotman, Beza, and Mornay* (1969). Three defenders of the right to resist tyranny.

J. GUY, *Tudor England* (1990). The standard history and a good synthesis of recent scholarship.

D. LOADES, *Mary Tudor* (1989). Authoritative and good storytelling.

G. MATTINGLY, *The Armada* (1959). A masterpiece resembling a novel in style.

J. E. NEALE, *The Age of Catherine de Médicis* (1962). Short, concise summary.

A. SOMAN, ED., *The Massacre of St. Bartholomew's Day: Reappraisals and Documents* (1974). Essays from an international symposium on the anniversary of the massacre.

C. WEDGWOOD, *William the Silent* (1944). Eloquent political biography of William of Orange.

A. B. WEIR, *The Life of Elizabeth I* (1998). Detailed portrayal of a successful ruler.

J. WORMALD, *Mary, Queen of Scots: A Study in Failure* (1991). Mary portrayed as out of touch with her country and her times.

## Chapter 13

W. BEIK, *Louis XIV and Absolutism: A Brief Study with Documents* (2000). An excellent collection by a major scholar of absolutism.

T. Blanning, *The Pursuit of Glory: Europe 1648–1815* (2007). The best recent synthesis of the emergence of the modern European state system.

J. BREWER, *The Sinews of Power: War, Money and the English State, 1688–1783* (1989). An important study of the financial basis of English power.

P. BURKE, *The Fabrication of Louis XIV* (1992). Examines how Louis XIV used art to forge his public image.

C. CLARK, *The Rise and Downfall of Prussia 1600–1947* (2006). A stunning survey.

R. CUST, *Charles I* (2007). The definitive biography.

P. COLLINSON, *The Religion of Protestants: The Church in English Society, 1559–1625* (1982). Remains the best introduction to Puritanism.

N. DAVIS, *God's Playground: A History of Poland: The Origins to 1795* (2005). The recent revision of a classic survey.

J. DE VRIES AND A. VAN DER WOUDE, *The First Modern Economy* (1997). Compares Holland to other European nations.

P. G. DWYER, *The Rise of Prussia 1700–1830* (2002). An excellent collection of essays.

S. FAROQHI, *The Ottoman Empire and the World Around It* (2006). Emphasizes the various interactions of the empire with both Asian and European powers.

R. I. FROST, *The Northern Wars: War, State and Society in Northeastern Europe, 1558–1721* (2000) A survey of an often neglected subject.

D. GOFFMAN, *The Ottoman Empire and Early Modern Europe* (2002). An accessible introduction to a complex subject.

T. HARRIS, *Restoration: Charles II and His Kingdom, 1660–1685* (2006). A major exploration of the tumultuous years of the restoration of the English monarchy after the civil war.

L. HUGHES, *Russia in the Age of Peter the Great* (2000). A major overview of the history and society of Peter's time.

C. IMBER, *The Ottoman Empire, 1300–1650: The Structure of Power* (2003). A sweeping analysis based on a broad range of sources.

C. J. INGRAO, *The Habsburg Monarchy, 1618–1815* (2000). The best recent survey.

J. I. ISRAEL, *The Dutch Republic: Its Rise, Greatness, and Fall, 1477–1806* (1995). The major work of the subject.

M. KISHLANSKY, *A Monarchy Transformed: Britain, 1603–1714* (1996). An important overview.

J. A. LYNN, *The Wars of Louis XIV* (1999). The best recent treatment.

J. LUKOWSKI AND H. ZAWADZKI, *A Concise History of Poland* (2006). A straightforward survey.

D. MCKAY, *The Great Elector: Frederick William of Brandenburg–Prussia* (2001). An account of the origins of Prussian power.

P. K. MONOD, *The Power of Kings: Monarchy and Religion in Europe, 1589–1715* (1999). An important and innovative examination of the roots of royal authority as early modern Europe became modern Europe.

G. PARKER, *The Military Revolution: Military Innovation and the Rise of the West (1500–1800)* (1988). A classic work on the impact of military matters on the emergence of centralized monarchies.

H. PHILLIPS, *Church and Culture in Seventeenth-Century France* (1997). A clear examination of the major religious issues confronting France and their relationship to the larger culture.

S. PINCUS, *England's Glorious Revolution 1688–1689: A Brief History with Documents* (2005). A useful collection by an outstanding historian of the subject.

G. TREASURE, *Louis XIV* (2001). The best, most accessible recent study.

**Chapter 14**

R. ASHCRAFT, *Revolutionary Politics and Locke's Two Treatises of Government* (1986). A major study emphasizing the radical side of Locke's thought.

J. BARRY, M. HESTER, AND G. ROBERTS, EDS., *Witchcraft in Early Modern Europe: Studies in Culture and Belief* (1998). A collection of recent essays.

M. BIAGIOLI, *Galileo Courtier: The Practice of Science in the Culture of Absolutism* (1993). A major revisionist work.

J. A. CONNER, *Kepler's Witch: An Astronomer's Discovery of Cosmic Order Amid Religious War, Political Intrigue, and the Heresy Trial of His Mother* (2005). Fascinating account of Kepler's effort to vindicate his mother against charges of witchcraft.

P. DEAR, *Revolutionizing the Sciences: European Knowledge and Its Ambitions, 1500–1700* (2001). A broad-ranging study of both the ideas and institutions of the new science.

M. FEINGOLD, *The Newtonian Moment: Isaac Newton and the Making of Modern Culture* (2004). A superb, well-illustrated volume.

S. GAUKROGER, *The Emergence of a Scientific Culture: Science and the Shaping of Modernity* (2007). A challenging book exploring the differing understanding of natural knowledge in early modern European culture.

S. GAUKROGER, *Francis Bacon and the Transformation of Early-Modern Philosophy* (2001). An excellent, accessible introduction.

J. GLEIK, *Isaac Newton* (2003). Highly accessible to the general reader.

I. HARRIS, *The Mind of John Locke: A Study of Political Theory in Its Intellectual Setting* (1994). The most comprehensive recent treatment.

J. L. HEILBRON, *The Sun in the Church: Cathedrals as Solar Observatories* (2000). Explores uses made of Roman Catholic cathedrals to make astronomical observations.

K. J. HOWELL, *God's Two Books: Copernican Cosmology and Biblical Interpretation in Early Modern Science* (2002). The clearest discussion of this important subject.

L. JARDINE, *Ingenious Pursuits: Building the Scientific Revolution* (1999). A lively exploration of the interface of personalities, new knowledge, and English society.

A. C. KORS AND E. PETERS, EDS., *European Witchcraft, 1100–1700* (1972). Classics of witch belief.

T. S. KUHN, *The Copernican Revolution: Planetary Astronomy in the Development of Western Thought* (1957). Remains the classic work.

B. LEVACK, *The Witch Hunt in Early Modern Europe* (1986). Lucid survey.

P. MACHAMER, ED., *The Cambridge Companion to Galileo* (1998). Essays that aid the understanding of the entire spectrum of the new science.

J. MARSHALL, *John Locke, Toleration and Early Enlightenment Culture* (2006). A magisterial and challenging survey of the background of seventeenth-century arguments for and against toleration.

J. R. MARTIN, *Baroque* (1977). A classic introduction to baroque art.

M. OSLER, *Rethinking the Scientific Revolution* (2000). A collection of revisionist essays particularly exploring issues of the interrelationship of the new science and religion.

R. POPKIN, *The History of Scepticism: From Savonarola to Bayle* (2003). A classic study of the fear of loss of intellectual certainty.

L. PYENSON AND S. SHEETS-PYENSON, *Servants of Nature: A History of Scientific Institutions, Enterprises, and Sensibilities* (1999). A history of the settings in which the creation and diffusion of scientific knowledge have occurred.

J. REPCHECK, *Copernicus' Secret: How the Scientific Revolution Began* (2007). A highly accessible biography of Copernicus.

L. SCHIEBINGER, *The Mind Has No Sex? Women in the Origins of Modern Science* (1989). A major study of the subject.

S. SHAPIN, *The Scientific Revolution* (1996). A readable brief introduction.

W. R. SHEA AND M. ARTIGAS, *Galileo in Rome: The Rise and Fall of a Troublesome Genius* (2003). Argues that Galileo in part brought about his own condemnation.

T. SORELL, *The Cambridge Companion to Hobbes* (1994). Excellent essays on the major themes of Hobbes's thought.

**Chapter 15**

J. BLUM, *Lord and Peasant in Russia from the Ninth to the Nineteenth Century* (1961). Remains a classic discussion.

J. BURNET, *Gender, Work and Wages in Industrial Revolution Britain* (2008). A major revisionist study of the wage structure for work by men and women.

P. M. DEANE, *The First Industrial Revolution* (1999). A well-balanced and systematic treatment.

P. EARLE, *The Making of the English Middle Class: Business, Community, and Family Life in London, 1660–1730* (1989). The most careful study of the subject.

M. W. FLINN, *The European Demographic System, 1500–1820* (1981). Remains a major summary.

E. HOBSBAWM, *Industry and Empire: The Birth of the Industrial Revolution* (1999). A survey by a major historian of the subject.

K. HONEYMAN, *Women, Gender and Industrialization in England, 1700–1850* (2000). Emphasizes how certain work or economic roles became associated with either men or women.

O. H. HUFTON, *The Poor of Eighteenth-Century France, 1750–1789* (1975). A brilliant study of poverty and the family economy.

A. KAHAN, *The Plow, the Hammer, and the Knout: An Economic History of Eighteenth-Century Russia* (1985). An extensive and detailed treatment.

D. I. KERTZER AND M. BARBAGLI, *The History of the European Family: Family Life in Early Modern Times, 1500–1709* (2001). Broad-ranging essays covering the entire Continent.

S. KING AND G. TIMMONS, *Making Sense of the Industrial Revolution: English Economy and Society, 1700–1850* (2001). Examines the Industrial Revolution through the social institutions that brought it about and were changed by it.

F. E. MANUEL, *The Broken Staff: Judaism Through Christian Eyes* (1992). An important discussion of Christian interpretations of Judaism.

K. MORGAN, *The Birth of Industrial Britain: Social Change, 1750–1850* (2004). A useful brief overview.

M. OVERTON, *Agricultural Revolution in England: The Transformation of the Agrarian Economy, 1500–1850* (1996). A highly accessible treatment.

J. R. RUFF, *Violence in Early Modern Europe 1500–1800* (2001). An excellent survey of an important and disturbing topic.

P. STEARNS, *The Industrial Revolution in World History* (2007). A broad interpretive account.

D. VALENZE, *The First Industrial Woman* (1995). An elegant, penetrating volume.

E. A. WRIGLEY, *Continuity, Chance and Change: The Character of the Industrial Revolution in England* (1994). A major conceptual reassessment.

**Chapter 16**

F. ANDERSON, *Crucible of War: The Seven Years' War and the Fate of Empire in British North America, 1754–1766* (2001). A splendid narrative account.

B. BAILYN, *The Ideological Origins of the American Revolution* (1992). An important work illustrating the role of English radical thought in the perceptions of the colonists.

C. A. BAYLY, *Imperial Meridian: The British Empire and the World, 1780–1830* (1989). A major study of the empire after the loss of America.

I. BERLIN, *Many Thousands Gone: The First Two Centuries of Slavery in North America* (1998). The most extensive recent treatment emphasizing the differences in the slave economy during different decades.

R. BLACKBURN, *The Making of New World Slavery from the Baroque to the Modern, 1492–1800* (1997). An extraordinary work.

M. A. BURKHOLDER AND L. L. JOHNSON, *Colonial Latin America* (2004). A standard synthesis.

L. COLLEY, *Britons: Forging the Nation, 1707–1837* (1992). Important discussions of the recovery from the loss of America.

D. B. DAVIS, *Inhuman Bondage: The Rise and Fall of Slavery in the New World* (2006). A splendid overview by a leading scholar.

D. B. DAVIS, *The Problem of Slavery in the Age of Revolution, 1770–1823* (1975). A major work on both European and American history.

J. ELLIOTT, *Empires of the Atlantic: Britain and Spain in America 1492–1830* (2006). A brilliant and accessible comparative history.

J. J. ELLIS, *His Excellency: George Washington* (2004). A biography that explores the entire era of the American Revolution.

R. HARMS, *The Diligent: A Voyage through the Worlds of the Slave Trade* (2002). A powerful narrative of the voyage of a French slave trader.

H. S. KLEIN, *The Atlantic Slave Trade* (1999). A succinct synthesis based on recent literature.

P. LANGFORD, *A Polite and Commercial People: England, 1717–1783* (1989). An excellent survey covering social history, politics, the overseas wars, and the American Revolution.

P. MAIER, *American Scripture: Making the Declaration of Independence* (1997). Replaces previous works on the subject.

A. PAGDEN, *Lords of All the World: Ideologies of Empire in Spain, Britain, and France, 1492–1830* (1995). One of the few comparative studies of the empires during this period.

M. REDIKER, *The Slave Ship: A Human History* (2007). An exploration of the harrowing experience of slave transportation across the Atlantic.

M. REDIKER, *Villains of All Nations: Atlantic Pirates in the Golden Age* (2008). A serious historical treatment of the subject.

J. THORNTON, *Africa and the Africans in the Making of the Atlantic World, 1400–1800*, 2nd ed. (1998). A discussion of the role of Africans in the emergence of the transatlantic economy.

J. WINIK, *The Great Upheaval: America and the Birth of the Modern World, 1788–1800* (2007). Sets the founding of the American republic in a transatlantic political context.

G. S. WOOD, *The American Revolution: A History* (2002). A major interpretation.

**Chapter 17**

D. D. BIEN, *The Calas Affair: Persecution, Toleration, and Heresy in Eighteenth-Century Toulouse* (1960). The standard treatment of the famous case.

T. C. W. BLANNING, *The Culture of Power and the Power of Culture: Old Regime Europe 1660–1789* (2002). A remarkable synthesis of the interaction of political power and culture in France, Prussia, and Austria.

P. BLOOM, *Enlightening the World: Encyclopedie, The Book That Changed the Course of History* (2005). A lively, accessible introduction.

J. BUCHAN, *Crowded with Genius: The Scottish Enlightenment* (2003). A lively, accessible introduction.

L. DAMROSCH, *Rousseau: Restless Genius* (2007). The best recent biography.

I. DE MADARIAGA, *Russia in the Age of Catherine the Great* (1981). The best discussion in English.

S. FEINER, *The Jewish Enlightenment* (2002). An extensive, challenging pan-European treatment of the subject.

P. GAY, *The Enlightenment: An Interpretation*, 2 vols. (1966, 1969). A classic.

D. GOODMAN, *The Republic of Letters: A Cultural History of the French Enlightenment* (1994). Concentrates on the role of salons.

C. HESSE, *The Other Enlightenment: How French Women Became Modern* (2004). Explores the manner in which French women authors created their own sphere of thought and cultural actiavity.

J. ISRAEL, *Enlightenment Contested: Philosophy, Modernity, and the Emancipation of Man 1670–1752* (2006). A challenging major revisionist history of the subject.

J. I. ISRAEL, *Radical Enlightenment: Philosophy and the Making of Modernity* (2001). A controversial account of the most radical strains of thought in Enlightenment culture.

C. A. KORS, *Encyclopedia of the Enlightenment* (2002). A major reference work on all of the chief intellectual themes of the era.

J. P. LEDONNE, *The Russian Empire and the World, 1700–1917* (1996). Explores the major reasons for Russian expansion from the eighteenth to the early twentieth centuries.

G. MACDONAGH, *Frederick the Great* (2001). A thoughtful and accessible biography.

D. MACMAHON, *Enemies of the Enlightenment: The French Counter-Enlightenment and the Making of Modernity* (2001). A fine exploration of French writers critical of the *philosophes*.

J. V. H. MELTON, *The Rise of the Public in Enlightenment Europe* (2001). Explores the social basis of print culture with an excellent bibliography.

S. MUTHU, *Enlightenment Against Empire* (2003). A challenging volume covering the critique of the empire.

R. PEASON, *Voltaire Almighty: A Life in Pursuit of Freedom* (2005). An accessible biography

R. PORTER, *The Creation of the Modern World: The Untold Story of the British Enlightenment* (2000). Seeks to shift the center of the Enlightenment from France to England.

P. RILEY, *The Cambridge Companion to Rousseau* (2001). Excellent accessible essays by major scholars.

E. ROTHCHILD, *Economic Sentiments: Adam Smith, Condorcet, and the Enlightenment* (2001). A sensitive account of Smith's thought and its relationship to the social questions of the day.

J. SHEEHAN, *The Enlightenment Bible* (2007). Explores the Enlightenment treatment of the Bible.

S. SMITH, *Spinoza, Liberalism, and the Question of Jewish Identity* (1997). A clear introduction to a challenging thinker.

A. M. WILSON, *Diderot* (1972). A splendid biography of the person behind the *Encyclopedia* and other major Enlightenment publications.

L. WOLFF, *Inventing Eastern Europe: The Map of Civilization on the Mind of the Enlightenment* (1994). A remarkable study of how Enlightenment writers recast the understanding of this part of the Continent.

**Chapter 18**

D. ANDRESS, *The Terror: The Merciless War for Freedom in Revolutionary France* (2006). The best recent survey of the reign of terror.

N. ASTON, *Christianity and Revolutionary Europe c. 1750–1830* (2002). Continent-wide survey of the impact of revolution on religion.

T. C. BLANNING, *The Revolutionary Wars, 1787–1802* (1996). Essential for understanding the role of the army and the revolution.

S. DESAN, *The Family on Trial in Revolutionary France* (2004). An important analysis of how the revolution impacted French domestic life.

W. DOYLE, *The Oxford History of the French Revolution* (2003). A broad, complex narrative with an excellent bibliography.

A. FORREST, *Revoltionary Paris, the Provinces and the French Revolution* (2004). A clear presentation of the tensions between the center of the revolution and the provinces.

C. HAYDEN AND W. DOYLE, EDS., *Robespierre* (1999). Essays evaluating Robespierre's ideas, career, and reputation.

P. HIGONNET, *Goodness beyond Virtue: Jacobins During the French Revolution* (1998). An outstanding work that clearly relates political values to political actions.

D. JORDON, *The King's Trial: Louis XVI vs. the French Revolution* (1979). A gripping account of the event.

E. KENNEDY, *A Cultural History of the French Revolution* (1989). An important examination of the role of the arts, schools, clubs, and intellectual institutions.

S. E. MELZER AND L. W. RABINE, EDS., *Rebel Daughters: Women and the French Revolution* (1997). Essays exploring the role and image of women in the revolution.

S. NEELY, *A Concise History of the French Revolution* (2008). The best of the numerous brief accounts.

C. C. O'BRIEN, *The Great Melody: A Thematic Biography of Edmund Burke* (1992). A deeply thoughtful biography

R. R. PALMER, *The Age of Democratic Revolution: A Political History of Europe and America, 1760–1800*, 2 vols. (1959, 1964). Still an impressive survey of the political turmoil in the transatlantic world.

M. PRICE, *The Road from Versailles: Louis XVI, Marie Antoinette, and the Fall of the French Monarchy* (2004). A lively narrative that brings the personalities of the king and queen into focus.

R. SCURR, *Fatal Purity: Robespierre and the French Revolution* (2007). A compelling analysis of a personality long difficult to understand.

T. TACKETT, *Becoming a Revolutionary: The Deputies of the French National Assembly and the Emergence of a Revolutionary Culture (1789–1790)* (1996). The best study of the early months of the revolution.

**Chapter 19**

M. H. ABRAMS, *The Mirror and the Lamp: Romantic Theory and the Critical Tradition* (1958). A classic on romantic literary theory.

E. BEHLER, *German Romantic Literary Theory* (1993). A clear introduction to a difficult subject.

D. BELL, *The First Total War: Napoleon's Europe and the Birth of Warfare as We Know It* (2007). A consideration of the Napoleonic conflicts and the culture of warfare.

G. E. BENTLEY, *The Stranger from Paradise: A Biography of William Blake* (2001). Now the standard work.

N. BOYLE, *Goethe* (2001). A challenging two-volume biography.

M. BROERS, *Europe under Napoleon 1799–1815* (2002). Examines the subject from the standpoint of those Napoleon conquered.

T. CHAPMAN, *Congress of Vienna: Origins, Processes, and Results* (1998). A clear introduction to the major issues.

P. DWYER, *Napoleon: The Path to Power, 1769–1799* (2008). A major study of the subject.

P. DWYER, *Talleyrand* (2002). A useful account of his diplomatic influence.

S. ENGLUND, *Napoleon: A Political Life* (2004). A thoughtful recent biography.

C. ESDAILE, *The Peninsular War: A New History* (2003). A narrative of the Napoleonic wars in Spain.

A. FORREST, *Napoleon's Men: The Soldiers of the Revolution and Empire* (2002). An examination of the troops rather than their commander.

H. HONOUR, *Romanticism* (1979). Still the best introduction to romantic art, well illustrated.

F. KAGAN, *The End of the Old Order: Napoleon and Europe, 1801–1805* (2006). A masterful narrative.

S. KÖRNER, *Kant* (1955). A classic brief, clear introduction.

J. LUSVASS, *Napoleon on the Art of War* (2001). A collection of Napoleon's own writings.

J. J. MCGANN AND J. SODERHOLM, EDS., *Byron and Romanticism* (2002). Essays on the poet who most embodied romantic qualities to the people of his time.

R. MUIR, *Tactics and the Experience of Battle in the Age of Napoleon* (1998). A splendid account of troops in battle.

T. PINKARD, *Hegel: A Biography* (2000). A long but accessible study.

N. ROE, *Romanticism: An Oxford Guide* (2005). A series of informative essays.

P. W. SCHROEDER, *The Transformation of European Politics, 1763–1848* (1994). A major synthesis of the diplomatic history of the period, emphasizing the new departures of the Congress of Vienna.

I. WOLOCH, *Napoleon and His Collaborators: The Making of a Dictatorship* (2001). A key study by one of the major scholars of the subject.

A. ZAMOYSKI, *Rites of Peace: The Fall of Napoleon and the Congress of Vienna* (2007). A lively analysis and narrative.

**Chapter 20**

B. ANDERSON, *Imagined Communities*, rev. ed. (2006). An influential and controversial discussion of nationalism.

M. S. BELL, *Toussaint Louverture: A Biography* (2007). An outstanding new biography.

M. BERDAHL, *The Politics of the Prussian Nobility: The Development of a Conservative Ideology, 1770–1848* (1988). A major examination of German conservative outlooks.

A. BRIGGS, *The Making of Modern England* (1959). Classic survey of English history during the first half of the nineteenth century.

A. CRAITU, *Liberalism under Siege: The Political Thought of the French Doctrinaires* (2003). An outstanding study of early-nineteenth-century French liberalism.

M. F. CROSS AND D. WILLIAMS, EDS., *French Experience from Republic to Monarchy, 1792–1824: New Dawns in Politics, Knowledge and Culture* (2000). Essays on French culture from the revolution through the restoration.

D. DAKIN, *The Struggle for Greek Independence* (1973). An excellent explanation of the Greek independence question.

L. DUBOIS, *Avengers of the New World: The Story of the Haitian Revolution* (2004). An analytic narrative likely to replace others.

E. J. EVANS, *Britain Before the Reform Act: Politics and Society, 1815–1832* (2008). Explores the forces that resisted and pressed for reform.

W. FORTESCUE, *Revolution and Counter-Revolution in France, 1815–1852* (2002). A helpful brief survey.

E. GELLNER, *Nations and Nationalism* (1983). A classic theoretical work.

L. GREENFELD, *Nationalism: Five Roads to Modernity* (1992). A major comparative study.

R. HARVEY, *Liberators: Latin America's Struggle for Independence* (2002). An excellent, lively treatment.

E. J. HOBSBAWM, *Nations and Nationalism since 1780: Programme, Myth, Reality*, rev. ed. (1992). Emphasizes intellectual factors.

C. Jelavich and B. Jelavich, *The Establishment of the Balkan National States, 1804–1920* (1987). A standard survey.

G. A. Kelly, *The Humane Comedy: Constant, Tocqueville, and French Liberalism* (2007). The best introduction to the subject.

M. B. Levinger, *Enlightened Nationalism: The Transformation of Prussian Political Culture, 1806–1848* (2002). A clear and expansive coverview on the most recent scholarship.

J. Lynch, *Simon Bolivar: A Life* (2006). Now the standard biography.

C. A. Macartney, *The Habsburg Empire, 1790–1918* (1971). Remains an important survey.

N. V. Riasanovsky, *Nicholas I and Official Nationality in Russia, 1825–1855* (1959). Remains a lucid discussion of the conservative ideology that made Russia the major opponent of liberalism.

J. Sheehan, *German History, 1770–1866* (1989). A long work that is now the best available survey of the subject.

A. Sked, *Metternich and Austria: An Evaluation* (2008). A thoughtful restoration of Metternich to the position of leading diplomat of his age.

A. B. Ulam, *Russia's Failed Revolutionaries* (1981). Contains a useful discussion of the Decembrists as a background for other nineteenth-century Russian revolutionary activity.

B. Wilson, *The Making of Victorian Values: Decency and Dissent in Britain: 1789–1837* (2007). A very lively overview of the cultural factors shaping early-nineteenth-century British society.

**Chapter 21**

B. S. Anderson and J. P. Zinsser, *A History of Their Own: Women in Europe from Prehistory to the Present*, vol. 2 (1988). A wide-ranging survey.

I. Berlin, *Karl Marx: His Life and Environment*, 4th ed. (1996). A classic introduction.

R. B. Carlisle, *The Proffered Crown: Saint-Simonianism and the Doctrine of Hope* (1987). The best treatment of the broad social doctrines of Saint-Simonianism.

J. Coffin, *The Politics of Women's Work* (1996). Examines the subject in France.

I. Deak, *The Lawful Revolution: Louis Kossuth and the Hungarians, 1848–1849* (1979). The most significant study of the topic in English.

R. J. Evans, *The Revolutions in Europe, 1848–1849: From Reform to Reaction* (2002). A series of essays by major experts.

J. F. C. Harrison, *Quest for the New Moral World: Robert Owen and the Owenites in Britain and America* (1969). The standard work.

D. I. Kertzer and M. Barbagli, eds., *Family Life in the Long Nineteenth Century, 1789–1913: The History of the European Family* (2002). Wide-ranging collection of essays.

K. Kolakowski, *Main Currents of Marxism: Its Rise, Growth, and Dissolution*, 3 vols. (1978). A classic, comprehensive survey.

D. Landes, *The Unbound Prometheus: Technological Change and Industrial Development in Western Europe from 1750 to the Present* (1969). Classic one-volume treatment of technological development in a broad social and economic context.

H. Perkin, *The Origins of Modern English Society, 1780–1880* (1969). A provocative attempt to look at the society as a whole.

J. D. Randers-Pehrson, *Germans and the Revolution of 1848–1849* (2001). An exhaustive treatment of the subject.

W. H. Sewell, Jr., *Work and Revolution in France: The Language of Labor from the Old Regime to 1848* (1980). A fine analysis of French artisans.

J. Sperber, *The European Revolution, 1841–1851* (2005). An excellent synthesis.

E. P. Thompson, *The Making of the English Working Class* (1964). A classic work.

F. Wheen, *Karl Marx: A Life* (2001). An accessible work that emphasizes the contradictions in Marx's career and personality.

D. Winch, *Riches and Poverty: An Intellectual History of Political Economy in Britain, 1750–1834* (1996). A superb survey from Adam Smith through Thomas Malthus.

**Chapter 22**

V. Aksan, *Ottoman Wars, 1700–1870: An Empire Besieged* (2007). Explores the impact of war on the weakening of the Ottoman Empire.

R. Aldous, *The Lion and the Unicorn: Gladstone vs. Disraeli* (2008). An accessible volume tracing the great political rivalry of the mid-Victorian age.

I. T. Berend, *History Derailed: Central and Eastern Europe in the Long Nineteenth Century* (2003). The best one-volume treatment of the complexities of this region.

P. Bew, *Ireland: The Politics of Enmity 1789–2006* (2007). A major, new, outstanding survey of the sweep of modern Irish history.

E. F. Biagini, *British Democracy and Irish Nationalism 1876–1906* (2007). Explores impact of the Irish question on British political structures themselves.

D. Blackbourn, *The Long Nineteenth Century: A History of Germany, 1780–1918* (1998). An outstanding survey.

R. Blake, *Disraeli* (1967). Remains the best biography.

J. Breuilly, *Austria, Prussia and Germany, 1806–1871* (2002). Examines the complex relations of these states leading up to German unification.

C. Clark, *Iron Kingdom: The Rise and Downfall of Prussia, 1600–1947* (2006). Now the standard survey.

M. Clark, *The Italian Risorgimento* (1998). A brief overview.

R. B. Edgerton, *Death or Glory: The Legacy of the Crimean War* (2000). Multifaceted study of a mismanaged war that transformed European politics.

C. J. Eichner, *Surmounting the Barricades: Women in the Paris Commune* (2004). Explores the impact of women's journalism and organizing in the Commune and wider radical political tradition.

B. Eklof and J. Bushnell, *Russia's Great Reforms, 1855–1881* (1994). A clear analysis.

M. A. HANIOGLU, *A Brief History of the Late Ottoman Empire* (2008). An accessible introduction.

R. KEE, *The Green Flag: A History of Irish Nationalism* (2001). A lively, accessible account.

D. LANGEWIESCHE, *Liberalism in Germany* (1999). A broad survey that is particularly good on the problems unification caused for German Liberals.

H. C. G. MATTHEW, *Gladstone, 1809–1898* (1998). A superb biography.

D. MOON, *Abolition of Serfdom in Russia: 1762–1907* (2001). Analysis with docments.

W. G. MOSS, *Russia in the Age of Alexander II, Tolstoy and Dostoyevsky* (2002). Emphaises the cultural background.

N. M. NAIMARK, *Terrorists and Social Democrats: The Russian Revolutionary Movement under Alexander III* (1983). Useful discussion of a complicated subject.

P. G. NORD, *The Republican Moment: Struggles for Democracy in Nineteenth-Century France* (1996). A major examination of nineteenth-century French political culture.

J. PARRY, *The Politics of Patriotism: English Liberalism, National Identity and Europe, 1830–1886* (2006). An excellent overview of English Liberalism and how its values determined mid-Victorian relations with the Continent.

J. P. PARRY, *The Rise and Fall of Liberal Government in Victorian Britain* (1994). An outstanding study.

O. PFLANZE, *Bismarck and the Development of Germany*, 3 vols. (1990). A major biography and history of Germany for the period.

R. PRICE, *The French Second Empire: An Anatomy of Political Power* (2001). This volume along with the following title are the most comprehensive recent study.

R. PRICE, *People and Politics in France, 1848–1870* (2004). Examines the rise of Louis Napoleon Bonaparte and his use of political power.

E. RADZINSKY, *Alexander II: The Last Great Tsar* (2005). An accessible biography.

L. RIALL, *Garibaldi: Invention of a Hero* (2007). An exploration of a nationalist hero's reputation in his own day and later.

A. SCIROCCO, *Garibaldi: Citizen of the World: A Biography* (2007). An admiring account.

D. SHAFER, *The Paris Commune: French Politics, Culture, and Society at the Crossroads of the Revolutionary Tradition and Revolutionary Socialism* (2005). Excellent in relating the Commune to previous and later revolutionary traditions.

A. SKED, *Decline and Fall of the Habsburg Empire 1815–1918* (2001). A major, accessible survey of a difficult subject.

D. M. SMITH, *Cavour* (1984). An excellent biography.

## Chapter 23

A. ASCHER, *P. A. Stolypin: The Search for Stability in Late Imperial Russia* (2000). A broad-ranging biography based on extensive research.

P. BIRNBAUM, *Jewish Destinies: Citizenship, State, and Community in Modern France* (2000). Explores the subject from the French Revolution to the present.

T. W. CLYMAN AND J. VOWLES, *Russia through Women's Eyes: Autobiographies from Tsarist Russia* (1996). A splendid collection of relatively brief memoirs.

G. CROSSICK AND S. JAUMAIN, EDS., *Cathedrals of Consumption: The European Department Store, 1850–1939* (1999). Essays on the development of a new mode of distribution of consumer goods.

D. ELLENSON, *After Emancipation: Jewish Religious Responses to Modernity* (2004). A volume that explores numerous examples of this response across Europe.

A. GEIFMAN, *Thou Shalt Kill: Revolutionary Terrorism in Russia, 1894–1917* (1993). An examination of political violence in late imperial Russia.

R. F. HAMILTON, *Marxism, Revisionism, and Leninism: Explication, Assessment, and Commentary* (2000). A contribution by a historically minded sociologist.

J. HARSIN, *Policing Prostitution in Nineteenth-Century Paris* (1985). A major study of this significant subject in French social history.

G. HIMMELFARB, *Poverty and Compassion: The Moral Imagination of the Late Victorians* (1991). The best examination of late Victorian social thought.

E. HOBSBAWM, *The Age of Empire, 1875–1914* (1987). A stimulating survey that covers cultural as well as political developments.

S. S. HOLTON, *Feminism and Democracy: Women's Suffrage and Reform Politics in Britain, 1900–1918* (1986). An excellent treatment of the subject.

T. HOPPEN, *The Mid-Victorian Generation, 1846–1886* (1998). The most extensive treatment of the subject.

S. KOVIN, *Slumming: Sexual and Social Politics in Victorian London* (2004). Explores the complexities of the extension of charity and social services in late Victorian London.

M. MALIA, *Russia under Western Eyes: From the Bronze Horseman to the Lenin Mausoleum* (2000). A brilliant work on how Western intellectuals understood Russia.

E. D. RAPPAPORT, *Shopping for Pleasure: Women in the Making of London's West End* (2001). A study of the rise of department stores in London.

H. ROGGER, *Jewish Policies and Right-Wing Politics in Imperial Russia* (1986). A learned examination of Russian anti-Semitism.

M. L. ROZENBLIT, *The Jews of Vienna, 1867–1914: Assimilation and Identity* (1983). Covers the cultural, economic, and political life of Viennese Jews.

R. SERVICE, *Lenin: A Biography* (2002). Based on new sources and will no doubt become the standard biography.

D. SORKIN, *The Transformation of German Jewry, 1780–1840* (1987). An examination of Jewish emancipation in Germany.

G. P. STEENSON, *Not One Man! Not One Penny!: German Social Democracy, 1863–1914* (1999). An extensive survey.

N. STONE, *Europe Transformed* (1984). A sweeping survey that emphasizes the difficulties of late-nineteenth-century liberalism.

A. THORPE, *A History of the British Labour Party* (2001). From its inception to the twenty-first century.

J. R. WALKOWITZ, *Prostitution and Victorian Society: Women, Class, and the State* (1980). A work of great insight and sensitivity.

## Chapter 24

C. ALLEN, *The Human Christ: The Search for the Historical Jesus* (1998). A broad survey of the issue for the past two centuries.

M. D. BIDDIS, *Father of Racist Ideology: The Social and Political Thought of Count Gobineau* (1970). Sets the subject in the more general context of nineteenth-century thought.

P. BOWLER, *Evolution: The History of an Idea* (2003). An outstanding survey.

J. BROWNE, *Charles Darwin*, 2 vols. (1995, 2002). A stunning biography.

J. BURROW, *The Crisis of Reason: European Thought, 1848–1914* (2000). The best overview available.

F. J. COPPA, *The Modern Papacy since 1789* (1999). A straightforward survey.

F. J. COPPA, *Politics and Papacy in the Modern World* (2008). A broad-ranging exploration.

B. DENVIR, *Post-Impressionism* (1992). A brief introduction.

M. FRANCIS, *Herbert Spence and the Invention of Modern Life* (2007). Now the standard biography.

P. GAY, *Modernism: The Lure of Heresy* (2007). A broad interdisciplinary exploration.

R. HARRIS, *Lourdes: Body and Soul in a Secular Age* (1999). A sensitive discussion of Lourdes in its religious and cultural contexts.

R. HELMSTADTER, ED., *Freedom and Religion in the Nineteenth Century* (1997). Major essays on the relationship of church and state.

J. HODGE AND G. RADICK, *The Cambridge Companion to Darwin* (2003). A far-ranging collection of essays with a good bibliography.

A. HOURANI, *Arab Thought in the Liberal Age 1789–1939* (1967). A classic account, clearly written and accessible to the nonspecialist.

J. KÖHLER, *Zarathustra's Secret: The Interior Life of Friedrich Nietzsche* (2002). A controversial new biography.

W. LACQUEUR, *A History of Zionism* (2003). The most extensive one-volume treatment.

M. LEVENSON, *The Cambridge Companion to Modernism* (1999). Excellent essays on a wide range of subjects.

B. LIGHTMAN, *Victorian Popularizers of Science: Designing Nature for New Audiences* (2007). A study that adds numerous new dimensions to the subject.

G. MAKARI, *Revolution in Mind: The Creation of Psychoanalysis* (2008). A major, multidimensional survey.

A. PAIS, *Subtle Is the Lord: The Science and Life of Albert Einstein* (1983). The most accessible biography.

P. G. J. PULZER, *The Rise of Political Anti-Semitism in Germany and Austria* (1989). A sound discussion of anti-Semitism and central European politics.

F. QUINN, *The Sum of All Heresies: The Image of Islam in Western Thought* (2008). An interesting and clear overview of this important subject.

R. ROSENBLUM, *Cubism and 20th Century Art* (2001). A well-informed introduction.

C. E. SCHORSKE, *Fin de Siècle Vienna: Politics and Culture* (1980). Classic essays on the creative intellectual climate of Vienna.

W. SMITH, *Politics and the Sciences of Culture in Germany, 1840–1920* (1991). A major survey of the interaction between science and the social sciences.

F. M. TURNER, *Contesting Cultural Authority: Essays in Victorian Intellectual Life* (1993). Explorations in issues relating to Victorian science and religion.

D. VITAL, *A People Apart: The Jews in Europe 1789–1939* (1999). A broad and deeply researched volume.

A. N. WILSON, *God's Funeral* (1999). Explores the thinkers who contributed to religious doubt during the nineteenth and twentieth centuries.

## Chapter 25

M. ADAS, *Machines as the Measure of Men: Science, Technology, and Ideologies of Western Dominance* (1989). The best single volume on racial thinking and technological advances as forming ideologies of European colonial dominance.

R. ALDRICH, *Greater France: A History of French Overseas Expansion* (1996). Remains the best overview.

C. BAYLY, *Imperial Meridian: The British Empire and the World: 1780–1830* (1989). Places the British expansion in India into larger imperial contexts.

D. BROWER, *Turkestan and the Fate of the Russian Empire* (2003). A concise treatment of a case study in Russian imperialism in Asia.

A. BURTON, *Burdens of History: British Feminists, Indian Women, and Imperial Culture, 1865–1915* (1994). Explores the relationship of women in Britain's Indian empire.

A. CONKLIN, *A Mission to Civilize: The Republican Idea of Empire in France and West Africa, 1895–1930* (2000). An in-depth analysis of a case history of the civilizing mission.

F. COOPER AND A. L. STOLER, EDS., *Tensions of Empire: Colonial Cultures in a Bourgeois World* (1997). Explores difficulties of accommodating ideas and realities of empire to domestic middle-class values and outlooks.

J. COX, *Imperial Fault Lines: Christianity and Colonial Power in India, 1818–1940* (2002). The best treatment of British missionaries in India.

J. P. DAUGHTON, *An Empire Divided: Religion, Republicanism, and the Making of French Colonialism, 1880–1914* (2008). A superb discussion of the interaction of religion, empire, and domestic French politics.

N. P. DIRKS, *The Scandal of Empire: India and the Creation of Imperial Britain* (2006). An elegant study of the interaction of British political sensibilities and the emergence of the British empire in India.

R. DRAYTON, *Nature's Government: Science, Imperial Britain, and the "Improvement" of the World* (2000). The best volume on the relationship of science and imperialism.

M. H. EDNEY, *Mapping an Empire: The Geograhical Constuction of British India, 1765–1843* (1997). Discusses how the science of cartography contributed to the British domination of India.

N. ETHERINGTON, ED., *Misions and Empire* (2005). An excellent collection of essays.

D. HEADRICK, *The Tools of Empire: Technology and European Imperialism in the Nineteenth Century* (1981). Remains an important work of analysis.

A. HOCHSCHILD, *King Leopold's Ghost: A Study of Greed, Terror, and Heroism in Colonial Africa* (1999). A well-informed account of a tragedy.

I. HULL, *Absolute Destruction: Military Culture and the Practices of War in Imperial Germany* (2006). Excellent account of destructive German actions in East Africa.

R. HYAM, *Britain's Imperial Century 1815–1914: A Study of Empire and Expansion* (2002). The single best one-volume analysis.

T. JEAL, *Livingstone* (2001). This and the following title recount the lives of the two persons most associated in the popular mind with the exploration of Africa.

T. JEAL, *Stanley: The Impossible Life of Africa's Greatest Explorer* (2008). A fascinating portrait of the famous explorer.

A. KAPPELLER, *The Russian Empire: A Multiethnic History* (2001). A straightforward overview that is very clear on the concepts behind Russian expansionist policy.

D. C. LIEVAN, *The Russian Empire and Its Rivals* (2001). Explores the imperial side of Russian government.

K. E. MEYER AND S. B. BRYSA, *Tournament of Shadows: The Great Game and the Race for Empire in Central Asia* (1999). A lively account of the conflict between Great Britain and Russia.

W. J. MOMMSEN, *Theories of Imperialism* (1980). A study of the debate on the meaning of imperialism.

M. A. OSBORNE, *Nature, the Exotic, and the Science of French Colonialism* (1994). Explores the impact of French horticultural gardens and imperialism.

B. PORTER, *The Absent-Minded Imperialists: Empire, Society, and Culture in Britain* (2006). Discusses the relatively few people actually involved in Britain imperialism and how imperialism often had a low profile in the British Isles.

B. PORTER, *The Lion's Share: A Short History of British Imperialism, 1850–2004* (2004). A lively narrative.

L. PYENSON, *Civilizing Mission: Exact Sciences and French Overseas Expansion, 1830–1940* (1993). A major work of the history of both science and imperialism.

R. ROBINSON, J. GALLAGHER, AND A. DENNY, *Africa and the Victorians: The Official Mind of Imperialism* (2000). A classic analysis that continues to bear rereading.

P. J. TUCK, *French Catholic Missionaries and the Politics of Imperialism in Vietnam, 1857–1914* (1987). Includes both narrative and documents.

H. L. WESSELING, *Divide and Rule: The Partition of Africa, 1889–1914* (1996). A clear narrative and analysis of a complicated topic.

H. L. WESSELING, *The European Colonial Empires: 1815–1919* (2004). The best recent overview of the entire nineteenth-century European colonial ventures.

E. R. WOLF, *Europe and the People Without History* (1990). A classic, highly critical account.

A. ZIMMERMAN, *Anthropology and Antihumanism in Imperial Germany* (2001). Discusses the manner in which anthropology in conjunction with imperialism challenged humanistic ideas in German intellectual life.

## Chapter 26

L. ALBERTINI, *The Origins of the War of 1914*, 3 vols. (1952, 1957). Discursive, but invaluable.

V. R. BERGHAHN, *Germany and the Approach of War in 1914* (1973). Stresses the importance of Germany's naval program.

S. B. FAY, *The Origins of the World War*, 2 vols. (1928). The best and most influential of the revisionist accounts.

N. FERGUSON, *The Pity of War* (1999). An analytic study of the First World War with controversial interpretations, especially of why it began and why it ended.

O. FIGES, *A People's Tragedy: The Russian Revolution: 1891–1924* (1998). The best recent analytic narrrative.

F. FISCHER, *Germany's Aims in the First World War* (1967). An influential interpretation that stirred an enormous controversy by emphasizing Germany's role in bringing on the war.

D. FROMKIN, *Europe's Last Summer: Who Started the Great War in 1914?* (2004). A lively and readable account of the outbreak of the war based on the latest scholarship.

D. FROMKIN, *A Peace to End All Peace: The Fall of the Ottoman Empire and the Creation of the Modern Middle East* (1989). A well-informed narrative of a complicated process.

R. F. HAMILTON AND H. H. HERWIG, *The Origins of World War I* (2003). An extensive collection of recent essays examining the subject from a number of differing perspectives.

H. HERWIG, *The First World War: Germany and Austria, 1914–18* (1997). A fine study of the war from the losers' perspective.

J. N. HORNE, *Labour at War: France and Britain, 1914–1918* (1991). Examines a major issue on the home fronts.

J. JOLL, *The Origins of the First World War* (2006). Most recent revision of a classic study.

J. KEEGAN, *The First World War* (1999). A vivid and readable narrative.

P. KENNEDY, *The Rise of the Anglo-German Antagonism, 1860–1914* (1980). An unusual and thorough analysis of the political, economic, and cultural roots of important diplomatic developments.

D. C. B. LIEVEN, *Russia and the Origins of the First World War* (1983). A good account of the forces that shaped Russian policy.

M. MACMILLAN, *Paris 1919: Six Months That Changed the World* (2003). The most extensive recent treatment.

E. MANELA, *The Wilsonian Moment: Self Determination and the International Origins of Anticolonial Nationalism* (2007).

A major exploration of how Wilson's foreign policy at Versailles raised colonial expectations and revolts in Egypt, India, China, and Korea.

A. MOMBAUER, *The Origins of the First World War: Controversies and Consensus* (2002). A discussion and evaluation of historians' shifting views regarding the responsibility for the outbreak of the war.

Z. STEINER, *Britain and the Origins of the First World War* (2003). A perceptive and informed account of British foreign policy before the war.

D. STEVENSON, *Cataclysm: The First World War as Political Tragedy* (2004). Analyzes the bankruptcy of reason that precipitated the war and kept it going.

N. STONE, *The Eastern Front 1917–1917* (2004). A study of the often neglected region of the war.

H. STRACHAN, *The First World War* (2004). A one-volume version of the massive three-volume magisterial account now underway.

S. R. WILLIAMSON, Jr., *Austria-Hungary and the Origins of the First World War* (1991). A valuable study of a complex subject.

**Chapter 27**

L. AHAMED, *Lords of Finance: The Bankers Who Broke the World* (2009). A lively narrative of the banking collapse leading to the Great Depression.

W. S. ALLEN, *The Nazi Seizure of Power: The Experience of a Single German Town, 1930–1935*, rev. ed. (1984). A classic treatment of Nazism in a microcosmic setting.

A. APPLEBAUM, *Gulag: A History* (2003). A superbly readable account of Stalin's system of persecution and resulting prison camps.

I. T. BEREND, *Decades of Crisis: Central and Eastern Europe before World War II* (2001). The best recent survey of the subject.

R. J. BOSWORTH, *Mussolini* (2002). A major new biography.

R. J. BOSWORTH, *Mussolini's Italy: Life Under the Fascist Dictatorship, 1915–1945* (2007). A broad-based study of both fascist politics and the impact of those politics on Italian life.

M. BURLEIGH AND W. WIPPERMAN, *The Racial State: Germany 1933–1945* (1991). Emphasizes the manner in which racial theory influenced numerous areas of policy.

I. DEUTSCHER, *The Prophet Armed* (1954), *The Prophet Unarmed* (1959), and *The Prophet Outcast* (1963). Remains the major biography of Trotsky.

B. A. ENGEL AND A. POSADSKAYA-VANDERBECK, *A Revolution of Their Own: Voices of Women in Soviet History* (1998). Long interviews and autobiographical recollections by women who lived through the Soviet era.

R. EVANS, *The Coming of the Third Reich* (2004) and *The Third Reich in Power, 1933–1939* (2005). Superb narratives.

G. FELDMAN, *The Great Disorder: Politics, Economics, and Society in the German Inflation, 1914–1924* (1993). The best work on the subject.

S. FITZPATRICK, *Stalin's Peasants: Resistance and Survival in the Russian Village After Collectivization* (1994). A pioneering study.

F. FURET, *The Passing of an Illusion: The Idea of Communism in the Twentieth Century* (1995). A brilliant account of how communism shaped politics and thought outside the Soviet Union.

R. GELLATELY, *Lenin, Stalin, and Hitler: The Age of Social Catastrophe* (2007). A major new study of the Soviet and Nazi dictatorships.

R. GELLATELY AND N. STOLTZFUS, *Social Outsiders in Nazi Germany* (2001). Important essays on Nazi treatment of groups the party regarded as undesirables.

J. A. GETTY AND O. V. NAUMOV, *The Road to Terror: Stalin and the Self-Destruction of the Bolsheviks, 1932–1939* (1999). A remarkable collection of documents and commentary on Stalin's purges.

R. HAMILTON, *Who Voted for Hitler?* (1982). An examination of voting patterns and sources of Nazi support.

J. JACKSON, *The Popular Front in France: Defending Democracy, 1934–1938* (1988). An extensive treatment.

P. KENEZ, *The Birth of the Propaganda State: Soviet Methods of Mass Mobilization, 1917–1929* (1985). An examination of the manner in which the Communist government inculcated popular support.

B. KENT, *The Spoils of War: The Politics, Economics, and Diplomacy of Reparations, 1918–1932* (1993). A comprehensive account of the intricacies of the reparations problem of the 1920s.

I. KERSHAW, *Hitler*, 2 vols. (2001). Replaces all previous biographies.

C. KINDLEBERGER, *The World in Depression, 1929–1939* (1986). A classic, accessible analysis.

B. LINCOLN, *Red Victory: A History of the Russian Civil War* (1989). An excellent narrative account.

M. MCAULEY, *Bread and Justice: State and Society in Petrograd, 1917–1922* (1991). A study that examines the impact of the Russian Revolution and Leninist policies on a major Russian city.

R. MCKIBBIN, *Classes and Cultures: England, 1918–1951* (2000). Viewing the era through the lens of class.

R. PIPES, *The Unknown Lenin: From the Secret Archives* (1996). A collection of previously unpublished documents that indicated the repressive character of Lenin's government.

P. PULZER, *Jews and the German State: The Political History of a Minority, 1848–1933* (1992). A detailed history by a major historian of European minorities.

R. SERVICE, *Stalin: A Biography* (2005). The strongest of a host of recent biographical studies.

J. STEPHENSON, *Women in Nazi Germany* (2001). Analysis with documents.

A. TOOZE, *The Wages of Destruction: The Making and Breaking of the Nazi Economy* (2006). A wide-ranging, accessible study of the politics and ideology behind Nazi economic policy.

E. WEBER, *The Hollow Years: France in the 1930s* (1995). Examines France between the wars.

L. YAHIL, *The Holocaust: The Fate of European Jewry, 1932–1945* (1990). A major study of this fundamental subject in twentieth-century history.

## Chapter 28

O. BARTOV, *Mirrors of Destruction: War, Genocide, and Modern Identity* (2000). Remarkably penetrating essays.

A. BEEVOR, *The Spanish Civil War* (2001). Particularly strong on the political issues.

R. S. BOTWINICK, *A History of the Holocaust*, 2nd ed. (2002). A brief but useful account of the causes, character, and results of the Holocaust.

C. BROWNING, *The Origins of the Final Solution: The Evolution of the Nazi Jewish Policy* (2004). The story of how Hitler's policy developed from discrimination to annihilation.

W. S. CHURCHILL, *The Second World War*, 6 vols. (1948–1954). The memoirs of the great British leader.

A. CROZIER, *The Causes of the Second World War* (1997). An examination of what brought on the war.

J. C. FEST, *Hitler* (2002). Probably the best Hitler biography.

R. B. FRANK, *Downfall: The End of the Imperial Japanese Empire* (1998). A thorough, well-documented account of the last months of the Japanese Empire and why it surrendered.

J. L. GADDIS, *We Now Know: Rethinking Cold War History* (1998). A fine account of the early Cold War using new evidence emerging since the collapse of the Soviet Union.

J. L. GADDIS, P. H. GORDON, AND E. MAY, EDS., *Cold War Statesmen Confront the Bomb: Nuclear Diplomacy since 1945* (1999). Essays on the effect of atomic and nuclear weapons on diplomacy since World War II.

M. GILBERT, *The Holocaust: A History of the Jews of Europe during the Second World War* (1985). The best and most comprehensive treatment.

M. HASTINGS, *The Second World War: A World in Flames* (2004). A fine account by a leading student of contemporary warfare.

A. IRIYE, *Pearl Harbor and the Coming of the Pacific War* (1999). Essays on how the Pacific war came about, including a selection of documents.

J. KEEGAN, *The Second World War* (1990). A lively and penetrating account by a master military historian.

W. F. KIMBALL, *Forged in War: Roosevelt, Churchill, and the Second World War* (1998). A study of the collaboration between the two great leaders of the West.

M. KNOX, *Common Destiny, Dictatorship, Foreign Policy, and War in Fascist Italy and Nazi Germany* (2000). A brilliant comparison between the two dictatorships.

M. KNOX, *Mussolini Unleashed* (1982). An outstanding study of fascist Italy in World War II.

S. MARKS, *The Illusion of Peace* (1976). A good discussion of European international relations in the 1920s and early 1930s.

W. MURRAY, *The Change in the European Balance of Power 1938–1939* (1984). A brilliant study of the relationship among strategy, foreign policy, economics, and domestic politics.

W. MURRAY AND A. R. MILLETT, *A War to Be Won: Fighting the Second World War* (2000). A splendid account of military operations.

P. NEVILLE, *Hitler and Appeasement: The British Attempt to Prevent the Second World War* (2005). A defense of the British appeasers of Hitler.

R. OVERY, *Why the Allies Won* (1997). An analysis of the reasons for the Allied victory with emphasis on technology.

N. RICH, *Hitler's War Aims*, 2 vols. (1973–1974). The best study of the subject in English.

D. VITAL, *A People Apart: The Jews in Europe, 1789–1939* (1999). A major survey with excellent discussions of the interwar period.

R. WADE, *The Russian Revolution, 1917* (2000). A fine account that includes political and social history.

G. L. WEINBERG, *A World at Arms: A Global History of World War II* (1994). An excellent narrative.

## Chapter 29

A. AHMED, *Discovering Islam. Making Sense of Muslim History and Society*, rev. ed (2003). An excellent and readable overview of Islamic–Western relations.

C. BAYLY, *Forgotten Wars: Freedom and Revolution in Southeast Asia* (2007). An important volume on decolonization by a master historian of the region.

R. BETTS, *France and Decolonization* (1991). Explores the complexities of the French case.

A. BROWN, *The Gorbachev Factor* (1996). Reflections by a thoughtful observer.

C. ELKINS, *Imperial Reckoning: The Untold Story of Britain's Gulag in Kenya* (2005). A study of the violence involved in Britain's eventual departure from Kenya.

M. ELLMAN AND V. KONTOROVICH, *The Disintegration of the Soviet Economic System* (1992). An overview of the economic strains in the Soviet Union during the 1980s.

G. FULLER, *The Future of Political Islam* (2003). A good overview of Islamist ideology by a former CIA staff member.

J. L. GADDIS, *The United States and the Origins of the Cold War, 1941–1947* (1992). A major discussion.

M. GLENNY, *The Balkans, 1804–1999: Nationalism, War and the Great Powers* (1999). A lively narrative by a well-informed journalist.

D. HALBERSTAM, *The Coldest Winter: America and the Korean War* (2007). A superb narrative by a gifted journalist.

M. I. GOLDMAN, *Petrostate: Putin, Power, and the New Russia* (2008). A thoughtful, but critical analysis.

W. HITCHCOCK, *Struggle for Europe: The Turbulent History of a Divided Continent, 1945–2002* (2003). The best overall narrative now available.

A. HORNE, *A Savage War of Peace: Algeria 1954–1962* (1987). A now dated but still classic narrative.

R. HYAM, *Britain's Declining Empire: The Road to Decolonization, 1918–1968* (2007). The best one-volume treatment.

T. JUDAH, *The Serbs: History, Myth and the Destruction of Yugoslavia* (1997). A clear overview of a complex event.

J. KEAY, *Sowing the Wind: The Seeds of Conflict in the Middle East* (2003). A thoughtful account.

N. R. KEDDIE, *Modern Iran: Roots and Results of Revolution* (2003). Chapters 6–12 focus on Iran from 1941 through the 1978 revolution.

J. KEEP, *Last of the Empires: A History of the Soviet Union, 1945–1991* (1995, 2007). An outstanding one-volume survey.

G. KEPEL, *Jihad: The Trail of Political Islam* (2002). An extensive treatment by a leading French scholar.

Y. KHAN, *The Great Partition: The Making of India and Pakistan* (2008). An important recent study of a difficult issue.

P. KHANNA, *The Second World: Empires and Influence in the New Global Order* (2008). A volume that seeks to provide a broad global analysis of recent events.

W. R. LOUIS, *Ends of British Imperialism: The Scramble for Empire, Suez, and Decolonization* (2007). A major study that captures the intensity and passions of the events.

R. MANN, *A Grand Delusion: America's Descent into Vietnam* (2001). The best recent narrative.

K. E. MEYER AND S. B. BRYSAC, *Kingmakers: The Invention of the Modern Middle East* (2008). A lively narrative of the past two centuries of British and then American influence in the Middle East.

D. E. MURPHY, S. A. KONDRASHEV, AND G. BAILEY, *Battleground Berlin: CIA vs. KGB in the Cold War* (1997). One of the best of a vast literature on Cold War espionage.

W. E. ODOM, *The Collapse of the Soviet Military* (1999). A study more wide ranging than the title suggests.

M. OREN, *Power, Faith, and Fantasy: America in the Middle East: 1776 to the Present* (2007). A thoughtful, balanced analysis.

B. PAREKH, *Gandhi: A Very Short Introduction* (2001). A useful introduction to Gandhi's ideas.

T. R. REID, *The United States of Europe: The New Superpower and the End of American Supremacy* (2004). A journalist's exploration of the impact of the European Union on American policy.

T. SHEPARD, *The Invention of Decolonization: The Algerian War and the Remaking of France* (2008). Explores the impact of the Algerian War on French politics.

L. SHEVTSOVA, *Russia—Lost in Transition: The Yeltsin and Putin Legacies* (2007). A major analysis and meditation on the past two decades.

J. SPRINGHALL, *Decolonization since 1945: The Collapse of European Empires* (2001). Systematic treatment of each major former colony.

B. STANLEY, *Missions, Nationalism, and the End of Empire* (2003). Discusses the often ignored role of Christian missions and decolonization.

M. THOMAS, *The French Empire Between the Wars: Imperialism, Politics and Society* (2005). Useful background to postwar decolonization.

M. VIORST, *In the Shadow of the Prophet: The Struggle for the Soul of Islam* (2001). Explores the divisions in contemporary Islam.

L. WRIGHT, *The Looming Tower: Al Qaeda and the Road to 9/11* (2007). A compelling narrative.

## Chapter 30

G. AMBROSIUS AND W. H. HUBBARD, *A Social and Economic History of Twentieth-Century Europe* (1989). An excellent one-volume treatment of the subject.

B. S. ANDERSON AND J. P. ZINSSER, *A History of Their Own: Women in Europe from Prehistory to the Present*, vol. 2 (1988). A broad-ranging survey.

G. BOCK AND P. THANE, EDS., *Maternity and Gender Politics: Women and the Rise of the European Welfare States, 1880s–1950s* (1991). Explores the emergence of welfare legislation.

E. BRAMWELL, *Ecology in the 20th Century: A History* (1989). Traces the environmental movement to its late-nineteenth-century origins.

P. E. CERUZZI, *A History of Modern Computing* (2003). A comprehensive survey.

S. COLLINSON, *Beyond Borders: West European Migration Policy and the 21st Century* (1993). Explores a major contemporary European social issue.

R. CROSSMAN, ED., *The God That Failed* (1949). Classic essays by former communist intellectuals.

D. DINAN, *Europe Recast: A History of the European Union* (2004). A major overview.

C. FINK, P. GASERT, AND D. JUNKER, *1968: The World Transformed* (1998). The best collection of essays on a momentous year.

B. GRAHAM, *Modern Europe: Place, Culture, Identity* (1998). Thoughtful essays on the future of Europe by a group of geographers.

H. S. HUGHES, *Sophisticated Rebels: The Political Culture of European Dissent, 1968–1987* (1988). Thoughtful essays on recent cultural critics.

P. JENKINS, *Mrs. Thatcher's Revolution: The Ending of the Socialist Era* (1988). The best work on the subject.

P. JENKINS, *The Next Christendom: The Coming of Global Christianity* (2002). A provocative analysis.

T. JUDT, *Past Imperfect: French Intellectuals, 1944–1956* (1992). An important study of French intellectuals and communism.

T. JUDT, *Pastwar: A History of Europe Since 1945* (2005). The most recent authoritative overview.

R. MALTBY, ED., *Passing Parade: A History of Popular Culture in the Twentieth Century* (1989). Essays on a topic just beginning to receive scholarly attention.

R. MARRUS, *The Unwanted: European Refugees in the 20th Century* (1985). An important work on a disturbing subject.

D. MEYER, *Sex and Power: The Rise of Women in America, Russia, Sweden, and Italy* (1987). A lively, useful survey.

N. NAIMARK, *Fires of Hatred: Ethnic Cleansing in Twentieth-Century Europe* (2002). A remarkably sensitive treatment of a tragic subject.

M. POSTER, *Existential Marxism in Postwar France* (1975). An excellent and clear work.

H. ROWLEY, *Tête-á-Tête: Simone de Beauvoir and Jean-Paul Sartre* (2005). A highly critical joint biography.

S. STRASSER, C. McGOVERN, AND M. JUDT, *Getting and Spending: European and American Consumer Societies in the Twentieth Century* (1998). An extensive collection of comparative essays.

F. THEBAUD, ED., *A History of Women in the West*, vol. 5: *Toward a Cultural Identity in the Twentieth Century* (1994). A collection of wide-ranging essays of the highest quality.

**Sejm** Central legislative body to which the Polish nobles belonged.

themselves. Most of the Polish monarchs were foreigners and the tools of foreign powers. The Polish nobles did have a central legislative body called the *Sejm*, or diet. The diet, however, had a practice known as the *liberum veto*, whereby the staunch opposition of any single member, who might have been bribed by a foreign power, could require the body to disband. Such opposition, termed "exploding the diet," was most often the work of a group of dissatisfied nobles rather than of one person. Nonetheless, the requirement of unanimity was a major stumbling block to effective government. The price of this noble liberty would eventually be the disappearance of Poland from the map of Europe in the late eighteenth century.

## THE HABSBURG EMPIRE AND THE PRAGMATIC SANCTION

The close of the Thirty Years' War marked a fundamental turning point in the history of the Austrian Habsburgs. Previously, in alliance with their Spanish cousins, they had hoped to bring all of Germany under their control and back to the Catholic fold. In this they had failed, and the decline of Spanish power meant that the Austrian Habsburgs were on their own. (See Map 13-2.)

After 1648, the Habsburg family retained a firm hold on the title of Holy Roman Emperor, but the power of the emperor depended less on the force of arms than on the cooperation he could elicit from the various political bodies in the empire. While establishing their new dominance among the German states, the Habsburgs also began to consolidate their power and influence within their hereditary possessions outside the Holy Roman Empire, which included the Crown of Saint Wenceslas, encompassing the kingdom of Bohemia (in the modern Czech Republic) and the duchies of Moravia and Silesia; and the Crown of Saint Stephen, which ruled Hungary, Croatia, and Transylvania.

In each of their many territories the Habsburgs ruled by virtue of a different title—king, archduke, duke—and they needed the cooperation of the local nobility, which was not always forthcoming. They repeatedly had to bargain with nobles in one part of Europe to maintain their position in another. Their domains were so geographically diverse and the people who lived in them of so many different languages and customs that almost no grounds existed on which to unify them politically.

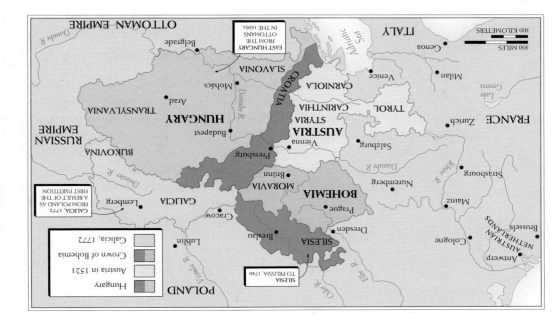

**MAP 13-2 The Austrian Habsburg Empire, 1521-1772** The empire had three main units—Austria, Bohemia, and Hungary. Expansion was mainly eastward: eastern Hungary from the Ottomans (seventeenth century) and Galicia from Poland (1772). Meantime, Silesia was lost after 1740, but the Habsburgs remained Holy Roman Emperors. **Why was** expansion of the Austrian Habsburg Empire mostly eastward?

organized a monopoly, called the Mississippi Company, on trading privileges with the French colony of Louisiana in North America.

The Mississippi Company also took over the management of the French national debt. The company issued shares of its own stock in exchange for government bonds, which had fallen sharply in value. To redeem large quantities of bonds, Law encouraged speculation in the Mississippi Company stock. In 1719, the price of the stock rose handsomely. Smart investors, however, took their profits by selling their stock in exchange for paper money from Law's bank, which they then sought to exchange for gold. The bank, however, lacked enough gold to redeem all the paper money brought to it. In February 1720, all gold payments were halted in France. Soon thereafter, Law himself fled the country. The Mississippi Bubble, as the affair was called, had burst. The fiasco brought disgrace on the government that had sponsored Law. The Mississippi Company was later reorganized and functioned profitably, but fear of paper money and speculation marked French economic life for decades.

**Renewed Authority of the *Parlements*** The duke of Orléans made a second decision that also lessened the power of the monarchy. He attempted to draw the French nobility once again into the decision-making processes of the government. He set up a system of councils on which nobles were to serve along with bureaucrats. The experiment failed. Nonetheless, the chief feature of eighteenth-century French political life was the attempt of the nobility to use its authority to limit the power of the monarchy. The most effective instrument in this process was the *parlements*, or courts dominated by the nobility.

*parlements* French political institutions with customary rights of consultation and deliberation.

Throughout the eighteenth century, *parlements* succeeded in identifying their authority and resistance to the monarchy with wider public opinion. This situation meant that until the revolution in 1789, the *parlements* became natural centers not only for aristocratic, but also for popular resistance to royal authority. In a vast transformation from the days of Louis XIV, the *parlements* rather than the monarchy would come to be seen as more nearly representing the nation.

By 1726, the general political direction of the nation had come under the authority of Cardinal Fleury (1653–1743). He worked to maintain the authority of the monarchy, including ongoing repression of the Jansenists, while continuing to preserve the local interests of the French nobility. Like Walpole in Britain, he pursued economic prosperity at home and peace abroad. Again like Walpole, after 1740, Fleury could not prevent France from entering a worldwide colonial conflict. (See Chapter 17.)

## CENTRAL AND EASTERN EUROPE

WHAT WERE the main characteristics that defined the Polish, Austrian, and Prussian states in the seventeenth and eighteenth centuries?

Central and eastern Europe were economically much less advanced than western Europe. Except for the Baltic ports, the economy was agrarian. There were fewer cities and many more large estates worked by serfs.

During the sixteenth and early seventeenth centuries, the political authorities in this region, which lay largely east of the Elbe River, were weak. During the last half of the seventeenth century, however, three strong dynasties, whose rulers aspired to the absolutism then being constructed in France, emerged in central and eastern Europe. They were Austria, Prussia, and Russia. By contrast, Poland during the eighteenth century became the single most conspicuous example in Europe of a land that failed to establish a viable centralized government.

### POLAND: ABSENCE OF STRONG CENTRAL AUTHORITY

In no other part of Europe was the failure to maintain a competitive political position so complete as in Poland. The Polish monarchy was elective, but the deep distrust and divisions among the nobility usually prevented their electing a king from among